FROM LATIN TO MODERN FRENCH WITH ESPECIAL CONSIDERATION OF ANGLO-NORMAN

PHONOLOGY AND MORPHOLOGY

BY

M. K. POPE, M.A., Litt.D.

*Docteur de l'Université de Paris ; Docteur, honoris causa, de l'Université de Bordeaux ;
Emeritus Professor of French Language and Romance Philology in the University
of Manchester ; Honorary Fellow of Somerville College, Oxford*

MANCHESTER UNIVERSITY PRESS

Published by the University of Manchester at
THE UNIVERSITY PRESS
316–324, OXFORD ROAD, MANCHESTER, 13

First Published . . . 1934
Reprinted . . 1952, 1956, 1961

PRINTED IN GREAT BRITAIN BY
ABERDEEN UNIVERSITY PRESS, 1934

REVISED EDITION PRINTED BY
BUTLER & TANNER LTD.
FROME AND LONDON, 1952

PUBLICATIONS OF THE UNIVERSITY OF MANCHESTER
No. CCXXIX

FRENCH SERIES No. VI

FROM LATIN TO MODERN FRENCH WITH ESPECIAL CONSIDERATION OF ANGLO-NORMAN

PREFACE TO FIRST EDITION

THE subject of this book is the evolution of sound and flexion that has led from Latin to Early Modern French, the French of the educated Parisian Society of the seventeenth century. No attempt has been made to present in detail subsequent changes in pronunciation and flexion, but the main modifications in pronunciation that have taken place in the course of the Modern period are indicated summarily in the general surveys of linguistic development and included in the tables of sound-changes. The outline sketch of the history of orthography has been brought up to the end of the seventeenth century, the time when the publication of the *Dictionary of the Academy* (1694) settled definitely the main lines of modern spelling. Throughout the book a relatively large space has been accorded to the language of the later sixteenth century in order to provide a basis for the observation of later changes, and the verb tables include the forms of verbs in the sixteenth century as well as those of Old French. I would add that the book on the French language recently published by Professor Ewert contains a survey that may serve as complementary to this book in that it includes the modern period and treats of vocabulary and syntax as well as pronunciation and flexion.

In compiling this work I have had in mind primarily the needs of University students, of learners, that is to say, and not the learned, and though I hope I may have been able to elucidate here and there a few of the minor problems of the development of the French language, my chief aim has been to present to the student the history of French pronunciation and flexion in such a way that the main processes underlying their evolution may stand out unobscured. With this end in view I have given more space than is usual in books of this type to the description of these processes and treated the ordinary sound-changes as far as possible under such heads as *palatalisation, nasalisation, influence of stress, of position,* etc. Typographical variation is

v

employed to bring into relief the general lines of development, con-
troversial questions, details and dialectal variants being thrown into
small print, and the paragraphs dealing with these last being distinguished by the use of a double asterisk.

To make it easier to follow the course of sound-change, sound and
spelling are rigorously distinguished, italics being used to represent all
forms given in ordinary spelling, phonetic symbols to represent the
pronunciation. In the examples cited to illustrate development of
sounds the pronunciation of the word in Old or Modern French is
ordinarily given as well as its pronunciation at the stage reached in the
history of the sound whose development is being traced. The symbols
employed are those approved by the Copenhagen International Confer-
ence of 1926, but to facilitate the use of the book by those familiar with
other systems, the corresponding symbols of the *Association Phonétique
Internationale* and a few of those used by other scholars are included in
the key list of words (pp. xvii, xviii). I am much indebted to Professor
Daniel Jones for suggestions about various points and for permission to
reproduce some of the figures included in his own books (cf. below,
pp. 121, 122).

In the belief that the history of a language should be related as
closely as possible to the study of texts the changes in sound and
flexion are documented as frequently as possible from texts or from the
utterances of contemporary grammarians. A select list of these is included (pp. xxv, xxvi) as well as short summaries of the various authorities
available at the early periods of the language (pp. 7, 8, 21, 22, 48), but
the bibliography proper is narrowly selective, confined in the main to
the mention of the work dealing most recently with the subject under
discussion or the one that is of special importance for it. For a
completer list of older works readers should consult the lists given in the
modern grammars cited on pages xxvii, xxviii. A detailed subject-index
and full word-lists are included, and these contain not only the words and
forms whose development is described but also a considerable number
of those cited as illustrative examples, more especially those drawn from
the oldest French Monuments or from important or much read texts
such as the *Chanson de Roland, Aucassin et Nicolete* and the works of
Villon.

The main features of the Mediaeval French dialects are noted in
their appropriate places in the body of the book and summarised in the
Appendix, but as the book is intended more especially for English-
speaking students I have paid most attention to the dialects of the west

and north of France and have worked out more fully than has yet been attempted the development of French speech in England, the relation between Anglo-Norman pronunciation and spelling, and in particular the influence exercised by the English speech habits on the language of their conquerors. To secure a sound basis for the treatment of these questions I have set out with some fullness the probable Western French pronunciation and flexion in the late eleventh century and included a summary description of the Early Middle English sound-system and the more important Middle English sound-changes. For advice in this part of the work I am greatly indebted to Professor Wyld and Miss D. Everett.

On the works of my predecessors I have drawn very freely, more especially on the grammars of Professors Brunot, L. Jordan, Meyer-Lübke, Nyrop, Suchier, and on the verb treatises of Professors Tanquerey and Wahlgren and in the final revision on that of Professor Fouché also. My conscious borrowings find acknowledgment but there remains much unconscious plagiarism—for this my apologies, and for all I owe to these and others whose work I have utilised, my grateful thanks.

To my colleagues, pupils and friends my debt is also great; to the late Professor Waters, to Professor Ewert, Miss D. Paton and Miss D. Legge, for useful suggestions; to my friends Mrs. Somerset and Mrs. Geldart who have given assistance, the one in the typing of the first draft of the MS., the other in the task of compiling the word index; to my pupils C. Craven, M. Lucas, M. Sorrell for their help in checking references. Chiefly, however, is my gratitude due to Miss O. Rhys .o whom a great part of the work has been submitted in MS. and in proof, with whom a great many points of detail have been discussed and whose exact scholarship and vigilance have saved me from more blunders than I care to remember.

And finally I should not close this list of benevolent contributors of help without mentioning with gratitude my own College, whose generous subvention encouraged the publication of the work, and the Secretary of the Manchester Press and its printers, who have borne with my inconsistencies and vagaries with exemplary patience.

M. K. P.

PREFACE TO SECOND EDITION

THIS is a reprint by photo offset of the original 1934 edition. It incorporates in the text a number of minor corrections and additions which have been made under the supervision of Professor T. B. W. Reid. Those that it has not been possible to include in the text have been listed on a page of Addenda. I should like to express my thanks to Professor Reid for his work in supervising the corrections and to Professor R. C. Johnston for compiling the Supplementary Bibliography.

M. K. P.

LIST OF CONTENTS.

[References are to paragraphs unless otherwise indicated.]

CONTENTS

PART II.

PHONOLOGY.

CHAPTER I.

PHONETIC INTRODUCTION.

CHAPTER II.

CHRONOLOGICAL SURVEY OF SOUND-CHANGES.

CHAPTER III.

ISOLATIVE CHANGES.

CHAPTER IV.

INFLUENCE OF POSITION IN THE WORD.

CHAPTER V.

INFLUENCE OF EXPIRATORY WORD-ACCENT.

CHAPTER VI.

PALATALISATION OF CONSONANTS.

CHAPTER VII.

VOICING AND OPENING OF SINGLE BREATHED AND PLOSIVE CONSONANTS IN VOCALIC ENVIRONMENT.

CHAPTER VIII.

REDUCTION OF LENGTHENED CONSONANTS AND INTERVOCALIC CONSONANTAL GROUPS.

CHAPTER IX.

DEVELOPMENT OF THE l-SOUNDS AND r.

CHAPTER X.

INFLUENCE EXERCISED BY PALATAL SOUNDS ON VOWELS.

CHAPTER XVII.

INFLUENCE OF SYNTACTICAL PHONETICS.

CHAPTER XVIII.

LOAN-WORDS.

CHAPTER XIX.

SOUND TABLES, 661-687.

PART III.

ORTHOGRAPHY.

CHAPTER I.

PERIOD I—OLD FRENCH.

CHAPTER II.

PERIOD II—THIRTEENTH CENTURY, MIDDLE AND EARLY MODERN FRENCH.

CONTENTS

PART IV.

MORPHOLOGY.

CHAPTER I.

CONTAMINATION AND ANALOGY.

CHAPTER II.

SUBSTANTIVES AND ADJECTIVES.

CHAPTER III.

PRONOUNS.

CHAPTER IV.

VERBS.

CONTENTS XV

PART V.

ANGLO-NORMAN.

CHAPTER I.

INTRODUCTORY.

CHAPTER II.

PHONOLOGY.

CHAPTER III.

ORTHOGRAPHY.

CHAPTER IV.

DECLENSION.

CHAPTER V.

VERBS.

APPENDIX.

CONSPECTUS OF DIALECTAL TRAITS.

LIST OF PHONETIC SYMBOLS WITH KEY-WORDS.

The symbol standing first is the one employed in this book; those following are alternative symbols adopted either by the *Association Phonétique Internationale* or by other scholars.

The key-words given are Modern French, unless otherwise indicated.

a	ʀatte	pat	æ	*English* fat	fæt
ɑ	ʀas	pɑ			
ẹ, ɛ	fête	fɛt			
ẹ, e	fée	fẹ			
ẹ	*German* Gabe	gɑbẹ	ə	le	lə
ị	*English* it	ịt			
ị or i	pli	plị, pli			
ọ, ɔ	bosse	bọs	ọ, ɔ:	*English* saw	sọ
ọ, o	sot	sọ	ọ̈, œ	œuf	œ̈f
			ọ̈, ø	feu	fọ̈
ụ	*English* put	pụt			
ụ or u	coup	kụ, ku			
ü, y	plus	plü	ụ̀, ü	*Norwegian* hus	hụ̀s

Nasalisation is indicated by the *tilde*, the symbol ～ placed above the vowel or diphthong nasalised, e.g. ã, Modern French *an*, ọ̃, Modern French *on*, ọ̈̃, Modern French *un*, etc.

CONSONANTS.

b	*bout*	bu	β, ƀ	*Spanish* lobo	lọβọ
d	*doux*	du	ð, δ, d̦	*English* then	ðen
f	*fou*	fu			
g	*goût*	gu	γ	*N. German* Lage	Lɑγẹ
h	*English* hit	hịt			
J or j, y	*yeux*	jọ̈, jọ̈	ç	*German* ich	iç
k	*coup*	ku	χ, x	*Scotch* loch	lọχ
				German ach	ɑχ
l	*loup*	lu	ʝ, ʎ, lı	*Italian* figlio	fiʝọ
				Spanish llamar	ʝamar
			ɫ	*English* old	ọuɫd
m	*mou*	mu			
n	*nous*	nu	ŋ, ɲ, nı	agneau	aɲọ
			ɴ, ŋ	*English* king	kịɴ
p	*pas*	pɑ			

xvii

b

r	provincial French rue	rü		ɹ	Southern English rose		ɹouz
	English rose	rọuz					
R	Parisian French rue	Rü		ʁ	Parisian French	rue	ʁü
s	sou	su		š, ∫	chou		šu
				tš, t∫	English chin		tšįn
t	tout	tu		θ, þ, ṭ	English thin		θįn
					Spanish cruz		kruθ
v	vous	vu					
w	oui	wi		ẘ, ɥ	lui		lẘi
z	oser	ọzę		ž, ʒ	joue		žu
				dž, dʒ	English gin		džįn
∫	French patois qui	ʃi		ɟ	French patois	gaie	ɟę

Palatalised Consonants. The palatalisation of consonants is indicated by the use of the symbol ⌒ placed above the sound palatalised, e.g. r̂, ŝ, t̂ (cf. p. 57).

Accentuation.

The *tonic* syllable is indicated by a prae-posed perpendicular dash ', the *counter-tonic* by a prae-posed double dash ", e.g. 'pĕdem, 'ā̆mo, 'hŏmĭnĕm, "hă̆'bēre, "dormi'tōriŭm.

The stressed element of a diphthong is sometimes indicated by a prae-posed dash, e.g. pʰieθ, bʰuef.

Quantity.

Vowel length is indicated by a superposed horizontal dash, e.g. Middle French tŏt, pā̆tę.

Use of Asterisks.

A single asterisk prae-posed to a Latin word or form indicates that the word or form is Late Latin, attested or conjectural, e.g. *auca, *dolus, *dŭi.

A single asterisk prae-posed to a Germanic word indicates that it is conjectural, e.g. *helm, *hatjan.

A double asterisk prae-posed to a word in the body of the book indicates that it is a conjectural Gallo-Roman form, e.g. **baɣa (baca), **sęvęt (sapit).

A double asterisk is prae-posed to a paragraph to indicate that it is concerned with a dialectal variant.

Use of Brackets.

In the body of the book *round brackets* are used in words: (1) to enclose terminations that are analogical, e.g. *sent* (*ant*); (2) to enclose sounds that are moribund or varying in pronunciation according to position, e.g. mę(ð)lęr, portę(θ); Middle French vi(f), vi(s).

[For use in tables and indexes cf. headings of tables and indexes.]

Use of Italics and Phonetic Script.

In the examples cited in the body of the book italics are used to indicate the ordinary spelling of the word, phonetic script, the pronunciation. Italics are used ordinarily in words cited from texts, e.g. Villon, *Troies : trois*, etc., and in the names of works, e.g. *Roland, Thebes*, etc.

In the citations taken from the works of grammarians their own spelling is retained, in those drawn from Thurot the system adopted by him is followed.

Abbreviations.

frk.	= frankish.	frpr.	= franco-provençal.
L.L.	= Late Latin.	V.L.	= Vulgar Latin.
O.F.	= Old French.	Mid. Fr.	= Middle French (§ 16).
Mod. Fr.	= Modern French.	M.E.	= Middle English.

E.O.F. = Early Old French = O.F. I (§ 16).
L.O.F. = Later Old French = O.F. II (§ 16).
Early Modern French = cent. xvii.

> denotes *becomes.*
< denotes *comes from.*
± denotes *on the model of.*

LIST OF WORKS CITED, WITH ABBREVIATED TITLES.

Illustrative Texts.

CLASS. FR., Les Classiques Français du Moyen Age, publiés sous la direction
de Mario Roques, Paris, 1910-
S.A.T.F., Publications de la Société des Anciens Textes Français, 1875-
For the Gallo-Roman Period, cf. § 39.
For the Early Old French Period, cf. § 40.

Later Old French.

(For Anglo-Norman Texts (A.N.), cf. below, pp. 483-485.)

ADAM, A.N.
ADGAR, A.N.
ANGIER = *Dialogues et Vie de St. Grégoire* (XIII¹) ; MS. Paris, Bibl. Nat.
24766 fonds français.
ANGIER ET. = *Etude sur la Langue de Frère Angier*, par M. K. Pope, Paris,
1903 (Thèse).
AUBAN, A.N.
AUC. = *Aucassin et Nicolete*, ed. (*a*) H. Suchier, Paderborn, 1878 ; ninth
edition, revised by W. Suchier, 1921 ; French translation of fifth
edition by A. Counson ; (*b*) F. W. Bourdillon, Manchester, 1919 ;
(*c*) M. Roques ; Class. Fr. No. 41.
BERNARD = *Die Predigten des h. Bernhard in Altfrz. Uebertragung*, ed. A.
Schulze, Tübingen, 1894 (Extract 43 in Studer-Waters = Ex. BERN.).
BEROUL = *Le Roman de Tristan*, par Beroul, ed. Muret, (*a*) S.A.T.F., 1903 ;
(*b*) Class. Fr. No. 12.
BEST. GUILL. = *Le Bestiaire* de Guillaume le Clerc (XIII¹), ed. Reinsch, 1890.
BESTIAIRE, A.N.
BOEVE, A.N.
BOILEAUE = *Le Livre des Métiers* d'Etienne Boileaue (XIII), ed. Lespinasse et
Bonnardot, Paris, 1879.
BRENDAN, A.N.
CAM. PS., A.N.
CHARDRI, A.N.
CHRISTIAN V. TROYES, *Sämtliche Werke*, hgg. v. W. Foerster u. A. Hilka, Halle,
1884-1932.
CREST. *CL.* = *Cliges*, 1888, and Rom. Bibl. No. 1.
CREST. *E.* = *Erec et Enide*, 1890, and Rom. Bibl. No. 13.
CREST. *IV.* = *Der Löwenritter* (*Yvain*), 1887, and Rom. Bibl. No. 5.
CREST. *L.* = *Der Karrenritter* (*Lancelot*), 1899.
CREST. *P.* = *Der Percevalroman* (*Li Contes del Gral*), ed. A. Hilka, 1932.
CHRON. NORM. = *La Chronique des Ducs de Normandie* (XII²), par Benoit, ed.
F. Michel, Paris, 1836-1844.

CLEF D'AMOURS (XIII), ed. A. Doutrepont, Halle, 1890.
COMPUT, A.N.
COURONNEMENT. LOUIS = *Le Couronnement de Louis* (XII), 2me ed., revue
    par E. Langlois ; Class. Fr. No. 22.
DIAL. GREG. = *Li Dialoge Gregoire lo Pape*, ed. W. Foerster, Halle, 1876 ;
    (Extract 42 in Studer-Waters = Ex. GREG.).
DOOMSDAY BOOK, cf. A.N. MSS.
ENEAS = *Eneas* (XII²), ed. J. Salverda de Grave ; Class. Fr. Nos. 44, 62.
ERACLES = *Eracles*, par Gautier d'Arras (XII²), ed. Löseth, Paris, 1890.
ESCOUFLE = *L'Escoufle* (XIII¹), ed. H. Michelant et P. Meyer ; S.A.T.F.,
    1891.
ESTIENNE = *Epistre St. Estienne* (XII¹), ed. Foerster u. Koschwitz, Altfrz.
    Uebungsbuch.
FAITS ROM. = *Li Fait des Romains*, Ex. 27 in Studer-Waters.
FANTOSME, A.N.
FAUVEL = *Le Roman de Fauvel*, par Gervais de Bus (XIII-XIV), ed. A.
    Långfors ; S.A.T.F.
FEUILLÉE, *Le Jeu de la Feuillée*, par Adam le Bossu (XIII²), ed. E. Langlois ;
    Class. Fr. No. 6.
GAIMAR, A.N.
G. DÔLE = *Le Roman de la Rose ou Guillaume de Dôle* (XIII¹), ed. G. Servois ;
    S.A.T.F.
GERBERT = *Gerbert de Montreuil* (XIII²), *La Continuation de Perceval*, ed.
    Mary Williams ; Class. Fr. Nos. 28, 50.
GORMONT = *Gormont et Isembart* (XII¹), ed. A. Bayot ; Class. Fr. No. 14.
GUERNES = *La Vie de St. Thomas le Martyr* (XII²), par Guernes de Pont Ste.
    Maxence, ed. E. Walberg, Lund, 1922.
GUILLELME = *La Chançun de Guillelme* (XII¹), ed. H. Suchier, Halle, 1911 ;
    (Bibliotheca Normannica, VII).
GUIOT = *Les Oeuvres* de Guiot de Provins (XII-XIII), ed. J. Orr, Manchester,
    1915.
JEU ROB. = *Le Jeu de Robin et Marion*, par Adam le Bossu (XIII²), ed. E.
    Langlois ; Class. Fr. No. 36.
JOINVILLE = *Histoire de St. Louis, Credo et Lettre à Louis IX* (XIII-XIV),
    par Jean, Sire de Joinville, ed. N. de Wailly, Paris, 1867.
LAPIDARIES, A.N.
LIVRE MAN. = *Le Livre des Manieres*, par Estienne von Fougieres (XII²), ed.
    J. Kremer, Marburg, 1887 ; (*Ausgaben und Abhandlungen* XXXIX).
MACÉ = *La Bible* de Macé de la Charité (xiii² ; cf. *Rose*, vol. I, p. 188).
MARIE FR. FABLES = *Die Fabeln* der Marie de France (xii²), ed. Warnke,
    Halle, 1898 ; (Bibl. Norm. 6).
MARIE FR. LAIS = *Die Lais der Marie de France*, 3rd edit., ed. Warnke, Halle,
    1925 ; (Bibl. Norm. 3).
MIRACLES CHARTRES = *Le Livre des Miracles de Notre-Dame de Chartres*
    (XIII), par Jehan le Marchant, Chartres, 1855.
MOUSKET = *Chronique Rimée de Philippe Mousqués* (XIII²), ed. von Reiffenberg,
    Bruxelles, 1836-38 ; (Extract 39 in Studer-Waters = Ex. MOUSKET).
OAK BOOK, A.N.
OMBRE = *Le Lai de l'Ombre*, par Jean Renart (XIII¹), ed. J. Bédier ; S.A.T.F.
OXF. PS., A.N.
P. MOR. = *Poème Moral* (XII-XIII), ed. Cloetta, Erlangen, 1886.
PURG. PATR., A.N.
Q.L.R., A.N.
RAOUL CAMBR. = *Raoul de Cambrai* (XII²), ed. P. Meyer et A. Longnon ;
    S.A.T.F.
RENART = *Le Roman de Renart* (XII²-XIII), ed. E. Martin, Strassburg, 1882-
    1885.
RENCLUS = *Li Romans de Carité et Miserere* du Renclus de Moiliens (XII²), ed.
    A. G. van Hamel, Paris, 1885.

ROLAND, ROL. = *La Chanson de Roland* (XII[1]) ; Oxford MS., ed. (*a*) Groeber, Bibl. Rom. 53, 54 ; (*b*) Bédier, Paris ; (*c*) Laborde, Edition Phototypique, (1932, Roxburghe Club ; 1933, S.A.T.F.).

RÔLES DE TAILLE = *Les Rôles de Taille Parisiens* (1292, 1296-1300) ; cited from the work *Etude sur les Noms de Personne Français d'après les Rôles de Taille Parisiens*, par Karl Michaëlsson, Uppsala, 1927.

ROM. HAM = *Le Roman de Ham* (1278), ed. Peigné Delacour, 1854.

ROSE I = *Le Roman de la Rose* (XIII[1]), par Guillaume de Lorris,

ROSE II = *Le Roman de la Rose* (XIII[2]), par Jean de Meung, ed. Langlois ; S.A.T.F.

ROU = Maistre Wace's *Roman de Rou et des Ducs de Normandie*, Pt. III (XII[2]), ed. H. Andresen, Heilbronn, 1879.

RTBF. = Rustebuef's *Gedichte* (XIII[2]), ed. Kressner, Wolfenbüttel, 1885 ; *Le Miracle de Théophile*, ed. G. Frank ; Class. Fr. No. 49.

ST. BERNARD = Li Sermon St. Bernard (XIII[2]), ed. W. Foerster, Erlangen, 1885 ; (Extract 43 in Studer-Waters = Ex. ST. BERN.).

ST. EDMUND, A.N.

ST. GILLES, A.N.

ST. MARTIN = *Das altfrz. Martinsleben* des Péan Gatineau aus Tours (XIII), ed. W. Söderhjelm, Helsingfors, 1899.

ST. NIC. = *Le Jeu de St. Nicolas*, par Jean Bodel (XII-XIII), ed. A. Jeanroy ; Class. Fr. No. 48.

STE. EUPHROSINE = *La Vie de Ste Euphrosine*, ed. R. Hill, *Romanic Review*, X.

SERMON EN VERS = *Reimpredigt*, ed. H. Suchier, Halle, 1878 ; (Bibl. Norm. I).

SIMUND FREINE, A.N.

THEBES, *Le Roman de Thèbes* (mid. XII), ed. L. Constans ; S.A.T.F.

TROIE, *Le Roman de Troie* (XII[2]), par Benoit de Ste. Maure, ed. L. Constans ; S.A.T.F.

Middle French.

G. ALEXIS = *Oeuvres Poétiques* de Guillaume Alexis (XIV[2]), ed. Piaget et Picot ; S.A.T.F.

BLACK PRINCE = *Life of the Black Prince*, by the Herald of Sir John Chandos (XIV[2]), ed. M. K. Pope and E. C. Lodge, Oxford, 1910.

BOZON, A.N.

CHANSONS XV = *Chansons françaises du XVe siècle*, ed. G. Paris ; S.A.T.F.

CHARLES D'O. = *Poésies* de Charles d'Orléans (XV[2]), ed. P. Champion ; Class. Fr. Nos. 34, 56.

CHRISTINE PIS. = *Oeuvres Poétiques* de Christine de Pisan (XV[1]), ed. M. Roy ; S.A.T.F.

CRETIN = *Oeuvres Poétiques* de Guillaume Cretin (XV[2]), ed. K. Chesney, Paris, 1933.

DEGUILEVILLE = *Le Pélerinage de Vie Humaine* (XIV[1]), par Guillaume de Deguileville, ed. J. J. Stürzinger, London, 1893 (Roxburghe Club) ; (Extract 34 in Studer-Waters = Ex. DEGUILEVILLE).

DESCHAMPS = *Oeuvres Complètes* d'Eustache Deschamps (XIV[2]), ed. Le Marquis de Queux de St. Hilaire ; S.A.T.F.

DIV. MUNDI, A.N.

FROISSART = *Chroniques* de Froissart (XIV[2]), ed. S. Luce et G. Raynaud, Paris, 1869 ff. ; (Extract 41 in Studer-Waters = Ex. FROISSART).

FROISSART, MEL. = *Meliador*, par Jean Froissart, ed. A. Longnon ; S.A.T.F.

GREBAN = *Le Mystère de la Passion* d'Arnold Greban (XV[2]), ed. G. Paris et G. Raynaud, Paris, 1878.

GUIART = *Branche des royaux lignages* (XIV[1]), ed. Buchon, 1828 ; (Recueil des Hist. des Gaules, V).

GUISE LETTERS = *Foreign Correspondence with Marie de Lorraine* (1537-48, ed. M. Wood, Edinburgh, 1923 ; (Pub. Scottish Hist. Soc., 3rd series, Balcarres Papers).

M. D'AUVERGNE = *L'Amant rendu Cordelier à l'Observance d'amour* (XV), poème attribué a Martial d'Auvergne, ed. A. de Montaiglon ; S.A.T.F.

MIR. N.D. = *Miracles de Nostre Dame par personnages* (XIV), ed. G. Paris et U. Robert ; S.A.T.F.

MYSTERES XV = *Mystères et Moralités du ms.* 617 *de Chantilly* (XV), ed. G. Cohen, Paris, 1920 ; (Bibl. du XVᵉ siècle).

PELETIER, ART P. = *L'Art Poétique* de Jacques Peletier du Mans (1555), ed. A. Boulanger, Paris, 1930 ; (Publications de la Faculté des Lettres de Strasbourg, 53).

PLSGR. = Palsgrave, see p. xxv.

PS. LORRAIN = *Lothringischer Psalter* (XIV²), ed. F. Apfelstedt, Heilbronn, 1881 ; (Altfr. Bibl. iv).

RABELAIS = *Oeuvres* de François Rabelais (XVI¹), éd. critique sous la direction d'Abel Lefranc, Paris.

REGNIER = *Les Fortunes et Adversitez* de Jean Regnier (XV), ed. E. Droz ; S.A.T.F.

RONSARD = *Oeuvres complètes* de P. de Ronsard (XVI²), ed. P. Blanchemain, Paris.

RYMER, A.N.

ST. JOAN = *St. Joan of Orleans*, scenes from the fifteenth century *Mystère du Siège d'Orléans*, selected and edited by J. Evans and P. Studer, Oxford, 1926.

VILLON = *Oeuvres* de François Villon (XV), ed. Auguste Longnon ; 3rd edit. rev. par L. Foulet ; Class. Fr. No. 2.

YEAR BOOKS, A.N.

CHRONOLOGICAL LIST OF MIDDLE AND EARLY MODERN FRENCH GRAMMARIANS.

LINGUISTIC WORKS.

Select chronological list of Grammatical Treatises compiled before the end of the seventeenth century.

A. Treatises composed in England for the English.

Late Thirteenth Century,

TRACT. ORTH. : *Tractatus Orthographiae* of T. H. Parisii Studentis, ed. M. K. Pope, *Modern Language Review*, V, pp. 185-193.
ORTH. GALL. : *Orthographia Gallica*, ed. Stürzinger, 1884 (Altfrz. Bibliothek, VIII).

Middle French.

COYFURELLY : *Tractatus Orthographiae* (a re-casting of the work of T.H.), ed. Stengel, *Zts. nfrz. Spr. u. Lit.* I, pp. 16-22.
BARTON, Jean : *Donait François*, c. 1400, ed. Stengel, *ibid.*, pp. 25-187.
BARCLEY, Alexander : *Introductory to write and pronounce Frenche*, London, 1521 (ed. in part by Ellis in his work *On Early English pronunciation with especial reference to Shakespere and Chaucer*, London, 1870).
PALSGRAVE, Jean : *Lesclarcissement de la Langue Francoyse*, 1530 ; reprinted by Génin in *Documents inédits de l'histoire de France*, Paris, 1852.
DEWES, Giles (de Vadis) : *An Introductorie for to lerne to rede, to pronounce and to speke French trewly*, 1532.
ST. LIENS : Claudii a Sancto Vinculo, *De pronuntiatione linguae gallicae libri duo*, Londini, 1580.

B. Treatises written and published in France.

Sixteenth Century.

1521.   FABRI, Pierre (of Rouen) : *Le second livre de vraye rethorique*, Rouen.
1528.   ERASMUS : *De recta latini graecique sermonis pronunciatione*.
1529.   TORY, Geoffrey (of Bourges) : *Champfleury auquel est contenu lart et science de la deue et vraye proportion des lettres Attiques, quon dit autrement lettres antiques, et vulgairement lettres romaines, proportionnees selon le corps et visage humain*, Paris.
1531.   SYLVIUS, Jacobus (Jacques Dubois of Amiens) : *In linguam gallicam Isagoge una cum eiusdem grammatica latino-gallica, ex Hebraeis, Graecis et Latinis authoribus*, Paris.

1540. DOLET, Estienne (of Orléans) : *Les accents de la langue françoyse*, Paris.
1542. MEIGRET, Loys (of Lyons) : *Traité touchant le commun usage de l'escriture françoise* and *Le tretté de la grammère françoèze*, 1550, re-edited by W. Förster, Heilbronn, 1888.
1548. GUILLAUME DES AUTELS, cf. Thurot, I, p. xxviii.
1549. ESTIENNE, R. : *Dictionaire François-latin, contenant les motz et manieres de parler François, tournez en Latin*, Paris, 1539 (enlarged and corrected in 1549) ; *Traicté de la grammaire françoise*, 1569, Paris.
1549. PELETIER, Jacques (du Mans) : *Dialogue de l'ortografe é prononciacion françoèse, departi en deus livres*, Lyons.
1562. RAMUS, Pierre (of Cuth, Vermandois) : *Gramère ; Grammaire de P. de la Ramee, lecteur du roy en L'Université de Paris*, 1572.
1568. MEURIER, cf. Thurot, I, p. xxxiii.
1582. ESTIENNE, H. : *Traicté de la conformité du langage françois auec le grec*, reprinted by L. Feugère in 1853 ; *Deux Dialogues du nouueau langage françois italianizé et autrement desguizé, principalement entre les courtisans de ce temps*, Genève, 1578, re-edited by Ristelhuber, Paris, 1885 ; *Projet du livre intitulé de la Precellence du langage françois*, 1579, reprinted by L. Feugère in 1850 and by E. Huguet in 1896, Paris.
1584. BÈZE, Théodore (of Vézelay) : *De Francicae linguae recta pronuntiatione*, Genevae, reprinted by Tobler, Berlin, 1868.
1587. TABOUROT, Estienne (of Dijon) : *Dictionnaire des rimes françoises ; Les Bigarrures et touches du seigneur des Accords auec les Apophthegmes du sieur Gaulard et les escraignes dijonnoises*, Rouen, 1616 ; re-edited 1625.
1596. LANOUE, Odet : *Le Dictionnaire des rimes françoises, selon l'ordre des lettres de l'alphabeth. Auquel deux traitez sont ajoustez : L'un des coniugaisons françoises, L'autre, de l'orthographe françoise.*

Seventeenth Century.

1606. MALHERBE (of Caen) : Annotations on the work of Desportes, printed in vol. IV of Lalanne's edition of the *Oeuvres de Malherbe* (Paris, 1862) ; cf. also Brunot, F. : *La Doctrine de Malherbe*, Paris, 1891.
1625. MAUPAS, Charles (of Blois) : *Grammaire et Syntaxe françoise, contenant reigles bien exactes et certaines de la prononciation, orthographe, construction et usage de nostre langue en faveur des estrangiers qui en sont desireux.* English translation by AWFEILD, W., London, 1634.
1632. MARTIN, Daniel (of Sedan) : *Grammatica Gallica sententiosis exemplis ceu fragrantibus floribus referta.*
1633. OUDIN, Antoine : *Grammaire françoise rapportée au langage du temps.*
1647. VAUGELAS, Claude (of Chambéry) : *Remarques sur la langue françoise, utiles a ceux qui veulent bien parler et bien escrire*, reprinted by A. Chassang, Paris, 1880.
1659. CHIFFLET, Laurent (of Besançon) : *Essay d'une parfaite grammaire de la langue françoise*, Anvers.
1673. CAHIERS : *Cahiers de remarques sur l'orthographe françoise pour estre examinez par chacun des Messieurs de l'Académie*, ed. by Ch. Marty Laveaux, Paris, 1863.
1674. BOUHOURS, Dominique : *Remarques nouvelles sur la langue françoise ; Suite des Remarques nouvelles sur la langue françoise*, 3rd edit., 1682.
1687. HINDRET, J. : *L'art de bien prononcer et de bien parler la langue françoise.*
1694. DIC. ACAD. : *Le Dictionnaire de l'Académie françoise.*
1694. DANGEAU, cf. Thurot, I, p. lxxi.
1696. DE LA TOUCHE, cf. Thurot, I, p. lxxii.
[For full list, cf. Thurot, I, pp. v-lxxiii.]

BIBLIOGRAPHY

Modern Linguistic Works—General.

(For monographs, cf. sections dealing with the subject.)

APPEL = *Provenzalische Lautlehre*, von C. Appel, Leipzig, 1908.

BEARDWOOD = *Rhymed Latin and French Words in Old French*, by J. Beardwood, Diss. Philadelphia, 1930.

BEAULIEUX = *Histoire de l'Orthographe Française*, par Charles Beaulieux, Paris, 1927.

BEHRENS = *Unorganische Lautvertretung innerhalb der formalen Entwicklung des frz. Verbalstammes*, von D. Behrens, Heilbronn, 1882 ; (Frz. St. III, 6).

BRUNOT, cf. H.L.F.

CHATELAIN = *Recherches sur le Vers Français au xve siècle*, par H. Chatelain, Paris, 1908.

DAUZAT = *Histoire de la Langue Française*, par A. Dauzat, Paris, 1930.

DREVIN = *Die frz. Sprachelemente in den lateinischen Urkunden des 11ten und 12ten Jahrhunderts (aus Hte. Bretagne und Maine)*, von H. Drevin, Halle, 1912.

EWERT = *The French Language*, by A. Ewert, London, 1933.

FOUCHÉ = *Le Verbe Français, Etude Morphologique*, Paris, 1931 ; (Publications de la Faculté des Lettres de l'Université de Strasbourg, No. 56).

GG. = *An Introduction to Vulgar Latin*, by C. H. Grandgent, Boston, 1907.

GOERLICH, N.W. = *Die Nordwestlichen Dialekte der Langue d'Oïl*, von E. Goerlich, Heilbronn, 1886.

H.L.F. = *Histoire de la Langue Française des Origines à 1900*, par F. Brunot, Paris, 1924 ff. ; vol. I, Old and Early Middle French ; vol. II, Sixteenth Century ; vols. III and IV, Seventeenth Century.

JONES = *Outlines of English Phonetics*, by Daniel Jones, London, 1932.

JORDAN = *Altfrz. Elementarbuch*, von L. Jordan, Bielefeld u. Leipzig, 1923.

JURET = *Manuel de Phonétique Latine*, Paris, 1921.

KASTNER = *A History of French Versification*, by L. E. Kastner, Oxford, 1903.

LINDSAY = *The Latin Language*, by W. M. Lindsay, Oxford, 1894.

LONGNON = *Les Noms de Lieu de la France, Résumé des Conférences d'Auguste Longnon*, ed. P. Maréchal et L. Mirot, Paris, 1920-29.

MARCHOT, PH. = *Petite Phonétique du Français Prélittéraire*, Fribourg, 1901.

MATZKE, L MOUILLÉ = *Dialektische Eigentümlichkeiten in der Entwicklung des Mouillierten L im Altfrz.*, von J. E. Matzke, P.M.L.A., V.

MEILLET E.L.L. = *Esquisse d'une Histoire de la Langue Latine*, par A. Meillet, Paris, 1928.

MEILLET LG. HIST. = *Linguistique Historique et Linguistique Générale*, par A. Meillet, Paris, 1921.

MILLARDET = *Linguistique et Dialectologie Romanes, Problèmes et Méthodes*, par G. Millardet, Montpellier et Paris, 1923.

M.L. EINF. = *Einführung in das Studium der Rom. Sprachwissenschaft*, von W. Meyer-Lübke, Heidelberg, 1909².

M.L. GR. = *Historische Grammatik der frz. Sprache*, von W. Meyer-Lübke, vol. I, Laut- und Flexionslehre, Heidelberg, 1908.

NYROP MAN. = *Manuel Phonétique du Français Parlé*, par K. Nyrop, tr. et remanié par E. Philipot, 1914³.

NYROP GR. = *Grammaire Historique de la Langue Française*, par K. Nyrop ; vol. I, Phonétique, Copenhague, 1904² ; vol. II, Morphologie, Copenhague, 1903.

PARIS MÉL. = *Mélanges Linguistiques*, publiés par M. Roques, Paris, 1909.

RISOP STUDIEN = *Studien zur Geschichte der frz. Konjugation auf -ir*, von A. Risop, Halle, 1891.

ROSSET = *Les Origines de la Prononciation Moderne, étudiées au XVIIᵉ siècle*, par T. Rosset, Paris, 1911.

ROUSSELOT = *Principes de Phonétique Expérimentale*, par Rousselot, Paris, 1897-1908.

RYDBERG = *Zur Geschichte des frz. ə*, von G. Rydberg, Uppsala, 1907.

SCHWAN-BEHRENS = *Geschichte des Altfranzösischen*, von E. Schwan, neubearbeitet von D. Behrens, 1914¹⁰.

SUCHIER GR. = *Altfrz. Grammatik*, von H. Suchier, Halle, 1893.

SUCHIER PROV. = *Die frz. und prov. Sprache und ihre Mundarten*, von H. Suchier, Strasburg, 1906 ; (Sonderabdruck aus dem Grundriss der Rom. Philologie).

THOMAS, E. = *Essais de Philologie Française*, par A. Thomas, Paris, 1897.

THOMAS, N.E. = *Nouveaux Essais de Philologie Française*, Paris, 1904.

THUROT = *De la Prononciation Française depuis le commencement du XVIᵉ siècle*, d'après les Témoignages des Grammairiens, par Ch. Thurot, Paris, 1881.

TOBLER MÉL. = *Mélanges de Grammaire Française*, traduction fr. par M. Kuttner et L. Sudre de la deuxième édition des ' *Vermischte Beiträge I* ' d'Adolf Tobler, Paris, 1905.

VENDRYES = *Le Langage*, par J. Vendryes, Paris, 1921.

VOSSLER = *Frankreichs Kultur im Spiegel seiner Sprachentwicklung*, von K. Vossler, Heidelberg, 1913.

WAHLGREN (W.) ET. = *Etude sur les Actions Analogiques Réciproques du Parfait et du Participe Passé*, par E. Wahlgren, Uppsala, 1920.

WAHLGREN PARFAITS FAIBLES = *Observations sur les Verbes à Parfaits Faibles*, Uppsala, 1931.

ZACHRISSON = *A contribution to the study of A.N. influence on English place-names*, by R. Zachrisson, Lund, 1909.

Collected Papers.

BECKER VOL. = *Hauptfragen der Romanistik*, Festschrift für Ph. Aug. Becker, Heidelberg, 1922.

VISING VOL. = *Mélanges de Philologie* offerts à Johan Vising, Göteborg, 1925.

Dictionaries.

BLOCH = *Dictionnaire Etymologique de la Langue Française*, par O. Bloch avec la collaboration de W. von Wartburg, Paris, 1932.

GAMILLSCHEG = *Etymologisches Wb. der frz. Sprache*, von E. Gamillscheg, Heidelberg, 1928.

GF. = *Dictionnaire de l'Ancien Français*, par F. Godefroy, Paris, 1881-1902.

HUGUET = *Dictionnaire de la Langue Française du seizième siècle*, par E. Huguet, Paris, 1925-

TOBLER-LOMMATZSCH = *Altfranzösisches Wörterbuch*, Berlin, 1925-

WARTBURG = *Frz. Etymologisches Wb.* : Eine Darstellung des gallo-romanischen Sprachschatzes, von Walther von Wartburg, Bonn, 1928-

Periodicals.

ARCH. ROM. = *Archivum Romanicum*, ed. Giulio Bertoni, Genève.

KR. JB. = *Kritischer Jahresbericht über die Fortschritte der romanischen Philologie*, ed. K. Vollmöller, 1892-98.

MEM. SOC. LG. PAR. = *Mémoires de la Société Linguistique de Paris.*
M.L.R. = *Modern Language Review,* Cambridge, 1906-
PUB. M.L.A. = *Publications of the Modern Language Association of America,*
    ed. J. W. Bright, Baltimore, 1885-
R. LG. R. = *Revue de Linguistique Romane,* Paris, 1925-
REV. L.R. = *Revue des Langues Romanes,* Montpellier et Paris, 1870-
R.P.F. = *Revue de Philologie Française et de Littérature,* p.p. L. Clédat et
    J. Gilliéron, Paris.
ROM. = *Romania,* Paris, 1872-
ZTS. FRZ. SPR. = *Zeitschrift für (neu)französische Sprache und Literatur,*
    Oppeln, 1879-
ZTS. ROM. PH. = *Zeitschrift für romanische Philologie,* Halle, 1876-

SUPPLEMENTARY BIBLIOGRAPHY

THE following list includes some of the most important publications which have
appeared since 1934 in the fields covered by the present work. Further
bibliographical indications will be found in *The Year's Work in Modern
Language Studies* (Oxford, 1931-35 ; Cambridge, 1936-) ; R. L. Wagner,
Introduction à la linguistique française (Société de publications romanes et
françaises, XXVII, Lille and Geneva, 1947) ; *Où en sont les études de français,*
ed. A. Dauzat (2nd ed., Paris, 1949) ; G. Rohlfs, *Romanische Philologie,
Teil 1 : Allgemeine Romanistik ; Französische und provenzalische Philologie*
(Heidelberg, 1950).

General Linguistics.

BALLY, Ch. *Linguistique générale et linguistique française,* 2nd ed., Berne,
    1944.
BATTISTI, C. *Fonetica generale,* Milan, 1938.
BLOOMFIELD, L. *Language,* revised ed., New York, 1946.
GRAMMONT, M. *Traité de phonétique,* 3rd ed., Paris, 1946.
GRAY, L. H. *The Foundations of Language,* New York, 1939.
JABERG, K. *Aspects géographiques du langage,* Paris, 1936.
MAROUZEAU, J. *Lexique de la terminologie linguistique,* 2nd ed., Paris, 1943.
MAROUZEAU, J. *La Linguistique ou science du langage,* 2nd ed., Paris, 1944.
MEILLET, A., and others. 'Le Langage,' in *Encyclopédie française,* vol. i,
    pt. 2, Paris, 1937.
STURTEVANT, E. H. *An Introduction to Linguistic Science,* New Haven, 1948.
WARTBURG, W. von. *Problèmes et méthodes de la linguistique,* Paris, 1946.

Late Latin and Romance.

BOURCIEZ, E. *Eléments de linguistique romane,* 4th ed., Paris, 1946.
IORDAN, I., and ORR, J. *An Introduction to Romance Linguistics,* London,
    1937.

FOUCHÉ, P. 'De quelques changements de quantité dans le latin parlé,'
    Mélanges de philologie romane offerts à Ernest Hoepffner, Paris, 1949.
MEIER, H. *Die Entstehung der romanischen Sprachen und Nationen,* Frankfurt,
    1941.
PERROCHAT, P. *Pétrone, Le Festin de Trimalcion : Commentaire exégétique et
    critique,* Paris, 1939.
VÄÄNÄNEN, V. *Le Latin des inscriptions pompéiennes,* Helsinki, 1937.
WARTBURG, W. von. *Les Origines des peuples romans,* Paris, 1941.

General Evolution of French.

BRUNOT, F., and BRUNEAU, Ch.   *Précis de grammaire historique de la langue française*, 3rd ed., Paris, 1949.
COHEN, M.   *Histoire d'une langue : le français*, Paris, 1947.
DAUZAT, A.   *Le Génie de la langue française*, Paris, 1943.
WARTBURG, W. von.   *Evolution et structure de la langue française*, 3rd ed., Berne, 1946.

Early History and Regional Features.

ALESSIO, G.   *Le Origini del francese : introduzione alla grammatica storica*, Florence, 1946.

BOLELLI, T.   ' Le voci di origine gallica del Romanisches etymologisches Wörterbuch di W. Meyer-Lübke,' *L'Italia Dialettale*, xvii (1941), 133-194 ; xviii (1942), 33-74, 203-207.
BRUN, A.   ' Linguistique et peuplement,' *Revue de Linguistique romane*, xii (1936), 165-251.
BRUN, A.   *Parlers régionaux : France dialectale et unité française*, Paris and Toulouse, 1946.
DAUZAT, A.   *La Toponymie française*, revised ed., Paris, 1946.
GRENIER, A.   *Les Gaulois*, Paris, 1945.
MULLER, H. F.   *L'Epoque mérovingienne : essai de synthèse de philologie et d'histoire*, New York, 1945.
REMACLE, L.   *Le Problème de l'ancien wallon*, Liége, 1948.
WARTBURG, W. von.   *Bibliographie des dictionnaires patois*, Paris, 1934.

Early Phonetic Developments.

BRUNEAU, Ch.   ' La Diphtongaison des voyelles françaises,' *Zeitschrift für romanische Philologie*, lvii (1937), 170-192.
FOUCHÉ, P.   ' Diphtongaison et tendances phonétiques,' *Archives néerlandaises de phonétique expérimentale*, viii (1933), 247 ff.
FOUCHÉ, P.   ' De l'action dilatrice du yod en gallo-roman,', I, *Revue des Langues romanes*, lxviii (1937-39), 1-64 ; II, *Romania*, lxvii (1942-43), 433-490.
RHEINFELDER, H.   *Altfranzösische Grammatik*, I : *Lautlehre*, Munich, 1937.
RICHTER, E.   *Beiträge zur Geschichte der Romanismen*, I : *Chronologische Phonetik des Französischen bis zum Ende des 8. Jahrhunderts*, Halle, 1934.
VERRIER, P.   ' Origine et évolution des anciennes diphtongues françaises,' *Romania*, lxii (1936), 289-301.

The Earliest Texts.

EWERT, A.   ' The Strasbourg Oaths,' *Transactions of the Philological Society*, 1935, 16-35.
LOT, F.   ' Le Dialecte roman des Serments de Strasbourg,' *Romania*, lxv (1939), 145-163.
ROQUES, M.   ' Les Serments de Strasbourg,' *Medium Aevum*, v (1936), 157-172.

LINSKILL, J.   *Saint Léger, Étude de la langue du ms. de Clermont-Ferrand, suivie d'une édition critique du texte avec commentaire et glossaire*, Paris, 1937.

STOREY, C. *Saint Alexis, Étude de la langue du ms. de Hildesheim, suivie d'une édition critique du texte d'après le ms.* L, Paris, 1934.

WEERENBECK, B. J. H. ' Le Système vocalique français du XIe siècle, d'après les assonances de la *Vie de Saint Alexis*,' *Archives néerlandaises de phonétique expérimentale*, viii (1933), 252-262.

Later History of French.

STREICHER, J. *Vaugelas, ' Remarques sur la langue françoise' : Fac-similé de l'édition originale, avec introduction, bibliographie et index,* Paris, 1934.

STREICHER, J. *Commentaires sur les ' Remarques ' de Vaugelas,* Paris, 1936.

Collected Papers.

GAMILLSCHEG, E. *Ausgewählte Aufsätze*, Supplementheft XV der Zeitschrift für französische Sprache, Jena and Leipzig, 1937.
  Especially : ' Beiträge zur Geschichte der Romanismen ' ; ' Zum romanischen Artikel und Possessivpronomen ' ; ' Zur sprachlichen Gliederung Frankreichs ' ; ' Zur u > ü-Frage ' ; ' Zum französischen h-Laut ' ; ' Uber Lautsubstitution '.

HUGUET, E. *Mélanges offerts à E. H.*, Paris, 1940.
  Especially : Ch. Beaulieux, ' L'Orthographe de Montaigne ' ; J. Bourciez, ' La Triphtongue ou diphtongue *eau* en fr. et spécialement au 16e siècle ' ; N. Dupire, ' Le Suffixe latin *-alis* en fr.'

MELANDER, J. *Mélanges de philologie offerts à M. J. M.*, Uppsala, 1943.
  Especially : T. Sävborg, ' Les Sources de la préposition *dès* ' ; R. Ekblom, ' Die Wörter vom Typus *spatulam > épaule*.'

POPE, M. K. *Studies Presented to M. K. P.*, Manchester, 1939.

ROQUES, M. *Études romanes dédiées à M. R.*, Société de publications romanes et françaises, XXV, Paris, 1946.
  Especially : J. Vendryes, ' Sur le Suffixe *-is* du fr. ' ; A. Ernout, ' Les Noms latins en *-tus* ' ; C. Brunel, ' Le Préfixe *ca-* dans le vocabulaire picard.'

Dictionaries.

MEYER-LÜBKE, W. *Romanisches Etymologisches Wörterbuch*, 3rd ed., Heidelberg, 1935.

DAUZAT, A. *Dictionnaire étymologique de la langue française*, 3rd. ed., Paris, 1946.

Periodicals.

Archivum Linguisticum : A Review of Comparative Philology, Glasgow, 1949-.
Lingua : Revue internationale de linguistique générale, Haarlem, 1947-.
Romance Philology, Berkeley and Los Angeles, 1947-.
Studia Linguistica : Revue de linguistique générale et comparée, Lund, 1947-.
Vox Romanica, Zürich, 1936-.

ADDENDA

§ 17. For recent divergent views on the significance of the place-
names mentioned in this paragraph, cf. the article of F. Lot :
' De l'Origine et de la Signification Historique et Linguistique
des Noms de Lieu en -ville et en -court,' *Rom.* LIX, pp. 194-246.

§ 21. Cf. M. Pei, *The Language of the Eighth Century Texts in Northern,
France*, New York, 1932.

§ 47. On the use of French in the South, cf. A. Brun, *Recherches
Historiques sur l'Introduction du Français dans les Provinces
du Midi*, Paris, 1923.

§§ 126-132. For a fuller treatment of the processes *Assimilation, Dissimilation
Differentiation*, cf. M. Grammont, *Traité de Phonétique*, Part II,
sections II, III, VI.

§ 324, l. 1. *add* (cf. Meyer-Lübke, *Zts. Rom. Ph.* XLV).

§ 341 (i), l. 3. insert **džǫu** > *before* **džu.**

p. 159, l. 4. *after monsieur* insert ; *piqueur* (hunting-term), *rebouteur.*

§ 425. For a fuller account of the raising influence exercised by the
tongue-position of nasal consonants on vowels, cf. M. Grammont, *Traité de Phonétique*, pp. 217-222.

§ 449. For a variant explanation of the forms *faner, ramer*, etc., cf.
Brüch, *Zts. Fr. Spr.* LVI, pp. 359, 360.

§ 759, l. 27. *add after* *sias, etc. [but cf. J. U. Hubschmied, *Zts. Rom. Phil.
Beiheft* 58, 6.]

§ 931, l. 8. *insert after* (F. 61 ; Mgr. p. 110 : " *mettons, mettez* . . . l'*e* se tourne
en *e* clos e brief . . . de sorte qe nou' ne dizon' pas *mẹttons,
mẹttez* ").

§ 938, ll. 16, 17. *after* colgant *add* **koldžänt** and *after* jugant *add* **džüdžänt.**

p. 405, l. 2. *add after* M. mětons, cf. above § 931, l. 8.

§ 1232, l. 6. *add* The graphical similarity of *c* and *t* contributed to the confusion of these symbols.

p. 483 : *under Middle XII, after* V. 61. Gaimar *add* V. 331. Leis
Guillaume, ed. Matzke.

p. 486. For modern patois, cf. also A. Dauzat, *Histoire de la Langue
Française*, 550-564.

§ 1320, l. 1. *add after* Rom. xvii-xix, Jean Haust, *Dictionnaire liégeois.*

p. 487, § iii, l. 4. *add after* § 636, and cf. Barbier, Notes on Germanic initial **w** in
French, *Zts. Fr. Spr.* liii, pp. 1-25, lv, pp. 385-424, lvi,
pp. 210-233, 333-358).

§ 1321 (xviii), l. 3. *in bracket read* (cf. § 1028 and Suchier, article there cited).

p. 551, col. 2. *insert a new entry after* ea :
ẹau, 388, 538, 539, 540, A.N. 1165, N. § viii.

p. 565, col. 1, l. 9. *insert entry :*
Present Tenses : radical, cf. Pt. IV, chap. 4, sections 8-10,
A.N. 1311 ; terms. : pres. ind. 887-902 ; pres. subj. 903-
910, A.N. 1266, 1272-1276, 1283, 1293-1303 ; anomalous
forms, 951-963 ; dial. variants : N. §§ xxviii, xxix,
E. §§ xxvi, xxix, xxxi, S.C. §§ xvi, xviii, xix, xx,
W. §§ xv, xvii ; cf. infixes, syllabic and vocalic alterna-
tion, first, second and third person.

p. 571, col. 1. *insert before* Weak perfects, *entries :*
wẹ, wẽ, cf. **uẹ, uẽ.**
wẽ : source, 476 ; devel. 476.
insert at end of column, entry :
wĩ : sources, 514 ; date 515 ; devel. 515, 516, A.N. 1160 ;
dial., 517.

PART I.

EXTERNAL HISTORY OF THE LANGUAGE.

CHAPTER I.

LATE LATIN.

Meillet, A. : *Esquisse d'une Histoire de la Langue Latine*, Paris, 1928.
Grandgent, C. H. : *An Introduction to Vulgar Latin*, Boston, 1907.
Hofmann, J. B. : *Lateinische Umgangssprache*, Heidelberg, 1926.
Marouzeau, J. : *Le Latin*, Toulouse and Paris, 2nd ed., 1907.

Section 1.—Classical and Vulgar Latin.

§ 1. In 120 B.C. South-East Gaul was constituted a Roman Province : *Gallia Transalpina ;* seventy years later, by 51 B.C., Caesar had completed the conquest of North Gaul, and out of the later acquisitions there were constituted by Augustus the three provinces, *Aquitania, Gallia Lugdunensis (la Lyonnaise)* and *Gallia Belgica,* in 27 B.C.

'Peaceful penetration' had preceded military occupation, and Romanisation was rapid : 'Dans le siècle qui suivit la conquête de César . . . la vie en Gaule se transforme à l'instar de Rome : il se crée une société gallo-romaine, qui pour l'habitation, le costume, l'embellissement des villes et le service des routes, même pour les mœurs et pour l'esprit est plus romaine que gauloise.' (Vendryes, *R. Lg. ˙R.* I, 266.) The schools established early in Narbonne, Arles, Vienne, Toulouse, Lyons, Autun and Bordeaux, and later on in all the larger towns, were mainly attended by young nobles, but inscriptions show that the corporations of merchants, i.e. the trading class, adopted Latin rapidly also ; in the rural districts the use of Celtic lingered on, but by the fifth century it appears to have died out completely, even in the remote country districts.[1]

---

[1] The survival of the Gallic language into the third century is attested by a passage in the *Digesta* of Ulpian, composed between 222 and 228 : ' Fideicommissa quocumque sermone relinqui possunt, non solum Latina vel Graeca, sed etiam Punica vel Gallicana vel alterius cujuscumque gentis ' (31. 11). St. Jerome's comparison of the language of the Treviri to the language of the Galatians (*Ep. ad Galat.*, Migne, *Patrologia*, xxvi, col. 357*a*), appears to indicate that in the vicinity of Trèves Celtic was still in use at the end of the fourth century (cf. Vendryes, ' Celtique et Roman,' *R. Lg. R.* I, 268-270). Breton, the Celtic speech of Brittany (Armorica), is a fifth-century importation from Great Britain, and is consequently closely related to Cornish and Welsh (cf. J. V. Hubschmied, *Teuthonista* 19, p. 186).

§ 2. Officially the language introduced in the wake of the conquest was the written language of Rome, the language of law, literature and education. The inscriptions of Gaul, from the time of Augustus and Tiberius on, are for the most part couched in a Latin as correct as Italian ones of the same period. In Gaul, however, as in Italy and the other parts of the Roman Empire, the official written language is not the only form of Latin in use. With the constitution of 'literary' Latin in the third century B.C. archaic Latin necessarily bifurcated. Side by side with the new development of the Latin that was to become the language of Caesar, Cicero and Vergil, the real 'urbanitas,' our 'classical' Latin, there lived on unfettered, unimpeded in development, the older uncultivated Latin, the plainer, humbler speech of everyday life, the *lingua quotidiana, usualis, rusticalis, vulgaris*, the Latin from which French and all the other Romance languages are derived. This Vulgar Latin, as it is termed, is of infinite shade and variety, varying from the colloquial usage of the educated (exemplified in a polished form in Cicero's letters, and later in the Christian fathers) to the 'patois' of the country dweller or the vulgarity of the baser sort, a Latin as free and picturesque, unconstrained and simple in structure as its counterpart, the precisely regulated and defined language of the rhetoricians, orators and poets, is ultra-conservative, jealously guarded, balanced and complex.

§ 3. Some such bifurcation of language indeed is familiar to all of us : it is the necessary concomitant of the development of a great literature and is exemplified to a greater or less degree in all modern civilised countries. The use of a language by the great poets and thinkers, the forging of a tool to represent the deeper thoughts, aspirations and emotions of men of genius, must inevitably lead to a differentiation of the language of a nation, and the rise of an educated class jealously anxious to maintain the standard and preserve the traditions set, must also infallibly deepen the breach, because their natural conservatism opposes a barrier to those newer developments that find free course in the speech of the people. 'La langue parlée,' writes one of the French classical scholars of to-day, 'vit et se transforme, la langue littéraire se fixe et meurt.' (Marouzeau, 'Notes sur la formation du latin classique,' *Mém. Soc. Lg. Par.* xxii, 263.)

§ 4. Several causes, however, combined to make the difference between the two types of language exceptionally wide in the days of the later Roman Empire :—

    (i) The influence under which the literary language was created.
    (ii) The rigidity of tradition.
    (iii) The history of the Empire.

(i) In most countries the literary language is a slow elaboration of the native speech, out of which it is gradually created by the genius and persistent efforts of the great thinkers, poets and artists of phrase. In Rome—and this from the very outset—violence was done to the native tradition and foreign influence was dominant, for its literature arose not spontaneously but under Greek influence.[1] The alphabet is Greek; Greek influence is traceable in the almost sacred language of the early law; and from the third century on, from the time of Ennius and his school, subjugated by the splendour of the Greek civilisation, philosophers, poets, orators, rhetoricians, grammarians put themselves literally to school with Greece, endeavouring by all means in their power to change their rather simple, straightforward, uncouth speech into a language that could at a bound rival the complexity and subtlety, the cadencies and harmonies, the elegance and decorations of the Greek poets and philosophers, and most of all of the later Greek rhetoricians, their contemporaries.

True it is that in France of the sixteenth century the poets and thinkers were strongly influenced by the splendour of classical Latin, and that Rabelais and Ronsard, Amyot and Montaigne go to school with the classics and forge a language that is far removed from the speech of the unlearned, but (a) the influence of Latin on French—its lineal descendant—is less foreign than that to which archaic Latin was subjected, (b) owing to the influence of the Church and of education it was more pervasive of all ranks of society, and lastly (c) the influence was brought to bear on the language only when the native idiom had for generations been exercised in literary composition, and had already gained an individuality too strong to be overridden.

(ii) The second factor that contributed to emphasise the difference between the language of law and letters and that of the everyday life of the people was the jealous care with which the classical tradition was guarded. Rhetoricians and grammarians strove to uphold the 'purity' of the language, and education was largely a training in grammar and rhetoric. Neologism, provincialism and vulgarism were held equally blamable and in vocabulary and turn of sentence, as much as or more than in pronunciation, the written usage came to differ from the spoken. The position of things in modern French, the language which most has reproduced the Latin fixity of tradition, in which, according to competent opinion:[2] 'Langue écrite et langue parlée sont tellement éloignées l'une de l'autre qu'on ne parle jamais comme l'on écrit et qu'on écrit rarement comme on parle,' affords in this respect a close parallel to the relative position of written and spoken Latin in the later days of the

---

[1] Monceau, *Rev. deux Mondes*, lxi, p. 432; Marouzeau, pp. 111-119; Meillet, *E.L.L. passim.*

[2] Vendryes, *Le Langage*, p. 171.

Empire. The traditional language had become alien to some extent to
the newer outlook ; then as now people turned from the older, stereotyped words, forms and constructions to secure more direct, emotional
and vivid methods of speech.

(iii) Lastly, the vast extension of the Roman Empire in its later days,
its contact with peoples of varied character and language and the
acquirement of Latin by these tended directly to weaken linguistic
tradition wherever it was not reinforced by school training, and this
contributed not only to the expansion of the vocabulary but also to the
modification of pronunciation and even more to the simplification of
the flexional system. Rarely do the differences show themselves in the
Latin documents, for all who learned to write were trained also in
spelling and grammar, but it is almost impossible not to believe that in
the later days of the Empire there were as many varieties of vocabulary,
of shades of 'accent,' of slight modifications of sounds and intonations
as there were provinces, just as there are, in the course of a much shorter
period, already 'colonial accents' of every type in the British Common-
wealth ; impossible not to believe also that much of the complication
of the older flexional system was being jettisoned in speech. 'Servant
en quelque sorte de *lingua franca* à un grand empire, le latin a tendu à
se simplifier, à garder surtout ce qu'il avait de banal . . . le latin
vulgaire est devenu quelque chose que les hommes les plus variés et les
moins cultivés pouvaient manier, un outil commode, bon pour toutes
mains . . . le verbe a changé de structure, le nom, de caractère, et il
est résulté de là une construction différente de la phrase. Sans que
l'aspect extérieur de la langue se soit beaucoup modifié, le latin est devenu
au cours de l'époque impériale une langue nouvelle.' (Meillet, *E.L.L.*
pp. 270, 273.)

§ 5. The extent to which the vocabulary of the educated was at times influenced
by the colloquial usage, even in the early days of the Empire, is illustrated interest-
ingly by the account that Suetonius gives us of the usage of Augustus: 'He
cultivated a style of speaking that was chaste and elegant, avoiding the vanity of
an artificial order . . . making it his chief aim to express his thought as clearly as
possible. With this end in view he did not hesitate to use prepositions with names
of cities, nor to repeat conjunctions several times, the omission of which causes
some obscurity, though it adds grace. . . . That in his everyday conversation he
used certain favourite and peculiar expressions appears from letters in his own
hand. . . . ' Urging his correspondent to put up with present circumstances, such
as they are, he says: 'Let's be satisfied with the Cato we have'; and to express
the speed of a hasty action : 'quicker than you can cook asparagus'. He continually used *baceolus* (dolt) for *stultus* (fool), *pulleiaceus* (darkish) for *pullus* (dark) and
vacerrosus (blockhead) for *cerritus* (mad) ; also *vapide se habere* (feel flat) for *male se
habere* (feel badly) and *betizare* (be like a beet) for *languere* (be weak), for which the
vulgar term is *lachanizare*.' (Vol. I, Bk. II, chaps. 86 and 87, Loeb Library
Translation.)

Here we have in germ the main tendencies of later colloquial speech : the premium set on direct intelligibility, the preference for the longer, heavier forms, the pursuit of the striking and picturesque and the willingness to accept formations of foreign origin.

Section 2.—LOCAL DIFFERENTIATION.

§ 6. The amount of influence exercised by the linguistic substrata of the conquered countries on Latin and the extent of local differentiation thus produced in the language, are far from being determined with any certainty.

Vocabulary.—The stock of *loan-words* undoubtedly differed from province to province, varying with the speech of the conquered peoples.   In the countries inhabited by a predominantly Celtic population (Rhaetia, Gaul and Northern Italy), a considerable number of Celtic words were taken up ; the majority of these were place-names, but there were also words denoting natural features, customs, apparel, implements and some others.   A few of these loan-words gained currency in other parts of the Empire, e.g. **alauda, *braca, *camminus, *carrum, *pettia*, but the greater number were restricted to the Celtic-speaking countries.

Examples of Celtic loan-words in French are :—

arpent $<$ *arepennis* (**arependis*), *brueil* $<$ **brogilum*, *bruiiere* $<$ **bruc-aria*, *charue* $<$ **carruca, choan* $<$ **cavannum, changier* $<$ **cambiare, encombrer* $<$ **combros, lieue* $<$ **leuga, vassal* $<$ **vassallum, veltre* $<$ **vertrăgum.*

Cf. also the place-names formed with *dunum* (mountain), e.g. *Verdun, Laon, Lyon ;* with *dŭrum* (fortress), e.g. *Auxerre* (O.F. *Aucuerre* $<$ *Altessiŏdŭrum*) ; with *brĭga* (fortress), e.g. *Deneuvres* and *Denevre* (O.F. *Denuevre* $<$ *Donŏbrĭga*), *Escaudoeuvres* ($<$ *Scaldŏbrĭga*) ; with *măgos* (field), e.g. *Caen* (O.F. *Cauem* $<$ *Catŏmăgos*), *Rouen* (O.F. *Ruuem* $<$ *Rotŏmăgos*) ; and with the suffixes -*ăcum,* -*oiălum*, e.g. *Cambrai* ($<$ *Cameracum*), *Aubigny* ($<$ *Albiniacum*), *Bailleul* ($<$ *Ballioialum*).   Cf. Longnon, *Les Noms de Lieu de la France,* Paris, 1920-29 ; Hölscher, *Die mit dem Suffix* -acum, -iacum *gebildeten frz. Ortsnamen,* Strasbourg, 1890 ; W. Kaspers, *Etymologische Untersuchungen ueber die mit* -acum *gebildeten nordfrz. Ortsnamen,* Halle, 1918.

[For contaminations cf. §§ 748-750.]

According to the latest investigations of the scholars who are in a position to utilise the new linguistic atlases, local differentiation of vocabulary in the later days of the Empire went much further than has hitherto been supposed and affected already very considerably the Latin element of the language as well as the loan-words. 'L'étude de l'histoire des verbes signifiant *éteindre* dans les langues romanes,' writes M. J. Jud, 'nous oblige à admettre qu'au moment où l'Empire romain se désagrégeait, l'unité lexicale du latin de Rome et des provinces était compromise ; les crises qui naissaient dans le latin parlé pouvaient encore être réprimées par la capitale au Ier ou au IIe siècle, grâce à l'obéissance facile des provinces ; mais aux IIIe, IVe et Ve siècles, le latin provincial se soustrayait de plus en plus aux ordres linguistiques venus de la métropole. . . . Le latin de Rome, n'ayant plus réussi à rétablir l'unité lexicale de *l'imperium romanum* . . . laisse une Romania lexicographiquement désorganisée.' (J. Jud, ' Problèmes de Géographie Linguistique Romane,' *R. Lg. R.* I, 235.)

§ 7. *Flexion.*—In the history of flexion, on the other hand, the direct influence of the conquered peoples appears to be very slight ; the important changes of the period being the outcome or continuance of the earlier changes that Latin was undergoing, or the result of the loosening of tradition.   Cf. Meillet : ' Les langues qu'a éliminées l'extension du latin sont multiples et très diverses ; il n'y a pas d'apparence qu'aucune ait joué un rôle particulièrement décisif dans les formes

que le latin a prises au cours de l'époque romaine. . . . Les innovations communes
résultent de la structure du latin et du fait qu'un mécanisme délicat et complexe a été
manié par des gens nouveaux de toutes sortes.' (*E.L.L.* 240-241.)

§ 8. *Pronunciation.*—The extent of local differentiation in pronunciation, in other
words, the extent to which the organic basis (the linguistic substratum, § 117) of the
conquered peoples exercised an influence on the formation of sounds and intonation
is still a very vexed question. In Gaul there is no indication of any sudden violent
change, but Celtic predispositions may count for something in the long series of
later Gallo-Roman changes. Cf. Meillet : ' Telle action a pu se produire dès le
début. . . . Mais le changement initial n'est pas toujours bien appréciable. Il n'en
résulte pas que le substrat n'agisse pas ; il y a des faits plus délicats, et sans doute
plus importants : pour avoir changé de langue, les sujets parlants n'ont pas changé
leurs tendances internes. . . . Il faut donc tenir compte de l'influence des " substrats "
en tant qu'elle exprime l'action des tendances héréditaires.' (*E.L.L.* 233-234 ; cf.
also Vendryes, *R. Lg. R.* I, 272.)

§ 9. The influence of the Celtic organic basis has been utilised by scholars to
explain the following Gallo-Roman sound-changes, but only the first two are generally
accepted :—

(i) Differentiation of **kt** to χ**t**, e.g. *factum* **faktum** > **faχtu̬*.
This differentiation is attested by the spelling *Rextum* for Rectum ; it is co-ex-
tensive with the region which has a Celtic substratum, i.e. Gaul, Rhaetia and North
Italy, and is corroborated by parallel changes in Celtic languages.

(ii) *The Weakening of Intervocalic Consonants.*—This development shows itself
in Late Latin in many parts of the Roman Empire, but was carried furthest in Gaul
and Rhaetia. Fragmentary documentary evidence indicates similar treatment of
intervocalic consonants in the Gaulish idiom :—

(*a*) In a fifth-century Gallo-Roman Glossary (the so-called ' Glossary of
Endlicher ') older Gaulish intervocalic **g** is written *i* in the word *broialo*, diminutive
of *brogi* (O.F. *brueil*).

(*b*) Gallic inscriptions contain isolated examples of the interchange of

> **d** intervocalic with **ð** or **dz,**
> **t** intervocalic with θ,
> **b** intervocalic with **v** (*Cevenna* beside *Cebenna*),

and of the loss or weakening of intervocalic **g**, e.g. *bria* for *briga*, *Rotomo* for *Roto-
măgum*, *vertrahum* < *vertragu* (Vendryes, *R. Lg. R.* I, 273).

(iii) *The Palatalisation of* **u** *to* **ü**.—The geographical extension of this change is
broadly co-extensive with the Celtic substratum. Complete palatalisation of **u** to **ü**
was, however, a very slow process : the loan-words of Frankish and Norse origin share
in the change, and it appears never to have been completed in the extreme north-east
of France (cf. § 183). It is, however, possible, as Professor Vendryes has recently
pointed out, that the tendency to form rounded front vowels, which is common to
Celtic and French, may be a ' heritage from the Celtic speech of Gaul ' (*R. Lg. R.*
I, 272). [For the arguments against Celtic influence cf. Meyer-Lübke, *Gr. Fr.*
§§ 48, 50, and *Zts. frz. Spr. u. Lit.* xli, 1-7, xliv, 75-84, xlv, 350-357.]

(iv) *The Nasalisation of Vowels.*—For a discussion of this question cf. Meyer-
Lübke, *Einführung*, § 221.

AUTHORITIES :

J. Vendr es : ' Celtique et Roman,' *R. Lg. R.* I, 262-277.
G. Dottin : *La Langue Gauloise*, Paris, 1920.
Meyer-Lübke : *Einführung*,[2] pp. 207-216.

Section 3.—SOURCES OF KNOWLEDGE.

§ 10. The chief sources of information about the pronunciation and morphology of colloquial Latin, more especially in the later period, are the following :—

(1) The remarks of grammarians, rhetoricians or other writers on 'vulgar' expressions or pronunciations; cf. H. Keil, *Grammatici Latini*, 1857-80.

The most important for our purpose is the *Appendix Probi*, a list of correct and incorrect spellings drawn up probably in the third century, ed. Keil, iv ; Foerster und Koschwitz, *Altfranzösisches Uebungsbuch*, 3rd edition, Leipzig, 1921 ; a selection is contained in the *Historical French Reader* of Studer and Waters and in Paul Meyer's *Recueil d'Anciens Textes*, Part I, *Bas-Latin*.

Cf. also the works of Consentius, *Ars Consentii, de Barbarismis et Metaplasmis* (fifth century, Gaul), ed. *Altfrz. Uebungsbuch*, p. 234, and of Virgilius Maro, *Epitomae* (seventh century, South Gaul), ed. A. Mai, *Class. Auct.* 5. 1 ; J. Huemer, Leipzig, 1886 (cf. Th. Stangl, *Virgiliana*, München, 1891 ; Manitius, *Gesch. der Lat. Lit. des Mittelalters*, I, pp. 119-127 ; Sandys, *A History of Classical Scholarship*, p. 437).

§ 11. (2) The works of writers who have but a moderate amount of education or who for some reason or other allow themselves to be influenced by colloquial usages. Among the former the most important for our purpose is the *Peregrinatio Aetheriae*, the work of an abbess of the late fourth or early fifth century (ed. P. Geyer in *Itinera Hierosolymitana*, saec. iv-viii, Wien, 1898; N. Heraeus, Heidelberg, 1908 ; E. A. Bechtel, 1902, in *Chicago Studies in Classical Philology*, iv, i : cf. also E. Löfstedt, *Philologischer Kommentar zur Peregrinatio Aetheriae*, Uppsala, 1911).

Deliberate use of colloquial usage is acknowledged by St. Jerome (331-420) and St. Augustine (354-430) ; cf. St. Jerome : 'Volo pro legentis facilitate abuti sermone vulgato'; St. Augustine : 'Melius est reprehendant nos grammatici quam non intelligant populi.' The earlier translators of the Bible, the men whose extant writings form the version called the *Itala*, are even more strongly influenced by the speech of their day than St. Jerome allowed himself to be in his translation, the *Vulgate*, (cf. Rönsch, *Itala und Vulgata; H.* Goelzer, *Étude lexicographique et grammaticale de la latinité de St. Jérôme*, 1884; Regnier, *De la latinité des Sermons de St. Augustin*, 1886).

§ 12. (3) Greek transliterations, e.g. *Guario* for *uario, kreskens* for *crescens, Patrikious* for *patricius* (cf. Marouzeau, *Le Latin*, p. 56).

§ 13. (4) Graphies in inscriptions and manuscripts that betray the influence of the colloquial speech. Of the inscriptions those that are of the greatest interest from this point of view are the Pompeian (before A.D. 79) and the later Christian. Cf. *Vulgärlateinische Inschriften*, ed. Ernst Diehl, Bonn, 1910 (*Kleine Texte für Theologische und Philosophische Vorlesungen und Uebungen*, 62), and Pirson, *La Langue des Inscriptions de la Gaule*, 1901. Slotty's *Vulgärlateinisches Uebungsbuch*, Bonn, 1918, contains a convenient selection of inscriptions and extracts.

§ 14. (5) The pronunciation of words borrowed from Latin by the surrounding peoples, as these afford occasionally some slight clue. Thus :

(a) Celtic *gwin*, O.E. *win*, Gothic *wins* < *vinum ;*
     Eng. *wall* < *vallum* and *-wick* < *vicum*,

clearly indicate the labio-velar pronunciation of the **w** at the time these words were taken over (Lindsay, p. 51).

(b) In the German loan-words *Keller* < *cellarium*, *Kelch* < *calicem*, the velar pronunciation of **k** before **e** is retained, but Welsh *tengl* < *cingula*, Frankish *tins* <

census, indicate that the palatalisation of **k** to **t̯** had begun at the time these words were borrowed, i.e. probably before the sixth century (cf. M.L. *Einf.* § 126 and below, §§ 290-297).

(*c*) The Breton place-name *Messac* < *Metiacum* indicates the vogue of the pronunciation **tʃ** for **tj** at the time when the insular Celts migrated to Armorica (fifth century) (cf. M.L. *Einf.* § 143 and below, § 304).

§ 15. (6) Most important of all are the indications afforded by the Romance languages themselves : Roumanian, Rhaetian (Ladin), Italian, Sardinian, Spanish, Portuguese, Catalan, Provençal, Northern French, Franco-Provençal.   Where complete agreement among all the Romance languages occurs, or where agreement exists in all the western varieties of Romance, it is fairly safe to premise a widespread Late Latin pronunciation or form.   When agreement is less general, the possibility of a separate similar development must always be taken into account.   The probability of the reconstructed form is naturally increased if it is one that is in accordance with what is known otherwise to be a tendency of the earlier Latin.   Examples are :—

(i) The differentiation of the vowels into *closed* and *open*, a trait common to all Romance languages.

(ii) The falling together of **į** and **ę** and of **u̧** and **ǫ**, a development common to all but the Sardinian and Corsican dialects, which were romanised late and were early cut off from the Empire (cf. M.L. *Einf.* §§ 97-99).

(iii) The loss of the intervocalic labial consonant in the termination of the perfect of the first conjugation—a loss common again to all the Romance languages and parallel to the loss of **w** that had already taken place in the fourth conjugation (§ 989).

CHAPTER II.

FORMATION OF FRENCH.

Period I.—Gallo-Roman and Early Old French.

Section 1.—Period Division.

§ 16. The long stretch of time that extends from the end of the fifth century to the end of the sixteenth falls into two main periods :—

Period I extends roughly from the end of the fifth century to the end of the eleventh (from the Germanic invasions to the first Crusade). It is, broadly speaking, the formative period of the French people and the French language.

Period II extends roughly from the end of the eleventh century to the beginning of the seventeenth (from the first Crusade to the end of the Wars of Religion). It is, broadly speaking, the period of the formation of educated French society, of French literature and the French literary language.

Both these periods may conveniently be subdivided into two: Period I into :—

(1) *Gallo-Roman*, the period extending from the end of the fifth century to the middle of the ninth, i.e. to the appearance of the written vernacular in the *Strasbourg Oaths* of 842.

(2) *Early Old French* (*Old French I*), extending roughly from the middle of the ninth century to the end of the eleventh.

Period II into :—

(1) *Later Old French* (*Old French II*), extending roughly from the end of the eleventh century to the beginning of the fourteenth.

(2) *Middle French*, comprising roughly the fourteenth, fifteenth and sixteenth centuries.

The customary division of the period is into three :—

(1) Gallo-Roman.
(2) Old French—from the middle of the ninth to the fourteenth century.
(3) Middle French.

This division, though time-honoured, is to some extent factitious and misleading. It masks the most important turning-point of the older language, and creates a division where no division exists, for in their linguistic development the ninth and

tenth centuries are closely linked with the preceding age and it is the eleventh century that marks an epoch in the history of French civilisation, the twelfth that sees the creation of the first French literary language.

Section 2.—GALLO-ROMAN, LOW LATIN, AND EARLY OLD FRENCH.

§ 17. In the fifth century the barriers that held back the incoming tide of Germanic invasion were swept away and the Germanic peoples poured into Gaul. In the early part of the century the Visigoths established themselves in the south-west, with Toulouse as their capital; in the latter part of it the Burgundians settled in the Rhône valley, with Lyons, taken in 469, as their capital. The Franks, a Low German tribe or confederation of tribes, occupied first and most intensively the northern and north-eastern region, that comprising roughly Artois, Picardy and modern Belgium; their enterprising monarchs, Childerich (d. 481), Chlovis (d. 511) and their descendants carried conquest much farther south and extended their sway over almost the whole of Gaul. Their settlements, however, according to the evidence of the place-names ending in -court, -ville, -villers, etc., rarely extend south of a line drawn from Mont St. Michel through Orléans to Burgundy.[1]

§ 18. In the strongly romanised south, under the relatively mild sway of the Goths, Roman civilisation was maintained at first to an almost surprising extent,[2] and Roman law and much of Roman municipal administration persisted into the Middle Ages. North of the Loire civilisation was not so deeply rooted and under the fiercer assaults of the ruder Franks broke down rapidly. Outside the Church, which maintained to some extent its organisation and traditions, the political, social and economic life of the country was destroyed, and it was only slowly that that new order of society, known to us as the 'feudal system,' emerged from the amalgamation of the freer, ruder customs of the conquerors with those elements of the Gallo-Roman civilisation that persisted. Outside the Church education and literature perished, and even in the Church their existence was threatened.

The Merovingian dynasty petered out miserably in the eighth century. Its successors, the Carolingians, were drawn from an East Frankish (Austrasian) family. The capable early rulers of this dynasty, (Charles Martel, 715-741, Pepin le Bref, crowned king in 751, and above all Charlemagne, Pepin's younger son, (768-814)), repulsed the Saracen invaders (e.g. at Poitiers, 732), overthrew the Lombard kingdom

---

[1] Cf. Longnon, p. 226, R. Lg. R. II, p. 45, and Addenda, § 17.
[2] Cf. the letters of Sidonius, bishop of Clermont (d. circa 489), ed. and tr. O. Walton, Oxford, and H. F. Muller, A Chronology of Vulgar Latin, Beiheft Zts. rom. Ph., 78 (1929).

in Italy (756-777), subdued the Saxons (772-799), and brought all Gaul under their sway; they restrained the turbulent nobility, reformed the administration and laid the foundations of law and order and education (cf. § 21).

The Carolingian 'renaissance' was, however, but short-lived. The curve of civilisation never dipped so low again as in the evil days of the seventh century, but the family dissensions and weakness of the later Carolingians in the ninth and tenth centuries, the ravages of the Danes (*c.* 800-911), the turbulent beginnings of the feudal states, undermined the shallow-rooted stability of the empire established by Charlemagne and brought local disintegration in northern Gaul to its height. The settlement of the Danes (the *Northmen, Normanni*) in 'Haute Normandie' in 910, in 'Basse Normandie' in 923, the accession of the stronger Capetian dynasty in 987, the rise of the bigger feudal states, gradually brought relative peace to the distracted country and made possible the great movements that had their beginnings in the eleventh century.

§ 19. *Development of Gallo-Roman.*—With the dissolution of the Roman Empire and its civilisation perished gradually the unity of the common Latin speech that, despite ever-increasing local differences, had up till then linked together the inhabitants of its various parts.[1] The language used in the common intercourse of everyday life, exposed to disintegrating foreign influence (cf. below), freed from the shackles of tradition, was modified with increasing rapidity and its nascent local characteristics emphasised. Thus the Romance languages in their early stage, Gallo-Roman, Hispano-Roman, Italo-Roman, etc., slowly took shape.

The Gallo-Roman styled himself *romanus;* by his conquerors he was called *walah,* the term from which is derived the later adjective *wallon.* From the phrase *loqui romanice* was drawn the O.F. adjective *romanz,* the word used to designate at first the vernacular language as opposed to Latin (cf. *Sermon en vers : Por icels enfanz le fis en romanz, qui ne sont letré ; car mielz entendrunt la langue dunt sunt des enfance usé*), and later on, concretely, the French works (cf. Crestien, *Cl. Cest romanz fist Crestiiens,* 24, and *Li Romanz de Renart, de Rou (Rollo), de la Rose,* etc.). The Germanic tribes were at first without any common appellation : in the ninth century the adjective *theotiscus,* i.e. *national,* emerges (cf. Council of Tours, 813, *lingua theotisca*) and this gave O.F. *tieis, tiois.* In the *Glossary of Reichenau* (c. viii.) *Gallia* is glossed as *Francia.*

§ 20. *Low Latin.*—Literary Latin, however, continued to be in intention the official language both of Church and State even in northern Gaul, but amidst the endless wars and dissensions of the Merovingians

---

[1] Cf. F. Lot, 'A quelle époque a-t-on cessé de parler latin ?' *Arch. Lat. Med. Aevi,* 1931, pp. 97-159.

and the general confusion and misery of the times, instruction even of the most elementary kind became rare and the quality of written Latin deteriorated rapidly.[1]   In the sixth century Gregory of Tours, a bishop, is conscious of the enormities he perpetrates,[2] but the more uninstructed of his time and the later writers and copyists appear to employ in almost haphazard fashion a flexional system but half acquired and constructions only partially understood, and make shift with a vocabulary of a curiously hybrid description.   A typical sentence from the *Formulae Andegavenses* (c. vii.) runs : *cido tibi caballus cum sambuca et omnia stratura sua, boves tantus, vaccas cum sequentes tantas* . . . (H.L.F. I, 136).

§ 21. In the eighth century, with the advent of the Carolingian dynasty, came an improvement in the quality of this debased literary Latin, *Low Latin* as it is commonly called.   Pepin, the first of the family to don the royal crown (751), was a man of some education and a staunch supporter of the reforms of the Church inaugurated under his predecessor Carloman by the Saxon monk Boniface (Wynfrith).   With the help of another English monk, the schoolmaster, Alcuin of York, called to Aix la Chapelle in 782, Pepin's son Charlemagne succeeded in raising the standard of education in the Church and among the nobles through reforms of spelling, grammar and last, but perhaps not least, handwriting, for it is the reformed half capital writing taught at Alcuin's school at the church of St. Martin of Tours that replaced the almost unintelligible cursive Merovingian script, and lies at the base of our modern printed characters.[3]

§ 22. *Emergence of Old French.*—A natural outcome of the improvement of the quality of the written Latin that resulted from the Carolingian reforms was the more conscious separation between the spoken and the written language.   In the eighth century it already seemed advisable to a clerk in the north of Gaul to draw up a list of the difficult (i.e. obsolete) words of the *Vulgate* with their vernacular equivalents, the so-called *Glossary of Reichenau*, and in 813 the Council of Tours specifically enjoined on priests the duty of putting their sermons 'in rusticam linguam aut theotiscam, quo facilius cuncti possint intelligere quae dicuntur.'   In the latter part of the ninth

[1] In the early fifth century the imperial schools disappeared ; private ones were carried on longer, but M. Roger notes that we possess no single sixth-century classical MS. (M. Roger, *L'enseignement des lettres classiques d'Ausone à Alcuin*, Paris, 1905, cf. also F. Lot, *op. cit.* pp. 134-144).

[2] Cf. the preface to his *Liber in gloria confessorum*, cited Studer and Waters, p. 6.

[3] For the influence of the Carolingian reforms on Latin spelling and pronunciation, cf. §§ 646, 647.

century Charlemagne's grandson, Nithard, the historian of Louis le Pieux, deemed it worth while to preserve in the vernacular form in which they were sworn the famous *Oaths of Strasbourg* of 842, and a copyist of the last quarter of the century has saved for us, sandwiched in between a Latin *Eulalia* sequence and a contemporary German poem, the French *Eulalia*, the first extant metrical Old French composition. This was written in all probability at the abbey of St. Amand les Eaux, near Valenciennes, before the end of the ninth century.

From the tenth century there is nothing extant in the northern French vernacular except fragmentary notes on a sermon on *Jonah* and two short poems, one on the *Passion*, the other on the life of *St. Legier*, both markedly childish in construction. It is only towards the end of the period, in the *Vie de St. Alexis* (*c.* 1050), that the potential strength of the French language reveals itself.

Section 3.—LINGUISTIC DEVELOPMENT IN PERIOD I.—INFLUENCE OF GERMANIC SPEECH-HABITS.

(Cf. J. Brüch, *Der Einfluss der Germanischen Sprachen auf das Vulgärlatein*, Heidelberg, 1913, and ' Die bisherige Forschung über die Germanischen Einflüsse auf die Romanischen Sprachen,' *R. Lg. R.* II, 25-98.)

§ 23. The course of linguistic development was profoundly influenced by the events of the period. The disintegration of political, social and economic life led directly to a rapid and general local differentiation of speech ; Germanic speech-habits exercised a direct and strong influence on vocabulary and pronunciation, and contributed, together with the general confusion of the times and the low ebb of education, to a weakening of linguistic tradition, which left free play to the disruptive forces of sound-change and counterbalancing analogical creations, and made the period one of markedly rapid linguistic change.

§ 24. In Austrasia (the territory between the Rhine and the Moselle) the Frankish speech became predominant ; in Neustria, the province comprising roughly Flanders, Normandy, Champagne and Central France as far as the Loire, Gallo-Roman remained the language of the people, but the court and the aristocracy were for a time German-speaking or bilingual. The court, indeed, remained so into the ninth century, for the Frankish speech received fresh impetus from the advent of the Caro-lingian dynasty, Austrasian and German-speaking.

Charlemagne is extolled by his biographer, Eginhart, for his bilingualism : ' Not content with his native tongue, he took trouble to learn foreign languages ; among which he so learned Latin that he could talk in that tongue as well as in his native

tongue.' (*Vita Karoli*, § 25.)   German appears still to have been the mother tongue of his son, Louis le Pieux, to judge from the death-bed utterance attributed to him, ' *huz, huz* quod significat *foras, foras*.'   Two or three of the saints of the period are credited with knowledge of both the *lingua romana* and the *lingua teutonica*, e.g. St. Adalhard (d. 826), cf. F. Lot, *op. cit.* p. 104.

§ 25. *Frankish Influence in Vocabulary.*[1]—The invaders from the sea, the Saxons and Northmen, influenced directly only the vocabulary of the Gallo-Romans, the Saxons contributing a few place-names, the Normans, place-names and also a sprinkling of nautical terms, e.g. *crique, eschipre, hune, sigle, tillac, touer*, etc., and a few others, e.g. *gab, cane* (*jaw*), *jolif* (< *jol, yule*).

The Frankish element was of considerable importance in Old French. It comprised not only military and feudal terms, but also words of more general and abstract type as well as many names of persons.

Examples are : *atgier, broigne, dart, escharguaite, eschiec, espie, espieu, estrif, fuerre, gonfanon, hache, halsberc, herberge ; blecier, boter, eschiver, guarir, nafrer ; aleu, ban, baron, fief, guarant, plevir ; espelir, guaaignier, haïr, hardi, honir, jehir, marir, orgueil, teche ; balt, bleu, franc, graim, isnel ; Charles, Huon, Legier, Aëlis, Berte.*

§ 26. *Frankish Influence on Word Formation.*—More important and more significant of the hold the Franks acquired on the country is the influence they exercised on *word formation* and on *pronunciation*.

The Frankish suffix *-ing* gave rise to the O.F. *-enc*, cf. *balcenc* < *balteus, jaserenc* < Arabic *g'azair, paisenc, Loherenc ;* numerous Germanic names in *-hart* and *-wald* were introduced, e.g. *Eginhart, Nithart, Reginhart, Grimwald, Herwald,* and from these were drawn the suffixes *-art* and *-alt,* employed to form derivatives both from Germanic and Romance radicals, cf. *bastart, (bastarda ≠ tarda), coart* (< *cauda*), *hagart, gaillart, richart, vieillart ; cortaut, lordaut, ribaut* (< *hriba*).

From the Frankish adjectives *frankisk, thiudisk* was drawn the suffix *-escum, -esca,* employed to form derivatives from names of countries, e.g. *angleis—anglesche, daneis—danesche, franceis—francesche, grieis— griesche.*   The similarity in the masculine form of this suffix and of the Romance suffix *-eis* < *-*ese* < *-ense*, fem. *-eise* led to the early replacement of the feminine by *-eise* (§ 783 (ii)).

In the prefix of the O.F. words : *forbannir, forconseillier, seï forfaire, forjugier,* etc., there survives the Frankish prefix *fir-*, contaminated with Romance *fors*, and in the prefix *mes-*, e.g. *mesamer, mesconseillier, mesdire, mesprendre,* the Frankish pejorative prefix *mis-*, (cf. Baist, *Rom. Forsch.* xii, pp. 650, 651 ; Lozinski, *Rom. L.* 515-540 ; Brüch, *op. cit.* pp. 47-48.)

The most probable explanation of the abnormal development of the Latin suffix *-arium* lies in the hypothesis of Frankish influence.   It is based on the following facts :—

[1] For Germanic loan-words in Late Latin and in French, cf. Ewert, pp. 290-296.

(1) The irregularity of the development is confined to the suffix; as an integral part of a word the series of sounds -*arium*, -*aria*, develops on normal lines, cf.

O.F. vair < **βar̥ < warium *varium*, airę < arĕa, feirę < feria.

(2) In the Frankish language a number of names are formed with the elements -*charī*, -*garī*, -*harī*, e.g.

Autchari (Ogier), Hlothari (Lohier), Walthari, Liutgari (Legier).

(3) In the development of the Germanic languages the phenomenon known as *mutation* (§ 419) is more widespread than in Romance and under its influence in the Gallo-Roman period the tonic vowel **a** in Frankish words of this type was raised to ę. It is therefore suggested that the resemblance in function and form between the endings of these Frankish names and **-ar̥**, the Gallo-Roman form of the suffix -*arium* (cf. § 313), provoked the replacement of **-ar̥** by **-ęr̥**, whence **-ier** by the normal diphthongisation of the tonic free vowel ę (§ 225). This theory receives some corroboration from the forms *paner* and *sorcerus* (<*sortiarius*) in the *Glossary of Reichenau*, *Berhero* for *Berhario* in a charter of 766, and *Ludher* (<*Hlothari*) in the *Oaths of Strasbourg*, this latter being the only word in the document in which tonic free **a** has changed to **e** (cf. Thomas, *Nouveaux Essais*, pp. 119-147).

In Middle French the O.F. suffix -*er* =ę(r) (<-**arem**) was occasionally replaced by -*ier*, **ję(r)**, cf. § 495.

§ 27. *Frankish Influence on Gallo-Roman Pronunciation.*—*Accentuation.*—The Frankish system of accentuation was a strong expiratory one and it was in the intensifying of the weak Latin tonic stress that the Germanic speech-habits, and in particular the Frankish, exercised their strongest influence on pronunciation.   Directly resultant were :

(*a*) The diphthongisation of the long (free) vowels ę and ǫ (§ 225).

(*b*) The reduction or effacement of the unstressed vowels (Part II, chap. v, sect. 8).

(*c*) The closing of secondary stressed ę and ǫ (Part II, chap. v, sect. 6).

The effacement of unstressed vowels brought into juxtaposition consonants that formed groups of unfamiliar type and these in turn were for the most part reduced or modified by various processes (Part II, chap. viii, sect. 2).

The strength of the expiratory accent contributed to the suppression of the vowels of unstressed monosyllabic words, i.e. to the widespread use of *enclisis* that characterised the language in its early stages (§ 602).

§ 28. *Sound System.*—*Reintroduction of* **h.**—The laryngal sound **h** which disappeared from the sound system in Late Latin (§ 185) was reintroduced in *initial* position in the numerous Germanic words beginning with this sound : in the interior of words it was early effaced:

O.F. *hache* < *hapja, *haste* < *haifst, *halsberc* < *halsberg, *helme* < *helm, *herberge* < *heriberga.

Bernart < *Bernhart*, *Renart* < *Reginhart*, *jehir* < *jehan*, cf. *geïne*.

Under the influence of the German words *hôh, hand, the pronunciation of Latin altum, (h)asta was also modified, cf. O.F. halt, hanste.

O.F. osberc (< ausberc < *halsberc) and elme, Mid. French auberge (< *hariberga) are loan-words from the south, where **h** was never re-established.

[For the effacement of **h** in Middle French, cf. § 196; for the influence of Germanic initial **w** cf. §636; for the treatment of Germanic sounds cf. §§ 634-637.]

§ 29. *Frankish Influence on Flexion.*—Contact with a flexional system of another type undoubtedly accelerated the disintegration and remodelling of the Latin flexional system in Gaul (cf. the rapid flexional changes in England after the Norman Conquest), the phonological changes caused by the heavy Frankish stress induced a levelling of termination and modification of the radical that provoked much analogical re-formation, but the amount of direct influence exercised by the Frankish flexional forms on Gallo-Roman forms is still a matter of controversy and was certainly slight.

§ 30. (i) *Imparisyllabic Declension in* '-a, -'ane.—In documents of the Gallo-Roman period an imparisyllabic type of declension in '-o, -'onem (masculine), -a, -'anem (feminine) is frequent, especially among proper nouns of Germanic origin. The masculine type comprised Latin imparisyllabics in '-o, -'onem (latro—latronem) and Germanic words in '-o, -ûn (Hugo—Hugûn, baro—barûn), remodelled under Latin influence. The starting-point of the feminine type appears to have been the Frankish feminine declension in '-a, '-ûn (Berta—Bertûn), remodelled under the influence of the masculine imparisyllabic type. (Cf. J. Jud, *Recherches sur la genèse et la diffusion des accusatifs en -ain et en -on*, Halle, 1907; Brüch, *op. cit.* pp. 58-60.)

(ii) The old French termination *-omes* (§ 895), a variant of the termination of the first person plural, is held by some to have been influenced by the Frankish termination *-umês*. (Cf. Brüch, *op. cit.* p. 61.)

Section 4.—LOCAL DIFFERENTIATION.

§ 31. *Langue d'Oc and Langue d'Oil.*—Between the spoken language of southern and northern Gaul the beginnings of divergence may have existed even in Late Latin, for the south differed to some extent from the north both in the organic basis of its inhabitants, Iberian, Ligurian, Celtic in the one, predominantly Celtic in the other,[1] and in the date and intensity of its Latin culture. To Pliny the 'Provincia Narbonensis'

---

[1] At the time of the Roman Conquest of Gaul the oldest inhabitants were the *Iberians*, Caesar's *Aquitani*, who then occupied the region between the Pyrenees and the Garonne. (After the invasion of the Spanish *Vascones*, at the end of the sixth century A.D., the Aquitani took the name of *Gascons* or *Basques*.) The next comers, the Ligurians, must have held at one time a considerable part of Gaul, but at the time of the Roman invasion most of the territory they had occupied and all the more northern part of Gaul was in the hands of the Celtic peoples, divided by Caesar into two main groups, *Celtae* and *Belgae*, the latter established north of the Seine and the Marne.

was ' Italia verius quam Provincia,' [1] and the rather late northern writer, Sulpicius Severus, fears to offend the ears of the Aquitanians by the rusticity of his speech. [2]

These differences must have been accentuated by the course of political events, which tended to keep south and north apart, and by the varying intensity of the Germanic influence, less strongly felt in the countries south of the Loire (§ 17), and in the twelfth century the vernaculars of the south and the north (the *Langue d'Oc* and the *Langue d'Oïl*, as they were called after their particles of affirmation) were held to be distinct languages.

The social and political differences that underlay and strengthened the linguistic differences between south and north in the eleventh century are summarised by Luchaire in the following terms : ' Ces deux France étaient alors profondément distinctes . . . La France méridionale, fragmentée par tant d'obstacles naturels, n'a pas de centre ; . . . L'énorme barrière du Plateau Central force le Midi à s'orienter de préférence vers la Méditerranée, l'Italie et même l'Espagne. Là se trouvent ses affinités les plus fortes, ses rapports de commerce, ses relations d'art, de littérature et d'amitié. . . . Les rois mérovingiens et carolingiens n'y séjournèrent que rarement : ils la tenaient pour un pays étranger. . . . Au ixe siècle, le régime féodal s'y répandit comme ailleurs, mais l'esprit aristocratique et militaire y était moins intense. . . . Une civilisation moins rude, plus tolérante pour les inférieurs, même pour les juifs ; les différences de condition moins tranchées entre les classes sociales ; l'usage du droit romain conservé dans les coutumes locales et dans les actes judiciaires ; l'importance politique plus grande des bourgeoisies riches : tout enfin distinguait " les Aquitains " des Français proprement dits. Autres mœurs, autre organisation sociale, on peut presque dire autre nation. Hommes du Nord et hommes du Midi se fréquentaient peu, s'entendaient mal et ne s'aimaient pas.' (Lavisse, *Hist. Fr.* II, 2, p. 40.)

§ 32. No hard and fast line of demarcation exists between the two languages, but scholars have agreed to make the retention of tonic **a** free (e.g. in *talhar* < **taleare*), the criterion of *Provençal*, the modern name of the language of the south, and in accordance with the retention or modification of this sound in present-day speech a line, or rather a zone of division has been drawn that runs, curving considerably north in its central part, from the mouth of the Gironde on the west to Puy St. André on the east.

Several other characteristics of Provençal coincide roughly with this line, e.g. the termination of the imperfect indicative and the use of the verb *anar* for *aller* (cf. C. Appel, *Provenzalische Lautlehre*, pp. 4, 5 and map). The causes determining the course of the line of division are as yet undiscovered.

§ 33. *Franco-Provençal.*—In the Suisse romande (cantons of Valais, Vaud, Fribourg, Neuchâtel and Geneva), in the Val d'Aosta and some valleys of Piedmont, in the departments of Savoie, Haute-Savoie, Ain, Rhône, Loire and Isère, there is in use an intermediate variety of southern French, designated by modern scholars *Franco-Provençal* or *Middle-Rhône*. In this region **a** tonic free is retained as **a** except after palatal and palatalised consonants : after these the northern develop-

---

[1] *Nat. Hist.* III, § 31.
[2] *Dial.* I, 27 I, quoted by Meyer-Lübke (*Becker vol.* p. 140).

ment is followed and **a** becomes **ie**.   Thus **amare** becomes **amar** in both Provençal and Franco-Provençal, but **amẹr** in Old French ; ***taleare** becomes *talhar*, **tajar** in Provençal but **tajier** (*talhier, taillier*) in Franco-Provençal and Old French.

On the west and south Franco-Provençal is roughly conterminous with the boundaries of the mediæval bishoprics of Lyons and Vienne, and these were based on Roman administrative divisions (cf. Morf, *Zur sprachlichen Gliederung Frank-reichs*, Berlin, 1911, and A. Duraffour, *R. Lg. R.* viii, 259-261).

§ 34. *Poitevin.*—In modern times the speech of the south-west, i.e. of Poitou, goes with northern French in its treatment of the sounds derived from tonic **a** *free*, but this appears to be due to an extension of the northern speech southwards, for in the Middle Ages the treatment of this sound appears to have been akin to that in the south-east, i.e. **a** tonic free was retained unless it followed a palatal or palatalised consonant and then it was raised to **ẹ**: this sound was not, however, diphthongised, cf. Poitevin **amar** and **tajer** (*tailler*), (cf. Gamillscheg, ' Zur sprachlichen Gliederung Frankreichs,' *Becker vol.* pp. 50-74).

§ 35. *Dialects of the Langue d'Oil.*—In north Gaul, despite the existence of two Celtic peoples, the Belgae and the Celtae (Galli), the local divergences observable in later times afford no ground for holding that any marked local differentiation had taken place as early as the fifth century.   The divergences that appear to be oldest are certain northern, north-eastern and eastern traits, e.g. the absence of the palatalisation of **k** and **g** before **a** (§§ 298-302) : and of the 'breaking ' of tonic **ẹ** and **ǫ** (§§ 410-412) : these may well have their origin in the sixth century.   On the other hand, the earliest monuments, the ninth century *Oaths* and the poem of *Ste Eulalia*, the tenth-century poems of *St. Legier* and the *Passion* and the *Jonas* fragment all show distinctive local features, and by the twelfth century north Gaul was covered by a network of local variations, some confined to a relatively small area, others in use over whole provinces or rather regions, for the political divisions of the time appear to have exercised but little influence over the diffusion of ' dialectal ' traits.

The main causes of the rapid local differentiation of the speech of northern Gaul appear to have been :—

(i) The chaotic political and social conditions and consequent weakening of all restraining linguistic tradition.

(ii) The variations in the intensity of the Frankish influence (cf. § 17).

(iii) The absence of all centralised government and large cities and the intensely local life of the time.

(iv) The many difficulties in the way of communication.

This last factor, important in the creation of local forms of speech, is even more important in determining their extension.   Mountains and, still more, trackless forests, extensive swamps, unfordable and unnavigable rivers, the things that impede communications, impede also the spread of linguistic changes ; on the other hand, the absence of such physical features, the existence of good roads and navigable rivers, the things

that facilitate intercourse, facilitate the extension of local traits and so level linguistic differences.

In French speech in Period II the most strongly marked dialectal divergence is between the northern zone and the region south of it, cf. § 37, but the eastern region is also characterised by a set of strongly marked dialectal traits whose extension is largely attributable to the existence of the great trade route that ran right up the valleys of the Rhône and Saône from Lyons through Langres to Metz, and thus linked together the eastern side of Gaul. In the west, on the other hand, no trunk road ran from north to south, and the river valleys of the Seine and Loire offered comparatively easy lines of communication between the centre and the coastal region : the result is that western speech is less cohesive and less markedly dialectal than eastern ; it is linked more closely with the speech of the central region in some of its developments and possesses fewer characteristics that connect it with the speech of the south, although these are not entirely lacking (cf. §§ 319, 371, 382, 616, 894, 921, S.W. § viii).

§ 36. It is difficult to determine the region in which linguistic changes began and the lines along which they were propagated, but the dialectal differences observable in Old and Middle French afford the following indications :—

The palatalisation of u to ü and the raising of ǫ to u appear to have spread northward from the south-west and to have reached the north-east last (§§ 183, 184). The differentiation of diphthongs spread from the north-east southwards and failed to reach the western region (§ 230) ; the counterpart of this movement, the tendency to level diphthongs, began in the south-west and spread northward and eastward (§ 508). The diphthongisation of tonic ę and ǫ under palatal influence (*breaking*, §§ 410-412), a process more characteristic of the Langue d'Oc than the Langue d'Oïl, appears to have followed much the same path, for here again the north-east is least affected.

The lowering influence of nasalisation appears to have been strongest in Old French in the south-central, south-eastern, central and eastern regions (§ 450). The effacement of final r appears to have begun in the south-eastern region and it is in the south-central region that the replacement of intervocalic r by z first appeared (§§ 399-402) ; the effacement of præ-consonantal s began in the south-west (§ 378).

In the early period of the language few wide-spread linguistic changes appear to have originated in Paris or its neighbourhood—an indication of the relatively small importance of the town at this date—but in Later Middle and Early Modern French various changes are attributed to the Parisian populace, e.g. the broadening of wę to wa and wɑ, the reduction of ɟ to ʒ and the substitution of R for r, (cf. also § 62).

§ 37. Much controversy has arisen over the question whether or no dialects have ever had any *real* existence in France, i.e. whether or no the linguistic usage of one region has ever been sharply marked off from that of adjacent regions by linguistic boundaries, by the convergence along the frontier line of a district of a set of distinctive local traits.

It is true that local divergence was marked enough to attract the attention of the mediæval observers, witness Roger Bacon's often-quoted remark in his *Opus Majus* : ' Nam et idiomata ejusdem linguae variantur apud diversos, sicut patet de lingua Gallicana quae apud Gallicos et Normannos et Burgundos multiplici variatur idiomate. Et quod proprie dicitur in idiomate Picardorum. horrescit apud Burgundos, imo apud

Gallicos viciniores.' The designations used by him suggest, moreover, that these local forms of speech were conterminous with the political provinces.

Close study of Old French and the investigation of the modern patois disprove this theory conclusively. It is clear that the east, west, centre, south possess different linguistic characteristics that serve broadly to differentiate their speech, but ordinarily in such a way that it is impossible to draw any definite lines of demarcation between region and region. To quote the picturesque comparison of Gaston Paris : ' Nos parlers populaires étendent une vaste tapisserie dont les couleurs variées se fondent sur tous les points en nuances insensiblement dégradées '. (Paris, *Mél.* pp. 435, 436.) The extension of individual ' local ' traits may thus be delimited but not the extension of the dialects : a map may be made of the extension of the western traits, e.g. the retention of **ei** as **ei**, of **ē** as **ē**, etc., but west French itself merges into central French.

In the north, however, the position is somewhat different, and there, if anywhere in French, it is possible to speak of a definite dialect. In this region a variety of causes has combined to separate off linguistic usage from that of the region south of it :—

(1) The part of Gaul comprising north Normandy, Picardy and French Flanders, the territory of the Belgae, was constituted by the Romans a separate administrative area, and this division was continued in the Merovingian episcopal dioceses, which were based on the Roman administrative areas.

(2) In this region the Franks settled more thickly than in the central and western regions (§ 17).

(3) The different parts of this region were linked together by the great trade route that ran from the mouth of the Seine over Beauvais, Amiens, Arras, Cambrai to Cologne.

It is not altogether surprising therefore to find a set of important local charac-teristics (cf. N. §§ i, xx(*a*)) terminating along a frontier zone that extends from Gisors to Trélon, through the departments Oise and Aisne, and which divides to this day ' Picard ' from ' Francien,' the local speech of the Île de France. In the west this northern linguistic boundary was obliterated already in the Middle Ages by the formation of the duchy of Normandy in the tenth century, for from that time on the development of the speech of northern Normandy was linked more closely with that of South Normandy and the centre, than with the northern region, of which it had previously formed a part ; in the east the line of demarcation was never strongly marked because there the Germanic influence was as strong as in the north, and the whole eastern side of Gaul was to some extent knit together by the great eastern trade route that ran up to Metz and Trèves.

Gaston Paris : *Les Parlers de France, Mél. Ling.*, p. 432 *et seqq.*

H. Morf : *Zur Sprachlichen Gliederung Frankreichs (Abhl. kgl. Preuss. Akad.,* 1911).

[For synopsis of dialectal traits cf. Appendix.]

✱✱ § 38. *Linguistic Geography.*—Modern local forms of speech, the patois, are now being studied systematically, as they afford much information about various linguistic questions. A method now much followed is the compilation of linguistic atlases : series of maps, each one giving a word, form or locution in a number of selected localities. The originator of this form of inquiry was the late Professor Gilliéron, and the *Atlas Linguistique de la France,* compiled by M. Edmont, under his direction, consists of 1920 maps of words, etc., each containing 639 localities. These maps throw much light on the history of individual words, their survival, disappearance and replacement, and on the vocabulary in use at the different periods of the language, (cf. § 6), on the expansion of Late Latin and of the Germanic languages, etc. They illustrate also the relations obtaining between social centres and the surrounding region and are occasionally of much value in the history of sounds and flexion.

[For a fuller account of this branch of investigation, cf. the works of M. Gilliéron, e.g. *L'Abeille* and also the summaries and bibliography given by Professor Terracher in the Zaharoff Lecture for 1929, *L'Histoire des Langues et la Géographie Linguistique*, Oxford, or by A. Ewert, p. 400.]

Section 5.—SOURCES OF KNOWLEDGE OF GALLO-ROMAN AND OLD FRENCH I.

§ 39. (1) *Latin Documents.*—(i) *Glossaries.*

Glossary of Reichenau, eighth century (cf. § 22), ed. Foerster und Koschwitz, *Altfrz. Uebungsbuch*; selection in Studer and Waters' *Historical French Reader*; cf. Hetzer, *Die Reichenauer Glossen*, *Zts. R. Ph.*, Beiheft VII.

Glossary of Cassel, eighth or ninth century, drawn up apparently to assist Bavarians in the acquirement of a romance language, perhaps that of northern Gaul : ed. *Altfrz. Uebsb.*, cf. *Zts. R. Ph.* XXVI, 521-531.

These glossaries, particularly that of Reichenau, supply much information about the vernacular vocabulary and incidentally throw some light on pronunciation and flexion (§§ 260, 505, 790, 792).

(ii) *Works in Low Latin.*—The tendencies of the vernacular may often be discerned in the spelling and forms of the Low Latin of the period, particularly in the charters and works written before the introduction of the Carlovingian spelling reforms. Among these may be cited :—

Gregory of Tours, sixth century, ed. W. Arndt and B. Krusch, *Mon. Germ. Hist. Scriptores rerum Merovingicarum*, t. I, 1884 ; *Historia Francorum*, ed. R. Poupardin, Paris, 1913 (*Collection des Textes pour servir à l'étude de l'histoire*) ; cf. M. Bonnet, *Le Latin de Grégoire de Tours*, Paris, 1890.

Fredegarius, seventh century, ed. *Scriptores rerum Merovingicarum*, II, 1888 ; cf. O. Haag, *Die Latinität Fredegars*, Diss. Freiburg-im-Breisgau, Erlangen, 1898, *Rom. Forsch.* x. 5.

Inscriptions chrétiennes de la Gaule antérieures au VIIIe siècle, ed. Le Blant, Paris, 1856.

Formulae Andecavenses, 514-676, cf. E. Slyper, *de Formularum Andecavensium latinitate disputatio*, Amsterdam, 1906.

Capitulare de Villis Imperialibus, ninth century, ed. Boretius, *Mon. Germ. Hist.*, Legum, sect. II, t. I, 1883, p. 82 (Selection in the *Historical French Reader* of Studer and Waters).

On the language and bibliography of the Merovingian documents, cf. J. Pirson, *Le Latin des Formules Mérovingiennes*, *Rom. Forsch.* xxvi. pp. 837-945 ; Vielliard, *Le Latin des Diplômes Royaux et chartes privées de l'époque Mérovingienne*, Paris, 1927.

In the Latin charters it is often the spelling of the names, place and personal, that affords the best clue to the vernacular pronunciation of the time. Their origin is often unknown and the spelling consequently reproduces directly the current pronunciation of the word. As examples of investigations based wholly or largely upon material of this kind may be cited :—

H. Drevin : *Die frz. Sprachelemente in den lateinischen Urkunden des 11. und 12. Jhte*, Diss. Halle, 1912.

E. Goerlich : *Die nordwestlichen Dialekte der Langue d'Oïl* (Bretagne, Anjou, Maine, Touraine) ; *Die südwestlichen Dialecte der Langue d'Oïl* (Frz. Studien, V, 3 ; III, 2), Heilbronn, 1882, 1886.

F. Hildebrand : *Ueber das französische Sprachelement im Liber Censualis Wilhelms I von England* (*Zts. R. Ph.* VIII, 321-362).

F. Lot : 'Date de la chute des dentales intervocales en français' (*Rom.* XXX, 481-488).

S. Weigelt: 'Französisches oi aus ei auf Grund lateinscher Urkunden des 12ten Jhts.' (*Zts. R. Ph.* XI, p. 85).

Cf. also A. Longnon: *Les Noms de Lieu de la France*, Paris, 1920-29.

§ 40. (2) *Texts in the Vernacular.*

(For editions and bibliography cf. *Altfranzösisches Uebungsbuch*, W. Foerster and E. Koschwitz, sixth edition, Leipzig, 1921; *Arch. Rom.* xiii, Rajna, Un nuovo testo parziale del 'Saint Alexis' primitivo.)

Ninth Century:

The *Strasbourg Oaths*, 842, provenance still in dispute, but probably the Rhône valley.

The *Sequence of Ste Eulalia*, eighth decade, provenance the north-eastern region.

Tenth Century:

Poem on the *Passion*, preserved in a strongly provençalised form.

The *Life of St. Legier*, provenance eastern or north-eastern, but also provençalised by the copyist.

Notes of a *Sermon on Jonah* in the Tironian script, the mediæval shorthand; provenance north-eastern.

Eleventh Century:

Life of St. Alexis, *c.* 1050, ascribed conjecturally by its first editor, Gaston Paris, to Thibaut, canon of Vernon (Eure).

Other texts have been ascribed to the end of the century but none with complete certainty.

§ 41. (3) *Extant Old French Forms.*—Extant Old French forms enable us not infrequently to make deductions about the relative order of the sound changes in the earlier period. For example, the O.F. form *onz*, **ãnts**, from **annos** indicates that the reduction of double consonants was subsequent (i) to the diphthongisation of the tonic vowels, ct. **mains** < **manus**, and (ii) to the slurring of the final unstressed vowels, because no partial de-nasalisation of **n** to **t** takes place when a single nasal consonant comes in contact with flexional **s**, ct. *mains*, *chiens*, etc.

(Cf. also §§ 229, 295, 299, 308, 349-354, 356, 366, 373.)

§ 42. (4) *The Form assumed by Loan-words.*—The form assumed by loan-words affords sometimes chronological data, e.g.

(i) The palatalisation of **u** to **ü** in the Norse loan-word **bū** > **bü** (*Bû-sur-Rouvres*) indicates that in this region this palatalising movement was continuing in the tenth century (cf. M.L. *Gr.* § 48);

(ii) The O.F. learned loan-words *empeechier*, *preechier*, *vochier* indicate that the tendency to palatalise **k** before **a** continued after the period in which intervocalic **k** was voiced to **g** (§ 640 (5)).

§ 43. (5) *The Comparative Study of French and Provençal.*—(i) The Langue d'Oc which developed more slowly than the Langue d'Oïl retained sometimes into the twelfth century stages left behind by the more rapidly developing northern language, e.g. the voicing of intervocalic **p** and **t** to **b** and **d** respectively:

cf. O.F. *saveir*, *balee*; Prov. *saber*, *balada*.

(ii) There is some probability that developments common to the whole of Gaul, (e.g. the breaking of tonic **ę** and **ǫ** by following palatal consonants, § 410, the closing of the o-*sounds* by nasal consonants, § 426), began relatively early and those proper to one region only relatively late, e.g. the northern levelling of **au** to **ǫ**, cf. O.F. **ǫr**, Provençal **aur** < **aurum**, the opening and effacing of **g** *intervocalic* < **k** and of **d** *intervocalic* < **t**, cf. O.F. **seür**, **balęę**, Prov. **segür**, **balada** < **securum**, ****ballata**.

CHAPTER III.

FORMATION OF STANDARD FRENCH.

Period II.—LATER OLD AND MIDDLE FRENCH.

Section 1.—LITERARY FRENCH IN THE TWELFTH CENTURY.

§ 44. The eleventh and twelfth centuries in France were characterised by an amazing activity and force of initiative in almost every sphere of human life: in rapidity of development, religious, economic, political, social, intellectual, artistic and literary, these centuries are second to none in the history of the country. With the eleventh century the "Dark Ages" are left behind, together with the haunting apprehensions that darkened the years before 1000. France was freed from the most turbulent of the nobles and their followers by a great series of expeditions and conquests outside the country: the Norman conquest of Sicily and South Italy (between 1016 and 1075), the Norman Conquest of England, 1066, the Spanish Crusades from 1018 on, the first Crusades to the Holy Land (1095, 1146, 1189). These extended commerce, widened experience, stimulated intellectual curiosity, promoted literary intercourse between northern and southern France. Political life was settled on a firmer basis: the Capetian monarchy established itself, weak in possessions but heir to a traditional and almost religious reverence; national feeling was fostered; large and relatively stable feudal states emerged from the welter of the preceding age; chivalry was instituted; monasticism and the Church were reformed under the high inspiration of the great monastery of Cluny; monastic and cathedral schools were revived or founded, Rheims first, under the scholar Gerbert (d. 1003), then Laon, Bec, Angers, Orléans, Chartres, St. Benoît sur Loire, Paris, to name only the more outstanding, and in the beginning of the thirteenth century the university of Paris emerged, (its first written statutes about 1209). In quick succession France created two great forms of religious architecture, the *romane* (our Norman) and the *française* (Gothic), and in the twelfth century a great and varied literature took shape, in Latin first and more slowly in the vernacular. In its wake the earliest form of literary French came into being.

§ 45. Up to the close of the preceding period the use of the vernacular in northern France had been so narrowly restricted to the

intercourse of everyday life that it had remained simple in construction and concrete in vocabulary. The early epic, the first great literary creation of northern France, in its bareness and simplicity still reflected closely the colloquial usage of the period, for the epic, in the main the product of the eleventh and early twelfth centuries, voiced the ideals and aspirations of the time when lay society was as yet undifferentiated, and when the baron and his followers lived and thought alike, the code of 'cortoisie' being as yet unformulated, and knightliness, 'chevalerie,' consisting in the performance of high deeds of valour, not in the observance of a strict code of manners. With the extension of education among clerk and lay, with the steadily expanding use of the vernacular in literary composition by Latin-trained writers, with the rise of 'society' in the narrow sense of the word, the meeting together of men and women on equal terms for the purpose of social intercourse and amusement, with the adoption of the ideals and code of *cortoisie* formulated at the brilliant southern courts, the social life of the north lost its former homogeneity, class distinctions emerged and linguistic usage was differentiated. In the *Roman de Thèbes*, the earliest but one of the great romances, the ideal of social exclusiveness is expressed with brutal frankness : *Or s'en voisent de tot mestier, Se ne sont clerc et chevalier*, and a like note is often struck in lyric poetry although the northern poets never employed the *trobar clus*, the côterie language of their southern compeers. In the brilliant court of Champagne, the literary centre of highest polish in the north, the poets, e.g. Crestien de Troies, Gautier d'Arras, Bertrand de Bar-sur-Aube, were evidently at pains to slough off the most marked of their local idiosyncrasies,[1] and Conon de Bethune plaintively laments the ridicule poured on his *mos d'Artois*, his rougher northern speech. The widening of the scope of vernacular writing led to the importation of learned words ;[2] subtler thought and interest in psychological analysis produced greater complexity of construction ; the study of Latin and the influence of the Provençal lyric inspired an ideal of *bel parler* that led to the use of various forms of rhetorical embellishment. The magnitude of the change may be measured by a comparison of the diction of the tenth-century poem on *St. Legier* with the *Chanson de Roland* and this poem with the subtle soliloquies in the *Tristan* of Thomas, written about fifty years later, or with the love lyrics of the trouvère, Gace Bruslé.

§ 46. Like the precocious court society that gave birth to it, this first development of literary French was, however, but short-lived : the ideal adumbrated in the brilliant court societies of the later twelfth and early

---

[1] Cf. Foerster, *Cligès*, Intr. p. lv ; M.L. *Gr.* § 10.
[2] Cf. below, § 53.

thirteenth centuries attained formulation in the sixteenth century, realisation only in the modern period.   After the twelfth century political and social conditions became less favourable to the cultivation of literature ; Latin continued too dominant in education and too wholly the medium of original thought to allow full scope or range to the vernacular ; education and literary taste were too narrowly diffused, lay society too illiterate to permit the formation of permanent tradition ; centralisation made headway but slowly and local life long remained too vigorous and individual to allow of any thorough-going unification of linguistic usage. Thus the processes that had begun their work in the twelfth century— the extension of the use of the vernacular, the expansion of vocabulary, the social differentiation of speech, the unifying and standardising of linguistic usage—made way but slowly and reached their term only in the seventeenth century.

Section 2.—POLITICAL AND SOCIAL CONDITIONS AFTER THE TWELFTH CENTURY.

§ 47. In the course of the thirteenth century the brilliant court life of northern France was ruined by the extravagance of the nobles ; in the south it was extinguished in the early part of the century by the ferocious Albigensian Crusade (1208-13), which deprived the south of political independence, destroyed its prosperity and sapped its literature.[1] In the following period the relative stability and prosperity that had characterised the life of the country in the twelfth and thirteenth centuries gave place to alternating periods of war and peace : literary production was hampered, linguistic development became slow and chequered.

§ 48. The expeditions that took the French out of France, notably the Italian wars (1494-1514), which brought them in contact with a culture far more advanced than their own, widened their outlook, quickened their appreciation of art and antiquity and thus contributed directly, as well as indirectly, to the advancement of the French language (§§ 56, 57).

The wars waged within the country itself, the Hundred Years' War and the Religious Wars of the sixteenth century (1562-98) exercised a *direct* influence of a very different kind.   The long-drawn-out wars

---

[1] Provençal literature was cultivated into the sixteenth century, buttressed up in the early fourteenth by the institution of the *Jeux Floraux* of Toulouse.   In the early sixteenth century, however, French secured a footing in these poetic compositions, and even before this, from the time of Antoine de la Salle on, the more ambitious of the southern writers migrated north and wrote in French instead of in their native idiom.

with the English (1334-1453) were the more disastrous ; they ruined trade and prosperity and lowered very generally the standard of life and learning : literary production sank to a low ebb, linguistic tradition was weakened and the rapid modifications of the language of the late fourteenth and early fifteenth centuries reflect the uncertainty and disorders of the life of the times. The havoc wrought by these wars went beyond the recuperative power of the short period of peace, (the reign of Charles V, 1364-1380), that intersected it, and France, the country that in the twelfth and thirteenth centuries had dominated the culture of western Europe,[1] in the later fifteenth century had become a laggard and had to put itself to school with Italy.

To the revival of learning and art that marks the early part of the sixteenth century religious dissensions and wars again brought a check : prosperity was impaired, the conditions of life made uncertain, education and all artistic activity hampered, the attempts of the educated to constitute a firm linguistic tradition thwarted : Montaigne at the end of the century repeats in stronger terms the lament made by Tory at the beginning.

The *indirect* influence exercised on linguistic development by the wars waged within the country was not, however, wholly unfavourable. The disorders and miseries attendant on them provoked in the fifteenth and later sixteenth century a desire for peace and strong government that strengthened national sentiment and the royal power and facilitated a centralisation that paved the way for a more rapid development of a unified language (§ 67). The relatively rapid disappearance of provincial literary French in the sixteenth century, the readiness of the seventeenth century to accept discipline, its submission to authority in linguistic matters, its subordination of individual practice to use and wont, find their explanation very largely in the experience of the troublous times preceding these epochs.

Section 3.—USE AND DISPLACEMENT OF LATIN.

§ 49. Latin remained at first the language of scholars, the medium of education, the vehicle for the expression of all serious thought, ceding its place step by step only, until the changed conditions of the sixteenth century turned its slow retreat into a rout. Until then no appreciable progress was observable in the use of the vernacular in learned works, except in legal documents and in translations.

In private legal documents the vernacular began to be used in the thirteenth century ; in the first quarter, in the great towns of the north,

---

[1] Cf. below, Section 8.

later on in the Île de France ; and it is not till the reign of Philippe le
Bel that the vulgar tongue is of any frequent use in the royal chancellery,
and only in the fifteenth century does Latin there become rare.[1]

In the law courts of the south Latin remained the official language
up to the celebrated ordinance of Villers-Cotterets (1539) ; in the north,
depositions of witnesses and pleadings began to be taken down and
sentences given in the vernacular in the fourteenth century.   In the
thirteenth century various compilations of local legal customs were made
in French, but the manuals of jurisprudence and the instruction given in
the schools of Law continued to be in Latin till after the sixteenth
century.[2]

With the exception of the years from 1340-75, the official chronicles
of France were compiled in Latin until after the reign of Charles VIII ;
in the chronicles of the Burgundian court the vernacular made its
appearance officially at the beginning of the fifteenth century.

§ 50. The translation, or rather adaptation, of saints' lives preceded
all other kinds of translation ; in the twelfth century a considerable
number of didactic works (saints' lives, books of the Bible, moral
treatises, chronicles, pseudo-scientific works) were translated, the largest
contribution being made in England, where translation was stimulated
by the zeal of the Normans for learning, and the prestige that attached
to French, the language of the conquerors.   The history and literature
of antiquity were at first regarded mainly as a storehouse of tales, of
plots that could be amplified and embroidered at will to suit the taste of
the audiences of the day (cf. the romances of antiquity, *Alexandre*, *Thebes*,
Troie, *Eneas* and the spirited thirteenth-century prose work *Li Fait des
Romains*).   With the later thirteenth century a more utilitarian view
was taken and poets and princes alike begin to value antiquity as a
source of knowledge and of moral instruction, cf. Jean de Meung :
Car en leur jeus et en leur fables Gisent deliz mout profitables ; Eustace
Deschamps : *Sur tous tresors que princes peut avoir C'est d'apprendre
les livres et savoir Les faiz des anciens.*

Little attempt was made, however, to give any exact rendering of
any classical author before the fourteenth century.   Then Jean le Bon
commissioned Pierre Berçuire to translate Livy, and Charles V set to
work a whole band of translators, chief of whom was Nicole Oresme,
charged with the translation of Aristotle in 1370.

§ 51. *Displacement of Latin in the Sixteenth Century.*—Throughout
the fifteenth and early sixteenth centuries, however, Latin retained its
dominance, with even heightened prestige, and it remained for the

---

[1] Giry, *Manuel de Diplomatique*, 469, 470.
[2] For the use of French in legal documents in England, cf. §§ 1072, 1076.

century most closely associated with the revival of antiquity, the one most successful in the cultivation of elegant latinity, to oust it from its pride of place and accord to the vernacular the right to express the highest thoughts and inspirations and the most highly-prized knowledge of its age.

The factors that combined to produce this unexpected result are the following :—

(i) *Political policy*, for it appears that the displacement of Latin in the law courts of the south (in 1539, §§ 49, 67) was induced more by the desire to secure the unification of the country than to avoid ambiguity in the interpretation of the Latin phraseology.

(ii) *The Protestant movement*, with its enforcement of Bible reading and its appeal to private judgment.

(iii) *The discovery of the art of Printing*, for printers and authors, both in their own interests and for the disinterested spread of knowledge, encouraged the use of the vernacular in order to reach as wide a public as possible.

(iv) *The strict purification of the Latinity*.—Mediaeval Latin, which had served as a general medium of communication for scholars in all countries and for all subjects, had been ordinarily a comfortable, easy-going kind of Latin, ' une langue vivante dont chacun disposait à son gré, usant avec une liberté sans limite du droit de fabriquer des mots et de les construire à volonté.' The scholar of the Renaissance was contented with nothing less than Latin of the purest type, Ciceronian by preference in vocabulary and construction, and this sublimated Latin proved a far less suitable vehicle for the expression of modern thought and scientific discoveries than the earlier ' *bon et gros latin.*'

(v) *National sentiment*, stimulated by the desire to emulate the Italians and the nations of classical antiquity. The first note was struck by Claude de Seyssel, in the preface of his translation of Justinian (1509, cf. H.L.F. II, 30) ; it was repeated by Tory in his *Champ Fleury* in 1529, expressed with more fullness and precision by Jacques Peletier du Mans in the introduction to his translation of the *Ars Poetica* of Horace (1549),[1] more flamboyantly in Du Bellay's *Deffence et Illustration de la langue francoyse.*

---

[1] '. . . ie veux bien dire qu'a une langue peregrine il ne faut faire si grand honneur que de la requeillir et priser, pour regretter et contemner la sienne domestique. I'ai pour mes garens les anciens Rōmains, lesquelz bien qu'ilz eussent en singuliere recommandation la langue Greque, toutesfois apres i avoir emploié un etude certain, se retiroint a leur enseigne et s'appliquoint a illustrer et enrichir leur demaine hereditaire. . . . Autant en est des souuerains poetes, Dante, Sannazar, aussi Italiens . . . Il est bien vrai que ces auteurs la ont aussi bien voulu escrire en Latin, pour la maiesté et excellence d'icelui . . . Mais quant a ceux qui totalement se vouent et adonnent a une langue peregrine . . . il me semble qu'il ne leur est possible

§ 52. In philosophy Latin held its ground until the next century; in theology, thanks to Protestantism, in medicine, science and the applied arts a beginning was made in vernacular writing in the sixteenth century, cf. Calvin's *Institution de la Religion Chrestienne, composee en latin par Jean Calvin et translatee en francois par luy mesme*, 1541, Bernard Palissy's *Recepte veritable, par laquelle . . . ceux qui n'ont jamais eu cognoissance des lettres pourront apprendre une philosophie necessaire a tous les habitans de la terre*, and the works of the great physician, Ambroise Paré.

The first protest against the domination of Latin in the schools was raised (in Latin) by the celebrated lawyer, Jean Bodin, in 1559 : *Fateor equidem magnum aliquid ac praeclarum futurum, si apud nos, ut iam apud Italos fieri coeptum est, artes scientie lingua vernacula doceantur ;* (H.L.F. II, 11), and at the Collège de France two or three professors, notably Ramus and Loïs Le Roy, ventured to lecture in French in the latter part of the century. The hold of tradition, however, was too strong for their boldness to take effect, and Latin, solidly entrenched, remained dominant in education until the eighteenth century (cf. H.L.F. VII, bk. II).

Section 4.—EXPANSION OF VOCABULARY.

§ 53. *Latin.*—Throughout the history of French, Latin was a storehouse on which the learned drew to supplement the vernacular, weak as it was in abstract and general terms. The relatively short *Life of St. Alexis* contains no less than thirty learned loan-words (*mots savants*) [1] and with the increase in translation and adaptation of Latin originals the number of such words increased rapidly in the next century.

In the early adaptations of classical works the translators and adaptors had, however, at first little scruple about using current terms to render their originals, however misleading these might be, and when in the later fourteenth century translators began to aim at exactitude of rendering they were consequently hard put to it to find the appropriate term, the more so that they themselves were often quite unaccustomed to using the vernacular in written composition. 'Une science qui est forte . . . ne peut pas estre bailliee en termes legiers a entendre, mes y convient souvent user de termes ou de mots propres en la science qui

---

d'atteindre a celle naïue perfection des anciens non plus qu'a l'art d'exprimer Nature.' (*L'Art Poetique d'Horace*, quoted H.L.F. II, pp. 81, 82 ; on all this section cf. H.L.F. II, pp. 1-159.

[1] Adiutorie, affliction, alienes, ampirie, ancienour, anfermetet, apostolie, avuegle, celeste, candelabre, escole, fecunditet, felix, fraile, grabatum, graciet, habiter, humilitet, imagine, leprus, memorie, miracle, nobilitet, palasinos, palie, paradis, regenerer, sacrarie, saintismes, savies, sazit, servise, servitor, trinitet, vochie.

ne sont pas communellement entendus ne cogneus de chascun, mesme-
ment quant elle n'a autrefois este traictee et exercee en tel langage,'
and in accordance with these principles Oresme introduces the words:
aphorisme, aristocratie, architecte, democratie, extase, heroïque, mon-
archie, monopole, symphonie, and others, taking the precaution to
explain these 'fors mots' in a glossary.[1]

In this way the borrowing of learned loan-words, which had been an
infiltration in Old French,[2] became a stream in the fourteenth century
and almost a deluge in the fifteenth and sixteenth centuries, when
latinisation of language began to confer social distinction (§ 71).[3]

§ 54. *Provençal.*—Loan-words from the south filtered into northern
French at all periods of the language, often with the articles they
designated. The southern forms *osberc* and *elme* are in the *Chanson
de Roland*; in the course of Later Old French the words *aigle,
becasse, figue, fleute, langouste, notuner, velos, viguier, viole, abrier, egal,*
were introduced, later on *auberge, aigrette, barrique, bigorne, brague,
cabane, câble, cadastre, cadenas, cadeau, cadet, caisse, cap, escalier, fadaise,
gabelle, garer, goujat, mistral, palefrenier, radeau, rôder, tocsin,* etc.
Literary French of the later twelfth century was also enriched by not
a few terms in vogue in the southern *cortois* literature, e.g. *abelir,
donneier* (formed on *donna* < *domina*), *donnei, cembel, gai, rossignol, solaz,
tose, balade, tenzon,* and the vogue of Provençal poetry contributed to the
acceptance of the west French pronunciation of the words *amour* (**amur**)
and *jalous* (**džalus**), in lieu of **ameur** and **džaleus**.

(Cf. G. Braun, *Der Einfluss des südfrz. Minnesangs u. Ritterwesens
auf die nordfrz. Sprache bis zum 13 Jh., Rom. Forsch.* xliii. Erlangen,
1929.)

§ 55. *Italian.*—An infiltration of Italian words, mainly connected
with navigation and commerce, began in Later Old French, the words
often finding their way north through Provençal. The list of words
borrowed in Later Old and Early Middle French includes: *falot* (< *falo*
< Gk. *pháros*), *galerie, golfe; calibre, carat, casenier, casse, cassette,
magasin, page* (< *paggio* < Gk. *paidion*), *pourcelaine.*

§ 56. In the fifteenth century Italian influence gained in strength,
largely owing to the policy of Louis XI and the growing importance of

---

[1] Cf. also the translator of the *Lorraine Psalter:* 'Quar pour tant que laingue
romance . . . est imperfaite . . . il n'est nulz tant soit boin clerc ne bien parlans
romans, qui lou latin puisse translateir en romans, quant a plusour mos dou latin, mais
couuient que per corruption et per diseite des mos francois en disse lou romans
selonc lou latin, si com: *iniquitas, iniquiteit; redemptio, redemption; misericordia,
misericorde.*'

[2] H.L.F. I, 514.

[3] Cf. for the importation of learned words in the sixteenth century, H.L.F. II,
pp. 215-241, and Sainéan, *La Langue de Rabelais*, II, pp. 64-82.

Lyons, where at that time 'more than half the inhabitants were foreigners and nearly all these Italians.'[1] It was, however, the Italian wars and the occupation of Milan (1499-1512) that led to the 'discovery of Italy,' that is the discovery of a civilisation, art, and literature considerably in advance of the French, but like enough in kind and ideal to render assimilation possible. France, restored by the recent years of peace and good government, was emerging from the torpor into which she had fallen in the later Middle Ages, and Italy was already in the full tide of the Renaissance.

The numerous visits of French notables to Italy, the residence of Italian architects, artists and poets in France, the many translations from the Italian, did much to make Italian culture widely accessible, and the marriage of Cathérine de Médicis with Henry II led to a very complete italianisation of the court when she became regent in 1560.[2]

In the new attitude taken by the sixteenth century to vernacular literature, in its vision of French as a language fit to take its place beside the language of antiquity, and in its 'defence and illustration' of the vernacular, the ideals and example of Italy counted for much. The intercourse between French and Italian humanists encouraged the attempts of the scholars to free the pronunciation of Latin from the strong vernacular influence that still dominated it and the new pronunciation of Latin was not without affecting in its turn the pronunciation of the vernacular (§§ 653-655).

§ 57. The more direct influence exercised by Italian on French may be summarised as follows :—

(i) The court craze for Italian may have helped to accredit among educated people the reduction of the earlier wẹ (< oi) to ẹ (§ 523) and may have contributed to a partial restoration of the group *s + consonant* (§ 379).

(ii) Its influence may have increased the vogue of one or two constructions that had appeared but made relatively little progress before the sixteenth century, e.g. the use of the reflexive as a passive, and of the verb *estre* in sentences of the type : *Les dieux se sont voulu venger*.

(iii) On vocabulary alone was its influence potent and durable, so strong indeed that in the later part of the century the invasion of Italian words and phrases roused the wrath of the scholar grammarian, Henri

---

[1] Tilley, *Dawn of the French Renaissance*, p. 167.

[2] Charles VIII brought Italian architects to Amboise in 1495 ; François I had the famous Sebastian Serlo at Fontainebleau in 1541 ; Benvenuto Cellini, Andrea del Sarto, Leonardo da Vinci and Tasso were all guests of François I ; the great French architect, Philibert de l'Orme, Rabelais and most of the great French writers of the century travelled in Italy ; all read Italian and some composed in this language. (Cf. Tilley, *Dawn of the French Renaissance*, Cambridge, 1918, and *The Literature of the French Renaissance*, Cambridge, 1904.)

Estienne, who in his *Deux Dialogues du Nouveau Langage italianisé et autrement desguizé principalement entre les courtisans de ce temps*, makes a violent onslaught on the 'gaste-francois' of these 'Gallo-italicques.'

Estienne's attack miscarried, and with reason, for the invasion that he deplored was not, as he thought, a mere literary fashion, a craze for novelty of expression, it was the result of the assimilation by the more backward of the two nations concerned of the conceptions and ideals, the sciences, arts and craftsmanship of the other.   With but few exceptions (e.g. *balzan*, O.F. *baucent ; canaille*, O.F. *chiennaille ; ghirlande*, O.F. *garlande ; inamouré*, O.F. *enamouré*) the words imported were not simple doublets ; they were terms with new connotations, words introduced with the novelties they designated : *réussir* is, like O.F. *reissir*, a derivative of *re-exire*, but it is the Italians who linked together the idea of escape with initiative and success ; the word *courtisan* which appears first in the translation of Castiglione's *Il Cortegiano* was introduced with a new ideal of social life, an ideal which is responsible also for the introduction of such words as *banquet, carnaval, concert, festin, bouffu, burlesque, pedant*.   The influence of literature brought in the words : *cadence, sonnet, stance*.   The new organisation of the army, the recasting of the art of military tactics and of fortification that are owed to Italy, are reflected in the loan-words : *caporal* (whence, contaminated with *corps, corporal*), *colonel, cavalerie, infanterie, arquebuse, attaquer, alarme, alerte* (< *all'erta, on the hill*), *barricade, bastion, citadelle, esplanade, parapet*.   It is computed that out of the fifty-five military terms pilloried by Estienne forty were naturalised, and it is clear that Pasquier had a better appreciation of the situation than Estienne when he wrote : 'et de malheur . . . quittames nous nos vieux mots de fortification, pour emprunter des nouveaux italiens, parceque en telles affaires les ingénieurs Italiens sçavent mieux debiter leurs denrées que nous aultres François.' (*Recherches, ed.* Feugère, II, p. 111).

Highly instructive is the treatment of the terms of architecture by Rabelais. In *Gargantua* (i.e. in 1532), the abbey of Thelema is constructed in accordance with the highest native French building traditions and the vocabulary employed by Rabelais is composed of the older consecrated terms, the only innovations being the two words of general significance, *architecture* and *symetrie*, first used in Tory's *Champfleury*.

In 1534, 1540 and again in 1548 Rabelais visited Italy ; in 1541 the Italian architect Serlo, ' qui a donné le premier aux François, par ses livres et desseings, la cognoissance des edifices antiques et de plusieurs fort belles inventions '[1] took charge as architect at Fontainebleau, and in 1545 Jean Martin translated Serlo's treatise *De Architectura* and in 1548 Colonna's translation of Vitruvius.

It is not then surprising that in the later books of Rabelais, especially the fifth, the buildings described are all of the new style and that he employs the words : *architrave, cornice, crotesque, frise, pedestal, peristile, plinthe, portique*, all Italian in origin. (Cf. L. Sainéan, *La Langue de Rabelais*, Paris, 1922 ; H.L.F. II, 198-215.)

[1] Philibert de l'Orme, quoted Sainéan, *op. cit.*, p. 58.

§ 58. *Spanish Influence.*—The introduction of Spanish words, never copious, only reached its height in the seventeenth century. Among words introduced in the sixteenth century or earlier are : *alezan, algarade, camarade, cédille, escamoter, fanfaron, genêt,* *hâbler* (< *hablar* < *fabulari*), *mermelade, picorer.*

The words in -*ade* swelled the number already borrowed from Italian and Provençal and the suffix was naturalised, cf. *oeillade, secouade,* etc.

(For complete list cf. H.L.F. II, pp. 206-214; for Arabic loan-words cf. Ewert, p. 296.)

Section 5.—Unification of the Language—Extension of Francien.

§ 59. *Use of Dialect in Later Old French.*—The wandering life led by many of the Old French poets resulted undoubtedly in a considerable mingling of dialectal forms in written French and some obliteration of local peculiarities.[1] Texts quite consistently dialectal are rare and for the most part consist of local documents, e.g. charters or abbey chronicles.

Ordinarily, however, throughout the twelfth and thirteenth centuries the local speech of all regions of northern France was freely used in literary productions, provided only that it was not the insular brand of French, for so strongly had the English accent and usage modified the French in England that the later twelfth-century writers of Continental origin, like Guernes de Pont Ste. Maxence and Marie de France, emphasise the fact that their language is of superior quality because it is ' of France.' (Cf. Guernes, *Mis lengages est bons car en France fui nez,* 6165.)

In the later thirteenth century, however, a more definite ideal of unified linguistic usage began to be formulated and the words of Jean de Meung indicate clearly that this ideal is already being identified with the speech of Paris :—

' Si m'escuse de mon langage   Rude, malostru et sauvage,
  Car nes ne sui pas de Paris,   Ne si cointes com fut Paris . . .
  Ne n'ay nul parler plus habile   Que celui qui keurt a no vile.'
                                     (*Boece,* quoted Nyrop, I, p. 22.)

§ 60. *Extension of Francien.*—The dominant position that ' francien,' the speech of the Île de France, gradually assumed among the dialects of the Langue d'Oïl, seems to be in no way due to the part that the capital or its province played in literary production, for few of the great provinces appear to have been so little represented in the literature of the first great period as the Île de France.[2] The growing prestige of the speech of Paris is rather to be ascribed to the geographical situation

---

[1] Cf. G. Wacker, *Ueber das Verhaeltniss von Dialekt und Schriftsprache im Altfranzoesischen,* Halle, 1916.

[2] Rustebuef, even, often called the first Parisian poet, may have been of Burgundian origin.

of the town, to its commercial preponderance, its University and its
political and social importance as the seat of the royal administration
and of the law courts.

§ 61. *Geographical Situation of Paris.*—No great trade route of the
Roman Empire led through Paris, but its central position and comparatively easy accessibility from all parts of northern and southern France
and England led to its gradual rise to importance as a trading centre,
especially after the Norman Conquest had brought England into close
relations with the Continent.   It was, however, only in the later thirteenth
century, after the annexation of Champagne by the Crown, that the fair
of St. Denis became more important than the fairs of Champagne.

   ' Entre cette ramification coordonnée de cours d'eau et de vallées et la Manche
où vient aboutir l'artère principale qu'est la Seine, Paris joue un rôle naturel de
liaison.   C'est la station par laquelle la région comprise entre l'Yonne et la Marne
communique avec la mer. . . . Le bassin de la Seine s'ouvre aisément sur ceux qui
l'avoisinent (i.e. the basins of the eastern Loire and upper Moselle).   Paris deviendra
ainsi tout naturellement par la simple exploitation de sa situation géographique,
le port de France le plus important. . . . Au commencement de Paris est le chemin,
la voie naturelle de passage.' (Poète, *Une Vie de Cité*, Paris, 1926, pp. 8 and 21.)

§ 62. Central and easily accessible from most of the adjacent regions,
Paris became the meeting place of many provincialisms and its speech
not infrequently served as a bridge between them.   Linked at first most
closely by facility of communication with the region to the north-east
and east, the pronunciation of the Île de France in the late eleventh
century was speedily affected by changes such as the differentiation of
the diphthongs **ei** and **ou** that appear to have originated in that region
(§ 230).   The consolidation of the royal domain and the annexation
of Normandy, Maine and Touraine in the early thirteenth century
opened the way for closer relations with the south-central and western
speech, and in the thirteenth century it was reached by the tendency
to level diphthongs that was characteristic of western speech (§ 1326),
and transmitted this movement in turn to the eastern and northern
regions.   In the later thirteenth century the verbal ending -*ions* arose
from the contamination of eastern -*iens* with central -*ons* (§ 907), and
the Parisian vulgarisms of the sixteenth century (§§ 75, 76) afford a
considerable number of examples of the connection between Parisian
speech and that of the surrounding regions.   The lowering of ē to ā in the
ending -*ien* appears, for instance, to have worked up from the Orléanais
(§ 472), the differentiation of **eau** to **iau** and of **ọu** to **eu** came down
from the north (§§ 539, 549), the broadening of **ẹ** before **r** is first met
with in the eastern region (§ 496), and the effacement of final **r** (§ 401)
and the replacement of intervocalic **r** by **z** in the south-east (§ 399;
cf. also §§ 36, 245, 391 (1), 445, 454, 1008).

§ 63. *The University.*—Paris was the home, first of the chief theological schools of France, later on of the university that held pride of place not only in France but also in Europe, and its speech must have become the ideal and in large measure the common property of the youth that thronged its streets and halls, for it must be remembered that the student life of the Middle Ages began early and closed late and that consequently local idiosyncrasies of speech must have been rubbed off more completely than in these days. The estimation in which the university was held by its members is eloquently expressed by more than one of them and it is not surprising to find a monk of Ste Geneviève describing Paris in 1206 as *the rich city, queen of towns, the soul of France.*

§ 64. *Political importance.*—The early Capetian monarchs had no fixed capital,[1] but once the royal residence was fixed at Paris the town shared in the rise of the royal dynasty to dignity and importance, a rise to which the idealisation of clerk and epic poet contributed in no small measure,[2] and which was so rapid that by the death of Philip Augustus (1223) the royal domain had been widely extended and the royal authority was being exercised up to the frontiers of the kingdom.[3]

§ 65. *Law Courts.*—From the thirteenth century on, the law courts of Paris contributed perhaps more potently than any other factor to the unification of the language : ' La langue des légistes du Palais et de la Chancellerie fut naturellement le modèle qu'on tâcha d'imiter dans les autres juridictions parisiennes et notamment au Châtelet, où affluaient les jeunes gens désireux de s'initier à la pratique, et qui rapportaient chez eux, dans toutes les parties de la France, la connaissance de la langue. Les conseillers aux Parlements, légistes, prélats et grands vassaux, ainsi que leurs clercs qui allaient remplir de hautes fonctions en province, qui la parlaient et l'écrivaient, étaient imités par les habitants de leur nouvelle résidence. Les agents innombrables que le roi délègue dans tout le royaume, baillis, prévôts, procureurs, avocats, sergents etc. parlent sa langue et exercent aussi une grande influence sur les populations au milieu desquelles ils vivent. Les ordonnances royaux qu'on publiait partout, les arrêts du Châtelet . . . habituèrent les practiciens et les lettrés à cette langue si rapidement que, dans l'espace d'un peu plus d'un demi-siècle, soit de la fin du XIIIᵉ siècle au milieu du XIVᵉ, les particularités dialectales qu'on remarquait dans les actes des juridictions et chancelleries de province disparaissent.

[1] Cf. Longnon : ' Les quatre premiers Capétiens . . . étaient bien plutôt des rois orléanais que des rois parisiens ' (*La Formation de l'Unité Française*, p. 38).

[2] Cf. Vossler, *Frankreichs Kultur*, pp. 27-51.

[3] Cf. Luchaire, *Hist. Fr.* III, 1, p. 284.

'Depuis le milieu du XIVe siècle . . . la langue du Palais était la langue officielle de toute la France de langue d'oïl et était comprise des practiciens de langue d'oc . . . Ce sont les légistes de la Chancellerie et surtout du Parlement qui . . . ont fait de la langue de la Cour du roi la langue du royaume.' (C. Beaulieux, *Histoire de l'Orthographe française*, pp. 131, 127.)

The extension of the use of French among law students in the provinces is attested by the indignant outburst of the fourteenth century lawyer, J. Faber: 'On dit qu'il y a eu à l'université d'Orléans des lecteurs qui parlaient dans leurs cours partie en français partie en latin; il leur eût mieux valu se servir d'un grossier patois angoumois ou poitevin et savoir parler latin, et comprendre les textes, que de mépriser le latin et s'imaginer faussement que le français peut atteindre au summum de l'éloquence.' (Beaulieux, p. 137.)

§ 66. *Use of Dialect in Middle French.*—In literary works provincial speech held its ground for a while tenaciously, in part owing to the disintegration of national life caused by the Hundred Years' War.

With the Valois (i.e. from 1328 on) court patronage of authorship began in Paris, and under Charles V (1364-1380) encouragement of literature, particularly didactic literature and translation, was generous (§ 50). The reign of Charles was, however, but short and his immediate successors were too fully occupied with the last stages of the Hundred Years' War, the final struggle with feudality, and the political and economic recuperation of the country, to concern themselves much with literary patronage; thus the literary centres of the fifteenth century are again provincial, and neither in the courts of the Valois nor in those of the dukes of Burgundy nor at Orléans were provincialisms meticulously avoided. Jehan le Bel and Froissart, travelled as they are, employ without apology their northern speech; the numerous 'picardisms' in the work of the court poet Eustace Deschamps aroused no comment; the writers of the western and eastern regions do indeed appear to avoid local characteristics too narrowly circumscribed, but, to mention a few writers almost at random, neither Guillaume Deguilleville (Norman of the fourteenth century), nor Jean Regnier (Auxerrois of the fifteenth century), nor Cretin, one of the grands rhétoriqueurs and also Norman, appear to have any scruple about introducing some of their more ordinary provincialisms into their works.

§ 67. *Attitude of the Sixteenth Century to Dialect.*—It is indeed only in the sixteenth century, when the royal policy had reduced the powers of all the great princely houses, and national feeling had become more conscious, that Paris and its speech secured general acceptance. It was then that the importance of the part that linguistic unity might play in the constitution of national unity was first recognised and the use of

French in the south enforced by the celebrated ordinance of Villers-Cotterets (1539). Under François I the Parisian court first became a brilliant social and literary centre and its preponderance was greatly strengthened when the brilliant group of writers at Lyons, the one important provincial literary centre of the age, made the French of Paris their medium : ' Désormais les arts et les lettres n'auront plus guère qu'une patrie et aussi qu'un marché : la Cour et ses environs.' [1]

It is significant also that provincialisms are condemned by almost all the sixteenth-century grammarians, and for all, except Palsgrave, it is the speech of Paris that is the norm.

Cf. Fabri (1521) : ' Il advient mainteffoys que lon barbarise en pronunçant comme en faisant faulx accent ou aspiration, comme communement font tous nos vulgaires parciaulx, comme trop picart, trop normant, trop breton, etc., barbarisent en leur accent.' (Th. I, lxxxviii.)

Palsgrave : ' . . . in all this worke I moost folowe the Parisyens and the countreys that be conteygned betwene the ryver of Seyne and the ryver of Loyrre, . . . for within that space is contayned the herte of Fraunce, where the tonge is at this day moost parfyte, and hath of mooste auncyente so contynued . . . there is no man, of what parte of Fraunce so ever he be borne, if he desyre that his writynges shulde be had in any estymacion, but he writeth in suche language as they speke within the boundes that I have before rehersed ' (p. 34).

Estienne, *Precellence*, 170 : ' Nous donnons tellement le premier lieu au langage de Paris, que nous confessons que celuy des villes prochaines, qui sont aussi comme du cœur de la France, ne s'en esloigne guere.   Et pour ce que Orleans voudroit bien avoir le second lieu, Tours aussi, pareillement Vandosmes, et qu'il est demandé aussi par Bourges, et Chartres d'autre costé y pretend, et quelques autres villes des plus prochaines de Paris ; à fin que les unes ne portent point d'envie aux autres, nous laissons ceste question indecise.'

(Cf. also Nyrop, I, § 28.)

§ 68. Notwithstanding the official reprobation of the use of dialect a considerable use of it is still made in the sixteenth century. The great writers from south of the Loire, e.g. Rabelais, Montaigne, make little or no effort to avoid provincialisms. Montaigne confesses : ' Mon langage françois est alteré et en la prononciation et ailleurs par la barbarie de mon creu ' (*Essais*, II, xvii), and it was the editors of 1595 who made it part of their business to eliminate locutions and forms ' qui sentent leur vieux temps, qui sentent la province.' [2]

In accordance with the practice of the fifteenth century deliberate use of provincialisms was made in drama and romance to give local colour,[3] and the Pleiade, as is well known, went further, for they stoutly defended the poet's right to make use of words culled from all parts of France, if

[1] Brunot, *La Doctrine de Malherbe*, p. 300.
[2] Cf. Strowski, *Essais*, I, p. 463, Voizard, *Etude sur la Langue de Montaigne*, and Sainéan, *La Langue de Rabelais*, II, pp. 132-201.
[3] Cf. Villon, G. T., xciv, Rabelais, *passim*.

he thought good : 'Tu sçauras dextrement choisir et aproprier a ton
œuvre les mots les plus significatifs des dialectes de nostre France.'
(Ronsard, *Abrégé*, VII, p. 321) ; 'Le Poëte pourra aporter de mon conseilh
moz Picars, Normans et autres qui sont souz la Couronne ; Tout ę̃t
Françoę̃s puisqu'iz sont du païs du Roę̃.' [1]

No part of the Pleiade's recipes for securing a copious and varied
diction went more speedily out of fashion, however, for no part was more
out of harmony with the spirit of the age of Henri IV.   Du Perron is
evidently voicing the feeling of his times when he relegates the use of
dialect to the 'estats populaires et aristocratiques, ou l'on s'y doit
accommoder' and tells his contemporaries 'qu'on s'estudie à parler le seul
langage de la cour, en laquelle se trouve ce qu'il y a de politesse dans le
royaume.'   (Quoted Brunot, *La Doctrine de Malherbe*, p. 301.)

§ 69. Elimination of provincialisms was naturally more easily accomplished in
written French than in speech, and it may be noted that both Palsgrave and Meigret
appear to have been misled in their accounts of sounds by their provincial origin :
Palsgrave in prescribing a velarised pronunciation of ā and the labialisation of final e
(Norman traits of his time, §§ 275, 446), Meigret in his description of the o-sounds
(§ 584).   Vaugelas himself is said to have retained his Savoyard accent to the end of
his life.

The first extant treatise written expressly to combat provincialism in speech is
said to have appeared in 1624 in Hainault : *Ecloge praecipuarum legum gallicae
pronunciationis ex primis gallicae linguae auctoribus.*

Section 6.—SOCIAL DIFFERENTIATION.

§ 70. In the fifteenth century social differentiation of linguistic usage
made itself evident in two directions. [2]

(1) *Argot.*—At the bottom of the social scale, among the numerous
bands of vagrants, thieves and wastrels that were the dreary heritage of
the Hundred Years' War, the *Coquillards, Caimans, Egyptiens*, there was
forged a specialised language, a jargon, that received the name of *argot*.
In its earliest form this argot was distinguished chiefly by a fantastic
corruption of the meanings of words.   It found its way into literature in
the mystery plays, where it is used to characterise the part of exe-
cutioners, thieves and gamblers, and it is employed by not a few poets,
including Villon, who has left seven ballads in 'iargon ou iobelin.'
Mediaeval argot has bequeathed a few words, e.g., *bribe, duper, gueux,
narquois* (cf. Sainéan, *L'Argot Ancien*, Paris, 1907).

§ 71. (2) Among the educated writers, more especially those at the
court of Burgundy, there came into fashion a pretentious latinisation of

---

[1] Peletier du Mans, *L'Art Poétique*, p. 124 ; cf. also Estienne, *Precellence*, pp. 167-
183, Vauquelin de la Fresnaye, I, 361-364, but ct. II, 907-910.

[2] For the beginnings of social differentiation in the twelfth century, cf. § 44.

language, employed largely to confer social prestige on the users. An amusing illustration of the estimation in which this pompous diction was held, is furnished by the mystery plays, for in them a latinised diction is always accorded to dignitaries such as angels, bishops and allegorical figures, and one still more pretentious to God the Father.[1]

The exaggeration and pretentiousness of these 'escumeurs de latin,' these 'sottelets glorieux' who make a 'fricassée de grec et de latin' (Dolet) did not escape the ridicule of their contemporaries. The sentence that Rabelais (*Pant.* V) puts in the mouth of his 'tout jolliet escholier limousin' had already been pilloried by Tory in his *Champfleury* (1529): 'Despumons la verbocination latinale et transfretons la Sequane au dilicule et crepuscule, puis deambulons par les Quadriues et Platees de Lutece, et comme verisimiles amorabundes, captiuon la beniuolence de l'omnigene et omniforme sexe feminin.' It is probable that both authors were drawing upon a parody that was circulating orally in the 'Quartier Latin': and indeed reality is hardly outdone by the parody.

§ 72. It is, however, only in the sixteenth century that any social differentiation in ordinary linguistic usage is attested. The first explicit mention is made in 1529 by Geofroi Tory in his *Champfleury*, where he twice mentions the pronunciation of the 'dames de Paris' (cf. §§ 497, 623), and few of the later grammarians[2] fail to reprobate some trait or other of the 'vulgus,' the 'plebs,' the 'populace,' the 'menu peuple,' although they are not by any means always at one in their animadversions. A few also mention, with approval or disapproval, the usage of the court (§§ 82, 523).

Social divergence of this kind may indeed have existed earlier, but no overt condemnation of vulgarisms is attested previously and Villon makes use of the very pronunciation that offended the taste of the 'dames de Paris,' for he rhymes together *terre : Barre ; appert : part* (T. liii, lxvi, etc.), i.e. he lowers ę to a before r: his pronunciation appears, however, to have passed without remark.

Palsgrave also is still oblivious of the existence of any such distinctions and admits pronunciations that we find later French grammarians rejecting as 'vulgar,' e.g. the lowering of ųę (<oi) to ųa before s, t, l and r, e.g. *troas* (pp. 13, 14; cf. § 525), and of ję̃ to jã, e.g. *mianne* (p. 3 ; cf. § 472) and the use of intervocalic z for r (pp. 34, 456; cf. § 399).

§ 73. It is indeed the reign of François I that marks a turning-point in this matter. His court in becoming the centre of polite society

<hr>

[1] Cf. Vossler, *op. cit.*, pp. 149-152.
[2] Cf. H. Estienne: 'or ie presuppose, quand ie parle ou de nostre langage Parisien ou de ceux que i'appelle les dialectes, qu'on entende qu'il faut premierement oster toutes les corruptions et depravations que luy fait le menu peuple': (*Precellence*, p. 170).

set up a standard of social and linguistic usage which for a time became the ideal of all who sought social distinction, cf. Peletier: ' J'é tousjours été de l'opinion de ceus qui ont dit qu'an notre France n'i a androèt ou l'on parle pur françoès, fors la ou èt la court, ou bien la ou sont ceus qui i ont été nourriz: ie m'i suis voulontirs geté toutes les foès qu'an é u l'ocasion . . . m'aprochant dés pèrsonnages qui auoèt crédit, faueur é manimant d'afères: qui sont ceus qui parlet le mieus.' (Th. I, pp. lxxxviii, ix.) And social differentiation once established remained, though later on in the century the court, strongly italianised, ceased for a while to set the standard of educated usage (cf. below § 82).

§ 74. The most notable of the 'vulgarisms' prevalent in the middle of the century were parodied in the poem *Epistre au Biau Fils de Pazys* (1549, attributed falsely to Marot), and the salient characteristics of the court fashion towards the end of the century by Henri Estienne in his *Remontrance aux autres Courtisans*.

Short citations from these works may serve to illustrate the outstanding characteristics considered vulgar or fashionable by contemporaries:—

(1) *Vulgar Pronunciations:*

(i) **a** + **r** for **ę** + **r** (§§ 496-498).
(ii) Intervocalic **z** for **r** (§ 399).
(iii) Effacement of final consonants and of **r** + consonant (§§ 617, 623, 397).
(iv) **iau** for **eau** (§ 540).
(v) Lowering of **ī** to **ę̄** (§§ 452-454).
(vi) Use of the first person plural for the first person singular.
(vii) Use of the perfect forms of the second conjugation for the first (§ 1008).
(viii) Adoption of pronunciation -**ę** in the imperfect indicative (§§ 522-524).

Du jour de la Sin Nicoula,
D'avoir dancé? Vou commensite,
C'est au jardin: mon peze entry,
Aupres de vous, et sy avoy
Laquelle me sembly depui
May se Piar nou regardet,
Et quan il m'eu bien espié,
Si fort, en me sarran la main,

A propo, vou souvien ty poin
Que j'etien tou deux si tresla
Aussi trèsbien vou rachevite;
Davantuze me recontry
Touriou l'yeu dessu vostre voy,
Aussi claize que l'iau de puy.
Qui de gran jalourie ardet,
Vou me marchiste sur le pie
Que j'en clochy le lendemain.

(2) *Court Pronunciation:*

(i) **u** for **ǫ** (§ 581).
(ii) **ua** for **uę** (§ 525).
(iii) **a** + **r** for **ę** + **r** (§ 496).

Si tant vous aimez le son doux,
De dire Chouse, au lieu de Chose.
Et pour Trois mois dire Troas moas?
En la fin vous direz La guarre,

N'estes vous pas bien de grands fous,
De dire J'ouse, au lieu de J'ose?
Pour Je fay, vay, Je foas, je voas?
Place Maubart, et frère Piarre.

§ 75. Subjoined is a list, mainly culled from Thurot, of the traits stigmatised as vulgar by the grammarians of the sixteenth century:—

A. PRONUNCIATION.

(1) *Traits accepted wholly or partially in educated speech in the course of the sixteenth or seventeenth centuries:*—

(i) Lowering of ę before r to a, I, 3 *et seq.* (§ 496).

(ii) Reduction of wę ($<$ oi) to ę and the beginnings of the lowering of wę to wa before s and r (e.g. troas, *trois*, voarre, *voirre*), I, 375, 356 (§§ 522-525).

(iii) Effacement of final consonants:

(*a*) Effacement of r accepted in -ęr and -ɟęr, II, 150-157; rejected finally in -ir, -ör -*eur* (except in *monsieur*), II, 162-170 (§§ 400, 401).

(*b*) Effacement of final s at a pause and of final z after ə in prevocalic position, accepted in the seventeenth century, II, 36, 24, 28 (§§ 621-623).

(*c*) Effacement of final f, k, l, p, t, accepted variably, II, 133, 130, 141, 124, 97 (§§ 611-620).

(iv) Effacement of initial h *aspirée*, II, 395, 6 (§ 196).

(2) *Traits rejected:*—

(i) Use of iau for *eau* : biau, iaue, I, 439 (§ 540).

(ii) Lowering of ɟēn to ɟān, II, 49 (§ 472).

(iii) Substitution of z for intervocalic r, II, 271 (accepted in *chaise* and *besicles* (§ 399)).

(iv) Assimilation of r to l in the group rl, e.g. *paller*, II, 289 (§ 397). Effacement of r in *toujours*, II, 83, (§ 397).

(v) Lowering of ī to ę before intervocalic nasal consonants, e.g. in *cousine*, II, 479, (§ 454).

(vi) Use of the shortened form *dornavant* for *dorenavant*, I, 103, and of nasalised *ainsin* for *ainsi*, II, 498, (§ 455).

It should be noted that the first three of these traits are provincial in origin.

§ 76. B. FLEXIONAL FORMS.

(1) *Forms accepted:*—

(i) The replacement of *fol, mol, col* by analogical *fou, mou, cou*, II, 186 (§ 814).

(ii) The reduction of fęz-, the weak radical of *faire* to fəz-, e.g. fəzā for fęzā faisant, I. 312-313, (§ 961).

(2) *Forms rejected:*—

(i) The analogical extension of the endings of the perfect and imperfect subjunctive of the second conjugation to the first conjugation was proscribed by the grammarians (§ 1008, cf. Nyrop, *Gr.*, II, § 71).

(ii) A certain number of older forms retained in popular usage were rejected:

(*a*) The etymological feminine *quel*, I, 176.

(*b*) The etymological future of *baillir, baura* (Picardism for *baudra*, cf. § 370).

(*c*) The termination -ęs ($<$ -oĭs) in the second person plural of the future, I, 50 (§ 967).

(*d*) The shortened forms *aga* $<$ *agart*, a'vous, sa'vous $<$ *avez vous, savez vous*, I, 118, 119, (§ 937).

Section 7.—REGULATION OF LANGUAGE.

§ 77. The first treatises on the French language were compiled for those most in need of such instruction, the English, who desired to secure enough French to be unhampered in their travels or military expeditions in France, and to enable them to read the language and copy it with tolerable accuracy (cf. §§ 1072, 1073). They are therefore

of the nature of modern spelling treatises or phrase-books. The first grammatical treatise proper is the *Donait Francois* of Jean Barton, compiled *c.* 1400, the most complete is Palsgrave's great work *L'Esclarcissement de la Langue Francoyse* (1530). These treatises, especially Palsgrave's, supply much information, but their French, especially that of the earlier work, is often markedly insular (cf. § 69), and none, not even the *Esclarcissement*, had any vogue in France or exercised any influence on the language.

§ 78. The first French writer to make lament over the instability of the vernacular is the fourteenth-century translator of the Psalms : 'Aucune fois li latin warde ses rigles de gramaire et ses congruiteiz et ordenances . . . en nombres, en temps, en declinesons, en causes, en muef . . . que en romans ne en francoiz on ne puet proprement wardeit (§ 401), pour les uarieteiz et diuersiteiz des lainguaiges et lou deffault d'entendement de maint et plusour, qui plus souuent forment lour mos et lour parleir a lour uolenteit at a lour guise que a ueriteit et au commun entendement ; et pour ceu que nulz ne tient en son parleir ne rigle certenne, mesure ne raison, est laingue romance si corrompue qu'a poinne li uns entent l'aultre et a poinne puet on trouueir a iour d'ieu persone, qui saiche escrire . . . ne prononcieir en une meismes menieire, mais escript . . . et prononce li uns en une guise et li aultre en une aultre.' (*Ps. Lorr.*, p. 2.)

§ 79. The protest of this Lorraine translator is not renewed until the sixteenth century is reached. Then the contrast between the stability and well-ordered regularity of the classical languages and the shifting and motley character of the vernacular aroused attention, and the success of the Italians in stabilising their own tongue incited to emulation. The first sixteenth-century French writer to voice the need of stabilisation and to encourage regulation is the printer Geofroi Tory in his *Champfleury* (1529) :—

'O Deuotz Amateurs de bonnes Lettres, Pleust a Dieu que quelque Noble cueur semployast a mettre et ordonner par reigle nostre Langage Francois ; Ce seroit moyen que maints Milliers d'hommes se esuertu-roient a souuent user de belles et bonnes paroles. Sil ny est mys et ordonne, on trouuera que de Cinquante Ans en Cinquante Ans La Langue Francoise, pour la plus grande part, sera changee et peruertie . . . Le Langage dauiourdhui est change en mille facons du Langage qui estoit il y a Cinquante Ans ou enuiron . . .'

Tory's own precepts are meagre and concerned mainly with ortho-graphy and it is to the learned doctor Jacques Dubois, Silvius Ambianus, that is ascribed the first French Grammar compiled in France. The cumbersome title of the grammar affords sufficient indication of its

character : ' Iacobi Syluii Ambiani in linguam gallicam Isagoge, una cum eiusdem Grammatica Latino-gallica, ex Hebraeis, Graecis et Latinis authoribus ' (1532, new style).   The work is etymological in aim, dominated by the theory that French is mangled Latin and that the touchstone of a ' true ' French form is its similarity to Latin (e.g. Picard *mi* is superior to French *moi ; j'ame* to *j'aime*, etc.).

' I shall have realised my desire, if the native brilliance of the French language, for so long tarnished and almost destroyed by rust, is somewhat brightened and restored by a return home, as it were, to its pristine purity, assisted by my study of the origin of its words in Hebrew, Greek and Latin, from the which sources our speech is almost completely drawn.' (Quoted H.L.F. II, 137.)

§ 80.   Dubois was followed by many other scholars and grammarians, of whom the most outstanding are *Louis Meigret* of Lyons and the brilliant and versatile printer-scholar *Henri Estienne*.[1]   This latter, vigorous, combative, unsystematic, is more of a comparative philologist than a grammarian and was chiefly concerned about the relation in which the vernacular stood to the classical languages (cf. his *Traicté de la Conformité du langage françois auec le grec*) and its defence against the craze for italianisation (cf. *Deux Dialogues du nouueau langage françois, italianizé et autrement desguizé, principalement entre les courtisans de ce temps* (1578)).   Louis Meigret, born at Lyons *c.* 1510, resident at Paris from about 1538, is a translator and grammarian of high intelligence, good sense, and initiative.   He had most at heart the reform of spelling, and boldly advocated the adoption of a semi-phonetic system which, unfortunately for posterity, found little favour with his contemporaries, but he is a pioneer in other directions also.   His most complete grammatical work, *Le Tretté de la Grammęre Françoęze, fęt par Louis Meigręt Lionoęs*, 1550, is mainly concerned with flexions, but deals shortly also with spelling and pronunciation, including the problem of intonation and musical accent in French, a problem that has had to wait for its solution to the present time.   Syntax is only mentioned incidentally, ' par rencontres,' but his treatment of the questions he touches on is often suggestive.   Unlike Dubois, Meigret definitely refuses to bring French under the dominance of Latin, and though occasionally too autocratic in his decisions he is quite ready as a rule to recognise the authority of usage.[2]   His remarks in the concluding chapter on the relation of

[1] For these and other sixteenth-century grammarians cf. also H.L.F. II, pp. 133-159.

[2] ' Je ne m'amuze pas fort ao' formęzons dęs deriuatifs : d'aotant qe çela reqiert la lęcture dę' Grammęres Gręcqes, ę Latines ; ao'qęlles çeluy se deura addresser qi lę' voudra ęntęndre ; sans toutesfoęs se prescrir' aocune loę contre l'uzaje de la prononçiaçion Françoęze : come font pluzieurs, qi dizet nou' dussions dir' einsi suyuant lę' regles Latines e Gręcqes ; ao'qels pour toute satisfaççion il faot repondre, qe nou' deuons dire, come nou' dizons, puis qe jenerallemęnt l'uzaje de parler l'a reçu einsi.' (fol. 26 v° p. 35.)

language to the order of nature contain an interesting anticipation of the eighteenth century attitude to grammar.

§ 81. *Influence of the Grammarians.*—It is difficult to estimate how far the attitude of the grammarians and the educated public affected the linguistic developments of their time, for the final settlement of most of the changes they sought to advance or check lay with the next period. They and their successors achieved success in their immediate aims most completely when Latin usage or spelling was on their side, or when the traits they rejected were provincial in origin and presumably not in general use in Paris. Thus it appears to be largely due to their efforts that the pronunciation of learned loan-words (§§ 653-655) and a few others (§ 582) was modified, that the tendency to use the termination of the first plural for the first singular (§ 74) and the terminations of the perfect indicative of the second conjugation for those of the first (§§ 74, 1008) was checked, that the terminations *-assions, -assiez* were generalised (§ 1044), and that the following provincialisms were rejected : the use of **iau** for **eau** (§§ 74, 75, 540), of **ʝā** for **ʝē** (§§ 75, 472), of **u** (*ou*) for **ǫ** before **ž, š, d, z,** (§§ 74, 581-583), of **z** for **r** intervocalic (§§ 74, 75, 399), and of the termination **-ęs** for **-ęs** in the second person plural of future (§§ 75, 967).

The influence that they exercised on the more important and general sound-changes, however, e.g. the reduction of **wę** (< **ǫi**) to **ę** (§§ 74, 75, 523), or its broadening to **wa** (§§ 74, 75, 525), the broadening of **ęr** to **ar** (§§ 74, 75, 496), the effacement of final consonants (§§ 74, 75, 400-401, 615-623), the effacement of aspirated **h** (§§ 75, 196), the restriction of the use of analogical **-s** in the first person singular (§§ 901, 902), was sufficient to check and perturb these changes, but not entirely prevent them.

§ 82. In the ultimate aim that the grammarians had in view, the defining and fixing of linguistic usage, the attempts of these pioneers, interesting as they are, met with little success, and linguistic usage remained fluctuating.

This is doubtless attributable in part to the fact that in their formulation of usage they often misconceived the part that grammar can play and were not always sufficiently in touch with the linguistic tendencies of their time. Some, as we have seen, like Jacques Dubois, were desirous of pressing French into the mould of Latin ; others, like Meigret, were too much in advance of their contemporaries, and indeed Meigret's spelling reforms ran counter to the only body of linguistic tradition that already had some claim to fixity. The greater number tended to impose rules rather than to observe practice and formulate usage.

It is, however, in the main the political and social conditions of their

age and the prematurity of their attempts. that occasioned their failure. The fixing of linguistic usage, the codification of grammatical rule, is only possible when conditions of life are stable, when there is existent some recognised authority to make decisions, backed up by a sufficient weight of public opinion to enforce them. In the sixteenth century these conditions were almost entirely absent.

The disorders attendant on the religious dissensions and wars were probably sufficient in themselves to frustrate their efforts, but it must also be borne in mind that throughout the century education was but sparsely diffused, and that educated opinion was lacking in weight, because it was vacillating and without any generally accepted court of appeal. Turn by turn the *royal court*, the *parlement, the people* are cited as arbiters of 'bel usage,' none with general acceptance or permanence.

Under François I authority was attributed by some to the court, Marot's 'maîtresse d'école,' either alone or in conjunction with the law courts. Tory, for instance, maintains that 'le stile de Parlement et le langage de la Cour sont tres bons': Peletier, as we have seen, § 73, is for the court alone, but his contemporary, Guillaume des Autels, is of quite another opinion: 'Tes labeurs,' he writes to Meigret, 'et les miens . . . seroient a mon auis autant inutiles que si nous auions basti sus le sable : quand nous ne voudrons establir et confirmer nostre langue autrement qu'à l'appetit des courtisans : veu leur tant estrange et tant variable mutation : ioint que la court est un monstre de plusieurs testes, et consequemment de plusieurs langues, et plusieurs voix.' (Th. I, p. lxxxix.)

The italianisation of the court under Catherine de Medicis completed its discredit, and this not only in the eyes of a scholar of Protestant upbringing like Henri Estienne. In 1562 Ronsard, court poet as he was, excepts from his recommendation of dialects the language of the court, 'sans affecter par trop le parler de la Cour, lequel est quelquefois tres-mauvais pour estre langage de Damoiselles, et ieunes Gentils-hommes qui font plus profession de bien combattre que de bien parler.' (*Abrégé*, p. 321.)

In 1584 Bèze summed up the position as follows : 'There was a time, that of François I, who may rightly be called 'parentem bonarum litterarum,' when the pure French pronunciation was to be sought at the court. But it is known how in France since his death the language has gradually changed with the manners, so that it is less and less apparent where it can be found in its purity. All that remains is preserved in some families faithful to ancient traditions, and in the parlement of Paris, although there also the contagion of an incorrect pronunciation is spreading.' (P. 8.)

Alone in his time Ramus anticipates Malherbe in making the people the arbiter of linguistic usage : 'Le peuple est souuerain de sa langue

et la tient comme un fief de franc aleu, et n'en doit recognoissance a aulcun seigneur. L'escolle de cest doctrine n'est point es auditoires des professeurs Hebreus, Grecs et Latins en l'Uniuersite de Paris ; elle est au Louvre, au Palais, aux Halles, en Greue, a la place Maubert.' (*Gramaire*, 2nd edition, 1572, p. 30 ; cf. H.L.F. II, p. 154.)

Section 8.—EXPANSION OF FRENCH ABROAD.[1]

§ 83. The pride taken by the twelfth century in its language is pleasantly illustrated by a passage in the translation of *Genesis* made by the clerk Evrat for Eleanor of Aquitaine's famous daughter, Marie de Champagne :—

Chascune tere, vils et chiere,	A son langage a sa maniere. . . .
De quelque part que l'on l'aprenge	Tuit sunt et divers et estrange
Fors que li languages franchois	C'est cil que Deus entant au chois
K'il la fist et bel et legier.	(P. Meyer, *Recueil*, p. 339.)

The conquests of the French and the admiration felt by other nations for their language and literature carried French into all the countries with which they were in contact.

§ 84. In the states founded by the Crusaders in the East, i.e., the four states that resulted from the first Crusade—Jerusalem, Antioch, Edessa, Tripoli—and those founded after the fourth, French was the language of the courts, and the official and legal language. In Cyprus the domination of the Lusignans lasted two centuries (1291-1489) and there in the thirteenth century Philippe de Novare, Italian by origin, wrote in French his Memoirs and the important feudal treatise *Livre de forme de plait* that was afterwards incorporated in the *Livre des Assises et des bons usages dou roiaume de Jerusalem*. But it is only in Cyprus that the use of French left much trace, elsewhere the Christian states were too ephemeral and the civilisations with which they were in contact, whether Arab or Greek, too advanced for the use of French to be established among the subject populations. Hence there resulted nothing but a slight influence on vocabulary, as marked on French as on Arabic or Greek.

Significant are the words of the chronicler, Foucher de Chartres (cf. Lavisse, II, 2, pp. 246-247): ' Behold our Western men transformed into dwellers in the East . . . the man of Rheims or Chartres has become the man of Tyre or Antioch . . . We make use of the languages of all the countries where we have settled . . .'

§ 85. Jongleurs and pilgrims carried early into northern *Italy* (Lombardy, Venetia and Emilia) the *chansons de geste* and the Arthur stories (cf. the mention of Ganelon on the lapidary inscription of Nepi of 1131, and the twelfth-century carvings of Arthurian personages on the Cathedral of Modena), but the main period of expansion of the French language in this region extends from about 1230-1350. In that period the vogue of French is attested by the number of copies of French works that were made (e.g. three MSS. of the *Roland* are of Italian provenance, six of the *Roman de Troie*), by the number of original compositions in French,[2] and also by the curious hybrid Franco-Italian language. In Piedmont, French was used as the

---

[1] For the use of French in England cf. Part V.

[2] Cf. the much-quoted remark of Brunetto Latini, the master of Dante, in the preface of his book *Li Tresors* (c. 1265): ' et si aucuns demandoit por quoi cist livres est escriz en romanz selonc le langage des François, puisque nos somes Ytaliens, je diroie que ce est por ij raisons, l'une car nos somes en France, et l'autre por ce que la parleure est plus delitable et plus commune a toutes gens.'

official language after the displacement of Latin until it was ousted by Italian (in 1577), and in some parts of the province it remained in use until the modern period.[1]

§ 86. *Germany*.—In Germany a translation of the *Alexander* of Alberic de Besançon, was made by the priest Lamprecht (about 1130), and of the *Roland* by the priest Konrad about 1131,[2] and these were followed towards the close of the twelfth century and the beginning of the next by the translation cr adaptation of several of the greatest old French poems.

The infatuation of the German nobles for French is described by the trouvere, Adenet le Roi, in his poem *Berte aus grans pies* (*c.* 1280) :—

> 'Avoit une coustume ens el tiois pais
> Que tout li grant seignor, li conte et le marchis
> Avoient entour aus gent françoise tous dis
> Pour aprendre françois lor filles et lor fil..
> Li rois et la roïne et Berte o le cler vis
> Sorent pres d'aussi bien le françois de Paris
> Com se il fussent né au bourc a Saint Denis.'   (ll. 148-154.)

Many French words were borrowed by the MHG. writers, e.g., *barun*, *betscheler* (*bacheler*), *hartschierer* (*archier*), *tschahtel* (*chastel*), *prinz*, *mütze* (*aumuce*), *shanze* (*chance*), *foreht* (*forest*), *vassal ;* the greater number were, however, short-lived, and the most permanent trace of French influence on German is seen in the verbal suffix *-ieren*, abstracted from loan-words such as : *allieren* (<*allier*), *embrazieren*, etc., and the substantival suffix *-ie*, cf. H. Suolahti, *Der frz. Einfluss auf die Deutsche Sprache im dreizehnten Jahrhunderte* (*Mém. Soc. Néo-philologique de Helsingfors*, VIII).

§ 87. *Flanders and the Netherlands*.—French was the dominant language in Flanders, Hainault and Brabant, their rulers were the patrons of French poets (e.g. the *Perceval* of Crestien de Troies was written for Philip of Flanders), many French works of all types were translated into Middle Dutch, and thus it is not surprising that the influence of French on both Dutch and Flemish is strong and abiding. 'Dès le moyen âge . . . le français imposa au néerlandais une partie de son lexique, quelques-uns de ses procédés de dérivation, et quelques-uns des traits essentiels de sa syntaxe. Sur le flamand, il continuera longtemps d'exercer son influence.' (H.L.F. I, 398).

§ 88. In the sixteenth century the continuance of the vogue of French abroad is frequently attested, cf. Peletier : 'On sét qu'au pais d'Artoès é de Flandre iz tiénet tousiours l'usance de la langue é i plédent leurs causes, é i font leurs écritures é pro-cédures an Françoès. An Angleterre, au moins antre les Princes é an leurs cours, iz parlet Françoès an tous leurs propos, An Espagne, on i parle ordinéremant Françcès es lieus les plus célébres . . . An la court de l'ampereur . . . on n'use, pour le plus, d'autre langage que Françoès. Que diré je de l'Italie, ou la langue Françoèse èt toute commune ? '   Writing more flamboyantly the Fleming Mellema, in the dedicatory epistle of his French-Flemish dictionary (1591), ranks with the ' trois langues souveraines ' (Hebrew, Greek and Latin), 'la tresnoble et tresparfaite langue Françoise, laquelle apres les trois susdictes (maugré que m'en sçaura l'Italienne) regne et s'use pour la plus commune, la plus facile, voire la plus accomplie de toutes autres en la chrestienté.' (Cited Thurot, I, xiv.)

---

[1] P. Meyer, *De l'Expansion de la Langue Française en Italie pendant le Moyen-Âge*, Roma, 1904 (Atti del Congresso Internazionale di Scienze Storiche).

[2] This date is now questioned, cf. *Rolandslied*, ed. C. Wesle, *Intr.* pp. xi, xii.

Section 9.—SOURCES OF KNOWLEDGE OF PERIOD II.

§ 89. *Assonance, Rhyme and Metre.*—From the study of the *assonances* information may be obtained about the pronunciation of the tonic vowels, e.g. the extent of nasalisation (§§ 433, 434), differentiation of the e-sounds (§ 573), levelling of diphthongs (Pt. II, chap. xiv).

The use of *rhyme* (used first in the vernacular French in the *Comput* of Philippe de Thaon, *c.* 1119) adds further information about the pronunciation of consonants standing after the stressed vowel. From the systematic use of *rime leonine* or *rime double*, as in the second part of the *Roman de la Rose* (cf. Introduction, pp. 237-262), or the work of Cretin (15th cent.), some indication is furnished of the value of the consonants and vowels that stand before the tonic syllable (cf. §§ 275, 611).

The numbering of syllables supplies some information about consonantalisation (§ 241), the use of ę etymological or analogical (cf. §§ 243-247, 265-272, 780, 898) and of final consonants standing after ę, e.g. the use of θ (§ 347), of analogical s (§ 805).

§ 90. *Orthography.*—In the earlier part of the period changes in pronunciation continued to be reflected in the spelling, and serve to some extent to date changes in pronunciation, e.g. the substitution of *eu* for *ou*, of *oi* for *ei*, of *e* for *ai*, of *u* for vocalised *t*, etc. When spelling becomes more fixed changes are indicated more and more only in the spelling of the unlettered and of words whose origin is unknown. Documents which provide information of this kind are the letters of unlearned people, e.g. those included in the *Foreign Correspondence of Marie de Lorraine,* 1537-1548 (Balcarres Papers, third series), the fifteenth-century *Mystery Plays*, and the spellings of proper names, e.g. those in the Parisian *Rôles de Taille.*

Throughout the period the occasional use of intruded inorganic letters and of symbols with unusual value, the so-called ' graphies inverses,' often furnishes useful clues, cf. the spellings *neuold* (Rol.), *Colstentinoble* (Auc.), which indicate the equation of the value of the symbols *l* and *u*, i.e. the vocalisation of *l*, the graphy *boin* for *buen* and *moille* for *moelle*, etc., cf. §§ 716-732.

§ 91. *The Notation of French Words in Foreign Alphabets.*—(i) The transliteration of French words into Hebrew, cf. the early thirteenth-century glosses published by Neubauer in *Rom. St.* I, p. 165, and the late thirteenth-century Hebrew *Elegies* published by Darmesteter, *Rom.* III, p. 474 (cf. below the subject-index, and the bibliography given by Nyrop, *Gr.* I, p. 497).

(ii) The signature of Queen Anne in Cyrillic characters in 1063, cf. Thomas, *Essais*, pp. 159-167 (§ 235).

§ 92. *Loan-Words.*—Middle English and Middle High German loan-words of the twelfth century indicate the value of the symbols *z*, *ch*, *g* and of the group *s* + consonant (cf. below, § 378 and the bibliography given by Nyrop, *Gr.* I, pp. 495-496).

The French loan words : *artichault* < Italian *articiocco*, *haubby* < English *hobby*, corroborate the reduction of **au** to **o** in stressed syllables in the sixteenth century, and the graphy *aulogier* for *orlogier* in 1292 indicates its still earlier reduction in a weak syllable (§ 535 ; cf. also § 627).

[For Spelling Treatises and Grammars cf. above p. xxv, xxvi and §§ 77-80.]

PART II.

PHONOLOGY.

CHAPTER I.

PHONETIC INTRODUCTION.

Section 1.

§ 93. The basis of language is physical, for its raw material consists of sounds, the products of the movements of the organs of speech; its function is psychological: speaking broadly, it exists to enable the individual to make intelligible to others his needs, emotions, thoughts and experiences. In all parts of linguistic study, therefore, the psychological and the physical are linked together. Physical factors, the structure and movements of the organs of speech, are dominant in the formation and modification of sounds; sound changes profoundly influence flexions and affect, though in less degree, the history of constructions and the life of words. Psychology, dominant in the history of construction and vocabulary, i.e. in *syntax* and *semantics*, is a factor as important as sound change in the history of flexion, i.e. in *morphology*; in *phonology*, the history of pronunciation, it also plays a part, though a minor one, for in speech, it must be remembered, sounds are not used in isolation but in sequences, linked together in significant patterns, in words, locutions, sentences; and moreover, in speech, emotion and the desire for intelligibility may at any time modify habitual pronunciation.

The intelligent comprehension of the evolution of sound and flexion in any given language demands therefore a certain amount of preliminary knowledge, for it is necessary to understand clearly the character of the organs of speech, the place and mode of production of the sounds of the language studied and to comprehend something of the psychological processes that underlie or influence changes in sound and flexion. In this book, therefore, the study of the history of the sounds is prefaced by a chapter dealing with the formation of those that are or have been employed in French and Latin, and with the main processes and predisposing conditions of sound-change, and the study of Morphology begins with a chapter dealing with contamination and analogy, the

4

psychological processes that most strongly affect the development of flexions. The treatment of these subjects is necessarily summary, and students who have received no previous training in phonetics are strongly advised to consult one of the manuals of this subject mentioned below. All those interested in the more general linguistic questions will find a more detailed discussion and bibliography in the authorities quoted at the end of this introductory chapter.

Nyrop : *Manuel Phonétique du Français Parlé, traduit et remanié par E. Philipot*, 3ᵐᵉ édition, 1914.

M. Grammont : *Traité Pratique de Prononciation Française*, Paris, 1920.

Paul Passy : *The Sounds of the French Language*, translated Savory and Jones, second edition, Oxford, 1924.

L. E. Armstrong : *The Phonetics of French*, London, 1932.

Section 2.—CLASSIFICATION OF SOUNDS.

§ 94. Sounds are made by the modification of the breath by the varying positions of the organs of speech. They are differentiated in various ways : by the amount of vibration of the vocal chords, by the position of the velum, by variations in the extent to which the breath passage is constricted, and by variations in the place where this constriction is made, i.e. by the point of articulation of the sound.

§ 95. (1) *Vibration of Vocal Chords. Voiced and Voiceless (Breathed) Sounds.*—A sound is said to be *voiced* when it is produced with vibration of the vocal chords, the two membranes which, when stretched taut across the larynx, are set vibrating by the breath expelled from the lungs : when there is no vibration sounds are called *voiceless* or *breathed*.

Normal vowels are all voiced : consonants may be either voiced or voiceless, cf. **b, v, d, z, g** and their breathed counterparts **p, f, t, s, k.**

§ 96. (2) *Position of the Velum. Oral and Nasal Sounds.*—The velum or soft palate may be raised so as to block the nose passage and thus allow the main stream of air to pass through the mouth and form the *oral* sounds, e.g. the vowels **a, e, i, o, u,** etc., and the consonants **k, g, t, d, p, b,** etc., or it may be lowered so as to open the nasal passage and allow the main stream of air to pass through the nose and thus produce the *nasal* sounds, e.g. the nasal consonants **n** and **m** and the nasal vowels heard in Modern French :

an ā   fin fẽ   on ǫ̃   un œ̃.

§ 97. (3) *Variations in the Extent of Constriction of Passage.*—The air-stream may either pass through the throat, mouth or nose unimpeded,

or the passage may be wholly or partially closed at one or more points. From the passage of unimpeded air, modified by the vocal chords, the shape of the mouth and a slight raising of the tongue, are formed the *vowels*, oral and nasal; out of air constricted or stopped at some point of its passage through the throat or mouth, are developed the *consonants*.

§ 98. According to the amount and kind of constriction several varieties of consonants may be formed :—

(i) Consonants made with constriction of the passage sufficient to cause friction but not wholly to check the stream of air are called *fricative* consonants :

e.g. f, v, s, z, h.

Constriction is ordinarily produced in the mouth; **h** is ordinarily a breathed *glottal* fricative.

(ii) Consonants made with a complete closure of the air-passage at some point or other are called *plosive* or *stopped* consonants :

e.g. p, b, t, ḍ, k, g.

(iii) *Nasal* consonants, the **m**- and **n**- sounds, are those made with complete closure in some part of the mouth and the nose passage open but, possibly, slightly constricted.

(iv) *Trilled* consonants, the **r**- *sounds*, are those formed by a rapid succession of taps of the tip of the tongue or of the uvula.

(v) In making the *lateral* consonants, the **l**- *sounds*, the raising of the tongue obstructs the central passage, but leaves room for voice or breath to escape at the sides.

(vi) *Affricates.*—Plosive consonants produced with slow separation of the articulating organs of speech, so that the corresponding fricative sound becomes audible as the operation takes place, are called *affricates*. Examples are the initial sound of English *jerk, chance, tsetse*. [Cf. for all these affricate consonants chap. xviii in the third edition of *An Outline of English Phonetics*, by Daniel Jones.]

It is not always easy to distinguish between these affricated sounds and the consonantal groups consisting of plosive consonant and the corresponding fricative consonants, i.e. between the sounds indicated in the above words and the combinations of: **d** with **ž**, **t** with **š**, **d** with **z**, **t** with **s**, and the same symbols are ordinarily used for both. The groups **d** + **ž**, **t** + **š**, **d** + **z**, **t** + **s** are mentioned so rarely in the book that the usual symbols **dž**, **tš**, **dz**, **ts** are employed to denote the affricated consonants and should always be so interpreted. Where confusion seems possible, the special symbols **dž, tš, dz, ts**, in which the symbols are linked by a ligature, are employed.

§ 99. Vowels may be differentiated by the extent to which the tongue is lifted and the mouth opened, two movements which ordinarily go together. The classification most convenient to adopt in French recognises five main types of vowels differentiated in quality in this way :—

(*a*) A primary division into *low*, *high*, *mid*, i.e. vowels formed with the tongue lying flat, with the tongue raised relatively high and with the tongue in an intermediate position.

(*b*) A secondary division of the mid and high vowels into *closed* (i.e. *relatively high*) and *open* (i.e. *relatively low*). This secondary differentiation is symbolised in this book by the use of ͏ subscript to mark the open vowels and by . subscript for the closed vowels, e.g.

ẹ for e open   ẹ for e closed
ọ for o open   ọ for o closed

The subjoined diagram illustrates this classification.

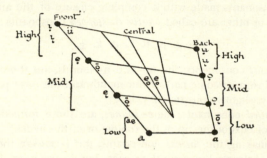

Examples of *low* vowels are the two Modern French vowels ɑ and a heard in *pas* pɑ and *patte* pat ; *mid* vowels are the Modern French o- ö- and e- sounds : ọ, ọ, ȫ, ȫ, ẹ, ẹ, heard in :

fol	fọl	*beau*	bọ
peur	pȫR	*peu*	pȫ
tête	tẹt	*nez*	nẹ

high vowels are the Modern French sounds u, ü, i, heard in :

fou fu   *du* dü   *si* si

and the Modern English sounds ͏u and ͏i heard in :

put p͏ut   *fit* f͏it

Between the positions assumed by the tongue in making these sounds there are many intermediate ones, as, for example, the English vowel sounds æ and ǭ heard in *pat* and *law*, the one intermediate between ẹ and a, the other between ọ and ɑ.

§ 100. The lift of the tongue required to make the high vowels is considerable, but not so high as to narrow the mouth passage enough to produce friction, or in other words to turn the vowels into consonantal sounds. Between the high vowels **u, ü, i,** and the consonantal sounds **w, w̌, ɪ,** there is, however, no solution of continuity, and it is often hard to tell whether one of these sounds is vocalic or consonantal, cf. for example, the pronunciation of the initial sound in Modern French *hier, oui.* In such cases the terms *semi-vocalic* and *semi-consonantal* are often used. The symbol used to denote these sounds is ⌣ subscript, e.g. **i̯, u̯.**

(For the processes *vocalisation* and *consonantalisation,* cf. § 135.)

§ 101. (4) *Point of Articulation.*—Vowels and consonants may both be differentiated by variations in their point of articulation.

Vowels.—Vowels are formed by raising either the back or front of the tongue. Those vowels formed at the back of the mouth by raising the back of the tongue towards the soft palate (the velum) are called *back* or *velar* vowels; those formed more to the front of the mouth by raising the front (middle) of the tongue towards the hard palate are called *front* or *palatal* vowels; those that are intermediate in position, i.e. between back and front, are called *central* or *mixed* vowels. The raising may be accompanied by lip-rounding or -spreading or by the opening of the nose passage.

Examples of *unrounded* or *buccal* vowels, i.e. of vowels made without lip-rounding, are the palatal vowels **a, ẹ, ę, i̦,** heard in Modern French *patte* **pat,** *tête* **tẹt,** *nez* **nẹ,** *si* **si̦,** the velar vowels heard in Modern French *pas* **pɑ** and in Modern English *duck.*

Examples of vowels made with lip-rounding, i.e. of *labial* or *rounded* vowels, are the front vowels **ȯ, ȯ̈, ə, ü,** heard in Modern French *peur* **pȯR,** *peu* **pȯ̈,** *de* **də,** *du* **dü,** the back vowels heard in the Modern French *or* **ǫR,** *beau* **bǫ,** *fou* **fu,** and the central vowel **u̇,** heard in Modern Swedish *hus.*

§ 102. All languages spoken with a relatively heavy expiratory accent tend to reduce unstressed vowels to a weak neutral sound. In English and German the sound ordinarily employed is *central* and *unrounded* (cf. English *actor,* German *gabe*): the Modern French counterpart, the so-called *e muet* is a weak *front* vowel, slightly *rounded* (e.g. *le, premier*). The phonetic symbol used in all three languages is ordinarily **ə, æktə, gabə, lə, prəmi̯e** : in this book the symbol **ę** is ordinarily employed in the older language, in which the vowel is usually of undetermined value, **ə** in Modern French and when the vowel has presumably the Modern French value (cf. § 275).

§ 103. Vowels pronounced with the nose passage open, i.e. with the velum lowered, are called *nasal* vowels. If the nose passage is open throughout the period of the emission of the vowel, nasalisation is clearly audible; a vowel may, however, be nasalised *partially*, at the beginning or end of its emission, and then its nasal character is acoustically little evident. Experiments of phoneticians have shown conclusively that vowels are always partially nasalised in the vicinity of a nasal consonant, that, for instance, the vowels in the English *maid, mutter, bin, king* are all partially nasalised, slightly at the beginning in the first two words, at the end in the last two.

The symbol used to denote complete (audible) nasalisation is $\sim$. Examples of nasal vowels are the four in use in Modern French, often disguised under very varied traditional spellings :—

ã	e.g. in *an, lent, Jean*	ã, lã, žã
ę̃	in *fin, plein, main*	fę̃, plę̃, mę̃
ǫ̃	in *un, emprunter*	ǫ̃, ãprǫ̃tę̃
ọ̃	in *on, compte*	ọ̃, kọ̃t

In the modern pronunciation ã is a nasalised low back sound inclining towards ǫ̃; ọ̃ lies between ọ̃ and ǫ̃.

In the older language **a** was palatal and the high vowels **i, ü, u** were also susceptible of nasalisation as well as many diphthongs (cf. chap. xi).

§ 104. *Consonants.*—The constriction or stoppage of voice or breath that produces *consonants* may be made by the *uvula*, or by the raising of one or other part of the *tongue*, or by the closing of the *lips*, wholly or partially, or by the combined action of the tongue and lips or of two parts of the tongue. The point of articulation of consonants may thus be either *single* or *double*.

§ 105. The consonants formed with a single point of articulation are the following :—

(i) *Labials.*—Those consonants made by the action of the lips are called *labials*. They may be either *bi-labial*, i.e. formed by the use of the two lips, or *labio-dental*, i.e. formed by the contact of lip and teeth. The Modern French sound system comprises the two labio-dental fricatives **f** and **v**, the two bi-labial plosives **p** and **b**, and the bi-labial nasal **m**. In the earlier stages of the language there were also in use the bi-labial fricative sound β (**ƀ**), a sound still employed in Spanish, e.g. *eso basta* esǫ βasta, *lobo* lǫβǫ.

§ 106. (ii) *Linguals.*—The long series of consonants made by the raising of different parts of the tongue are named *linguals*. The names given to the parts of the tongue used are :—

          (*a*) the *point* or *tip*,
          (*b*) the *blade*,
          (*c*) the *middle* or *front*,
          (*d*) the *back*.

(*a*) *Dentals.*—Those consonants made by raising the *point* (tip) or *blade* of the tongue up to or towards the *teeth* or *teeth-ridge* are called *dental* or *point* consonants, subdivided into *dental* and *alveolar*. The most advanced are the interdental fricatives θ and ð, the initial sounds of the English *think* and *the ;* formed further back are the plosives t and d, the affricates ts and dz, the fricatives s and z (the final sounds in the English *bass* beɪs and *raise* reɪz), the lateral l, the nasal n, the fricative r-sound ɹ (cf. southern English *red* ɹed) and the trilled r, a sound still heard in some parts of England and France and used in Old and Middle French (cf. chap. ix). The slight raising of the *front* of the tongue that accompanies the articulation of s and z is usually more marked in the articulation of ts and dz.

(*b*) *Denti-palatal* (*palato-alveolar*).—When the point or blade of the tongue is raised towards the hinder-part of the teeth-ridge and the main part of the tongue towards the forepart of the hard palate, the *denti-palatal* consonants are formed, sub-divided into the *post-alveolar* and the *prae-palatal*. The former include the fricative sounds š and ž, the initial sounds of the French *cher* šęR and *juge* žüž, the latter are the affricate consonants represented by tš and dž or tš and dž, cf. § 98, the initial and final sounds heard in English *church* and *judge*.

(*c*) *Palatal.*—The consonants formed by raising the *front* (middle) of the tongue up to or towards the hard palate are called *palatal* (*front*) consonants. In the educated speech of Paris to-day only two palatal consonants are employed, the voiced fricative sound j (*jod*), heard in *bien* bję, *paille* pa·j, and partially unvoiced in *pied* pję, *feuilleter* fȯjtę, and the palatal nasal, n *mouillé*, represented in this book by ŋ and written ordinarily *gn*, e.g. *digne* diŋ.

The *palatal lateral* consonant l *mouillé* is still heard in Swiss and Belgian French, but in the greater part of France this sound has been simplified to j, a simplification which appears to have begun with the *petite bourgeoisie* of Paris in the seventeenth century, although it was only accepted in the nineteenth century (cf. Nyrop, *Gr.* § 351).

The *plosive palatal* consonants, represented in this book by ɟ and ɟ and the *breath fricative* ç were also in use in the early stages of the language, and are now again found in many of the patois.

(*d*) *Velar.*—The consonants formed by raising the back of the tongue up to or towards the velum or soft palate are called *velar* or *back* consonants. In modern educated French the only velar consonants in use are the plosives, breathed and voiced, k and g, the initial sounds

heard in *camp* kᾶ, *qui* ki, *gout* gu, *guetter* gẹtẹ, but in the earlier stages of the languages the fricative velars χ and γ (the sounds heard in the Scotch *loch* lǫχ or German *ach* aχ, and often in German *Wagen* vayən) were also employed, as also the velar nasal ɒ, the final sound heard in English *king* kiɒ.

§ 107. (iii) *Uvular.*—Modern French has developed two forms of *uvular* consonants, the trilled and fricative *r*-sounds R and ʁ. The former is first attested at the end of the seventeenth century; the latter is one of the more recent developments of Parisian speech (cf. Nyrop, *Man.* §§ 56-58).

§ 108. (iv) The laryngal fricative consonant **h** was used in Old French in words of Germanic origin, e.g. *haïr*, *helme*, and in words influenced by Germanic words, e.g. *halt*, *hanste*. The '**h** *aspiré*' of Modern French, which is the lineal descendant of this sound, is now no sound in standard French but only a symbol used to prevent elision of the preceding vowel (§ 196).

§ 109. The consonants formed with a *double* point of articulation, a main and a secondary, are the following :—

(i) *Velarised Labial and Dental Consonants.*—*Labial* and *dental* consonants may be *velarised* by the combination of a lift of the back of the tongue toward the soft palate with the ordinary labial or dental articulation. The two velarised consonants that are in commonest use are: **w** and ɫ :

(*a*) **w** is a fricative *bi-labial* with *velar* modification, i.e. it is a sound made with a rounding of the two lips accompanied by a raising of the back of the tongue towards the soft palate.

(*b*) ɫ, the so-called *dark* l, is a velarised *lateral* consonant, formed with the point of the tongue pressed against the teeth or teeth-ridge and the back raised towards the soft palate. It is the sound heard in English when the l is final or prae-consonantal, e.g. *full* fuɫ, *field* fiˑɫd, and it was also in use in Latin and in Period I of French (§§ 380-389). The raising of the back of the tongue gives this l-sound acoustic resemblance to the vowel **u**.

§ 110. (ii) *Palatalised Labials.*—Corresponding to **w** is ẅ, a fricative bi-labial consonant made with *palatal* modification: it is the fricative bi-labial consonant or semi-vowel formed with a rounding of the two lips accompanied by a raising of the front of the tongue towards the hard palate, the initial sound heard in the French *huit* ẅit.

§ 111. (iii) *Palatalised Dentals.*—Dentals made with *palatal* modification result from the combination of the lift of the point or blade of the tongue towards the teeth or teeth-ridge with a raising of the front of the tongue towards the hard palate; ordinarily in the articulation of these sounds 'the two articulations merge into a single articulation of unusually extensive area,' (Rousselot, *Principes,* p. 618; Trofimov and D. Jones, *The Pronunciation of Russian,* pp. 322-324). The acoustic difference between the palatal and palatalised nasal and lateral consonants is slight.

In this book the symbol ⁀ is used to denote these palatalised consonants, i.e. r̂, ŝ, ẑ, etc. In the early stages of the language the *denti-palatals* as well as all the dentals were susceptible of palatalisation.

§ 112. (iv) *Labialised Dentals.*—In the pronunciation of the post-alveolar consonants š and ž the main denti-palatal articulation is not infrequently combined with a *rounding* of the lips. This is often seen in the pronunciation of these sounds in Modern French and English (cf. Jones, *English Phonetics,* § 726).

§ 113. *Double Consonants.*—In words like *Allah, illégal,* or Latin *Appius, bucca, canna, mille,* we speak currently of 'double' consonants, but the term is something of a misnomer, for in reality the intervocalic sound pronounced here is a modified *lengthened* complete consonant. Every complete consonantal sound consists of three parts, for it is the result of three articulatory movements :—

  (i) The putting of the articulatory organs into position, the 'on-glide.'
  (ii) The keeping of the organs in position, the 'stop.'
  (iii) The release of the articulatory organs from the position of the given sound, the 'off-glide.'

In the pronunciation of syllables and words, the juxtaposition of sound with sound normally brings curtailment of consonantal sounds, and the distinguishing feature of the double consonants is just that they retain the complete triple movement together with a slight lengthening modification of the middle movement, the stop. In Modern English or Modern French double consonants are rarely pronounced, except when words are combined or run together, cf. *home-made* **hoummeid,** *là-dedans* **laddã,** *une noix* **ünnwa** (Nyrop, *Man. Ph.,* § 127).

§ 114. *Diphthongs and Vowels in Hiatus.*—Combinations of two vowel sounds in *one* syllable are called *diphthongs,* of three vowels *triphthongs,* cf. English : *house* **haus,** *they* ðei, *no* **nou,** *I* ai ; Latin : *aurum, causae ;* Italian : *buoi.*

In these combinations one element, normally the higher of the two, is always the weaker, the less sonorous : the diphthongs in which the first element is the more sonorous are called *falling* or *descending* diphthongs, e.g. **aṷ, aị, oṷ**, those with a more sonorous second element *rising*, e.g. **ịe, ṵe**.

In the Old French sound system diphthongs and triphthongs (e.g. **eau, ieu**) were strongly represented (§ 507). In Modern French, although the traditional spelling has often been retained, cf. *peine* **pẹn**, *heure* **ö̧R**, *bien* **bịẹ̃**, *roi* **Rwa**, *foin* **fwẹ̃**, *puits* **pẅi**, etc., no true diphthongs survive (cf. § 508).

§ 115. Vowels juxtaposed in *two successive* syllables are said to be *in hiatus*, e.g. *béant* **bẹ.ɑ̃**, *trahir* **tra.ir**, *ouvrier* **uvri.ẹ** ; Latin : **dĕ.ŭs, fīlĭ.ŭs, fīlĭ.ŏlŭm**.

§ 116. *Variability of Sounds.*—In the classification of sounds made above, for obvious reasons of convenience, a definite single value has been attached to each sound. This simplification, however, is purely theoretical. In reality every sound has varying values, i.e. may be made in slightly varying ways. This is obvious in the case of the trilled sound, which, as we saw, may be either dental or uvular, but it is equally true, though less markedly so, of all others. To English students of foreign languages, indeed, the difference between the values of the vowels familiar to us and those of other languages is quickly apparent. But the variations of position taken up by the organs of speech in making consonants of nominally the same acoustic value, though not always so obvious, are in reality hardly less marked. The formation of an English **l** or **t** differs from French **l** or French **t** probably about as much as English vowel sounds from French vowel sounds. Rousselot has noted at least six variations of the sound **t** in the French patois, variations ranging from a **t** so advanced as to be near **θ** to one so retracted as to be almost **t̂**.

What, in fact, we call a 'sound,' whether vowel or consonant, is in reality rather a sequence or chain of sounds, a closely-related series of very slightly differentiated movements of the organs of speech. For purposes of representation in writing a more or less arbitrary number of recognised positions have been selected and named, but it must always be remembered that the fixity of the value of the symbols of the alphabet is entirely fictitious, and that between adjacent lingual sounds there is a real continuity.

In the consideration of sound changes the variability of the individual sound and the continuity of the sequences that constitute recognised sounds must never be lost sight of.

§ 117. *Organic Basis.* — The abundance of possible sounds is ordinarily utilised but very incompletely in any one language, for out of the great variety available each speech community includes only a very limited number in its sound system. The choice made is not entirely haphazard but appears to be always guided by certain tendencies or pre-dispositions that have become habitual to the people speaking that language : the Modern French vowel system, for instance, tends to be characterised by 'tenseness, purity, strong lip-action, nasalisation and a forward pronunciation with a convex position of the tongue' (*Sounds of the French Language*, 169), while in the English pronunciation vowels are diphthongised, the lips in neutral position, the tongue flattened, lowered and retracted (cf. Sweet, *Primer of Phonetics*, p. 69).

This complex of loosely connected pre-dispositions is called by English phoneticians the 'organic basis' of the language, and it is the organic basis that makes the adult's chief difficulty in acquiring a foreign language and is responsible for what in common parlance is called 'accent.' It is the difference between the French and English organic basis that renders for us the acquirement of each other's language so difficult, just as it was the influence of the English organic basis that made Anglo-Norman the laughing stock of the French of France in the Middle Ages (cf. § 1077).

Section 3.—ACCENT.

§ 118. The word *accent* varies greatly in significance, but in linguistic study the definition most commonly accepted is 'prominence given to a syllable.' Prominence may be obtained either by variations of *pitch* (*ton*), produced by the varying degree of tension of the vocal chords, or by variations of *stress* (*intensité*), produced by variations in the force with which the air is expelled from the lungs. Hence arise two forms of accent : the *musical* and the *expiratory* or *stress* accent (*accent d'intensité*). A third method of giving prominence is the difference in *quantity* or *length* of sound, but this method is not usually included in the term 'accent.'

§ 119. *Word and Sentence Accent.*—The accent may be a *word* accent, i.e. it may be attached to a definite syllable in a word, and thus help to constitute its individuality, or it may vary from word to word according to the function in which words are being used in a sentence or phrase, i.e. it may be a *sentence* accent. The musical and expiratory accents are both ordinarily present in speech, but with different functions and varying importance. In modern Romance and Germanic languages it is stress, the expiratory accent, that is the word accent, but in ancient Greece and probably also in ancient Rome (§ 210), it was the musical

accent that fulfilled this function.   In the Modern French sentence accent, i.e. in the *accent d'insistance*, both pitch and stress (the musical and expiratory accent) are employed (cf. Grammont, *op. cit.*, pp. 121-160).

Section 4.—INFLUENCE OF SPEECH ON SOUNDS.

§ 120. The foregoing sections have treated of sounds in isolation, but in speech it is in combination that they are used, in groups or rather sequences of sounds linked together more or less closely in syllables, words, phrases and sentences uttered at varying rates of speed with varying degrees of stress and pitch, and many modifications are thereby induced.   The strongest influence is exercised by word stress and position within the word, but speed of utterance, sentence stress and position in the sentence (i.e. 'syntactical phonetics') may also play a part (cf. chap. xvii).   Moreover, since words come up into consciousness as wholes, modifications are not infrequently induced by the influence of sounds not immediately juxtaposed (cf. §§ 128, 129).

§ 121. *Influence of Expiratory Accent.*—Under the influence of the expiratory accent, whether word or sentence accent, consonants may be lengthened, vowels lengthened or diphthongised, diphthongs differentiated (cf. for instance the pronunciation of English *no*, *ale*, *I*, **nou, eil, ai**, and below, §§ 225, 226).   In the less stressed syllables vowels are not infrequently raised, for high vowels can be produced with rather less force of breath than low ones (cf. Meillet, *Mém. Soc. Lg. Par.* XI, p. 168). Thus **a** unstressed tends to pass to **ẹ, ę** to **ẹ, ę** to **i, ọ** to **ǫ, ǫ** to **u.** Compare the pronunciation in Modern English of the words : *riches* **ritšiz,** *Magdalen* **Mǫ:dlin,** *sausage* **sǫsidž,** *vineyard* **vinjǝd.**

In the unstressed syllables a tendency is often observable to reduce the vowel to a weak sound, that is often gradually effaced, cf. English *butler* from O.F. *bouteillier*, *pantry* from O.F. *paneterie*, *proctor* from *procuratorem*.   When words are unstressed in a sentence curtailment is sometimes more violent and consonants may be discarded as well as vowels, cf. for instance the shortenings of words used as title words, e.g. English *miss* < *mistress*, *ma'am* < *madam*, Late Latin **sejor* for *senior* (§ 600), or of verbs much used or functioning as auxiliaries, e.g. English *ain't* for *am, not;* Latin *sis* for *si· vis*, *ain* for *ais ne ?*, Late Latin **va* for *vade*, **at* for *habet*, etc. (cf. §§ 946, 953, 959).   Effacement of vowels in hiatus is generally accompanied by compensatory lengthening of the remaining juxtaposed vowel, cf. §§ 561, 562.

Old and Modern French illustrate the effects of stress very differently. The older French language, like Modern English, possessed a strong expiratory word accent, and this induced diphthongisation among the

stressed vowels, raising, reduction and effacement among the less stressed (cf. chap. v) ; in the modern language, in which the expiratory word accent has become very slight, it is the sentence stress, compounded of pitch and stress, that modifies most strongly the pronunciation of sounds. Under its influence 'la durée de la voyelle augmente d'une manière très sensible . . . la durée de la consonne, qui précède cette voyelle est toujours très nettement augmentée, en général plus que doublée.' Thus words like *épouvantable*, phrases like *c'est désolant ! c'est épatant !* are pronounced emotionally :

ẹp'puvā̆tabl sẹd'dẹzolā̆ sẹtẹp'patā̆

[For the difference between lengthened single consonants and double consonants cf. Grammont, *Tr. Phon.*, pp. 52-56.]

§ 122. *Influence of Juxtaposition and Proximity.*—The modifications produced among sounds by their juxtaposition or proximity are very varied, for effacements, shortenings, lengthenings, metatheses, glide developments, assimilations and dissimilations of many types may result. The modifications induced by the influence of sound on sound are grouped together under the name 'combinative,' in contradistinction to 'isolative' changes, the modifications which a sound undergoes independently of accent and of all other sounds (cf. chap. iii). Underlying most of these combinative phenomena is the very human tendency designated somewhat euphemistically 'economy of effort,' for just as water finds for itself the easiest path, so quite unconsciously the organs of speech tend to assume the most convenient positions, and thus facilitate the passage from one sound to another by one or other of the adjustments enumerated above.

It must be borne in mind that convenience is relative, always determined by the position in which the organs of speech are placed in the given sequence of sounds, and that it is possible for the shifting of the point of articulation of a sound to produce gradually one that is in itself more difficult to articulate than the one from which the move started. When the juxtaposition of **k** and **g** to the front vowels **e** and **i** in Late Latin, induced the forward move of **k** and **g,** the move was for convenience, but the plosive palatal sounds that were in consequence gradually reached are in themselves much more difficult to articulate than the plosive velars **k** and **g** from which the evolution started.

§ 123. *Glide Development.*—The name 'glide,' 'son transitoire,' is the name given to the weak transitional sounds produced during the passage from one sound to another, or before or after a sound, these latter being known as *on-* and *off-glides.* These weak sounds may be either vocalic or consonantal, and develop frequently into an independent vowel or consonant. It is a vocalic glide-development between the high

vowel **i** and the low consonant **r** that ultimately produced the Modern English pronunciation of the word *friar* **fraię** < **frȩrȩ** < O.F. **frȩrȩ**, and it is an off-glide that is responsible for the vulgar pronunciation of the phrase *idea of* as **aidjȩrov.** In the course of the development of Latin into Modern French every kind of glide-development is exemplified : *on-glides* in the L.L. *i-scriptu*, etc. (§ 361) ; *off-glides* when the consonantal groups **bl, ŏr, jr,** etc., became final as in O.F. **ēnsēmble, frȩŏrȩ** < **frater, mairȩ** < **major** (§ 258) ; interconsonantal in **estrȩ** < ***ess(e)re, lazdrȩ** *lasdre* < ***laz(e)re** < **Lazarum, mo+drȩ** < **mol(e)re,** etc. (§ 370), **hanap** < *hnapp,* **kanif** < *knif;* intervocalic in *épouvanter* **epuvātȩ** < O.F. **espu(w)āntȩr,** *pays* **pȩjl** < **peis** (§ 531), O.F. **pieus** < **pįᴜs,** O.F. **bȩaᴜs, tieᴜs** (§ 388) ; between vowel and consonant as in *vierge* **vierdžȩ** < **virdžȩ** (§ 500).

§ 124. *Metathesis.*—Metathesis is the name given to the transposition of sounds. It takes place ordinarily between juxtaposed sounds, but may, like assimilation and dissimilation, affect sounds in the vicinity of one another only, and may then lead either to a simple transposition or to an interchange of position among the sounds. This latter process is known as *reciprocal* metathesis.

The consonantal sound most frequently transposed is **r** (for the intervocalic group **sk + o** or **u** cf. § 325).

Simple Metathesis :—

brebis < *vervecem, fromage* < **formaticum, por* < *pro,* O.F. *proumener* < *pourmener, tros* < **tursum (thyrsum), troubler* < *torbler (turbulare), breuvage* < *beuvrage (*biberaticum), frange* < *fimbria, tremper* < *temprer, moelle* < *meole (medulla), ruisseaus* < **riuscellus, suit* < *siut* (§ 328), *suif* < *siuf, tuile* < *tiule* (§ 641 (i)), O.F. *espalde* < ***espadla* (< *spatula,* § 765).

Reciprocal Metathesis :—

*alenare < *anhelare, beluter (bluter)* < O.F. *buleter, *colyrum* < *corylum,* O.F. *ireter* < *eriter,* O.F. *lasne* < *nasle* (frk. *nastila), *stincella* < **scintilla,* O.F. *tonlieu* < **tonoleum* < *teloneum.*

§ 125. *Shortenings and Lengthenings.*—When vowels are pronounced in the same syllable as a following consonant, in other words, when they are *blocked,* they tend to shorten ; when they end their own syllable, i.e. when they are *free,* they tend to lengthen, cf. the difference in pronunciation of the English *shadow* and *shade, throttle* and *throat* (cf. Jespersen, *M.E. Gr.* pp. 114-117, and below, §§ 197, 198).

Lengthening of a vowel is also often produced by the coalescence or effacement of contiguous sounds, whether vowel or consonant, for the vibrations of the effaced sound may be added to those of the vowel,

cf. in Late Latin the lengthening of vowels that took place when **n** and **r** were assimilated to **s** (§ 359 and Juret, *Ph. Lat.* pp. 333 *et seqq.*) and the vowel lengthenings in Middle French, chap. xv.

(For shortenings and lengthenings due to variations in stress cf. §§ 219, 229.)

§ 126. *Assimilation and Dissimilation.*—By the term *assimilation* is meant normally the appropriation by one sound of the articulatory movements proper to another, a process which results in the production of a close or complete resemblance between the two sounds, cf. the modern English pronunciation of **v** and **s** in the words *fivepence* **faifpens** or **fippens**, *dogs* **dogz**, and of Modern French **d** and **v** in *médecin* **mẹtsẹ**, *oisiveté* **waziftẹ**.

The complete assimilation of one consonant to another ordinarily produces a lengthened consonant, which is subsequently often reduced to a single one, cf. the pronunciation of English *lamb*, *comb*, in which **mb** became **mm** and then **m** ; (cf. §§ 359, 372, 373).

The gradual disappearance of a sound (*amuïssement*) induced by assimilation or other process, is called in this book *effacement.*

Occasionally an assimilatory influence may lead to the introduction of a wholly new sound, cf. O.F. *perdriz* < *perdiz*, *fortrece* < *fortece*, *tertre* < *termitem.*

§ 127. *Dissimilation* is the converse process. Broadly speaking it is the rendering of two sounds unlike each other and leads ordinarily to a modification of the articulatory movement of one or both the sounds concerned :—

O.F. *pelerin* < ****pelerinu** < **peregrinum*, *gonfalon* < **gundfanon*, *deviser* < *dīvīsare*, *devin* < *dīvīnum*, O.F. *secorre* < *socorre.*

It may also provoke the elimination of a sound :—

O.F. *flambe* < *flamble* < *flammula*, *feible* < *flebilem ;* **kinque* < *quinque ;* **abea* < *habebam* (§ 916), *viande* < *vivenda*, *guarait* < *vervactum.*

The sounds that most frequently suffer dissimilation are **l, n,** and **r.**

§ 128. *Varieties of Assimilation and Dissimilation.*—Both assimilation and dissimilation may take place either between sounds juxtaposed, or between sounds in the vicinity of one another only. Assimilations between sounds that are not in contact with one another are called *harmonic assimilations :*—

L.L. **aramen* < **eramen* < *æramen*, **gagante* < *gigantem*, **salvaticum* < *silvaticum*, **toloneum* < *teloneum.*

O.F. *cherchier* **tšertšier** < *cerchier* **tsertšier** (< *circare*), **brẹbis** < ****βerbiʃe** (§ 189) (*vervecem*).

§ 129. The counterpart of *simple* assimilation, the tendency to avoid the continuance of the same articulatory movement among juxtaposed sounds, is called by some scholars *differentiation* (cf. the Cockney English pronunciation of *lady* **leidi** as **laidi** or **loidi** and § 226), and the name *dissimilation* is then reserved for the counterpart of *harmonic* assimilation, the form of dissimilation that takes its rise in the tendency to avoid the repetition of like articulatory movements among sounds that are in the vicinity of one another, but not in contact, cf. O.F. *Bologne* < *Bononia*, *contralier* < *contrarier*, *esquarteler* < *esquarterer*, *ensorceler* < *ensorcerer*; **varactu* < *vervactum*; **devisare* < *divīsare*, *devinum* < *divinum*.

§ 130. Assimilation and dissimilation in its narrower sense both take their rise in the instinct to economise effort : differentiation is at times due to the same instinct, as for instance when *plosive + plosive* is differentiated to *fricative + plosive*, e.g. **kt** > χt, **faktu** > faχtu (§ 359). At other times it appears to be induced by a subconscious desire to strengthen a sound which is emphatic or in a key-position in a word, as for instance when diphthongs are differentiated (cf. Grammont, *Assimilation*, pp. 35, 64; Meillet, ' De la Différenciation des Phonèmes,' *Mém. Soc. Lg. Par.* XII, 14-34).

§ 131. Broadly speaking, it is the sound which is most prominent in the mental picture of a word which exercises assimilating or dissimilating force and among vowels it is ordinarily the tonic vowel that is dominant and assimilates or dissimilates, cf. O.F. *aage* < *eage*, *soür* < *seur*, *enour* < *onour*, *sejorn* < *sojorn* (§§ 244, 484, 490); L.L. *agostu* < *augustum* (§ 505), *devinum* < *divinum*.

In languages in the flexional stage, however, it is not infrequently the flexional termination that is important in the mental picture and exercises the associative influence, and this explains the phenomenon known as *mutation* (*Umlaut*), the modification of the tonic vowel of a word under the raising influence of a final high unstressed flexional vowel. The English plural forms *feet*, *geese* and others, and the German plurals *Männer*, *Häupte*, etc., are more or less directly the result of this phenomenon (cf. also below § 419).

Again, in Late Latin it was the tonic vowel that was differentiated if juxtaposed to a final flexional vowel that was homophonous or almost homophonous :—

L.L. **tous*, **toum* < **tous*, **toum* < tŭŭs, tŭŭm, **mea* < **mea* < mĕa, **dies* < **dies* < dĭēs (M.L. *Einf.* § 109).

§ 132. Assimilations and Dissimilations may be either *regressive* or *progressive*, i.e. a sound may be modified in anticipation of a sound following, or the articulatory position of one sound may modify the pronunciation of a later one.

The pronunciation of the modern French word *absoudre* **apsudrə** illustrates the regressive type, the modern English pronunciation of *absolve* **əbzolv** the progressive.

In French regressive assimilations are the more usual type.

§ 133. All forms of articulatory movements may be modified by assimilation or dissimilation. The commonest types of assimilation are the following :—

(i) The *voicing* or *unvoicing* of juxtaposed breathed and voice consonants : cf. Modern English *gooseberry* **guzberi**, *dogs* **dogz**, *stopped* **stopt** ; Modern French *savetier* **saftję**, *tête dure* **tęddür**, etc., and §§ 372, 377.

§ 134. (ii) The *voicing* of consonants under the influence of juxtaposed vowels (all *voiced* sounds), cf. Modern English *dessert* **dizə·t** < O.F. **desęrte** *desserte*, *flagon* **flæɡən** < O.F. **flakun**, *flacon*, and below, chap. vii.

§ 135. (iii) The *opening of consonants* under the influence of juxtaposed vowels (all *open* sounds) :—

(*a*) *Plosive* consonants standing between vowels often open into *fricatives*, cf. English *father* **faðə** < **fader** and chap. vii.

(*b*) The voiced fricative consonants ɉ, γ, w, ẇ, β and the voiced velar lateral ɫ often *vocalise*, i.e. open into semi-vowel sounds ɉ to ı̣, γ, w, β, ɫ to u̯, ẇ to ü̯. *Vocalisation* takes place most frequently when these sounds end their own syllable, i.e. are *prae-consonantal* or *final* of the word but ɉ, γ and w are sometimes vocalised when intervocalic.

Examples are :—Latin **naufragium** < **nawifragium** ; Late Latin **auca* < ** awica*, *avica*, **paraula* < **paraβla*, **sauma* < **saγma* < **sagma** (§ 359) ; Old French **mais** < ***majes* (§ 404), *forge* **fǫrdžę** < ***faurga* < **fabrika** (§ 359), **ãntiu** < ***antiw(ę)* < **antikwum** (§ 328), **autrę** < **aɫtrę** (§ 385).

Consonantalisation, the converse process, the closing of a vowel into a consonant, is due mainly to the influence of rapidity of speech. The process occurs most frequently when a relatively weak, high or mid vowel stands immediately before a stronger, lower (more sonorous) vowel ; in these conditions i and e are apt to close to ɉ ; u and o to w ; ü to ẇ. Examples are :—L.L. **filjus* < **filius**, **monjo* < **monĕo** (§ 220) ; Later Old and Middle French : **pję** < **pieθ**, **frwęsję** < **frųęsier** *fruissier*, **lẇi** < **lüi**, **wi** < **uï(l)** < **oïl**, cf. below, §§ 241, 267, 503, etc.

§ 136. (iv) *The Raising and Lowering of Vowels.*—The tongue may be *raised* or *lowered* in the articulation of a vowel under the influence of another sound formed with a high or low point of articulation. Thus the relatively high lift of the front of the tongue required in the formation of *palatal* consonants tends to *raise* juxtaposed vowels (chap. x., sect. 4), and conversely the relatively low position of the main part of the tongue in the articulation of the *dental* consonants l and r tends to lower sounds in contact with them, cf. the modern English pronunciation of *clerk*, *Derby*, *Cherwell* and chap. xiii. (Cf. also § 425 and Addenda, § 425.)

5

§ 137. (v) *The Opening and Closing of the Nose Passage.*—The nose passage may be opened or closed under the assimilatory or dissimilatory influence of adjacent sounds, i.e. sounds may be *nasalised* or *denasalised*, cf. chap. xi., the nasalisation of **g** to **ŋ** in Latin *dignus* **diŋnus,** *agnus* **aŋnus,** etc. (Juret, p. 180), and the denasalisation of Mid. Fr. *aîné*, ẹnẹ < ẽnẹ < O.F. āin(ts)nẹ *ainzne*.

§ 138. (vi) *The Shifting of the Point of Articulation.*—(*a*) Under the influence of a *lip* sound, vowel or consonant, the lips may be rounded or protruded in the pronunciation of a buccal sound, i.e. a sound may be *labialised* (*rounded*): for example, **n** may be labialised to **m,** γ to **w** or **ŭ,** cf. Latin *impejorare* < *in-pejorare;* Eng. *hamper* < **hanaper;** O.F. ēmfẹs < ēnfẹs, ēmmẹner < ēn(t)mener, etc. (§§ 371, 435, 610); **rover** < ****rower** < ***royare** < **rogare** (§ 341).

The buccal vowels **i, e, a, ɑ** may all be pronounced with rounded lips and so turned into the lip vowels that are nearest their point of articulation: thus **i** > **ü, e** > **o** or **ö, a** and **ɑ** > **ǫ** or **ǭ,** cf. English **wǫr** < **war,** *wall* **wǭɫ** < **waɫ,** Late Latin ***wǫkẹtŭ** < ***wɑkẹtŭ** **vacitum,* O.F. **soür** < **sẹür,** chap. xii, sect. 2 and § 527.

§ 139. (*b*) A palatal sound may *palatalise*, i.e. may induce a palatal pronunciation in another sound and thus draw the velars forward, the dentals backwards (either completely or by extending their point of articulation backwards on to the hard palate), cf. chap. vi and the Modern English pronunciation of words like *measure, ocean, nature,* in which ordinarily the dentals **z, s, t** are moved back and become **ž, š, tš** respectively, i.e. denti-palatals. Palatal sounds may also *raise* low vowels (§§ 413, 421) and occasionally unround lip ones, cf. chap. x, sect. 7.

§ 140. Similarly velars may *velarise* and dentals *dentalise*, i.e. may induce a velar or dental pronunciation of a sound made with another point of articulation: in Latin, for example, **m** was velarised to **ŋ** when brought in contact with **k,** cf. *princeps,* **priŋkeps,** formed from **primus;** in Gallo-Roman **m** dentalised to **n** when brought in contact with non-nasal dental consonants, cf. O.F. *singe,* **sindžẹ** < **simium,** āint < **amet.**

Section 5.—Characteristics of Sound Change and Sound Substitution.

§ 141. All sound changes are normally *involuntary, gradual* and *uniform* in operation within the conditions that determine them.

They may be, as we have seen, induced by the tendency to economise effort, but there is no *deliberate* attempt to do this, still less to obtain 'euphony.' The only periods at which conscious effort and ideals of euphony play a part are those comparatively rare ones in which

the cultivation of language has become the ideal and pre-occupation of a lettered class, and when there has associated itself with certain pronunciations the stigma of provincialism or vulgarity. Then indeed deliberate resistances to change are found, and reactions and mannerisms may appear (cf. Pt. I, chap. iii, sect. 6).

§ 142. *Sound Change and Sound Substitution.*—The normal sound changes are *gradual,* the result of imperceptible movements of the articulatory organs which bring them successively through the intermediate points that lie between sound and sound: the mouth or nose passage closes or opens a little more or less, the vocal chords vibrate more or less strongly or weakly, the lips round a little more or less, the lift of the tongue is made slightly further forward or backward or increased or diminished and thus a sound is quite gradually voiced or unvoiced, nasalised, labialised, palatalised, etc.

Many of the combinative modifications mentioned above, however, and many others due to psychological causes, are of a quite different type, *sudden* and at once complete: *sound substitutions* and not *sound changes.* Of this order are the varied forms of metathesis (§ 124), all forms of harmonic assimilation (§ 128), many dissimilations, e.g. all sudden eliminations or additions of sounds (§ 127, etc.).

Sound substitutions are particularly frequent in the accommodation of the unusual sounds of loan-words to the sound-system of the borrowers, cf. the treatment of Greek sounds in Latin, of Frankish sounds in Gallo-Roman and learned words in Old and Middle French (Pt. II, chap. xviii). They may be induced by the acoustic similarity of certain sounds, e.g. the modern French substitution of the uvular sound R for r, the Gallo-Roman substitution of ts for t + s (§ 367), the Latin substitution of kl for tl (§ 360). Occasionally onomatopeia plays a part, e.g. in the aspirated pronunciation of the words *haleter* (< *ala*), *hennir* (< *hinnire*), *hurler* (< *ululare*).

[For the substitutions occasioned by psychological (associative) influences, cf. Pt. IV, chap. i.]

§ 143. *Uniformity of Sound Change.*—A further fundamental characteristic of sound change proper is that of uniformity of operation within the conditions determining it. Ill-formulated in the phrase, 'Sound laws admit of no exception,' this principle has often been misunderstood and in consequence disputed. The use of the term 'law' in respect of sound change is misleading, for neither moral nor physical obligation governs the development of sounds; the so-called 'sound laws' are merely *rules,* or better still *formulæ,* summary statements of the changes that sounds have undergone under certain conditions, in a particular locality and at a particular time: 'Ce sont des formules qui résument des procès, des règles de correspondance,' (Vendryes, *Le Langage,* p. 51).

If, however, the rules are rightly formulated and if in addition sufficient account be taken of the psychological element always present in speech, it may rightly be

said that the rules admit of no exception and this necessarily so, owing to the involuntary and unconscious character of sound change proper. Whoever indeed
comes to pronounce a sound in a slightly different way from those before him or
around him, will pronounce that sound in that way wherever the conditions that
induced the change obtain, for he himself will be unconscious of his own deviation
from the norm, and so in all probability will those around him.

§ 144. It must, however, always be borne in mind that the complexity of conditions often makes correct formulation very difficult. The commonest sources of
error in formulation are the neglect to take into account (a) the whole sequence of
sounds in a word or phrase, and (b) the exact conditions of time and place. Thus :
(i) a change induced by one factor may be thwarted by the influence of some other,
e.g. the raising influence of a palatal may be neutralised by the lowering influence
of another sound such as l or r (cf. below, the development of countertonic a free
after palatals, § 417 and §§ 234, 261-264).

(ii) The condition that originally provoked a change may be modified before
the sound change reaches its conclusion : the difference in the development of *dēbet*
and *dēbita*, O.F. **deit** and **dẹtẹ**, is not an indication of a lack of uniformity in the
diphthongisation of ẹ tonic free, but is due to the early effacement of the unstressed
vowel in *dēbita* and the consequent early blocking of the tonic vowel ; (cf. also the
development of Latin t final (chap. vii, sect. 5) and of O.F. ei and countertonic ẹ
before a nasal, §§ 439, 449).

§ 145. Again the physical, the sound change, may be dominated by psychological factors, for social influence, function, significance, the desire for intelligibility
play a part, more important than appears on the surface, in the modification of pronunciation as well as in the history of construction and vocabulary.

The influence exercised on pronunciation by speed of utterance, sentence stress,
etc., are considered in chap. xvii ; the associative influences (*analogy*, *contamination*,
etc.) in Part IV, chap. i ; here mention will only be made of two factors in which
scholars have begun recently to attribute influence on linguistic development—one
mainly social, the dominance of a standard language, the other psychological, the
sub-conscious desire for intelligibility.

§ 146. (1) When a 'standard' language is formed linguistic development is
often perturbed as well as slackened, particularly when, as is the case in French,
the influence of the standard language is strengthened by the influence of orthography and learning. It may then so happen that sounds and forms that had
become almost obsolete in the spoken language of everyday life are *restored*—first in
the more emphatic or precise speech and then generally—and then traditional
sounds are sometimes replaced by others under a misapprehension, under the idea
that the really 'correct' sound is being employed.

The *restoration* of moribund traditional sounds or forms is called *regression ;* the
replacement of a traditional sound under a misapprehension is called *false regression*.

The definition of *regression* given by Professor Dauzat runs as follows : 'La
restitution dans une série fonétique sous l'influence d'un parler directeur ou de forces
conservatrices (grammairiens, ortografe, etc.),—d'un son que le geu normal des lois
fonétiques avait transformé ou éliminé.' (*Rev. Ph.*, 1923, p. 125.)

Examples of regression are seen in the reinforcement of final s and t in the Latin
of Northern Gaul (§ 205) and of final consonants in the late sixteenth and seventeenth
centuries (§§ 618-623). False regression is exemplified in Middle French by the
substitution of ẹr for ar (§ 497) and of ǫ for u *countertonic*, § 582.

§ 147. (2) Professor Gilliéron has shown recently that a sub-conscious desire
for intelligibility is a factor in the evolution of pronunciation as well as in the life-

history of words. Its influence is strongest when for any reason there has developed a fluctuating pronunciation of a given sound, for in such a condition of things it is the readier intelligibility of one form of the word which may lead to its final adoption by the community. When, for example, in Middle French, the effacement of the final consonants produced forms of words which lost almost completely their individuality, as was the case with most of the mono-syllables, the form selected from the competing forms for general use was ordinarily the longer one, with sounded final consonant (cf. *chef, oeuf, coc, mer*, etc., § 619).   Again, when in Middle French there developed the fluctuating pronunciation wẹ and ẹ out of the older sound oẹ < oi (cf. §§ 522, 523), advantage was taken to differentiate homonyms that were misleading, and in this way

foin	**fwẹ̃**	*moins*	**mwẹ̃**	*l'avoine*	**lavwẹ̃nə**

were successfully differentiated from

faim	**fẹ̃**	*main*	**mẹ̃**	*la veine*	**lavẹ̃nə**

as also

froids	**frwẹ(s)**	*poele*	**pwẹlə**	*je vois*	**žə vwẹ(s)**

from

frais	**frẹ(s)**	*pelle*	**pẹlə**	*je vais*	**žə vẹ(s)**

(§§ 487, 523).

Cf. Gilliéron, *L'Abeille*, p. 205 : ' Le flottement wẹ : ẹ n'a pas été un caprice de la langue, mais, comme celui de ar : er . . . le résultat d'une lutte entre deux parlers, de laquelle lutte la langue en triomphant a su sémantiquement tirer souvent parti au bénéfice de son intelligibilité et de sa clarté, conditions premières de toute langue qui doit vivre et ne pas être inférieure aux exigences de la pensée qu'elle représente.'

Section 6.—CAUSES OF SOUND CHANGE.

§ 148. The immediate cause of some kinds of sound change is, as has been mentioned (§ 121), a strong expiratory accent; the immediate cause of many combinative changes lies in the principle of economy of effort (§ 122) ; a few isolative changes may result from the same cause, e.g. the shift forward of the plosive palatals ɟ and ɟ (§ 191), for these consonants being made with a markedly high lift of the most flaccid part of the tongue are relatively difficult to articulate : in the simplification of compound consonants, such as w and of the palatalised dentals, this same principle also plays a part.

Whole sets of changes, further, may be the outcome of previous changes, e.g. the wholesale modification of consonants in later Gallo-Roman was largely the result of the previous effacement of unstressed vowels, which had brought them into unfamiliar and often difficult positions.   There remain, however, many changes, particularly among the isolative ones (e.g. the palatalisation of Latin u to ü in French) which can be explained in none of these ways, and rarely is it obvious why changes begin when they do, (why, for instance, should k and g palatalise before e and i in Late Latin and not earlier ?), or why one speech community should retain its pronunciation tenaciously while another changes rapidly, or why the pace of change should alter in the history of one and the same community.

These questions and kindred ones are still under discussion and students interested should consult the general books on linguistics which deal with them (cf. below). Here all that can be attempted is a slight indication of the chief factors that affected the development of Latin in Gaul.   They may be summarised as follows :—

§ 149. (1) *Foreign Influence.*—Foreign influence is directly provocative of sound change, and this in two ways :—

(*a*) The ' organic basis,' the fixed speech habit of a people, is bound to exercise an influence on any other language acquired (cf. § 117).   The effect may be direct

and immediate, and tends to be so if the organic bases differ widely: for example, the 'French of Paris,' or rather of west and north-west France, was speedily modified in the mouths of the English (cf. Part V). Direct and also relatively rapid was the influence of the Frankish invaders of Gaul on the Gallo-Roman speech they adopted (§§ 25-30).

The influence of the foreign contact may, however, assert itself more slowly, producing at first a certain instability, giving rise to modifications so slight as only gradually to affect the direction of change. Tnis would seem to be the case when the speech habits of the peoples concerned are closely akin, as were apparently those of the Celts and the Latins—the two branches of the Indo-European family that were most closely related, cf. § 8.

(b) The influence of one language on another does not stop here, nor, in all probability, is it only felt when one nation exchanges its language for another. Close contact of any kind with a foreign speech is likely to some extent to weaken linguistic tradition, and so give freer play to the ever-present possibilities for variations and fluctuations: the pace of change may thereby be accelerated and possibly influenced in direction. The extraordinary conservation of the pronunciation and flexion of the Lithuanians is ascribed by Professor Meillet in part to the homogeneity of the Lithuanian population, in part to its isolation from all foreign influence. The rapidity of the evolution of Late Latin, on the other hand, may be in part due to the weakening of linguistic tradition that came with its widespread diffusion and manifold contact with foreign speech (cf. Meillet, E.L.L. p. 255, and § 4 (iii)).

§ 150. (2) The key to the problem of acceleration or retardation of sound change is often furnished by the history of the speech communities concerned. Language is a social institution and its vicissitudes must be, in consequence, determined to some extent by the vicissitudes of the society that uses it. Stability of economic and social conditions, ease of communication within the speech-community, the strengthening of tradition that comes with the spread of education and the formation of ideals of social conduct and right speech, the creation of a national literature, undoubtedly make for the stiffening of linguistic conservatism and so conduce to uniformity and stability of language. On the other hand, disturbed economic conditions and insecurity of communications, social upheavals, overthrowal of social standards and education are all factors that tend to weaken linguistic tradition and leave free course to the ever-present tendencies to change and thus foster and accelerate sound changes.

The history of French with its early period of social, political and economic confusion—the 'Dark Ages'—and concomitant rapid phonetic evolution, its later periods of comparative social, political and economic stability, of literary culture and the concomitant slackening of phonetic change, affords abundant illustration of the connection between linguistic change and historical and social conditions.

It must also, however, always be remembered that the effects of the perturbation of social and economic conditions are not *immediately* perceptible in linguistic development, for this is always affected indirectly by such factors, through the interruption of communications occasioned, and above all by the slackening of tradition that gives free play to the latent forces of change. Present-day colloquial French, so widely different from the French of the pre-Revolution period, is affording interesting evidence of the way in which mass movements, social, political, economic, come in time to affect the speech of a people even at a period of its history when tradition is strong.

§ 151. (3) *Acquirement of languages.*—Lastly, in the consideration of these questions, the conditions in which the language is acquired must never be lost sight of.

One speaks ordinarily of the transmission of language, but the term is a misnomer. Language is no 'thing,' no possession to hand on from father to son. What a child inherits is the capacity to acquire speech, the faculty of audition and the organs of speech that allow him to hear and imitate the speech of those around him. 'Une langue ne se transmet pas comme un outil, c'est une capacité qu'ont un certain nombre d'hommes de parler suivant un certain système.' (Meillet, *Les Langues dans l'Europe nouvelle*, p. 152.) The process is thus rather one of creative imitation than of transmission. This imitation, this perpetual re-creation of language, is normally accomplished, as far as the acquirement of sounds and flexions are concerned, in infancy or early childhood, and is rendered particularly difficult by the fact that the sounds which strike upon a child's ear are not isolated but in use in connected speech. It is consequently safe to say that a completely accurate imitation is practically never achieved, that no generation ever reproduces with absolute faithfulness the pronunciation of the preceding one. One need only note with some care the pronunciation of those around to convince oneself of the amount of variation in the pronunciation even of 'standard' English. And it is not only in England that pronunciation varies from generation to generation and from group to group. In France also, despite the greater strength of tradition and regulation, trained observers can always detect slight variations : 'Chaque fois,' says Rousselot, 'que j'ai pu grouper les membres d'une même famille, les grands-parents, les pères, les mères, les enfants, ou des personnes issues de villages voisins, j'ai toujours vu se renouveler le même spectacle : diverses étapes phonétiques très rapprochées se révélaient à mon oreille, et d'ordinaire j'ai pu les faire remarquer aux sujets intéressés, tout surpris de ne s'en être pas aperçus plus tôt.' (*Principes*, I, p. 43.)

One must, however, be careful not to exaggerate. Language is a human product and consequently ever mobile and pronunciation, it is true, can never remain completely set, but the slight differences observable in the speech of individuals may not always result in the modification of the sound in the speech of the community ; the fluctuations observable may, and often do, counterbalance one another ; association with others is a great leveller of differences, for peculiarities in speech lead to ridicule : tradition is a very potent retarding force. 'Toute forme linguistique se maintient naturellement ; pour vaincre l'inertie de la tradition il faut des conditions favorables et du temps.' (Meillet, *E.L.L.* p. 272.)

AUTHORITIES :

F. de Saussure : *Cours de Linguistique Générale*, 2me ed., Paris, 1922.

J. Vendryes : *Le Langage*, Paris, 1921 (cf. Bibliography).

O. Jespersen : *Language, its Nature, Development and Origin*, London, 1922.

L'Abbé Rousselot : *Principes de Phonétique Expérimentale*, Paris, 1897-1908.

L. Roudet : *Éléments de Phonétique Générale*, Paris, 1910.

P. Fouché : *Etudes de Phonétique Générale* (Publications de la faculté des Lettres de Strasbourg, fasc. 39).

M. Grammont : *Traité de Phonétique*, Paris, 1933 (cf. also § 93).

CHAPTER II.

SURVEY OF SOUND CHANGES.

Section 1.—INTRODUCTORY.

§ 152. The sound changes that gradually turned Latin into French were sometimes isolative, sometimes combinative, sometimes due to the influence of the expiratory accent, sometimes occasioned by the position of the sound in the word or sentence. The order of treatment adopted in this book is as follows :—

Isolative changes.
Influence of Position in the word.
Influence of Expiratory word-accent.
Combinative Changes, (1) Consonants, (2) Vowels.
Influence of Syntactical Phonetics.
Treatment of Loan-words.

To make it easier to follow the general trend of the evolution of pronunciation and the approximate chronological sequence of the changes, the more detailed account of the various changes is preceded by a synopsis of the more important ones, period by period, with appended tables of the sound-systems of the different periods.

The changes considered in Late Latin are those that affected Latin speech in Gaul.

Section 2.—LATE LATIN.

§ 153. The Classical Latin Accentual System and the Sound System were both profoundly modified in the course of Late Latin and the pronunciation of many words simplified by combinative changes.

Accentual System.—The whole rhythm of the language was gradually modified by the replacement of the older musical accent by a weak expiratory accent (§ 210).

§ 154. *Sound System.*—The simple Latin sound system was gradually modified by isolative and combinative change, the isolative being more important among the vowels, the combinative among the consonants.

Vowels.—(1) Among the mid and high vowels a *qualitative* difference gradually associated itself with the earlier *quantitative*, long vowels becoming closed, short vowels open (§ 179) : ē > ẹ, ĕ > ę, ī > ị, ĭ > ị,

ŏ > ǫ, ŏ > ǫ, ū > ų, u > ṷ. Subsequently ị and ṷ were lowered to ẹ and ǫ respectively (§ 180).

(2) Later on, in the stressed syllables, short vowels lengthened when free, long vowels shortened when blocked, **bŏnu** > **bǫnų*, **mĕl** > **mẹl*, **scriptum** > **ẹscriptų* (cf. § 125).

(3) The diphthongs **æ** and **œ** were levelled to **ẹ** and **ẹ** respectively (§ 504).

§ 155. *Consonants.*—(1) The laryngal fricative **h** was discarded (§ 185).

(2) The voiced bi-labial fricative *β* was developed: (*a*) from **b** *intervocalic* and + **r** (§ 333); (*b*) from **w**, which, when retained (§ 187), lost its velar articulation except after **k** (§ 186).

(3) The voiced velar fricative *γ* was developed from **g** *intervocalic* + **a**, **aṷ**, **o**, **u** and + **r** (§§ 323, 333).

(4) The voiced palatal plosive **ɟ** opened to **ȷ** when *intervocalic* (§ 297).

(5) New consonants were formed by the palatalisation of dental and velar consonants :—

(i) The breathed plosive palatal **ɟ** by the palatalisation of **k** by following **e**, **i**, **ȷ** (§§ 290, 306).

(ii) The voiced plosive palatal **ɟ** by the palatalisation of **d** by **ȷ** (§ 309) and of **g** by following **e**, **i**, **ȷ** (§§ 290, 307).

(iii) The alveolar affricate **ts** from **t** + **ȷ** (§ 308).

(iv) **ȷ** and **ŋ** from **l** + **ȷ** and **n** + **ȷ** (§§ 311, 312).

§ 156. The more important of the other changes are the following :—

(i) The introduction of the expiratory accent led to the consonantalisation of unstressed **ĕ**, **ĭ**, **ŏ**, **ŭ** in hiatus before a vowel to **ȷ** and **w** respectively (§ 220), to the occasional effacement of the unstressed penultimate vowel of proparoxytons (§ 221) and to the gradual shortening of all unstressed long vowels (§ 222).

(ii) In words of more than one syllable final **m** was effaced (§ 205).

(iii) The reduction of consonantal groups by combinative processes continued (§ 359): **ns** and **rs** > **s(ss)**, **kst** > **st**, **ɒkt** > **ɒt**, **ks** > *χ***s**, **kt** > *χ***t**, **gm** > **ṷm**.

(iv) Before initial groups consisting of **s** + *cons.* an initial glide sound was developed, unless the word was preceded by one ending in a vowel (§ 361).

(v) **kʲl** was substituted for **tʲl** (§ 360).

(vi) Countertonic vowels were not infrequently dissimilated or assimilated by the tonic vowels, thus countertonic **ị** was often dissimilated to **ẹ** by tonic **ị** (§ 127), countertonic **aṷ** to **a** by tonic **u** (§ 505), countertonic **e** assimilated to **a** by tonic **a** (§ 128).

(vii) Tonic vowels were differentiated from unstressed final vowels to which they were juxtaposed, if their articulation was similar or nearly so, e.g. *díes > díes, *mea > mea, *toum, > toum (§§ 131, 854).

§ 157. VOWEL SYSTEMS.

<table>
<tr><td>Classical Latin.</td><td>Late Latin.</td></tr>
</table>

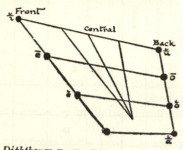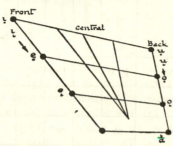

Diphthongs æ, œ, au.   Diphthong au.

In the pronunciation of the diphthong au, the first element was strongly emphasised, cf. the interpretation of *Cauneas* as *caue ne eas* (Juret, p. 30). The complete absence of the palatalisation of velar consonants before *a* and the velarisation of β to u between a – a (§ 345) make it clear that the variety of this vowel in use in Latin was *velar*.

§ 158. CLASSICAL LATIN CONSONANT SYSTEM.

	Labial.		Dental.				Denti-Palatal.		Palatal.	Velar.	Uvular.	Laryngal.
	Bi-labial.	Labio-dental.	Dental.	Alveolar.	Palatalised Dental.	Palatalised Alveolar.	Post-alveolar.	Prae-palatal.				
Plosive	p b		t d							k g		
Affricate												
Nasal	m		n							ŋ		
Lateral			l ɫ		î					(ɫ)		
Trilled				r								
Fricative	{ w (u) }	f	s					{ j i }	(w)	u	h
Semi-vowel												

LATE LATIN CONSONANT SYSTEM.

[Sounds queried in process of development.]

	Labial.		Dental.				Denti-Palatal.		Palatal.	Velar.	Uvular.	Laryngal.
	Bi-labial.	Labio-dental.	Dental.	Alveolar.	Palatalised Dental.	Palatalised Alveolar.	Post-alveolar.	Prae-palatal.				
Plosive	p b		t d						ɟ ɟ	k g		
Affricate						t͡s						
Nasal	m		n						ŋ (?)	ɳ		
Lateral			l̩ ɫ			î			ʎ (?)	(ɫ)		
Trilled			r									
Fricative	β	f	s						j	χ γ		
Semi-vowel	{ w (ɥ) }								{ j ʎ }	{ (w) ɥ }		

The Classical Latin consonant system, like the Modern English, was relatively rich in velar consonants, for it comprised not only k and g but also ɫ and ɳ. Dental l was employed at the beginning of words, but it is probable that it was a palatalised variety of this sound that was in use before i and in the lengthened sound (e.g. in *millia*, *mille*) and a velar variety (ɫ) that was employed elsewhere (e.g. aɫterum, soɫ, noɫo, pɫenum) (cf. Juret, p. 31); ɳ was employed before k and g, e.g. in *quinque* kwiɳkwe, *tango* taɳgo, *sanctum* saɳktum and in words of the type *agnus*, *dignus*, aɳnus, diɳnus, in which g had been nasalised to ɳ (Juret, p. 180); t, d and n appear to have been dental (Juret, p. 32); it is often uncertain whether the symbol u denotes w or ɥ. [Cf. A. Lloyd James, *Historical Introduction to French Phonetics*, London, 1929, pp. 82-95.]

Section 3.—PERIOD I: GALLO-ROMAN AND EARLY OLD FRENCH: FORMATION OF THE FRENCH LANGUAGE.

§ 159. The conditions that obtained in Gaul in Period I were precisely those most favourable to linguistic change (§§ 17-19): instability of political, social and economic conditions, local disintegration, weakness of means of communication, intensive foreign influence. Rapidity of evolution is therefore the outstanding characteristic of the linguistic

evolution of the period. Modifications begun in Late Latin were intensified and accelerated, and in turn provoked many others. Combinative
and isolative changes united in producing a more forward articulation
of many of the sounds. The frankish influence, especially its strong
expiratory accent, modified the pronunciation of the mid and low vowels
and provoked so much curtailment of unstressed syllables that the whole
rhythm of the language was altered (§ 223).

The more important changes may be summarised as follows :—

§ 160. *Consonants.*—(1) The *palatalisation* of consonants was extended further and affected : (i) *velars* before new-formed **a**, § 298,
(ii) the remaining *dentals* before **j**, §§ 313-315, (iii) the intervocalic
groups of *velar + dental*, §§ 319-326, and *velar + w*, §§ 327-330,
(iv) **s** *final* after **ʃ** and **ŋ**, § 318.

The *velar nasal* **ŋ** was thus eliminated from the sound-system,
§§ 293, 320, 321.

(2) The *voicing* and *opening* of intervocalic consonants was extended
to all single plosive and fricative consonants, §§ 332-335, and led ultimately to the effacement of the new-formed dentals **ð** and **θ**, § 346, and
of *β* and *γ*, under certain conditions, §§ 342, 344 ; when retained, *β* > **v**,
§ 189 ; **θ** *final* was also gradually effaced, § 346.

(3) The plosive palatals **ɟ** and **c** became denti-palatal affricates
(**dž** and **ts** or **tš**) in Gallo-Roman, § 191.

(4) All consonants brought into a *final* position in the word by the
slurring of unstressed final vowels were unvoiced, § 206.

(5) *Double* consonants were reduced in Old French I, § 366.

(6) Many *consonantal groups*, whether inherited from Latin or new-
formed by the effacement of unstressed vowels (§§ 249-256), were reduced
or modified by glide developments, effacement or some form of assimilatory process (chap. viii, section 2) : the middle of three consonants was
often slurred, the first of a group often assimilated to the following
consonant.

Towards the end of the period prae-consonantal **z** was modified or
effaced, § 377, and prae-consonantal **ł** and **ʃ** began to vocalise §§ 383-388.

§ 161. *Vowels.*—(1) *Isolative* changes continued : **α** and **u** palatalised
to **a** and **ü** respectively, §§ 182-183 : **ǫ**, already a high close sound in
Gallo-Roman, moved up to **u** in the course of early Old French, § 184.

(2) Under the influence of the intensified *tonic stress* vowels were
strongly modified : the tonic mid vowels were diphthongised in Gallo-
Roman when *free*, § 225 ; the new-formed diphthongs **uo, ei, ou**, were
subsequently differentiated to **ue, oi, eu** in the course of early Old
French, § 226 ; tonic **a** free passed to **ę**, § 231, unless influenced by a
juxtaposed *palatal, labial* or *nasal* consonant.

In *countertonic* syllables (§§ 211, 217) ẹ and ǫ closed ordinarily to ẹ and ǫ (§ 234), and subsequently ẹ *free* became ẹ and ǫ passed to **u** (§§ 184, 234).

Unstressed vowels were all either slurred or reduced to ẹ, §§ 249-256, and thus all words became oxyton or paroxyton, and always oxyton unless the last syllable contained ẹ.

Sentence stress induced much enclisis, § 602.

(3) Countertonic vowels were often modified by the assimilatory or dissimilatory influence of tonic vowels, §§ 131, 244, 421, 484.

(4) Vowels were strongly influenced by sounds adjacent or in their vicinity : they were often raised or diphthongised under the influence of *palatals* (chap. x), sometimes rounded by *labials* (§§ 481-484), and in the latter part of the period the low vowels were *nasalised* completely by following *nasals*, chap. xi.

As compared with Latin and Modern French the sound-system of the early part of the period was characterised by its abundance of *palatal* sounds, in its later part by its wealth of vowel sounds, diphthongal and pure.

An approximately chronological list of the sound changes of this period is appended.

[For a discussion of specific Celtic and Germanic influence, cf. §§ 6-9, 24-30.]

§ 162. *Chronology of Sound Change in Period I.*—The extent of the changes and the scarcity of documentary evidence of the spoken language make it difficult, and at times impossible, to determine the chronology of the Gallo-Roman sound changes with complete accuracy, but the evidence available from the sources mentioned above (§§ 39-43), makes it possible to arrange the more important changes in groups of more or less contemporary happenings. Some tendencies were persistent and consequently some processes recurred whenever the conditions inducing them reappeared, e.g. the diphthongisation of ẹ and ǫ *free* and *tonic*, the assimilation of labial and dental consonants, the voicing and opening of single intervocalic breath or plosive sounds, the palatalisation of consonants juxtaposed to palatal sounds.

§ 163. *Group I.—Changes mainly attributable to the Sixth and Seventh Centuries.*—This group consists mainly of changes that are continuations or extensions of processes begun in Late Latin :—

(1) Mutation of tonic ẹ and ǫ, § 419.
(2) Palatalisation of **a** to **a**, § 182.
(3) Effacement of penultimate ẹ before **r** and **l**, § 262.
(4) Shift of Late Latin **ʄ** and **ɟ** to **t͡s** and **d͡z**, § 191.
(5) Voicing of intervocalic **k to g**, § 335.

(6) Effacement or labialisation of intervocalic γ ($<$ g) before the back vowels **a, o, u**, § 341.

(7) Effacement of Late Latin β ($<$ intervocalic **b**) before labial vowels and after tonic **u**, § 343.

(8) Continuation of the palatalising movements :—

(i) Palatalisation of **rj, sj, zj**, §§ 313-315, and of *dentals + palatals*, § 293.

(ii) Palatalisation of *dentals* preceded by *palatals*, § 316.

(iii) Palatalisation of intervocalic groups of *velar + dental*, §§ 319-326.

(9) Assimilation of plosive labials to juxtaposed following dentals, § 373.

(10) First diphthongisation of **ę** and **ǫ**, § 225.

(11) Raising of **a** free to **ę** and of **ę** tonic free to **i** by preceding velar or palatal consonants, §§ 414-418.

(12) Breaking of **ę** and **ǫ** by following palatal consonants, §§ 410-411.

§ 164. *Group II.—Changes mainly attributable to the Seventh Century* :—

(1) Palatalisation of **k, g,** γ before **a** and **ę** ($<$ Latin **a**), §§ 413-415, and before **a, e** and **i** in Gallo-Roman loan-words, § 298-302.

(2) Shift of Gallo-Roman **ƫ** and **ɟ** to **tš** and **dž**, § 191.

(3) Resolution of **ř, ŝ, ẑ, ť, ď** into **r, s, z, t, d,** preceded by a palatal glide, § 190.

(4) Opening of Latin *intervocalic* **d** to **ϑ**, § 333.

(5) Voicing of breathed consonants **p, t, ts** when *intervocalic*, §§ 334, 335.

(6) Opening of Gallo-Roman **b** $<$ *intervocalic* **p** to β, § 335 ; shift of β to **v**, § 189.

(7) Opening of Latin **t** *final unsupported* and of **d** $<$ *Latin* **t** *intervocalic* to **θ** and **ð**, §§ 335, 355, 356.

(8) Closing of **j** *initial* to **dž**, § 203, and of **w** *initial* to **gw**, § 636.

(9) Introduction of **h** in initial position in Germanic words, § 28.

(10) Gradual complete effacement of the unstressed penultimate vowel, § 250.

(11) Reduction of unstressed **e, i, o, u** *final* and *intertonic* to **ę**, § 256.

(12) Closing of **ǫ** and **ǫ** to **u** by following nasal consonants, § 426.

(13) Diphthongisation of tonic free **ę** and **ǫ** to **ei** and **ou**, § 225, and of tonic free **a** to **ae** (?), § 233.

(14) Second bout of diphthongisation of **ę** tonic free, § 225.

(15) Raising of countertonic **ę** and **ǫ** to **ę** and **ǫ**, § 234.

Changes (10), (11), (13), (14), (15) and the first two in the next group are directly attributable to the influence of the intensified tonic stress.

§ 165. *Group III.—Changes mainly attributable to the Eighth and Ninth Centuries :—*

(1) Effacement of final and intertonic ẹ (< e, i, o, u), § 256.

(2) Reduction of final and intertonic a to ẹ, § 251.

(3) Unvoicing of all voiced consonants become final of the word, § 206.

(4) Palatalisation of s *final* by preceding ŋ and ʃ, § 318.

(5) Levelling of Latin and Gallo-Roman aṳ to ǫ, § 505.

(6) Levelling of tonic ae (< a *tonic free*) to ẹ, § 231.

(7) Gradual reduction of unfamiliar consonantal groups and of double consonants, chap. viii, sections 2, 3, 4.

(8) Resolution of prae-consonantal ŋ to ịn, § 279 (iv).

§ 166. *Group IV.—Changes mainly attributable to Early Old French :—*

(1) Completion of the palatalisation of u to ü, §·183.

(2) Shift of ǫ to u, § 184.

(3) Differentiation of uo to ue, § 226, 227.

(4) Beginning of differentiation of ei to oi and of ou to eu, §§ 226, 227.

(5) Reduction of countertonic ẹ free to ẹ, §§ 234, 235.

(6) Nasalisation of the vowels a and e and of the diphthongs ai and ei, §§ 434 ; beginnings of the lowering of ē to ã, § 439.

(7) Gradual effacement of ð and θ, §§ 346-347.

(8) Reduction of kw and gw to k and g, § 192.

(9) Beginnings of the velarisation of prae-consonantal ʃ and of the vocalisation of ɫ to ṳ, §§ 383-391.

(10) Gradual assimilation or effacement of prae-consonantal z, § 377.

§ 167   VOWEL SYSTEMS.

A.
Early Gallo-Roman, VI-VII.

B.
Late Eleventh Century.

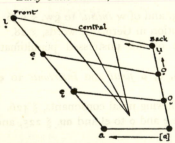

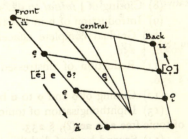

Diphthongs and Triphthongs :

ʹie, ʹuo, (ae ? cf. § 233)	ʹie, ʹue, ueu ?
aṳ, ʹǫu, ʹǫu, ʹieu, ʹuou	au ?, ẹu ?, ǫu ?, ʹeau ?, ʹẹeu ?, ʹieu, ʹüeu
[aj, ej, ǫj, ǫ̣j, uj]	ai, ei > ǫi, ǫi, ǫi > ui, üi

In Early Gallo-Roman the vowels ę and ǫ were high and close (§ 180).

In the later eleventh century it is uncertain how far the vocalisation of prae-consonantal ɫ and ĵ had advanced.

In the northern region u was not yet fully palatalised and there and in the east the opening of *jod* was possibly less advanced, especially after a, § 404 ; in the western region the diphthong ie had probably already passed to ịe or ịę.

§ 168. PROBABLE CONSONANT SYSTEM OF EARLY GALLO-ROMAN (VI-VII).

[Sounds queried those in process of development.]
[Sounds in square brackets those becoming obsolete.]

Consonants.	Labial.		Dental.				Denti-palatal.		Palatal.	Velar.	Uvular.	Lar-yngal.
	Bi-labial.	Labio-dental.	Dental.	Alveolar.	Palatalised Dental.	Palatalised Alveolar.	Post-alveolar.	Prae-palatal.				
Plosive	p b		t d		t̂ d̂				ɟ ɖ	k g		
Affricate					t͡s d͡z		d͜ž					
Nasal	m		n		ñ				ŋ	[ɳ]		
Lateral			l ɫ		l̂				ʎ	(ɫ)		
Trilled				r		r̂						
Fricative	[β] w	f v	s z ð		ŝ ẑ				ç j	[x] [γ] (w)		h
Semi-vowel	(ɥ)								ị?	ʮ		

CONSONANT SYSTEM OF THE LATE ELEVENTH CENTURY.

[Sounds queried those in process of development.]
[Sounds in square brackets those becoming obsolete.]

	Labial.		Dental.				Denti-palatal.		Palatal.	Velar.	Uvular.	Lar-yngal.
	Bi-labial.	Labio-dental.	Dental.	Alveolar.	Palatalised Dental.	Palatalised Alveolar.	Post-alveolar.	Prae-palatal.					
Plosive	p b		t d								k g		
Affricate				ts dz				tš dž					
Nasal	m		n							ŋ			
Lateral			l [ɫ]		[ĺ]					ʎ	[ɫ]		
Trilled				r									
Fricative	w	f v	s z [θ ð]							j	(w)		h
Semi-vowel	(ɥ)									i̯	u̯		

It is uncertain how far the vocalisation of prae-consonantal ɫ and ĺ had been carried at this date: in the northern region ŝ and ẑ were retained and ts and dz were possibly already passing to s and z; in the (south)-western region i̯ was developing from ˡie, § 512.

Section 4.—PERIOD II: LATER OLD AND MIDDLE FRENCH: FORMATION OF STANDARD FRENCH.

§ 169. Period II is the period in which standard Modern French is slowly formed. At its outset a period of relative peace and prosperity and of almost unexampled creative force (§ 44) led to an outburst of literary production that provoked a short-lived stabilisation of linguistic usage at the provincial courts in which literature was most cultivated (§ 45). These literary centres had, however, but an ephemeral existence and it is the dialect of Paris and the Île de France, a dialect relatively unrepresented in the literary work of the twelfth century, that ultimately developed into the standard language of France, and whose development is traced in this book.

6

The continued dominance of Latin as a medium of thought and learning (Pt. I, chap. iii, sect. 3) and the unfavourable political, social and economic conditions of the Middle French period hampered the development of literature and the unification and stabilisation of linguistic usage, but throughout this period Paris, already favoured by its geographical situation (§§ 61, 62), became steadily more important as a political, legal, economic and learned centre (§§ 63-65). By the end of the period the pre-eminence of its speech is recognised by all (§ 67).

Towards the end of the period the advance in culture and education began to differentiate with increasing strength the speech of educated and uneducated (Pt. I, chap. iii, sect. 6), and this differentiation was considerably increased in the sixteenth century by the influence that orthography and the knowledge of Latin began to exercise on the linguistic usage of the educated (§§ 740-746).

§ 170. The dominant factors in the evolution of pronunciation in Later Old and Middle French are the gradual lessening of the heavy tonic stress that characterised Period I and a new tendency to link closely together words closely connected in thought.

In the earlier period, when the tonic stress was intense, words remained, broadly-speaking, the unit of the phrase but, in Later Old and Middle French, words closely connected in thought, word-groups consisting of substantives and articles or adjectives—verbs and subjects, objects or adverbs—auxiliaries and participles, etc., were more and more run together and thus the phrase or locution became the sentence-unit instead of the word.

'Nous joignons tellement nos mots ensemble par une mutuelle liaison et proportion de voyelles et consonantes qu'il semble que chasque comma n'est qu'un mot : car encore qu'il y en ait quelquefois sept ou huict, ils sont si bien mariez et enchainez ensemble, qu'on ne les peut desjoindre, sans rompre les reigles de la vraye et naturelle prononciation.' [Delamothe (1592), quoted Thurot, II, p. 7.]

This new tendency, combined with the levelling of stress, modified profoundly the rhythm of the language.

§ 171. The main changes in pronunciation that ensued are the following :—

(1) The lessening of tonic stress led to the levelling of the diphthongs that were so marked a feature of Early Old French: shift of stress with subsequent consonantalisation of the weaker element or mutual assimilation reduced many of them in the course of Later Old French, and the last surviving—**au, ęau, uī**—were levelled in the course of the sixteenth and early seventeenth centuries (chap. xiv). One result of the levelling of the diphthongs and triphthongs in **ɥ** was the introduction

of the vowel ö into the sound system of the twelfth century (§§ 542, 545, 551, 555).

(2) With the diminution of stress the juxtaposition of monosyllabic unstressed words became less repugnant and their enclitic use became obsolete (§ 602).

(3) The running together of words in the phrase modified profoundly the pronunciation of consonants at the ends of words, for in this position they began to be treated very much as previously consonants had been treated in the interior of words : single fricative consonants before vowels, i.e. in intervocalic position, were voiced, s becoming z and f, v ; plosives and fricatives, supported and unsupported, became mute before words beginning with a consonant, i.e. when they were middle of three or prae-consonantal. ' And here upon it ryseth why the frenche tong semeth so short and sodayne in pronounsyng ; for after they have taken away the consonantes . . . by reason of the wordes folowyng, they joyne the vowels of the wordes that go before to the consonantes of the words folowynge in redyng and spekyng without any pausyng, save only by kepyng of the accent : as though fyve or syx wordes or somtyme mo made but one worde : whiche thyng, though it make that tong more hard to be atteyned, yet it maketh it more pleasant to the eare : for they put away all maner consonantes, as often as they shulde make any harshe sounde, or let ' (i.e. prevent) 'theyr sentences to flowe and be full in soundyng.' (Palsgrave, p. 40 ; cf. chap. xvii, sect. 5.)

(4) This close linking together of words in the group appears also to have increased the speed of emission of words within the phrase, and there began in the thirteenth century a gradual reduction or contraction of the weaker vowels juxtaposed to others, whether countertonic or atonic (chap. v, sects. 7 and 9). By the end of the period ę in hiatus was everywhere effaced and the juxtaposition of other vowels was almost entirely eliminated in the interior of words.

§ 172. The other sound changes of the period were largely continuations or extensions of movements begun earlier :—

(1) In the course of Later Old French the simplification of consonants and consonantal groups was carried further :—

(a) Before the middle of the twelfth century θ and ð were wholly eliminated from the sound-system (§§ 346, 347).

(b) Before the end of the thirteenth century the denti-palatal affricated consonants tš, dž, ts, dz moved forward, opened and became the fricatives š, ž, s, z (§ 194).

(c) Before the middle of the twelfth century ł (and ļ in prae-consonantal position) was effaced or vocalised to u̯, which combined to form diphthongs and triphthongs with the low and mid-vowels (§§ 383-388).

(*d*) In the course of Later Old French prae-consonantal s was effaced, often with compensatory lengthening of the previous vowel (§ 377).

(*e*) In the thirteenth century, in the pronunciation of some regions, r in every position except initial sometimes lost its trill and was sometimes effaced, sometimes shifted to z (chap. ix, sect. 4).

(*f*) In Middle French a tendency to eliminate the voiced fricative element in the combinations je̯, we̯, ẅi gained considerable ground, (§§ 510, 522, 516).

(2) Nasalisation was slowly extended to the earlier diphthongs je̯ (< ie), u̯e̯, ui and to the higher vowels u, i, ü, which were gradually lowered under its influence; when nasalisation became complete, the nasal consonant was absorbed, unless it was intervocalic; when it was not absorbed a differentiating movement began which led to the gradual denasalisation of the preceding vowels, roughly in order of height. These processes continued during the whole period and only reached their conclusion in the seventeenth century (chap. xi).

§ 173. New and important movements began among the vowels :—

(1) The lengthening of the vowel sound that ordinarily accompanied the effacement or absorption of consonants in prae-consonantal or final position (chap. xv) and the reduction of vowels in hiatus (chap. v, sects. 7, 9), and was sometimes induced by the influence of single consonants, e.g. z and v (§ 579), introduced a new quantitative difference among vowels (chap. xv), and these lengthenings led to a considerable amount of modification of quality :—

(*a*) ǫ *lengthened* ordinarily closed to o̦ and thus this sound was brought back into the sound-system of the thirteenth century (§§ 579, 580).

(*b*) tonic ę *lengthened* ordinarily opened to e̦ (§§ 575, 576).

(*c*) a *lengthened* tended to velarise to ɑ towards the close of the period (§ 586).

Thus by the end of the period almost all the vowels of the Modern French sound-system were in use.

(2) Adjustments of quality were not infrequently also induced by the influence of consonants and of position in the word, r and l exercising a lowering influence (chap. xiii), final position a closing one (§ 529). The three e-sounds of Old French (e̦ < L.L. ę *blocked*, ę̌ < L.L. ę *blocked*, ę̂ < L.L. a *tonic free*) were thus reduced to two, and by the end of the period their distribution was very much that of Modern French, except that in educated speech ę̂ (< a *tonic free*) was still given *close* value before intervocalic r (§ 495). Among the countertonic vowels

there was considerable hesitation between **u** and **ǫ** or **ǫ** and between **ẹ** and **ę** (§§ 581, 582, 591).

(3) In the course of the period the weak vowel **ę** was gradually labialised to weak **ö** (§ 275).

§ 174. Vowel Systems.

Early fourteenth century.   *Early seventeenth century.*

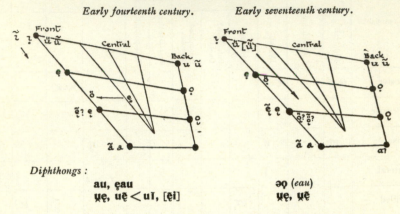

Diphthongs :

    au, ęau   **əǫ** *(eau)*

    ųę, uę < uĭ, [ęĭ]   **ųę, ųę**

§ 175. Consonant System of the Early Fourteenth Century.

[Sounds in square brackets those becoming obsolete.]

Consonants.	Labial.		Dental.				Denti-palatal.		Palatal.	Velar.	Uvular.	Lar-yngal.
	Bi-labial.	Labio-dental.	Dental.	Alveolar.	Palatalised Dental.	Palatalised Alveolar.	Post-alveolar.	Prae-palatal.				
Plosive	p b		t d							k g		
Affricate												
Nasal	m		n							ŋ		
Lateral			l							ʎ		
Trilled				r								
Fricative		f v	s z				š ž					[h]
Semi-vowel	{ w ẅ (ɥ)(ü) }								{ (ẅ) j ü ʎ }	(w) ɥ		

Consonant System of the Early Seventeenth Century.

[Sounds in square brackets those becoming obsolete.]
[Sounds queried those developing.]

Consonants.	Labial.		Dental.				Denti-palatal.		Palatal.	Velar.	Uvular.	Glottal.
	Bi-labial.	Labio-dental.	Dental.	Alveolar.	Palatalised Dental.	Palatalised Alveolar.	Post-alveolar.	Prae-palatal.				
Plosive	p b		t d							k g		
Affricate												
Nasal	m		ıı						ŋ			
Lateral			l						ʝ			
Trilled				r							R ?	
Fricative		f v	s z					š ž				
Semi-vowel	{ w ẅ } { (ɥ) (ᶙ) }								{ (ẅ) ɟ } { ü i }	{ (w) } { ɥ }		

§ 176. The pronunciation of the early seventeenth century is reasonably well illustrated in the partially phonetic representation given in the grammar compiled by Martin for the use of Germans in 1632 (cf. Th. II, pp. 757-759).

Value of Symbols.—*Vowels :* ä = ę, äh = ē̦, eh = ē̦, oh = ǫ, i + n = ē̦. i, ö, u, ü have their ordinary phonetic values ; wę (< oi) is represented by oä. No attempt is made to distinguish nasal vowels, ə, or differences of quality or quantity other than those mentioned above.

Consonants : in intervocalic position *ss* functions as **s**, *s* as **z** ; *sch* represents both **š** and **ž** : *nj* stands for **ŋ**, *lj* for **ʝ**.

O grand Dieu qui habite	O gran Diö ki habite
En ce haut firmament	An se hoh firmaman
Ie te pri' ne t'irrite,	Sche te pry ne tirrite
De quoy presentement	De koä presenteman
Un vermiceau de terre	Un vermisseoh de terre (*sic*)

A toy s'ose addresser	A toä sose adressehr
Pour sa requeste faire	Pur sa rekäte fähre
Et tes saincts pieds baiser.	E tä sin pieh bäsehr
Ie n'en aurois l'audace	Sche nan ohroä lodasse
N'estoit que mon sauveur	Nätoä ke mun sohvör
M'a donné de sa grace	Ma donneh de sa grasse
Des lettres de faveur	Dä lettre de favör
M'enjoignant comme frere	Manschoenjan kunme frehre
Iesus pour moy percé,	Schesu (*sic*) pur moä persseh
De t'appeller mon pere	De tapelehr mun pehre
Certain d'estre exaucé.	Sertin dätre exosseh
En son nom donc escoute	An sun nun dunck äkute
Ton humble suppliant	Tun umble süplian
Seigneur et ne reboute	Senjör ä ne rebute
De ton fils le client	De tun fi le klian
Lorsque dans l'ombre espesse	Lorke dan lunbr äpässe
Des ames l'assassin	Däs ahme lassassin
Embuscade me dresse	Anbuskade (*sic*) me drässe
Empesche son dessein.	Anpäsche sun dessin.
Tiens bien courte la lesse	Tjin bjin kurte la lässe
Du lion rugissant . . .	Dü liun rüschissan . . .
Fay que mon esprit veille	Fä ke mun espry velje
Le corps dormant tout coy	Le kor dorman tu koä
Et songe à la merveille	E sunsch a la mervelje
De l'object de la foy.	De lobschä de la foä.
Puis ton immense torche	Püy tun inmanse torsche
Me venant esclairer	Me venant äklärehr
Serve à mon cœur d'amorche	Serva mun kör damorsche
Afin d'y allumer	Afin dy alumehr (*sic*)
Un feu inextinguible	Un fö inextingible
Du desir de loüer	Dü desir de luehr
Dieu l'incomprehensible	Diö linkunpreanssible
Et à luy me voüer	E a lüy me vuehr
Ainsi soit-il	Inssy soäty
Fay—moy aussi la grace	Fä moä ossi la grasse
Qu'en fait ou en penser	Kan fät uh an panssehr
Ie n'aye onque l'audace	Sche n'äy unke lodasse
Seigneur, de t'offenser.	Senjör, de toffansehr.
Mais qu'ayant pour boussole	Mä kayan pur bussole
En ceste trouble mer	An sette truble mer (*sic*)
Ta sacrée parole	Ta sakree parole
Ie ne puisse abysmer.	Sche ne püiss abymehr.

Section 5.—MODERN FRENCH.

§ 177. In the modern period sound changes have slowed down under the influence of education and printing. Parisian speech is still the recognised norm but with the increase of the reading public spelling has come to play a more and more important part.

It is as yet difficult to assess the extent of the influence of the great social and political movements of the late eighteenth and nineteenth century.

The nasalising and denasalising processes of the preceding period were completed (chap. xi), and two of the more important movements of the preceding period continued to extend :—

(1) The effacement of final consonants. The modern usage in respect to consonants in prae-consonantal position and at the pause was established in the main in the seventeenth century, but the practice of liaison has suffered and is suffering continual diminution (cf. A. Langlard, *La Liaison dans le Français*).

(2) The effacement of ə has been extended to ə in every position, and the current practice is, roughly, to pronounce it only when its effacement would bring three consonants into juxtaposition (cf. Grammont, *Traité*, pp. 105 et seqq. ; Nyrop, *Manuel*, §§ 86-92).

These movements are in turn affecting considerably the pronunciation of vowels, whose quality in Modern French is largely determined by the position in which they stand in the word and the point of articulation of the following consonant (§ 571). There has resulted considerable instability in the quality of vowels and this is increased by the tendency to velarise ã (§ 443) and also a under certain conditions, and to give ö open and close value (§§ 585, 586).

The Middle French vulgar pronunciation of wę as ę was established in a considerable number of words in the seventeenth century : the broadening of wę to wa (wɑ), which was rejected in the seventeenth century (§ 525), found acceptance after the French Revolution.

Among consonants two important isolative changes, the reduction of ʎ to j and the substitution of R for r, had their beginning in vulgar Parisian speech in the seventeenth century but were also only accepted finally in the later nineteenth (§§ 106, 107).

[Cf. Rosset, *Les Origines de la Prononciation Française étudiées au XVIIe Siècle*, Paris, 1911 ; H.L.F. IV, i, pp. 190-215, and the general works mentioned in the bibliography.]

CHAPTER III.

ISOLATIVE CHANGES.

Section 1.—INTRODUCTORY.

§ 178. The vowel system was affected strongly by isolative changes in the early period of the language, the consonantal system at various periods. Consonantal changes were mainly due to the tendency to eliminate the weaker fricative sounds, e.g. h, β, ð, θ, and to modify sounds relatively difficult to articulate, e.g. w and many palatal and palatalised sounds. Isolative change among the vowels induced a more forward pronunciation and it is possible that Celtic influence plays a part in this movement, cf. § 9 (iii).

Section 2.—VOWELS MODIFIED IN LATE LATIN.

§ 179. (1) The mid and high vowels, which in classical Latin were mainly differentiated by *quantity*, began to be differentiated more strongly by *quality*, the long becoming closed, the short open.

Thus ī > ị, ĭ > ị̣, ē > ẹ, ĕ > ẹ, ŏ > ọ, ō > ọ, ŭ > ụ, ū > ụ:

filŭm > *filụ, illum > *ịllụ, mē > *mẹ, pĕdĕm > *pẹdẹ, bŏnŭm > *bọnụ, mōrēs > *mọrẹs, gŭla > *gụla, dūrŭm > *dụrụ.

§ 180. (2) Subsequently ị and ụ were lowered to ẹ and ọ respectively and thus ịllụ > *ẹllọ, fidēs > *fịdẹs > *fẹdẹs, gụla > *gọla, ŭrsŭm > *ụrsụ > *ọrsọ.

[For tables of vowel systems cf. § 157.]

The lowering of ị to ẹ was earlier and more general than that of ụ, which has retained its value, particularly in the final unstressed syllable, in parts of the Roman Empire up to the present time. In Gaul in the Gallo-Roman period ẹ and ọ were markedly close varieties of these sounds: frk. ō is equated with ọ and not ọ (§ 637), and ẹ is often written *i* and ọ *u*, by Merovingian scribes, cf. § 691.

Section 3.—VOWELS MODIFIED IN PERIOD I.

§ 181. The vowels modified by isolative change in Period I were the lowest and highest of the velar vowels—a and ụ. These both shifted forward, a palatalising to **a** in Early Gallo-Roman, ụ to ü in the course of Period I.

§ 182. ɑ > a. In Early Gallo-Roman ɑ palatalised to a in every position in all words of more than one syllable. The palatal pronunciation of the sound persisted unmodified through Old French and remained dominant into Modern French but velarisation to ɑ appears to have begun under certain conditions in Later Middle French (§ 586).

In monosyllables palatalisation was tardier (cf. M.L. *Gr.* § 60) but appears to have been accomplished in the course of Period I, as monosyllabic words (e.g. *va*, *esta* (< *stat*)) assonate freely with words in blocked **a**:

aɩɑ > **ala,	pɑtrem > **padre,	gɑmbɑ > **gamba,
pɑstɑ > **pasta,	kɑstĕllum > **kastę̣llu̧,	stɑt > **estɑt (> estɑθ).

In the course of Period I the sound **a** was modified by *stress* in words in which it was *tonic* and *free* (§ 231), and often by the influence of *palatals* (§§ 404, 413-417, 423), *nasals* (§§ 427, 443), *labials* (§§ 481, 483, 484 (ii)) : in the course of Period II by combination with u̧ (< *praeconsonantal* ɫ and]), (§§ 387, 388) and by *lengthening* (§ 586).

[For the O.F. palatalisation of **a** to ę̣ in the eastern and northern region cf. § 423.]

§ 183. u̧ > ü. u̧ (Late Latin and Germanic) palatalised to ü (whenever it was not previously reduced or slurred) in the course of Period I alike before oral and nasal consonants. The sound **u** thus disappeared for a while out of the francien sound-system but was brought in again by the raising of ǫ to **u** (§ 184):

dūrŭm > *du̧ru̧ > dür, fūstem > füst, dūrɑre > dürę̣r, pūrgɑre > pürdžier, *u̧stɩu̧ (for *ǫstɩu̧) > üis, ūnŭm > ün, *bru̧mɑ > brümę̣, *bru̧nu̧ > brün.

[For the later development of üi cf. §§ 514-517; for ü + *nasal*, cf. §§ 456-458.]

✻✻ The palatalisation of **u** appears to have spread slowly from the south, reaching last the northern and eastern region. Norse words were affected by it, (cf. modern *Etainhus* > *Steinhūs*), rhymes between ü and **u** are occasional in mediaeval northern texts and the sound **u** is still retained in Eastern Walloon, (cf. above, §§ 9 (iii), 42, N.E. § ii, and E. Jacoby, *Zur Geschichte des Wandels von* **u** *zu* ü, Berlin, 1916).

§ 184. ǫ > u. In the course of the eleventh and twelfth centuries, ǫ, already a high close sound in Gallo-Roman, § 180, when not previously diphthongised, § 225, moved upwards in all positions to **u**, i.e. to the place left vacant by the palatalisation of **u** to ü. The graphy, when it was not etymological, was at first *u* in Norman and Anglo-Norman MSS., *o* elsewhere : the di-graph *ou* appears first in the late twelfth century (§ 698).

The sound ǫ thus disappeared for a while out of the sound-system, but was brought in again in the thirteenth century and Middle French by the tendency to close lengthened ǫ, §§ 579, 580 :

*tǫttụ (for *tōtum*) > tǫt > tut   úrsum > ǫrs > urs
genŭculum > džęnǫ] > džęnụ] *genoil*   *bŭrgụ > bǫrk > burk *borc*
angŭstia > āngǫisę > ānguisę *angoisse*   krŭkem > krǫits > kruits *croiz*
dŭbitare > dǫtęr > dutęr *doter*   úrtica > ǫrtię > urtię (§ 582)
dǫlour < dŏlōrem (§ 234) > duleur *doleur*   lǫer < lŏkare > luęr *loer*
tǫrmēnt < tŏrmentum (§ 234) > turmānt *torment*

[For the development of ǫ + *nasal*, cf. §§ 459-465; for the later development of **ui** (< ǫi), cf. §§ 519-525; for modifications of **u** *counter-tonic* in Middle French, cf. § 582.]

The early use of the symbol *u* (for earlier ǫ) in the western region and the western levelling of the diphthong **ou** to **u**, § 230, indicate that the shift to **u** must have been accomplished in that region in the course of Early Old French : elsewhere it appears to have taken place rather later.

Section 4.—Consonants Modified in Late Latin.

§ 185. (1) The laryngal fricative **h** was gradually effaced, e.g. hŏminem > *ǫmne, prehendere > *preendere > *pręndere.

Effacement began early in the interior of words, cf. *App. Pr. adhuc non aduc*, and as in Modern English social stigma became attached to the misuse of **h**, cf. St. Augustine, ' it was deemed a greater offence to drop the *h* of *hominem* than to disregard the law of Christian charity.' (*Conf.* I, 181.)

§ 186. (2) **w** > *β*. Except after **k** (i.e. in *qu*) Classical Latin **w** (ụ ?), initial and intervocalic, where retained, lost its velar articulation and simplified to *β*, the bi-labial fricative sound that is still preserved in Spanish : *vinum* wīnŭm > *βịnụ, *vivere* wiwere > *βịβęrę, *viva* wiwα > *βịβα, *salvia* saɫwia > *saɫβịa, *servum* sĕrwum > *sęrβụ.

Inscriptions in Greek letters attest this simplification in the Early Empire, e.g. Νερβα for *Nerva* (cf. also *App. Probi, baculus non vaclus* and GG. § 322) ; as intervocalic **b** also opened to *β* (§ 333) complete confusion arose between the symbols *v* and *b* (§ 336).

§ 187. Before this simplification took place **w** appears to have been sometimes either effaced or opened to ụ and combined in a diphthong with the preceding vowel.

(i) If made prae-consonantal by the slurring of an atonic vowel, **w** vocalised to ụ. cf. *aucellu* *auɬęllụ < awikęllum *avicellum*, *auka < awïka *avica*.

(ii) **w** was effaced : (*a*) when intervocalic before the labial vowels **o** and **u**, cf. *App. Pr. avus non aus, rivus non rius, pavor non paor* and spellings such as *aunculus* for *avunculus* (O.F. *oncles*).

(*b*) When standing between **k** and either **u** or **o**, cf. *App. Pr. equs* (i.e. *equus*) *non ecus, coqus non cocus, coquens non cocens* and the later spellings *cot* for *quot*, *condam* for *quondam* (cf. Lindsay, p. 300).

(*c*) Before *jod* (< *consonantalised* ĕ, ĭ, § 220), e.g. in *atavia* *atawịa, O.F. taię ; *aviolum* *awịǫlụ, O.F. *aiuel*; *caveola* *kawịǫla, O.F. *jaiole*; *plovia* *plǫwịa, O.F. plüię ; *laqueum* *lakwịụ, O.F. **lats** *laz*; cf. the spellings *Flaius* for *Flavius*, οκταιος for *Octavius* (Juret, p. 162) and the place-names *Noyon*, *Noyant*, etc. (Longnon, pp. 45 and 63).

§ 188. Under the influence of associated forms in which **w** stood under different conditions the labial consonant was, however, not infrequently retained by preservative analogy (§ 765), cf. O.F. **uef** < *$\varrho\beta\mu$, *ovum,* **vif** < *$\beta_l\beta\mu$ *vivum, cage* **kadžę** < *kaβja *cavea, legier* **ledžier** < *leβjarʃμ *leviarium,* the L.L. forms being due to the influence of associated form such as *ova, ovis, viva, vivere, cava, levis.*

Section 5.—CONSONANTS MODIFIED IN GALLO-ROMAN.

§ 189. β. In the course of Gallo-Roman the bi-labial fricative consonant β, a sound that is always relatively unstable, shifted to **v** (**f** when final), unless previously eliminated, cf. § 344:

vivere	*$\beta_l\beta$ere (< wiwere) > vivrę		*ovum*	*$\varrho\beta\mu$ (§ 188) > uef	
lavare	*laβare (< laware) > lavęr		*navem*	*naβe > nęf	
habere	*aβere (< habère) > aveir		*bibe*	*bęβe > beif	
saponem	*sapone > **saβone > savun		*sepem*	*sępe > **seiβe > seif	

Sources of β: Gallo-Roman β was derived: (i) from L.L. β < w, § 186; (ii) from L.L. **b** *intervocalic* and + r, §§ 333, 372; (iii) from L.L. **p** *intervocalic* and + r, §§ 335, 372.

β initial of a syllable after r and n was sometimes strengthened or differentiated to **b**, cf. O.F. *corber* **kurbęr** < **korbare < *kurβare < kŭrware *curvare*; **brębis** < *βerβįʃe (*vervecem*), § 128; **ēmbler** < *emβolare < inwolare *involare* (cf. the spelling *imbolet* for *involat*, 7th cent. (*Mél. Wilmotte*, p. 503).

§ 190. Many of the new-made palatal and palatalised sounds were relatively difficult to articulate, for the *palatalised dentals* have a double point of articulation (§ 111), and the *plosive palatals* are made with a markedly high lift of the front, the more flaccid part of the tongue, § 106 (*c*): all these sounds were modified in the course of Gallo-Roman.

(i) The new-formed palatalised dentals r̂, ŝ, ẑ, t̂, d̂, n̂, formed in Gallo-Roman from simple dental consonants in contact with *jod* (§§ 313-315), were resolved again into simple dentals preceded by a palatal glide which merged in preceding i and combined with other vowels in a diphthong, i.e. r̂ > įr, ŝ > įs, ẑ > įz, t̂ > įt, d̂ > įd, n̂ > įn, cf. O.F. **airę** < **afa < *arja < aréa; *baissier* **baisier** < **baŝare < *bassiare; *baisier* **baizier** < **baẑare *basiare*; **meitie** < **mejîate < *medjetatem; **aidier** < **aj(u)dare *adjutare.*

✱✱ In the northern region, and more particularly the north-eastern, ŝ and ẑ were retained into Old French, cf. N. § xvi.

§ 191. **ɟ** *and* **ʃ** > **dž, ts** *or* **tš**.—The plosive palatal **ɟ**, whether formed in Late Latin or Early Gallo-Roman (§§ 290, 300), shifted forward to **dž**, cf. O.F. *gent* **džēnt** < *ɟente < gentem, O.F. *jambe* **džămbę** < G.R. **ɟamba < *gamba (§§ 291, 300): the plosive palatal **ʃ**, formed in Late Latin, shifted forward to **ts**, but **ʃ**, formed in Gallo-Roman,

shifted forward to **tš**, cf. O.F. *cent* tsēnt < *ţentu̧ < kentum *centum*, O.F. *chier* **tšier** < G.R. **ţaru̧ < karum *carum* (§§ 291, 300).

The passage of the sounds ţ and ɡ to **ts, tš, dz, dž** respectively, is sometimes termed *assibilation*.

Section 6.—Consonants Modified in Early Old French.

§ 192. **w(u̯?).** Dislike of the sound w persisted into Middle French and led often to the modification or elimination of the sound both in the words in which it was traditional and in those in which it was developed anew.

(i) Latin *qu* ku̧?, initial of the word, appears to have been simplified to **k** before **e** and **i** in Gallo-Roman (cf. *Eulalia, chi* for *qui* 6, 12) and before **a** in Early Old French (cf. Rydberg, I, pp. 328-331).

(ii) Initial **gw** from Germanic initial **w** and in Latin words influenced by this sound (§ 636) appears to have been simplified to **g** before the later twelfth century : ****wardɑre > gwardęr > gardęr, *wisɑ > **gwizɑ > gizę,** *vespa* wěspɑ + *frk.* *wespɑ > **gwęspę > gęspę** (cf. § 1180 and the English loan-words *guard, guise,* etc.).

(iii) Gallo-Roman intervocalic **w**, ordinarily opened to **u̯**, but if it persisted in intervocalic position into Early Old French it then shifted to **v** :

*hawa > hǫu̯ę, *pava* **pawa > pǫu̯ę,** estšewęr (< *skiuhan*) > **estševęr** *eschever,* ****estšiwet** (§418) > **estšiut** *eschiut (eschieut,* §121).

[For G.R. intervocalic **ww** cf. §§ 374, 1024-1027 ; for Latin *qu* ku̧ intervocalic cf. §§ 327-330 ; for Late Latin **kw** initial cf. § 1180.]

w and **ẅ,** developed out of the diphthongs oę, ue, üi in the course of Later Old French, were also sometimes slurred (§§ 475, 503, 516, 522).

§ 193. The dental fricatives **ð** and **θ** were gradually effaced in the course of Early Old French (§§ 346, 347).

Section 7.—Consonants Modified in Later Old and Middle French.

§ 194. **ts, dz, tš, dž > s, z, š, ž.** In the course of the thirteenth century the affricated consonants **ts, dz, tš, dž** opened and thus became simple fricatives :

ts > s. O.F. *cent* **tsēnt > sānt,** *poiz* **poits > pu̯ęs,** *faz* **fats > fas,** *fiz* **fits > fis,** *bainz* **bāints > bęins,** *parz* **parts > pars,** *granz* **grānts > grāns.**

dz > z. *doze* **dǫdzę > duzę,** *treze* **trędzę > tręzę,** *unze* **undzę > ūnzę.**

tš > š. *char* **tšar > šar,** *chier* **tšier > šįęr,** *arche* **artšę > aršę,** *sache* **satšę > sašę.**

dž > ž. *jambe* **džānbę > žānbę,** *argent* **ardžēnt > aržānt,** *ruge* **rudžę > ružę,** *lange* **lāndžę < **lɑnɟɑ > lānžę,** *eage* **eadžę > ęažę.**

The sources of **ts** are : (i) **k** (+ **e** and **i**) initial, and intervocalic become final, §§ 291, 295 (iii) ; (ii) **k** + *jod*, § 306 ; (iii) **s** final palatalised by preceding **ʃ** and **ŋ**, § 318 ; (iv) **d** and **t** combined with final **s**, § 367 ; **t** initial + *jod*, § 308.

The sources of **tš** are : (i) **k** initial before **a**, § 300 ; (ii) **k** initial before **e** and **i** in Gallo-Roman loan-words, § 300 ; (iii) Late Latin *jod*, initial after **p**, § 305.

The sources of **dž** are : (i) **g** initial, before **e, i, a**, §§ 291, 299 ; (ii) Latin *jod*, initial of words, § 203 ; (iii) Late Latin *jod*, initial of a syllable after **b, w, m**, § 203 ; (iv) Gallo-Roman *jod*, initial of a syllable after consonants, § 203.

[For representation of **ts, dz, tš, dž** cf. §§ 692-694 ; for use of symbols in Middle French, cf. §§ 722, 723, 724, 731.]

§ 195. *Date of Shift of* **ts, dz, tš, dž** to **s, z, š, ž**. The affricated pronunciation of these sounds was retained ordinarily through the twelfth century but rhymes between **ts** and **s** are already occasional in the work of Crestien de Troyes (e.g. E. 2249, 3870). The affricated pronunciation is attested (i) by the M.E. and M.H.G. loan-words, e.g. M.E. *Fitz* (-*James*, etc.), *chapel, chief, judge, jury*, etc., M.H.G. *tschevalier, tschapel, Mütze* (<*almuce*), *Schanze*, etc. ; (ii) by the value **ts** accorded to *c* in the word *force* and to *z* in the word *fiz* in the transcriptions of these words in the Hebrew glosses of the early thirteenth century ; (iii) by early spellings, cf. § 700.

✶✶ In the northern region the shift of **ts** to **s** took place early, and the symbol **z** is not used in the MS. of *Aucassin* (late thirteenth century), cf. N. § xxi.

§ 196. *Effacement of* **h**.—In the course of Later Middle French **h**, retained in Old French in words of Germanic origin or influenced by such (§ 28), gradually became mute in uneducated speech, cf. H. Estienne, 'Many people say *un'onte* . . . *un'arpe* . . . *il m'ait*, (for *il me hait*),' Tn. II, 396.   Under the influence of the grammarians and the reformers of Latin pronunciation (§ 654) effacement was checked in educated speech and only recognised officially in the later seventeenth century, and not even then in the conservative *Cahiers* of the Academy (1673) : 'Dans tous les autres mots qui ne viennent point du latin, l'*h* aspire fort, quoyque le mauvais usage introduit par les gens du province d'outre Loire, et mesme par le peuple de Paris s'efforce de l'abolir tout à fait.' (Th. II, 396.)   The influence of the grammarians remained strong enough to prevent acceptance of the elision of the preceding vowel (cf. Rosset, pp. 288-291).

[For the modern reduction of **ʃ** to **jod**, cf. § 106 (*c*) ; for the modern substitution of **R** for **r** cf. § 107.]

CHAPTER IV.

INFLUENCE OF POSITION IN THE WORD.

[For influence of position in the sentence cf. chap. xvii.]

Section 1.—INFLUENCE OF POSITION ON VOWELS.

§ 197. In words of more than one syllable the most important point to consider in the position of a vowel is whether it is *free* or *blocked*, i.e. whether it ends its own syllable or is pronounced together with a following consonant, for in the one position a vowel tends to lengthen, in the other to shorten (cf. § 125). The *blocked* vowels (*voyelles en-travées*) are those that stand before double consonants and all con-sonantal groups, excluding those consisting of *plosive* + l and r, e.g. ter-ra, bel-la, mit-tere, mis-sa; por-tam, per-dere, or-na-men-tum, *saṗja (< *sapiam*).   *Free* vowels are those that stand in the following positions :—

(i) Final of a word, e.g. amo, mensa, mensae.

(ii) In hiatus with a following vowel, e.g. de-us, di-es, su-us.

(iii) Before a single consonant, e.g. pe-dem, i-ni-mi-cus.

(iv) Before a group consisting of *plosive* consonants (labial, dental or velar) + l or r, e.g. du-plum, pa-trem, ni-grum.

§ 198. The influence of position began to affect the length of vowels toward the end of the Late Latin period, *after* the quality of vowels had been determined (§ 179).   In early Gallo-Roman it is probable that all the *short* tonic vowels that were *free*, had been lengthened and all the *long* ones, that were *blocked*, had shortened.   In monosyllabic words ending in a single consonant the vowel was also lengthened :

'pĕdem > *'pĕdẹ > **'pēdẹ, minŭs > *'mĕnụs > **'mēnọs, 'lătŭs > **'lātọs
'dĕus > *'dĕụs > **'dēụs, 'sŭa > *'sụa < **'sọa,
'dŭplum > **'dọplụ, 'fĕbrem > **'fēbre, mĕl > *mĕl > **mēl,
frūctum frŭktŭm > **frụ̆χtụ, *cohortem* *kọrte > **kọ̆rte.

This lengthening is of importance because with the increase in the strength of the expiratory accent in Gallo-Roman (§§ 27, 213) it led to the diphthongisation of the mid and low vowels, §§ 224, 225, 231, 233.

Before the palatal consonants ļ and ŋ lengthening appears to have been checked, for before them the tonic vowels a, ọ, ẹ, remained undiphthongised under

the tonic stress in Gallo-Roman (§ 231), cf. O.F. **guverna]** < **gŭbernakŭlŭm,**
orẹlẹ < au'**rikŭla,** *genoil* **džẹnu]** < **genuculum; montagne* **mŭntāŋẹ** <
**montaŋa. [For the later development of ẹ + ŋ cf. § 407 (ii); for the diphthongisation of ẹ and ǫ before palatal consonants cf. §§ 410, 411.]

§ 199. In Later Old French, when many vowels previously blocked
had been made free by the simplification of double consonants (§ 366)
and the effacement of prae-consonantal s and z (§ 377), the same
tendency again asserted itself and the lengthenings that appear to have
taken place then and in Middle French were a factor in the modifications of the quality of vowels in subsequent periods (cf. chap. xvi).

§ 200. Position at the end of a word may also exercise an influence
on vowel development, for vowels that are in this position tend to *close*
both in Later Old French (cf. §§ 529, 578), and in the modern period
(cf. Nyrop, *Manuel*, §§ 97, 101).

Section 2.—Influence of Initial Position on Consonants.

§ 201. Consonants may stand in *initial* or *final* position, in *groups* or
between vowels (*intervocalic*), and the position occupied by them in the
word exercised a very considerable influence on their development.

§ 202. Consonants are said to be *initial :* (i) when they stand at the
beginning of a word, (ii) when they stand at the beginning of a syllable,
if preceded immediately by a consonant, e.g. in the word **portare** both **p**
and **t** are termed *initial.* Consonants may be initial in Latin or become
so in the course of development, e.g. **t** in the words hospitalem, hospitem,
became initial in the Gallo-Roman forms owing to the effacement of the
preceding unstressed v̄owel : **hospitalem** > ****osptale, hospitem** > ****ospte.**

The *initial* position of the word and the syllable was the *strongest*
and the consonants standing in that position, with the exception of the
weak fricatives **w** and **j**, ordinarily remained unchanged unless affected
by palatalisation (chap. vi) or by isolative changes (chap. iii, sects. 4-7).
Cf. O.F. **barbẹ** < **barba,** *cuer* **kuer** < **kŏr, dür** < **dūrum, mānḍẹr** <
mandaɾe, fẹrir < **feriɾe, gǫst** < **gŭstum,** *lẹz,* **lẹts** < **latus, mür** < **mūrum,**
nül < **nūllum, pẹr** < **pɑ̄rem, ta+pẹ** < **ta+pa, sẹl** < **salem, ǫrsẹ** < **ŭrsa,**
tǫst < **tŏstum, fẹstẹ** < **festa.**

In Gallo-Roman there was a tendency to voice **k** initial of the word before **r** and
l, cf. *Glodoveus* for *Chlodoveus* (Fred.), O.F. *glas* < **classicum, gras* < *crassum, greïlle*
< *craticula.*

§ 203. **j** and **w.** In the early Gallo-Roman period, in which the
strong articulation of initial consonants that characterised Vulgar Latin
(cf. Meillet, *E.L.L.* p. 252), still persisted, the weak fricative consonants **j**

and **w** were strengthened when in initial position, **ɟ** closing to **dž, w**
Germanic to **gw** (§ 636) : **ɟam > dža** *ja*, **ɟungere > džuindrę** *joindre* ;
*rǫbjǫ > rǫdžę *roge*, ***sɪmjǫ > sindžę** *singe*, ***waddjǫ > gwadžę** *guage*.
[For **tš** from **ɟ** cf. § 305.]

Sources of Gallo-Roman Initial jod.—Gallo-Roman *jod initial* might
be initial of the word or of the syllable. It was derived from :—

(i) Latin *jod initial* of the *word*, e.g. *jam, jungere, Jerusalem.*

(ii) *Jod* formed in Late Latin by the consonantalisation of **ĕ** and **ĭ** in
hiatus with a following vowel and preceded by a *labial* consonant, e.g.
*rǫbjǫ < rŭbĕŭm, *sɪmjǫ < sīmiŭm (§ 220).

(iii) *Jod* formed in Gallo-Roman : (*a*) by the consonantalisation of the
unstressed penultimate vowel in the terminations *-aticum, -eticum, -oticum*,
in which it was brought into hiatus by the effacement of the following
velar consonant (§ 352), e.g. O.F. *eage*, **ęadžę < aetaticum**; (*b*) by the
consonantalisation of unstressed **ĕ** and **ĭ** in hiatus in Gallo-Roman loan-
words (§ 640 (2)), cf. O.F. *lange* **lāndžę < lanea**, *gage* **gadžę < **waddjǫ**;
(cf. also O.F. *gie* **džįę < **ieu < ego**, § 829).

[For the strengthening of β, initial of the syllable after **r** and **n,** cf.
§ 189.]

Section 3.—INFLUENCE OF FINAL POSITION ON CONSONANTS.

§ 204. Consonants are said to be *final* when they end a word. They
may be final in Latin, e.g. **t** in debe**t**, deben**t** or become final in the
course of development by the effacement of an unstressed final vowel,
cf. **t** in Old French part < partem, **r** in Old French per < parem.
Final consonants preceded by another consonant are called *supported*,
preceded by a vowel, *unsupported*, e.g. **t** in Latin debent is supported,
t in Latin debet is unsupported. Consonants unsupported in Latin may
become supported in Gallo-Roman by the effacement of the preceding
unstressed vowel ; thus the effacement of the final unstressed **e** in **tenet**
and **debet** made the **t** supported in the Gallo-Roman forms of these
words : ****tient, **deift.**

§ 205. Final consonants were in a *weak* position, liable to be influenced in Period I by sounds preceding them, in Period II by sounds
preceding and following.

(i) In Late Latin when, as in Classical Latin, the ends of words were
pronounced weakly (§ 211, Juret, pp. 214-217) unsupported final consonants tended to weaken and disappear.

m *final*. In Late Latin **m** *final*, already weak in Classical Latin
(cf. Juret, pp. 214-217), was effaced in words of more than one syllable,
cf. *App. Pr. : passim non passi, numquam non numqua, olim non oli.*

In Italy unsupported final **s** and **t** were also weakly pronounced, cf. the graffiti
of Pompeii, *valia. ama* and later inscriptions. The speech of Southern Gaul was

affected by the weakened pronunciation of **t**, but in Northern Gaul, where pronunciation was influenced by the teaching in the schools, both **t** and **s** were maintained in final position into Gallo-Roman (cf. Juret, pp. 208-213, 204-206; Lindsay, pp. 103, 119, 124).

(ii) In Gallo-Roman unsupported **t** and **k** were opened to θ and χ respectively (§§ 355-357) and effaced.

(iii) In Period II, when the phrase had become the sentence unit, § 177, final consonants were strongly influenced by syntactical phonetics (Pt. II, chap. xvii, sect. 5).

§ 206. In later Gallo-Roman, a period in which words still remained the unit of the sentence (§ 170), all voiced plosives and fricatives, brought into final position by the effacement of final unstressed **e, i, o, u**, were unvoiced and thus final **g > k, d > t, ð > θ, z > s, v > f, b > p**. The etymological spelling was sometimes retained in Old French and ordinarily made usual in Middle French :—

lŭngum > lunk *lonc, long*, *burgum > bǫrk, *borc*, sŭrgo > sork, *sorc*, grandem > gränt, deǫnde > dunt, perdo > pęrt, nudum > nüθ, risum > *rizų > ris, *servum* serwum > **sęrvę > sęrf, bibe > **beivę > beif, corvum *kǫrbųm (§ 189) > korp *corp*, *Job* džob > džop (Rtbf. *Job: cop*, p. 5, 20).

[For the dentalisation of final **m** cf. § 435; for the palatalisation of final **s** cf. § 318; for the isolative change of **ts** to **s** cf. § 194; for the replacement of **t + s** by **ts** cf. § 367; for the pronunciation of final consonants in Middle French cf. chap. xvii.]

Section 4.—CONSONANTS IN INTERVOCALIC POSITION AND IN GROUP.

§ 207. *Intervocalic Position.*—Consonants standing between vowels are called *intervocalic*. They may be either *single*, e.g. **m** and **t** in amata, *lengthened* (*double*), e.g. **nn** in annata, **ll** in bella, or *in group*, e.g. **tr** in patrem, **sp** in hospitem, **mbr** in umbra.

§ 208. *Position in Group.*—Consonants may be combined in groups of two or three consonants, e.g. patrem, umbra. Consonantal groups may be *initial* of a word or of a syllable after a consonant, e.g. **tr** in trans, **cr** in crassus, **br** in umbra, or *final* of a word, e.g. **nt** in portant, vident, or *intervocalic*, e.g. **tr** in patrem, **mbr** in umbra. Consonantal groups may exist in Latin or be formed in the course of development by the effacement of an unstressed vowel, cf. *posta < pos(i)ta, **deift < deb(e)t.

§ 209. *Single* consonants in *intervocalic* position, the *first* consonant of intervocalic or final groups and the *middle* consonant of three were all in a *weak* position, readily dominated by sounds in their vicinity, liable to combinative change of various types: for their development cf. below, chaps. vii and viii.

[For the *last* consonant of intervocalic groups cf. § 202.]

CHAPTER V.

INFLUENCE OF EXPIRATORY WORD-ACCENT.

Section 1.—Nature and Position of Latin Accent.

§ 210. In Early Latin the accent in use appears to have been the musical one, but at some period or other an expiratory accent gradually associated itself with the musical one and by the fourth century at latest had become dominant.

The exact nature of the accent in the classical period is still a matter of controversy: the French scholars, Professors Meillet and Juret, hold that it was still musical (cf. *E.L.L.* pp. 241-246, Juret, chaps. iii and iv), Professor Lindsay that it was already expiratory (chap. iii, § i).

Section 2.—Position of the Accent in Latin and French.

§ 211. *Position of Accent in Classical Latin.*—The syllable most strongly accented, the *tonic* syllable, was ordinarily the last but one or last but two (the *penultimate* or *ante-penultimate*) and dissyllabic words were consequently always accented on the first syllable, e.g. ˈbo-nos, ˈpor-to, ˈpor-tat, ˈpor-tant, the *final* syllable being always relatively weak (cf. Juret, § 103). A *secondary* accent emphasised the *initial* syllable of words that contained one or more pre-tonic syllables: ‖mŏ-ˈnē-re, ‖nĕ-ˈpō-tem, ‖or-na-ˈmen-tum. The syllable that receives this secondary accent is called the *countertonic* syllable.

§ 212. In Classical Latin the tonic syllable of a word of more than two syllables was always the *penultimate*, if that syllable was *long*, i.e. if it contained a diphthong or a long vowel or a *blocked* vowel, i.e. a vowel (short or long), followed by a double consonant or any group of consonants other than those consisting of *plosive* + l or r, e.g. mŏ-ˈnē-re, vir-ˈtū-tem, a-ˈlau-da, an-ˈnĕl-lum, or-na-ˈmen-tum. If the penultimate syllable was short or doubtful, i.e. if it contained a short *free* vowel, one ending its own syllable, i.e. followed by another short vowel or by a single consonant or by one of the groups consisting of *plosive* + r or l, the accent fell on the *ante-penultimate* syllable, e.g. ˈfi-lĭ-us, ˈrē-gĕre, fi-ˈlĭ-ŏ-lum, ˈho-mĭ-nem, ˈca-lă-mum, ˈin-tĕ-grum, ˈte-nĕ-bras, dor-mi-ˈtō-rĭ-um. Words in which the *penultimate* syllable is tonic are

called *paroxytone*, those with a tonic *ante-penultimate* syllable, *pro-paroxytone*, those with a tonic *final* syllable *oxytone*.

§ 213. Certain types of words (conjunctive particles, prepositions, pronouns), might be used with little or no independent word accent, forming a unity with a word that preceded or followed them (*itaque, vosmet, propatre*, etc., cf. Juret, pp. 79-90), and in Late Latin among dissyllabic words used with slight stress there was often a displacement of the tonic accent (§§ 837, 855).

§ 214. *Position of Tonic Accent in Late Latin.*—The change in the nature of the accent produced ordinarily no change in its position ; the main tonic accent, expiratory now, continued to emphasise the penulti-mate or ante-penultimate syllable, e.g. aˈmĭcum, aˈmare, ˈamo, ˈamant, ˈhominem, dormiˈtorium, and apart from the changes that were occasioned among pronouns by syntactical phonetics (§§ 837, 855), in numerals (§ 823) and in verbs (e.g. §§ 990, 991) by associative influences, its position only shifted in two small groups of proparoxytone words, which both became paroxytone.

(1) In accordance with a very general tendency to stress more heavily the *lower* of two juxtaposed vowels the accent moved forward on to the lower vowel in words of the type, mŭˈlĭĕrem, fīˈlĭŏlum, i.e. in words in which the penultimate syllable was short ĕ or ŏ in hiatus with an ante-penultimate short ĭ or ĕ : subsequently the ante-penultimate ĭ and ĕ (now unstressed), consonantalised to j (§ 220); thus mŭˈlĭĕrĕm > *mŭli̯ˈĕrĕm > *mol̩i̯ˈere, fīˈlĭŏlum > *fịlị̯ˈŏlŭm > *fịlị̯ˈolụ.

This shift is attested by the metrical practice of the Christian poets of the third and fourth centuries and sanctioned by an anonymous grammarian : ' *mulierem* in antepenultimo nemo debet acuere, sed in penultimo potius.' (cf. Lindsay, III, § 11).

(2) In proparoxytones of the type ˈintĕgrum, ˈtŏnĭtrum, i.e. those con-taining a penultimate syllable of ' doubtful ' length, (one consisting of a short vowel preceding the consonant group *plosive* + r), the stress was ordinarily moved forward on to the penultimate syllable, ˈintĕgrum > ẹnˈtẹgrụ, ˈtŏnĭtrum > toˈnẹtrụ.

As a result of this change the rule for the position of the tonic stress is simplified, for in Late Latin it may be said that the penultimate syllable is stressed whenever it contains a long vowel, a diphthong or a vowel of any kind followed by any two consonants or a double consonant.

The early Old French loan-words *entre* < ˈ*integrum, fiertre* < ˈ*fĕrĕtrum, poutre* < * ˈ*pullĕtra, paupres* < ˈ*palpĕbras*, indicate that the traditional accentuation was retained late among the educated in Gaul.

§ 215. Under the Frankish influence the intensity of the tonic stress was considerably increased (§ 27), but its position remained unchanged, and it is consequently a fundamental rule of the French language that in all traditional words *the syllable that bore the tonic word-accent in Late*

Latin continues to bear it in French, cf. O.F. a'mi, por'tęr, 'portes, 'portent, dor'toir, to'noire, Modern French a'mi, por'tę, 'port(es), 'port(ent), dor'twaʀ, to'nęr(re).

Shift of stress in any word (not occasioned analogically) is one of the surest criteria of the class of words called *learned loan-words* (*mots savants*)—those Classical Latin words which were brought into the language by the learned, e.g. *fabrique, fragile, facile, idole, rigide,* etc. (cf. §§ 53, 648).

§ 216. *Position of Countertonic Accent in Late Latin.*—In Late Latin, as in Classical Latin, the *secondary (countertonic)* accent continued to emphasise normally the *initial* syllable of a word that had one or more pretonic syllables, e.g. ''amicum, ''amare, ''debere, ''ornamentum, ''dormitorium.

In a few words in which the initial syllable was weak and followed by a relatively strong intertonic syllable or consisted of a vowel in hiatus with a following vowel, the secondary stress slid forward on to the second syllable, and the first vowel, become unstressed, was gradually effaced or consonantalised, cf. O.F. *drecier<*directiare, cachier<*coacticare, caillier<coagulare, queit<quietum.*

§ 217. *Accentuation of Derivatives and Compound Words.*—In Classical Latin the accentuation of derivatives and compound words conformed to that of simple words: ''collŏ'care, 'collŏcat, ''interrŏ'gare, ''in'tĕrrŏgat, ''invŏ'lare, 'invŏlat, ''adjū'tare, 'ad'jūtat, 'consŭo, 'ĕrĭgo, 'exĕo, 'adjăcens, 'infans, ''in'tĕrea, 'undĕcim, 'quŏmŏdo. In the formation of verbal derivatives in Late Latin this system was modified, the accentuation of the simple verb being ordinarily retained in the derivative and the prefix given a second half-strong stress, e.g. ''ad-''li-gare, ''ad-'ligat, ''ad-''lo-'care, ''de-''me-'nare, ''de-'menat. A few derivative verbs in which the connection between the simple verb had become obscured retained the earlier accentuation, e.g. ''ad-ju-'tare, ''col-lŏ'care, 'collŏcat, ''in-vŏ-'lare, 'invŏlat, ''in'terrŏgat, 'collĭgit, 'consŭit (cf. O.F. *aidier, colchier, colche, embler, emble, enterve, cueilt, cost*), but ordinarily the older Latin derivatives were re-compounded on the new system.

§ 218. *Position of Accent in Compound Words in French.*—Compound words continued to lose their double stress as soon as they coalesced into simple words, cf. O.F. ''Bone'val < 'Bone'val, ''ains'nez < 'ainz'nez, ''porte'rai < por'tare * 'ajo, etc. (cf. § 965).

In the adverbs formed from adjectives combined with *mente* (*fortimente,* etc.) the compound retained its independence into Early Old French and the adjectives show the normal development of tonic vowels in Gallo-Roman, cf. O.F. *fierement* (< *fĕra mente*), *pleinement, rerement* (< *rara mente*).

Section 3.—INFLUENCE OF EXPIRATORY ACCENT IN LATIN.

§ 219. The expiratory accent introduced in Late Latin, slight as it appears to have been, contributed to the lengthening of free tonic vowels (§ 198) and to some modifications among unstressed syllables.

§ 220. (1) Unstressed ĕ, ĭ, ŏ, ŭ, standing in hiatus with a following vowel, gradually lost syllabic value and consonantalised, ĕ and ĭ to j, ŏ and ŭ to w (cf. earlier Latin *solvo*, **solwo** < **solŭo**) : **fīlium** > ***filjụ**, **monĕo** > ***monjo**, **dĭŭrnum** > ***djọrnŭ**, **annŭalem** > ***annwale**, **habui** > ***abwi**, **koagŭlare** > ****kwaglare**.

[For the later development of **j** and **w** cf. §§ 303-315, 192 and 374.]

Consonantalisation was begun early. It is attested by the confusion of the spellings *cu* and *qu* and of *ĕ* and *ĭ* in hiatus, cf. *App. Pr. vacua non vaqua, vinea non vinia, cavea non cavia*, but the date at which it was carried through varied according to the point of articulation of the preceding consonant, labials tending to retard the change, **l** and **n** to accelerate it : **konsiljum** was accepted in classical verse. **ịẹ**, especially after consonants that exercised a retarding influence, was ordinarily levelled to **ẹ** before the process was concluded and thus **parịētem** > ***parẹte, sapientem** > ***sapẹnte, kapịēbam** > ***kapẹβa**, etc.

§ 221. (2) Among proparoxytones there showed itself a tendency to generalise the shorter of two forms, where two existed, e.g., *angulus* and *anglus*, *tabula* and *tabla*, *vetulus* and *vetlus*, and occasionally to slur the unstressed penultimate vowel that stood between consonants that readily combined in a group (cf. § 262).

§ 222. (3) Very gradually unstressed long vowels were shortened and thus all quantitative differences were obliterated in unstressed syllables.

Section 4.—INTENSITY AND INFLUENCE OF EXPIRATORY ACCENT IN FRENCH.

§ 223. The Germanic accent was a strong expiratory one, and its influence intensified considerably the stress accorded to the *tonic* syllable and lessened in proportion that placed on the others, especially those in its immediate vicinity : thus the relatively level accentuation of Early Gallo-Roman was changed into a more up and down system, very like that of Modern English except that it was still the syllable that was last but one or two that was the strongest. The influence of this increased intensity was rapidly felt ; the tonic mid and low vowels were diphthongised when long, i.e. free (§§ 197, 233), unstressed vowels were reduced or slurred, secondary stressed sometimes raised—all phenomena that are closely paralleled in Modern English (§ 121).

The wholesale reduction and elimination of atonic syllables made of Old French a language in which all words were either *oxytone* or *paroxytone*, and, if paroxytone, then always ending in a syllable containing **ẹ**.

In Early Old French, as far as extant documents enable us to judge, there was little diminution in the intensity of the tonic stress : some diphthongs were differentiated further (§ 226), countertonic ẹ was reduced to ę when free (§§ 234, 235), and in the sentence the practice of enclisis remained frequent (§ 602).   In Period II, on the other hand, the whole rhythm of the language was gradually changed : the intensity of the tonic stress was gradually diminished, and there manifested itself with increasing strength a tendency to link closely together words closely associated in thought (§ 170).   Diminution of stress led to a relatively rapid levelling of diphthongs (chap. xiv) and the disappearance of enclisis (§ 602) :   the tendency to run words together increased speed of speech within the group ; and this, combined with the strength of stress remaining, led to a gradual reduction of syllables among weaker vowels juxtaposed to stronger ones (§§ 236-246), and finally to the gradual effacement of atonic ę (§§ 268-273).

By the end of the seventeenth century these processes were completed and French had become a language of almost level word-stress.

The strengthening of the tonic stress in north Gaul appears to have varied somewhat with the intensity of the Frankish settlement (§ 17), and was consequently strongest in the north-east and east (i.e. in Belgium and Lorraine), weakest in the south-west (i.e. in Anjou, Maine, Touraine).   The differentiation of the tonic vowels (§ 226), the reduction of the atonic (§ 261), and the levelling of the diphthongs (chap. xiv), were all affected by this variation.

Section 5.—INFLUENCE OF STRESS ON TONIC VOWELS IN PERIOD I.

§ 224. The tonic vowels whose development was affected by intensified expiratory accent in Period I were the *mid* and *low* vowels that had been lengthened either because they were *free* (§ 197) or because they stood in monosyllabic words before a single consonant (§ 198).

[For the diphthongisation of tonic ę and ǫ before a palatal consonant cf. §§ 410-411.]

§ 225. *Diphthongisation of the Tonic Mid Vowels*, ẹ, ọ, ę, ǫ.—Unless previously modified by palatal or nasal consonants (chaps. x, xi), the tonic mid vowels ẹ, ọ, ę, ǫ, diphthongised under the influence of the tonic stress when *free*, and when before a single consonant in a mono-syllabic word.

ẹ > ʹie	ǫ > ʹuo
pĕdĕm > *pēdĕ > pieθ,	sŏrŏr > *sọ̄rŏr > suor,
ę > ʹei	ǫ > ʹou
mē > *mę̄ > mei,	flōrĕm > *flǭrę > flour.

ę *tonic free*, developed in Early Gallo-Roman from a *tonic free* preceded by a palatal (§ 414), shared in this diphthongisation: *carum* karŭm > **ʃērµ > tšʲier *chier*.

These diphthongs were all *descending*, i.e. all stressed on the first element: all were formed before final unstressed vowels were slurred (§ 256), or double consonants simplified (§ 366); thus *tĕnĕt > tient, *plĕnọs > plēins but *bĕllµ > bęl, *tĕrra > tęrę, *mĕttere > mętrę.

[For the checking of diphthongisation in proparoxytones cf. § 229; for ǫ tonic *free* before a nasal consonant cf. § 426.]

✱✱ In the north-eastern region and Lorraine tonic ę and ǫ were diphthongised in *blocked* syllables also, ę generally, ǫ before r and s, cf. *fier* < *ferrum*, *castiel* < *castellum*, *iestre* < *essere*, *muert* < *mortem*, *tuest* < *tostum* (cf. N.E. § iii (*a*) and Wahlgren, *Vising vol.*, pp. 311 *et seqq.*).

§ 226. *Differentiation of* 'uo, 'ei *and* 'ou *to* 'ue, 'oi *and* 'eu.—In the course of Early Old French, while the tonic stress was still strong, the diphthongs 'uo 'ei, 'ou were further differentiated. Before the end of the period 'uo had passed to 'ue (often written *oe*, especially when initial); before the middle of the twelfth century 'ei had been differentiated to 'oi, except before nasal consonants (§ 439), and 'ou to 'eu, except before labial consonants (§ 489).

The differentiation of **ei** to **oi** affected the diphthong **ei** from all sources, i.e. included the diphthong formed by the combination of an **e**-sound with *jod* in countertonic and intertonic as well as in tonic syllables.

§ 227.   ę > 'ie

				ę > 'ie					
hĕrī	> *ērį	> ier		kārŭm	> **kārµ	> ** ʃērµ	> tšier *chier*
sĕdĕt	> *sēdęt	> siet		pākāre	> **pakāre	> paiier
pĕtră	> *pētrà	> pieðrę		traktāre	> **traχtāre	> traitier
tĕpĭdŭm	> *tēpędµ	> tiedę		pietātem	> **piʃtatę	> pitie
bĕnĕ	> *bēnę	> bien		kănĕm	> **kānĕ	< tšien *chien*
dĕŭm	> *dēµ	> dieu				

ǫ > 'uo > 'ue

sŏrŏr	> *sǫrǫr	> suor	> suer
mŏrĭtŭr;	*mǫręt	> muort	> muert
G. fōdr	> *fǫdrµ	> fuoðrę	> fuerrę
*mŏwĭta	> *mǫβęta	> muotę	> muetę
bŏnŭm	> bǫnµ	> buon	> buen
fŏkŭm	> fǫkµ	> **fuou	> fueu

[For the subsequent development of the diphthong 'ie cf. §§ 510-513, of 'ue cf. §§ 550-553, of ieu cf. §§ 544-546, of ueu cf. §§ 556-558. For the influence of the nasal consonants cf. chap. xi.]

Attesting Graphies:

ie, Eul., *ciel* 6, *chielt* 13, *pagiens* 12, *chief* 22.

uo, Eul., *buona* 1, *ruovet* 24, *Al. MS. L. quor* 34 (a) (cf. Suchier, *Gr.* § 28 (c)).

ue (*oe*), Jonas, *foers, Domesday Book* (1084) *buen, mueles, Rainbued,* (*Zts. Rom. Ph.*, viii, p. 359).

§ 228.

$$\text{ę} > \text{'ei} > \text{'oi}$$

mē	> *mę	> mei	> moi
bĭbit	> *bęββet	> beit	> boit
flēbilem	> *flęblę	> feiblę	> foiblę
tŏnĭtrŭm	> *tǫnętrų	> toneiǒrę	> tunoirę
[plēnŭm	> *plęnų	> plein	> plēin, § 439]
[mĭnŭs	> *męnųs	> meins	> mēins, §§ 439, 487]

$$\text{ę} + \text{ı} > \text{'ei} > \text{'oi}$$

tēktŭm	> *tęχtų	> teit	> toit
pĭkĕm	> *pęɟę	> peits	> poits
nĕkāre	> *nękāre	> neiier	> noiier
*empęɟorāre, *impejorare*	> empeirier	> empoirier	
*dǫmnęɟĕlla, *dominicella*	> dāmeizęlę	> dāmoizęlę	

$$\text{ǫ} > \text{'ou} > \text{'eu}$$

sōlum	> *sǫlų	> soul	> seul
gŭla	> *gǫla	> goulę	> geulę
mōres	> *mǫręs	> mours	> meurs
sŭa	> *sǫa	> souę	> seuę
[lŭpa	> *lǫpa	> louvę, § 489]	
[dŭplum	> *dǫplų	> doublę, § 489]	

[For the later development of **oi** cf. §§ 518-525, of **eu** cf. §§ 541-543.]

Attesting Graphies and Rhymes:

ei, Eul., *sostendreiet* 15, *concreidre* 21.

oi, Jonas, *noieds* 13; *Soifridus* (< *Seifridus* < *Sigfridus*) 1078, dept. Meuse, *Poissiacum* (< *Pissiacum*) 1137, dept. Seine (cf. Weigelt, *Zts. R. Ph.* xi, 106): Crest. E., *soie : joie* 2337, *poise : boise* 3305 : *noise* 4423; Gt. d'Arras *oi : moi* 1079, *oient : voient* 3237.

ou, Eul. *bellezour* (< *bellatiorem*) 2, *soure* 12, *souue* 29.

eu, Doomsday Book, *Vis de leuu* (*visum de lupu*), *Froisseleuu, Dreuues* (< *Durocăsses*), (*Zts. rom. Ph.*, viii, pp. 334, 359).

Crest. E., *jeus : seus* 2835 : *corageus* 3391, *preu : leu* (*locum*) 1041 [cf. *Auc.* § 17, *lę* (< *lęu* < *lupum*) : *fossé, cler*].

§ 229. *Process and Date of Diphthongisation.*—It is thought that the diphthongal stage attested in the development of the open mid vowels ę and ǫ was preceded by one in which those sounds were lengthened and differentiated, i.e. that ę > ē̦ > ęe > 'ie and ǫ > ō̦ > ǫo > 'uo. The beginnings of this process, at any rate the lengthening, appear to fall in Late Latin (cf. § 198), for the diphthongs 'uo and 'ie are common to Central Italy and Spain as well as north Gaul. In

south Gaul, however, in the region south of the Loire, the process was not carried through and in Old Poitevin and Old Provençal the vowels remained undiphthongised (cf. Appel, p. 31, and Gamillscheg, *Becker Volume*, p. 61). In north Gaul the tendency to diphthongise these vowels continued in Early Gallo-Roman, for tonic ę in loan-words, both Frankish and Latin, is affected by it, and also those Latin words in which tonic a was raised to ę by the influence of a preceding palatal (§ 414).

The diphthongisation of ę and ǫ is on lines familiar in Modern English, where the energetic utterance of a vowel sound is apt to produce a lengthening which leads to the closing of the end of the articulation (cf. § 121). The diphthongisation of these vowels was confined to the region in which Germanic influence was strong, i.e. north Gaul, the Rhaetian dialects and northern Italy. It was later than the diphthongisation of ẹ and ọ, as is shown by the difference in the development of the tonic vowels in proparoxytone words, for in these ę and ǫ are diphthongised, if free in Latin, but not ẹ and ọ (cf. O.F. **tiedę** < **tĕpidum, muetę** < ***moβetɑ, dętę** < **dēbitɑ,** *cude* **kudę** < **cúbitum**), the fall of the unstressed penultimate vowel taking place early enough to block the *closed* vowels before their diphthongisation began, but not the open vowels, ę and ǫ.

✱✱ § 230. (i) The differentiation of the diphthongs **ei** and **ou** was confined to the region in which the Frankish influence was strongest, i.e. the northern and eastern region of north Gaul, including the Île de France and north Normandy, and was first attested in the north-east (§ 228). The western region was not reached by the movement and here **ou** levelled to **u** in the course of Early Old French, **ei** to ẹ in the course of Later Old French (W. §§ v, vi).

✱✱ (ii) Before **r** the diphthongisation of ǫ to **ou** was checked very generally in the eastern and north-eastern region (E. § xviii), and poets who show little dialectal influence couple not infrequently words containing **u**(< ǫ tonic free) with those containing **u**(< ǫ tonic blocked), e.g. Rtbf., *pecheors, ors : cors* (< *cursum*). The combined influence of provincial pronunciations, of the Provençal love lyric and code of courtoisie led to the use of the forms **amur** *amour,* **džalus** *jalous* over almost the whole of northern France.

[For Middle French **lu** *loup,* cf. § 343; for Eastern **oi** < **ei** + *nasal,* cf. E. § xix.]

✱✱ (iii) The differentiation of **uo** to **ue** appears to have been checked often by following *labials* and by **l, ɉ** and **k** and then **uo** was levelled to **u** or **o** (spellings *u, o, ou*), cf. O.F. *moble, mouble, ovre, ouvre, dol, dul, voil, vuil, avoc, illoc, illuc* (cf. § 554).

§ 231. *Development of Gallo-Roman* **a** *tonic free.*—[Gallo-Roman **a** included Latin and Germanic **ɑ** in polysyllables (§ 182).]

In the course of the Gallo-Roman period Gallo-Roman **a**, when *free*, passed to ẹ̄, unless it was preceded or followed by a *palatal* consonant (§§ 198, 414), or followed by a *nasal* consonant (§ 427), or by **w** (**u̯**) (§ 481):

**āla	> ęlę	****grātu̯**	> grẹθ	****āpes**	> ęs
**sāpa	> sęvę	****nāsu̯**	> nęs	****ad sātes**	> asęts *assez*
**brāza	> bręzę *brese*	****māre**	> męr	****portātes**	> portęts *portez*
**lāβra	> lęvrę	****portāre**	> portęr	****portātos**	> portęts *portez*
**pātre	> pęðrę	****sāle**	> sęl	****sāpęt**	> sęt

The passage of tonic a free to ẹ̄ preceded the fall of unstressed final vowels (cf. O.F. **sęt** < *sapit*): it was, like the diphthongisation of ẹ and ǫ *tonic free,* checked by a following lengthened consonant and in proparoxytones by the fall of

the unstressed penultimate vowel, cf. O.F. **bal** $<$ *ballu, radę $<$ rapidum, a⧧vę $<$ *alapa : it was also checked by the following group **bl**, cf. O.F. **tablę** $<$ *tabla. Documentary evidence is first found in the ninth century, cf. *nodelis* for *natalis* (M.L. *Gr.* § 62), *Eul. presentede*, 11, *spede*, 22, etc.

✱✱ § 232. Before **l** (⧧?) **a** was retained in the south-western region, § 502 (ii), S.W. § ii; before intervocalic **u** it was rounded to **ǫ** in the western region (§ 483). Throughout the eastern and northern region **ę̄** ($<$ **a** *tonic* free) diphthongised to **ei** in the course of Old French: this diphthongisation is attested in the eastern and north-eastern region in the later twelfth century (N.E. § iv), in the north-western in the late thirteenth, and is most widespread when **ę̄** is *final* of the word.
[For authorities, discussion of the question and later history of the diphthong, cf. Wahlgren, *Vising vol.*, pp. 290-301, and *Parfaits Faibles*, pp. 43, 48-50, 71-74, 98-105.]

§ 233. *Process of Development.*—Scholars have not yet succeeded in determining either the exact value of the sound in Old French nor the process by which the stage **ę** was reached. In the twelfth century the sound differed both from **ę** from Latin **ĕ** blocked and from **ę** from **ĭ** and **ē** blocked, for by Continental poets it is coupled in assonance not with these sounds but with **e** in loan-words (e.g. *de* $<$ *deum*, *valé*, etc.). The difference between this e-sound and the others may be partly quantitative, the **e** from **a** tonic free being long, and the other two, both blocked, being short (§ 198); the range of e-sounds is, however, varied enough to allow a qualitative difference also, and the close pronunciation of **e** in learned loan-words (cf. Th. I, 76), the later development of the sound (cf. § 576), and the character of the glide formed between it and **u** ($<$ vocalising ⧧), e.g. in **pęęus** $<$ **pę⧧s** $<$ **palos**, cf. **bęaus** $<$ **bę⧧s**, § 388, indicate a very high, close pronunciation of the **ę** (cf. M.L. *Gr.*, § 62; otherwise Nyrop, *Gr.*, § 171).
The limitation of this development of **a** to the tonic free syllable and the diphthongal character retained by **a** free before nasals (§ 427), make it probable that **a** tonic free passed through a diphthongal stage **ae**, parallel to that formed by the tonic free mid vowels **ę** and **ǫ** (cf. Marchot, *Petite Phonétique Pré-litteraire*, § 12; otherwise M.L. *Gr.* § 62).
[For later development of **ę̄** cf. §§ 494, 495, 576.]

Section 6.—INFLUENCE OF EXPIRATORY ACCENT ON COUNTERTONIC VOWELS IN PERIOD I.

§ 234. The strengthening of the stress on the tonic syllable in Gallo-Roman (§ 223) was accompanied by a lessening of the secondary stress sufficient to cause a modification of the pronunciation of the mid open vowels **ę** and **ǫ** (cf. § 121); **ę** countertonic closing to **ę** except when followed by **r** or ⧧ + *consonant*, i.e. by **r** or ⧧ pronounced in the same syllable as itself, **ǫ** countertonic closing to **ǫ**, unless followed by ⧧ + *consonant*.

In the course of Early Old French both **ę** and **ǫ** countertonic were further modified: **ǫ** moved up to **u**, in this syllable as elsewhere (§ 184), **ę** *free* (from all sources) was ordinarily reduced to **ę**. Tonic vowels frequently exercised an assimilatory or dissimilatory influence on countertonic vowels, cf. §§ 244, 421, 484, 490:

nĕpŏtem > *nępǫte > nęvouθ > nęveu
sĕkūrum > *sękųrų > sęür > sęür
tĕnēre > *tęnęre > tęn[īr] > tęnir
pĕrsōnα > *pęrsǫnα > pęrsunę > pęrsūnę
dēbēre > *dęβęre > dęveir > dęvoir
laetitiα > *lętętsɪα > lę(ð) ętsę > lietsę (§ 308 (ii))

dŏlōrem > *dǫlǫre > dǫlour > duleur
lŏcαre > *lǫkāre > lǫęr > luęr
mŏrīri ; *mǫrire > mǫrir > murir
fŏrmīcem > *fǫrmɪʃe > fǫrmits > furmits

[For the later development and value of ę cf. below §§ 243-247, 275 ; for Middle French modifications of countertonic u cf. § 582 ; for Middle French rounding of ę to ö and closing to ü cf. § 486 ; for Middle French opening of lengthened ę̄ cf. § 574.]

Derivatives and weak radicals of verbs were sometimes re-modelled on stressed forms in which ǫ blocked was retained, cf. O.F. mǫrtel (≠ mǫrt), pǫstel (≠ pǫstę), dǫrmir (≠ (il) dǫrt, etc.), pǫrter (≠ pǫrtę) ; late Mid. Fr. mętā *mettant*, etc. was formed on (il) męt, etc., F. 61.

When ę *countertonic* was in hiatus with tonic ę or ǫ́ (u) in the eleventh century there was a tendency to differentiate it to i, cf. O.F. *crier* krięr < kręęr *creer*, piun < pęǫn, (< pĕdōnem), lięsę < lęętsę *liece*.

§ 235. The reduction of ę to a neutral vowel (ę̨?) is indicated for the late eleventh century by the signature appended by Anne of Russia, wife of Henry I, to a document of 1063, for in the Cyrillic characters she used, the symbol for the first vowel of the word *reina* is the one used to denote an obscure vowel (Thomas, *Essais*, pp. 159-165).

Section 7.—Reduction of Countertonic Vowels in Period II.

§ 236. In the later thirteenth century and Middle French Period the weaker countertonic vowels were very generally reduced : ę interconsonantal was sometimes slurred and all types of vowels juxtaposed to the tonic vowel tended to lose syllabic value (cf. § 223).

[For the weakened value of countertonic syllables, standing second in the word, e.g. O.F. *achater* ǁaǁtša'tęr, cf. § 266.]

Vowels in Hiatus.

§ 237. The frequent effacement of single intervocalic consonants in the earlier period brought countertonic vowels very frequently into hiatus with the tonic vowels, and this juxtaposition led to a variety of developments in countertonic syllables in the thirteenth century and Middle French. Hiatus was sometimes retained, but more usually the juxtaposition of the two vowels was obviated by the development of a consonantal glide, or eliminated by some process or other.

§ 238. *Retention of Hiatus.*—Hiatus was retained: (i) in later loan-words, e.g. *féodal, laïque, théologie, théâtre,* etc.; (ii) by the action of preservative analogy (§ 765) in some derivatives and verbal forms, e.g. (*a*) *naïf, crieur, lueur, sueur, boueux, noueux, bluet, fluet, flouet, rouet, jouet, fouet, Noël, criard, douaire;* (*b*) *haïr, trahir, fier, lier, prier, ouïr, vouer, jouer, ruer, suer, tuer, béant, échéant, séant.*

In many of these words syllabic value was uncertain in the speech of the sixteenth century and is lost in Modern French.

§ 239. *Glide Developments.*—In Late Middle and Early Modern French the palatal glide, ɹ, developed: (*a*) between countertonic **wę < oi** (§ 519) and a juxtaposed tonic vowel, e.g. *boyaux* **bwęɹǫ̈(s) < bwęǫs,** *joyeux* **žwęɹö(s) < žwęös,** *loyal* **lwęɹal < lwęal,** *monnayeur* **mūnwęɹör < mūnwęör,** *voyelle* **vwęɹęlę < vwęęlę,** and similarly in the weak forms of *veoir* and all verbs in *-oyer,* e.g. *voyant* **vwęɹã(t) < vwęã(t)** (§ 931), *aboyant* **abwęɹã(t) < abwęã(t);** (*b*) more variably between countertonic **ę** (< **ai**) and a juxtaposed tonic vowel, e.g. *ayant* **ęɹã(t) < ęãn(t),** *payer,* (§ 531). In some words of this type, however, **ai** was levelled to **ę** and remained in hiatus, e.g. *céans, léans, géant.*

A labial glide developed between **u** and **ã** in *espouvanter,* **epuvãtę < O.F. espu(w)ãntęr,** a palatal glide between **ü** and **ę** in *essuier, huier.*

[For labial and palatal glides in the north-eastern region cf. N.E. § xiv.]

§ 240. *Reduction of Hiatus.*—In the course of the thirteenth century and Middle French the juxtaposition of the countertonic and tonic vowels was elsewhere eliminated by one of the following processes: (i) Consonantalisation of the first vowel, (ii) Contraction, the coalescence of two vowels in hiatus in a diphthong or long single vowel (*syneresis*), (iii) Effacement of the countertonic vowels.

§ 241. *Consonantalisation* took place (as in Late Latin) when the countertonic vowel was the higher of the two juxtaposed and in Later Middle French the consonantalisation of countertonic **i, u, ü** standing in hiatus with a lower tonic vowel was very general, although fluctuations in the syllabic value of this syllable continued into Modern French (cf. Kastner, *A History of French Versification,* pp. 21-38). Grammarians of the sixteenth century accept reduction of syllabic value (i.e. consonantalisation of the countertonic vowel), in the words *diable, diantre, fiacre,* and attribute fluctuating value to *lien, lion, pion, viande, violet; fouace, fouet, moelle* (cf. § 124), *ouaille, ouy* (< *oïl*), *poele* (< *paele* < *patella*), *poeme, poete, souef, touaille; fuir, fui* (perfect and past participle), *juif, ruine.*

Cf. Vaugelas, 'Le sentiment de tous les bons grammairiens est que *fuir, ie fuis (pf.), i'ay fuy* sont de deux sillabes . . . Les poetes n'ont garde de les faire que d'une sillabe,' II, 178, 181.

§ 242. *Contraction.*—The coalescence of the countertonic vowel with the tonic took place ordinarily : (*a*) when the two vowels were homophonous or nearly so, (*b*) when countertonic **a** stood in hiatus with the tonic vowel. The resultant vowel was always long. Examples are :

(*a*) a—a > ā *acabler* akablẹr < akaablẹr, *baillier* baʝẹr < baaʝẹr.

a—ā > ã *Caen* Kãn < Kaãn.

e—ẹ > ẹ̄ *chaire* šẹrẹ < šẹẹrẹ (§§ 409, 531), *sceller* sẹlẹr < sẹẹlẹr.

u—u > ū *coule* kulẹ < kuulẹ (< *cucullum*).

u—ū > ũ *rogner* rũɲẹr < ruũɲẹr (< **rotundiare*), *rond* rũnt < ruũnt.

(*b*) a—ẹ > ẹ̃ *chaine* šẹ̃nẹ < šaẹnẹ, *gain* gẽn < gaẹn < O.F. gaãiɲ.

a—i > ai > ẹ̄ *maistre* mẹtrẹ < maistrẹ, *traitre* trẹtrẹ < traïtrẹ.

a—ī > aī (aẹ̃ § 454) > ẽ *train* trẽn < traïn, *haine* hẹ̃nẹ < haïnẹ, *gaine* gẽnẹ < gaïnẹ (< *vagina*).

a—ū > ã *paon* pãn < paũn, *taon* tãn < taũn.

a in hiatus with oral **u** appears to have been simply effaced in *aoust* ū(t) < aust, *saoul* sū(l) < saul.

Contraction began in the thirteenth century and was established in most words by the sixteenth.

The preposition **a** coalesced not infrequently with the initial **a** of a following word, cf. Regnier, ' *Escript a⌒Auxerre, sans seiour,* xi, 2 ; in the locutions *a aise, guet a apens, ja a dis,* this contraction became stereotyped; cf. also O.F. *leur, leu* < *illac ubi,* G. Paris, *Mél. Ling.,* pp. 247, 560.

§ 243. *Effacement of Countertonic* ẹ (§ 275) *in Hiatus.*

Sources of Countertonic ẹ:—
(i) Late Latin ẹ and ẹ́ free, § 234 : *seür, veïs.*
(ii) Late Latin ɑ free preceded by a velar or palatal consonant, § 417 : *cheü.*
(iii) Early Old French **a** and ọ free in hiatus with tonic ü, §§ 421, 490 : *meür, mëu.*

Effacement of ẹ in hiatus began in the thirteenth century and had become very usual in the sixteenth century, but the traditional spelling was often retained :

greïlle grẹiʝẹ (< **cratīcula,* § 202) > griʝẹ, *veïs* vẹis > vis, *veisse* vẹisẹ > visẹ, *meur* mẹür > mür, *deumes* dẹümẹs > dümẹs, *deu* dẹü > dü.

§ 244. Countertonic ẹ in contact with tonic **a** was ordinarily assimilated, and **aa** contracted to ā: *meaille* mẹaʝẹ > maaʝẹ > māʝẹ, *eage* ẹažẹ > aažẹ > āžẹ.

§ 245. In the development of countertonic ẹ (ə) + ü there was considerable local divergence. In the Île de France reduction to ü appears to have been the normal process, but in some other regions (e.g. the western and north-western) eü contracted to ö (cf. Ch. d'Orléans, *Ballades,* cxi, *maleurs : ardeurs; Cretin, l'heur : leur, seur : successeur,* etc., *Intr.* p. xliii), and this pronunciation has left its mark

on the pronunciation of *feu* fö (< fẹü < **fatutum**), *heur* ör (< ẹür < **augurium**), *jeûne* žön (< žẹün < **jejunium**), *jeûner* žönẹ (< žẹünẹr < **jejunare**).   The influence of *heure* örẹ < **hora** may have facilitated the adoption of the pronunciation ör for ẹür, and the lowering of ü̃ to õ (§ 456), the acceptance of žõnẹ and žõnẹ. According to Bèze (p. 67) : ' French people who pronounce correctly omit the letter *e* as if *hureuse* were written,' but according to Hindret (1687), 'Ce seroit parler en badaut que de dire *bonur*, comme quantité de gens disent à Paris.'   (Th. I, 515.)

[For the rounding of countertonic ẹ to ọ and ö cf. § 484.]

§ 246. The development of the words ending in **-in, -inẹ** was influenced by the relatively early nasalisation and lowering of i to ẹ̃ found in some regions (cf. § 454). The spellings *trahain, gaaignes* are found for *traïn* and *gaïnes* (Gf.) and *geïner* is written *geesner* in a letter of Louis XI (Gf.); cf. also Palsgrave, ' *Je gehynne* which I fynde also written *je gehenne*,' R. Estienne, ' *geine, gehenne, genne*.' The spelling and pronunciation of *reine* was further influenced by that of *roi* (pronounced rwẹ), cf. the spellings *roine, roiene, royenne*, cited by Gf. and *roieine* in Boileaue, p. 11. In the sixteenth century the pronunciation of this word fluctuated between rẹnẹ and rwẹnẹ, cf. Peletier, ' Les uns disent *reine*,' i.e. rẹnẹ, ' les autres *roene*,' i.e. rwẹnẹ; the pronunciation rẹnẹ was violently opposed by Henri Estienne on the ground that it confused *reine* and *raine* (< *rana*).

§ 247. *Countertonic* ẹ *in Interconsonantal Position.*—When ẹ *countertonic* stood between two consonants that combined readily in a group it was sometimes effaced ; the process began with the words in which it was placed between a *fricative* or *plosive* consonant and **r** or **l**, cf. Later O.F. **vrai** < **verai.**

In Middle French there was hesitation between *pelote* and *plote*, *pelouse* and *plouse*, *peluche* and *pluche* and in other words of this kind, and the beginnings of a more widespread reduction is indicated by the shortened forms cited by grammarians of the sixteenth century, e.g. *ch'val, d'ssus, s'la, s'pendant* (cf. Th. I, 146-162, and for Modern French, Nyrop, *Man.*, §§ 86-93 ; Grammont, *Traité*, pp. 105-111).

Section 8.—INFLUENCE OF EXPIRATORY ACCENT ON ATONIC VOWELS IN GALLO-ROMAN.

§ 248. *Atonic* (*unstressed*) syllables may be either *post-tonic* or *praetonic* or rather *intertonic*, for the praetonic unstressed syllables always stand between the secondary stressed (countertonic) syllables and the tonic, e.g. ‖can-**ta**-ˈto-**re**, ‖dor-**mi**-ˈto-**ri-um**, ‖do-**mi-ni**-ˈcel-**la**. Unstressed pretonic syllables are sometimes called *counterfinal* because they stand in the same relation to the countertonic syllables as the final to the tonic. In this book the term *intertonic* will be used.

There may be *two* unstressed syllables either before or after the tonic stress, but while unstressed penultimate syllables are relatively frequent their counterpart before the tonic syllable is rare and has received no distinguishing appellation.

Atonic syllables all varied slightly in the amount of stress they received, the weakest being the unstressed penultimate:

$$\overset{\shortparallel}{\text{dor}}\text{-mi-}{}^{\shortmid}\text{to-ri-um.}$$
$$\underset{2}{}\quad\underset{4}{}\quad\underset{1}{}\;\underset{5}{}\;\underset{3.}{}$$

The final syllables of *proparoxytones*, which were separated from the tonic syllable by the penultimate, received more stress than the final syllables of *paroxytones*, which followed immediately on the tonic (§ 223).

The value of the *intertonic* syllables approximated so nearly to that of the *final* unstressed syllables of *paroxytones* that they followed, broadly speaking, the same development.

§ 249. Under the influence of the intensified tonic stress of the Gallo-Roman period atonic vowels in every type of syllable were ordinarily either effaced or reduced to ę, unless previously consonantalised (§ 220). The main lines of the process may be formulated simply; but the varying amounts of stress received by the syllables, the varying degrees of sonority among the vowels and the varying point of articulation of the surrounding consonants induced some variation in the extent of reduction and much variation in the pace at which the process was carried on (cf. below).

§ 250. *Effacement of the Unstressed Penultimate Syllable.*—In the weakest of the syllables, the unstressed penultimate syllable, *all* vowels were effaced in the course of Gallo-Roman, unless previously consonantalised (§ 220):—

pĕrdĕre > pęrdrę, tęnĕrum > tēndrę, tĕpĭdum > tiedę, dēbĭta > dętę, arbŏrem > arbrę.

kompŭtŭm < kuntę, sĭmŭlo > sēmblę, alapa > a+vę, balsamŭm > ba+mę, Lazarŭm > lazdrę *lasdre*, *adjace *ajaɟe > aizę *aise*.

§ 251. *Reduction and Effacement of Final and Intertonic Vowels.*—a, the most sonorous vowel, was reduced to ę, which retained ordinarily syllabic value into Modern French, except when it was juxtaposed to another stronger vowel or stood between n, r or l and other consonants (§§ 253, 268-272):—

femina > fēmę, tĕrra > tęrę, ūna > ünę, porta > portę.

portas > portęs, portat > portęθ, portant > portęnt.

armata > armęðę (> armę, § 271), plaga > plaię (> plę, § 271).

ornamentum>ornęmēnt, sakramentum>sairęmēnt (§ 272), *portarajo > portęrai, *trapaliare > travęɟier, *traveillier* (§ 275), armatūra > armęðürę (> armürę, § 269), ĭmperatōrem > ēmpęręðour (< ānpęrör, § 269).

[For the value of ę cf. § 275; for its graphical representation cf. § 697.]

§ 252. With juxtaposed following **j** intertonic **e** combined to form the diphthong **ei** which was differentiated to **oi** and levelled in the normal way (§§ 519-525), O.F. **oreizun** > **oroizūn** (*orationem*), **veneizun** > **venoizūn** (*venationem*); cf. also **dāmeizẹlẹ** (§ 257) > **dāmoizẹlẹ**.

[For *damisele, orison, venison*, etc., cf. § 422.]

§ 253. Between **n** and **r** and **r** and **r**, **ẹ** < **a** *intertonic* was ordinarily slurred in the course of Early Old French and **n** assimilated to **r**, cf. O.F. **dēnrẹẹ** (> **derrẹẹ**) < **den(ẹ)rẹðẹ** < *denarata*, **dọrrai** < **dọn(ẹ)rai**, **dürrai** < **dür(ẹ)rai**.

§ 254. **e, i, o, u.** Final unstressed **i, ọ** and **ụ**, in hiatus with the tonic vowel in Late Latin or brought into hiatus in Early Gallo-Roman by the effacement of an intervocalic consonant (§§ 341, 343), became semi-vocalic and combined in a diphthong with the preceding vowel:

a + i > ****aͤi**, cf. O.F. **amai** < **amawi** *amavi*.

ū + i > ****ụͤi**, cf. O.F. *cui* **kũi** < **kūi**, ****dũi** (< ***dụị** for **dŭọ**, § 822).

a + ŭ > ****aͤu**, cf. O.F. **klọͤu** < ****klaͤu** < **klawum** *clavum*.

ẹ̄ + ŭ > ****ieͤu**, cf. O.F. **dieu** < ***dẹu** > **dĕŭm**, **grieu** < ****grie(γ)ụ** < **graecum.**

ọ̄ + ŭ > ****ọͤu**, cf. O.F. **dọus** < ***dọọs** < **dŭŏs.**

ẹ̄ + u > ****ụͤoͤu**, cf. below § 555.

[For the subsequent development of the diphthongs and triphthongs cf. chap. xiv.]

In O.F. **tüit** < ***tọttị** (for **tōtī**) and **voil** < ****vollị** < **voluī** (§ 374) **ị** final appears to have suffered metathesis.

✱✱ § 255. In the south-western region **ịe-ụ** appears to have been reduced to **ịe**, cf. O.F. *fieθ* (< Germ. *fehuod*), *estrie* (< G. *streupu*), *espieθ* (< G. *speut*), *gie* (< *ĕgo*, § 829), *cie, ce* (< *caecum*), (*St. Martin, ce* 5010, *cee : apelee* 4897).

§ 256. *Final* **ĕ, ĭ, ŏ, ŭ,** in all other positions in L.L. *paroxytones* (cf. §§ 262, 263) and *intertonic* **ĕ, ĭ, ŏ, ŭ,** and **au** in all positions were reduced to **ẹ** and effaced before the ninth century, unless required to facilitate the articulation of preceding or following groups of consonants:

rēgĕm > **rei, dēbēt** > **deit; audīt** > **ot, mūrī** > **mür; mūrŏs** > **mürs; minŭs** > **mēins, frūctūm** > **früit.**

libĕrᾱre > **livrer,** ***dēbĕrajo** > **devrai; firmitᾱtem** > **fertẹ, dormitorium** > **dortoir,** ***audīrajo** > **ọrrai;** ***masịŏnᾱta** > **maizniee,** ***impẹjŏrᾱre** > **ēmpeirier; pistŭrire** > **pestrir, mandūkare** > **mᾱndžier** *mangier ;* ***paraulᾱre** > **parlẹr.**

§ 257. The consonants and groups of consonants that required a vowel sound to facilitate their articulation, i.e. a *supporting vowel*, (*voyelle d'appui*) are the following :—

(1) *Intertonic.*—In the intertonic syllable **ẹ** (**ẹ**, § 275) was retained

(*a*) after the groups *consonant* + **r** or **l** (*not* **rr** and **ll**);

(*b*) before **l, ŋ, ts** and any particularly heavy group of consonants:

ẹ, when retained, was nasalised in Old French by a following nasal and combined in a diphthong with following *jod :*

8

karrefọrk<*kwadrịfụrkụ *quadrifurcum*, nọ̆ŏrẹ̆ŏürẹ̆<*nụtrịtụra, *ladrecin* laŏrẹtsiŋ > latrokinium;
paveillon pavejun < *papiliōnem*, *champeignon* tšãmpẹŋun < kampiniōnem, *sospecon* sospẹtsun > *suspektionem, *correcier* kọrrẹtsier > korruptiare, *chalengier* tšalẽndžier<*kalumniare, *dameisele*, dãmeizẹlẹ>*dominikella.

The stress-value of juxtaposed intertonic syllables appears to have been so nearly equal that the persistence of one or other was determined by the nature of the vowels and the surrounding sounds, a persisting ordinarily as ẹ and e, i, o, u being retained as ẹ in the syllable requiring a supporting vowel, whichever it was, cf. *palefrei* < *pắrăv(e)rēdŭ*, *Ostedun* < *Aug(ŭ)stŏdūnŭm*, *ancessour* < *ant(e)cessorem*, *dameisele* < *dom(i)nicella, *otreiier* < *auct(o)ricare*. Analogical influences often modify the form assumed.

[For the later development of e before j, ŋ, cf. § 422; of ei cf. §§ 226, 519-525, of ẽ cf. § 448; for the effacement of ẹ cf. §§ 272, 273.]

§ 258. (2) *Final.*—Among *paroxytones* a supporting vowel was retained in the final syllable :—

(*a*) Before the final group -nt, cf. O.F. deivẹnt, diẹnt, veiẹnt, vēndẹnt.

(*b*) After the denti-palatals tš and dž and the groups consisting of *consonant* + r and l (*not* rr and ll), +m, +n; (for mn cf. M.L. *Gr.*, § 117).

O.F. *ache* < atšẹ< ắpĭum, *roge* rọdžẹ < rŭbĕum, *singe* sindžẹ<sĩmium, pẹ̆ŏrẹ < pắtrem, *fievre* < fĕbrem, feiblẹ < flēbilem, dọblẹ < dŭplum, hẹ+mẹ < *hĕ+mụ, a+nẹ < a+num.

If the effacement of a final vowel resulted in the formation of a final group consisting of a *consonant* + r or + l, ẹ developed as an off-glide: cf. O.F. sẽmprẹ< semper, mairẹ < major, pirẹ < **piejrẹ < pejor, ēnsẽmblẹ< in simul.

§ 259. Among *proparoxytones* a final vowel was retained in all words except those made paroxytone in Late Latin or Early Gallo-Roman by the slurring of the unstressed penultimate vowel at that date (cf. §§ 248, 260-263) :—

asne aznẹ < asinum, *beivre* < bibere, kuntẹ < kŏmitem, *disme* dizmẹ < dẹkimum, *piege* piedžẹ < pĕdicum, *polce* pọ+tsẹ < pŏllikem, *porche* portšẹ < portikum, dutẹ < dubito; but *ueil* uej < *ọk(ŭ)lụ, *chalt* tša+t < *kal(i)dụ, nẹt < *nẹt(e)dụ < nĭtĭdŭm.

[For the value of ẹ cf. § 275; for its graphical representation cf. § 697; for its effacement in final syllables in Middle and Early Modern French cf. §§ 268-273.]

§ 260. *Date of Reduction and Effacement of Final and Intertonic Vowels.*—Effacement of final and intertonic e, i, o, u is indicated for the eighth century by the spellings *carcati* for *carricati*, *avortetiz* for *abortaticius* in the *Glossary of Reichenau;* cf. also *Strasbourg Oaths*, *amur*, *comun*, *dreit*, etc., and M.L. *Gr.* § 127.

The reduction of intertonic **a** to **e** is attested in the above mentioned word *avortetiz*; the reduction of final and intertonic **a** to **e** is frequent in *Eulalia*, cf. *auret, elle, eskoltet, manatse; preiement, bellezour.*

§ 261. *Date of Reduction and Effacement of the Unstressed Penultimate Vowel.*— The reduction of the unstressed penultimate began in Late Latin, but the process was carried out mainly in the Gallo-Roman period, and the scarcity of documentary evidence makes it difficult to fix with any accuracy the chronology of a process which was influenced by a variety of factors, long drawn out and locally variable. The main factors that retard or accelerate the process are :—

(i) The greater or lesser facility with which the various consonants fall into groups.

(ii) The varying sonority of the vowels : **a,** the lowest vowel, possessing sonority enough to retard its own effacement and to accelerate the reduction of other unstressed vowels in adjacent syllables.

(iii) Local variations in the intensity of the tonic stress, due to the variations in the intensity of the Germanic settlement (§ 17). Thus in the north-eastern region a strongly syncopated form of proparoxytone appears, e.g. *teve* < *tepidum, maleve* < **malehabitum* (N.E. § v), while in the south-western region the effacement of the unstressed penultimate occurred relatively late (S.W. § ix).

§ 262. *Effacement of* **e, i, o, u** began in Late Latin : (i) among words used unstressed in the sentence, e.g. *dominus*, and (ii) among words in which the unstressed penultimate syllable stood between two consonants that readily combined in a group. These included :—

(a) Proparoxytones ending in *-ŭlus, -ŭla, -ŭlum*, e.g. *capulus, fabula, populus, vapulo, genuculus, oculus, *plumaculus, *soliculus, vetulus, vitulus*. The *Appendix Probi* condemns the use of the shortened forms *oclus, tabla, vaplo* and the replacement of **tl** by **kl** : ' *vetulus non veclus, vitula non vicla.*'

The unshortened form of some words appears to have been either retained under the influence of preservative analogy (§ 765), or to have been reintroduced under clerkly influence, cf. (a) O.F. **espaðlę** < **spatulam, roðlę** < **rotulum,** (b) **reulę** > **riulę** < **rēgula,** doublet of **relę,** *reille,* **teulę** > **tiulę** < **tēgula, seulę** < **saeculum** (replaced by *siegle, siecle*).

[For the development of these words cf. §§ 372, 641.]

(b) Proparoxytones ending in *-ĭdus, -ĭdis, -ĭtus*, e.g. **kalidus, frigidus, matidus, nitidus, positus, plakitus, plikitus, solidus, wiridis,** which were shortened to ***kaɫdus, *mattus, *nettus,** etc.; (cf. also § 353).

(c) Proparoxytones in which the penultimate vowel stood between **n** or **l** and **r**, e.g. *gĕnĕrum, tĕnĕrum, cŏlўrum.*

§ 263. Proparoxytones in which the unstressed penultimate vowel was followed by a velar consonant which was early effaced or palatalised also early became paroxytone, cf. *sar'cŏphăgum, Ro'tŏmăgum,* '*cŏllĭget* which were early shortened to ****sar'kǫ(f)ʉ, **Ro'dǫmʉ, **kǫllĭęt.**

§ 264. **a.** Reduction of unstressed penultimate **a** is attested for the seventh century by the spellings *Bonogelum* for *Bonoialum, Spinogelum* for *Spinoialum* (cf. Longnon, pp. 66, 68) and *Isera* for *Isara, Segona* for *Sequana* in Fredegarius (cf. Haag, 23). The syncopated forms *Segna, Isra* are attested in the eighth century (cf. Haag, 34) ; *-omo* for *-omagum* before the seventh century (Longnon, p. 43).

[For the relation between the slurring of the unstressed vowels and the development of intervocalic consonants cf. §§ 348-354.]

Section 9.—REDUCTION OF ATONIC VOWELS IN PERIOD II.

§ 265. After a period of relative stability unstressed vowels began to lose value again in the thirteenth century and Middle French period. The process began with vowels juxtaposed to other vowels and in this position the high vowels i and ü were consonantalised and ę ordinarily slurred before the end of the period.   When final of a word after a consonant ę ordinarily retained syllabic value into early Modern French (§ 273), but it was sometimes slurred when interconsonantal (§ 272).

§ 266. Among words in which the countertonic syllable was not the initial of the word it not infrequently lost value and was treated like an intertonic in this period : (i) Words of which prosthetic ę had become an integral part, e.g. ''eküęlę < Early O.F. ''(e)''sküęlę, ''estęüst < Early O.F. ''(ę)''stęüst, § 361 ; (ii) Derivative verbs which had lost connection with the word from which they were formed, e.g. ''ašętęr < ''a''tšatęr (*adcaptare), ''barętęr < ''ba''ratęr.

§ 267. *Consonantalisation of i and ü* : (i) i *intertonic* stood in hiatus : (*a*) in learned loan-words such as *ancïien, crestïien, champïon*, (*b*) in the terminations of the first and second persons plural of the imperfect indicative and conditional (§ 919), *-ï-iens, -ï-ons, -i-iez*, (*c*) in the verbal derivatives in *-ïer, oublier, magnefier* (§ 640) ; (ii) ü *intertonic* stood in hiatus : (*a*) in loan-words, e.g. *circüit, sontüeus*, (*b*) in words such as *escüele*, § 266.

Except in (i) (*c*), consonantalisation of i̯ to j and of ü to w̌ began in the later thirteenth century (rather earlier in the northern region (N. § xi)) : *anciien* āntsii̯ēn > ānsi̯ēn, *champion* tšāmpiun > šānpi̯ūn, *-i-iens* ii̯ēns > -i̯ēns, *-iuns* > -i̯ūns, *i-iez* -ii̯ęts > -i̯ęs, *escuele* esküęlę > ękw̌ęlę, *circuit* tsirküit > sirkw̌it.

Under the influence of preservative analogy (§ 765) syllabic value was often maintained in derivative words, e.g. in the weak radical of the verbs in *-ïer*, etc. and sometimes hiatus was obviated by the development of a palatal glide : cf. O. Fr. *essuyer*, esüi̯ę < esüęr, *oublier* ublii̯ę < ublięr.   It is uncertain whether the form parvis is derived from O.F. parẹis by the development of a labial glide (parẹis > parẹwis > parẹvis, cf. St. *Martin*, 2495, *Parevis : le vis*), or is the result of an earlier development (cf. Gamillscheg, *Et. Wb.* under *parvis*).

§ 268. *Effacement of ę in Hiatus.*—By the end of the sixteenth century ę in hiatus had lost syllabic value very generally : the process began with the effacement of ę *intertonic*, in hiatus with the *following* tonic vowel, and affected last ę *final* in hiatus with the *preceding* tonic vowel : the juxtaposed tonic and countertonic vowels were ordinarily lengthened.

✱✱ The greater intensity of the stress in the northern region (§ 223) led to the earlier instability of ę in that region (N. § x).

§ 269. ę *Intertonic in Hiatus with the Tonic Vowel.*—Effacement began in the thirteenth century and was carried through before the sixteenth : *esteüst* ętęüt > ętüt, *armëure* armęürę > armürę, *pechëeur* pęšęör > pęsör, *mirëoir* miręuęr > mirüęr, *treslëiz* tręlęis > tręli(s), and similarly all words formed with the Latin suffixes, *-atura, -atorem, -atorium, -aticium.*

§ 270. ę *Intertonic in Hiatus with the Preceding Vowel.*—Shortened forms such as *prirai* < *prierai, oblirai, pairai, vraiment* (< *vraiement*), *aveuglement* (< *aveugleement*), *aisement, espressement, privement, cririe* (< *crierie*), made their appearance in the fourteenth century or even earlier, and the effacement of intertonic ę in this position was general in the sixteenth century and accepted by the grammarians, although the spelling was rarely altered.

§ 271. ę *final in Hiatus after the Tonic Vowel.*—The effacement of ę *after* the tonic vowel began in the thirteenth century in the verbal terminations *-oie, -oies, -oient* and in the forms *soie, soies, soient, aie, aies, aient* under the analogical influence of the third person singular of these tenses, but the general effacement of ę final in hiatus with the tonic vowel only became frequent in the later fifteenth and sixteenth centuries. Although this pronunciation was accepted in educated speech and by the poets in the sixteenth century, the grammarians of the early seventeenth century continued to insist on retention of its syllabic value, especially in verse, except in the verbal forms mentioned above.

The lengthening of the preceding vowel, which was a marked feature of the pronunciation at the time of effacement (§ 562), gradually disappeared when the word stood in the interior of the phrase but remained so clearly audible at the pause that it was possible in the seventeenth century to distinguish clearly the feminine forms of past participles from the masculine (§ 562, cf. Rosset, pp. 130-136).

Villon accords ordinarily syllabic value to *-ę* final in hiatus—metrically attested in the Testament forty-one examples of *-ę* in hiatus with syllabic value to six of ę slurred—but he allows *oue (auca)* to rhyme with *ou*, l. 1338 and *Troies* with *trois*, l. 614. The word *eaue*, which was early shortened, is always monosyllabic in his work, (cf. *Rose* II, *eauz : seauz*, 10431 and *Rom.* xxx, 356).

Attesting Remarks.—Meigret (1548) gives *-oęt* as the termination of both the third singular and third plural of the imperfect indicative and adds this remark : ' la tięrse, qe vous ecriuez par *-oyent*, qi ęt merueĦeuzemęnt etranje de la prononçiaçion, laqęlle ne la fęt point aotre q'ao singulier, sinon d'aotant qe l'ę ouvęrt du plurier ęt de plu longe prolaçion,' p. 114. Ronsard and Péletier recommend the effacement of ę in hiatus : ' . . . Tu dois oster la derniere *e* foeminine, tant des vocables singuliers que pluriers, qui se finissent en *-ee* et en *-ees*, quand de fortune ils se rencontrent au milieu de ton vers . . . Si tu veux que ton poeme soit ensemble doux et savoureux, ¦pour ce tu mettras " *rou*," " *jou*," " *nu*," contre l'opinion de tous nos maîtres, qui n'ont de si pres avisé à la perfection de ce mestier ' (*Art. Poët.*, pp. 327, 328). ' J'é usé de *gru's* e *oę's* pour *grues* é *oęes*' (*oies*) . . . 'dęmandant cę conge-la, e an donnant dę mȩmȩ.'

(Peletier, *Art P.*, p. 212). This pronunciation is rejected by others, cf. Sebillet (1548) : ' Prononçant *aimée, desestimée*, tu sens bien le plein son du premier *é* masculin . . . et le mol et flac son du second *e* femenin en la syllabe derniere.' (Th. I, 163) ; Malherbe : ' . . . jamais ne dis *Proté* ni *Promethé*, mais *Prothée* et *Promethée*.' (Th. I, 177) ; Awfeild (1634) : ' You shall find *e* doubled in many words, e.g. *portee*, which are both distinctly sounded,' p. 16.

§ 272. *Effacement of ę interconsonantal.*—Shortened forms of words in which intertonic ę stood between **n, r** or **l** and other consonants began to appear in the late twelfth and thirteenth centuries, e.g. *denree* (> *derree*) < **denarata, donrai* (> *dorrai*) < *donerai* (§ 253), *dernier* < *derrenier, controlle* < *contrerolle, napron* < *naperon, persil* < *perresil, sairment* < *sairement*, etc. Forms like these became very general in Middle French, but pronunciation was long hesitating, and in the sixteenth century doublets were still in use for many words of this type, cf. *calçon* and *caleçon, carfour* and *carrefour* (< *quadrifurcum*), *chaperon* and *chapron, charretier* and *chartier, esperon* and *espron, contrerolle* and *controlle, horiloge* and *horloge, larrecin* and *larcin, maletote* and *maltote* (< *mala *tollita*), *mairerie* and *mairie, souspeçon* and *souspçon*.

§ 273. *Effacement of ę final post-consonantal.*—The elision of ę *post-consonantal* before a word beginning with a *vowel* was usual already in the Oldest French (*Eul. Ell'ent*, 15, *Qu'elle*, 17), but in the educated speech of Paris syllabic value was retained by ę *final* in prae-consonantal position and at a pause into the later sixteenth century : at that period people appear to have begun to reduce it to an indistinct sound, an 'off-glide,' which rapidly lost syllabic value in colloquial speech and served only to reinforce the preceding consonant. In oratory and declamation syllabic value was maintained.

Monosyllabic words such as *ce, le, que*, etc., were still coupled freely with the last syllable of polysyllabic words in the later fifteenth and early sixteenth century, cf. Villon, *promesse : jamais ce* T. 887, Cretin, *en ce : insolence, querez le : querelle.*

Bèze, in 1564, describes the sound as 'weak and barely perceptible' and Aufeild, in 1634, recommends a pronunciation of *e* feminine 'like *uh* in English, . . . *famuh*, pronouncing *uh* very gently like a sick man's short breathing,' but Van der Aa (1622) already states categorically that ' short *e* is treated as if it were not written, so for *lire* read *lir*.' (Th. I, 168.)

[For the modern pronunciation, cf. Nyrop, *Man.* §§ 86-93, Grammont, *Traité*, pp. 105-120.]

✱✱ In the north-eastern and eastern region, where the tonic stress was heavier (§ 223) the effacement of ę final was more rapid, cf. Th. I, 166, Cohen, *Mystères*, pp. lv-lvii, N.E. § vi.

[For ę in Anglo-Norman, cf. Part V, Section 8.]

§ 274. In some words the use of ę final was optional in Later Old and Middle French. The origin of these doublets is diverse :—

(1) *Arrier, derrier, seur* (< *supra*), *encor, or, onc*, doublets of *arriere*, etc., were all originally prae-vocalic forms (§ 604).

(2) *Donque* (*donques*) was created on the model of *onque*; *avecque* (*avecques*) and *illecque* (*illecques*) on the model of *donque(s)* and *onque(s)* (§ 604).

(3) *Come* is thought to be an early contraction of *com + et* (< *como* < 'quomodo + et*, ' also '), and was at first only used in elliptical comparisons such as *Rol.* 20, ' *Conseillez mei cume mi savie hume.*'

(4) In many learned loan-words the use of ẹ was very vacillating, e.g. *brut— brute, exact—exacte, fidel—fidele, inutil—inutile*, etc. (Th. I, 187 *et seq.*).

Section 10.—Pronunciation of ẹ.

§ 275. The obscured neutral vowel in use in Modern English is buccal and central, the one in Modern French is a slightly rounded front sound (cf. § 103), and it is difficult to determine which of the two was in use in Old and Middle French. The sixteenth-century grammarians describe the sound only in general terms: ' son mou et imbecille,' ' flac,' ' un peu obscur,' but a variety of considerations make it probable that it was at first predominantly a buccal sound :—

(1) In the leonine rhymes of the period ẹ is freely coupled with ẹ and ẹ, cf. Rose II : *sera : plaira, chevaus : et vaus, entrepris : esté pris, ambedeus : volenté d'eus, anemis : ai mis, Rome rei : desrei, onques point : les point, simples on : saison, le pris : e pris, le sent : et sent, le chief : meschief, te fier : e fier, de gris : amaigris*, etc. (*Intr.* pp. 247, 248), Cretin, *a quelle fin : Ha qu'il est fin*, lxii, 39, and Tabourot equates *parlez bas* with *par le bas*.

(2) In the Hebrew glossary of the thirteenth century e tonic and countertonic are represented by the same symbol (*Rom. St.* I, 165).

(3) In the countertonic syllable in Middle French there was much hesitation between ẹ and ẹ (§ 591).

(4) In the interrogative form of the first person singular of the present indicative of the first conjugation ẹ gradually passed into ẹ (cf. § 898).

(5) Poets rhyme frequently words ending in ẹ with Latin words ending in e, e.g. Cretin, *Exite : Et si te*, lxii, 54, Beardwood, *Ite : di te, milites : eslites, quoque : mocque*, p. 64.

It is, however, probable that ẹ when juxtaposed to a labial sound (e.g. in **dẹü, mẹür, emperẹör**) was early labialised slightly, and this pronunciation is occasionally attested in the later ' rimes leonines,' cf. Cretin : *renom : peu, non*, 206, 87, *ung peu : repeu*, 282, 119. After the effacement of vowels in hiatus this pronunciation must have gained extension rapidly, because in the early seventeenth century it is already being described by Deimier (1610): ' L'*e* feminin se prononce non comme en l'alphabet, mais bien ainsy qu'une lettre qui tient de la nature de ce mot *ou* et de cest mesme lettre *e* . . . ' (Th. I, 164). Oudin in 1633 prescribes *deu, ceu, queu* for *de, ce, que*, but Hindret, in 1687, though recommending *ampakeuter, keunouille* in verse, still prefers ' *anvoyez-laí* ' to ' *anvoyez-leu* ' (Th. I, 157, 158, 207).

It is also probable that the value of the sound was affected to some extent by the sounds in its vicinity and that it remained more palatal before palatal or denti-palatal consonants and the *e-sounds*, e.g. in *paveillon* **pavẹ̣un** (cf. § 422), *seel* **sẹẹl** *abbeesse* **abẹẹsẹ**.

✱✱ In Normandy ẹ final was nasalised (under the influence of the termination *-ent ?*), § 1328 (5 *e*).

CHAPTER VI.

PALATALISATION OF CONSONANTS.

Section 1.—Nature and Characteristics of Palatalisation in
Gallo-Roman.

§ 276. In simple general terms *palatalisation* may be described as
the process in which a non-palatal sound comes to be made, wholly or
partially, in the position in which a palatal sound is articulated, i.e. with
the characteristic lift of the middle or front of the tongue up to or
towards the hard palate (§ 106 (*c*)).   Vowels and consonants may both
be palatalised (cf. §§ 413, 421) but in this chapter it is only consonants
that will be considered.

When, for instance, there is a palatalisation of a plosive velar consonant, i.e. of a sound made with a lift of the *back* of the tongue up to
the *soft* palate, the lift of the tongue is advanced until it comes about
that it is the *front* of the tongue that is in contact with the *hard* palate,
and thus the velar plosives **k** and **g** become the palatal plosives **ɟ** and **ɟ**.
In a similar way the fricative velar **γ** palatalises to the fricative palatal **ʝ** :
the nasal velar **ŋ** to the nasal palatal **ɲ** : the lateral **ɬ** to the palatal **ʎ** :
each velar consonant passing into a palatal consonant of its own kind.
The palatalisation of a dental involves a like process in a reverse direction.
These processes are illustrated by the subjoined figures, which give :—

(*a*) The tongue position of **k** as a velar (fig. 1).
(*b*) The tongue position of **k** articulated in a forward position (fig. 2).
(*c*) The tongue position of the plosive palatal **ɟ** (fig. 3).
(*d*) The tongue positions of **ŋ**, **ɲ** and **n** (figs. 4-6).

§ 277. *Palatalisation in Latin and Gallo-Roman.*—The general lines
followed in the palatalising of consonants in Latin and Gallo-Roman are
simple :—

(1) The palatalisation of consonants in this period is always a *combinative* phenomenon, induced by the assimilative influence of a juxtaposed sound.

(2) Only the consonants made with a movement of the tongue, the
linguals, were palatalised, i.e. the dentals and velars, including the labio-
velar **w**; the labials neither induced palatalisation nor underwent it.

(3) Since the palatalisation of a *velar* implies the shifting *forward* of the point of articulation, it follows that it was always caused by the influence of a juxtaposed lingual sound made further *forward* than itself, either palatal or dental ; the palatalisation of a *dental*, on the other hand, was always due to the influence of a juxtaposed lingual sound articulated further *back* than itself and most frequently by a palatal sound.

(4) *Velar* consonants were palatalised by palatal *vowels* as well as by palatal and dental *consonants ; dentals* were only palatalised by consonants.

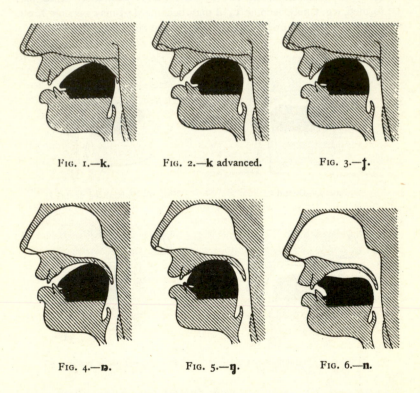

FIG. 1.—**k.**   FIG. 2.—**k** advanced.   FIG. 3.—**ʃ.**

FIG. 4.—**ȵ.**   FIG. 5.—**ŋ.**   FIG. 6.—**n.**

§ 278. The process of palatalisation is, however, complicated in the history of French by several factors :—

(1) *The Number and Variety of Palatal Sounds.*—It must be borne in mind that the palatal sounds comprise the *front* vowels **i, e, a, ü, ö** and three types of consonant : palatals proper, denti-palatals and palatalised dentals, those consonants which combine with their dental articulation a lift of the tongue up to or towards the hard palate (§ 111).   When

velars palatalise they normally do so completely and simply, i.e. they move slowly forward into a palatal position :—

k and **g** becoming **ʄ** and **ɟ**, **χ** and **γ** becoming **ç** and **ʝ** respectively, **ɲ** becoming **ŋ**, and **ʎ**, **ʝ**.

When *dentals* palatalise results are apt to be more variable because the point of articulation of a dental may either be moved right back to *palatal* position, e.g. **t** may become the breath plosive palatal **ʄ**, **d** may become **ɟ**, **l** may become **ʝ**, etc., or it may shift only to *denti-palatal* or *alveolar* position, e.g. **t** may become **ts** or **tš**, **d** may become **dz** or **dž**, or again the palatalisation may be only *partial* and a *palatalised-dental* may be formed, e.g. **t** may become **t̂**; **d** may become **d̂**; **l** may become **l̂**, etc.

The subjoined figures illustrate these three last possibilities for **t**.

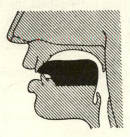

Fig. 7.—Dental **t**.

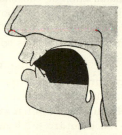

Fig. 8.—Palatalised dental **t**.

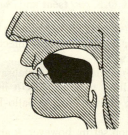

Fig. 9.—Tongue position of plosive element in **ts**.

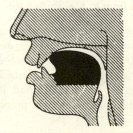

Fig. 10.—Tongue position of plosive element in **tš**.

§ 279. (2) *The Instability of the Palatal Consonants.*—Both palatal and palatalised consonants are difficult to articulate (§ 190) and tend in consequence to be unstable: **ʝ** and **ŋ** persisted under certain conditions into modern French, all others were modified in the course of Gallo-Roman, and in quite modern times **ʝ** has been simplified to **ʒ** (§ 106).

(i) The *plosive palatals* **ɟ** and **ʄ** ordinarily shifted forward or opened, **ɟ** passing to **dž** or **ʝ**, **ʄ** to **ts** or **tš** and the affricates subsequently opened (§§ 191, 194).

(ii) The *palatalised dentals* were all resolved into simple dentals preceded by a palatal glide, i.e. r̂ > i̯r, ŝ > i̯s, etc. (§ 190).

(iii) The *fricative palatal* i̯ closed to dž when initial (§ 203), opened ordinarily to i̯ and combined with preceding vowels when intervocalic, prae-consonantal or final (§ 404).

(iv) In the course of Gallo-Roman ŋ, if brought into contact with a consonant, was resolved into i̯n ; i̯ in this position was ordinarily velarised and vocalised to u̯ before the middle of the twelfth century (§§ 383-391).

(v) In the course of Period II ŋ final of the word was dentalised and absorbed into the preceding nasal vowel (§ 435 ; cf. also § 406).

§ 280. (3) *The Long Duration of the Palatalising Phenomena.*—The palatalising movements extended over several centuries. The beginnings of the palatalisation of consonants lie in Late Latin (about the fourth century, § 304), and the last bout took place in Late Gallo-Roman, after the fall of the unstressed final vowels (§ 318). The protraction of the movement provoked various complications :—

§ 281. (i) The palatalisations that took place in Gallo-Roman were not always carried out on exactly the same lines as those followed in the palatalisation of the earlier period. For example : **dj** palatalised completely in Late Latin but **i̯d** only partially in Gallo-Roman : **radi̯u̯ > *radu̯ > rai, adi̯uta̯re > **ai̯dare > **ai̯d̂are > aidier.**

The plosive palatal t̡ formed in Late Latin from **k + e** and **k + i** shifted forward to **ts** in early Gallo-Roman ; but t̡, formed in Gallo-Roman from **k + a,** shifted forward to **tš,** cf. O.F. *cent* **tsēnt** and *char* **tšar.**

§ 282. (ii) Concurrently with the long drawn-out palatalising movements other sound changes were taking place which often affected the course followed by the consonants palatalised :—

(*a*) a, being velar in Late Latin, § 157, induced no palatalisation at that period, but after it had itself palatalised to **a** (§ 182), it induced the palatalisation of the preceding velar consonants in Gallo-Roman (§§ 298-302).

Before this second bout of palatalisation set in, however, **k** and **g** in intervocalic position had been opened and voiced to γ and the palatal sound that resulted in this position was consequently not one of the plosive palatals t̡ and d̡, but the fricative voiced palatal i̯ (§ 302), e.g. *baca* **baka > **baγa > **baje > baie̜, riga > **reγa < **reje > reie̜.**

(*b*) The slurring of unstressed vowels in Gallo-Roman (§§ 250-256) brought about frequent changes in the position of consonants, intervocalic becoming initial, final or first of a group and the development of the consonants palatalising was necessarily affected. For example, in the development of words of the type *manducare* the fall of the unstressed

intertonic vowel brought the velar into initial position, but only after it had voiced to **g** (§§ 335, 349), and therefore the O.F. form of the word is *mangier*, with *voiced* denti-palatal sound :

> mandukαre > **mandugare > măndžier *mangier*.

[Cf. also the development of *plangere*, *fulgere, *carcerem*, etc., § 293.]

Section 2.—Survey of Palatalising Phenomena.

To facilitate the understanding of the many-sided process the detailed description of the various kinds of palatalisation is preceded by a summary account of the chief palatalising phenomena.

§ 283. (1) Before **e** and **i** the breathed plosive velar consonant **k** palatalised to **ʄ** in Late Latin, shifted forward early and opened, becoming first affricated and then fricative ; when *intervocalic* the affricated sound **ts** was voiced (§ 334) :

> **k** *initial* > **ʄ** > ts > s (cent. xiii) : *centum* kentum > *ʄentu > tsēnt > sănt *cent*.
>
> **k** *intervocalic* > **ʄ** > **ts** > **dz** > **ɀ** : *placere* plαkēre > *plαʄere > plaizir *plaisir*.

§ 284. (2) Before **e** and **i** the voiced plosive velar consonant **g** palatalised in Late Latin to **ɟ** : in *initial* position **ɟ** shifted forward to denti-palatal position and then opened to **ž** ; when *intervocalic* **ɟ** opened to **ɪ** which was often effaced :

> **g** *initial* > **ɟ** > dž > ž (cent. xiii) : *gentem* gentem > *ɟente > džēnt > žănt *gent*.
>
> **g** *intervocalic* > **ɟ** > **ɪ** : *regina* *reɟina > *reɪina > *reïna.

§ 285. (3) Before Gallo-Roman **a, e, i**, the plosive velar consonants **k** and **g** palatalised, shifted forward and opened :

> **k** *initial* > **ʄ** > tš > š (cent. xiii) : *carrum* karrum > *karrų > **ʄarrų > tšar *char ;* *carum* karum > tšier *chier*.
>
> **g** *initial* > **ɟ** > dž > ž (cent. xiii) : *gαmbα **ɟamba > džămbę > žănbę *jambe*.

§ 286. (4) Before Gallo-Roman **a, e, i**, the voiced fricative **γ** (< **k** and **g** *intervocalic*), when preceded by **a, e,** or **i**, palatalised to **ɪ**, which merged in preceding **i** and combined with other preceding vowels in a diphthong :

> *baca* bakα > **baga > **baγa > baię, *negare* > **neγare > neiier, *mica* mikα > **miga > **miγa > mię.

§ 287. (5) When juxtaposed to following **ɪ** all *lingual* consonants palatalised, cf. sect. 4.

§ 288. (6) All intervocalic groups consisting of *velar* consonants (other than **4**) + *dental* consonants palatalised by mutual assimilation, cf. sect. 6.

§ 289. (7) s *final*, juxtaposed to **ȷ** and **ŋ**, palatalised to ts (§ 318):

filius > ***fiȷu̧s** > **fiȷts** > **fits** *filz, fiz.*

Section 3.—PALATALISATION OF k AND g BY FRONT VOWELS IN
LATE LATIN.

(For the subsequent development of the diphthongs produced cf. chap. xiv.)

§ 290. In Late Latin, when the velar consonants **k** and **g** preceded the front vowels **e** and **i**, they palatalised before the end of the period:

The breathed plosive velar **k** > breathed plosive palatal **ȶ**,
The voiced plosive velar **g** > voiced plosive palatal **ɟ**,

e.g. *centum* **kentum** > ***ȶentu̧, plakēre** > ***plaȶere**
gentem **gentem** > ***ɟente,** *legem* **legem** > ***leɟe.**

The subsequent development of **ȶ** and **ɟ** was modified by position.

§ 291. *Development of* **ȶ** *and* **ɟ** *initial.*—In early Gallo-Roman the plosive palatals **ȶ** and **ɟ** in initial position shifted forward and opened, the breath plosive **ȶ** becoming **t͡s**, the voiced palatal **ɟ** becoming **dž**:

*ȶentu̧ > ****t͡sentu̧** ***ɟente** > ****džente.**

t͡s was depalatalised but the affricates **ts** and **dž** both persisted into Later Old French, opening to **s** and **ž** in the course of the thirteenth century (§ 194):

*ȶentu̧ >	****t͡sentu̧** >	**tsēnt** >	**sānt**	*cent*
merkēdem >	***merȶede** >	**mẹrtsiθ** >	**mẹrsi**	*merci(t)*
radikīna >	***radiȶına** >	**ratsinẹ** >	**rasīnẹ**	*racine*
pŏllikem >	***pọlleȶe** >	**pọ4tsẹ** >	**pusẹ**	*polce*
falkem >	***fa4ȶe** >	**fa4ts** >	**faus**	*falz*
*ɟente >	**džente** >	**džēnt** >	**žānt**	*gent*
argentum >	***arɟentu̧** >	**ardžēnt** >	**aržānt**	*argent*
gemellos >	***ɟemẹllos** >	**džẹmẹ4s** >	**žẹmẹaus** (§ 486)	

[For intervocalic **sȶ** < **sk** + **e** and **i** cf. § 315; and for intervocalic **nɟ** (< *ng* + **e** and **i**) cf. § 311.]

§ 292. The divergence in the development of the two sounds appears to be due to the fact that the voiced palatal **ɟ** is articulated a little farther back than the breathed one (cf. Grammont, *Assimilation*, p. 65).

The stage **ts** appears to have been preceded by an intermediate stage **t͡s**, **ts** palatalised, i.e. pronounced with its point of articulation, the area of contact between the blade of the tongue and the teeth-ridge, continued rather farther back on to the hard palate and thus covering a rather larger extent. This palatalised pronunciation explains the palatal glide that appears in the development of **t͡s** intervocalic (cf. § 294) and also the

northern development of the sound to **tš** (*ch*), e.g. *chent* **tšĕnt**, N. § i, for the sound **tš** appears to be more readily reached from **tʃ** than from **ts**, and rarely, if ever, develops out of **ts**, cf. K. Ringenson, ' Etude sur la Palatalisation de **k** devant une voyelle antérieure en Français,' pp. 143-147.

§ 293. *Initial become Middle of Three Consonants.*—In words of the type *plangere, vincere,* *folgere (*fulgur*), *culcita, nascere,* *adergere (*aderigere*), *torkere (*torquere*) the initial velar consonants **g** and **k** palatalised in the normal manner to **ɟ** and **c** and in their turn palatalised preceding **ɲ, ʎ** and **s** :

plangere	**plaɲɟĕre** > ***plaɲɟĕre**,	*culcita*	**kŭʎkita** > ***kŭʎcta**,	
nascere	**naskĕre** > ***nascĕre**,	*torquere*	***torkĕre** > ***torcĕre**.	

At this stage the unstressed penultimate vowel was slurred and **ɟ** and **c** being thus brought into contact with **r**, a dental consonant, were replaced by **d** and **t**, instead of developing to **tʃ** and **dž** (§ 291). Subsequently **ɲ** was disintegrated in the ordinary way to **in** (§ 279 (iv)), **ʃ** to **is** (§ 279 (ii)) and **ʎ** was velarised and vocalised to **u** (§§ 385-390) :

****plaɲd(e)re** > **plāindrę**	****kŭʎt(e)ta** > **koʎtę** > **kutę** *coilte, coute*
****nast(e)re** > **naistrę**	****tort(e)re** > **tortrę**

Cf. also O.F. **vēintre** < *vincere* **wiɲkĕre** (> ***βeɲtĕre**), *foildre* **foʎdrę** < ***fŭʎɟĕre** (for *fulgurem*), *aerdre* < ***aderɟĕre** (for *aderigere*).

✱✱ In the south-western region **r** appears to have been palatalised sufficiently strongly to cause the diphthongisation of preceding tonic **ǫ** (§ 410).

§ 294. *Development of* **c** *in intervocalic Position.*—When **c** was in intervocalic position it shifted forward to **tʃ** which voiced to **dž** (§ 334) and **dž** ordinarily opened to **ẑ** which was resolved into **iz** (graphy *is*) ; **i** merged in **i** and combined with other preceding vowels in a diphthong :

placere	**plakĕre** > ***placĕre** > ****platʃire** > ****pladžire** > **plaizir** *plaisir*
	vicinum	**wikīnum** > ***βecinu** > **veizin** *veisin* (§ 131)
	dicentem	**dīkentem** > ***dicente** > **diz(ānt)** *disant*

§ 295. *Modifying Conditions.*—With the gradual effacement of unstressed vowels (§§ 250, 256) the position of the palatalised sound was altered and its develop ment modified.

(i) In words of the type *pollicem, rumicem,* the early fall of the unstressed penultimate vowel (§ 250) brought **tʃ** into *initial* position and it developed accordingly (§ 292).

(ii) In words of the type *tacet,* **amicitatem,* *cicinum the rather later fall of the unstressed vowels (§§ 249, 256) brought **dž** into *prae-consonantal* position and it developed into **is** before breath consonants, **iz** before voiced ones :

taket > **taist**, ***amicitate** > **amistie**, ***cicinu** > **tsiznę** *cisne*.

[For the effacement of **s** and **z** cf. § 377.]

(iii) In words of the type *nucem, picem,* etc., the fall of the unstressed final vowel (§ 256) made **dž** final of the word and it unvoiced to **its** (§ 206) :

pikem > **peits** *peiz*, **nŭkem** > **noits** *noiz*.

[For the passage of **ts** > **s** cf. § 194 ; for *pais* cf. § 639.]

Under the influence of **sis** (< ***sĕks** *sex*), *diz* **dits** was often replaced by **dis**.

§ 296. *Relation of Palatalisation and Assibilation to Fall of Unstressed Vowels.*—
Palatalisation and assibilation (§ 191) appear to have ordinarily antedated the
slurring of unstressed vowels, cf. O.F. *taist < tacet, cerst < circet, amistie <
amicitatem, disme < decimum, Aisne < Acinum.*

Deviations are of two types:

(1) When the slurring of an unstressed penultimate vowel produced a group of
consonants easy to articulate together, e.g. **kt, kr, kl** (cf. § 262), these groups
were ordinarily formed before the palatalisation of **k** before **e** or **i** had set in, and
consequently palatalisation in words of this type followed the lines of the palatalisation of **k** juxtaposed to a dental consonant (§§ 323, 324):

placitum **plakitum** < ***plaktu** > **plait,** *facere* **fakĕre** > ***fakre** > **fairę.**

(2) In words of the type *placitare, vocitare* in which **k** stood between a secondary
stressed *velar* vowel and intertonic **i**, the palatalisation of **k** appears to have been
delayed and to have taken place only after the voicing and opening of intervocalic
k to **g** and **γ** (§ 335):—

plakitare > ****plaγĕdare** > **plaidier, wŏkitare** > ****βογγedare** > **voidier.**

[For analogical verbal forms cf. §§ 939-943.]

§ 297. *Development of* **g** *in intervocalic Position.*—When **g** was in
intervocalic position it opened to **j** which was ordinarily early effaced,
unless brought into contact with a consonant by the fall of an unstressed
vowel:

rēgina	> *reḍina	> *reɪina	> reinę
*segęllu	> sęęl	> *fūgire	> foir
plantagĭnem	> plāntāin	triginta	> trēntę
*kūgitare	> küidier	frigida	> freidę

Between countertonic **a** and tonic **e, ɪ** appears to have been maintained, cf.
O.F. **païs** < ****pajis** < ***paḍęse** (***pagensem), saiętę** < **sagitta.** It is uncertain
whether the diphthong **ei** in O.F. **lei, rei,** etc., is to be attributed to the diphthongisation of tonic **ę** free or to the combination of the tonic vowel with *jod.*

(For a discussion of the dates of the palatalising processes cf. M.L.
Einf. pp. 125-128.)

Section 4.—PALATALISATION OF **k, g** AND **γ** BEFORE FRONT VOWELS
IN GALLO-ROMAN.

§ 298. In Gallo-Roman, after intervocalic **g** and **k** had passed to **γ**
(§§ 333, 335), there set in a second bout of palatalisation before front
vowels, which now included Latin **a** and **au**, palatalised to **a** and **au**
(§ 182) and **a, e** and **i** in loan-words, Latin, Germanic and Arabic.

k, g and **γ** were all affected, but **γ** only under certain conditions
(cf. below).

§ 299. *Date of Palatalisation.*—The palatalisation of **k** and **g** in words of
Frankish origin shows that this second bout was subsequent to the Frankish invasions; the palatalisation of the intervocalic velar to **j** (and not to **t** or **g**) shows
that it took place after **k** voiced and opened (§ 335); since, however, **k** and **g**

palatalised before **aʉ**, the beginnings of the process must have preceded the level-ling of **aʉ** to **ǫ**, i.e. must have taken place before the end of the eighth century (§ 505).

§ 300. *Palatalisation of* **k** *and* **g** *in initial Position.*—**k** and **g** initial before **a, au, e, i** palatalised to **ʃ** and **ɟ**; **ɟ**, like the Late Latin **ɟ**, moved forward to **dž** (§ 191), and in the thirteenth century to **ž** (§ 194; graphies *j* and *g*); **ʃ**, now following a parallel course, moved forward to **tš** (§ 191), and in the thirteenth century opened to **š** (§ 194; graphy *ch*) :

	carrum, **karrum** ＞ ****ʃarrʉ** ＞ tšar ＞ šar, *char*		
cantare	**kantare** ＞ tšãntęɲ	＞ šãntęr	*chanter*
arca	**arka** ＞ artšę	＞ aršę	*arche*
bucca	**bŭkka** ＞ bǫtšę	＞ bušę	*boche*
carum	**karum** ＞ tšier	＞ šįęr	*chier*
circare	**kirkare** ＞ tsertšier	＞ seršįęr	*cerchier*
causa	**kausa** ＞ tšǫzę	＞ šǫzę	*chose*
***(e)skina*	****(e)skina** ＞ estšinę	＞ ešĩnę	*eschine*
**franca	****franka** ＞ frãntšę	＞ frãnšę	*franche*
ar. *meskin*	****meskinʉ** ＞ mestšin	＞ mešĩn	*meschin*
galbinum	**ga╋binum** ＞ dža╋nę	＞ žaunę	*jalne, jaune*
*gamba	***gamba** ＞ džãmbę	＞ žãnbę	*jambe*
larga	**larga** ＞ lardžę	＞ laržę	*large*
gaudia	***gaudja** ＞ džoįę	＞ žʉęę	*joie*
manducare	****mandugare** ＞ mãndžįęr	＞ mãnžįęr	*mangier*
**gardinum	****gardinʉ** ＞ džardin	＞ žardĩn	*jardin*

§ 301. ✱✱ In Provençal and the northern region **k** and **g** in initial position retained their velar articulation, e.g. *car, kier, cose; gaune, ganbe, gardin*, N. § i.

§ 302. *Palatalisation of* γ *intervocalic.*—If in Gallo-Roman the velar fricative γ stood before **a** and was preceded by any one of the front vowels **i, e, a,** it palatalised to **j**: if a velar vowel preceded, palatalisa-tion was hindered and γ was effaced or labialised (§§ 340-342): jod merged in preceding **i**, combined ordinarily (§ 404) with other preceding vowels in a diphthong :

baca	**baka** ＞ ****baga** ＞ ****baγa** ＞ ****baję** ＞ baię (§ 531)			
mica	**mika** ＞ ****miga** ＞ ****miγa** ＞ ****miję** ＞ mię			
pacare	**pakare** ＞ paiier (§ 531)	*pacas*	**pakas** ＞ paięs (§ 531)	
secare	**sĕkare** ＞ seiier	*sĕcas*	**sĕkas** ＞ sięs (§ 418)	
decanum	**dĕkanum** ＞ deiien	*paganum*	**paganum** ＞ paiien (§ 531)	
ligare	**ligare** ＞ leiier	*ligas*	**ligas** ＞ leięs	

In Latin *caecum* and *graecum*, Gallo-Roman ****tsʼieγʉ, **grʼieγʉ** and in the suffixes -*aticum, -ēticum* (§ 352) γ was effaced as usual before atonic -**ŭ**, but in the

Latin endings -*licum* and -*lucum*, palatalisation of γ appears to have been induced in Gallo-Roman by the preceding un-diphthongised tonic palatal vowels **i** and **a**, and -**īkum** > -**i**, -**ākum** > ****-aγμ** > -**ai**, -**iakum** > ****-ιεγμ** > -**i** (§ 415): **amicum** > **āmi**, **spicum** > **espi**, **Tornacum** > **Tornai**, **Sabiniacum** > **Saviɲi**, *Savigni*, cf. M.L. *Zts. R. Ph.*, xxxix, 398.

In O.F. *çaienz, laienz, oïl*, locutions formed in Gallo-Roman from *ecce hac intus, illac intus, hoc ille*, the velar consonant, which had been opened to χ while still final of the word (§ 357), was also palatalised to **ɉ** which merged in -**i** and combined in a diphthong with **a**.

✳✳ In the south-eastern, south-central and south-western region γ was palatalised to **ɉ** when it stood between ****au** and ****a** and thus **pauca** > **pǫię** and ***auca** > **ǫię** (S.C. § ix, S.W. § 5).

Section 5.—PALATALISATION OF VELARS AND DENTALS BY JOD.

§ 303. The group *consonant + jod* was formed in Late Latin by the consonantalisation of unstressed **e** and **i** in hiatus before a vowel (§ 220). In the course of Late Latin and Early Romance all preceding *lingual* consonants in such groups, whether dental or velar, were palatalised wholly or partially.

Palatalisation of **t, d, g, k** and probably also of **l** and **n** began in Late Latin, the partial palatalisation of **s, z, r** followed in early Gallo-Roman. The result was often modified when the group stood in intervocalic or prae-consonantal position.

§ 304. *Date of Palatalisation.*—Palatalisation appears to have begun with the groups **tɉ** and **dɉ** for the pronunciation **tsɉ** is attested for **tɉ** in the fourth century by the remark of the grammarian, Papirius: *iustitia cum scribitur, tertia syllaba sic sonat quasi constet ex tribus litteris t, z, i;* it may have begun considerably earlier, (cf. M.L. *Einf.* § 143). The palatalisation of **dɉ** was probably contemporaneous with that of **tɉ** (*Einf.* § 144), that of **kɉ** and **gɉ** began a little later (*Einf.* §§ 142-143). The palatalisation of **ssɉ** is indicated by the spelling *Sexsionas* for *Sessionas* (*Suessionis*) in Gregory of Tours (Haag, § 53).

§ 305. *Labials* juxtaposed to *jod* were ordinarily unaffected by palatalisation, but *jod*, being in initial position, closed and shifted to **dž** (**tš** after a breathed labial, § 203) and the resultant groups **bdž** and **ptš** simplified, § 373 :

> **rŭbĕum** > ***rǫbjμ** > ****rǫbdžę** > **rǫdžę** *roge*
> ***cavea kaβja** > **kadžę** *cage* **sapiam** > ***sapja** > ****saptšę** > **satšę** *sache*
> **sīmium** > ***sɪmjμ** > **sindžę** *singe* **sŏmnium** > ***sǫmnjμ** > **sundžę** *songe*
> **commĕātum** > ***kommjatμ** > **kundžieθ** *congiet*

[For the passage of **dž** and **tš** to **ž** and **š** cf. § 194; for the effacement of **w** before **ɉ** cf. § 187 (*c*); for the treatment of *jod* groups in loan-words cf. § 645.]

§ 306. *Palatalisation of Velars.*—**kɉ** in initial and intervocalic position alike was palatalised to **ɉ** and shifted forward to **ts**, which

was opened to s in the thirteenth century (§ 194), graphy *c* when initial or intervocalic, *z* when final of the word.

(i) *Initial :*

arcionem	*arkɪǫne	> *arʃǫne	> artsun > arsūn	*arcon*
*dulcium	*dǫ+kɪɥ	> dǫ+ts	> dus	*dolz, douz*

(ii) *Intervocalic :*

faciam	*fakɪa	> fatsę	> fasę	*face, fasse*
minacia	*męnakɪa	> męnatsę	> męnasę	*menace*
brachium	*brakɪɥ	> brats	> bras	*braz*

[For skɪ cf. § 315 ; for the effacement of s final cf. chap. xvii, sect. 5.]

When **kɪ** was intervocalic the first element appears to have been lengthened and consequently escaped voicing (**kɪ** intervocalic > ʄʄ > tts > ts).

✳✳ In the northern region t͡s and t͡ts (§ 292) shifted to t͡š (graphy *ch*), e.g. *Franche, fache, fach* < *franciam, faciam, facio*, etc. (N. § i).

§ 307. **gɪ.**—(i) **g** *initial* + ɪ palatalised to **ɟ**, which shifted forward to **dž** and was opened to **ž** in the thirteenth century (§ 194), graphy *g* :

gĕorgĭus   ɟorɟęs > džordžęs > žoržęs   *Georges*

(ii) **g** *intervocalic* + **ɪ.**—When **gɪ** was intervocalic it palatalised to **ɟ** which opened to **ɪ** (§ 333), and combined in a diphthong with the preceding vowel :

corrigia *korręgɪa > kǫreię,   *exagium* *esagɪɥ > esai *essai*

§ 308. *Palatalisation of the Plosive Dentals* tɪ *and* dɪ.—The development of both these groups was modified by voicing and opening when they were in intervocalic position.

(i) **tɪ** *initial* > tsɪ > t͡s (§ 292) > ts which opened to s in the thirteenth century (§ 194) :

fortia	*fortɪa	> *fortsɪa > fortsę	> forsę	*force*
factionem	*faktɪǫne	> fatsun	> fasūn	*facon*
suspectionem	*sǫspektɪǫne	> sǫspętsun	> supęsūn	*sospecon*
*sortiarium	*sortɪarɪɥ	> sortsier (cf. § 26)	> sorsɪer	*sorcier*

(ii) **tɪ** *intervocalic* > tsɪ > t͡s > d͡z > ɪz, (ɪs when *final*) :

rationem *ratsɪǫne > raizun   *potionem* *potsɪǫne > poizun
pretiare *prętsɪare > preizier   *pretiat* *prętsɪat > prizę (§ 411)
pretium *prętsɪɥ > pris (§ 411) *palatium* *palatsɪɥ > palais

[For stɪ cf. § 315 ; for ts in loan-words cf. § 640.]

The intervocalic group **t** + **ɪ** and **ʄ** < *intervocalic* **k** + **e** and **i** (§§ 291, 294, 295) appear thus to have developed along lines that were similar but not quite contemporaneous : **t** + **ɪ**, palatalising earlier, reached the stage -ɪz before final unstressed

vowels were effaced, and was consequently unvoiced to -įs (§ 206), but t͡s < k + e and i having only reached the d͡z stage at that period unvoiced to įts (§ 295 (iii)).

In the suffixes -*itia*, -*itium*, under the influence of -*icia*, -*icium*, **tsj** lengthened and became **tts**, whence **ts**, cf. O.F. *perece* **perętsę** < *pigritia*, *chevez* **tšęvęts** < *capitium* : **ts**, become prae-consonantal, opened early to **s**, cf. O.F. *chast*, **tšast** (< **captiet*).

[For a variant explanation cf. M.L. *Gr.* § 157.]

§ 309. (i) **dj** *initial* > **ɟ** > **dž**, which opened to **ž** in the course of the thirteenth century (§ 194) :

diŭrnum	*djǫrnų > *ɟǫrnų > **džǫrn**; **žur** (§ 811)	*jor, jur*
dĕorsum	*djǫsų (§ 359) > **džüs** (§ 749)	*jus*
hŏrdeum	*ǫrdjų > **ǫrdžę** > **ǫržę**	*orge*

(ii) **dj** *intervocalic* > **ɟ**, which opened to **j** (§ 333) and combined with preceding vowels in a diphthong, § 404 :

radium	*radjų > **rai**	*gaudia*	*gaudja > **džǫię**	*joie*
audio	*audjo > **ǫi**	*podium	*pǫdjų > **püi** (§ 411)	

[For early loan-words such as *envire* (< *invidiam*) cf. § 645.]

§ 310. The equivalence of **dj**, **gj** and **j** in some positions led to confusions in Low Latin spelling which occasionally influenced the pronunciation of words taken from written sources, cf. Fredegarius : *Madio* for *Majo*, *Remidium* for *Remigium*, *corridiae* for *corrigii*, *Trogiae*, *Troge* for *Troiae*, *Pompegius*, etc. (Haag, pp. 867, 868), and the loan-word *diaspre* < *diasprum*, a derivative of *jaspis*.

§ 311. **nj**, **nɟ** (< **ndj**), **ŋɟ** (< **ŋg + e, i,** § 290) > **ŋ**.—In intervocalic position **ŋ** persisted, elsewhere it was gradually resolved into **įn** (§ 279 (iv)), or dentalised to **n**, (§ 406) ; graphies *gn, ign, ingn, ing* (§§ 695, 696) :

linea *lįnja > **liŋe** *ligne*, *montanea* *montanja > **mūntãŋę** *montagne*,
teneam *tęnja > **tięŋę** *tiegne*, *verecundia* *βerekųnɟa > **vergüŋę** *vergogne*,
plangit *plaŋɟet > **plãint** *plaint*, *balneos *banjos > **bãints** *bainz*,
lŏnge *lǫŋɟe > **luŋ** (§ 426) > **luįŋ** > **lųę(n)** *loing, luign*,
balneum *banjų > **baŋ** > **baįŋ** > **bę̃(n)** *baing, baign*.

§ 312. **lj**, **llj**, **ɫɟ**, **ɫɟ** (§ 293) > **j**; *graphies ill, il*.—When *prae-consonantal* in Early Old French **j** was effaced after **i**, velarised and vocalised to **ų** elsewhere (§§ 384-388) :

filia	*filja > **fiɫę**	*fille*	*meliorem*	*męljǫre > **meĵeur**	*meilleur*
palea	*palja > **paɫę**	*paille*	*bulliam*	*bǫllja > **bǫɫę**	*boille*
allium	*alljų > **aj**	*ail*	*tripalium	*trępaljų > **travaj**	*travail*
filius	*filjųs > **fiɫts**	*filz*	*tripalios	*trępaljos > **travauts**	*travauz*

§ 313. **rj** palatalised to **ř**, which was early resolved into **įr** (§ 279) :

area	*arja > **ařa > **airę**	*feria*	**fęrja > **feřa > **feirę**
corium	*kǫrjų > **küir** (§ 411)	*cuir*	*morio *mǫrjo > **müir**

Cf. also O.F. *repairier* < *repatriare*, *mairrien* < *materiamen*, *uistre* < *ŏstrea*, *cuivre* < **cŏprium*. [For the suffix -**arium** cf. § 26.]

§ 314. zɪ (< s *intervocalic* + ɪ) palatalised to ẑ which was early resolved into ɪz (§ 279); graphy *is* :

mansionem *masɪǫ́ne > **maizun** *maison*   *nausea* *naʋsɪa > nǫizę̀ *noise.*

§ 315. sɪ (< ss intervocalic + ɪ), sʃ (< sk + ɪ, § 306, sk + e, i, § 291), sʃs (< st + ɪ, § 308), palatalised to ŝ (ŝs), which was early resolved into ɪs (§ 279): graphy *iss*, *is* when final or prae-consonantal :

messionem *messɪǫne > **meisun** *meisson*   *angustia* *aɴgǫstɪa > ãngoisę̀
piscionem *pęsʃǫne > **peisun** *peisson*   *ūstium ʋstɪʋ > üis
nascentem *nasʃente > **nais(ãnt)** *naissant*

✱✱ In the western region ŝ and ẑ in final position were depalatalised to s after ü, cf. **üs** < *ūstium*, **pertüs** < *pertūsium* (cf. W. § x).
✱✱ In the north-eastern and eastern region palatalised ŝ and ẑ remained longer than elsewhere and passed to š and ž (cf. N. § xvi).

Section 6.—PALATALISATION IN THE INTERVOCALIC GROUPS PALATAL + d, t, s.

§ 316. (1) *Palatal* + d and t.—When d and t were brought into contact with a preceding palatal consonant by the effacement of an un-stressed vowel in Gallo-Roman, they palatalised to đ and t̂, which were resolved into ɪd and ɪt (cf. § 279); d becoming final unvoiced to t (§ 206) :

frigidam   *freɪ(ę)da > **freidę̀**   *frigidum*   *freɪ(ę)dʋ̧ > **freit**
medietatem   *mejętate   > **meitie**   *adjutare*   **aɪ(u)dare > **aidier**
*cūgitare   *kʋjętare   > **küidier**   *pietatem*   **piɪtate > **pitie**
cf. *amicitatem *amiʃetate > **amiʃstate > **ãmistie**

§ 317. A similar incomplete and ephemeral palatalisation of n to ñ and of r to r̂ was also occasionally produced in Gallo-Roman, for example in **masɪ(o)nata (< *mansionata), whence O.F. **maiznieðę̀** *maisniede*, **ępęɪ(o)rare ĕm-**peirier**. In these words, as in the majority of those above, it is the form taken by the tonic a free that attests the existence of an ephemeral palatalisation, cf. § 414.

§ 318. (2) *Palatal* + s *final*.—s *final*, when brought into contact with ɪ and ɳ by the effacement of an unstressed final vowel in Gallo-Roman was shifted to ts (graphy z) : ts > s in the thirteenth century (§ 194) :

filius > **fiɪ(ę)s > **fiɪts** *filz*   *trepalɪos > **travaɪ(ę)s > **travaɪts** *travailz*
plaɴgis > **plaɳ(e)s > **plãints** *plainz*   *baɴɪos > **baɳ(e)s > **bãints** *bainz*

Section 7.—PALATALISATION IN THE INTERVOCALIC GROUPS VELAR + DENTAL.

§ 319. In the intervocalic groups of *velar* + *dental* (ɬ + dental excepted) the palatalisation of both elements took place in Gallo-Roman

by mutual assimilation.   The velar consonants were drawn forward into a palatal position by the influence of the juxtaposed dentals and in their turn palatalised the dentals : thus, for example, ɒn > ŋn > ŋ.

The palatalisation of dental l and n was complete and absorbed the palatalising consonant; that of r, d, t, s was partial and ephemeral, but sufficiently marked to modify the development of *following* a *tonic free* (§ 414).   These palatalisations all took place after the *plosive* velars had become *fricative*, e.g. after kr had become γr, kt, χt (§§ 359, 362), and consequently it was the fricative palatal (ȷ) that was formed out of them, remained when not absorbed and was subsequently merged in preceding i, combined with other preceding vowels in a diphthong.

✳✳ In the south-western region the group +t palatalised to ɟ t, which in that region was usually simplified to ȷt (§ 391, S.W. § vii): *volutulare* **ßo+t(ṳ)lare > voɟtrer > voitrer, cf. *culcita* *ko+ȷĕta > koɟtę > koitę.

§ 320.   ɒs and ɒt (< ɒks, ɒkt, § 359) > ŋs, ŋt > ȷns, ȷnt :

planxi	*plaɒsi > **plaŋŝi > plāins	*planctum*	*plaɒtṳ > plāint
finxi	*feɒsi > fēins	*finctum*	*feɒtṳ > fēint

§ 321.   ɒn (*gn*) > ŋ.—The intervocalic group ɒn (written *gn*, § 158), palatalised to ŋ, which persisted when intervocalic, elsewhere was gradually resolved into ȷn (§§ 279, 406) :

agnellum *aɒnęllṳ>aŋęl *agnel*, *insignare* ęnsęɒnare>ānsēiŋier *enseignier dignitatem* *dęɒnętate>dēintie *deintie*, *insignet* ęnsęɒnęt>ānsēint *enseint pugnos* *pṳɒnos > puints *poinz*, *pugnum* pṳɒnṳ > puȷŋ *poing* (406)

cognoscere *kǫnǫsȷere (Juret, p. 112), O.F. *conoistre*, appears to have been influenced by *nosco* nǫsko.

§ 322.   k'l and g'l > ȷ: graphies *il*, *ill*, cf. §§ 695, 696 :

pariculum	*paręklṳ > paręȷ *pareil*,	*oculum* *ǫklṳ > ueȷ *ueil*
genuculum	*dęnǫklṳ > džęnǫȷ *genoil*,	*vetulum* *ßęklṳ (§ 360), > vieȷ *vieil*
vigilare	*ßęȷelare > vęȷier *veillier*,	*regula* *ręgla > ręȷę *reille*

[For the vocalisation of *prae-consonantal* ȷ cf. §§ 383-389; for k'l and g'l in loan-words cf. § 641.]

§ 323.   kr and gr > γr (§ 362) > ȷr̂ > ȷr :

lacryma *lakrĕma > lairmę	*sacramentum* *sakramentṳ > sairęmēnt
fragrare > flairier	*lĕgere* > lirę *nigrum* > neir

In words in which Late Latin γr (< gr) was pretonic after e, γ appears to have been effaced before palatalisation set in, cf. O.F. *perece* peretsę < *pigritia*, pęlęrin < **pererin < **peregrinum**.

§ 324. **kt** > χt (§§ 130, 359) > jî̯t > i̯t.

In the Latin group **kt** (*ct*) **k** was differentiated to χ which palatalised to ç (> i̯) and occasioned a partial and temporary palatalisation of **t** : *tractare* **traktare** > *** tra**χ**tare > **** tra**i̯**t̂are > traitier, *** adfa**k**tare > afaitier, fa**k**tum > fait, te̜**k**tum > teit, pla**k**i̯tum > plait (§ 296).

[For **kt** in learned loan-words cf. §§ 650, 655, 745.]

In Italy **kt** was assimilated to **tt** and this pronunciation appears to have had some vogue in Gaul where **flectikare** > fletŝier *flechier* (< **flettekare*) and **jectare* appears in double form, cf. Old French *geitier (jitier)* —(il) *gite (giete,* S.W. § 1), *jeter* —(il) *jete* (cf. also *Atlas Lg.* 36 and 718).

✱✱ [For the south-western effacement of final **t** cf. S.W. § viii.]

§ 325. *Early Gallo-Roman* χs (< ks, § 359) > jŝ > i̯s.

The Early Gallo-Roman group **χs** included :—

(i) Latin **ks** (*x*), e.g. *axem* **aksem** (cf. § 359).

(ii) Gallo-Roman **ks** derived by metathesis from **sk** before **u** and **o**, e.g. ******kre̜kso** < kre̜sko *cresco* (cf. G.G. § 255) :

laxare **laksare** > **laχsare > ***lajŝare > laisier *laissier*	
exire **eksire** > eisir *eissir,*	*exit* **e̜ksit** > ist (§§ 410, 411)
texere **te̜kse̜re** > tistre̜,	*coxa* **ko̜ksa** > küise̜ *cuisse*
axem **aksem** > ais,	*cresco* ******kre̜kso** > kreis *creis*

[For *x* in learned loan-words cf. §§ 650, 655.]

✱✱ In the north-eastern and eastern region ŝ persisted longer than elsewhere and passed to š and ž (N. § xvi).

§ 326. *Later Gallo-Roman* **ks** > s.

When the final group **ks** was formed in Later Gallo-Roman by the effacement of unstressed final vowels, there was no palatalisation and **k** was effaced :

coccus **ko̜kkus** > ko̜ks > kos *cos, cocs*	**bo̜rgos* > bo̜rks > burs *bourgs*
saccos **sakkos** > saks > sas, *sacs*	*siccos* **sïkkos** > se̜ks > se̜s *secs*

[For Late Middle French pronunciation of *x* cf. §§ 740-746.]

Section 8. DEVELOPMENT OF LATIN *qu* (**ku̯**) INTERVOCALIC.

[For Late Latin **kw** intervocalic < k + *consonantalised* ŭ and ŏ (§ 220), cf. § 379; for *qu* and *gu* initial cf. § 192.]

§ 327. In words in which Latin intervocalic *qu* was preserved in Late Latin (cf. § 186), the velar consonant in the course of Gallo-Roman was opened and palatalised to i̯ after the tonic front vowels **i, e, a** ; elsewhere it was assimilated to the labial element.

§ 328. When the velar element was *palatalised*, u̯ was ordinarily retained when *prae-consonantal* or *final* and combined in a diphthong with the preceding vowel ; when *intervocalic* or before **r** it consonantalised ordinarily to **w** (especially in the western region), and shifted to **v**. The tonic vowel, if e̜, was broken to **ie** and raised by *jod* to **i** (cf. §§ 410, 411) :

antiqua   ɑntikʉɑ > **antiʉɑ > āntivę, āntiuę (> āntieuę, § 123).
antiquum   ɑntikʉum > *ɑntikʉ > ānti (§ 187 (*b*)).
ēqua   ĕkʉɑ > **iejʉę > ivę.
*sequam   sękʉɑ > **siejʉę > sivę, siuę.
*sequere   sękʉere > **siejwrę > siurę or sivrę (by contamination *suivre*).
*sequit   sękʉet > **siejʉet > siut (by metathesis süit).
*sequo   sękʉo > sieu > siu (by metathesis *sui*).
**lĕgua (by metathesis from **leuga) > liwę > livę, liuę.

✳✳ In the northern and eastern region the velar element was not palatalised and consequently **sequere* sękʉere > seure or sieure; **sequit* sękʉet > seut or sieut (N.E. § xii).

✳✳ In the south-western region, where local variants of ę + ȷ developed (S.W. § i), other forms of -ękʉ- are found, e.g. **sequit* gave *seit, siet, set, seut* and *sieut*, cf. *St. Martin*, 1994, *seit (sapit)* : *seit (*sequit)*; Ber. 2155 *aqeut : porseut*.

§ 329.   When kʉ was preceded by a secondary stressed vowel, the velar element was voiced and assimilated to ʉ; the strengthened labial sound that resulted sometimes rounded preceding ę to ǫ and merged in the resultant labial vowel (§ 484):

sequenter   sękʉenter > **sęwentrę > soventrę, soentrę
aequalem   ękʉɑle > **ęwale > owęl, oęl

The more usual forms *iwel, iuel* are unexplained; the loan-word *egal* may be of southern French origin and *igal* arose from its contamination with *iwel, ingal* from the influence of the prefix *in* on *igal*.

The weak forms of **sequere* (*sevant, seveie*, etc.) were early replaced by forms made cn the model of the strong radical : siv-, siu-, sui-, suiv-.

§ 330.   *Development of aqua* akʉɑ.—In accordance with the ordinary development of kʉ intervocalic, *aqua* **axʉɑ (<ɑkʉɑ) passed to aiʉe which levelled to ęuę, ęwę in the western region in the eleventh century (§ 533, cf. English *ewer*).

In the central region ę + ʉ (like ę + ʉ, in bęaʉs < bę+s, § 388) developed a low vocalic glide and passed to ᶦęaʉę, ᶦeawę, which followed along the lines of the triphthong ęau and passed through ęᶦauę to ęᶦǫ (xvi), and ǫ (xvii); (for early effacement of ę final cf. § 271).

✳✳ Local variants of *aqua*.—In the northern region ᶦęaʉę, like the triphthong ᶦęaʉ in bᶦęaus, etc., was differentiated to iauę, a form still used in vulgar Parisian in the sixteenth century, N. § viii.

In the western region ęwę passed to ęvę (§ 192, cf. *evier*) : *St. Martin, eve : desve* 83; Rtbf. *eve : leve* (< *lavat*) *Compl. d'Outre Mer* 71/2.

In the east the velar element was not palatalised but assimilated to the following labial, i.e. *aqua* *axʉɑ > awę, N.E. § xii.

A form of a different type *aigue* (*egue*) is found in Old French poems of very varied provenance (e.g. *Chanson de Willelme*, cxli, ccii, xix; *Alexis*, MS. L. *egua* 54 b; Estienne de Fougieres, *aigue* 1113, *eigue* 493; *Raoul de Cambrai*, and other northern and eastern texts). Like the ordinary southern French form (cf. *Aigues-Mortes*) *aigue* may be derived from a widely attested Late Latin form *acqua* with lengthened velar consonant, but its sporadic use in O.F., combined with its complete disappearance from the Modern French patois, make it probable that it was in the north of Gaul a loan-word from the south or from Latin (Hürlimann: *Die Entwickelung von* aqua *im Romanischen*. Diss. Zürich, 1903).

CHAPTER VII.

VOICING AND OPENING OF SINGLE BREATHED AND PLOSIVE CONSONANTS IN VOCALIC ENVIRONMENT.

Section 1.—INTRODUCTORY.

§ 331. Vowels are all voiced and open, and in the early period of the language their characteristics exercised a marked influence on the pronunciation of single breathed and plosive consonants that stood either between vowels or ended a word after a vowel. In the inter-vocalic position all single *breathed* consonants were *voiced*, in both positions all single *plosives* became *fricative* (cf. §§ 134, 135).

[For the closely similar development of these consonants in the interior of words before r, cf. § 372.]

Section 2.—VOICING AND OPENING OF SINGLE BREATHED AND PLOSIVE CONSONANTS IN INTERVOCALIC POSITION.

§ 332. The gradual accommodation of single breathed and plosive consonants to their vocalic environment began in Late Latin with the opening of intervocalic **b**. In Gaul the process gained ground rapidly (possibly under Celtic influence, § 9), and in the course of Gallo-Roman all single *plosive* consonants in this position became *fricative*, all single *breathed* consonants were *voiced* and subsequently the voiced fricative consonants thus developed were often either effaced or turned into semi-vowels.

As a result of these changes the only *single plosive* consonants in use in intervocalic position in traditional words in French are those derived from lengthened consonants (*gaber, chape, tote*) or Gallo-Roman intervocalic groups (*rote* (< *rupta*), *tiede*), and the only *single breathed fricative* consonants in use in this position are those derived from lengthened consonants, Gallo-Roman intervocalic groups or O.F. affricates (*passer, chasser, façon, hache*).

§ 333. (i) *Opening of Latin Voiced Plosives.*

Latin **b** > L.L. *β* :

faba > *fa*β*a,   trabem > *tra*β*e,   tabonem > *ta*β*ǫne

Late Latin **ǧ** (< **g** + **e, i, gj, dj,** §§ 297, 307) > L.L. **ȷ** :

*paǧęse < pagensem > *pajęse

Latin g (+ a, o, u) > Early G.R. γ :

> rūga > **rųγa, nĕgāre > **nęγāre

Latin d > G.R. ð :

> audire > **auðire, nūda > **nųða

§ 334. (ii) *Voicing of Breathed Fricatives and Affricates.*
Latin s > G.R. z :

> risum > **rizų, pausare > **pauzare

Early Gallo-Roman ȶs (< k + e, i (§ 291) and tj (§ 308)) > d͡z :

> **diȶsente (< dikentem) > **di͡dzentę (O.F. *disant*)

Latin f > G.R. v :

> *malefatiŭs > Early Old French ma‡vais

§ 335. (iii) *Voicing and Opening of Latin Breathed Plosives.*
Late Latin k (+ a, o, u) > G.R. g > G.R. γ :

> baca > **baga > **baγa, securum > **segųrų > **seγųrų

Late Latin p > G.R. b > G.R. β :

> ripa > **riba > **riβa, saponem > **sabone > **saβonę

Late Latin t > G.R. d > G.R. ð :

> fata > **fada > fęðę, portata > portada > portęðę

[For the relation between the voicing of intervocalic consonants and the slurring of unstressed vowels, cf. §§ 348-354.]

§ 336. *Date of Voicing.*—The voicing of the plosives appears to have begun in the fifth century, k being first affected; it became general in Gaul before the end of the sixth century, cf. g for k, Greg. *negatum, negari*; Fred. *negat, iogundus, pagandum, mediogrebus* (Haag, § 39); b for p, *coberturio* (cent. vi, Nyrop, § 371), Greg. *lebrosus, crepras* for *crebras* (B. p. 160), Fred. *occubauit, cubidus* (Haag, § 40); v for f, Fred. *pontivecem, aedevecationem* (Haag, § 46); d for t, Fred. *Adaulfus* for *Ataulphus, idemque* (Haag, § 41; cf. also GG. § 256).

Date of Opening.—The early opening of intervocalic b to β is indicated by the confusion of the symbols *b* and *u* in inscriptions, *e.g. iuuente* for *iubente* (second century, cf. GG. § 318 and § 186). The fricative pronunciation ð (for d < t) is attested by the graphy *dh* in the *Oaths of Strasbourg* and by the A.N. graphy *th* (§ 347). The relatively early opening of g is indicated by the forms with effaced velars cited in § 341.

Section 3.—DEVELOPMENT OF SINGLE VOICED FRICATIVE CONSONANTS
IN LATER GALLO-ROMAN AND EARLY OLD FRENCH.

§ 337. The voiced fricative consonants, β, ð, z, j, γ, were all unstable except z and in the course of Period I either shifted their point of articulation or opened further and became semi-vocalic or were effaced. In this way the voiced fricative sounds β, ð, j, γ, disappeared out of the

sound-system, β, ð and γ permanently, ʒ until the sound was brought back by the consonantalisation of i in Later Old French (§§ 241, 511).

All were unvoiced if brought into final position by the slurring of final unstressed vowels (§ 206).

[For Early O.F. w cf. § 192.]

§ 338. z.   The voiced dental z persisted ordinarily when it remained intervocalic, unvoiced to s when made final:

pausare > **pauzare > pozer *poser*	*pesare > **pezare > pezer *peser*
*nasu > **nazu > nes	*risu > ** rizu > ris

If made prae-consonantal by the slurring of unstressed vowels z was gradually effaced (§ 377).

[For the effacement of s *final* in Middle French cf. chap. xvi, sect. 4; for loss of s in s- perfect forms cf. § 1019.]

§ 339. ʒ.   Gallo-Roman ʒ gradually opened to į which merged in preceding i, combined with other preceding vowels in a diphthong:—

Sources of ʒ *intervocalic:*

(1) Classical Latin ʒ intervocalic, e.g. **majum.**

(2) Late Latin ʒ intervocalic < (i) earlier dʒ, gʒ intervocalic (§§ 307, 309); (ii) g + e, i preceded by ct. a (§ 297), e.g. raʒu (<radium), flaʒęllu.

(3) Gallo-Roman ʒ intervocalic < Gallo-Roman γ palatalised (§ 302), e.g. **baʒa (<**baγa < baka *baca*), **nejare (< *neʒare < nĕgare):

*maʒu > mai	*raʒu > rai	*flaʒęllu > flaieł
*neʒare > **nejare > neiier	**baʒa > baię	**mija > mię

The opening of G.R. *intervocalic* ʒ and of G.R. ʒ after a *final* appears to have been very generally retarded, cf. §§ 404, 530, 531.

§ 340. *Development of Gallo-Roman* γ *and* β.—Gallo-Roman γ and β were both strongly influenced by the point of articulation of the vowels in their vicinity, especially those following them: both consonants tended to open further and disappear before homophonous vowels, γ before *velar* vowels, β before *labial* vowels.

It must always be borne in mind that the vowel a was *velar* in Latin and only became *palatal* in the course of Gallo-Roman (§ 182).

[For the palatalisation of γ cf. § 302.]

§ 341. *Early Gallo-Roman* γ (< Latin intervocalic g + o, u, a, au) was ordinarily *effaced:*

(i) When it stood before o or u, *tonic* or *atonic*:

augŭstum **aγostu (§ 505) > aost, fagum **faγu > **fou (§ 481), *sarcophăgum* **sarko(făγ)u > sarkueu, jŭgum **joγu > dʒu *jou* (§ 740).

(ii) When it stood between y and ɑ :

rūga > **ruɣa > rüę, sangyisūga > **sangyęsuɣa > sān(k)süę

Between o and ɑ ɣ appears to have been labialised to w which shifted to v, cf.
O.F. dǫvę < dōga, rǫvęr < rŏgare, entervęr < interrŏgare, corvee korvęę
< korrŏgatam.

Effacement of ɣ (< g) preceded the reduction of unstressed final y, cf. the forms
for Rotomagus, Rotomaus (Greg. Tours), Rothomo (Fred.) and O.F. fǫ < faū.

§ 342. *Later Gallo-Roman* ɣ (< Latin k before o, u, ɑ, ɑu) was
effaced :

(i) When it stood before *tonic* o or u :

Saukōna > saǫnę	*cuculla* kŭkŭlla > kǫǫllę, *coole*	
sekūrum > sęür	*tacutu* * takūtu > tęü	

(ii) When it stood before *atonic* u and was preceded by a *velar*
vowel :

paucum pɑukum > pǫu   locum lŏkum > lieu (§ 556)

(iii) When it stood between o, u, ɑu and ɑ *tonic* or *atonic* :

locare lŏkare > lǫęr	*advocatum* ɑdwŏkatum > avǫę
auca ɑuka > ǫę (§ 302)	*lactuca* lɑktūka > laitüę

§ 343. Gallo-Roman β was either effaced or shifted to v: it was
effaced (i) when it was derived from classical Latin intervocalic b and
stood *before* the *labial* vowels u and o or *after* tonic y, (ii) when it
was derived from Latin and Germanic intervocalic p and stood between
diphthongs in y and unstressed final y :

*taβǫne < tabonem > taun   ** deβytu > deüθ *nyβa > nüę
**lǫuβy < lupum > lǫu > leu   ** estrieuβy (G. streup) > estrieu

Under the combined influence of the west French form lu *lou* (§ 230), and the
feminine luvę (§ 489), O.F. leu was replaced in Middle French by lu *loup*, the old
form only surviving in the locution à la queue leu (for le) leu and in place names,
St. Leu, Canteleu, etc.

§ 344. In all other positions β was shifted to v, § 189: v was unvoiced to f, if made final of the word (§ 206) :

*faβa < faba > fęvę	* iβerny < hībĕrnum > ivern	
**riβa < ripa > rivę	**alaβa < ɑlɑpa > a4vę	
*traβe < trabem > tręf	**seiβe < sēpem > seif	
*naβe < nawem > nęf	*breβe < brĕwem > brief	

[For the ending -ęa < -ēbam cf. § 917 ; for aud < ɑpud cf. § 597.]

§ 345. Gallo-Roman β *intervocalic* was derived from :—
(i) Late Latin β *intervocalic* developed from (a) Classical Latin b intervocalic
(§ 333), e.g. *faβa < faba, *taβǫne < *tabōnem, (b) Classical Latin w, when
preserved (§§ 186-188), e.g. *βiβa < wīwa (viva), *βiβy (vivu).
(ii) Late Latin p intervocalic (§ 335), e.g. **riβa < ripa.

The passage of β to ʋ is attested for the later seventh century by the spelling *seues* for *saepes* in the *Form. Andegavenses;* cf. also the spellings of the *Glossary of Reichenau : alaues* < *alapes, cauanna* < *capanna, trauis* < **trabes.*

✹✹ Between *tonic* and *atonic* a Early Gallo-Roman β (< **b**) was velarised to ʋ in the western region, cf. O.F. **portque** < **portabam** (§ 483).

§ 346. ð. The voiced fricative ð was unvoiced to θ when made final of the word and both ð and θ were effaced in the course of Early Old French, at latest by the middle of the twelfth century :

audire > ǫðir > ǫir		nūda > nüðę > nüę
**vida < wīta > viðę > vię		**finida < finīta > finiðę > finię
**feiðę < fidem > feiθ > foi		**finidę < finītum > finiθ > fini

Attesting Rhymes. Best. vie : Marie, mue : manjue, ni (nidum) : altresi, fei : lei, duné : De, (Intr. p. lvii).

§ 347. In intervocalic position between homophonous vowels ð began to be effaced in eastern and north-eastern French in the late ninth century, cf. the spellings in the Cluny charters, *Ermendrau* 878, *Freelaus* for *Fredelaus* 893, *Raulfo* 926, *Louuici* 943 ; *Tiericus* for *Tiudericus* appears in 961 (cf. Lot, *Rom.* XXX, 480). In final position in this region θ began to be effaced before homophonous consonants in the same period, cf. *Eulalia : perdesse sa* 17, *arde tost* 19, but in the west and in Anglo-Norman the process was later. The complete absence of elision of the unstressed termination -ęθ in the *Alexis* and the continued use of the analogical forms *sed* **seð**, *qued* **keð**, *ned* **neð** (§ 608), in this poem, indicate the maintenance of final θ and ð in Normandy in the middle of the eleventh century, and this is corroborated by the use : (*a*) of the graphy *th* (borrowed from English scribes), in the oldest A.N. MS. of the *Alexis,* e.g. *vithe* 69, *mustrethe* 71, *espethe* 72, and (*b*) of the symbol ð in French names in the Laud MS. of the A.S. *Chronicle,* e.g. *Caðun* (modern *Caen* < ***Cadomum** < *Catomagum*), *Roðem* (1124), *Loðewis* (cf. also Nyrop, I, § 383).

Section 4.—RELATION OF THE VOICING, OPENING AND EFFACEMENT OF INTERVOCALIC CONSONANTS TO THE SLURRING OF UNSTRESSED VOWELS.

§ 348. It is by no means easy to determine in detail the relation between the development of intervocalic consonants and the slurring of unstressed vowels : both processes were more or less contemporaneous and both long drawn out; local variations and analogical formations are frequent and the consonants brought into juxtaposition often exercise assimilative influence on each other. [For the influences determining the fall of unstressed vowels cf. §§ 248-264.]

§ 349. (i) *Voicing and Effacement of Intertonic Vowels.*—k normally voiced to g *before* intertonic vowels were slurred, cf. O.F. *mangier* **măndžier** < ****mandugare** < **mandukare**, *delgie* **dẹɫdžie** < **delikatum**.

Weak verb forms with the breath consonant **tš**, such as *chevauchier*, *colchier*, *esrachier* < *exradicare* (> *arachier*, § 496) are formed on the model of the strong forms: *chevauche* > (***ka'βall(ĕ)ka**), *colche*, etc.

§ 350. **t** normally voiced to **d** *after* intertonic vowels were slurred, cf. O.F. **buntę** < **bonitatem**, **ēnfertę** < **infĭrmĭtatem**, *cherte* **tšertę** < **karĭtatem**, **lointāin** < **loⁿgĭtanum**. If **t** was brought into contact with preceding **ɟ**, **b** or **β** it voiced ordinarily to **d**, cf. O.F. **aidier** < ****ajdare** < **adjutare**, *cuidier* **küidier**, **sọdāin** (< **sŭbĭtānŭm**), **bundir** (< ***bombĭtīre**); O.F. **dọtęr** and **sọtāin** were influenced by **dọtę** (< **dŭbĭto**, etc.) and **sọtę** (**sŭbĭtŭm**).

§ 351. (ii) *Voicing and Effacement of Unstressed Penultimate.*— **'-ĭkem.** In the termination **'-icem** the unstressed penultimate vowel was ordinarily effaced before the breath affricate **ȶs** (< **k + e**, § 291) was voiced to **dz**, cf. O.F. *polce* **pọɫtsę** (< **pŏllĭkem**), *ronce*, *Joce* (< *Jodoci*). In the numerals *onze* (**undzę**), *quatorze*, *quinze* voicing was due to the assimilative influence of the preceding voiced consonantal *group*, and *doze* (**dọdzę**), *treze*, *seze* followed suit.

§ 352. **'-ĭkum, '-ĭka.**—The development of the suffixes **'-ĭcum**, **'ĭca** differed because in words ending in **'-ĭka** the fall of the unstressed penultimate vowel, being accelerated by the sonority of the vowel **a**, occurred *before* **k** intervocalic was voiced, cf. O.F. *manche* **măntšę** < **manika**, *basoche* **bazọtšę** < ***bazęɫka** (< *basilǐca*), *diemanche* **diẹmăntšę** < ***dia *domenika**, *perche* **pertšę** < **pertika**, *pesche* **pestšę** < ***pesseka** < **persika**, *chevalche* **tševaɫtše** < ***kaβallĕkat**, *masche* **mastše** < **mastikat**, *venche* **vēntše** < **windĭkat**, *vindicat*.

In the ending **'-ĭkµm (-'atĭkŭm, -'ētĭkŭm)**, **k** voiced, opened and fell and the ante-penultimate vowel (**ę** < **ĭ**) brought thus into hiatus with the following final vowel consonantalised to *jod*, which being in initial position closed to **dž** (§ 203); thus **-atikum** > ****-ateɣµ** > ****-adę(ɣ)µ** > ****-adję** > **adžę** *-age*, **-ētikum** > **-ędžę** *-ege*, cf. O.F. *eage* **ęadžę** < ***aetaticum**, *fromage* **frọmadžę** < ***formaticum**, etc., *erege* **ęrędžę** < ***haereticum**. Divergent forms are sometimes dialectal, e.g. *basoge*, *grange* (south-western, cf. §§ 223, 259, S.W. § ix), sometimes due to the assimilative influence of the preceding consonant, cf. *porche* **portšę** < **portikum**, *piege* **piedžę** < **pĕdika**, or to the longer maintenance of the unstressed penultimate as the supporting vowel of a consonantal group, cf. *forge* **fọrdžę** < ***faβręga** < **fabrika**.

§ 353. ¹-ĭtum, ¹-ĭtem, ¹-ĭdum, ¹-ĭtɑ.—In the development of the words in ¹-item, ¹-itum, ¹-idum, as well as in those in ¹-itɑ, the unstressed penultimate vowel, if not effaced in Late Latin (§ 262), was normally effaced before t was voiced or d opened to ᵭ, cf. O.F. tertrę < *termitem, lintę < līmitem, sadę < sapidum, tiedę < tĕpidum, dętę < dēbitɑ, huntę < *haunitɑ, jate džatę < *gɑβĕtɑ. In O.F. boistę (< bŭxĭdɑ), flaistrę (< flaccidum) and moistę (< muccidum) d was unvoiced under the influence of the preceding consonants; in malade (< male habitum) and cude (< cubitum), t appears to have been voiced under the influence of preceding b (β), but cute is also frequent; jade for iate is presumably south-western (§ 261, S.W. § ix).

[For eastern and north-eastern development cf. N.E. § v; for loan-words cf. chap. xviii.]

§ 354. ¹-ătem, ¹-ădem, ¹-ăpem.—Penultimate a being more persistent than the other vowels, the development of the intervocalic consonants following it was carried some way before it was effaced. Thus dentals opened to ᵭ and fell, ʦ voiced to ᵭz and p became v, c.f. O.F. anę < **anęᵭę < ¹anătem, lampe < ¹lămpădɑ, sānvę < ¹sinăpi, aᵻvę < ¹alăpɑ. The loan-words sene (< *sęnǫdu, *synodum), pale (< pallidum), pieuvre (< polypum) show a like development [§ 640 (6)].

[Cf. Gierach, "Synkope und Lautabstufung," Beiheft, Z.R.Ph. XXIX; Gerhard, "Synkope des Pänultimavokals," Beiheft, Z.R.Ph. LV; Seifert, E., Zur Entwicklung der Proparoxytona auf ¹-ite, ¹-ita, ¹-itu im Galloromanischen.]

Section 5.—Opening of d, t, k in Unsupported Final Position.

§ 355. In Later Gallo-Roman d, t, k *final* of the word remained plosive when supported (i.e. preceded by a consonant), but became fricative when preceded by a vowel *at that period*.

§ 356. *Old French* t.—t final of the word was *supported* in Later Gallo-Roman and consequently remained unchanged in Old French when derived from :—

(i) Latin supported t, e.g. in *sunt, vadunt* and in the verb endings *-ant, -ent, -unt*, cf. O.F. sūnt, vūnt, portęnt < portɑnt and portent, porteręnt, portasęnt *portassent*, etc.

(ii) Latin final t preceded by unstressed e or i after a consonant, for the slurring of these vowels brought final t into supported position in Later Gallo-Roman, cf. O.F. tient < tĕnet, muert < *mǫręt, deit < **deift < dēbet, sęt < **sęft < sapit, kriet < **krieft < krĕpet, apęᵻt < ɑppĕllet, vit < wīdit *vidit*, ǫut < **awwet < hɑbŭit (§ 1025), pǫut < **pǫwwęt < pǫtŭit.

Old French θ.—In all other words and terminations t and d final were

opened to θ, cf. O.F. *ad* **aθ** < **ad**, *od* **οθ** < ****aud** < **αpud** (§ 597) ; *ad*
aθ < ***at** < **habet** (§ 953), **portęraθ** < ****portarat**, **portęθ** < **portαt**, **beivęθ**
> **bibαt**, **oięθ** < **audiαt**, **portaθ** < ***portαt** < **portαwit**, **sentiθ** < ***sentīt** <
sentīit, **mǫrüθ** < ****morǫt**, **ēntręθ** < **intret**.

It may thus be said that **d** and **t** final opened to **θ** when preceded
in *Late* Latin by (i) the tonic vowel, (ii) atonic **α**, (iii) atonic **e, i, o, u**
following a group of consonants needing a supporting vowel.

[For the subsequent effacement of **θ** cf. § 346, of -**t** cf. chap. xvii,
sect. 5.]

✱✱ In the northern region **t** final persisted after tonic vowels, cf. N. § xv ; for
the effacement of **t** *final* in *plai, vui*, etc., cf. S.W. § viii.

§ 357. **k** (*c*) *final* > χ.—Latin unsupported final **k** opened to χ,
which was effaced in words used unstressed in the sentence, cf. O.F.
ca **tsa** < ***eccehac**, *co* **tso** < ***eccehoc**, *la* < **illac**, **nę** < **nec ;** in the words
which had stressed position in the sentence χ closed again to **k** after
velar vowels but palatalised to ɹ after **a** and **i** (cf. § 286), cf. O.F. *avuec* <
ab hoc, poruec < *pro hoc, fai* < *fac, cai* **tsai** < *eccehac* (*stressed*) and **di** < *dic*,
si < *sic* with ɹ merged in **i**.

CHAPTER VIII.

REDUCTION OF LENGTHENED CONSONANTS AND INTERVOCALIC CONSONANTAL GROUPS.

[For the treatment of consonantal groups consisting of *consonant* + *jod*, *jod* + *consonant*, *velar* + *dental* and Latin **kụ** *qu*, cf. chap. vi.]

Section 1.—LATE LATIN.

§ 358. In Classical Latin consonantal groups had already been greatly simplified (cf. the forms *sedecim* < *segzdecim*, *tostus* < *torstus*, *tortus* < *torctus*, etc., Juret, pp. 190, 191), and the tendency continued in Late Latin and French. In Late Latin intervocalic groups were simplified by assimilative processes or sound substitution and the pronunciation of some of the initial groups was facilitated by glide developments.

§ 359. *Assimilation.*—The more usual type of reduction of intervocalic groups in Late Latin was by the assimilation of the weaker first consonant to the dominant second (§§ 131, 209), but *voiced* consonants standing first of an intervocalic group were sometimes partially or wholly accommodated to vowel position, plosives being opened and voiced fricatives vocalised. In the group **kt** *ct*, possibly under Celtic influence (§ 9), the first consonant was differentiated from the second, i.e. **kt** > χt, *factum* **faktum** > *faχtụ*.

ns was early assimilated to **s**, with compensatory vowel-lengthening, e.g. **mensem** > *mēse*, **pensare** > *pēsare*, cf. *App. Pr.* ansa non asa, *mensa* non *mesa*.

The spelling *ns* came to be used simply to indicate the length of the preceding vowel or the pronunciation **s** (not **z**), cf. *App. Pr.* formosus non formunsus, occasio non occansio, Fred. thensarus, occansione, etc. (Haag, p. 870).

rs (< **rss**) was ordinarily assimilated to **ss**, after long vowels to **s**, e.g. **dorsus** > *dŏssus*, **sursum** > *sūsụ*, **deorsum** > *djǫsụ* (cf. § 749), cf. *App. Pr. persica* non *pessica*.

x **ks** + *consonant* was simplified to **s** + *consonant*, e.g. *dexter* **dĕkster** > *dẹster*, *extra* **ĕkstra** > *ẹstra*, *juxta* **jŭksta** > *jụsta*.

nx ŋks, *nct* ŋkt were assimilated to ŋs, ŋt, e.g. *franxi* fraŋksi >
*fraŋsi, *sanctum* saŋktum > *saŋtu, *punctum* pŭŋktum > *pǫŋtu.

ks opened to χs, e.g. *axem* aksem > *aχse.

g before m opened and vocalised to u̯, e.g. pigmentum > *piumentu.
sagma > sau̯ma, cf. *App. Pr. pegma non peuma.*

β and w brought in contact with a consonant by the fall of an unstressed vowel
vocalised to u̯, e.g. *parabola* *paraβ(ŏ)la > *parau̯la, *paraβ(ŏ)lare >
*parau̯lare, *avica awika > *auka; cf. also **faurga < fabrika.

§ 360. *Sound Substitution.*—The group t'l made by the slurring of
an unstressed penultimate vowel was replaced by kl (a sound group to
which it is acoustically very near), cf. *App. Pr. vetulus non veclus, vitulus
non viclus.*

[For *spatula, rotula,* etc., cf. § 262.]

§ 361. *Development of an Initial Vocalic On-glide.*—The pronunciation of words beginning with an initial group consisting of s + *consonant*
was facilitated by the development of a vocalic on-glide (written *e* or *i*),
whenever these words stood at the beginning of a phrase or after a word
ending with a consonant. The spellings *ispumosus, iscripta* go back to
the second century (cf. Juret, p. 164).

[For use in Old French cf. § 603.]

Section 2.—GALLO-ROMAN AND EARLY OLD FRENCH.

§ 362. The effacement of unstressed vowels in Gallo-Roman (chap.
v, sect. 8) produced many unfamiliar groups of consonants in the
interior and at the ends of words, and many of these, as well as some of
the groups that survived from Latin, were simplified in the course of
Period I. The processes adopted were various, *denasalisation, sound-
substitution* and *glide-developments* being employed, as well as *effacement*
and *assimilation.*

It should be borne in mind that the *last* consonant of an intervocalic
group is in a *strong* position and ordinarily remains unmodified except
by isolative change (chap. iii) and palatalisation (chap. vi), but the *first*
and *middle* consonants of a group are in *weak* position, especially the
middle consonant which was, as a rule, only preserved when the last
consonant was l or r.

Plosive consonants, standing first in a group, were all modified in
this period—the breathed plosives ordinarily voiced before voiced and
open consonants, the voiced either assimilated or opened—and the
groups of three consonants containing them all simplified unless the
third consonant was l, r or n. All *lengthened* consonants (except rr)
were also simplified in this period.

Section 3 —Groups of Three Consonants in Period I.

§ 363. In intervocalic groups of three consonants the middle plosive consonant was ordinarily retained when the group ended in **l** or **r**, because a plosive consonant can combine with these consonants in a group that can readily stand at the beginning of a syllable, cf. ar-**brę**, al-**trę**, sen-**glęr**. In other groups of three consonants the middle consonant was ordinarily either slurred or assimilated and thus disappeared.

[For **sts, nns, rns,** cf. § 365 ; for **nts, nds, rts, rds,** cf. § 367.]

§ 364. *Groups ending in* **l** *or* **r**.—*Middle Consonant Retained :* arbŏrem > **arbrę**, fĭndĕre > **fēndrę**, perdĕre > **perdrę**, rompĕre > **rumprę**, a4terum > **a4trę**, kĭŋgŭlŭm *cingulum* > **tsēnglę** *cengle*, kĭrkŭlum *circulum* > **tsęrklę** *cercle*, ĭnflare > **ēnflęr**, sĭngularem > **sēnglęr.**

[For *scl* **skl, rgl,** cf. § 365 ; for loan-words cf. § 642.]

By the subsequent vocalisation of prae-consonantal **4**, § 385, and the absorption of prae-consonantal **n** in the preceding nasal vowel, § 436, many of these groups were further reduced in the course of Later Old French and Middle French.

§ 365. *Groups ending in Consonants other than* **l** *or* **r**.—*Effacement of Middle Consonant :*

(i) *Middle Consonant Velar :*

porkos > **porks** > **pors,   longus** > **luns**

Similarly **skl** > **sl (zl), rgl** > **rl,** cf. O.F. *mesler* **mezlęr** < **mĭskŭlare, marlę** < **margŭla.**

(ii) *Middle Consonant Dental :*

aestimare > **ezmęr** *esmer,* testimŏnium > **tezmuŋ** *tesmoing* (§ 406), fortimente > **formēnt,**   pertika > **pertšę** *perche,* mastikare > **mastšier** *maschier,* partikella > **partsęlę,** *parcele,* mandukare > **māndžier** *mangier,* grandimente > **grāmēnt,** perdĭt > **pert.**

sts was early simplified by the dissimilation of the first **s, nns** and **rns** by the denasalisation of **n,** § 369, cf. O.F. :

ǫts *oz* < **hostes,** mats *maz* < **mastos,** pats *paz* < **pastos** ānts *anz* < **annos,** džǫrts *jorz* < **diŭrnos,** tǫrts *torz* < **tornes**

[For **ts** < **t** + **s** cf. § 367 ; for Latin **ks** + *consonant* cf. § 360.]

(iii) *Middle Consonant Labial :*

computare > **kuntęr** *conter,* hospitalem > **ǫstel, rumpĭt** < **runt,** carpinum > **tšarmę** *charme,* corpus > **kǫrs** *cors,* **tempus** > **tēns,** cambiare > **tšāndžier** *changier,* ga4bīnum > **dža4nę** *jalne,* absŏlvĭt **absŏ4wit** > **asǫ4t,** servĭs **sęrwīs** > **sęrs.**

Before its effacement a labial middle consonant, if fricative, labialised preceding **n** to **m,** cf. O.F. **ēmblęr** < ***enβolare** *involare* and the loan-word *giemble* (§ 643).

Section 4.—Lengthened Consonants in Period I.

§ 366. All the double, i.e. lengthened, consonants that were in use in Late Latin and all those formed by assimilation in the course of Period I (cf. below) were reduced to single consonants before the end of this period except **rr** in intervocalic position, and **rr** intervocalic was simplified to **r** before the end of Middle French, usually with compensatory vowel lengthening :

ɑbbɑs > ɑbẹs	cɑppɑ > tšɑpẹ *chape*	**addŭbbɑre > adọbẹr	
gŭttɑ > gọtẹ	mittĕre > mẹtrẹ (§ 575)	**rọttɑ (> rŭptɑ) > rọtẹ,	
tĕrrɑ > tẹrẹ	*fẹrrɑre > fẹrẹr	prĕssɑ > prẹsẹ *presse*	
bĕllɑ > bẹlẹ	illɑ > ẹlẹ (§ 575)	kĕssɑre > tsesẹr *cesser*	

The reduction of the double consonants took place later than the palatalisation of **k** *initial* + **a** to **tš**, (*sẹkka > sẹtšẹ, § 300), or the voicing of single intervocalic consonants, §§ 334, 335, or the diphthongisation of the tonic free vowels, § 225, and consequently the intervocalic single breathed consonants that resulted from them escaped voicing and the diphthongisation of the tonic free vowels that preceded them was always checked, cf. the examples above and O.F. **bẹl < bĕllum, tọr < tŭrrem, mẹtẹ < mittɑt**, etc.

Traditional spelling was very frequently maintained (§ 707).

[For the influence of this reduction on the pronunciation of tonic ę̆, cf. § 575.]

Lengthened consonants were occasionally formed in Later Old French when a monosyllabic word was closely linked to another beginning with a consonant, e.g. *affin, affaire* : these were also reduced to single consonants.

Section 5.—Groups of Two Consonants in Period I.

§ 367. *Sound Substitution.*—When **d** and **t** were brought in contact with **s** in Gallo-Roman by the fall of unstressed final vowels, the resultant group **t + s** was replaced by the affricated denti-palatal **ts**, (to which it is acoustically very near), and was opened to **s** in the course of Later Old French (§ 194) :

nɑt(u)s > nẹts > nẹs, *nez*	portɑt(i)s > portẹts > portẹs, *portez*
nūd(u)s > nüts > nüs	grɑnd(i)s > grɑ̃nts > grɑ̃ns, *granz*

Attesting rhymes.—Crest. E., *foiz : froiz* 947, *cerviz : serviz* 4469.

d in contact with **s** in Latin was assimilated to **s**, cf. O.F. *asaillir* (*adsalire*).

§ 368. *Consonant* + **l, r, n**. — Intervocalic groups consisting of *consonant* + **l, r, n** persisted ordinarily into Early Old French but were for the most part modified in Gallo-Roman by denasalisation, glide-development or assimilation.

§ 369. *Denasalisation.*—m + l, m + r, n + r.   When m and n
were brought in contact with l and r in Gallo-Roman by the effacement
of an unstressed vowel, pronunciation was facilitated by their partial
denasalisation and thus m'l > mbl, m'r > mbr, n'r > ndr :

cŭmulum > kumblę *comble*	sĭmulare > sēmblęr	insĭmŭl > ēnsēmblę
camera > tšāmbrę *chambre*	nŭmerum > numbrę	*crĕmĕre*>criembrę
generum > džēndrę *gendre*	pŏnere > pundrę	minor > mēndrę

In the pronunciation of Latin and early learned loan-words such as *damner* m
was sometimes partially denasalised to p, cf. O.F. *dampner, dampnedeu*, cf. also § 643.
    When n and r were brought in contact in Early Old French by the effacement
of intertonic ę < unstressed a, § 253, there was no partial denasalisation, but n was
ordinarily assimilated to r, cf. O.F. dunrai, durrai < dunęrai, mēnrai,
merrai < menęrai, dēnrę̄ę, derrę̄ę < denęrę̄ę (< *denarata).

✷✷ [For the variant development of m'l and n'r in the northern region cf.
N. § xiii.]

§ 370. *Glide Development.*—s, ŝ, z, l,], + r.   The pronunciation of
the groups consisting of s, ŝ, z, l,] and r was facilitated by the development of a glide, an intermediary plosive dental consonant, voiceless after
s and ŝ, voiced after z, l and]:

antecĕssŏr	antekęssor	>āntsęstrę	*essĕre* > estrę
dixerunt	ˈdīksĕrŭnt	> distręnt	ˈarsĕrunt > arstręnt (§ 981)
ˈmīsĕrŭnt >	**mįz(e)rųnt	> mizdręnt	ˈlazărum > lazdrę *lasdre*
solvere	*sŏ┼wĕre	> sǫ┼drę	**voleraio* > **βǫleraio > vǫ┼drai
melior *męlįǫr	> mieļdrę *mieildre*		*pŭlverem* pŭ┼wĕrem > pǫ┼drę

[For the subsequent effacement of s and z cf. below; for the vocalisation of prae-consonantal ┼ and] cf. §§ 383-391.]

✷✷ In the northern region there was no glide development in the group ┼ r,
cf. O.F. *pourre* purrę < pǫ┼rę (N. § xiii).

§ 371. *Assimilation.*—(i) m'n, n'm *and* mb.   In the groups consisting of mn, nm, and mb, m was the dominant sound and assimilated the
other consonants to itself; the resultant double consonant was reduced
to m in the course of Early Old French; (for the spelling cf. § 728):

        carmina > tšarmę *charme*, femina > fēmę, seminare > sęmęr
        anima > āmę (cf. § 643), Hieronymum > džeromę *Jerome*
        plŭmbare > plummęr > plūmęr, plŭmbum > plum > plūn (cf. § 435)

✷✷ In the southern zone, in south Normandy and across into south Champagne,
as well as in Provençal, mn was assimilated to nn, i.e. assimilation followed the
more usual lines and was dominated by the consonant that is initial of the following
syllable, cf. Beroul, *fenne : regne* 835 (MS. *feme : reigne*), St. Martin, *fenne : arrienne*
1169, Crest. E. *fane : sane* 4021, danner *Ep. St. Et.* 25.

§ 372. (ii) **t, d, + r, l, n.** t and d brought in contact with **r, l, n(m)** in Gallo-Roman were voiced and opened to **ð**, which was assimilated to the following consonant or effaced in the course of Early Old French.

[For Late Latin **kl** for **tl** cf. § 360; for **tr, dr** in Later O.F. cf. N. § xiii.]

fratrem > frẹðrẹ > frẹrẹ, *vitrum* *βẹtrụ > veiðrẹ > veirrẹ,

hĕdĕra > ieðrẹ > ierẹ   *iterare > ẹ(ð)rẹr > errẹr

*(e)spatula (§ 262)>espaðlẹ>espa+lẹ, ritmum>ri(ð)mẹ, retina>re(ð)nẹ

**Ruodlandụ (*Hruodland*) > Roðlant > Rollānt, mŏdŭlum moðlẹ > mo+lẹ

*Rodănụ (*Rhodanum*) > Roðnẹ > Rọnẹ, (cf. vẹðvẹ < *βẹdwa < widŭa)

ð appears to have been sometimes assimilated to **r**, sometimes simply effaced, and the conditions under which these processes take place have not yet been determined. In contact with **n**, **ð** was sometimes differentiated to **z**, e.g. *Rosne* (Rol. 1583, 1626), *bozne* (< *bodina*): the suffix -*udinem* appears to have been replaced by -*umine*, cf. O.F. *costume* kọstümẹ (< **kọstụmnẹ for *consuetudinem*).

The later forms **espaulẹ, mọulẹ** (> mulẹ) indicate a velarised pronunciation of **ll** in these words.

(iii) **p, b, β** (< w, § 186) **+ r, l.** p, b and β juxtaposed to r all passed to **v** (p > b > β > v, b > β > v, β > v): juxtaposed to l, **p** voiced to b but the group **bl** persisted:

aprilem > avril	lĕpŏrem > lievrẹ		ŏpĕra > uevrẹ
fĕbrem > fievrẹ	labra > lẹvrẹ		liberare > livrẹr
vivere *βiβere < wiwere > vivrẹ			
dŭplŭm > dọblẹ	flebilem > feiblẹ (§ 127)	tabŭla > tablẹ	

[For O.F. **soure, seurẹ** (< super) cf. § 597.]

�✶ In the northern region **b** in contact with **l** was opened and vocalised to **ụ**, cf. O.F. *peule, pule* pölẹ, pülẹ < pueulẹ *populum*, taulẹ < **tabla (> tọl), N. § xiv; for **vr** cf. N. § xiii.

§ 373. *Plosive Labial and Dental Consonants + Consonants other than* **l, r, n.**—In the course of Period I the *plosives, labial* and *dental*, were ordinarily assimilated or effaced whenever they were juxtaposed to following plosive, fricative or affricated consonants: Late Latin groups were reduced in Gallo-Roman, those formed in Later Gallo-Roman by the effacement of unstressed final or intertonic vowels in the course of Early Old French:

p, b, β, v + s, t, d > s, t, d.

capsa >tšasẹ *chasse*	apes > ẹs,	crẹpes > kries *cries*	
obscūrum > oskür *oscür*	**gabbos > gas	*vivis* *wiwis > vis	
*adcaptare > atšatẹr *achater*	rŭpta > rọtẹ	sapit >sẹt	
sŭbtilem > sọtil,	dĕbita > dẹtẹ	dĕbet > deit	
civitatem kiwitate > tsitẹ *cité*	*vivit* wiwit > vit	tĕpidum > tiedẹ	

p, b, β + ts, dž, tš > ts, dž, tš.

captiare *kaptjare >tšatsier *chacier*, *navicella* nawikẹlla >natsẹlẹ *nacele*

**saptše < *sapjа > satšẹ *sache* (§ 305) **rọbdže < *rọbjụ > rọdžẹ *roge*

d, t + p, t, d, dž, ts.

*adprĕssum > aprĕs,   radit > rĕt,   *hatit   > hĕt,   *potet > puet
adjudicare   > adžüdžier *ajugier*,   radikina > ratsinĕ *racine*

Date of Assimilation.—If the word *dist* in the *Strasbourg Oaths* is a scribal error for *dift*, as is generally held, it affords an indication that the assimilation of the groups of *labial* and *dental* that were formed in Gallo-Roman by the slurring of an unstressed final vowel only took place in the course of Early Old French ; the assimilation of the labials in the older groups occurred earlier, but the resultant double consonants were only reduced after the diphthongisation of tonic free vowels.

[For Latin *x*, **ks** and Gallo-Roman **k + s** cf. §§ 325, 326 ; for **kt** cf. § 324 ; for Middle French modifications cf. §§ 655, 744, 745.]

§ 374. *Consonant + w.*—A whole series of intervocalic groups consisting of *consonant + w* was formed in Late Latin by the consonantalisation of ŭ and ŏ in hiatus (§ 220) and all these groups were reduced or modified in the course of Gallo-Roman.

(i) **w** developed after a double consonant or a group of consonants was early slurred, e.g. ***battwo** < **battŭo** > ****batto**, ***febrwarjŭ** < **feb=rŭarium** > ***feβrarjŭ** (> **fevrier**).

(ii) The groups consisting of a *single consonant + w* were all reduced by assimilation except **nw**, which passed to **nv**, cf. O.F. **anvĕl**<***annwale** < **annŭalem**, *janvier* **džānvier** < ***janwarjŭ**.   In the groups **lw** and **sw** **l** and **s** were dominant and **lw** was assimilated to **ll**, **sw** to **s** (**ss** ?), e.g. ***βǫlwi** < **wǫlŭi** > ****vǫlli** (cf. § 1011), ***poswi** > ****posi** ; in the others **w** was ordinarily the dominant sound and the preceding consonants were first voiced (if breathed) and then wholly assimilated :

***aβwi** < **habŭi** > ****awwi**   ***deβwi** < **dēbŭi** > ****diwwi** (§ 993)
***plakwi** < **plakŭi** > ****plawwi**   ***sapwi** < **sapŭi** > ****sawwi**
***pǫtwi** < **pŏtui** > ****pǫwwi**   ***krĕdwi** > ****kriwwi** (§ 993)

[For the subsequent development of these forms and for analogical ***tĕni** for ***tĕnwi** cf. §§ 192, 1024-1027, 1011.]

In the word *vidua* ***wĕdwa d** opened to ð and the group ðv persisted into Early Old French, cf. O.F. *vedve* **vĕðvĕ**.

✱✱For dialectal ****pǫti** < ***pǫtwi** cf. § 1024.

Section 6.—DEVELOPMENT OF PRAE-CONSONANTAL ɫ, n, s, z IN
PERIOD II.

§ 375. In Gallo-Roman the open consonants ɫ, n, m, and the fricative dentals s, z, standing first of a group, ordinarily persisted but in the course of Old and Middle French these sounds also were modified or eliminated when prae-consonantal.

ɫ (l) vocalised to ʮ in the course of the eleventh and twelfth centuries (§§ 383-391).

n and m nasalised preceding vowels (§ 428) and merged in them in the course of Middle French (§ 436).

s and z, prae-consonantal, were modified and effaced in the course of the eleventh, twelfth and thirteenth centuries (cf. below).

As a result of the long series of reductions the only consonantal groups remaining in intervocalic position in traditional words at the end of the sixteenth century were those consisting of r + *consonant* and of a *consonant* or *consonants* + r or l.

In Later Old and Early Middle French prae-consonantal r was also often reduced to a weak fricative and effaced (§ 396).

§ 376. In spoken Modern French many new consonantal groups of very varying type are continually being formed, more or less ephemerally, by the effacement of ə, cf. Grammont, *Traité*, pp. 105 *et seqq.*

§ 377. *Prae-consonantal* s, z.—Prae-consonantal s was voiced to z before voiced consonants and f and first z then s gradually became mute in this position in the course of the eleventh, twelfth and thirteenth centuries, usually with vowel lengthening :

insŭla > *ĭsǫla > ĭzlę̨ > īlę̨   *blastemare (§ 749) > blazmę̨r > blāmę̨r
hispidum > hizdę̨ > hīdę̨   misculare > mę̨zlę̨r > mę̨̄lę̨r
fĕsta > fę̨stę̨ > fę̨̄tę̨   *frisca > frę̨stšę̨ > frę̨̄šę̨ *fresche*
nŏster > nǫstrę̨ > nǭtrę̨   *excappare ę̨stšapę̨r > ę̨šapę̨r *eschaper*
*sponsare > ę̨spǫzę̨r > ę̨puzę̨r   *(e)skütarjų > ę̨skü∂ier > ę̨küję̨r *escuyer*
[For st + s cf. § 365 (ii).]

The English pronunciation of words such as *aim* (< *ezmer*), *blame*, *hideous*, *isle*, *male*, *defeat*, on the one hand, and of *beast*, *feast*, *host*, *astonish*, *espouse*, *esquire*, on the other, indicates that at the time of the Norman Conquest the voiced sound z was already modified or mute when prae-consonantal while the breathed sound s was still intact. Rhymes of Old French poets also indicate that z was mute in the early twelfth century but that s was sounded into the thirteenth century (except in the western region): Ph. Th. *Best. ille : cocodrille*, Crest. E. *meïsmes : veïmes* 1138 : *primes* 685.

§ 378. Complete effacement of s and z was preceded by various transitional stages provoked by assimilation or differentiation :—

(i) Before voiced dentals the more usual transitional stage of z was ∂, graphy d, cf. the spellings, *adne, brudler, madle, medler, idle, vadlet* in MSS. of *Adam, Wace, Q.L.R.*, etc., and below § 1177. In the northern region z is transformed to r, cf. the Picard forms *dervę̨* (< *dezvę̨*), *varlet*, and possibly *bǫrne* < *bozne* < *bodina* (§ 372).

(ii) s before breathed dentals (more rarely z before voiced dentals) was differentiated to a fricative palatal or velar sound (ç or χ), written h in Walloon MSS. (e.g. *P. Moral, ehmaier, mahnie* < *maisniee*). These sounds are attested by the spelling and rhymes of French loan-words in German poems, e.g. *foreht : sleht, reht,́ tschahtel*, and by the explicit statement of the *Orthographia Gallica :* 'Quant s est joynt [a la t], ele avera le soun de *h*, come *est, plest* seront sonez *eght, pleght*.' (H. 35.)

This development often induced in the twelfth century the palatalisation of following **l** and **n**, especially after palatal vowels, cf. Ambroise, *s'esvelle : graisle, Escoufle, raigne : remaigne* 2221, and the use of the graphy **gn** for **sn** in words such as *cigne, digner, ignelepas* (< *isnelepas*), cf. Walberg, *Intr. Best*, lxiv-lxvii, Pope, *Et. Angier*, pp. 26-27, and below, § 1178.

✳✳ Effacement of prae-consonantal **s** appears to have begun in the south-western region and worked slowly northward, for rhymes attesting effacement begin in the south-western region in the later twelfth century and in the north-eastern region **s** has persisted before **p, k** and **t** into Modern French and **st** final was often reduced to **-s**, cf. N.E. § xiii and Herzog, *Nfrz. Dialekttexte*, § 329.

Thebes, maistre : sceptre 5117, *crisolites : ametistes* 4027, *Troie, destre : ceptre* 23057, *dit : fist* 14127, *saietes : prestes* 7867.

§ 379. *Re-introduction of* s *in the Sixteenth Century.*—s continued in use in spelling to indicate the lengthened pronunciation of the preceding vowel (§ 725) until the eighteenth century and this orthographical tradition combined with analogical influences, provincial variations, the influence of the new Latin pronunciation (§§ 652-655) and the introduction of numerous loan-words, learned, Italian and Spanish, produced considerable uncertainty about the pronunciation of many words containing the group s + *consonant* in the later sixteenth century and Early Modern French.

The words about which the sixteenth and seventeenth centuries showed hesitation may be grouped as follows :—

(1) *Traditional Words with effaced* s, *modified analogically.*—The pronunciation of the words *jusqu'à ce que, lorsque, puisque, presque*, in which s was ordinarily mute in Middle French, was modified in the sixteenth century under the analogical influence of the conjunctions *par(ce)que, pour(ce)que, puis ce que* (**parskə, purskə, pwiskə**), but the older pronunciation with s effaced was still in vogue in the next century, cf. Noel François (1654) : ' La douceur de la langue françoise fait que j'aimerois mieux dire . . . *puĭque, jŭqu'a ce que, prêque*.' (Th. II, 20.)

(2) Words influenced by learned pronunciation and spelling : *admonnester, blaspheme, cisterne, destrier, escarboucle, esclandre, estoc, honeste, jurisdiction, lester, ostruce, presbitere, pastourelle, registre, rescourre, rescousse, resplendir, restreindre, restriction, satisfaction, satisfaire, senestre, souscrire, soustraire, translation, transmettre.*

Many of these words were chiefly in use among the learned professions, and others (e.g. *destrier, senestre, rescousse*) were becoming obsolete.

(3) Late loan-words, learned or Italian, which were sometimes influenced by cognate traditional words, e.g. *bastonnade, destruction, rescript, tempestueux, spasme, sophisme.*

The consistent pronunciation of s in *esperer, espoir*, etc., may be due to Latin influence or to association with the loan-word *esprit* (Gilliéron, *Abeille*, p. 228).

CHAPTER IX.

DEVELOPMENT OF THE l-SOUNDS AND r.

Section 1.—VARIETY AND DISTRIBUTION OF THE l-SOUNDS.

§ 380. The l-*sounds*, it must be remembered, are very various: they comprise not only the simple dental and palatal lateral consonant l and ʎ but also the velarised and palatalised l-*sounds*, ɫ and ḷ, sounds made by combining the dental (alveolar) articulation with the raising of the back or the front of the tongue (§§ 109, 111).

The Latin sound-system appears to have comprised at least three varieties of the sound, l, ɫ and ḷ (cf. Juret, p. 31), and in the course of Late Latin there was developed in addition the palatal variety, ʎ (l *mouillé*) from the juxtaposition of an l-*sound* with a palatal consonant (e.g. in *fiʎu, *foʎdre, §§ 312, 322, 293). The subsequent history of these sounds is mainly one of simplification.

§ 381. In the course of Period I the *lengthened* l-*sound* ll was simplified (§ 366); in the course of Early Old French, at latest by the middle of the twelfth century, the velarised variety, ɫ, had vocalised to u (§§ 383-391): the palatalised variety, which appears to have survived into Old French after ḷ, was gradually either dentalised to l or effaced: in the course of Modern French ʎ has been reduced to ʝ. Thus it has come about that the sound-system of standard Modern French comprises l, the dental lateral, only.

§ 382. *Distribution of* l-*sounds in the eleventh century.*—In the eleventh century the distribution of the l-*sounds* appears to have been as follows:—

(1) The *dental* lateral l was the sound ordinarily in use when an l-*sound* was initial, final or intervocalic, e.g. in lit, bẹl, ẹlẹ.

(2) The *velarised* lateral ɫ was the sound ordinarily in use when an l-*sound* was prae-consonantal, e.g. in aɫtrẹ, bẹɫs, foɫs, nüɫs (but cf. (4) below).

(3) The *palatal* lateral ʎ was in use in intervocalic and final position wherever it was traditional, i.e. where formed by palatalisation in the earlier period (§§ 312, 322, 296), e.g. *fille* fiʎẹ, *bataille* bataʎẹ, *ail* aʎ, *ueil* 'ueʎ. In the words in which ʎ had become prae-consonantal, e.g. in *ailz* aʎts, *ueilz* ueʎts, it was probably already velarising after all vowels except ḷ (cf. below).

(4) The *palatalised* lateral ḷ was possibly still in use after ḷ, e.g. in fiḷ (< filum), iḷ < illi, *filcele* fiḷtsẹlẹ, for the rhymes between words ending in -iḷ and -iʎ are perceptibly more frequent than between those ending in l and ʎ after other vowels, cf. Crestien, *Cl. il : peril* 2413, 3789 : *fil* (< filum) 2437.

✳✳ It appears probable that the distribution of the ɫ-*sounds* varied locally and that this variation was a factor in the frequent local variants developed in Old French (§ 391). In some regions the velarised variety appears to have been employed instead of ʃ after i̯ in prae-consonantal position, e.g. in *filz* (§ 391 (iv)); in the south-eastern region ɫ was apparently used when intervocalic after a (ɑ ?), e.g. in *saule* (< *sala*) and after b, and in the south-western region, as in Provençal, when final after a (ɑ ?), cf. *St. Martin*, *au* 431, *ostau* 432, *beau* 250 (cf. M.L. *Zts. frz. Spr.* xli, p. 6, and E. § xvi, S.W. § ii).

Section 2.—DEVELOPMENT OF ɫ-SOUNDS IN PRAE-CONSONANTAL POSITION.

§ 383. Before the middle of the twelfth century all the *prae-consonantal* ɫ-*sounds* were either effaced or vocalised to y̨ and ɫ thus disappeared from the sound-system.

§ 384. *Effacement of Prae-consonantal* ɫ *and* ʃ.—After i prae-consonantal ɫ (ɨ?) and ʃ were both effaced, e.g. *filcele* fiɫtsęlę > fitsęlę *ficele*, *filz* fiɫts > fits *fiz*, (cf. English *Fitz-John*).

§ 385. *Vocalisation of* ɫ.—After all other vowels ɫ (<*prae-consonantal* ɫ and ʃ) vocalised to y̨ which merged in the preceding vowel or combined with it to form a diphthong or triphthong. Combination might be either direct or facilitated by the development of a vocalic glide.

§ 386. (1) After the high labial vowels, ü, u (< earlier ǫ, § 184) and eu (< ou, § 226), y̨ (< vocalised ɫ) was merged in the preceding vowel and thus disappeared :

nüɫɫus < nüɫs < nüs, müɫtum > mǫɫt > mut, *molt, mult,* ausküɫtare, *askǫɫtare (§ 505)>askǫɫtęr>askutęr, genukulos>džęnǫɫts > džęnuts *genuilz, genoilz,* sōɫus > souɫs > seus.

§ 387. (2) With preceding a, ę̆, ǫ, ie and ue, y̨ combined directly to form the diphthongs and triphthongs ¹au, ¹ęu, ¹ǫu, ¹ieu, ¹ueu :

aɫba > aubę, aɫterum > autrę, aɫtarem>autęr (cf. § 398), *alljos > aɫts > auts *auz*, fallit > faɫt > faut, *salvet* saɫwet > saɫt > saut. illos > ęɫs > eus, *fïɫtrų > fęɫtrę > fęutre, *konsęljos > kunsęɫts > künseuts *conseuz*, *konsęljet > kunsęɫt > künseut *conseut*. fǒllis > fǫɫs > fǫus, *colaphum* *kǫɫpų > kǫup, sǒɫwęre > sǫɫdrę>sǫudrę. mělius > mięɫts > mieuts, *mieuz, vetulos* *βęklos > vięɫts > vieuts *vieuz*, *volit *βǫlet > vueɫt > vueut, ǒkulos > ueɫts > ueutz *ueilz*.

§ 388. (3) The combination of the vowels ę and ę̨ (<a *tonic free*) with y̨ was facilitated by the development of a vocalic glide, a after ę, e after ę̨, and ęeu was speedily differentiated to ieu :

běllus > bęɫs > bęaus, pělles > pęɫs > pęaus, *hělmų > hęaumę, appěllet > apęɫt > apęaut, O.F. vęltrę (< *vertragum*) > vęautrę. tales > tęɫs > tęeus > tieus, palos > pęɫs > pieus.

[For the subsequent development of diphthongs and triphthongs cf. chap. xiv ; for the passage of ts to s cf. § 194.]

§ 389. *Process of Vocalisation.*—The velarised ɫ-*sound* combines with its dental (alveolar) articulation a lift of the back of the tongue which resembles the point of articulation of the vowel u and gives it the resonance of that vowel (cf. § 109), vocalisation to ụ is therefore readily intelligible. It is probable that the vocalisation of ļ was preceded by velarisation.

§ 390. *Date of Vocalisation and Effacement of ɫ.*—Isolated spellings indicate that the vocalisation of ɫ had its beginnings in the ninth century, e.g. *Caus dou Pont* (832-840), cf. M.L. *Gr.* § 169. The first rhymes attesting vocalisation or effacement fall in the middle of the twelfth century : *Adam, ascute : rute,* 240; Wace, *tout* (< *tollit*) : *plout* 4428; *Eneas, esmaus : Menelaus* 3139; Crestien, *Cl. seus : deus* 4505, *Iseuz : preuz* 5261; assonating poems afford no evidence as the articulation of the preceding vowel was not at first affected and consequently words containing in their tonic syllables vowels followed by these vocalising consonants continue to assonate with words containing in their tonic syllables these vowels preceding other consonants, cf. *Cor. Louis, altres : sages, aspres,* etc., xvi, *ciels : plaidier, mostier* xix, *Guillelme, tertre, bele* liv.

In Anglo-Norman the product of ę + ɫ is so frequently represented by *eu* (§ 1162) that it appears probable that at the time of the Norman Conquest the development of the vocalic glides had not proceeded far.

✶✶ § 391. *Local Variants.*—In the development of ɫ and ļ + *consonant* local variants were numerous :—

(1) Over a widespread region ɫ was effaced after the high vowel ẹ < a tonic free and thus **talis > tẹs, hospitalis > ostẹs**; cf. *Comput, cles : anves (annuales)* 49, *Troie, tes : remes* 19511, Crest. *E. ostes : remes* 5697, *Auc. tes* 10, 41, *canpes* 31, 8, Rtbf. *achatez : chatez (capitalis)* 189, 133, Cretin *lesquelz : alleguez, Intr.* p. xlv.

This pronunciation had some vogue in Paris in the sixteenth century ; rhymes such as *cruelz : tuez* are admitted by Sebillet, and Duez recommends the pronunciation of *quels* without ɫ ; **kẹkẹ** for *quelque* was also general, (Th. II, pp. 78 and 263).

(2) In a widespread region, including the north-east, east, south centre and Champagne *prae-consonantal* ɫ was effaced after ǫ; cf. *Rose* I, *trop : cop, los (laus). fos (follis), Intr.* p. 215; Crest. *fos (follis) : dos, Iv.* 5649.

(3) In the eastern region there was a tendency to efface ɫ after all vowels, e.g. **pames < paɫmes, Bẹfort < Bẹɫfort,** *miez* **miets < mieɫts** *mielz,* etc., E. § xx.

(4) In the northern region and in parts of the south-western there was a tendency to velarise and vocalise ɫ and ļ after i, cf. **fiuts, fius < fiļts** *filz,* and in some parts of the north *fieus* with a vocalic glide development, (§ 123) : this has been accepted in Modern French *essieu* (+ *essieus* < O.F. *aissils < *axiles*), N. § xix.

(5) In parts of the south-western region ļ *prae-consonantal* remained palatal and was reduced (like modern ļ) to ι (į): *conseilz* **kunsęļts > kunseits** *conseiz, murailz* **müraļts > müraits** *muraiz, ueilz* **ueļts > üits** *uiz,* cf. *Bestiaire, uiz : duiz* 2051; *Troie, conseiz : feiz, merveit : destreit; Intr.* p. 128, Beroul, *cuite : voitre* (< *voiltre* < *vol(u)tulat,* § 319) 3685; *St. Martin, moites* (< *moiste*) : *coites* (< *culcita*) 9851. *Coite* survives in Modern French *couette* (cf. S.W. § vii and Matzke, *l mouillé*).

Section 3.—TREATMENT OF ɫ AND ļ IN FINAL POSITION.

§ 392. In Period II when words ending in ɫ and ļ were closely linked in the sentence with words beginning with a consonant (§ 170), the ɫ-*sounds* were often treated like the ɫ-*sounds* in the interior of words and either effaced (after the *high front* vowels) or vocalised.

Effacement.—Spellings such as *i* for *il* make their appearance in the thirteenth century (§ 841), and in Later Middle French effacement was usual in the pronunciation of words in -il and -iḻ (e.g. *fil, peril*), -ęl (e.g. *mortel, quel*), -üil (e.g. *cul*), -ul *oul* (e.g. *saoul*), when they were prae-consonantal, and this effaced pronunciation, which was supported by the effacement of ɫ in the plural forms (*fis, mortes,* etc.), was often made use of at the pause. In educated usage, however, a restoration of the sound began in the latter part of the sixteenth century under the influence of spelling and Latin, and this was ordinarily successful in Early Modern French among words ending in -ęl, -üil, -ul, more rarely among words ending in -il and iḻ.

[For the pronunciation of the pronoun *il* cf. § 841, for *ni* and *si* cf. § 598, and for further details about other words cf. Th. II, pp. 140-146.]

Bèze ruled that ɫ should always be pronounced, but H. Estienne admitted *fusi* and *fusil, sourci* and *sourcil, gri* for *gril, sou* for *soul;* Tabourot permits rhymes between words ending in -üil (e.g. *consul*) and those in -ü (-*u*, -*ut*, e.g. *receut*); Palsgrave writes *mortéperil* for *mortel peril* and Duez mentions the suppression of final ɫ in *Michel, Noel* and *quel* in prae-consonantal position, e.g. in *quel livre.*

§ 393. *Vocalisation of* ɫ *Final* is found after low and mid vowels, but was confined ordinarily to words in stereotyped locutions such as *moyeu d'œuf, à mau chat, mau rat.*

Many words ending in ɫ in the accusative singular were however replaced analogically by words made on the model of the forms in which ɫ had vocalised before flexional s, e.g. *beau, seau, fou, cheveu,* etc. (cf. § 814).

[For *final* ɫ in liaison cf. §§ 621, 623.]

Section 4.—Pronunciation of r in Later Old and Middle French.

§ 394. The r-*sound* now in vogue in Paris is the uvular sound trilled or fricative R or ʁ; the use of this form of the consonant is, however, a relatively modern development; for the modifications the sound underwent in the earlier period and the type of influence it has exercised on vowels (chap. xiii) make it evident that the consonant in use in Old and Middle French was ordinarily the dental (alveolar) variety r.

[For the use of R in educated Modern French and its beginnings in the seventeenth century cf. Nyrop, *Manuel,* § 57.]

§ 395. When r was in a *weak* position in the older language, i.e. when it was *prae-consonantal, intervocalic* or *final unsupported* it often lost its trill and was sometimes effaced or replaced.

§ 396. *Effacement of prae-consonantal* r.—In Later Old and Middle French prae-consonantal r often became fricative and was assimilated to the following consonant or effaced, usually with compensatory lengthening of the preceding vowel (cf. the Southern English pronunciation of

words like *hard, force*, etc., **hɑ : d, fǫ : s**). Assimilation was especially frequent in the groups **rs, rl** (cf. *Rose, Intr.* p. 268).

Attesting Rhymes.—Ph. Th. *Best. sage : large* 7, *cors : enclos* 291, *parecus : jurz* 853; *Troie : braz : pars, lais : travers, Grezeis : veirs, sospirs : ententis* (Intr. pp. 130, 131); *Beroul : ars : pas, vet : sert, fiers : nies, voirs : Morrois, fors : clos, feurs* (MS. *fors*)*: deus* (Intr. p. xlvi); *G. Dôle : vert : vallet, estre : tertre, tierce : piece, ferme : meesme* (Intr. p. xli); *Rose*, II, *pelles* (*perles*)*: grelles* (*graciles*) 13561, 20965; Guiart II, 1208, *palle* (*parle*)*: malle*, Villon, T. cxiv, *courges : Bourges : rouges : bouges.*

[Cf. also Chatelain, *Le Vers Fr.* p. 51, and below § 721.]

§ 397. The pronunciation of s for **rs** and **ll** for **rl** was still current in the sixteenth century in Paris. Tabourot equates *chassieux* with *chats sieurs* and Bovelles attributes *paller* for *parler* to the Parisians: 'Infantes et Parrhisii . . . *paller* pro *parler* dicunt.' (Th. II, 289.) There was also hesitation about the pronunciation and spelling of a good many words, especially those containing **ar, or** and **ur** + *consonant*, e.g. *a(r)bre*, (cf. Lanoue: 'On écrit *arbre* quoy qu'on prononce *âbre*'), *ma(r)bre, o(r)fraie, rebou(r)s, toujou(r)s* and the loan-words *a(r)moniac, brouilla(r)s, dama(r)s, ma(r)sepain.*

§ 398. The effacement of **r** before **s** led occasionally to its intrusion before **s**, as for instance in *Nemours*, O.F. *Nemous*, and in *velours*, O.F. *velous*, a Provençal loan-word, and contributed to the confusion of the terminations *-eur* and *-eus* (§ 400).

The reduction of O.F. **fǫrburk < fǫrsbǫrk** to **fǫburk** led to its (graphical) replacement by *fauxbourg*, at the period when **faus** was being pronounced **fǭ(s)** (§§ 535, 536). The similarity in sound of the plural forms of **auter** and **(au)tel**, in the pronunciation of those who reduced -ę̄rs and -ę̄ls to -ę̄s (*Best. alters : tels* 2267, cf. § 391), led to the creation of the form *autel.*

§ 399. *Assibilation of Intervocalic* **r**.—In some regions, notably the central and the south-eastern, intervocalic **r** lost its trill and was assibilated to **z**.

Gesainvilla < Jerani villa 1201 (Eure-et-Loir), *Sezy < Seriacum* 1319 (Yonne); *Myst. d'Orléans, plaisa* for *plaira, conduisa*, etc., *chaese* (*< chaiere*)*: desplaise*, p. 191 of *St. Joan of Orléans.*

In the fifteenth and sixteenth century this pronunciation had some vogue in Parisian speech (cf. Villon *chaise : aise*, T. 1489), and was established gradually in the words *chaise* (*< chaire*), *besicles* (*< bericles*), *nasiller* (*< nariller*) and some place-names such as *Ozoir* for *Oroir* (*< Oratorium*).

Cf. Palsgrave: '. . . they of Paris sounde somtyme *r* lyke *z*, saying *Pasys* for *Parys* . . . ,' p. 34; Erasmus: 'Idem faciunt hodie mulierculae parisinae pro *Maria* sonantes *Masia*, pro ma *mere*, ma *mese*' (Th. II, 271); Bèze: 'Parisienses . . . ac multo etiam magis Altissiodorenses et mei Vezelii simplicem *r* etiam in *s* vertunt,'

p. 37. The tendency provoked a reaction and **r** was sometimes substituted for etymological **z** (*s*), cf. *Epistre du Biau Fys de Pazy*, § 74.

[For a survey of the extension of the phenomenon and its appearance in both the South and North of France and in the modern patois, cf. O. Bloch, ' L'Assibilation de *r* dans les patois gallo-romans,' *Rev. Lg. Rom.* III, 92-156 ; cf. also Th. II, 271-274.]

§ 400. **r** *Final*.—In the early sixteenth century there was evidently in Paris considerable divergence in the pronunciation of unsupported **r** at the end of words. Among the educated it was ordinarily sounded, (cf. Plsgr. : ' **r** in the frenche tonge shal be sounded as he is in Latin without any exception '), but among the uneducated a tendency to slur **r** final had gained much ground and **r** was being consistently effaced : (i) after the high vowels ẹ, (jẹ) and **i**, e.g. in *disner, bergier, plaisir*—**dinẹ, berž(ɪ)ẹ, plẹzi,** (ii) in the substantival terminations -*eur* -**ör** and -*oir* -**ụẹr,** e.g. in *porteur* **pọrtö,** *mouchoir* **mušụẹ**. In the first set the tendency was phonological in origin and probably provincial (cf. below, § 401), in the second effacement was due to the influence of the forms in which prae-consonantal **r** was effaced, (§ 396) i.e. the plural forms and locutions such as *mouchoir de poche, porteur d'eau, couppeur de bourses,* cf. Plsgr. *chastreux de truies* (for *chastreur*).

By the end of the century it is evident that in the speech even of the educated, 'the persons of very good parts and quality' (Awfield), the older tradition had to a very large extent given way and **r** was being left unsounded in these terminations, except in monosyllables or before vowels (cf. §§ 401, 611).

H. Estienne : ' The people say . . . *plaisi, mestié, papié, resueu,* for *plaisir, mestier, papier, resueur,* and in like manner leave out the *r* in *il faut parler bas.*' Duez : ' In conversation *r* is generally suppressed in *plaisir, desplaisir, loisir.*' Lanoue : ' Les verbaux en -*eur* se peuuent prononcer de ceste terminaizon [-*eus*], selon qu'on parle aujourd'huy, et se peut dire un *menteur* et *menteus* [i.e. **mätö**].' *L'Anonyme* de 1654 : ' Tous ces noms sont prononcez comme s'il n'y auoit point d'*r, mouchoi, parloi, dortoi, saloi.*' ' Tous ces mots ' (*menuisier, pommier,* etc.), ' se prononcent, mieux sans *r* ; d'autant que nos François estans devenus plus polis ont recherché de iour en iour la beauté et adoucissement du langage, qui consiste à euiter cette prononciation trop rude qui se rencontre à la fin de ces mots ou semblables à ceux-cy.' (Th. II, 149, 150, 157, 165.)

§ 401. The opposition of the grammarians was, however, persistent. Maupas in 1625 repeats Palsgrave's injunction to sound **r** clearly every-where and condemns strongly the vulgar practice of effacement : ' Ie trouve niaise la fantaisie d'aucuns, qui affectent une lasche prononciation du bas populas, d'obmettre et supprimer du tout toutes les *r* finales ; ainsi : *vous plaist il veni disné auec moy, vous me ferez plaisi,* au lieu de dire *venir, disner, plaisir* auec moderée prononciation de l'*r*.' (Th. II, 151.)   Later on in the seventeenth century the precepts of the grammarians together

with the influence of spelling (cf. § 740), Latin, the numerous loan-words, and the analogical influence of the infinitives in -*ire* (e.g. *dire* **dir**) and the feminines in -*eure* led to the restoration of the pronunciation of final *r* in all positions in the terminations **-ir, -ᶙer** *oir*, **-ör** *eur* (*monsieur* excepted) and to its retention : (*a*) in monosyllabic words in -ᶒr and -ᶖer in all positions, e.g. *mer*, *cher*, *cler*, *fier*, *hier* (and *amer* ≠ *mer*) and (*b*) in the terminations -ᶒr and -ᶖer in polysyllabic words in prae-vocalic position, cf. Hindret (1687) ; ' Pour dire *commencer une affaire* prononcez *commencé rune affaire.*' (Th. I, 59.)　In these last two terminations, however, the practice of effacement was too solidly established to be modified when polysyllabic words stood in prae-consonantal position or at the pause (cf. H.L.F. IV (1), pp. 208-212 ; Rosset, pp. 260-273).

When *r* followed one of the low vowels ᶒ, **a**, ǫ (e.g. in *fer*, *enfer*, *hiver*, *char*, *or*) effacement had less vogue among the uneducated and left educated speech entirely unaffected.

In prae-consonantal position the prepositions *pour* and *sur* were pronounced **pu, sü**, cf. Tabourot's puns : *poullets trespassés* for *pour les trespassés*, *a sué* for **a** *sur* **e** : this pronunciation led to the graphical confusion of *sur* and *sus*, also pronounced **sü** in prae-consonantal position (§ 611), cf. *Parisian documents : sus le chastel* 1260, *sus le gueit* 1273 (*Kr. Jb.* VI (1), 227).

✶✶ In the eastern and south-eastern region the effacement of r final after the high vowels ᶒ, (jᶒ), **i**, began in the thirteenth century, cf. the spellings in Lorraine documents, e.g. *ie me sui alier* (for *aliez*), 1268, *ai je fait offri mon fil*, 1278, *avons nous prier la justice ... de waranti a tous iours*, 1286 (Rydberg, *Kr. Jb.* VI (1), 246, and cf. *Rom.* xxxix, p. 530).　The spellings in the Parisian tax roll of 1292, *Nicolas le gantie, Robert le cordouanie, Colin le batelie*, show that the capital was also early affected by this development, but there is no evidence of it in the rhymes of Villon.

§ 402. -ᶒr *in the western region : '*Rimes Normandes.*'*—In the western region ᶒ before r was opened early to ᶒ (cf. § 495) and this led in the sixteenth century in Paris to three conflicting tendencies in speech in the pronunciation of the termination -ᶒr in polysyllabic words : (i) the vulgar Parisian effacement of r after ᶒ, (ii) the educated retention of r after ᶒ, and (iii) the western retention of r after ᶒ, i.e. **portᶒ**, **portᶒr, portᶒr**. In the terminations of the infinitive of the first conjugation the open pronunciation of **e** had much vogue in the later sixteenth and seventeenth centuries in spite of the opposition of the grammarians, in whose eyes this pronunciation remained provincial (according to Bèze ' Gascon,' to Vaugelas ' Normand '). According to the seventeenth century grammarian Hindret, its final discrediting was due to the combined influence of Vaugelas, who pronounced against it (*Rem.* II, 163), and of Molière and his troupe.

This fashion left its mark : (*a*) on the rhymes of the time in the so-called *rimes normandes*, found chiefly in the works of Norman poets but also elsewhere, e.g. Montchrestien, *rouler : l'air*, Malherbe, *philosopher : enfer*, Corneille, *air : donner*, Racine, *cher : arracher* (Kastner, pp. 7, 8), and (*b*) on the pronunciation of the word *cuiller* (O.F. **kuᶖier** < *cochlearium*), cf. Ménage (1672), ' Le petit peuple de Paris prononce *cueillié* . . . Les honnestes bourgeois y disent *cueillére* . . . Nous disons *cueillêr* en Anjou . . . On dit aussi plus ordinairement *cueillêr* à la cour.' (Th. I, 198.)

✶✶ In the south central region r final appears to have been lisped like r intervocalic, e.g. *Myst. d'Orleans, congnois : vois (voir)* 311, *aller : levez* 1638, *vous : poux* (*pavorem*) 258, cf. Coyfurelly (of Orléans): ' *R* vero aliquando in fine diccionis retinebit sonum *r* et aliquando sonum *z* ut *vuilez vous aler*, ou *voilez vous alez . . .*' (M.L.R. V, p. 191) and Bloch, *op. cit.*, pp. 106, 107.

CHAPTER X.

INFLUENCE EXERCISED BY PALATAL SOUNDS ON VOWELS.

Section 1.—SUMMARY.

§ 403. The development of vowels was modified in various ways by the influence of palatal sounds, juxtaposed or in their vicinity, more especially in the Gallo-Roman period.

(1) The diphthongisation of the free vowels **a, ẹ, ǫ**, induced ordinarily by tonic stress (§ 225), was checked and these sounds persisted ordinarily undiphthongised into Old French, cf. § 198.

(2) Diphthongs in -i̯ were formed :—

(i) In Late Latin and Early Gallo-Roman by the combination of tonic vowels with *unstressed final* i̯ or i̯, e.g. ****portai < porta(w)i̯, fų̄i̯,** (§ 254) **ai < *ai̯o, sai < *sai̯o** (cf. § 404 (i)).

(ii) In Period I by the combination of i̯ (i̯) derived from palatal or palatalised sounds (chap. vi) with preceding vowels (§ 404).

(iii) In the course of Old French by the development of a palatal glide (i̯ or i̯) before **l** and **ŋ**, under certain conditions (§§ 406-408).

(3) The relatively high lift of the tongue required to form palatal sounds, § 136, induced (i) in *Gallo-Roman* :—

(*a*) The diphthongisation of tonic **ẹ** and **ǫ**, blocked and free, by *following* palatal consonants (§§ 410-412).

(*b*) The raising of **a** free and of tonic **ẹ** free by *preceding* palatal consonants (§§ 413-418).

(*c*) The raising of **ẹ** and **ǫ** by following -i̯ *final* (§§ 419-420).

(ii) In *Later Old French* :—

(*a*) The raising of **ẹ** intertonic by following **ŋ** and **l** (§ 422).

(*b*) The raising of **a** countertonic to **ẹ** by juxtaposed tonic **ü** (§ 421).

(4) The unrounding of **u** and **ü** was occasionally induced by preceding i̯ (§ 424).

Section 2.—FORMATION OF DIPHTHONGS IN i̯.

[For later development of these diphthongs, cf. chaps. xi and xiv.]

§ 404. In the course of Period I, i̯, from all sources and in all positions, opened ordinarily to i̯ except when it was *initial* (§§ 203, 352) or *inter-*

vocalic or *final* in Later Gallo-Roman after **a** (e.g. in ****paȷant, **haȷę, **veraȷ,** §§ 528-532) ; **ȷ** combined in a diphthong with vowels of every point of articulation except **ı̣**, in which it merged : **maȷor**>**maırę**, *picem* ***pęȷę** > **peits,** *frūctum* ***frụxtu̧** > **früit,** *mīca* **mīka** > **mię,** cf. § 339.

** The passage of **ȷ** to **ı̣** was retarded somewhat after all vowels when **ȷ** was *intervocalic* (cf. the spellings in *Eulalia, veintre* 3, *preiement* 8, *laist* 28 and *regiel* 8 (= **reȷiel**), *pagiens* 12).

Sources of G.R. jod :—

(1) Late Latin *intervocalic jod* (< Classical Latin intervocalic *jod*, from **g** between **a** and tonic **e,** § 297, and from intervocalic **dȷ** and **gȷ,** §§ 307, 309), e.g. ***maȷu** < **maȷum,** ***saȷęta** < **sagitta,** ***raȷu̧** < **radium,** ***esaȷu̧** < **eksagiúm,** *exagium.*

(2) G.R. **γ** (< Late Latin **g** and **k,** *intervocalic* + **a,** § 302) *palatalised,* e.g. **nei-ier** < ****neγare** < **nekare** and **negare.**

(3) G.R. **dž** (< Latin intervocalic **tȷ** and **k** + **e, i,** §§ 308, 294), e.g. **raizun** < ****radzǫne** < **ratiōnem, plaizir** < ****pladzirę** < **plakěre.**

(4) G.R. *palatalised dentals,* **ř, ŝ, ẑ,** etc. (§§ 313-315), e.g. **airę** < ****ařa** < **arěa, üis** < ****u̧ŝu̧** < ***u̧stȷu̧.**

(5) Latin intervocalic groups of *plosive velar + dental* (§§ 323-326), e.g. **fait** < **faktum, ais** < **aksem** *axem.*

(6) G.R. **ŋ** resolved into **ı̣n** when prae-consonantal (§§ 311, 321), e.g. **plāindrę** < **plaŋgěre, dēintie** < **diŋnitatem** *dignitatem.*

(7) The palatal glide developed between **ę** countertonic or intertonic and **a,** e.g. **seiiens** < ****sęȷamǫs** < ***sęamus,** cf. § 919.

§ 405. *Old French.*—In the course of Old French diphthongs in -**ı̣** were sometimes formed by the development of a palatal glide before the palatal consonants **ŋ** and **ȴ** :—

§ 406. (1) **ŋ** *final.*—Before **ŋ,** final of the word, a glide developed in the course of Early Old French after **a, ę, u, ü** ; with the gradual nasalisation of the diphthongs formed **ŋ** was dentalised and merged in the nasal vowel (§§ 435-438) :

Early O.F. *baing* **baŋ** < ***banȷu̧,** *balneum* > **bāiŋ** > **bę(n)** ;
Early O.F. *poing* **puŋ** < **pu̧ənu̧m** *pugnum* > **puiŋ** > **pu̧ę(n).**

§ 407. (2) **ŋ** and **ȴ** *intervocalic :—*
(i) Before **ŋ** *intervocalic* a glide was developed after **ę** *tonic* or *countertonic* in the course of Early Old French :

Early O.F. *enseignet* **ęnsęŋęθ** > **ēnsēiŋę** (> **āsęŋę**) ;
Early O.F. *seignour* **sęŋour** > **sēiŋeur** (> **sęŋör**).

(ii) Before **ŋ** and **ȴ** intervocalic a glide was developed after **ü** *tonic* or *countertonic* :

Early O.F. *juignet* **džüŋęt** > **žüiŋęt** (> **žwiŋęt,** cf. § 476) ;
Early O.F. *aguille* **agüȴę** > **agüiȴę** (> **agwiȴę,** cf. Crestien E. 2643, *roïlle : aguille*) ; *cuillier,* **küȴier** > **kwiȴier.**

✷✷ § 408. A palatal glide was not infrequently developed before ɭ and ŋ after other vowels, but these forms, although often widely used in mediæval texts, have rarely been adopted in standard French. The region most affected appears to have been the southern and south-eastern but the eastern and south-western often share in the development.

(1) a + ŋ *intervocalic* > āiŋ (> ẹ̃ŋ > ęŋ): Early O.F **araŋẹ > arāiŋẹ > arẹŋẹ** *araigne;* cf. Rtbf. *eslǫingne : acompaingne,* 9, 12 (cf. § 445, E. § xxiii, S.C. § xiii).

(2) u (< ǫ) + ŋ > uiŋ > ụẹ̃ŋ: Early O.F. **vergụŋẹ > verguiŋẹ > vergwẹ̃ŋẹ,** cf. Rtbf. *besoingne : tiengne, G. Sar.* 144 (cf. § 445, E. § xxii).

These two developments affected mainly the eastern, south-eastern and south central regions.

(3) ẹ + ɭ > eiɭ (> oiɭ in the eastern region, E. § xxii, -ęiɭ (-ęɭ?) elsewhere, W. § vi), cf. *Rol. vermeil, conseil,* etc., in assonance with words in **ei** laisses vi, lxxix, etc., Crestien : *consoil, vermoil, Rose,* MS. Ab, *parail, mervaille (ai* graphy for ẹ).

(4) a + ɭ > aiɭ > ẹiɭ > ęɭ : Early O.F. **travaɭ > travaiɭ > travẹɭ,** cf. Macé, *travailles : veilles,* (Rose I, p. 230) ; Ch. d'Orl. II, *traveill : conseil* R. 32 : *apareil* R. 85 ; *traveilles : oreilles* R. 75 ; Cretin, *traveille : esveille,* LIX, 85, but cf. § 423 and E. § xxii.

[Cf. Matzke, *l-mouillé.*]

§ 409. In Later Old French diphthongs in - i̯ were also occasionally formed when palatal vowels were juxtaposed or countertonic vowels brought into contact with *jod* :—

(i) The diphthongs **ai** and **oi** developed when countertonic **a** or **o** were juxtaposed to i̯ẹ (< Early O.F. ʰie) and i̯au (< earlier ẹau, § 540), cf. Later O.F. *chaiere* **šai-ẹrẹ < tša-ieðrẹ,** *praiaus,* **prai-aus < pra-ẹaus < praẹ┼s,** *boiaus,* **boi-aus < bo-ẹaus < boðẹ┼s** (* bŏtẹllos).

(ii) The juxtaposition of palatal vowels led at times to the development of a palatal glide (§ 239) and this occasionally combined with the preceding vowel in a diphthong, cf. Later O.F. *essuyer,* **esẇiẹr < esüi̯ẹr < esüẹr** *(exsucare), huier.*

Section 3.—DIPHTHONGISATION UNDER PALATAL INFLUENCE—"BREAKING."

§ 410. When ẹ and ǫ, *blocked* or *free,* stood before a palatal consonant in Early Gallo-Roman, the front of the tongue appears to have been prematurely raised, in anticipation of the following high sound, and the vowels ẹ̈ and ọ̈, started thus too high, diphthongised to ʰie and ʰuo respectively, ʰuo being differentiated to ʰue in the course of Early Old French (§ 226). This process, to which various names have been assigned, is called in this book *breaking* or *fracture.*

(It should be borne in mind that Gallo-Roman ẹ included **a** free if raised to ẹ by preceding palatal consonants, § 414) :

mĕlius > *mẹɭǫs < mieɭts *mieilz, vetulus* ***βẹklǫs** (§ 360) > **vieɭts** *vieilz*
ingĕniat > ** endẹŋat > āndžieŋẹ *engiegne, mĕdium* ***mẹi̯ụ > **mieẹ** (§ 411)
folia > **fǫɭa > fuoɭẹ > fueɭẹ *feuille,* ****orgǫɭụ < orgueɭ** *orgueil*
kolliget > **kǫɭet > kuoɭt > kueɭt *cueilt,* **hŏdiĕ > *ǫi̯e > **uei̯ẹ,** (§ 411)

[For the later development of the diphthongs **ie** and **ue** cf. §§ 510, 551.]

In *niece*, **nietsẹ**, *piece* the diphthong **ie** may have been induced by the following consonant which was palatalised ephemerally in Early Gallo-Roman: **nĕptia > **nẹttsįa > **nẹtt̃sa > nietsẹ**, and similarly **ue**, *oe* in occasional *aprueche* (< *ad-prŏpiat*), *nuece* **nuetsẹ** (< *nǫptįa), **tuertrẹ** (< **tǫrtere**, **torkere*, § 293).

§ 411. When the following palatal sound was *jod* or disengaged a *jod* (§ 404), raising continued in Early Old French and ˈiẹj > iįj > i, ˈuẹj > ˈüįj > üi (§ 514):

**mieẹ < *mẹjo (*medium*) > mi   ****ueẹ < *ǫịe (*hodie*) > üi
prĕkat > **prieẹt > priẹθ   lĕktum > *lẹχtụ (§ 359) > **lieẹtẹ > lit
*mǫrjo > **mueẹrẹ > müir   nŏktem >*noχtẹ (§359)>*nueẹtẹ>nüit

Cf. also **pris** < prĕtium, *engint* ēndžint < ingĕniet, ēntir < *ẹntẹyrụ (*intĕgrum*, § 214(2)), **üistrẹ** < ŏstrĕa.

** § 412. Breaking is common to the whole of Gaul except apparently the north-eastern and eastern regions (the Walloon and Lorraine dialects), cf. N.E. § i.

[For the development of **ieẹ** and **ueẹ** in the south-western region cf. S.W. § i.]

*Section 4.—*RAISING INFLUENCE OF PRECEDING PALATAL SOUNDS IN GALLO-ROMAN.

§ 413. The vowels affected by preceding palatal consonants were **a** and **ẹ**, which were both raised when *free*, **a** in all types of syllables, **ẹ** when *tonic*. These changes took place in Early Gallo-Roman and are induced by all types of palatal consonants, palatalised as well as palatal.

§ 414. **a** *free*.—**a** *free* was raised by a preceding palatal consonant to **ẹ** which was always subsequently modified.

(i) *Tonic* **ẹ** (< **a** *tonic free*), like Late Latin **ẹ** *tonic free*, was diphthongised to ˈie under the influence of the heavy expiratory accent of the Gallo-Roman period, § 225:

carum **karŭm** > **karụ >**ẹẹrụ (§ 300) > tšier *chier*.
kalet > tšielt *chielt*, **pakare** > paiier, **kanem** > tšien *chien*,
pūrgare > pürdžier *purgier*, **ligare** > leiier, **paganum** > paiien,
adjutare > **ajdare** > aidier, *laxare* **laksare** > laisier *laissier*,
mĕdiĕtatem>meĵtate>meitieθ, *amicitatem* **amiʦ(e)tate>āmistieθ.

[For the subsequent development of ˈie cf. § 510, of ˈien cf. § 471.]

§ 415. (ii) Tonic **ẹ** (< **a** *tonic free*), like Late Latin **ẹ** tonic free (§ 411), was diphthongised to **ie** by a following palatal consonant and **ieẹ** raised to **i** (§ 411):

jacet **jaket** > **džệdzet** (§ 413) > **džieẹst** > džist *gist*,
cacat **kakat** > tšiẹ, *chie*   **Sabiniacum** (§ 302) > **Saviŋi** *Savigni*.

§416. The earliest documentary evidence of the raising of *tonic* **a** *free* under palatal influence to **ẹ** is furnished by the place-names *Criscecus*, *Erchrecus* (<*Crisciacus*, *Ercuriacus*), in the eighth century (Longnon, p. 84), but the fact that

the passage of tonic a to ę under these conditions is common to Franco-Provençal and Poitevin as well as northern Gaul (§ 34), indicates a relatively early origin of the development, and this is confirmed by the diphthongisation of the resultant ę to ie. This diphthongisation, one of the most characteristic features of Old French, did not, however, extend to the Poitevin region, a region which often went with Provençal in its treatment of tonic vowels under stress (cf. Gamillscheg, *Becker vol.* pp. 57-61).

The passage of a tonic free to ie was first delimited by the German scholar Bartsch, and its formula is consequently sometimes spoken of as ' Bartsch's Law.'

§ 417. (iii) a *free* in *countertonic* syllables was ordinarily raised to ę, which was subsequently obscured to ę in the course of Old French (cf. § 234):

$$caballum *ka\beta all\mu > **\dagger a\beta all\mu > tš\me val \; cheval.$$

kapillum > tšęvel *chevel*, kanutum > tšęnü *chenu*,
kapïtiŭm > tšęvęts *chevez* (§ 308), *kamisia > tšęmizę *chemise*.

Raising was checked by juxtaposed following l and r, the two consonants most prone to exercise a lowering influence (§ 491), and more variably by the dissimilatory influence of e in tonic syllables, cf. O.F. *chaleir* tšaleir < kalere, *charogne* tšaruɲe < *karŏnĕa, *chaeir* tšaeir < *kadęre, *chaeine* tšaeîne < katēna, *chaiere* tšaierę < *katędra.

The influence exercised by preceding palatals on *atonic* a is illustrated by the form *fazet* (< *faciat*) in the *Oaths of Strasbourg* but it is ordinarily obscured by the general reduction of atonic a to ę.

✱✱ In the region in which k remained velar (N. § i) a countertonic was ordinarily retained, e.g. *Auc. caviaus* 2, 12.

§ 418. ę.—In Early Gallo-Roman ę tonic free was raised to i by a preceding palatal or palatalised consonant:

$$cēra \; kēra > *\dagger era > tsirę \; cire.$$

merkēdem > mertsi *merci*, plakēre > *plaɟere > plaizir *plaisir*,
rakēmum > *raɟemμ > raizin *raisin* (cf. 451), pagensem < *paɟęse > paîs.

Among verbal forms and derivatives formed with the suffix *-ęse < -ensem analogical replacements are not infrequent, cf. *receivre, ceile (celat), borgeis*.

Section 5.—RAISING INFLUENCE OF FOLLOWING PALATAL SOUNDS IN GALLO-ROMAN.

§ 419. *Influence of* i̯ *final on tonic* ę *and* ǫ—Mutation.—In Early Gallo-Roman, before final atonic vowels were weakened, i̯ final exercised an assimilative influence on preceding tonic ę and ǫ, inducing a premature lift of the tongue which raised ę to i, ǫ to ü. This process, which is akin to that called ' Umlaut ' in Germanic languages, is termed in this book *mutation* (cf. § 131):

*ęlli (< illī) > il, *pręsi > pris, **dęwwi̯ < dēbuī > **diwwi̯ > düi
*dui̯ (for duo) > düi, *tǫtti̯ > tüit, *movi* *mǫwwi̯ > **müwwi̯ > müi.

Analogical re-formation obliterated all traces of mutated forms in the nominative plural of substantives and adjectives in the course of Period I.

§ 420. The influence of following palatal consonants may also account for the raising of ụ and ẹ in Early Gallo-Roman in some other words:—

(1) O.F. füi, füit, füitẹ (< *fụjo, *fụịet, *fụị(ẹ)ta), in which L.L. ụ was juxtaposed to *jod*, and in O.F. aür (< *aɣụrịụ *augurium*).

(2) O.F. *til* tiị < *tẹjụ < tilium (cf. M.L. *Gr.* § 52) and O.F. *bisse* bisẹ < **bẹs̄sa < *bẹstịa (cf. Rohlfs, *Zts. Rom. Ph.* xli, 354, Philipon, *Rom.* xlv).

(3) O.F. *linceul* lintsuel (< *lẹn͡tsịoịụ < lintĕŏlum), *pincel, estincele,* estin-tsẹlẹ (*stincella*, § 124), in which G.R. ẹ was juxtaposed to the palatalised group n͡ts.

Section 6.—RAISING INFLUENCE OF PALATAL SOUNDS IN FRENCH.

§ 421. When the effacement of intervocalic consonants brought countertonic a into juxtaposition with tonic ü, it was raised to ẹ which was subsequently reduced to ẹ:

$$\text{fatūtum} > \text{faðüθ} > \text{fẹü} \qquad \text{sabūcum} > \text{sẹü}$$
$$\text{matūrum} > \text{maðür} > \text{mẹür} \qquad \text{**aβụtụ} > \text{ẹüθ}$$

[For later development of ẹü cf. §§ 243, 245.]

§ 422. In the course of Old French intertonic ẹ (§ 275) was raised to i by a following palatal consonant:

papilionem > pavẹịon > pavijūn *pavillon,*
*campanịoịụ > tšampẹn̦uel > tšāmpin̦uel *champignuel.*

[For the terminations *-iiens, -iiez* cf. § 919; for verbs in *-iier (charrier,* etc.) cf. § 927.]

✱✱ In the northern and eastern region (N. § xviii, E. § ii) the palatalisation of ẹ was extended further and affected: (i) ẹ intertonic before palatalised ś and ź, cf. *damisele, orison, venison;* (ii) ẹ countertonic (a) *after* tš, (b) *before* ị, n̦ and ị, e.g. *chival, chivauchier; signeur, milleur,* sin̦eur, miịeur < sen̦our, meịour; *fiiee* fiieẹ < fẹịịeð̦ẹ (*vicata), nịēnt < nẹịēnt *neient.*

✱✱ § 423. In Later Old and Middle French there was widespread palatalisation of a to ẹ before the denti-palatals ś and ź (spelling *ai* or *e,* § 718), cf. E. § xv, S.C. § x.

The palatalised pronunciation of *-age* and *ache* was admitted by Palsgrave (e.g. *dommaige, langaige, saige, scayche, taiche*), but by none of the other sixteenth-century grammarians (cf. M.L. *Gr.* § 102, Th. I, 313-314).

It is possible that the Old French dialectal forms in *-eille* -eịẹ < -aịẹ *-aille,* (E. § xxii, S.C. § xii) result from the palatalisation of the vowel a by the following ị-*mouillé* and are not the outcome of a glide development as suggested in § 408.

Section 7.—UNROUNDING OF u AND ü.

§ 424. Unrounding of ü and u to i and e was occasionally provoked by juxta-posed preceding *jod,* cf. the Late Latin forms *jẹnẹpẹrụ < jūniperum, *jenitsịa < junicia (cf. M.L. *Einf.* § 119) and Old French laïs for la jüs (< *illac deorsum,* § 749), aït, aịe, etc. < ajüt, ajüẹ; cf. also Later Old French, *gienvle* džịēnvlẹ < džüenvlẹ *juenvle* (§ 643).

CHAPTER XI.

INFLUENCE EXERCISED BY NASAL CONSONANTS ON VOWELS.

Section 1.—CLOSING INFLUENCE IN GALLO-ROMAN.

§ 425. In the formation of the nasal consonants the nose passage is opened by the lowering of the soft palate and the mouth completely closed by the action either of the tongue or the lips, and these different movements led to divergent lines of influence on vowels. The more continuous and far-reaching was the form of assimilative influence known as *nasalisation ;* less general, but important in the early period, was the influence exercised by the tongue position of nasal consonants on some of the vowels that preceded them, for under this influence the o-*sounds* were raised and the development of *tonic free* ǫ and **a** modified (cf. Addenda).

[For the influence of ŋ on preceding vowels cf. §§ 198, 406-408.]

§ 426. ǫ *tonic blocked,* ǫ *countertonic, free* and *blocked,* ǫ *free* and *blocked, tonic* and *countertonic,* and late G.R. ǫ(< **au**) (§ 505), were raised to **u** by following nasal consonants, whether **m, n** or **ŋ,** and the diphthongisation of ǫ tonic free to ǫu was consequently prevented. The sound **u** was represented by *o* or *u,* more rarely *ou* :

pŏntem > *pǫnte > **pǫnte > punt, sŏnαre > sunęr, bŏnitαtem > buntęθ.
ŭmbra > *ǫmbrę > umbrę, fŭndĕre > *fǫndere > fundrę.
cŏrōna kǫrǫna > kǫrunę, dōnum > dun, dōnαre > dunęr.
Bŏnōnia > *Bǫnǫnja > Bǫluŋę *Bologne,* *ŭnionem ǫnjǫne > uŋun *oignon.*

[For the diphthongisation of ǫ *tonic free* cf. §§ 225-227; for the nasalisation of **u** cf. below.]

The closing of the o-*sounds* is indicated for later Gallo-Roman by spellings such as *spunte, sumpnus* in the *Glossary of Reichenau.* This closing influence appears to have been exercised early enough in French to prevent the *breaking* of tonic ǫ by following ŋ, (§ 410), cf. Early Old French *loing* **luŋ** < lŏngĕ, *cointe* **kuintę** < kŏɒnitum *cognitum ;* (ct. Prov. *luenh, cuende*).

§ 427. Before **n** and **m,** G.R. **a** (< L.L. α, § 182), when *tonic free,* developed into the diphthong **ai,** unless preceded by a palatal (§ 414) :

*mαnu < mαnum > main, mαnet > maint, fαmem > faim
[For the subsequent nasalisation of **ai** cf. §§ 466-469.]

The form *maent, Eulalia* 6, suggests that the diphthong **ai** developed out of earlier **ae** under the raising influence of the nasal consonant (cf. above § 233).

Section 2.—NASALISATION IN OLD AND MIDDLE FRENCH.

§ 428. It is difficult, if not impossible, in the emission of words to open and close the nose passage so rapidly that a clean cut is made between the nasal consonant and juxtaposed sounds, and in all speech the vowel sounds preceding or following a nasal consonant tend to be incompletely nasalised, i.e. articulated with the nose passage open either at the end or at the beginning of their emission. Ordinarily, however, as in standard English, the amount of nasalisation of the vowel sounds juxtaposed to nasal consonants is too slight to be audible, although strong enough to be detected by the delicate measuring instruments of modern phoneticians (cf. Jones, p. 176), and a vowel, and particularly a high vowel, may be nasalised to a considerable extent before its acoustic quality is much affected.

In the course of Early Old French the nasal consonants began to exercise an assimilative influence on the vowels preceding them and this led gradually to an earlier opening of the nose passage and thus to their complete and audible nasalisation, i.e. to the formation of nasal vowels and diphthongs. The process reached its height in Middle French, at which period it appears that all back and front vowels preceding nasal consonants were audibly nasalised; in Later Middle French a reaction was provoked which led to a considerable amount of denasalisation of nasalised vowels. From the eleventh century on, moreover, nasalisation led, when complete, to modifications in the quality of vowels that were only stabilised in the educated usage of Modern French.

The extant evidence, both in the Old and the Middle French period, is not easy to interpret and has provoked much controversy, but the history of the process has recently been elucidated by the experiments of phoneticians and the careful observation of the modern patois, in some of which conditions now obtain which are very similar to those in Old French (cf. Rousselot, *Principes*, pp. 536-542).

[For a possible Celtic influence in the beginnings of nasalisation cf. the authorities mentioned in § 9 (iv).]

Section 3.—CONDITIONS OF NASALISATION.

§ 429. (i) Nasalisation was ordinarily *regressive*, i.e. produced by the assimilatory influence of a juxtaposed following nasal consonant:

annum > ān, annata > ānẹ̃ɗẹ, grandem > grānt, manum > māin.

✲✲ In the eastern region *progressive* nasalisation also occurs, e.g. ami > amī *amin*, nēnil > nāni > nānī *nanin*, and this pronunciation had some vogue in vulgar Parisian in Early Modern French (cf. Rosset, p. 172, and below, § 464).

§ 430. (ii) Nasalisation was induced by all the three nasal consonants, m, n, ŋ : famem > fāim (> fāin), hŏminem > **ọmmẹ > ūmẹ, manum > māin, *ūniōnem > ūŋūn *oignon*, montanea > mūntāŋẹ *montagne*.

§ 431. (iii) *Low* vowels nasalise more readily than high ones because it is not quite easy to combine the lowering of the soft palate that is required to open the nose passage with the raising of the back or front of the tongue.

This fact is of great importance in the history of nasalisation in French, for it both determines the order in which vowels are nasalised and denasalised (cf. *below*) and explains the lowering influence exercised by nasalisation on the vowels nasalised (cf. *below*).

§ 432. (iv) Nasalisation set in most strongly when the nasal vowel was pronounced in the same syllable as the nasal consonant, i.e. when this consonant was final of a word or prae-consonantal, e.g. in O.F. **ān, plēin, grānt, fēndre**, etc., but it is important to bear in mind that in Old and Middle French nasalisation was not, as in Modern French, confined to vowels in these positions: in the earlier period the vowels and diphthongs, especially those that nasalised first and most completely, were nasalised audibly by the *intervocalic* nasal consonants following them, and thus **annata > āneᵈę, amare > āmęr, montanea > mūntāŋę, femina > fēmę, *ęnǫdjare > ēnoiier, amat > āimę, plęna > plēinę, pǫma > pūmę**, etc.

From the thirteenth century on the nasalisation of a vowel before an intervocalic nasal consonant was often indicated in the spelling by the use of the symbol ~ placed above the vowel or by the doubling of the nasal consonant, e.g. *ãnee annee, fẽme femme, plẽin pleinne, tiẽgne tiengne* (cf. § 715).

§ 433. *Evidence for Nasalisation before Intervocalic Nasals.*—(i) The assonating poems, in which ā and ē are segregated from oral a and e, introduce in the laisses with assonances in ā and ē, words in which a and e stand before intervocalic nasal consonants, e.g. *Roland*, lxxxvi, *aimet : Espaigne : estrange ; France*, cxxxv, *peine : feindre : temples*, etc.

(ii) Poets who make use of the 'rime leonine' rhyme together : *Adam né : condamné, don a : donna, bouton est : boutonnet, façon nees : faconnees (Rose* II, *Intr.* p. 257) ; *en mer : enmer* (for *amer*), St. *Martin*, 3753 ; *on ment : comment, maison nette : maisonnette, daulphin nay : daulphine*, Cretin, *Intr.* p. xliv.

(iii) The value of not a few puns in the sixteenth and seventeenth centuries depends on the likeness of sound between a word containing a vowel followed by an intervocalic nasal consonant and two words, the first ending in a nasal vowel, the second beginning with a nasal consonant, cf. Tabourot's pun on *sont nettes* and *sonnettes* **sūnętę(z)** and Molière's on *grand'mère* and *grammaire* (cf. § 444).

(iv) The modern pronunciation of words can sometimes only be explained by the assumption of the existence of a previously nasalised form. Thus the a of **fam** *femme*, **fanę < fenare** indicates earlier ā (< ę̄, § 447) denasalised ; the open ǫ of **pǫm** *pomme* **< pǫma** goes back to earlier ǭ (< ū, § 459); cf. also *aîné* **ęnę < ēnę < ēi(z)nę < āintsnę** *ainz ne*.

(v) The spelling with a double nasal finds its explanation here.

§ 434. *Date of Nasalisation.*—The complete nasalisation of the vowels and diphthongs appears to have been a slow process, occupying close on four centuries, from the tenth to the end of the thirteenth or later. The audible nasalisation of the low vowels began in Early Old French, first with ã and ãi (in the tenth century), then with ẽ and ẽi: the other vowels and diphthongs were gradually nasalised completely in the order of their height, i and ü last, the diphthongs ie, oi, ui only after shift of stress, i.e. after the middle or end of the twelfth century (§§ 510, 515, 474). At the beginning of the Middle French period it is probable that all vowels were nasalised audibly, though not all lowered, i.e. that u + *nasal* was pronounced ũ, i + *nasal*, ĩ, ü + nasal, ü̃ (cf. *below*).

Data for these conclusions are furnished mainly by the assonating poems, for in these the vowels that are audibly nasalised are kept apart from their oral counterparts. In the *St. Leger* (tenth century), ã and ãi are thus segregated; in the *St. Alexis* (eleventh century), ẽ and ẽi also, but in these poems, and in most of those with assonating laisses, the other vowels and diphthongs assonate freely with their oral counterparts, cf. *Roland*, laisses x, xii, xxxi, etc., i + *oral* consonant and i + *nasal* consonant; laisses l, lxviii, lxxiv, u + *oral* consonant and u + *nasal* consonant; laisses lxxxii, cxlvi, ü + *oral* consonant with ü + nasal consonant; laisses iii, viii, xviii, ie + *oral* consonant with ie + *nasal* consonant; laisse xxiii, ue + *oral* consonant with ue + *nasal* consonant; *Aucassin*, §§ 19, 29, i and in; §§ 27, 39, u and un; § 9, ie and ien. Towards the end of the twelfth century poets tend to segregate u + *nasal* and ie + *nasal*, an indication that the nasality of these vowels was becoming audible. The use of the symbol of nasality and the doubling of the nasal consonant indicate the beginnings of complete nasality of i in the thirteenth century; ę was apparently only fully nasalised in the ending -ęnt, cf. § 437. [For further details cf. §§ 442-478.]

Section 4.—INFLUENCE OF NASALISATION ON THE NASAL CONSONANTS.

§ 435. As the nasalisation of a vowel became complete the nasal consonant itself was affected when final of the word or prae-consonantal.

(1) The labial and palatal nasals, m and ŋ, were dentalised gradually to n when final of the word: m in the course of Early Old French, ŋ in the course of Period II:

Adam > Adãn, fãim < famem > fãin, num < nōmen > nũn.

O.F. *baing* bãiŋ < * banjy *balneum* > bęn *bain, tiegn* tjęŋ > tję̃(n).

O.F. *luing* luiŋ < longe (§§ 426, 407) > lµęn *loin.*

Cf. *Best.* Ph. *leun : num* 25, *Sathan : Adam* 753; Villon, *P.D.* iv *fain : foing : baing : poing;* G. Alexis, *faing* (*fingo*) *: fain* (*famem*), I, p. 32.

The beginnings of the dentalisation of m are attested for Early Old French by the spellings *Dinam* for *Dinan* 1065, *Brium* for *Brion* 1096 (Drevin, p. 170). While nasalisation of the vowel was still incomplete the dental nasal was sometimes labialised by a following labial consonant, cf. *Isembardus* 1075, *Seimfredus* 1067 (Drevin, p. 170), *Alexis*, MS. L. *emfes* 7(e), *amfant* 9 (b).

It is difficult to determine the date of the dentalisation of ŋ *final*. The notation gn (ng) persisted into the sixteenth century but rhymes between words ending in n and ŋ began in the thirteenth century, e.g. Rtbf. *gaaing : aing* (*amo*) 5, 38, *vain : vain* (*venio*) 142, 725: these, however, may be inexact.

§ 436. (2) **n** *final of the word* was maintained in *prae-vocalic* position into Modern French, but in the pronunciation of **n** *final* elsewhere and of **n**, *prae-consonantal* in the word, the tongue was gradually lowered and in the course of Middle French the consonant gradually merged in the preceding nasal vowel.

**grānt > grāt, pŭnt (< pŏntem) > pūt, fẹndre > fẹ̄drẹ, rūnpere > rūprẹ
ān > ā(n), fẽn (< fāim) > fẽ(n), dūn (< dōnum) > dū(n) > dǭ(n).**

§ 437. The *prae-consonantal* nasal was merged in the nasal vowel before the middle of the sixteenth century, at which time the lengthening of the preceding vowel which marks the completion of the process is mentioned by grammarians (§ 563).

Peletier states explicitly : ' Nous ne prononçons quasi point la lètre *n* apres une voyèle, quand èle èt acompagnée d'une tiérce lètre : comme an ces moz *bons, sons, conte* . . . é tous autres tèz.' (Th. II, 511.)   In the unstressed verbal ending **-ẹnt** absorption of the consonant goes back to the late thirteenth century, cf. the spellings *hateret*, etc., for *hasterent*, etc., in the Hebrew glosses of that date, (*Rom. St.* I, p. 167). It is expressly attested by Coyfurelly : ' N, autem, posita inter vocalem et consonantem in fine alicuius diccionis, que sit verbum tercie persone pluralis numeri . . . de jure non sonabitur, verb. gr. *ils aiment . . . ils amoient . . . ils amerent . . . ils distrent . . ils amassent.*' (*Zts. nfrz. Spr.* I, 18; cf. § 897.)

§ 438. In final position the absorption of the consonant was slower and at first only complete when the word was in prae-consonantal position. Bèze prescribes ' *Pierre s'en n'est alle, on m'en na parle,*' but warns foreigners that *n* when final ' has as it were only half a sound,' p. 35 ; Palsgrave's recommendation of a full sound ('*n* and *m* after the last vowel in a frenche worde lese never theyr sounde . . .' p. 24) is probably to be accounted for by influence of Norman pronunciation (§ 1328 (5a)).

Section 5.—INFLUENCE OF NASALISATION ON VOWELS.

§ 439. Nasalisation set in early enough to prevent in francien the differentiation of **ei** + *nasal* to **oi** (§ 226), and thus Early O.F. **peinẹ, plein,** etc., persisted (nasalised) into the twelfth century (cf. below). The chief effect of this process on vowels was, however, to induce a lowered tongue position in their articulation (cf. § 431).

The lowering of **ẽ** to **ã** began in the late eleventh century (§ 448) and before the end of the seventeenth century all the high and mid vowels that had remained nasalised were lowered, whether pure or diphthongal or preceded by one of the semi-vowels or voiced fricative consonants **i̯, u̯, ü̯, j, w, ẉ,** i.e. **i̇ > ẹ, ū > ǭ, ü̃ > ǭ̈, i̯ẽ > i̯ẹ, u̯i > wẹ, ü̯i > ẉẹ.** The last of the nasal vowels to be lowered were **ū** and **ũ̈.**

[For details cf. below, §§ 442-481 ; for eastern **oi** < **ei** + *nasal* cf. E. § xix.]

Section 6.—DENASALISATION.

§ 440. Nasalisation, an assimilatory process, was dominant in the Old and Early Middle French period, but in Later Middle French there

set in slowly its converse—*denasalisation*.   In that period there developed gradually a dislike to the juxtaposition of two nasal sounds, and wherever a nasal vowel was still in contact with a fully sounded nasal consonant it was gradually differentiated from that consonant, i.e. denasalised by the gradual closing of the nose passage.

When this tendency began to operate the nasal consonants that were in final or prae-consonantal position had already merged completely or to a considerable extent in the preceding nasalised vowels (§§ 436, 437), and the only nasal consonants that retained their full articulation were those that were at that period intervocalic, i.e. those not sounded in the same syllable as the preceding vowel, as, for instance, in *année* **ā-nę̣ę̣**, *pleinne* **plę̣-nę̣**, *homme* **ū-mę̣**, *finne* **fī-nę̣**, *chienne* **šję̣-nę̣**, *une* **ū-nę̣** : in words of this type the nasal vowels were gradually denasalised.   The process began with the vowels last and least strongly nasalised, i.e. the high vowels **ī** and **ū**, which were denasalised before they were lowered, and ended in Early Modern French with the low vowels **ā** and **ǫ̨**.

[For denasalisation in Norman cf. § 1328 (5*b*).]

Section 7.—Summary of History of Nasal Vowels.

§ 441.   Early Old French **a** + *nasal* > **ā** (c. x) (> **ɑ̃** in Modern French) : **ā**, denasalised, becomes **a** (xvi-xvii).

Early Old French **ẹ** + *nasal* > **ē** (c. xi) > **ā** (xi-xii) (> **ɑ̃** in Modern French) : **ā**, denasalised, becomes **a** (xvi-xvii).

Early Old French **ai** + *nasal* > **āi** (c. x) > **ę̣i** > **ę̣** in Period II : **ę̣**, denasalised, becomes **ẹ** in Later Middle French.

Early Old French **ei** + *nasal* > **ẹ̄i** (c. xi) > **ę̣i** > **ę̣** in Period II : **ę̣**, denasalised, becomes **ẹ** in Later Middle French.

Early Old French 'ie + *nasal* > **ɟẹ** (c. xii) > **ɟę̣** (c. xiii) > **ɟẹ́** in Period II : **ɟę̣**, denasalised, becomes **ɟẹ** in Later Middle French.

Early Old French **i** + nasal > **ī** in Later Old French > **ę̣** (c. xvi) : **ī**, denasalised, becomes **i** (c. xv).

Gallo-Roman **ǫ** + *nasal* > Early Old French **u** + *nasal* > **ū** in Later Old French > **ǭ** (c. xvii) : **ǭ**, denasalised, becomes **ǫ** (c. xvii).

Gallo-Roman **ǫi** + *nasal* > Early Old French **ui** + *nasal* > **uę̣** > **wę̣** (c. xvii) : **wę̣**, denasalised, becomes **wẹ** (> **wa** in Modern French).

Early Old French **ü** + *nasal* > **ǖ** > **ǫ̈̄** (c. xvii) : **ǖ**, denasalised, becomes **ü** in Later Middle French.

Early Old French **üi** + *nasal* > **ẅī** > **ẅę̣** (c. xvii) : **ẅī**, denasalised, becomes **ẅi** in Later Middle French.

Later Old French **ö** < **ue** + *nasal* > **ȫ** in Period II > **ǫ̈̄** (c. xvii) : **ǫ̈̄**, denasalised, becomes **ọ̈**.

Section 8.—DEVELOPMENT OF NASAL VOWELS AND DIPHTHONGS.

§ 442. Early Old French a + nasal > ã (c. x), (> ᾱ in Modern French); ã denasalised before intervocalic nasals to a (late xvi-xvii).

(i) G.R. a (< L. and G. ɑ) tonic and countertonic + n or m + oral consonant :

grandem > grãnt > grã(t)   kampum > tšãmp   > šã(p) champ
mandare > mãndẹr > mãdẹ   *kambiare > tšãndžier > šãzẹ changier

(ii) G.R. a (< L. and G. ɑ) tonic before intervocalic nn, mm, mn become final :

annum > ãn > ã(n)   *bannu > bãn > bã(n)   damnum > dam > dã(n)

(iii) G.R. a (< L. and G. ɑ) tonic before intervocalic nn, mm, mn, nm, denasalised to a :

anima > ãmẹ > amẹ   flamma < flãmẹ > flamẹ flamme

(iv) G.R. a (< L. and G. ɑ) tonic before intervocalic ŋ, denasalised to a :

mŏntanĕa > **montaɲa > muntãɲẹ > mũtaɲẹ montagne

(v) G.R. a (< L. and G. ɑ) countertonic before n, m, ŋ, nn, mm, nm, denasalised to a :

sanare > sãnẹr > sanẹ saner   amarum > ãmẹr > amẹr amer
annata > ãnẹðẹ > anẹ année   amikum > ãmi > ami
*agnellos aɲɲĕllos > ãɲẹɫs > aɲọ(z) agneaux

[Cf. also below ẽ.]

§ 443. ã, the first vowel to be nasalised completely (§ 434), persisted in francien into the seventeenth century; in the position in which it was retained, i.e. when final and prae-consonantal, it was lengthened by the absorption of the nasal consonant (§ 437) and gradually velarised to ᾱ in the Modern period, (cf. M. K. Pope, Kastner Volume, pp. 400, 401).

§ 444. Denasalisation.—In educated Parisian speech the denasalisation of O.F. ã appears to have begun in the later sixteenth century, but the nasality of the vowel standing before intervocalic nasals was maintained long in the provinces and in Paris itself it continued in the later seventeenth century in the adverbs in -emment pronounced -ãmã(t), in the word grammaire and in words whose initial syllable was ã, e.g. enivrer ãnivrẹ, emmener ãmǝnẹ, ennuyer ãnwijẹ : in most of these last the sound has persisted under the influence of words beginning with initial en- ã- preceding a consonant, e.g. entendre ãtãdrẹ.

The pronunciation grãmẹrẹ, ardãmã, prüdãmã is still prescribed by some grammarians at the end of the seventeenth century (Th. II, 453). The close acoustic similarity of the first syllable of the words grammaire and grand'mere is attested not only by Martine's pun (Femmes Sav. II, 6) but also by a remark of the grammarian Chifflet (1651), ‘Ne prononcez pas en é masculin’ (i.e. ẹ), ‘grammaire . . . autrement les petits escoliers diront je porte ma grand'mere dans mon sac.’

**§ 445. Local Variants.—(i) In the region in which a palatal glide developed between ã and ŋ (§ 408) and the diphthong ãi levelled to ẽ, -ãɲẹ passed through -ãĩɲẹ to -ẽɲẹ and is coupled in rhyme both with -ẽɲẹ (< -eiɲẹ) and -wẽɲẹ (< -oiɲẹ), cf. Rose I, Bretaigne : enseigne 1177, etc., Rtbf., Charlemaine : retiengne

p. 26, 126, *acompaingne : enseingne : esloingne*, p. 9, 9. Parisian speech was also affected, cf. Villon, T. 382, *Auvergne : Charlemaigne*, 1629, *Bretaigne : enseigne*.

In the sixteenth century this pronunciation had considerable vogue; Bèze gives two pronunciations for *baigner* and *gaigner* : beɲer, baɲer, geɲer, gaɲer (p. 47); Tabourot (Dijonnois) and Lanoue (Angevin (?)) also accept both, but in 1608 **-eɲ-** is violently rejected by Palliot ; ' Je sçay bien qu'il y a des diphthongues qu'il vauldroit mieux laisser et n'en retenir que la premiere voyelle plustost que de les escrire ny proferer : tant il s'y donne un mauvais air par des mal-embouchez et mauplaisants prononcears. Comme celle d'*ai* en *Bretaigne, montaigne, Champaigne, aigueau* ou ils semblent avoir le mords trop serré et se gourmer par trop, à en faire la petite bouche, les prononcantz en *ei, eigneau, Breteigne.* . . . J'aymerois autant leur faire avaller des champignons.' (Th. I, p. 330). **-aɲ-** was established in most words in the seventeenth century, **-eɲ-** survived in Modern *baigner, saigner, châtaigne*, etc., and *araignée*.

⚝✱ § 446 (ii). In the western and northern regions ã was strongly velarised and in Later Middle French, if not earlier, labialised to ǫ̃. Peletier's description is explicit : ' Vrèi êt qu'an Normandie, é ancous an Bretagne, an Anjou, é an votre Meine . . . iz prononcet l'*a* devant *n* un peu bien grossemant é quasi comme s'il i auoèt *aun* par diftongue; quand iz diset *Normaund, Nauntes, Aungers, le Mauns, graund chere.*' (Th. II, 430.) This pronunciation probably accounts for Palsgrave's diagnosis of the sound, although he may be influenced by home pronunciation (cf. § 69). ' If *m* or *n* folowe nexte after *a* in a frenche worde, all in one syllable, then *a* shall be sounded lyke this diphthong *au*, and somethyng in the noose, as these wordes *ambre, chambre, mander, amant, tant* . . . shall in redynge and spekynge be sownded *aumbre, chaumbre, maunder* . . .,' p. 2.

The isolated rhymes *manne : aune* (Froissart, I, p. 229), *sanle* (< *simulat*, MS. *samble*) ; *Maune* (the modern name *Mohun*, O.F. *Moion, Moon, Black Prince*, 569), indicate that both velarising and rounding were beginning to be current in the late fourteenth century in the northern region, and in the Mystery Plays of the fifteenth century *an* and *on* rhyme together freely, e.g. *Mahon : an* (cf. Cohen, *Intr.* p. xxiii and below, N. § xx and Part V, § 1152 ; for the spelling cf. § 536).

✗　§ 447. Early Old French ę + *nasal* > ẽ (c. xi) > ã (c. xi–xii) (> ɑ̃ in Modern French, cf. above, § 443) ; ã denasalised to a before intervocalic nasals (late xvi–xvii, cf. above, § 444).

(1) G.R. ę and ẹ (< L. and G. ĕ, ē) *tonic, countertonic* and *intertonic* + **n** or **m** + *oral consonant* :

pĕndĕre	> pēndrę	> pāndrę	> pãdrę	*pendre*
fīndĕre	> fēndrę	> fāndrę	> fãdrę	*fendre*
trĕmŭlo	> trēmblę	> trānblę	> trãblę	*tremble*
ĭn sĭmŭl	> ēnsēmblę	> ānsãnblę	> ãsãblę	*ensemble*
sĕntire	> sēntir	> sāntir	> sãtir	*sentir*

[Cf. also O.F. prüdēntmēnt > prüdãmānt > prüdamãt, § 444.]

(2) G.R. ę and ẹ *tonic* (< L. and G. ĕ, ē), before *intervocalic* **nn, mm, mn**, become final :
*sĭnnų > sēn > sãn > sã(n).

(3) G.R. ę and ẹ (< L. and G. ĕ, ē), *tonic*, before *intervocalic* **nn,** ᴵ **mm, mn**, denasalised to a :
pĭnna > pēnę > pãnę > pan(ę) *panne*, femina > fēmę > fãmę > fam(ę) *femme*.

(4) G.R. ę and ẹ (< L. and G. ĕ, ē), *countertonic* before intervocalic **n, m, nn, mm, mn**, denasalised to a (but cf. §§ 444, 449) :
fęnɑre > fēnęr > fãnęr > fanę *faner*, remɑre > rēmęr > rãmęr > ramę
hĭnnire > hēnir > hãnir > hanir *hennir*.

(5) *Countertonic* and *intertonic* e (< weakly stressed **o** (§ 257) before **n** and **m** :
*calumniare kalǫmnjare > tšalēndžier > tšalãndžier > šalãžę̆ *chalengier*
non *ęlli > nēnil > nãnil > nani *nenni* ; (cf. also § 601).

§ 448. e was nasalised to ę before nasal consonants in the course of Early Old French, § 434, and was gradually lowered to ã in the course of the late eleventh and twelfth centuries.

The lowering of ē to ã is attested in the *Roland* in which ē before prae-consonantal **n** is already assonating freely with ã (cf. laisses xix, xxii, xxx, etc.). Crestien not only admits rhymes of ē prae-consonantal with ã but also couples together ã (< ē) and ã (< a) before intervocalic nasal consonants, cf. *E. jame (gemma) : dame* 2410, *Iv. assane : barbacane* 4879.

§ 449. Before intervocalic single or double nasals there are variant developments of countertonic ę, cf. O.F. **męnęr** < ***menαre**, **sęmer** < **seminαre** and **fãnęr** < ***fęnαre**, **rãmer** < **remαre**. It is probable that in some regions ę was obscured to ę before nasalisation set in, in others after, but the question needs further elucidation.

✱✱ § 450. In the western, northern and north-eastern region ē remained unlowered before **n**, a characteristic of northern speech that did not escape the notice of sixteenth-century observers, cf. Pasquier : ' Que nous ne prononcions l'*e* pur ' (in words in -*ent*), ' j'en suis d'accord : il n'y a que le Picard qui le prononce, et par ceste prononciation on cognoist du premier coup qu'on est extrait de Picardie.' (Th. II, 431, N. § xx, W. § viii.)

Before **m**, even in this region, the sound was ordinarily lowered, cf. O.F. *essample, tans* (< *tempus*), cf. P. Meyer, *Mem. Soc. Lg.* I, 244-276.

✱✱ In the region in which diphthongs were levelled early, the south-central and south-western region, **ɥe** < ˡ**ie** (§ 512) was nasalised and lowered to **ɥã** (cf. § 478, S.C. § vi). Modern *taniere* may also find its explanation here: O.F. **taizniere** < ***taxonaria** > **tęnɥęrę** (§§ 377, 533) > **tãnɥęrę**.

§ 451. Later Old French **i** + *nasal* > **ĩ** (c. xiii) > ę̃ (c. xv-xvi) ; **ĩ** denasalised before intervocalic nasal to **i** in Late Middle French.

(1) **i** (< L. and G. **ī**) *tonic* and *countertonic* + **n** and **m** + *oral consonant* :
  principem **prīnkĭpem** > **printsę** > **prĩnsę** > **prę̃sę** *prince*.
  *cinquanta ***kĩɱkɥanta** > **tsĩnkãntę** > **sĩnkãntę** > **sę̃kãtę** *cinquante*.

(2) **i** (< L. and G. **ī**) *tonic* before **n** or **m** become final in Old French :
  fĭnem > **fĭn** > **fĩn** > **fẽ(n)** *fin*, **lĭnum** > **lĭn** > **lĩn** > **lę̃(n)**.

(3) **i** (< L. and G. **ī**) *tonic* and *countertonic* before intervocalic **n**, **m** and **ŋ** ; denasalised to **i** :
  lĭmα > **lĭmę** > **lĩmę** > **limę**, ***fĩna** > **fĩnę** > **fĩnę** > **finę**.
  lĭneα > ***lĭnɥa** > **liɲę** > **lĩɲę** > **liɲę** *ligne*.

(4) Latin ę *tonic free* raised to **i** by preceding palatal (§ 418) and followed by a nasal :
  rαkĕmum > **raizim** > **ręzĭn** > **ręzę̃(n)** *raisin*.

(5) Latin ę *tonic* + *præ-consonantal* **ŋ** (§§ 321, 411), e.g. *enginz, engint*.

§ 452. **i** appears to have been nasalised audibly to **ĩ** in the thirteenth century, but the lowered pronunciation ę̃ is not attested in Villon's rhymes and was not fully accepted in educated Parisian speech before the later sixteenth century : de-nasalisation before the intervocalic nasal ordinarily preceded lowering.

§ 453. H. Estienne (1582) professes still to detect a difference between ę̃ and **ĩ** : ' Indubitably one ought to pronounce *vain* and *pain* with the mouth more open than *vin, pin*.' Estienne may, however, have been biassed by spelling, for the lowered

pronunciation is accepted by Tabourot (1587) and Lyttelton (1566): ' Autres y a qui prononcent a la Parisienne *in* comme *ain* : Exemple *j'ay beu du bon uain a la pomme de pain* pour dire *j'ay beu du bon vin a la pomme de pin*.' (Tabourot, *Big*. p. 68.) ' We sound *ain* as *in*, say then insteed of *main, maintenant, demain . . . min, mintenent, demin*.' (Lyttelton, cited Zachrisson, p. 9.) Already, indeed, in 1533 Bovelles attributes the pronunciation ę̃ to the Parisians, for he speaks of words in which ' the Belgae use the diphthong *ai*, but the Parisians change it to a simple *i* ' (i.e. ę̃), ' thus *pain* with the Belgae, but with the Parisians *pin*.' (Th. II, 481.)

✳✳ § 454. In the north-western region ī was retained late, § 1328 (5); in the southern, especially the south-east (Burgundy), lowering appears to have begun in the later thirteenth century, cf. the spellings *Morin* for *Morain* 1278, *Cenin* for *Senain* 1485, in Burgundy (Thomas, *Essais*, p. 31, Rydberg, *Kr. Jb*. VI(1), 233) ; Regnier (Auxerre, c. xv) allows himself to rhyme *latin, matin* with *haultain*, p. 34, *latin : certain*, p. 198, *chemin : main*, p. 187, *jacinte : fainte*, 215 ; for the Orléanais cf. the spelling *letrain* 1461, and rhymes in *St. Joan*, e.g. *fins : mains*, 2110, *chemin : lointain* 1653.

Vulgar Parisian was also affected relatively early, cf. the spellings *roieine* (for *roine*), Boileaue, p. 11, *gindre* for **žēndrę** < **žwēndrę** *joindre* (< *junior*) and *Cochin* for *Cochein* in the *Rôle de Taille* of 1296 (Michaëlsson, p. 75).

Lowering preceded denasalisation in the southern region, cf. the spellings *saisene* for *saisine, cusene* for *cuisine* in the south-east (Philipon, *Rom*. xxxix, 522), and this tendency also affected vulgar Parisian, for the lowered pronunciation *cousaine, voisaine*, etc., is attributed to Parisians in 1604, and Hindret (1687) ascribes the pronunciation of ' *mainnuit* ' for *minuit* to the ' petite bourgeoisie de Paris.' (Th. II, 478, 501 ; cf. Rosset, 176-177.)

§ 455. Between i and ī the acoustic difference is relatively slight and in Early Middle French the two sounds were sometimes confused : Guiot, *Bible*, 174, *princes : crevices, G. Dôle coissins : assis* 1515. In Modern French *cingler* for O.F. *sigler* the nasalised sound was established.

The nasalisation of final i in Middle French *ainsi* (written *ainsinc, ainsint*, pronounced ę̃sę̃(n) ?) is due to the assimilative influence of the first syllable.

§ 456. Later Old French ü + *nasal* > ũ > ő (c. xvi-xvii) ; ũ denasalised before *intervocalic nasal* to ü in Late Middle French.

(1) G.R. ų (< L. and G. ū) *tonic and countertonic* + n *and* m + *oral consonant :*

O.F. **ümblę** > **ũmblę** > **őblę**, **lūnes diem > lün(z)di > lūndi > lődi.*

(2) G.R. ų (< L. and G. ū) *tonic before* n *or* m *become final in Old French :*

ūnum > ün > ũn > ő(n), Augustodunum > ǫstęün > ǫtũn > ǫtő(n).

(3) G.R. ų (< L. and G. ū) *tonic and countertonic before intervocalic* n, m, mn, denasalised to ü :

plūma > plümę̨ > plümę > plümę, luna > lünę > lũnę > lünę.

§ 457. ü nasalised completely relatively late (§§ 431, 439) and the lowered sound ö was only accepted in educated Parisian speech in the seventeenth century ; denasalisation ordinarily preceded lowering.

§ 458. *Attesting Remarks.*—(1) ũ. Cauchie (1540) : ' ü has a pure and simple sound and answers to the German sound marked by a trema as in *übel*, e.g. *vertu, fetu, bossu, chacun, emprunte, lundi*.' (Th. II, p. 543.) Tabourot (1587) still equates ' *Dieu tappe un nid* ' with ' *Dieu t'a puny*.' (*Big*. p. 15.)

(2) ő. Explicit recognition of the sound ő is late, first in D'Aisy (1674), ' *-un* a toujours le son confus et l'*u* sonne *eu . . .*' Lanoue, however, in 1596 classifies

ü among the vowels 'which thicken their sound' and admits *ieun* (**žõn**) among the rhymes in *un* (cf. Th. II, pp. 542-544).

In uneducated speech lowering certainly began in Late Middle French and affected **ü** before intervocalic nasals as well as elsewhere, cf. *Guise Letters* (1548), *heumble*, *heumblement*, *empreunte*, *eung*, p. 215, the hesitation in the sixteenth century between *aubun d'oeuf* and *aubin d'oeuf* (Th. II, 547) and the vulgar spellings *leune*, *pleume*, etc., cited by Rosset, p. 177.

§ 459. Early Old French **u** + *nasal* > **ū** > **ǫ̃** (c. xvii); **ǫ̃** denasalised before intervocalic nasal to **ǫ** (c. xvii).

(1) G.R. **u** (< L. and G. **ŏ, ō, ŭ**) *tonic* and *countertonic* + **n** or **m** + oral consonant :

ŭmbra	> **umbrę**	> **ūnbrę**	> **ǫ̃brę**
fŭndus	> **funts**	> **fūnts**	> **fǫ̃(z)** *fonds*
kŏmitem	> **kuntę**	> **kūntę**	> **kǫ̃tę** *comte*
pŏntem	> **punt**	> **pūnt**	> **pǫ̃(t)** *pont.*
fŭndare	> **fundęr**	> **fūndęr**	> **fǫ̃dę** *fonder*
fŏntana	> **funtāinę**	> **fūntę̃inę**	> **fǫ̃tęn(ę)** *fontaine*
bŏnitatem	> **buntęθ**	> **būntę**	> **bǫ̃tę** *bonté*
cŏmitatum	> **kuntęθ**	> **kūntę**	> **kǫ̃tę** *comté*

(2) G.R. **u** (< L. and G. **ō, ŭ**) *tonic free* before **n** and **m** become final in Old French :

dōnum	> **ɗun**	> **dūn**	> **dǫ̃(n)** *don*
latrōnem	> **laɗrun**	> **larūn**	> **larǫ̃(n)** *larron*

(3) G.R. **u** (< L. and G. **ō, ŭ**) *tonic free* before intervocalic **n** and **m**; denasalised to **ǫ** :

pōma	> **pumę**	> **pūmę**	> **pǫ̃m(ę)**	> **pǫm(ę)** *pomme*
kŏrōna	> **kǫrunę**	> **kurūnę**	> **kurǫ̃nę**	> **kurǫn(ę)** *couronne*

(4) G.R. **u** (< L. and G. **ŏ, ō, ŭ**) *tonic blocked* by *intervocalic* **mm, mn, nn** denasalised to **ǫ** :

sŭmma	> **sumę**	> **sūmę**	> **sǫ̃mę**	> **sǫm(e)** *somme*
hŏminem	> **umę**	> **ūmę**	> **ǫ̃mę**	> **ǫm(ę)** *homme*

(5) G.R. **u** (< L. and G. **ŏ, ō, ŭ**) *countertonic* + intervocalic **m, mm, mn, n, nn** ; denasalised to **ǫ** :

dōnare	> **dunęr**	> **dūnęr**	> **dǫ̃nę**	> **dǫnę** *donner*
sŏnare	> **sunęr**	> **sūnęr**	> **sǫ̃nę**	> **sǫnę** *sonner*

(6) G.R. **u** (< L. and G. **ŏ, ō, ŭ**) *tonic* and *countertonic* before intervocalic **ŋ** ; denasalised to **ǫ** :

*Bŏnōnja	> **Bǫluŋę**	> **Bulūŋę̃**	> **Bulǫ̃ŋę̃**	> **Bulǫŋ(ę)** *Boulogne*
*ǫnjǫne	> **uŋun**	> **ūŋūn**	> **ǫ̃ŋǫ̃n**	> **ǫŋǫ̃(n)** *oignon*

(7) G.R. **ǫ** (< au) + **n** or **m** + *oral* consonant.

*haunita > **hǫntę** > **huntę** > **hūntę** > **ǫ̃nt(ę)** *honte*

(8) O.F. unstressed *bon*, *on* (< *homo*), §§ 599, 870.

bun > **būn** > **bǫ̃(n)**

§ 460. Before the nasal consonants (**m, n, ŋ**), the **o**-*sounds* appear to have closed to **u** before the end of the Gallo-Roman period (§ 426) ; **u** was gradually nasalised to **ū** and this sound was retained throughout

Middle French.   In the course of the seventeenth century ū was lowered to ǫ̈ and denasalisation was carried through at that stage.

§ 461. The pronunciation ū (sometimes indicated by the use of the digraph *ou*, cf. *Auc. oume*, 14, 19) is formally attested by the grammarians of the sixteenth and early seventeenth centuries : Palsgrave : ' If *m* or *n* folowe next after *o* in a frenche worde both in one syllable, than shal the *o* be sounded almost lyke this diphthonge *ou* and some thyng in the noose : as these wordes *mon* . . . shalbe sownded *moun* . . . ; and in lyke wyse shall *o* be sownded though the next syllable followynge begynne with an other *m* or *n*, as in these wordes *home, somme, bonne, tonnerre*, whiche they sounde *houme, boune, soumme, tounner* ' (p. 7).   Behourt (1629) ' *o* se prononce tousiours en *ou* deuant *m*, comme *homme, houme, ombre, oumbre* . . . Aussi deuant *n* en mesme syllabe *ou* deuent deux *nn*, comme *ouncle, countre, dounne*.' (Th. II, 512.)   Awfeild (1634) also explicitly prescribes u : ' when in the middle of a word the Syllable after *o* begynneth with **m**, or **n**, these letters are commonly double and the first belonging to *o* maketh *o* to be pronounced like *ou* as *houme, coume, counoistre, douner*.   And so likewise is it though the consonant be not doubled ' (p. 26).

§ 462. In prae-consonantal and final position ū is still prescribed by Chifflet in 1659 ; the first mention of a lowered sound, ' un son mitoyen,' appears to be in d'Allais (1681) and it is Dangeau in 1696 who first clearly distinguishes ǫ̈ from ū (Th. II, 513).
Before intervocalic nasal consonants the lowered pronunciation developed earlier. Chifflet mentions a slightly lowered pronunciation of the sound in *-omme* and *-onne*, and already Oudin in 1633 condemned the higher sound : ' L'*o* français se prononce fort ouvert, contre l'opinion fort impertinente de ceux qui le veulent prononcer comme *ou* (**u**), quand il est devant **m** ou **n**; car ceux qui parlent bien ne disent iamais *houme, coume, boune*, etc. ' (Th. II, 521).

§ 463. *Denasalisation.*—Nasalisation of the vowel before intervocalic nasals is still indicated clearly by Martin in 1632, for he represents the words *personne, bonne, honneur, comme, commence*, etc., by *persunne, bunne, hunneur, kunme, kunmanse* (cf. § 176 and Th. II, 521), but Hindret (1687) blames provincials ' who pronounce the first syllable of the words *gomme, homme, pomme, bonne* like the words *pompe, bonté* (Th. II, 522).

§ 464. *Date of Nasalisation of* **u**.—The passage of **m** final to **n** after **u** is attested by rhymes in the early twelfth century (§ 435) and appears to indicate the nasalisation of the preceding vowel, but on the other hand in all the assonating poems, including *Aucassin and Nicolete* (c. xii-xiii) **u** + *nasal consonant* is admitted in assonance with **u** + *oral consonant* (*Auc.* laisse 27, *blons, parfont, arçon*, etc.: *amorous, amors, dox,* etc.).   It would thus appear that nasalisation at that date had not modified the *quality* of the **u**-*sound*.
Complete nasalisation, without modification of the vowel, is also indicated in Later Old and Middle French by the interchange of ū and **u**, cf. the spelling *mont* for *mout* in the Jewish Elegy of 1288, the rhymes between **u** + *nasal* + *oral consonant* and **u** + *oral consonant*, cf. Rtbf. *molt : mont*, p. 242, l. 877, G. *D ôle temoute* (< *tumultum*) : *honte* 2498 ; *Panthère d'Amour, contes : toutes*, 1880-81 ; G. Alexis, *dont ceste : doulcette*, I, p. 25, and the Middle French confusion of the locutions *tronc de chou* and *tros de chou*, i.e. **tru dę šu**.   In the words like *munt* (*multum*), *muntepleiier* (*multiplicare*), etc., in which **u** is preceded by a nasal consonant, progressive nasalisation may play a part (§ 429), but in the other words ū appears to have lost nasality after having been nasalised strongly enough to absorb the nasal consonant.
Continuance of the nasalising tendency into Middle French is indicated by

the fact that in the words *fromage* and *promener* nasalisation took place after the metathesis of **r** :

$$\textbf{furmažę} > \textbf{frumažę} > \textbf{frūmažę} > \textbf{frǫmaž(ę).}$$

§ 465. *-oigne* **-y̨ę̄ŋę̨** for **-ūŋę̨** *-ogne*.—In the region in which a palatal glide developed between **u** and **ŋ** intervocalic (§ 408) the diphthong **ui** followed the normal course of development to **y̨ę̨** (§ 475). This development does not seem to have affected Parisian speech, for it is the sound **ū** that is described by all the sixteenth-century grammarians before **ŋ** : in late Middle French, however, the diphthongal pronunciation began to be introduced under analogical influence in words which had derivatives or associated forms in which it was *normally* developed (i.e. when **ŋ** was final or prae-consonantal, § 279) and thus : (*a*) words like *eloigner* **ęlūŋę**, *soigner* **sūŋę**, *temoigner* **tęmūŋę** began to be pronounced **ęly̨ęŋę**, **sy̨ęŋę**, **tęmy̨ęŋę** under the influence of the substantives *loin*, *soin*, *temoin*, **ly̨ę̨(n)**, **sy̨ę̨(n)**, **tęmy̨ę̨(n)** ; (*b*) the verbal forms *-oignons, -oignez, -oignant*, etc., **-ūŋū, -ūŋę, -ūŋā**, (*joignons, joignez*), etc., began to be pronounced **-uęŋū, -y̨ęŋę, -y̨ęŋā** under the influence of *-oindre, -oint*, **-y̨ę̄drę, -y̨ę̨(t)**, etc. In many words there was hesitation for a considerable period.

Ramus (1562) ' Nous escripuons *tesmoingner, soingner, coingner ;* or il falloit escrire en escripture correcte *temonher, sonher, conher.*'

Lanoue (1596) ' Les motz de ceste terminaizon *ongne* reçoiuent triple orthographe selon qu'il plaist a celuy qui escrit, ou *ogne, oigne*, ou *ongne*, mais on les prononce de la derniere façon, car on n'y exprime point cet *i* de *oigne*, on ne baille pas aussi le son ordinaire de l'*o* pour prononcer *ogne*, mais un certain son sourd que luy donne ceste *n*. . . .' The pronunciation **ūŋū** is prescribed by Meigret for the verb form *oignons*, etc. (verbs which have *-dre* after *-oin* cast off *-dre* and turn *in* into *nh*, p. 109), but in 1632 Martin indicates the pronunciation **pwę̄ŋū** *poignons*, by his representation *poänjous*. Among words other than the weak forms of the verbs in *-oindre*, the analogical forms were adopted more slowly and only fully attested at the end of the century, cf. Chifflet (1659), ' *oi* devant *gn* sonne comme *on ;* c'est pourquoy les anciens ecrivoient *besongne, eslongner, songneux*, etc., au lieu de *besoigne, esloigner, soigneux*. Mais souvenez vous que l'*o* doit sonner clairement, presque comme s'il estoit seul, *eslogner*, etc. Exceptez-en *tesmoigner* ou l'*i* se prononce comme l'*é* ouvert et *joigne* avec ses composez *enjoigne, conjoigne.*' De la Touche (1696), ' *Oi* se prononce comme *oai* devant *g* et *n ;* exemple *témoigner, éloigner, foin, joindre*, etc., prononcez *temoaigner* . . . ; *oi* n'a pas le son si ouvert quand il est suivi d'une *n* que quand il l'est d'un *g*.' (Th. II, 525-528.)

§ 466. Early Old French **ai** + *nasal* > **ãi** > **ẽi** (c. xii)>**ę̃**; **ę̃** denasalised to **ę** before intervocalic nasal (c. xv-xvi).

Early Old French **ęi** + *nasal* > **ẽi** > **ẽi** > **ę̃** ; **ę̃** denasalised to **ę** before intervocalic nasal (c. xv-xvi).

(1) G.R. **a** (< L. and G. **ɑ**) + **ŋ** *prae-consonantal* (§§ 311, 321) and *final* (§ 406) :

saŋktum > **sãint** > **sę̃int** > **sę̃(t)** *saint,* **plaŋgit** > **plãint** > **plę̃int** > **plę̃(t).**
***baŋy̨s** > **bãints** > **bę̃ints** > **bę̃(z)** *bains.*
plaŋgĕre > **plaindrę** > **plę̃indrę** > **plę̃drę** *plaindre.*
***baŋy̨** > **baŋ** > **bãiŋ** > **bę̃(n)** *baing,* **plaŋge** > **plaŋ** > **plãiŋ** > **plę̃(n)** *plaing.*

(2) G.R. **a** (< L. and G. **ɑ**) *tonic free* before **m** or **n** (§ 427) become *prae-consonantal* or *final* :

manet > **mãint** > **mę̃int** > **mę̃(t)** *maint,* **amet** > **ãint** > **ę̃int** *aint.*
manum > **mãin** > **mę̃in** > **mę̃(n)** *main,* **famem** > **fãin** > **fę̃in** > **fę̃(n)** *faim.*

(3) G.R. a (< L. and G. a) *tonic free* + intervocalic nasal (§ 427) denasalised to ę :

plana > plāinę > plęinę > plęnę > plęn(ę) *plaine*.
amat > āimęθ > ęimę > ęmę > ęm(ę) *aime*.

(1) G.R. ę (< L. and G. ĕ, ĭ) + ŋ *prae-consonantal* and *final*, §§ 311, 321 :

piŋktum > pēint > pęint > pę(t) *peint*, piŋgit > pēint > pęint > pę(t) *peint*.
piŋgis > pēints > pęints > pę(z) *peins*.
piŋgere > pēindrę > pęindrę > pędrę *peindre*.
piŋge > pęŋ > pēiŋ > pęiŋ > pę(n) *peign*.

(2) G.R. ę (< L. and G. ĕ, ĭ) *tonic free* before n or m (§ 225) become *prae-consonantal* or *final* :

minus > mēins > męins (> mwę(z), cf. § 487), *moins*.
plēnum > plēin < plęin > plę(n) *plein*.

(3) G.R. ę (< L. and G. ĕ, ĭ) *tonic free* before intervocalic m and n (§ 225) ; denasalised to ę :

plēna > plęinę > plęinę > plęnę > plęn(ę) *pleine*.
strēna < estrēinę > estrēinę > ętręnę > ętręn(ę) *etrenne*.
minat > mēinęθ > mēinę > męnę > męn(ę) *mène*.

(4) G.R. ę (< L. and G. ĕ, ē, ĭ) *countertonic* and *tonic* before intervocalic ŋ (§ 407) ; denasalised to ę :

sĕniōrem > sēiŋour > sęiŋeur > sęŋör > sęŋör *seigneur*.
piŋgentem > pēiŋ[änt] > pęiŋänt > pęŋät > pęŋä(t) *peignant*.
insignat insïŋnat > ēnsēiŋęθ > ānsęiŋę > āsęŋę > āsęŋ(ę) *enseigne*.

§ 467. ăi (ai, § 529) was at first a descending diphthong, assonating with ā ; it passed to ęi in the course of the twelfth century.

ēi was at first a descending diphthong, assonating with ē : it was lowered under the influence of nasalisation to ęi and thus fell in with ęi < earlier ăi : in the course of Period II ęi was levelled to ę under the same influence.

Denasalisation took place before the middle of the sixteenth century :

-ain : *-an*—Rol. aimet : blasme, France, lxxxvi ; *plaindre* : *blanche* : *angele*, clviii.
-ein : *-en*—Rol. peine : aleine : feindre : temples : gente, cxxxv.
-ain : *-ein*—Troie, meins : mains 28691, esteinz : ainz 25585 ; Rose I, main : plein 1109, *plaindre* : *feindre* 3245, pleine : graine 3369.
-ain : *-ein* : *-en* (*-ien*)—Rtbf. meriens : Rains : rains 62, 95, regnes : raines 115, 69 ; Villon, *Veniciennes* : *Rommaines* : *lorraines*, T. 1516 ; Estienne : paine : sepmaine, T. clxvii, estrenes : Renes : regnes, T. xlii.

§ 468. The spelling *ai* is used for ę in documents from the end of the thirteenth century on (cf. § 454), and rhymes between the terminations *-ain*, *-ein* and *-(i)en* begin to appear in Later Old French ; these are, however, at first probably either only approximate or dialectal, for it is only in the later sixteenth century that the grammarians accept fully the monophthongisation of these sounds. Villon, however, uses them freely and it is possible that their formal recognition was delayed by the influence of spelling or of the northern dialect (§§ 469, 533).

Levelling to ę is accepted by St. Liens (1580) : ' In words ending in *-ain* and *-ein* we omit *a* and *e* and say . . . *demin, la min, sin, plin*,' by Bèze (1584) : ' This

diphthong *ei* differs little from simple *i*,' p. 50, and by Tabourot (cf. § 453) ; Meigret, however, still recognises a diphthongal pronunciation (Th. II, 483).

Denasalisation is clearly attested by a remark in the ' French Lyttelton ' of 1566 : '. . . *romain, certain, vilain, souverain* are pronounced as *romin, certin, vilin* ' (i.e. with ę̃), ' but add **e** to it and the pronunciation is cleane altered, so that *romaine* is as you sound *plainly* in English and such like, but more short.' (Zachrisson, p. 9.) The spelling of Robert Estienne, who no longer doubles the nasal consonant after *ai* and *ei*, and of Bèze who writes *plene*, corroborates this remark.

✳✳ § 469. In the south-western region **ãi** (like **ai**) monophthongised early to ę̃ (W. § iii) ; in the northern region **ãi** was (like **ai**, § 533) retained longer (cf. Matzke, *Pub. M.L.A.* xxi, pp. 637-676, § 453 and N. § ix) ; for the differentiation of **ei** + *nasal* to **oi** in the eastern region cf. E. § xix.

§ 470. Early Old French ˡie + *nasal* > ję + *nasal* (c. xii) > ję̃ (c. xiii) > ję̃ ; ję̃ denasalised before *intervocalic* nasal to ję (c. xvi).

(1) Early Old French ˡie (< L. and G. ĕ *tonic free*) + **n, ŋ, m** (§ 225) become final or + **n, m** become prae-consonantal :

bĕne > bien > bję̃n > bję̃(n),   rĕm > rien > rję̃n > rję̃(n),
tĕnet > tient > tję̃nt > tję̃(n)t > tję̃(t),   tĕnéo > tien > tję̃ŋ > tję̃(n) (§ 406).

(2) Early Old French ˡie (< L. and G. **ɑ** *tonic free* preceded by a palatal consonant) followed by a nasal, become final (§ 414) :

kɑnem > tšien > tšję̃n > šję̃(n) *chien.*
mĕdiɑnum > meiien > mɔiję̃n > mu̯ęję̃(n) *moyen.*

(3) Early Old French ˡie (< L. and G. ę *tonic free*), before intervocalic **n, m** (§ 225) and **ŋ** (§ 410) ;denasalised to ję :

O.F. mienę > mję̃nę > mję̃nę > mjęn(ę) *mienne.*
tĕnĕam > tieŋę > tję̃ŋę > tję̃ŋę *tiengne* (cf. § 950).

(4) Early Old French ˡie (< G.R. **a** *tonic free* preceded by a palatal) followed by an intervocalic nasal (§ 414) ; denasalised to ję :

mĕdiɑnɑ > meiienę > mɔiję̃nę > mu̯ęję̃nę > mwęjęn(ę) *moyenne.*

§ 471. **ie**, at first a descending diphthong, was nasalised after the stress had shifted to ję̃, i.e. in the course of Later Old French (§ 510) ; ję̃ was subsequently gradually lowered to ję̃, a pronunciation only finally accepted in the early seventeenth century ; denasalisation took place in the course of the sixteenth century.

Rhymes indicating the open value of the ẽ-sound begin in Later Old French (§ 467), but close quality is attributed to the nasalised vowel by Meigret, Peletier and Lanoue. Bèze retains ę in the feminine forms *chiene, miene*, etc., but admits open quality in monosyllabic words, e.g. in *bien, chien, mien, tien, vien* (p. 16) and ę̃ is admitted generally by the grammarians of the early seventeenth century.

Denasalisation and open quality of the e-sound are clearly indicated by Lanoue (1596) : ' l'*n* en la penultieme ' (-*ienne*), ' ne sert qu'à donner à l'*e* precedent la force de la diphthongue *ai*,' i.e. open ę (cf. Th. II, pp. 435-440, 450, 457).

✳✳ § 472. In the south-western and south-central region, the region in which the accent shifted early in the diphthong **ie** (§ 512) and the lowering of ẽ to ã took place (§ 448), ję̃ was also lowered to jã, cf. the place-name *Orléans*, O.F. **Orljãns** < **Orlję̃ns** < **Aurelianis**, and rhymes such as *lian* (<*ligamen*): *Gencian, meannes* (*medianas*) : *bannes* in Guiart (cf. *Rose*, I, p. 212, S.C. § vi).

In later Middle and Early Modern French this pronunciation had considerable vogue in Paris. Villon makes use of it, e.g. T. cxxxvi, *ancien : crestien : an*, and Palsgrave prescribes the lowered forms *mianne, tianne, sianne* (p. 3). Tabourot, however, the only other sixteenth-century grammarian to mention this pronunciation, ascribes it to the ' populace de Paris ' and adds : ' Selon le dialecte des Parisiens, on prononce *an* au lieu de *en*, et quelques poètes en ont usé, mais rarement et le faut remarquer comme une licence. Exemple *ie vy monsieur le Doyan Lequel se portoit tres bian*.' (Th. II, 436.)   The pronunciation was accepted in *fiente* **flãntẹ** < **fẹmitɑ**, (cf. § 75 and Rosset, pp. 166-168).

§ 473. Early Old French **uĭ** + *nasal* (< **ǫĭ** + *nasal*) > **wẽ** (c. xvii) ; **wẽ** denasalised before intervocalic nasal to **wẹ**: spelling *oi, ui*.

(1) Early Old French **u** (< L. and G. **ō, ŭ, ǒ**, § 426) *tonic* and *countertonic* before *prae-consonantal* **ŋ** (§ 279) :

punctum **pŭŋktum** > puint	> puĭnt	> pu̯ẽnt	> pwẽ(t) *point*.
pugnos **pŭŋnos** > puints	> puĭnts	> pu̯ẽns	> pwẽ(z) *poinz*.
pungere **pŭŋgẹrẹ** > puindrẹ	> pu̯ĭndrẹ	> pu̯ẽndrẹ	> pwẽdrẹ *poindre, puindre*.
cognitum **kǒŋnĭtum** > kuintẹ	> kuĭntẹ	> ku̯ẽntẹ *cueinte*.
punctura **pŭŋktūrɑ** > puintūrẹ	> pu̯ẽntūrẹ	> pwẽtūrẹ *pointure*.
*adcognitare **ɑdkǒŋnẹtare** > akuintier'	> aku̯ẽntjẹr'	> akwẽt[ẹ] *acointier, acuintier*.

(2) Early Old French **u** (< L. and G. **ō, ŭ**, § 426) + **ŋ** become *final* (§ 406) :

pugnum **pŭŋnum** > puŋ	> puiŋ	> pu̯ẽn	> pwẽ(n) *poing, puing*.
lŏnge **lŏŋge** > luŋ	> luiŋ	> lu̯ẽn	> lwẽ(n) *loing, luing*.

(3) Early Old French **u** (< L. **ǒ, ō, ŭ**) before **nj** in learned loan-words (§ 645) ; denasalised to **wẹ** (> **wa** in Modern French) :

O.F. **munjẹ** (< ***monicum** for *monachum*) > **muinẹ** > **mu̯ẽnẹ** > **mwẹn(ẹ)** *moine*.

[For *avoine, foin, moins*, cf. § 487 ; for analogical **wẽ** in *eloigner, temoigner, poignant*, etc., cf. § 465.]

§ 474. The diphthong **uĭ** (**ǫĭ**) + *nasal* at first assonated with **u** (**ǫ**) + *nasal* (e.g. *Alexis, cointes : Rome : encuntre* xliii, *Roland, luinz : barun : plurt* clviii) : it developed along the lines of the oral diphthong **uĭ** (**ǫĭ**), § 519, but more tardily, and the modern pronunciation **wẽ** is only officially recognised in the seventeenth century.

Sixteenth and early seventeenth century grammarians distinguish explicitly between the pronunciation of the oral and nasal diphthong *oi*, indicating for the latter a pronunciation in which the first element is more vocalic and the second higher than it is in **wẹ**, cf. St. Liens : ' *soin, besoin, moins, coins, point, pourpoint :* in these and their like **i** retains its nature ; speak them as if they were firmly divided : *pour-po-int*.' H. Estienne : ' The sound of the diphthong *oi* is ambiguous, as it were between *oi* and *oe* . . . in *coins, moins* . . . the letter *i* keeps its sound better.' Chifflet (1659) : ' in *oi* before *n* . . . pronounce clearly *i* and not open *e* . . . Read *lo-in*, etc.' (Th. II, 492, 493.) Awfeild, however (1634), prescribes *mweendre, pweent*, and Hindret (1687), ' *besoain, moains, soain* . . . *pourpoaint*.' (Th. II, 494.)

✳✳ § 475. In some regions, e.g. the southern and more especially the south-eastern, § 454, rhymes indicate a lowered pronunciation **u̯ẽ** from the mid-thirteenth century on, cf. *Rose* I, *essoine : saine* 2203, Rtbf. *jointes : saintes*, Th. 83, *besoingne : tiengne*, G. Sar. 144, *Mir. Chartres, seine : essoine*, p. 66, Regnier, *joinctes : plainctes* 56, 181, *St. Joan, oint : craint* 1012, *point : mains* 1282. Vulgar Parisian was also

affected, cf. Boileaue, *oens* for *oins*, p. 243 ; Villon, *essoyne : moyne : saine*, T. 338, *Anthoine : Saine*, L. xxix, *fain : foing : baing : poing, Ballade* IV.

w**ę** was sometimes reduced to **ę**, cf. *gindre* **žę̄drę** < **žwę̄drę** < **džuindrę** *joindre* < ˈj**ų̄nior** (< *jūnior* + *jŭvenem*), *flaine* **flę̄nę** < **flwę̄nę** < **floiznę** *fluxina*.

§ 476. Early Old French ˈ**üi** + *nasal* > **ü̧i** + *nasal* (c. xii-xiii) > **w̄ī** > **w̄ę̄** (ç. xvii) ; **w̄ī** denasalised before *intervocalic* nasal > **w̄į̄**.

Early Old French **ü** (> L. and G. **ū**) before **ŋ** *final* and *intervocalic* (§ 406) :

      ɟūnium > **džüŋ** > **žüiŋ** > **žw̄īŋ** > **žw̄ę̄(n)** *juing*.

The derivative word *juiguet* **žw̄īŋet** < **džüŋet**, § 407, was replaced by *juillet* **zw̄iJet** in Middle French.

§ 477. Later Old French **ö** (< ˈ**ue**) + *nasal* > **ö̃** ; **ö̃** denasalised before *intervocalic* nasal to **ö̧** ; spelling *ue, eu*.

Early Old French **ue** (< **uo** < L. **ǒ**, G. **ǒ**, **ö**) *tonic free* before **n** or **m** (§ 226) :

      juvenem *ˈɟǫβene* (§ 488) > **džuefnę** > **džönę** > **žönę** > **žö̧nę** *jeune*   *ˈStrömuų* > **Estruem** > **Etrön** > **Etrö̃(n)** *Etroeungt*

[For O.F. *bon* **būn** > **bonum**, *on* **ūn** < *homo*, cf. § 459.]

ˈ**ue** appears to have been ordinarily levelled to **ö** before it was nasalised and it denasalised to **ö̧**.

After **k** the accent slipped early on to the second element of the diphthong (§ 503), cf. O.F. *cuens* **kų̄ęns**.

✱✱ § 478. In a widespread region ˈ**ue** + nasal passed to **ų̄ę** (cf. § 553) and there the nasalised form of the diphthong was **ų̄ę̄**, which was lowered to **w̄ā** before **m** (§ 450) ; w**ę̄** and **w̄ā** were subsequently sometimes reduced to **ē** and **ā** respectively (§ 192, S.C. § vi).

bǫnum > b**ˈuen** > **bų̄en** > **bų̄ę̄n** *boin*, homo > ˈ**uem** > **ų̄ęm** > **ų̄ę̄n** > **ų̄ā(n)** *uem, en, an,* *ˈɟǫβene* > **džuefne** > **džų̄ę̄nę** > **žę̄nę** *jenne*, Rotˈ**ǫm(ag)um** > **Ruuem** > **Rų̄ų̄ęm** > **Rų̄ā(n)** *Rouen.*

Cf. *Troie*, *buen : Sicilien* 18599, *buens : sens* 18453, *suen : sen* 6413 ; *Rose* II, *l'en : Melan* ; G. *Dôle*, *soens : chamberlens* 6413 ; G. Guiart II, *jennes : Varennes* 11354 ; Martial d'Auvergne, *jenne : mondaine* 169 ; Ch. d'Orléans, *jenne, jennece.*

The form *juenne* (**žw̄ę̄nę**), *jenne* had some vogue in Paris, cf. *Tax Rolls of* 1292-1300, *Jaques de Montereul, le genne, Jehannot le genne, Guillaume de Saint-Denis, Le Jenne*, etc., *Jehan Augier le Juenne* (Michaëlsson, pp. 50, 54, 156, etc.).

[For O.F. *gienvle* < *juenvle* cf. § 424.]

CHAPTER XII.

INFLUENCE EXERCISED BY LABIAL SOUNDS ON VOWELS.

Section 1.

§ 479. The only consonant affected by the influence of labial sounds was **n** which was labialised to **m** in the early period of the language by juxtaposed labial consonants, cf. O.F. *emfes* < *infans, embler* < *involare* (§§ 365, 435); the articulation of vowels was, however, liable to modification by juxtaposed labial sounds in all periods of the language. The most direct and frequent form of influence exercised was *labialisation*, the *rounding* of buccal vowels, but the development of labial vowels was occasionally modified and labial glide-sounds occasionally induced.

Section 2.—LABIALISATION (ROUNDING).

§ 480. The strongest labialising influence was exercised by **w** and the semi-vowel **ṷ**, the labial sounds made with the most marked lip-rounding, but labialisation was also sometimes induced by the labial vowels and the other labial consonants and by **ž** and **š**, sounds often pronounced with considerable lip-rounding (§ 112). The vowels affected were mainly the low and mid, the **a-** and **e-***sounds*.

It should be borne in mind that a buccal vowel rounds ordinarily into the labial vowel that is nearest its own point of articulation (§ 138): thus the **a-***sounds* rounded normally into **ǫ**, the e-sounds to **ö** and **i** to **ü**; in the early period, however, when the mid-mixed vowel **ö** was not as yet in the sound-system, the **e-***sounds* rounded into **ǫ**.

§ 481. *Gallo-Roman.*—In *Gallo-Roman* it was the **a-***sound* that was mainly affected by labial consonants, **a** (**ɑ**?) being rounded to **ǫ** in the diphthong **aṷ** and whenever it was juxtaposed to following **ww** or unstressed final **-ṷ**: the simple vowel **ǫ** developed out of the diphthong **aṷ** (§ 505), the diphthong **ǫṷ** was formed when **a** or **aṷ** were juxtaposed to **ww** or unstressed final **ṷ**:

fa(γ)ṷ < **faɡum > **fǫu**	****eskla(γ)ṷ** < Frk. **slaɡ** > **esklǫu** *esclou*
clavum ***klaṷ** (§ 187) > **klǫu** *clou*	***blavum *blaṷ** > **blǫu**
cauua ***kawwa** > **tšǫṷę** *choue*	****awwet** (< **habŭit**, § 374) > **ǫut**
pau(γ)ṷ < **paukum > **pǫu**	***trau(γ)ṷ** < ***traukum** > **trǫu**

[For the subsequent development of **ǫu** cf. § 548; for the rounding of **i** to **ü** in the *u*-perfects cf. § 1027.]

✷✷ § 482. In the eastern and north-eastern regions no rounding took place before ww and thus **habŭit** > **aṵt, habuisti,** **abwịstị** (§ 994) > **awis(t),** **awwa** (< **akṵa** *aqua*, § 330) > **awę** (N.E. § xi).

✷✷ § 483. In the western region, tonic **a** was rounded to **ǫ** when it was followed by **ṵ** + unstressed **a** : (i) in the loan-word *blava* **blaṵa,** O.F. **blǫę,** (ii) in the termination *-abam, -abas,* etc., in which intervocalic **b** opened and velarised to **ṵ** (§ 345), cf. O.F. **amǫuę, amǫues,** etc. (§ 914).

§ 484. *Early Old French.*—(i) In the course of Early Old French, more particularly in the western region, **ę** countertonic was rounded to **ǫ** by following **w** and by juxtaposed tonic **ṵ,** cf. O.F. **sǫvēntrę** < **sewentrę** < **sekṵenter** *sequenter,* **owel, oel** < **ewale** < **ękṵale** *aequale,* **soür** < **sęür** < **securum,** **doüθ** < **dęüθ** < **dębṵtṵ, doüsę** < **dęüsę** *deusse,* etc.

(ii) It is possible that **ę** in contact with tonic **ü** was labialised to **ö,** but the spelling remained unchanged : **męür** < **maür** (§ 421) > **möür, ęür** > **öür** (cf. § 275).

§ 485. *Later Old and Middle French.*—(i) In the course of Period II. the unrounded stressed element of all diphthongs and triphthongs in **ṵ** was rounded under the influence of the labial element (cf. §§ 534-557).

§ 486. (ii) In Middle French there was a tendency to round e-*sounds* standing before a labial consonant to **ö** *eu,* more especially if the preceding consonant was also labial. The tendency established itself in the word *veuve* **vövę,** in countertonic syllables beginning with a labial or labialised consonant, e.g. **š** or **ž** (cf. § 112) and in *afubler* and *alumelle* (§ 606).

In the countertonic and intertonic syllables **ö** closed ordinarily to **ü** :

vevę < *βędwa* *vidua* > **vövę** *veuve*	**bęvānt** > **bövānt** > **büvā(t)** *buvant*
fęvrę < **fabrum** > **fövrę** *feuvre*	**bęvradžę** > **bövražę** > **brövažę** *breuvage*
trevę < **treuwa** > **trövę** *treuve*	**fęmier** > **fömįęr** > **fümįę** *fumier*
sṵęf < O.F. **soif** (§ 816) > **söf** *seuf*	**džęmęaus** > **žömęaus** > **žümǫ(z)** *jumeaux*

Palsgrave, '*nous beuvons, vous beuvez,*' Ramus, '*nous buvons* alias *beuvons*'; Guiart II, *veuve : preuve,* 11,354; Palsgrave, *vefve,* Tabourot, '*veufve* pour *vefve,*' Vaugelas, 'il faut escrire *veuve* ou *veufve* et non pas *vefve,* comme on dit en plusieurs provinces de France.' (II, 134); Villon, *esteuf: seuf,* T. 729; Tabourot, 'Ronsard a dit *seuf,* et rime avec *boeuf,* mais il le faut plus tost admirer en cela que de l'ensuyvre.' (Th. I, 373); cf. also Vaugelas, 'Deux mauvaises prononciations qui sont très-communes mesme à la cour. L'une . . . est de dire *cheuz vous,*' (**šö vu**) 'et ie ne puis comprendre d'où est venu cet *u* dans ce mot.' (II, 162.)

Section 3.—Development of Labial Glides.

§ 487. In Middle French, at the period when wę, the product of the diphthong oi, was being very generally reduced to ę in uneducated speech (§ 522), and there was much hesitation in the use of ę and wę, a tendency showed itself to develop a labial glide between the vowels ę, ȩ (ȩi?), and a preceding labial consonant; in this way armęrę < armairę > armwȩrę *armoire*, pęlę < paile (< palię, § 645) > pwęlę *poele*, ęmę < ezmai > emwę *emoi*, pęję < paię > pwęję *poie*, męns < meins > mwȩns *moins*, fęn < fēin > fwęn *foin*, avȩnę < avēinę > avwȩnę *avoine*.

Among verb-forms, e.g. *baye, paye, meine, peine*, the glide failed to secure acceptance owing to the influence of the weak radicals; it was established most solidly in the words which had homonyms, e.g. *moins* (cf. *mains*), *foin* (cf. *fin*), *avoine* (cf. *la veine*), *poele* (cf. *pelle*), but fluctuations continued into the seventeenth century (cf. Gilliéron, *L'Abeille*, 201-205, Dauzat, *R.Ph.F.* xxxv, 128-137 and § 147).

Rtbf. *moi : esmoi* 159, 69, *Mir. Chartres*, p. 18, *memoire : aumoire* (< *armoire*), Villon, P.T. 36, *memoire : aumoire*, T. 1493, *avoine : Babiloine*, B. 10, *foing* ; Cretin *moins : tesmoings* xxxviii, 449; Plsgr. *jaboye* 443, 451, *je aboye* . . and *je abaye* 586; (*aboyer* accepted under the influence of *abois*).

Vgl. 'Il faut dire *auoine* auec toute la cour et non pas *aueine* avec tout Paris,' *Rem.* I, 185; 'Une infinité de gens disent *mains* pour dire *moins* . . . ce qui est insupportable,' *Rem.* I, 184.

[For labial glides between vowels in hiatus in the north-eastern region cf. N.E. § xiv.]

Section 4.—Modification of Labial Vowels.

§ 488. In *Late Latin* there was a tendency to open ǫ (ṷ) to ǫ before labial consonants, cf. *ko̧ˈlǫbra* < ˈkŏlŭbra, *estǫpet* < stŭpet, *jǫβene* < jŭwĕnem *juvenem*. The open quality of ǫ in L.L. *ǫu, *oβṷ < ǭwum *ōvum* (§§ 187, 188), may be due either to the influence of the labial or to the differentiating influence of the final unstressed vowel (§ 131).

§ 489. In *Early Old French* the differentiation of *tonic* ǫu to eu was checked by following labial consonants and ou levelled to u, cf. O.F. luvę < lupa, Luvrę < Lupara, estublę < *stŭpŭla, dublę < **doublę < dŭplum, duvę < **douwe < *dōga.

§ 490. ǫ (u?) *countertonic* was sometimes dissimilated to ę under the influence of tonic ǫ (u) and ü, cf. O.F. enour < ǫnour, *sejorn* sędžǫrn < sǫdžǫrn, sęmūndrę < sǫmǫndrę, sęmūns < sǫmǫns, męü < mǫü.

[For the checking of the differentiation of ueu to ieu by a preceding labial consonant cf. § 557.]

CHAPTER XIII.

INFLUENCE EXERCISED BY THE l-SOUNDS AND r ON VOWELS.

Section 1.

§ 491. **r** and **l**, dental consonants in whose articulation the main part of the tongue lies relatively low, exercised not infrequently a *lowering* influence on vowels preceding them.

In the Gallo-Roman period this influence was felt chiefly *negatively*, in the neutralisation of raising influences, as, for instance, of preceding palatal consonants (e.g. *chaleur, charogne*, § 417), and of relatively weak stress (as in *persone*, § 234). In Later Old and Middle French the **l**-*sounds* and **r** tended to lower vowels preceding them, more particularly the **e**-*sounds ;* **r** and **ł** induced also the development of vocalic glides, under certain conditions.

Section 2.—Lowering Influence.

§ 492. **e**-*Sounds.*—In Old French three degrees of height were distinguished among the **e**-sounds in the tonic syllable : (i) a very open variety derived from L.L. **ę** *blocked,* (ii) a high, close sound (long) derived from L.L. **a** *free* (§ 233), (iii) an intermediate variety (short, § 198), derived from L.L. **ẹ** *blocked :* **bęl** < **bĕllu, **pẹl** < *pālu, **ĕlę** < ĕlla,* **tęre** < *tęrra,* **pẹ̄rę** < **pātre, messe* **mę̆sę** < **mę̆ssa* (< *mĭssa*).

The two closed varieties were both opened to **ę** under the influence of **l** and **r**, but at different periods, and in Middle French **ę**, from all sources, tended to open to **a** before **r**.

[For the opening of **ẹ̆** and **ę̄** before other consonants cf. §§ 575, 576.]

§ 493. O.F. **ẹ̆** < L.L. **ę** *tonic blocked* opened to **ę** before **l** and **r** in the course of the twelfth century, cf. Brendan, *cerne* (*cĭrcĭnem*) *: verne* 873, Crestien, *eles* (*illas*) *: dameiseles, Iv.* 2439.

§ 494. O.F. **ẹ̄** (< L.L. **a** *tonic free*) and **jẹ** (from all sources) before **l** and **ɟ** and O.F. **ẹ̆** (< L.L. **ę, ĭ**) before **ɟ** were opened to **ę** and **ję** respectively in the course of Middle French, cf. Villon, *telles : Vausselles : toiles* (i.e. **t(y)ęlęs**), T. 663, *criminel : isnel*, T. 1363. Open quality appears to have been only established fully in the sixteenth century.

Peletier (1549) still marks *tel, lequel, duquel*, etc., as e closed; Meigret gives both pronunciations before l; Lanoue couples *tel, quel, sel* with words in ę (Th. I, 55). Meigret gives ẹ and ę before l, Bèze ę (Th. I, 346).

✶✶ In the western and southern region ẹ̃ before l and ę̃ before l opened to ę in the thirteenth century, cf. *Rose* II *ele* (< *ala*) : *escuele* (< *scutĕlla*) 13401 (W. § ix; S.C. § vii).

§ 495. O.F. ę̃ *and* ję̃ (< a *tonic free*) + r.—In words like *amere, frere, mere, porterent* (§ 231), *chiere, legiere, laissierent* (§ 414), *fiere* (§ 225), and in loan-words like *chimere, sincere*, all words in which r, being inter-vocalic, was not pronounced in the same syllable as the preceding vowel, the closed pronunciation of the tonic vowel appears to have been maintained in educated speech in Paris into the later seventeenth century or even after, i.e. until the effacement of final ə brought the vowel into the same syllable as r, (cf. Corneille, *pére, frére, chére, formérent*, and Thurot, I, pp. 71-74). In mono-syllabic substantives and adjectives in -ęr and -ęr, however (e.g. *mer, cher, cler, fier, hier*), words in which r was pronounced in the same syllable as the vowel and maintained in educated speech (§ 401), ẹ opened to ę in the sixteenth century, i.e. męr > mẹr, fjęr < fjẹr, etc. ; when r was effaced, ẹ remained closed, e.g. *porter* pọrtẹ, *ouvrier* uvrjẹ.

Meigret attributes explicitly ę to *pere, mere*, etc., Lanoue also ; H. Estienne mentions that *pere* and *mere* are pronounced with a vowel ' less open than if they were written *paire, maire* ' and that the *e* in *mer, amer* is pronounced by some as in *aimer*, by others as in *fer, ver* (Th. I, 71, 55). Hindret (1687) allows ę in the adjectives *amère, chère*, etc. (÷ amẹr, šẹr), but hesitation about the value of the sound in words of this type continued into the eighteenth century (Th. I, pp. 72-75). The pronunciation of gẹrẹ < O.F. gairẹ was often assimilated to that of *chiere, legiere*, etc., and the spelling not infrequently changed to *guiere*, cf. *Mir. Chartres*, p. 58, *guieres : prieres*, Villon, T. 1531, *guieres : haranguieres ;* for *bachelier, sanglier*, cf. § 26.

✶✶ In the West and Orléanais ẹ < a tonic free opened to ę before r in the course of the thirteenth century, cf. *Rose* II, *joer : miroer* 1815, *merci : nomer ci* 5699, *amer ci* 7205 ; *Fauvel, pere : plere* 627, *mere : fere* (< *faire*) 954 ; Cretin, *air : enoiseller, trouver dure : verdure, tresorier : hier, Intr.* p. xlvi. The influence of this pronunciation and that of monosyllabic words affected Parisian speech in Late Middle French, cf. Villon, T. lxxiii, *chere : maschouere (maschoire).*

§ 496. ę + r > a.—Isolated instances of the lowering of ę to a by following juxtaposed r occur in the Gallo-Roman period, e.g. par < per, *marchie* martšie < mercatum, but it is in Middle French that this influence is strongest. The eastern region was affected first, but in the fifteenth and sixteenth centuries lowering of this sound was much in vogue in the uneducated speech of Paris and wę (< earlier ýę < lue, e.g. in *fuerre* < *fodrum*, § 553, and < oi, e.g. in *voirre* < *vitrum*, § 519) was affected as well as ę.

Villon, *Robert : Lombart*, T. lxiv, *aherdre : ardre*, T. lxxiii, *iverne : gouverne : Marne*, T. cxliv, *erre* (< *oirre*) : *Barre*, T. lxvi, *poirre* (< *pĕdere*) : *barre : carre*, T. xcviii, *fuerre : Barre*, L. xxiii. Cf. H. Estienne : ' Plebs praesertim parisina hanc literam *a* pro *e* in multis vocibus pronuntiat, dicens *Piarre* pro *Pierre*, . . . *guarre* pro *guerre*.' (Th. I. 3, cf. also §§ 74, 75.)

§ 497. This broad pronunciation of the sound provoked a reaction among people of higher social standing and they, to avoid the imputation of vulgarity in their speech, went too far in their avoidance of the lowered sound and often substituted ę for a in words in which a was traditional, e.g. in *asparge, sarcueil, boulevart, char*, etc.

Cf. Tory: '. . . les dames de Paris, au lieu de *a* prononcent *e* bien souvent, quant elles disent, *Mon mery est a la porte de Perys* . . .' In the later sixteenth century this pronunciation was taken up at Court and secured some vogue, (cf. H. Estienne: '. . . aulici *caterrhe* pronuntiant . . .').

§ 498. These opposing tendencies led to much vacillation in the distribution of **er** and **ar** and stability was only achieved in the next century. Broadly speaking it may be said that the 'vulgar' pronunciation, **a** for **ę** (if adopted), was established in words of colloquial type, in technical terms and in words of unknown origin, e.g. *boulevard* (< *bolwerk*), *dartre, écharpe* (< *skerpa*), *farouche* (< *ferotica*), *fuarre* (< *fuerre*, cf. § 553), *larme, sarcelle* (< *querquedula*), and that ę ousted **a** in a few words of more elevated diction or of infrequent use among the Parisian populace, e.g. *asperge, cercueil, chair* (šęr < šar, O.F. **tšarn** < **kɑrnem**, but cf. *charcutier*, derivative of *char cuite*), *épervier* (*sparwari*), *ergot, gerbe* (< frk. *garba*), *gercer* (O.F. *jarser*), *guérir* (< frk. *warjan*), *guérite, guéret* (O.F. *guarait*, cf. § 127), *serpe* (cf. H.L.F. IV (i), 174-6, Rosset 98-103).

The substitution of uvular R for dental r, a substitution that appears to have begun in the seventeenth century in uneducated speech in Paris and earlier in some dialects, may have contributed to the acceptance of ę in some of these words, for the influence of the uvular trilled sound, unlike that of **r**, tends to raise preceding vowels (cf. Grammont, *L'Assimilation*, pp. 89, 90).

§ 499. **u** *and* **ü** > ǫ *and* **ö**.—In Middle French there was a tendency in uneducated speech to lower **u** *ou* to ǫ and **ü** to **ö** in countertonic syllables before r + *consonant*, i.e. before r pronounced in the same syllable with these vowels. This tendency contributed to the uncertainty about the pronunciation of the sounds **u** and ǫ that was so marked a feature of the later sixteenth and seventeenth centuries (§ 582), but the lowered pronunciation was only established in a few words, e.g. *corvee, ortie, porcelaine* and *heurter* (örtę < ürtę < O.F. **hürtęr**).

R. Estienne, '*couruee*, alii scribunt *coruee*'; Richelieu, '*Nourrisse :* le peuple dit *norrisse* mais les gens d'esprit et tous les bons auteurs disent et écrivent *nourrisse*'; '*Fourbu, forbu*, l'un et l'autre se dit mais *fourbu* est plus en usage'; Plsgr. *pourselayne*, Richelieu: 'La plus part des faïenciers de Paris et presque tout le petit peuple dit *porceline* . . .' (Th. I, 253, 260, and 266.)

Section 3.—GLIDE DEVELOPMENT.

§ 500. In the course of Later Old French a vocalic glide (e) was developed between ɪ and r + *consonant*, i.e. before r pronounced in the same syllable as **ɪ**, and 'ie > ɪę : O.F. *cirge* (*cerea*) tsɪrdžę > tsɪęrdžę > sɪęržę *cierge*, O.F. *virge, virgene* (§ 644), vɪrdžę > vɪęržę *vierge*.

✷✷ For the extension of this glide in the south-central and western regions cf. S.C. § viii, W. § xi. For the development of a vocalic glide between u and *prae-consonantal* r in the north-eastern region cf. N.E. § xiv.

✷✷ *Section* 4.—INFLUENCE OF ⏧ IN EARLY OLD FRENCH.

§ 501. In the course of Period I the articulation of ẹ̆ (< L.L. ẹ blocked) was modified over a wide region by the influence of prae-consonantal ⏧ (< ⏧ and], § 389).

(1) *Lowering Influence.*—(i) In the northern (Picard) region ẹ̆ was lowered to ę before prae-consonantal ⏧ and e, when ⏧ vocalised, developed like L.L. ę in this position to the triphthong **iau** (< ęau), § 540 ; cf. *Auc. caviax* 2, 12, *ciax* (< *ecce illos*) 6, 33.

(ii) In the north-eastern, eastern, south-eastern and south-central region lowering was carried further and ẹ̆ and the e-element in the diphthongs ⁱie and ⁱue were lowered to **a**, cf. *Mis. paraus : maus* 126, *consaus : faus* 118 ; Crestien, *aus* (< *illos*), *solauz, miauz, viaut* (< *vuelt*). *iauz* (< *oculos*), *Intr. Cl.* p. lxviii ; *Rose* I, *meauz* (*melius*) : *Meaus* (*Meldis*), *deaus* (*dŏlus*) : *fardeaus, Intr.* pp. 233-234 ; Rtbf. *ciaus* (*caelos*) : *Citiaus*, 85, 87.

§ 502. (2) *Velarising Influence.*—(i) In the course of the first period of the language, in a region not as yet defined, the velar lateral ⏧ velarised and rounded ę < Latin ẹ̆, i to o (ǫ in tonic syllables, ǫ (> u) in countertonic), e.g. *basoche* < **bazǫtšę** < **bazǫ(⏧)tšę** < ***bazę⏧ka**, *basilica* **basilica**, *Isolt* **Izǫ(⏧)t** < **Ishilt**, *chevǫls* **tšęvǫ(⏧)s** < **kapillos**, *folgiere* **fo⏧džiere** < ***fel(ę)gaŕa *filikaria** (§ 26), **dou** < **dę⏧**, **nou** < **ne⏧** < **non illum** (cf. § 843).

Place-names containing *basoche, basoge, fougière*, in some form or other, are most thickly sprinkled in the western, south-western and south-central regions, but extend rather beyond these limits towards the north-east and east (cf. Longnon, pp. 334, 340). From documents of the south-west Drevin cites early forms such as 1092 *Basocis, Basogio*, 1110 *Basogis*, 1150 *Bazogers*, 1099 *Fougerolis*, 1146 *Fulgerosa*.

(ii) In the south-western region, where l following a appears to have remained velar (§ 382), the passage of tonic a *free* to ę was checked, cf. O.F. *tal, mortal, pal*, etc., *Thebes tal : cheval*, etc., *chevaus : comunaus, Intr.* p. lxxii, cf. S.W. § ii.

(iii) In the eastern region, where ⏧ appears to have remained velar between **a—a** and after **b**, e.g. in ***sa⏧a, tab(u)⏧a** (§ 382), the preceding a-sound was velarised (or remained velar (?), cf. E. § xvi).

[For the diphthongs and triphthongs formed by the combination of ṷ < *vocalised* ⏧ and] with preceding vowels cf. chapter ix, section 2.]

CHAPTER XIV.

LEVELLING OF ORAL DIPHTHONGS AND TRIPHTHONGS.

Section 1.

§ 503. The Classical Latin vowel system contained three diphthongs : **ae, oe, au** and these were all levelled to pure vowels before the close of the Gallo-Roman period, § 504.

Numerous diphthongs and triphthongs were formed in the course of Period I (cf. below), and these were all levelled to pure vowels or combinations of fricative consonants and pure vowels before the end of the seventeenth century.

The processes by which levelling was brought about are mainly *mutual assimilation, nasalisation, shift of stress with consonantalisation of the first element*, and these processes are often combined.

Assimilation was the process adopted ordinarily when the first element was the lower of the two : the point of articulation of each element was brought gradually nearer and nearer that of the other until complete similitude was reached and a long pure vowel resulted. In this way, for instance, **ai** levelled to ę and **au** to ǫ or ǫ.

Consonantalisation (§ 135) was the process ordinarily adopted when the first element was high. If the diphthong was *descending*, i.e. stressed on the first element, shift of stress always preceded consonantalisation, for it is only the weaker element that loses vocalic value. The weak fricative consonants (**w, ẅ, ɟ**) formed by consonantalisation were not infrequently effaced in the course of Middle French, §§ 510, 516, 522, 553.

The readiness with which **k** and **g** combine in a group with the semivowels **u** and **ü** facilitated shift of stress when descending diphthongs beginning with stressed **u** or **ü** followed **k** and **g**, cf. §§ 477, 515, 516.

[For the influence of *nasalisation* cf. chap. xi.]

Section 2.—LATE LATIN DIPHTHONGS.

§ 504. The Classical Latin sound-system included three diphthongs : **ae, oe, au**: all three were levelled to simple vowels by the mutual assimilation of their two elements before the ninth century.

ae and **oe** were levelled to ę end ę respectively in the Latin period, e.g. **saepe** > ***sępę, poena** > ***pęna** : graphical confusion of *ae, oe* and *e* begins in the first and second centuries. e.g. *questus* for *quaestus, equus* for *aequus, ceperint* for *coeperint, Phebus* (cf. GG., pp. 88, 90).

*fęnu for *faenum* and ***pręda** for **praeda** appear to be dialectal forms ; *coelum* is a graphical variant of *caelum*.

§ 505. *au* **ɑ̨** palatalised to **a̧ɥ** (§ 182) but remained diphthongal into Gallo-Roman; like **a** + **ɥ** or **w** (§ 481) it was levelled to **ǫ** before the end of the period, cf. *Gl. Reich.*, *sora* (for *saura*), *soma* (< *sauma* < *sagma*, cf. § 359), *Strasbourg Oaths, cosa, Eul. cose*, l. 9.

In ***agǫstu̧, *agu̧rju̧, *askǫltare**, **ɑ** was substituted for **ɑ̨ɥ** under the dissimilating influence of the tonic vowel.

Section 3.—ORAL DIPHTHONGS IN LATER OLD AND MIDDLE FRENCH.

§ 506. *Sources of Old French Diphthongs and Triphthongs.*—The main sources of the Later Old French diphthongs and triphthongs are the following:—

(1) The diphthongisation and differentiation of tonic free **ẹ, ọ, ę, ǫ** (§§ 225, 226): ˈie, ˈue (<ˈuo), ˈei, ˈǫi (<ˈei), ˈęu (<ˈǫu).

(2) The breaking of tonic **ę** and **ǫ**, §§ 410, 411: ˈie, ˈue. ˈüi.

(3) The combination of the vowels **a, ẹ, ǫ, ǫ (u), ü** with *jod* or **ɪ** (§§ 404-409): ˈai, ˈei, ˈǫi, ˈǫi (ˈui), ˈüi.

(4) The combination of unstressed final -ɪ with tonic **a** or **u̧** and of final -**u̧** with tonic **a, ɪ,** ˈie, ˈue (§ 254): ˈai, üi, au, iu, ˈieu, ˈueu.

(5) The combination of the vowels **a, ẹ, ę, ǫ,** ˈie, ˈue with **u̧** < vocalised **ɫ** and **ɟ** + *consonant* (§§ 385-388): ˈau, ˈęau, ˈęu, ˈǫu, ˈieu, ˈueu, üeu (§ 557).

[For the formation and development of nasal diphthongs cf. §§ 404 (6), 406, 407, 427, 439; 466-478.]

§ 507. The diphthongs ˈuo, ˈei, ˈǫu formed in Gallo-Roman were differentiated in the course of Early Old French to ˈue, ˈoi, ˈęu (§ 226), but the sound-system of twelfth century *francien* still comprised the following diphthongs and triphthongs: ˈie, ˈue; ˈai, ˈǫi, ˈǫi (> ˈui, § 184), ˈüi; ˈāi, ˈēi; ˈau, ˈęu, ˈiu, ˈǫu; ˈęau, ˈieu, ueu, üeu. These diphthongs and triphthongs were all at first *descending*, i.e. all stressed on the first element, e.g. ˈie, ˈue, ˈüi, ˈau, ˈęau, etc., and all except ˈei, ˈie, ˈue, ˈueu might be coupled in assonance with the pure vowel or diphthong that formed their first element, viz. **ai** and **au** with **a, ǫi** and **ǫu** with **ǫ, ǫi (ui)** with **ǫ (u), üi** with **ü, ieu** with **ie, iu** with **i, āi** with **ā, ēi** with **ē**.

§ 508. With the return to a more level intonation that characterised Later Old and Middle French (§ 223), these diphthongs were all slowly levelled to pure vowels or turned into combinations of pure vowels preceded by one of the semi-vowels or voiced fricative consonants: **į, ų, ü̧, ɟ, w, ẉ**. In the western region the levelling tendency showed itself in the eleventh century: in the northern and eastern regions the stronger expiratory tonic accent, that was the heritage of the more intensive Frankish settlement (§ 17), retarded and sometimes modified the development of diphthongs and triphthongs. The Île de France, which went with the northern and eastern regions in the differentiation of diphthongs in the eleventh century (§ 227), was affected later than the west by the levelling tendency, but followed ordinarily the same lines, and

by the beginning of Middle French the levelling process was far advanced in this region also.   Levelling was often retarded when diphthongs were in hiatus with other vowels, but Early Modern French was almost as free of true diphthongs as is the educated French of to-day, the oral diphthong ǝǫ and the nasal diphthongs uĩ, üĩ alone preserving diphthongal character in the early seventeenth century.

✱✱ Under the influence of the stronger expiratory tonic accent descending diphthongs were retained in the northern and eastern region longer than elsewhere, and not infrequently reduced by the effacement of their second (less-stressed) element, cf. N. §§ v-vii.

Section 4.—LEVELLING BY SHIFT OF STRESS AND CONSONANTALISATION OF THE FIRST ELEMENT : *diphthongs* ie, üi, ǫi, ǫi.

§ 509. (Early O.F.) ˈie > (Later O.F.) ję > (Middle French) } ję, ję̧ / ę̣, ę̧.

[For ˈieu cf. §§ 544-546.   For ˈie + *nasal* consonant cf. §§ 471-473.]

Sources of ˈie :—

(1) L.L. ę̣ (< L. and G. ĕ) *tonic free* (§ 225) : pieθ < pĕdem, bierę < *bęra.

(2) L.L. ę̣ (< L. and G. ĕ) *tonic before* ļ (§ 410) : *vieil* vieļ < *βęklu < wĕtŭlum (*vetulum*).

(3) G.R. a (< L. and G. ɑ) *tonic free* preceded by a *palatal* or *palatalised consonant* (§ 414) : *chier* tšier < karum.

(4) The suffix -arium (§ 26) : premier < primarium.

§ 510. The diphthong ˈie passed to ję in the course of Later Old French ; in the later fifteenth and sixteenth century ję was reduced to ę̣ after the palatal and denti-palatal consonants ļ, ŋ, š and ž, and by analogy ę̣ was adopted in all verbal terminations in ję (§ 877) ; in the course of Late Middle and Early Modern French ję and ę̣ were opened to ję̧ and ę̧ before sounded consonants, earliest before l and ļ (§§ 494, 576).

[For ę̧ and ję̧ before r cf. § 495.]

sĕdet > siet > sję *siet*, pietatem > pitieθ (§ 316) > pitję ;

primarium < premier > pręmję *premier* ;

hĕri > ier > jęr > ję̧r *hier*, fĕl > fiel > fję̧l, fĕbrem > fievrę > fję̧vrę ;

merkatum > martšieθ > maršę̧ *marché*, manducare > mãndžier > mãžę̧

consiliare konsęļare > künsęļier > künsęļę̧ *conseillier* ;

*kapum > tšief > šjęf > šęf > šę̧f *chief, chef*;

karum > tšier > šęr *chier, cher*, kara > tšję̧rę > šę̧rę > šę̧r(ę) (cent. xvii).

Attesting Rhymes and Remarks.—Villon still differentiates ordinarily ję and ę̣, but couples analogical *leve* (for *lieve*) and *grieve* with *greve*, T. 1042, *vuydez* and *cuidez* with *eschaudez*, T. 1695, *chiere* with *machouere*, T. 820.

Palsgrave admitted reduction in the verb forms : ' A generall thynge it was in Alayne Chartiers tyme to write the themes and infinityve modes of such verbes as nowe ende in *che, ge* or *sse* with an *i* as . . . *arrachier*, . . . But in this thyng Alayn Chartier at these dayes is nat folowed ' (p. 401).

In the pronunciation of substantives and adjectives Meigret in 1545 still recommended ję: ' En *cher*, *chef*, *danger* . . . indubitablement nous prononçons la diphthongue *ie* . . . I'entens bien que l'ung et l'autre sont en usage, mais celuy qui est proferé par diphthongue est plus armonieux, et plus usité ' ; but for Henri Estienne in 1582 the use of *ie* is only a matter of orthography (Th. I, 485).

§ 511. *Diaeresis of* ję.—In the pronunciation of the diphthong **ie** there began to show itself in Later Middle French a tendency towards the converse process, the division of the two elements of the diphthong into separate syllables.   This *diaeresis* shows itself first in the pronunciation of monosyllabic words, e.g. *fi-er*, *hi-er*, *mi-el ;* at the end of the sixteenth century it is sometimes found when **ie** is preceded by the group *consonant* + **r** or **l**, e.g. *levri-er*, *ouvri-er*.   In words of this latter type this pronunciation was established in the next century : cf. Menage : ' Tous nos vieux poètes, généralement, ont fait d'une syllabe l'*i* précédé d'une mute et d'une liquide, et suivi de la syllabe *-er*. . . . Aujourd'huy cet " *ier* " est constamment de deux syllabes. Nostre poésie a cette obligation avecque plusieurs autres à M. Corneille, qui, dans sa tragédie du Cid, a osé le premier faire le mot de *meurtrier* de trois syllabes.' (Th. I, 492.)

✱✱ § 512. (i) *Early shift of* ˡ**ie** *to* **ję** *in the western region* (W. § i).   Laisses in the *Epistre de St. Estienne* and in the *Roland* (e.g. xl, clx), in which the diphthong **ie** is admitted in assonance with **e**, indicate that the shift of stress in this diphthong had already taken place in these poems in the early twelfth century and this shift appears to have been quickly followed by the reduction of **ję** to **ę**, at least after the consonants **tš**, **dž**, **l̦** and **ŋ**, cf. St. *Martin*, *fondee : essaucee*, *renommee : drecee*, *loerent : nagierent*. In the more southern part of the western region the reduction may have been hastened by the influence of the Poitevin dialect, in which **ę** was not diphthongised to **ie**, and this would account for the early spellings of the suffix *-ier* noted by Drevin in documents of Maine and Brittany, e.g. 1060 *parcheminer*, *draper*, 1080 *Esclencher*, 1105 *Troter*, 1137 *Porcher* (p. 145) ; in the Orléanais (S.C. § vii) the reduction appears to have been accomplished by the end of the thirteenth century (cf. Bédier, *Rol. Commentaire*, pp. 126, 127, 280-293, and *Rose* I, p. 236, n. 1).

[For the early opening of (ɪ)ę to (ɪ)ę before **r** in this region cf. § 495.]

✱✱ § 513. (ii) In the northern and eastern regions, where stress was retained ordinarily longer on the first element (§ 508), it is the second element that was sometimes slurred, cf. *Auc. civres* 10, 7, *destrir* 10, 20, and N. § vii.   When ˡ**ie** was in hiatus with **ę** final, reduction was widespread and included north Normandy as well as the northern and eastern regions, (N. § v), and the pronunciation -ˡ**ię** is made use of by poets of other regions, e.g. *Rose* I-II, *cortoisie : proisie*, etc., *Intr.* p. 235, Rtbf. *mesnie : vie*, p. 184, 118.   The form **lię** < ˡ**ięę** < **laeta** was taken into standard French in the locution *chiere lie*.

§ 514. ˡ**üi** > **ẃi** (c. xiii), graphy *ui.*

Sources of **üi** :—

Late Latin *tonic* **ǫ** (< L. and G. **ŏ**) + **j(i̯)** (§ 411) : **püi** < *podjy* < **pŏdium.**
Late Latin *tonic* and *countertonic* **u̧** (< L. and G. **ū**) + *jod* or final **i̦** (§§ 404, 254) : **früit** < *fru̧χtu* < **fructum, füi** < *fu̧i.*
Late Latin tonic **u̧** or **ǫ** mutated + **i̦** (§ 419) : **tüit** < *tǫtti̦.*
Old French **ü** + palatal glide before **l̦** (§ 407) : **agüilę** < **agülę** < *acucula* *aku̧kula.*
Old French **iü** by metathesis : **tüilę** < **tlülę** < **tĕgǔla** (§§ 124, 641).

§ 515. ˡ**üi**, at first a descending diphthong assonating with **ü**, passed to **ẃi** in the course of the thirteenth century, earlier after **k** and **g** (§ 503) :

no̩ktem > nüit > nẅit *nuit*, hŏdie > üi > ẅi *ui, corium* ko̩rju̩ >
küir > kẅir *cuir* ; dükere > düire̩ > dẅire̩, *duire,* dükentem > düiz(ānt)
> dẅizānt *duisant, movi* *mo̩wwi̩ > müi > mẅi ; *sequit *se̩kwet >
siüt (§ 328) > süit > sẅit ; O.F. *aguille* agüile̩ > agẅile̩ (§ 407) ; *cui*
kūi > küi > kẅi *cui.*

Attesting Assonances and Rhymes.—**üi : ü.** *Rol.* xvi, *lui : plus : murs,* etc., cxxi,
luist : lui : escut : fust, etc.   Guiot, *murmure : luire* 1207, *rue : pluie* 2339 ; Rtbf.
Th., ordure : luire 118 ; *cure : nuire* 225.
    ẅi : i.   Wace, *Rou, qui* (∠*cogito*) : *ci, enemi,* etc., II, 3646 ; Crest. *E.,*
aguille : roïlle 2643, *Cl., luite : confite* 3363 ; Rtbf. *cuide : accide* 164, 29.

§ 516. **kẅi < küi** was reduced early to **ki** (§ 864) and a like reduction of the
diphthong is found not infrequently in Middle French, especially in the less stressed
syllables and after the group *consonant + r*, cf. Mid. Fr. *aprisme* **aprime̩ <
aprẅime̩ < aprüizme̩** (*approxĭmat), *desfrichier* **defrišje̩r < defꞛ wišje̩r < de-
früitšier** **defructicare, esfritier* **e̩fritje̩r < e̩frẅitje̩r, esfrüitier <** **exfructare,*
lāmbris < lāmbrẅis, tremie̩ < tremẅie̩, vidje̩r < vẅidje̩r, vide̩ < vẅide̩.
    In most of these words there was still hesitation in the sixteenth century, cf.
Th. I, 419-421.

✶✶ § 517. *Local Variants.*—In the western region the shift of stress in the
diphthong **üi** was relatively early (W. § iv), cf. *Gormont, iceli : fini, mis,* etc., *laisse*
viii : in the eastern region it was late (N.E. § vii) and **üi** was ordinarily reduced to **ü.**
This pronunciation influenced standard French in a few words, e.g. *charcutier, curec*
(< *cuiriee*), *lutter, lutin* (< *luitin,* earlier *nuiton,* alteration of *netun* < *neptunum*).

§ 518.   o̩i > oe̩ > u̩e̩   } (late xii-xiii) ; graphies *oi, oe, oue :*
            o̩i (ui, § 184) > u̩e̩ }
          u̩e̩ sometimes simplified to **e̩** (xiii²) ; graphies *oi, ai, e :*
          u̩e̩ occasionally opened to **u̩a** (xv-xvi) ; graphies *oi, oa.*

Sources of Later Old French **o̩i :**—
    (i) G.R **au̩** (< L. and G. **au̩**) *tonic* and *countertonic* + **j** or **i̩** from all sources
(§ 404) : *joie* **džo̩ie̩ < gau̩dia,** *choisir* **tšo̩izir <** G. **kau̩sjan.**
    (ii) Early Old French **ei** from all sources (§ 226) :
    (*a*) O.F. **ei** < G.R. **e̩** (< L. and G. **ē, ĭ**) *tonic free* (§ 225) : **mo̩i < mei < me̩,**
fo̩ible̩ < feible̩ < flēbilem.
    (*b*) O.F. **ei,** G.R. **e̩** (< L. and G. **ē, ĭ**) *tonic* and *countertonic* + **j(i̩)** (§ 404) : **toit**
< **teit < tēktum,** *loizir* < **leizir <** ***le̩t̬e̩re < likēre.**
    (*c*) O.F. **ei,** G.R. **e̩** (< L. and G. **ĕ**) *countertonic* + **j (i̩)** (§ 404) : **moitie̩ <
meitieθ <** ***me̩dje̩tate.**
    (*d*) O.F. **ei** < G.R. **e̩** (< L. **a, e, ĭ**) *intertonic* + **j (i̩)** (§ 404) : **damoize̩le̩ <
dameize̩le̩ <** ***do̩mne̩t̬e̩lla** **dominicella,* **oroizun < oreizo̩n < orātiōnem.**

Sources of **o̩i (ui) :**—
    (i) G.R. **o̩** (< L. and G. **ō, ŭ**) *tonic* and *countertonic* + **j (i̩)** (§ 404) : *noiz* **noits**
< ***no̩t̬e < nŭkem** *nucem* ; **poizun < pōtiōnem.**
    (ii) G.R. **o̩** (< L. and G. **ŏ**) *countertonic* + **j (i̩)** (§ 404) : **foiier < fŏkarĭum.**

§ 519. The diphthong **o̩i** assonated at first with **o̩** and the diphthong
o̩i (ui) with **o̩ (u),** cf. *Rol.* lxxxiii, *poi : esforz, corn,* etc. ; cxxiii, *bloie : volet,*

force, etc. ; *Al.* xl. *recunuissent : home, redutet,* etc. ; *Rol.* cl. *angoisset : tute, culchet,* etc.

In the course of the later twelfth and thirteenth centuries the less stressed high element of both diphthongs, under the influence of the lower first element, was lowered to ę, stress shifted and the first element, become the less stressed, consonantalised to ụ (> w) : thus ǫi > oę > uę > wę and ǫi (ui) > uę > wę.

*joie džǫię > žuęę, oiséls oizęls (*avicellos) > uęzęaus oiseaus.

mǫi > muę, tǫit > tuęt, fǫiblę > fuęblę, vǫirrę *(vitrum)* > vuęrrę. lǫizir > luęzir, mǫitię > muętię, damoizęlę > damuęzęlę. nǫits > nuęts, pǫizun > puęzūn, foiier > fuęięr, kǫistrę > kuęstrę.

Attesting Rhymes and Graphies.—*Ren.* XI (end XII-XIII), *Percehaie : joie,* 2701 : *coie* 13 : *voie* 3251, *envoit : ait* 259 ; *Rose* I, *recoeve : noeve* 39, *doeves : trueves* 2391 ; *G. Dôle, harnoes : oes (opus)* 2004 ; *Ren.* II *questres : mestres* 1129. *Boevin* (for *Boi(f)vin*) 1161 (Brittany, Drevin, p. 140) ; *laboer, razoer, Hebrew Gloss.* early XIII (northern region, *Rom. St.* I, pp. 180, 182) ; *βoet* (for *boit*), *Credo,* early XIII (*Rom.* XI, 608).

§ 520. The spelling *oe, ous* was employed most frequently in the terminations *-oir,* *-oire,* in which the lowering early become general under the influence of the **r** (chap. xiii) ; cf. Palsgrave, *arrousouere, machouere, miroer, mouchouer,* etc. It persisted in a few words whose origin was unknown to the sixteenth and seventeenth century printers, e.g. *bouee* (< *boie*), *couette* < *coite* (*culcita,* §§ 319, 391 (v)), *poele* < *poisle* (*pensilem*).

§ 521. When **oi** countertonic stood in hiatus with the tonic vowel or before *jod,* the whole process was retarded, the pronunciation uę being only established in the later sixteenth century : Meigret : 'En *royal, loyal* nous oyons euidemment en la prolation la diphthongue commencer par *o* et finir par *i.*' ; Baïf : '*oéians, loéial, loéier, moéienes, etc.*' (Th. I, 367, 368 ; cf. also § 404).

§ 522. uę > ę.—In the later thirteenth century there appeared in uneducated speech in Paris and adjacent regions to the east and south-east a tendency to slur the labial semi-vowel ụ, more particularly in the terminations of the imperfect indicative and conditional and after **r** and **l**.

Attesting Graphies.—*Hebrew Elegy* of 1288 (Champagne), *etet* iv, *tenret* vii, *avet* ix, etc. ; *Parisian Documents,* cited Rydberg, *Kr. Jb.* V (1), 224 : 1284 *cres* for *crois,* 1287 *cres, hers, crere ; Rôle de Taille, Danais, Englais, Galais, baudraier, pastaier,* etc. (Michaëlsson, pp. 46, 120, 90, 130) ; Boileaue, MS. xiii², *crestre, claie, sait* (for *soit*).

Palsgrave makes no mention of this pronunciation but it is implied in his spellings : *claye, craye, lampraye, arraye, le cressant, feble, monnaye, day* for *doibs.* R. Estienne gives *craye, cree* or *croye, effrai, feble* and *foible, frais* and *frez, soye* and *see, taye (thēca* 629) *raiz* and *retz, aulnay, chesnaye,* etc. (cf. Beaulieux, p. 296).

§ 523. The extension of this pronunciation was probably facilitated by the influence of the western dialect, in which the diphthong ei had been early levelled to ę (§ 230) ; its vogue in the sixteenth century among the higher ranks of Parisian society was increased by the influence of the court, where it was taken up on account of its resemblance to the then fashionable Italian pronunciation (§§ 56, 57). By the end of the century, in spite of the strenuous opposition offered by many of

the grammarians, the simplified sound was established in the terminations of the imperfect and conditional and in the adjectival ending -ois
(anglois, francois) and some other words.   Fluctuations, however, continued throughout the seventeenth century and the pronunciation
finally established was largely the outcome not so much of phonetic
conditions as of the long drawn out conflict between the simplifying
popular tendency and the conservatism of the grammarians.   It is
probable that the desire to distinguish homonyms played a part in the
final distribution of the sounds wę and ę (cf. § 147; Brunot, H.L.F. II,
255-257; Dauzat, Rev. Ph. Fr. xxxv, 128-137).

Attesting Remarks.—Sylvius (1531): ‘ *Vee, Pontese, Ese* ’ (for *voie, Pontoise, Oise*),
‘with the Normans: but even in the Parisian territory and among Parisians this
pronunciation is heard daily,’ Th. I, 375.   Guillaume des Autels (1531): ‘ Pourquoi
sera ce que quelque dame voulant bien contrefaire la courtisanne a l’entree de cest
yver dira qu’*il fait fret?* ’ (Th. I, 375.)   H. Estienne: ‘ Quant a *Francois, Anglois*
. . . il y a longtemps que plusieurs ’ (*sc.* Italiens) ‘ ont confessé n’avoir pas la langue
bien faicte pour les prononcer; et . . . ont esté fort ioyeux d’estre quittes pour dire
. . . en parlant . . . *Frances* , . . Et ie scay bien qu’entre vous courtisans trouvez
tous ces mots de trop meilleure grace, pour ce qu’ils sont plus mignards et quil ne
faut pas que les dames ouvrent tant la bouche.’ (Th. I, 376.)   ‘ *oi* should bee pronounced like *oe* . . . but the errour of late times hath made the pronunciation of it very
doubtfull and uncertaine.   For now it is a custome to sound *oi* like the open *e*. . . .
This Errour in my opinion is crept into the Court, by a foolish imitation of strangers
errours, which knowe not the pronunciation of our tongue.   And our Courtiers,
apishly seeking after all novelties, have left the true and ancient pronunciation, to
counterfeit the fustian language of strangers.   But Learned and best Speakers of
the Courts of Parliament and otherwhere, keepe themselves to the old naturall pronunciation.   Indeed the Errour is not growne generall; but chiefly is used in the
Praeter imperfect tense . . . they would saye *drait, frait, estrait*, etc.   But
they would not say *chaisir, lay, fay, ray, trais, mais*, for *choisir*, etc.   It may be
they would say *craire* for *croire*, but not *la crais* for *la croix*, nor *baire, naire* . . . nor
une fais, whereby you may see that this pronunciation is floting and uncertaine.’
(Awfeild, pp. 42, 43).

Vaugelas: ‘ A la cour on prononce beaucoup de mots escrits avec la diphtongue
oi, comme s’ils estoient escrits avec la diphtongue *ai*, parceque cette derniere est
incomparablement plus douce et plus delicate.   A mon gré c’est une des beautez de
nostre langue à l’ouïr parler, que la prononciation d’*ai* pour *oi*; *ie faisais*, prononcé
comme il vient d’estre escrit, combien a-t-il plus de grace que, *ie faisois*, en prononçant a pleine bouche la dyphtongue *oi*, comme l’on fait d’ordinaire au Palais?’
Rem. I, 183-187).

§ 524.   The representation of the simplified sound by *e* was adopted
early in a few words, e.g. *erre* (< *oirre*), *verre, tonnerre* (≠ *terre*), but
oi persisted into the eighteenth century, the adoption of *ai* being
secured finally through Voltaire’s advocacy in his preface to *Zaïre*.

§ 525. wę > wa.—In Late Middle French the modern lowered
pronunciation **wa** made its appearance in vulgar speech, at first
before **r**.   This broad pronunciation, however, found no favour with

the educated classes or the grammarians (Palsgrave excepted), in either the sixteenth or seventeenth century, and was not fully accepted until the upheaval of the Revolution had destroyed the old tradition (cf. Nyrop, I, § 160).

Attesting Rhymes, Graphies and Remarks.—

Chandos Herald (late xiv), *hoirs : Edwarz* 829; Villon, *quarre : poire* T. xcviii; Colletet *si ne qua* (= *quoi*) *: et reliqua* (cf. H.L.F. II, p. 257).

voars, voar for *voirs, v(e)oir,* XIII² (cited by Nyrop, I, § 160); R. Estienne, *voarre* (for *voirre, vitrum*), *foarre, poale* (for *poisle*), (Beaulieux, p. 296); cf. also § 74.

Palsgrave gives the rule, ' If *s, t* or *x* folowe next after *oy* in a worde of one syllable, in all suche the *i* shal be sounded in maner lyke an *a*, as for *boys, foys, soyt, croyst, uoix, croyx* they sounde *boas, foas, soat* ... and in lyke wyse, in wordes of many sillables if *oi* be the last vowel of the wordes, having *s* or *t* folowing them, all suche sounde theyr *i* of *oi* lyke an *a*, as *aincoys, francoys, disoyt, lisoyt, jasoyt* shal be sounded *aincoas, francoas* ... and so of alle suche other.' (pp. 13, 14), and he carries it out in his phonetic transcriptions, pp. 56-64. Bèze (1554): ' Corruptissimi vero Parisiensium vulgus . . . pro *voirre* sive ut alii scribunt *verre, foirre* . . . scribunt et pronuntiant *voarre* et *foarre*, itidemque pro *trois, troas* et *tras*.' (p. 54). Tabourot (end xvi): ' Item ils prononcent " a la Parisienne " *oua* quand il y a *ay* ou *oy*, comme pour dire: *ie ne vai iamais sans laquais*, ils diront *ie ne voua jamoy sans laqua* . . .' (Thurot, I, p. 357.) Hindret (1687): ' La plûpart des Parisiens prononcent ces mots des *noix, du bois, trois, mois, des pois, voir* comme . . . *des noüa, du boüa*. . . . Cette prononciation est fort irréguliere, et elle n'est pas à imiter, car elle sent son homme grossier et paresseux, qui ne daigne pas se contraindre en rien, ni s'assujettir à la moindre regle.' (Th. I, p. 358.)

✖✖ § 526. In the eastern and north-eastern regions **ụẹ** labialised to **ö** (graphy *eu*): cf. Jean d'Outremeuse, II, *meus* < *mensem* 806, *teux* < *tectos* 1000, (N.E. § ix).

Section 5.—LEVELLING BY ASSIMILATION : DIPHTHONGS **ai, au, eau, eu, ou, ieu, ue, ueu.**

§ 527. The diphthong **ai** was levelled by the mutual assimilation of its two elements; in the development of the diphthong **ue** and of the diphthongs and triphthongs in **ụ**, levelling was brought about by the assimilative influence of the labial element, which rounded the juxta-posed buccal vowels in the diphthongs **au, eau, eu, ieu, ue, ueu** and in **ọu** raised **ọ** to **u**, itself always merging in the labial vowel it induced.

§ 528. Early old French **ai** > **ẹ**, (**ẹ** when *final*); graphy *ai* or *e*.

Sources :—

(1) G.R. **a** (< L. and G. **ɑ**) tonic and countertonic + **ɟ** (**j̇**) *prae-consonantal* from all sources (§ 404): **mais** < **mɑgis, fait** < **fɑktum,** *maison* **maizon** < ***mɑsjone.**

(2) Late Latin tonic **ɑ** juxtaposed to **ī** final or *jod*: **portai** < **portɑ(w)ī, ai** < ***ajo.**

§ 529. **ai,** at first a descending diphthong assonating with **a,** (cf. *Alexis : lairmes : marbres*, etc., cvii, *Pel. abaisset : altres, place*, etc., xxvi, *mais, essai : -at* xxviii), was levelled in the course of Later Old French, first before *consonantal groups* and s.

(i) **ai** *prae-consonantal* $>$ ęi $>$ ę :

mais $>$ **męs, paistrę** $>$ **pęstrę, fait** $>$ **fęt, lairme** $<$ **lakrima** $>$ **lęrmę.**
maison **maizun** $>$ **męzūn, traitier** $<$ **traktare** $>$ **trętier, aidier** $>$ **ędier.**

[For *armoire, grimoire, poele,* etc., cf. § 487.]

(ii) **ai** *final* $>$ ęi $>$ ę.—When **ai** was final of the word monophthong-isation was tardier and the resultant vowel was ę (cf. § 200) :

$$\text{ai} < *\text{aჶo} > \text{ę,} \quad \text{porterai} > \text{portęrę,} \quad \text{sai} > \text{sę.}$$

Attesting Rhymes.—Crest., *Cl. mestre* ($<$*maistre*) : *estre* 945, *repestre : estre,* 2251, *lerme : terme* 4005, *mes : Cliges* 2857 ; *Rose* I, *amour ai : demouré, ostai : costé, Intr.* p. 190 ; *Fauvel, tendré* ($<$ *tendrai*) : *engendré* 1637, *livré* ($<$ *livrai*) : *enivré* 2358 ; Villon, *remiré : mueray,* T. xx ; Ronsard, *animay : renfermé.*

In the sixteenth century the pronunciation of ę in final position was often influenced by cognate forms and consequently variable ; cf. Meigret, '*j'ey* ou *j'é, je sey* ou *ie se*' ; Peletier, '*j'é, je sé*' ; Baïf, '*j'è, je sè*.' In the *passé défini* ę was prescribed, in the *future* there was hesitation (Th. I, pp. 302 *et seqq.*).

§ 530. Middle French **ai** (§ 404).

Sources :—

(1) G.R. **a + Ⳓ** (derived from a palatal sound) *final* or become *final :* Early Old French **fai, vęrai, gai.**

(2) G.R. **a + Ⳓ** *intervocalic* and remaining *intervocalic :* Early Old French **aჶę, paჶę, plaჶę, vęraჶę ; aჶānt, aჶuel** *aiuel,* **paჶier, laჶēnts** *laienz.*

(3) Later Old French **a** *countertonic* juxtaposed to *tonic* **Ⳓę** ($<$ ie, § 510) and **Ⳓau** ($<$ ęau, § 540) : *chaiere* **šaięrę** $<$ **tšaჶęrę, praჶaus** $<$ **praęaus.**

§ 531. **ai** *in Hiatus.*—When **ai** was in hiatus in Middle French either with the tonic vowel or with final ę (§ 404) levelling was late.

(i) **ai** *Tonic in Hiatus with* ę.—Before final ę the levelled pronunciation was frequent in the sixteenth century but only became consistent when ę was effaced.

$$\text{plaię} > \text{plę(ę),} \quad \text{vraię} < \text{vrę(ę),} \quad \text{aię} < *\text{aჶa} \ (habeam) > \text{ę(ę).}$$

(ii) **ai** *Countertonic in Hiatus with the Tonic Vowel.*—When counter-tonic **ai** was in hiatus with a tonic vowel monophthongisation was only established in the later seventeenth century and then not consistently (cf. Modern French *aïeul, cahier, payen* aჶȫl, kaჶę, paჶę).

paჶ'ier $>$ **paiჶer** $>$ **pęჶę,** *chaiere* **tšaięrę** $>$ **šęęrę** $>$ **šęrę, praiaus** $>$ **pręǫ(z).**

[For the development of Ⳓ between ę and the tonic vowel, cf. § 239.]

Attesting Remarks.—(1) -¹aię : Peletier (1549) gives -ę-ę, but according to Bèze three pronunciations of -*aie* were current, a-Ⳓę, ę-Ⳓę, ę-ę ; of these he himself preferred ę-Ⳓę, but a-Ⳓę was still in use in the early seventeenth century (cf. Maupas, p. 271, and Th. I, 291, 292). Strong verb forms were often influenced by the weak ones in which countertonic aჶ- was retained longer (cf. below).

(2) When **ai** *countertonic* was in hiatus with the tonic vowels hesitation between aჶ- ę- ęჶ- continued into Modern French, and except in a few words such as *céans,*

léans, fléau, géant, chaire (cf. above) **aɪ-** appears to have been preferred in educated speech both in the sixteenth and the seventeenth centuries, e.g. **aɪã(t)** *aiant,* **aɪę̣** *aiiez,* **aɪöl** *aieul,* **ę̣saɪę̣** *essayer,* **paɪę̣** *payer,* **paɪę̄** *payen,* **raɪū** *rayon.*

Tory mentions *peier* (i.e. **pęɪę̣**) as an affectation of the ' dames de Paris,' and Lanoue attributed this pronunciation to the courtiers, but Duez (1634) recommends **pęɪę̣**: the pronunciation **a-ɪūn** (*ayons*), **ra-ɪūn** is recommended by Maupas (1609) and in the later seventeenth century still insisted on by Hindret; ' Quelques personnes disent *payen, reyon, reyonner, eyons,* mais cette prononciation est mauvaise; il faut prononcer l'*a* et dire *payen, rayon,* etc.' (Th. I, 299).

D'Aisy (1674) attributes the pronunciation **ęɪã** for **aɪã** to the ' gens de province' and it is probable that the fluctuations in the pronunciation of this sound are to some extent due to dialectal influence, for to the north of Paris the diphthongal sound **ai** was long maintained (§ 533), and to the south-west it had long previously been levelled to **ę** (§ 533). O.F. **païs** was pronounced **pa-ĭ(s), pę-ĭ(s)** or **pai-i(s)** in the sixteenth century; **pęɪi(s)** appears in the seventeenth century.

§ 532. Middle French **ai** *final* (§ 404) levelled slowly to **ę**, accepted only in the seventeenth century.

fai > fę   gai > gę   vrai > vrę

Lanoue (1596) accepts **ę** in the verb forms *fai, brai, trai* but still prefers a diphthongal pronunciation (**-ęɪ** ?) elsewhere, e.g. in *bai, balai, gai, vrai,* and it is clear that the existence of two sets of words in *ai final,* with the diphthong levelled at different dates, led to much hesitation in pronunciation in Middle and Early Modern French, cf. Th. I, pp. 302-308, and also Wahlgren, *Observations sur les Verbes à Parfaits Faibles* I (1), Uppsala, 1931.

✱✱ § 533. *Local Variants.*—In the south-western, south-central and south-eastern regions **aɪ** from all sources and in all positions appears to have passed early to **ai** and levelled early: (i) *prae-consonantal* **ę** for **ai** began in the eleventh century: **ai** assonates already freely with **ę** in the *Roland* (cf. laisses iv, liii, lxv, etc.) and levelling is indicated even earlier in the spellings of documents from that region, e.g. *Fresneium* 1060 (*Fraxinetum*), *Grantamesnil* 1075, *Plesseio* 1075, *Ambesia, seisire* 1110 (Drevin, pp. 142-147); *Fresle, Greslet* (*Domesday book*); *palesio* (*Rom.* xxxi, p. 50). (ii) Early levelling of **ai** in hiatus to **e** is attested by the spellings *eol, eau, eiaus* for *aieul* in the *Livre de Jostise et de Plet,* (Orléanais, cent. xiii), *leanz, peant* (*Burgundian Docts., Rom.* XLI, pp. 559, 561; cf. Terracher, *Rev. Lg. R.* I, 452), and by the use of *ai* for **ę** (< **ei**) e.g. in *saie* (**sę̣ę**), *vaie,* etc., *donaie, corraie, etc., Rose,* MS. Ab., *Intr.* p. 199.

In the northern region **ai** was maintained later as a descending diphthong, cf. Coyfurelly (xiv), ' Romanici vero proprie et plena voce sonant *a* ut *faire, traire,* etc. '; Du Gardin (1620): ' Nous autres Wallons prononçons *ai* . . . en telle sorte, qu'on entend l'*a* et l'*i* . . . Les Parisiens les confondent.' (Th. I, 292); *geole* . . . le Picard dit *gayole* ou *geole.*' (R. Est. Th. I, p. 524, cf. N. §§ vii, ix.)

[For **a** + **ŝ** and **ẑ** in the northern region cf. § 315, N. § xvi, E. § v.]

§ 534. **au > ǫ** (c. xv-xvi) ; graphy *au.*

Source of **au.**—Old French **a** *tonic* and *countertonic* + **ɬ** and **ɟ** + *consonant* (§ 387), **autrę < aɬtrę < aɬterum, faukun < faɬkǫn < *falkǫne.**

§ 535. In the course of later Middle French the labial element of the diphthong **au** rounded **a** and merged in the rounded vowel. In the stressed syllables this monophthongisation was only accepted by the

grammarians in the sixteenth century but in less stressed syllables and in vulgar speech the levelled pronunciation had some vogue earlier (cf. Villon, *os : maulx, hospitaulx*, T. cxliii).

> aɫtĕrum > aɫtrę > autrę > ǫtrę, malos > maus > mǫ(z)
> *trępaljos > travaɟts > travauts > travǫ(z) *travauz*
> O.F. vaɫt > vaut > vǫt **valerajo > vaudrai > vǫdrai *vaudrai*

Attesting Graphies and Remarks.—*Rôle de Taille* (1292), *Jehan l'aulogier* (for *l'orlogier*); *Guise letters* (1537-1548), *otant, ocy (aussi), fodre (faudrai)*; loan-words, cent. xv and xvi, *haubby* from English *hobby, artichault* (Rabelais) from Italian *articiocco, rauder* (Palsgrave) < Provençal **rǫdar** (< *rǫtare*). Ramus (1561): ' En ces motz *aultre, autel* . . . nous prononçons une voyelle indivisible.' (Th. I, 427.)

§ 536. The stage ǫ appears to have been preceded in the tonic syllable by a stage in which ǭ, a more open long sound, was pronounced, the one heard in Modern English in the words *or, law*, cf. Palsgrave: ' *au* in the frenche tonge shalbe sounded lyke as we sounde hym in these wordes in our tonge, *a dawe, a mawe, a lawe*. Except where a frenche worde begynneth with this diphthonge *au*, as in these wordes *aulcun, aultre, au, aussi, aux* and *aucteur*, and all such lyke, in which they sounde the *au* almost lyke an *o*.' p. 14; cf. also the loan-words above and § 398.

✶✶ § 537. Fabri (1521) who rhymes *aubel* with *aoust bel* and Meigret, who insists on a diphthongal pronunciation **ao**, are probably influenced by their respective dialects, for both Normandy and the south-eastern region retained late a diphthongal pronunciation of this sound, cf. § 1328 (3) and Th. I, 425 et seqq.

§ 538. ˈęau > ęˈau (c. xii) > ęǫ (c. xvi) > ǫ (c. xvii); graphy *eau*.
Sources of **eau.**—Old French ę + ɫ + *consonant* (§ 388): **bęaus < bęɫs < bĕllos.** Old French ˈęauę (< ęuę < akųa, *aqua*, § 330).

§ 539. ˈęau was at first a descending triphthong and assonated with the vowel ę, but in the later twelfth century the stress shifted on to the more sonorous sound and ę was closed to ẹ: together with **au, ęau** was levelled to ęǫ in Later Middle French (§ 535). Complete monophthongisation to ǫ was not formally accepted till after the middle of the seventeenth century (latest in the word *eau*); it is, however, attested in vulgar speech and had some vogue at the court at the end of the sixteenth century.

bĕllos > bęɫs > bˈęaus > bęaus > bęǫs > bǫ(z) *beaux*, *sigęllos > sęęaus > sęǫs > sǫ(z) *seaux*, *hęlmų > hˈęaumę > hęǫmę > ǫmę *heaume.*

Attesting Rhymes, Graphies and Remarks.—ˈęau >ę ˈau: Marie, *reials : beals, Mil.* 213; *chevals : beals, El.* 645.
Erasmus: ' In some words you hear three vowels, as when the French say " *beau pere*," in *beau* you hear *e, a* and *u*, although the word is a monosyllable.' Bèze (1584): ' Auditur *e* clausum cum diphthongo *au*, quasi scribas *eo* ut *eau seau.* . . .' St. Liens (1580): ' The word *beau*, although it may seem to have two syllables, is pronounced as one by the courtiers, for they speak it as if it were written *bau* but very short; and likewise they say *vau* (i.e. **vo**) for *veau*, and instead of *chapeau, Izabeau* pronounce *chapau, Izabau*.' (Th. I, pp. 434-439.)

✳✳ § 540. In the northern and north-eastern region, including Champagne, but not the district to the north-east of Liége, ẹau was early differentiated to ịau (> ịau) (N. § viii). Vulgar Parisian speech was affected by this pronunciation, cf. Rtbf., *biaus : ciaus* (196, 41): Bèze: ' Vitanda est autem vitiosissima vulgi Parisiensis pronuntiatio in hac triphthongo, nempe *l'iaue* et *biau* pro *l'eau, beau* . . .' p. 58. In the extreme north-east the first element remained stressed and ẹau was reduced to ẹ (*Mystères*, XV, p. xvi, N.E. § viii).

§ 541. ẹu > öu (c. xii) > öı (c. xiii); *graphy eu, ueu, el* (§ 698).

Sources of eu :—

(1) Early Old French ọu < G.R. ọ (< L. ō, ŭ, G. ŭ) *tonic free* (§ 226): fleur < flour < flōrem, geulẹ < gọulẹ < gŭla, seus < sọu+s < sōlus.

(2) Early Old French ọu < G.R. ọ (< L. ō, ŭ) + ụ *final* (§ 254): deus < dọus < *dọụs < dŭŏs, leu < lọu < lŭpŭm (§ 343).

(3) Early Old French ẹ (< L. and G. ĭ, ĕ) + ɫ and ʃ + *consonant* (§ 387): eus < ẹ+s > illos, *pareilz,* pareuts < pareʃts < pariculos, feutrẹ < *fẹ+trụ (*filtir*).

§ 542. The first element of the diphthong eu was rounded to ö in the course of the twelfth century and öu monophthongised to ö in the course of the later twelfth and thirteenth centuries:

fleur > flör,	geulẹ > gölẹ,	seus > sös,	preuts < *prōdẹs > pröts.
deus > dös,	leu > lö (cf. § 343).		
eus > ös,	pareuts > parös *pareuz,*		feutrẹ < *fẹ+trụ > fötrẹ.

[For the quality of ö cf. § 585.]

Attesting Rhymes.—eu : ueu (öu : öu), *Troie, eus : dueus* 6167 : *vueus* 20173 *cheveus : dueus* 16747. Crestien, *preu : leu,* E. 1041, *jeus : seus* 2835, *corajeus* 3391.

eu : ue (ö : ö), *Troie, eus : bues* 27,917, G. Guiart II, *aveuent : peuent,* 11,902, *esqueuent* (*excūtunt*) : *peuent,* 7794.

§ 543. In secondary stressed syllables ö was often closed to ü in Middle French, e.g. in the contracted forms of the article dü < dö (< deu < de+) and ü < ö(< e+); cf. also blüet < blöet *bleuet* (§ 549), *prudhomme, prudefemme, mürier, buvant* (cf. § 486).

[For dialectal ou and au < ẹ+ cf. §§ 501, 502.]

§ 544. ịeu > jö (c. xiii); graphy *ieu, iel* (§ 698).

Sources of ịeu :—

(1) Early Old French ịie (< L. and G. ĕ *tonic free*) + ụ *final* (§§ 226, 254): dieu < dĕum.

(2) Early Old French ịie (< L. and G. ĕ *tonic free*) + ɫ + *consonant* (§ 387): *cieus* tsieus < tsie+s < kaelos.

(3) Early Old French ịie (L. and G. ĕ *tonic*) + ʃ + *consonant* (§§ 410, 387): *mieuz* mieuts < mieʃts < mēlius.

(4) Early Old French ẹ̈ (< L. and G. ạ *tonic free*) + ɫ + *consonant* (§ 388): tieus < tẹ+s < talis.

(5) Early Old French ịụ, with glide development (§§ 123, 391 (4)), e.g. pieus < plus.

§ 545. ịeu was at first a descending triphthong : in the course of the twelfth century the stress was shifted, ị consonantalised to j and ẹu labialised : ịeu > jöụ > jö :

dieu > djö *dieu*, kaekum > tsieu (§ 302) > sjö *cieu, cieus* tsieus > sjös, *mieuz* mieuts > mjös, *βęklos (*vetulus*, § 360) > vieuts > vjös *vieuz*, tieus > tjös *tieus, tiex*, pɑlos > pęɫs > pieus > pjös *pieus, piex*.

✶✶ § 546. In the northern region, where shift of stress was late, ˈleu was reduced to ˈiu, e.g. *diu, cius, mius* (*mix*), etc. (N. § vi).

[For reduction of ie + u *final* to ie in the south-western region cf. § 255; for lowering of ję to ja before ɫ and ɉ + *consonant*, cf. § 502.]

§ 547. ǫu > u (c. xiii); graphy *ou*.

Sources of ǫu:—

  (1) *Gallo-Roman* ǫu :

    (*a*) G.R. aʮ and aw + ʮ final (§ 481): trǫu < ✶✶ trɑʮɣʮ < *trɑukum, *clou* klǫu < klɑwum *clavum*.
    (*b*) Gallo-Roman a + ww (§§ 374, 481): tǫut < ✶✶ tawwet < tɑkŭit.
  (2) *Later Old French* ǫu < ǫ + ɫ + *consonant* (§ 387): fǫus < fǫ̈ɫs < follis.

[For the termination -ǫuę, -ǫut cf. §§ 483, 914.]

§ 548. ǫu, at first a descending diphthong assonating in ǫ (cf. *Rol.* ccxi, *Anjou : corn, fort*), was levelled to u in the course of the late twelfth and thirteenth centuries:

klǫu > klu *clou*, trǫu > tru *trou*, fǫus > fus *fous*, mǫudrę > mudrę *moudre*.

Cf. Gt. d'Arras, *fous : vous, Eracles* 1035; G. Guiart, *souz* (*solvitus): *desouz.*

✶✶ § 549. In the northern region there were two types of differentiation: (1) In the north-western region Gallo-Roman ǫ̈u was, like ǫu (§ 228), differentiated to eu and levelled to ö, e.g. *treu, cleu, peu, eut,* Mis. *peu : preu* xxxvi, *eut* (< *habuit*), *peut* < (*pavit*): *meut, veut,* xlviii, cf. *Eu* < **Augum.* In the speech of the Île de France both ö and u were current and the northern pronunciation of the words *peu, bleu, meunier,* was adopted, cf. Boileaue, p. 67, *meuniers, muniers;* R. Estienne, ' *munier voyez meusnier.*'

  (2) Elsewhere in the northern region ǫu (Gallo-Roman and Old French) was differentiated to au, cf. *Auc. trau,* 24, 89, *faus,* 3, 7, *saure* (< *solvere*), 24, 54, N. § viii.

§ 550. ˈue > ö (c. xii); graphies *ue, oe, eu, œu, el* (§§ 714, 698).

Sources of ue:—

  (1) Early Old French ˈuo < L. and G. ŏ *tonic free* (§ 226):

buef < buof < bŏwem, fuerrę < fuoðrę < *fǫdrʮ, duel < duol < *dǫlʮ.

  (2) Early Old French ˈuo < L. and G. ŏ *tonic, blocked and free,* + ɉ (§ 410):

fueille fuęlę < fuǫlę < fŏlia,   *orgueil* orguęɉ < orguǫɉ < *orgŏlium.
mueille muęlę < muǫlę < mŏlliat,   *ueil* uęɉ < uǫɉ < ŏkŭlum.

§ 551. ˈue, at first a descending diphthong, was monophthongised to ö in the course of the twelfth century:

buef > böf, fuerrę > förrę, duel > döl, uevrę < ŏpera > övrę.
fuęlę > föļę, orguęɉ > orgöɉ, muęlę > möļę, uęɉ > öɉ.

[For the quality of ö cf. § 585.]

Attesting Graphies and Rhymes.—1137 *Scaldeuvrium* < *Scaldŏbriga* (*Escaudoeuvres*, dep. Nord ; cf. Longnon, p. 41) ; A.N. MSS. of the late twelfth century : graphies, *eo*, e.g. *deol, Rol.* 929 ; *φ, Cam. Ps.. pφples. φures* (cf. Suchier, *Gr.* § 28).

Rhymes.—*ue* : *eu* : *Troie, bues* : *eus* 6977 ; Wace, *Bayeues* (*Bajŏcăsses*) : *lieues, Rou* III, 3247, G. Guiart II, *peuent* : *aveuent* 11902.

Attesting rhymes are relatively few and late because the words containing *ue* had only themselves to rhyme with until the diphthong *eu* (*ueu*) had monophthongised. The stages of the development have not been fully determined but appear to be ^{l}uö > ụö > ö.

✷✷ § 552. ^{l}ue in hiatus with ẹ was reduced to u in the northern, eastern and south-central regions (cf. N. § v, E. § iii and the parallel reduction of ^{l}iẹẹ, § 513) ; ruẹẹ < rueðẹ < rŏta > rụẹ (*Rose* I, *roe* : *boe*, 3989), puẹẹnt < pueðẹnt < *pŏtent > puẹnt ; the use of rụẹ was early extended but pǫẹnt < puẹẹnt was maintained in francien as it was supported by the forms, *peuz, peut*.

✷✷ § 553. *Western and Southern Development of* ^{l}ue.—Rhymes in several of the Later Old French poets indicate a divergent development of the diphthong ^{l}ue, one closely parallel to that followed by the diphthongs ^{l}ie and ^{l}üi, viz. shift of stress followed by the consonantalisation of the first element, ^{l}ue > ụẹ and ụẹ subsequently, particularly in less stressed syllables, was often reduced to ẹ.

Attesting Rhymes.—*Thebes, duel* : *fel* 1933 ; *Eneas, muert* : *requiert* 8789 ; *Marie, doels* : *cels Ch.* 7, *ilec* : *eschec El.* 177; *Rose* I, *noeve* : *recoeve* 39, II, *vueil* : *esveil* 10825, *vueille* : *vieille* 9689 ; *G. Dôle, soeil* : *conseil* 3346, *muelle* (*mŏlliat*) : *mervelle* 4753, *avoeques* : *arcevesques* 4987, *lues* : *entremes* 5424, (cf. also *jenne* < *juefne*, § 478).

The poets who make use of rhymes of this sort are predominantly in the western region and this fact, coupled with the distribution of place-names in which the modern terminations -*erre*, -*evre*, -*eil* are derived from O.F. -*uerre* (< -^{l}odŭrum), -*uevre* (< -^{l}ọbrĭga, -^{l}ovĕra), -*ueil* (-^{l}ọiălum), e.g. *Auxerre* < *Autessiodurum, Lingevres* (Calvados), *Dèvre* < *Dovera* (Cher), *Corbeil* (Seine et Oise), etc. (cf. Longnon, pp. 35-42, 65-69, 56), indicates that this pronunciation is not a stage in the passage of the diphthong ue to ö, but a divergent local development, one proper to the western, south-central and south-eastern regions.

In Middle French this pronunciation persisted and before ḷ secured such extension that it is mentioned and even prescribed by some of the sixteenth-century grammarians : cf. Palsgrave, '*fueille* .... shalbe sounded *feille*,' p. 10 ; H. Estienne, ' *oeil, dueil, accueil, orgueil* and others of the like are pronounced by some with an *e* long and a very slight *i*, by others with a kind of *u* . . . ; this second pronunciation, which is the more usual, would offend the ear in *orgueilleux* . . .' (Th. I, p. 463). The pronunciation ụẹ has left its mark in Modern French in the word *foarre* fwar < fụẹrrẹ (*fodrum*), and in reduced form in *avec, bienveillant, malveillant*.

§ 554. The spelling *o, u*, later *ou*, often found, especially before k, l, ḷ and labial consonants, e.g. *voil, vuil, ovre, ouvre* (cf. Philipon, *Rom.* L. pp. 386-412), apparently represents a pronunciation u, which may be derived from a reduction of the undifferentiated diphthong ^{l}uo to its first (stressed) element (cf. § 230 (iii) and Matzke, l *mouillé*).

§ 555. ueu > { jö; graphy *ieu, iel* (§ 698),
         { ö; graphy *ueu, oeu, eu, el* (§ 698).

Sources of ueu :—

(1) Early Old French ^{l}ueu (^{l}üeu ?) < L. ŏ *tonic free* + ụ *final* (§§ 226, 254) :

   **lueu < locum, **fueu < focum, **džueu < jocum.

(2) Later Old French ^{l}ueu (üeu ?) :

   (i) Early Old French ^{l}ue < Early Old French ^{l}uo (< L. ŏ, G. ǒ, ō *tonic free*) + l become *prae-consonantal* (§§ 226, 387) :

   dueus < dueɫs < duoɫs < *dọlọs, vueut < vueɫt < vuoɫt < *βǫlet.

(ii) Early Old French ˈue < Early Old French uo (< L. ŏ, G. ŏ, ǫ *tonic*) + ɟ
become *prae-consonantal* (§§ 410, 387):

> *ueilz* ˈueuts < ˈueɟts < ˈuoɟts < ŏkŭlos,
> *cueilt* kueut < kueɟt < kuoɟt < *kǫll(e)jet < kŏlligit.

§ 556. The triphthong ˈueu was at first descending : in the course of
the eleventh and twelfth centuries the middle element was rounded to
ö and stressed; the first element was ordinarily differentiated to i and
consonantalised to ɟ, which merged in dž but differentiation was ordinarily
checked by preceding labial and velar consonants :

> ueu > ɟö: ueuts > ɟös *ieuz*, lueu > lɟö *lieu*, džueu > džɟö > žö *jeu*.
> ueu > ö : vueut > vöt *vuet*, fueu > fö *feu*, kueut > köt *keut*.
>
> sarkueu (< *sɑrkǫ(f)ǔ) > sarkö *sarkeu* (cf. §§ 263, 497, 817).

Attesting Rhymes.—*Troie, ieuz : vieuz* 20221, *lieus : cieus* 13034, *gieus : cieus* 1625 ;
Crest. *feus : venimeus, Iv.* 3360, *jeus : deus E.* 2101 ; Angier, *voet : moet* 9*v*°, *qoelt :
moet* 111 *r*° ; Rtbf. *vues* (< *voles*): *Rustebues*.

§ 557. Anglo-Norman forms (§§ 1162, 1169) indicate that the differentiation of ueu
to ieu took place *after* the Norman Conquest when the triphthong was developed from
ue + vocalising ɫ and ɟ, *before* it when ueu was the product of ue + ǔ *final*, but the
development of this triphthong is not yet fully elucidated. Variants, possibly local, are
frequent : the differentiated form is sometimes found after velars and labials and is often
absent after dentals, e.g. *kieut, sarkieus, vieut—leu, deut* (cf. Crest. *leu : preu*, Cl. 359).
It appears also probable that u was palatalised to ü before being differentiated to i.

✶✶ In the northern region Early Old French ˈüeu and ˈieu were reduced to ü
and ˈiu respectively, e.g. *fu, sarku, liu, giu* (N. § vi).

[For *diaut, viaut, iauz*, etc., cf. § 501.]

CHAPTER XV.

VOWEL LENGTHENING IN MIDDLE FRENCH.

[For Vowel Lengthening in Gallo-Roman and Old French cf. §§ 198, 199, 233, 573.]

§ 558. No direct evidence of differentiation of quantity in vowels is afforded by the rhymes in Old or Middle French. Fifteenth-century poets like Villon couple together freely in rhyme words like *abbēsse : mĕsse*, *honnēstes : fillĕtes*, *maistre : mĕtre*, and the practice continued in the sixteenth century, though not without protests from grammarians and prosodists.

Protest appears to have been first raised by Bouchet in 1548, cf. also Du Bellay, *Def.* p. 133. Bèze is emphatic in his condemnation of any confusion of quantity : 'Nothing can offend the ear more than the lengthening of the short vowel and the shortening of the long, as those know that hear foreigners and some provincials speak, as for instance when we hear the people of Touraine and Picardy pronounce *mestresse* ∪ – ∪ for *maistresse* – ∪ ∪ or *messe* – ∪ for *messe* ∪ ∪ or say *feste* – ∪ for *faicte* ∪ ∪ . . .' (p. 84). In spite of Malherbe's strictures on the laxness shown by Desportes, the seventeenth-century poets, even Racine, allowed themselves complete freedom, and prosodists ended by condoning the licence (cf. Kastner, pp. 44, 45).

§ 559. Lengthening had, however, resulted from various causes : the levelling of diphthongs, the contraction of vowels in hiatus, the absorption or effacement of consonants and the influence of certain consonants on vowels preceding them, and it is evident from the remarks of the grammarians that the differentiation of quantity was strong enough to differentiate grammatical forms (cf. §§ 271, 562 564, 567, 567), and that it was already inducing a modification of the quality of some of the vowels (chap. xvi).

§ 560. *Diphthongs.*—The levelling of **au** and **eau** (§§ 535, 539) produced a lengthened vowel, cf. Bèze : 'The diphthong *au* (i.e. ǫ) is always long . . . whether penultimate as *aultre*, *autant*, *haultain*, or antepenultimate as *haultement*, or final in liaison as *hault et droict*.' (p. 89).

The earlier levelling of **ai** to ę may have also produced a lengthened vowel for some writers attribute length to the vowels in *faire*, *traire*, *baise*, etc.

§ 561. *Syneresis.*—(i) Lengthening resulted from the contraction of the vowels **aa, aā, aū, ee, uu** (§§ 242, 244), e.g. in *age* **āžę** < **aažę**, *chaire* **šērę** < **šęęrę**, *abbesse* **abēsę** < **abęęsę**, *paon* **pãn** < **paūn**.

§ 562. (ii) Compensatory lengthening accompanied the effacement of ę, juxtaposed to tonic or countertonic vowels, e.g. in **alūrę** < O.F. **alęürę**, *fisse* **fīsę** < **fęįsę**, *fi* **fī** < **fię**, *plaie* **plē** < **plęę**, *aloient* **alwēt** < **alwęę(n)t** ; cf. also *aiseement*, **ęzēmā** < **ęzęęmā(t)**, (§§ 243, 269-271).

Cf. Bèze: 'All words ending in *e* feminine juxtaposed to a preceding vowel lengthen the penultimate vowel, as *amie . . . fie, loue, . . .*' p. 88. Peletier: 'La troisieme personne singuliere' (of the imperfect indicative), 'ê brieue é la pluriére longue, comme *il aloèt* e *iz aloêt (alloient), il soèt* e *iz soêt (soient)*,' (Th. II, p. 584).

The extent to which this lengthening survived in the later seventeenth century (and incidentally the characteristic ignorance of the past history of the language) is shown by a curious passage of the grammarian Bouhours on the agreement of the past participle: '*J'ai receû vos lettres* . . . Voilà ce qui se fait régulierement et naturellement, selon la pure raison de la Grammaire. Mais il y a une autre raison, qui oblige de parler d'une autre maniere; c'est lorsque la prononciation ne seroit pas assez soustenuë. Car en ces rencontres, on donne des nombres et des genres aux participes, afin de soustenir le discours. On dit pour cette raison: "*La lettre que j'ai receûë.*" Cela est si vray que lorsqu'on ajoute quelque chose aprés, le participe redevient indéclinable, estant suffisamment soustenu par ce qui suit: comme il paroist dans les exemples de M. de Vaugelas: *Le commerce l'a rendu puissante, je l'ai veû partir, . . . la peine que m'a donné cette affaire.* Il arrive tout le contraire à l'égard du verbe estre; car son participe redevient indéclinable au milieu d'un sens, pour empescher la prononciation de languir et de traisner trop. C'est la raison pourquoi on dit: *elle s'est venu asseoir, ils se sont fait peindre; la liberté que je me suis donné de vous écrire*: quoy-qu'on dise: *la liberté que je me suis donnée.*' (Remarques, pp. 520, 521, 3rd ed., 1682; cf. Rosset, p. 132.)

§ 563. *Effacement of Consonants:* (i) **n** *prae-consonantal.*—The merging of prae-consonantal **n** in the preceding nasal vowel induced the lengthening of that vowel (§ 437). Cf. Bèze: 'Every syllable ending in the letter *m* or *n* that is not double but precedes another consonant is long by nature.' (p. 88).

Length ning was restricted to the *prae-consonantal* nasal consonant because it was only in this position that **n** was at that time completely absorbed in the preceding vowel (§ 438).

§ 564. (ii) **s** *prae-consonantal.*—The effacement of prae-consonantal **z** and **s** in later Old French was accompanied by compensatory lengthening of the preceding vowel, especially the tonic vowel (§ 377), e.g. **parlā < parlast, arę̄ < aręst, īlę < izlę, mī < mist, ǭtę < ǫstę, tǫt < tǫst, gū < gust, fū < füst, pwę̄lę < pųęzlę** (< ***pę̄sile, pensile**). Cf. Erasmus: '. . . when *s* is elided before a consonant, as in *est*, they sound a double or triple sound *eee*.' (Th. II, 593); Bèze: 'Every *s* mute before a consonant . . . lengthens the preceding vowel' (p. 90); H. Estienne: '*Afin qu'il gemist* . . . the interpolation of this letter *s* shows that this letter *i* is to be pronounced differently from the way it is pronounced in the present tense *il gemit*.' (Th. II, 639.) [For this use of *s* as a diacritic sign cf. § 725.]

In the seventeenth century the verbal endings **-ā < -ast, -āt(ę) < -astęs**, were shortened analogically (cf. Th. II, 597).

§ 565. (iii) **s** *final.*—As **s** final became mute in Middle French (cf. § 621) vowels preceding it were also lengthened; cf. Erasmus: 'The French suppress the *s* in *dominus* and then the *u* takes the place

of three vowels.' (Beaulieux, 121); Peletier: 'Mémes a la fin d'aucuns moz, qui se prononcet a part, la lètre *s* ne se sonne point que par une maniére d'alongemant é produccion de voès, nommémant après la lètre *r*, comme an *keurs, durs, obscurs.*' (Th. II, 621.)

§ 566. In the pronunciation of the first person singular of verbs, i.e. in a form in which *s* was a relatively late and often merely graphical addition (§ 902), there was considerable divergence in the sixteenth century. Peletier indicates a pronunciation that is mainly on traditional lines, for he marks as *short* the first persons that had in Old French neither flexional **s** nor **ę** in hiatus, e.g. *crein, di, mè (met), sè, tien, veu; appercu, repondi, vi*, etc., and as *long : f ē* (<*fais*), *soē, avoē* (<*soie, avoie*), as also all second persons singular, e.g. *tu peus, veus, dis, escris.* Levelling in favour of the long vowel had, however, already begun in his time and resulted in such complete oblivion of the historical development that in 1694 the rule formulated by the Academy runs: 'Comme les premieres personnes du présent de l'indicatif de tous les verbes sont fort longues, on est obligé d'y mettre un *s* pour faire sentir cette longueur. Ainsi il faut dire *je fais, je dis, je crains.*' (Th. II, 55.)

§ 567. It is probable also that the Old French effacement of the final consonants before flexional **s** had produced a lengthening that was still perceptible in the sixteenth century, for Meigret distinguishes between the length of vowel in the singular and plural of such words as end in the singular in a consonant that was mute in the plural, e.g. between *lac : lacs* (**lās**), *coc : cocs* (**kōs**), *hanap-hanaps* (**hanās**) and Peletier and Lanoue distinguish between the length of vowel in the plural of words of this type and in the plurals in which there was no such effaced consonant.

§ 568. *Lengthening Influence of Consonants.*—It is evident that some consonants were beginning to exercise a lengthening influence on the vowels that preceded them, but the difference of opinion among the grammarians on this point indicates that usage was not as yet fixed, the process being probably in an early stage. It is possible also that in some of their remarks observers confound quantity and quality, particularly in the **a**-*sounds.*

§ 569. The consonant about whose lengthening influence there is greatest agreement is **z** *intervocalic*, cf. Bèze: ' *s* intervocalic and pronounced as *z* lengthens a preceding vowel or diphthong, e.g. *chouse, cause, toise, bise, ruse, oser, saison, loisir, user* ' (p. 89). (For **rr** cf. § 366.)

§ 570. The consonants to which a lengthening influence is more variably attributed are **l**, **s** (< **ss**), **ž** :

(i) **l** in the ending **-alę**, cf. Bèze: '*A* before *ll* preceded by silent *i*, with *e* feminine following, is long, as *aille, baille, caille . . . paille*' (p. 89).

(ii) **s** < **ss**, e.g. in (a) **-āsę**, *basse, grasse, lasse*, the impf. subj. in *-asse, -asses*, etc., (b) **-ēsę**, e.g. *baisse*, (c) **-īsę**, e.g. the impf. subj. in *-isse*; also in borrowed words in *-ation, creātion, nātion* (Th. II, pp. 675, 680, 682, 721).

(iii) **ž** in the ending **-ažę**, e.g. *voyage* (Th. II, 669).

The vowel **a** is ordinarily given length in loan-words in the endings *-ane, -ame, -are*, e.g. *profāne, mānne, fāme, infāme, phāre, rāre, gāre* (Th. II, pp. 686, 691, 695).

CHAPTER XVI.

QUALITY OF VOWELS IN LATER OLD AND MIDDLE FRENCH.

Section 1.—QUALITY IN OLD AND MODERN FRENCH.

§ 571. Between the vowel system of the twelfth century and the system of Modern French the difference in respect of quality is wide. In the French of to-day differences in quality are perceptible in all vowels except the three highest (**i, u, ü**), and the qualitative differences observable in the mid and low vowels **e, o, ö, a**, though still determined to some extent by tradition (e.g. the **e**-sound derived from older **ai** and from older **oi** tends still to be open, the **o**-*sound* from **au** to be closed), are regulated with increasing frequency by quite other factors: (i) the position of the sound in the word, (ii) its length, and (iii) the point of articulation of the following consonant. Briefly summarised it may be said that the Modern French differentiation of quality among tonic *mid* vowels is determined as follows : vowels that end a word tend to be closed; those pronounced in the same syllable as a consonant, i.e. those that are now blocked tend to be open; those juxtaposed to a single intervocalic consonant vary with the extent to which they are lengthened and with the point of articulation of the consonant, **l** and **r** tending to open vowels.

The qualitative difference among the **e**-, **o**- and **ö**-*sounds* is mainly one of height, that observable in the **a**-*sounds* is mainly one of retraction, ' **a** being back and low and tending towards **ǫ**, **a** front and less open, tending towards **ę** ' (Grammont, p. 25).

[For details and for secondary stressed vowels cf. Grammont, *Traité, passim.*]

§ 572. The fluctuations in the quality of the modern vowels make it evident that the differentiation of quality is a movement still in process, but though it is difficult to get direct evidence or interpret the evidence forthcoming, it is also clear that the movement had its beginnings in the older language. No complete account of the subject has as yet been given and all that can be attempted in the limits of this book is to indicate briefly the chief modifications made in Later Old

and Middle French and describe summarily the pronunciation of the vowels at the end of the sixteenth century as far as their quality has been ascertained.

§ 573. *Differentiation of Quality in Old French.*—In the phonetic system of the twelfth century, the only vowel sound in which a difference of quality is observable is the e-sound. The (isolative) raising of ǫ to u (§ 184) had widened the difference of quality between ǫ and ǫ into a difference of vowel, and no qualitative distinction appears as yet to have developed in the vowels a, i, u or ü or in the newly forming sound ö. In the e-sounds in tonic syllables, however, the differences of quality were more finely differentiated than in the French of to-day, for the early Continental poets meticulously separated off from each other in their assonances and rhymes ę̆ from Late Latin ę tonic blocked (tęrę), ę from Late Latin ę tonic blocked (mętrę, dętę), and ę̄ from Late Latin ā tonic free (pę̄rę, tę̆l, bŭntę̄). The difference in the articulation of these vowels, whatever it may be (§ 233), was determined traditionally, i.e. in accordance with the development of the sounds from Latin.

Section 2.—MODIFICATIONS IN THE QUALITY OF THE OLD FRENCH
e- AND o- SOUNDS.

§ 574. In the course of Later Old French the factors that play a part in the differentiation of quality in Modern French began to exercise an influence on the Old French e- and o-*sounds*, viz.: the point of articulation of the following consonant, position in the word, and vowel lengthening. There showed itself also in Later Old French a tendency to *open* lengthened tonic ę and *close* lengthened ǫ, and in Later Middle French lengthened a begins to *velarise*.

[For the influence of following l and r cf. §§ 493-495 ; for modifications in the quality of nasal vowels cf. chap. xi.]

§ 575. *Opening of Tonic* ę̆ *and* ę̄ (ję).

(i) ę̆: By the reduction of lengthened consonants and intervocalic consonantal groups (chap. viii) vowels which had been blocked and consequently short in Gallo-Roman (§ 198) became free and relatively long, and consequently Early Old French ę̆ < L.L. ę blocked (§ 179), become free, opened to ę in the course of the twelfth century :

mętrę < mĭttĕre > mętrę,   mẹt < mĭttit > mętę,   evęskę > evękę *evesque*.

Cf. Beroul : *met : est* 2049 : *tret* 4409 ; *Rose* I ; *pretes* (*prestes*) *: saietes* 945 : *metes* 2249, *prete : petitete* 851.

✶✶ [For the development of ę̆ in the eastern region cf. E. § xvii.]

14

§ 576. (ii) ẹ, ı̯ẹ : In Late Middle French ę and ı̯ę (< L.L. a tonic free and ę tonic free, §§ 225, 231, 410) began to open to ẹ and ı̯ẹ when free, i.e. before single plosive and fricative consonants preceding ę, and also before final consonants if still sounded (chap. xvii), e.g. in words such as *feve, seve, treve, acheve, creve, leve, piege, siege, breise, chief, nef,* (O.F. fẹ̈vę, sẹvę, trı̯ẹvę, etc.), etc.   The quality of the vowel remained fluctuating into Early Modern French.

Peletier still attributes ẹ to *chef, souef, chevre* ; Baïf, ę to *chef, nef, greve,* ẹ to *chevre* ; Lanoue permits ẹ and ę 'indifferently' in *acheve, creve, leve* (Th. I, pp. 54, 69, 75).   In learned loan-words ẹ remained closed except before l and m (Th. I, 79).

✶✶ § 577. In the western and south-central region ẹ̈ opened to ę in the course of the thirteenth century, cf. Guiart I, *eve,* (*aqua* § 330) : *esleve* 3167 : *feve* 3435 : *soueve* II, 11882 and *Ét. Angier,* p. 9.

[For the opening of ę and ı̯ę by l and r cf. §§ 494, 495 ; for the lowering of ẹ to a before r cf. § 496 ; for the closing of ę < ai *final* cf. § 529 ; for ẹ and ę in countertonic syllables cf. § 591 ; for *rimes normandes* cf. § 402.]

§ 578. *Closing of o-sounds.*

Influence of Position.—ǫ (< Latin and Gallo-Roman aṷ, aw, §§ 481, 505), when final of a word or in hiatus, closed through ọ to u in the course of the thirteenth century :

O.F. lǫ < laudo > lu *lou.*

O.F. lǫẹr < laudare > luẹr *louer, joe* dʒǫẹ < *gauta > žuẹ *joue,* ǫẹ < *auca (§§ 187, 342) > uẹ *oue,*   pǫẹ < pawa *pava* > puẹ *poue.*

Cf. Adenet, *Berthe, roe* (*rauca*) : *renoe* (*renōdat*) ;   Villon, *oue* (*auca*) : *ou* (*ubi*) T. 1338.

§ 579. *Influence of Vowel Lengthening.*—(i) ǫ < Latin aṷ (§ 505) and in O.F. loan-words, lengthened and closed to ọ before z and v in the course of Middle French (§ 570) :

O.F. *chose* tšǫzę > šǫzę,   *ozer* ǫzẹr < *ausare* > ǫzẹr,   pǫvrę > pǫvrę, *rose* rǫzę > rǫzę.

§ 580. (ii) Old French ǫ < Latin ǫ *blocked,* gradually closed to ọ in words in which it had become *free* and *long* owing to the effacement of prae-consonantal or final s or z (§ 377) :

O.F. tǫst < tŏstum > tọt,   ǫstę < hospitęm > ọtę,   aumǫznę < *elimōzina > ǫmǫnę ;   grǫs > grǫ(s, z),   ǫs < ŏssem > ǫ(s, z).

These modifications brought back the sound ọ into the sound system (cf. § 184).

✶✶ § 581. In the southern region the closing of lengthened ǫ began earlier and was carried up to u, and ǫ before š was affected also, cf. G. Guiart, *arrouse : Toulouse* ; Rose II, *aprouche : bouche, reprouche : bouche* (*Intr.* 221) ; St. *Joan propoux : tous, doux*

(*dos*) : *vous, touche : poche* (*App.* p. 19).   This pronunciation had much vogue in the sixteenth century, when it became fashionable in court circles.   Ronsard made use of it occasionally in rhyme and recommended it 'pour faire ta rime plus riche et plus sonnante.'   It retained, however, a provincial taint and was not finally accepted.

Bovelles (1533): 'Superiores Galli, ut Aurelii, Turones . . . gallicas plerasque voces quas per *o* simplicem effamur, per *ou* eloquuntur: ut in his, *chose, chouse : gros, grous.*' Bèze: '*o* sounds not so obscurely as *ou* . . . and in this matter they of Bourges and Lyons and not a few other regions err, pronouncing *nostre, vostre, le dos* as *noustre, voustre, le dous.*' (Th. I, 240 ; cf. also § 74.)   Vaugelas : 'Depuis dix ou douze ans ceux qui parlent bien disent *arroser, fossé, chose*, sans *u*, et ces deux particulierement, *foussé* et *chouse*, sont devenus insupportables.' (Rem. II, 24-25.)

§ 582. *Modification of* u *in Middle French.*—In the course of Late Middle and Early Modern French, Old French **u** in *countertonic* syllables (<L.L. ǫ and ǫ countertonic, § 234) was either lowered to **o** or replaced analogically by **o** in a considerable number of words.   Discussion over the pronunciation became heated, people ranging themselves in two camps, the 'ouystes' and 'non-ouystes,' and pronunciation was only settled in the seventeenth century.   The modification of the sound appears to have been provoked by a variety of causes, phonetic conditions, analogy, pronunciation of Latin, spelling, provincial variations, all contributing to the confusion (cf. Beaulieux, I, 276; H.L.F. II, 251-252).

(*a*) Latin influence appears to have led to the replacement of the prefix **pru, prou** < **pur** *pour* by **pro** in *profit, profil, projet, proverbe*, etc., earlier *proufit, proufil, proujet, prouverbe*, cf. Cretin, *prouverbes : esprouve herbes*, lx, 47.

(*b*) Latin influence, combined with the lowering influence of **l** (§ 491), led to the lowering and opening of **u** to **ǫ** in *colonne, colombe, soleil, volonté*, earlier *coulonne, coulombe, souleil, voulonté*.

(*c*) The lowering influence of **r** (§ 499) induced opening and lowering in *corvée, forme, former, ortie, porcelaine*, earlier *courvee, fourme, fourmer, ourtie, pourcelaine*.

(*d*) The lowering influence of nasalisation (§ 460) induced the modern forms *commencer* **kǫmãsę,** *fromage* **frǫmaž,** *promener, promettre, promesse* for earlier *coumencer* **kūmãsę,** *froumage*, **frūmažę** (< **furmažę** < ***formɑtikum**), *proumener* **prūmęnęr** (< **purmęnęr**), *proumettre* **prūmętrę,** *proumesse* **prūmęsę** (cf. Cretin, *prou messe : promesse* xxxi, 91).

(*e*) The analogical influence of related forms accounts for the use of **ǫ** in *fossé, hôtel*.

[For further details cf. H.L.F. II, 251-252 ; IV, 1, 177.]

Section 3.—RECOGNITION OF QUALITATIVE DIFFERENCES IN THE SIXTEENTH CENTURY.

§ 583. The sixteenth-century grammarians, Latin trained, were alert to detect quantitative differences in the vowels, but their remarks on quality are meagre and sometimes misleading.   Discernment of the differences was in any case rendered difficult because so many of the vowel sounds were being affected by the important sound changes at that time in process : the effacement of final consonants and the elimination of hiatus.   Complications ensued also from the provincial varieties

represented in the speech of Paris and in the pronunciation of the grammarians themselves (Meigret being from Lyons, for example, Peletier from Le Mans, etc.). Their observations may be summarised as follows.

[For a fuller treatment of the subject cf. Beaulieux, I, pp. 260-271, II, 44-47.]

§ 584. *e feminine* ę (ə) was marked off from the other e-sounds both by Palsgrave and Fabri (1521), but it appears to have been Meigret who first recognised clearly a qualitative difference in the e-sounds proper and employed the terms *ouvert* and *clos ;* his analysis of the sounds was, however, unfortunately confused by quantitative distinctions. It was Meigret also who slowly and fumblingly in the course of his controversy with Peletier came to perceive the qualitative difference of the o-sounds, although here again his demarcation was not satisfactory, this time because he was misled by his provincial pronunciation.

§ 585. **ö-*sounds*.**—No qualitative difference in the ö-*sound* appears to have been observed in the sixteenth century. Meigret groups together *eur, peu, veu, eureus,* and describes the sound as consisting of '*e* close and *u*,' and the perception of a difference between ȫ and ȫ appears to have been first noted at the very end of the seventeenth century, cf. Dangeau (1694): ' J'avoue que ces deus sons ' (he is speaking of *serviteur* and *gouteux*), ' quoique samblables, ne laissent pas d'être fort difèrans.' (Th. II, 570.)

§ 586. **a-*sounds*.**—In the sixteenth century a appears certainly to have been still predominantly palatal; its affinity with *e* is stressed by Ronsard and some grammarians and finds corroboration in the interchange of e and a (e.g. before **r,** § 496); explicit recognition of a velar pronunciation is only found in the beginning of the eighteenth century (cf. Th. II, 570). It is, however, possible that some amount of differentiation of quality had begun earlier, for it is not without significance that the words in which in the sixteenth century a lengthening of a is noted (chap. xv) are those in which ordinarily the sound is velarised in Modern French, and this supposition finds some corroboration in a remark made in the *Dialogues françois pour les ieunes enfans* published by Plantin in 1567 : ' Il ' (l'accent circonflexe) ' se met quelquefois sur l'*a*, asçauoir lorsqu'il le faut prononcer ouuertement, comme en ce mot *theâtre* et *âtre*, ausquels les vulgaires auoyent accoustumé d'adiouster vn *s* après l'*a*.' (Beaulieux, II, p. 61.)

[For the velarisation of ā in western and northern French cf. § 446, of ā and ā in Anglo-Norman cf. § 1153 and also M. K. Pope, *Kastner Volume*, pp. 396-402 : for the pronunciation of *e* feminine cf. § 275.]

Section 4.—SOURCES OF e– AND o–SOUNDS OF THE LATE SIXTEENTH CENTURY.

§ 587. As a result of the modifications set forth in this chapter and preceding ones the sixteenth century sound-system contained two oral o–*sounds*, ǫ, ọ, two oral e–*sounds*, ę, ẹ and a weak sound ę or ə (cf. § 275).

§ 588. In *tonic* syllables in educated Parisian speech ẹ was derived from :—

(1) O.F. ẹ̄ and jẹ̄ (< L.L. ɑ tonic free, §§ 231, 414, 510) final of the word and before a final consonant ordinarily effaced at the pause (§§ 617-621), e.g. *bonté*, *pitié*, *porter*, *premier*, *chez*, *nez*, *bontés*, *portez*.

(2) Later O.F. ẹ (< Early Old French **ai**, § 529), final of the word in the verb forms *ai*, *sai*, *portai*, etc., *porterai*, etc.

(3) O.F. ẹ̄ and jẹ̄ (< L.L. ɑ tonic free, §§ 231, 414, 510) before intervocalic **r** (§ 495), e.g. *mere*, *chere*. [For the more open western French pronunciation cf. § 495.]

Before single plosive and fricative consonants the quality of this sound was vacillating (§ 576).

§ 589. In tonic syllables in educated Parisian speech ę was derived from :—

(1) O.F. ě̆ < L.L. tonic ę blocked, e.g. *perdre*, *nouvel*, *teste*.
(2) Early O.F. ě̆ (< L.L. ę blocked, § 575), e.g. *mettre*, *net*, *nette*, *elle*, *messe*.
(3) Early O.F. ě̆ (< L.L. ę) + ʝ (§ 494), e.g. *pareil*, *pareille*.
(4) O.F. ẹ̄ (< L.L. ɑ tonic free, § 231) + ʝ (§ 494), e.g. *tel*, *ele* (*aile*) < *ala*.
(5) O.F. ję (< Early Old French ʲie, § 510) + l and ʝ (§ 494), e.g. *fiel*, *vieil*, *vieille*.
(6) O.F. ẹ and jẹ (< L.L. ɑ tonic free) + r in monosyllabic words (§ 495), e.g. *mer*, *cher*.
(7) O.F. **ai** levelled to ę (§§ 529, 531), e.g. *faire*, *mais*, *plaie*.
(8) Later O.F. oę (< **oi**, § 519) levelled to wę and ę (§ 522), e.g. *roi*, *foible*.
(9) Middle French ę̄ and ję̄ (< O.F. **ãi**, **ẽi**, **jẽ**, §§ 467, 471), denasalised (§§ 467, 471), e.g. *vaine*, *pleine*, *chienne*.

Thus ę was ordinarily in use when final of the word, but it must be remembered that final consonants and post-consonantal ę were still being sounded more generally in educated speech than now (chap. xvii and § 273) and that the fluctuations in the pronunciation of these sounds produced fluctuations in the quality of the e–*sounds*.

§ 590. In *tonic* syllables ǭ was derived from :—

(1) **au** and **eau** levelled to ǭ (§§ 535, 539), e.g. *autre* ǭtrę, *beau* bǭ.
(2) O.F. ǫ < Latin **au** lengthened before z and v (§ 579), e.g. *chose* šǭzę, pǭvrę.
(3) O.F. ǫ before effaced prae-consonantal **s** and **z** or effaced final consonant (§ 580), e.g. *nostre* nǭtrę, *tost* tǭt, *gros* grǭ (grǭs).

In tonic syllables ǫ was derived from :—

(1) ǫ blocked < L.L. ǫ blocked, except before effaced s or effaced final consonant (§ 580), e.g. *mort* mǫrt, *mol* mǫl, *poche* pǫšę, *sot* sǫt (sǫ).
(2) O.F. ǫ < Latin **au** before r and l, e.g. ǫr, *Paul* Pǫl.

§ 591. In *countertonic* syllables ę was derived from :—

(1) G.R. e before r + *consonant* (§ 234), e.g. *personne* pęrsunę, *fermer* fęrmę.
(2) O.F. **ai** levelled to ę (§ 529), e.g. *maison* męzũ, fęlürę (< faielürę).
(3) O.F. **oi** levelled to wę or ę (§§ 519, 522), *froideur* frwędör, *roideur* rędör.
(4) O.F. ęę contracted, e.g. sęllęr, sęlę (< sęęlęr < sęęl (< *sigĕllum)).
(5) O.F. ę̄ (< ẽi and ãi) *denasalised* (§ 467), e.g. *peiner* pęnę, *aimer* ęmę.

Elsewhere O.F. ẹ (<L.L. ẹ, ę *blocked*) ordinarily remained ẹ and O.F. ę (<G.R. ę *free*, § 234) ę (ə ?), but there was some hesitation between ẹ and ę: (i) in words in which prae-consonantal s had been effaced, e.g. defẹrę and defęrę; (ii) before intervocalic z and r, dezọrdrę and dezọrdrę, pẹrir and pęrir. Analogical influences led frequently to the use of ę in the weak radicals of some verbs (cf. Th. I. 88-108).

§ 592. In the *intertonic* syllable the quality of the e-*sound* varied in loan-words before s, e.g. in *necessaire, profession*, but was usually open; e (< ęę) was closed in adverbs, e.g. in *aisement, infortunement*, etc., and also in *communement* (< O.F. *communelment*) and the loan-words *confusement, diffusement*.

§ 593. In *countertonic* syllables ọ was derived from :—

(1) O.F. au and eau levelled to ọ (§§ 535, 539), e.g. *aumone* ọmọnę, *beauté* bọtę.
(2) O.F. ọ before effaced prae-consonantal s or z (§ 580), e.g. *rostir* rọtir.
(3) O.F. ọ (< Latin au) before z (§ 579), e.g. *oser* ọzę.
[For the influence of related forms cf. § 582 (*e*).]

§ 594. In countertonic syllables ǫ was derived from :—

(1) O.F. ǫ (< Latin au) before r, e.g. *oreille* ǫręlę.
(2) O.F. ǫ preserved in derivatives of words containing ǫ in the tonic syllable (§ 234), e.g. *mortel, porter*, mǫrtęl, pǫrtę.
(3) Latin ŏ in learned loan-words, e.g. *potable* pǫtablę.
(4) Middle French u lowered to ǫ under special conditions (§ 582).

CHAPTER XVII.

INFLUENCE OF SYNTACTICAL PHONETICS.

Section 1.—INTRODUCTORY.

§ 595. The development of sounds, both vowels and consonants, was affected considerably by the influence of *syntactical phonetics*, i.e. by the influence exercised on the pronunciation of words by their position and use in the sentence.   In the early period the weakness or intensity of the sentence stress was the more important factor, and it was the vowels that were chiefly affected ; in both periods, but chiefly the later, the beginnings and ends of words were liable to be influenced by the way in which words were being closely linked in the phrase, and consonants were affected as much as vowels.

Section 2.—INFLUENCE OF SENTENCE STRESS ON VOWELS IN PERIOD I.

§ 596. (1) *Formation of Doublets.*—The words denoting grammatical relations : prepositions, adverbs, conjunctions, pronouns, auxiliary verbs —(the tool-words of speech)—appellations and a few much used adjectives and adverbs were sometimes so weakly pronounced in the sentence that they developed as secondary stressed or unstressed syllables, their vowels being left undiphthongised and sometimes weakened and slurred ; much used words weakly stressed were sometimes shortened by elimination of consonants, cf. § 121 : in these ways double forms—stressed and unstressed—were produced.   Rarely, however, were these doublets preserved for long : their use ordinarily soon became indiscriminate and then one or other form, more often the unstressed, was generalised.

[For pronoun doublets cf. §§ 826, 827, 837, 838, 855 ; for unstressed verb forms cf. §§ 951, 952, 953, 957, 959.]

§ 597. *Prepositions.*—Syntactical doublets of *foris* (**fuers** > **förs** *feurs* and **fŏrs**) and of *pro* (**puer** > **pör** *peur* and **pŏr** > **pur**) were still in use in twelfth-century French, but of *ad, de, in* unstressed forms only are attested ; *seinz* (the stressed form of *sine* + adverbial s) occurs in the Digby MS. of *Roland*, 571, 1607, 1775, etc., but elsewhere undiphthongised **sēns** > **sāns** is the only form in use ; O.F. *od* o**ð** is derived

from *aud, an unstressed shortened form of apud; O.F. seur sör (<seurę <sŭpra § 604) was closed to sür in Middle French, the influence of süs facilitating the adoption of the change, §§ 401, 543.

§ 598. *Conjunctions.*—The monosyllabic conjunctions kę (< *quia*), nę (< *nec*), sę (< *si*), when unstressed, became kę, nę, sę and ordinarily lost their vowel-sound when prae-vocalic, § 602 (for kęᵭ, nęᵭ, sęᵭ, cf. § 608). In later Middle French kę became obsolete and nę and nę, sę and sę were gradually replaced by ni and si, forms derived from earlier n'il and s'il, pronounced ni and si when prae-consonantal, e.g. *n'i(l) li plaist, s'i(l) li plaist, n'i(l) li convient, s'i(l) li convient*, etc. (cf. § 392 and Rydberg, II, pp. 979-987).

kę and sę developed in Early Old French and in *Roland* their vowel is more often than not slurred before a word beginning with a vowel ; nę was retained into the twelfth century and stands regularly in hiatus in *Roland* except in l. 3355, where *nę escut* coalesces into *nęscut*.

The generalisation of the forms ni and si was facilitated by the influence of the southern border dialects in which the forms ni and si developed out of nę and sę in prae-vocalic position, in accordance with the southern French tendency to raise ę countertonic in hiatus to i (cf. Rydberg, § 195), and these forms early obtained currency in Anglo-Norman, cf. *Rol.*, Digby MS., *si*, ll. 295, 423, 928, 3011, 3169, 3557.

§ 599. *Adverbs and Adjectives.*—Unstressed ᴣon was weakened to nen which was reduced early to nę in prae-consonantal position (cf. *Jonas, ne doceiet, ne dolreie*); nę weakened early to nę, cf. *Rol.* 4, *n'i ad ;* 5, *n'i est*, but nen was still employed before words beginning with vowels in the thirteenth century, and combined with il (nenil > nēni > nāni), survived into Modern French.

[For *naie* < *non ego* cf. § 831.]

mal is an unstressed form ; the stressed form męl is occasional early, cf. *Jonas* 25, *de cel mel, Rol.* 2006.   Buen, the stressed form of bŏnum, (§§ 226, 478), was longer lived (cf. *Troie, buens : perpens* 9283 : *tens* 25927), but already in the twelfth century unstressed bǫn, bun was more generally used (cf. *Troie, bon : gonfanon* 2518 : *sermon* 6453).

Both adjectives were strongly contracted in the locutions buer and mar derived from bona and mala hora.

✱✱ In the northern region, bųęn, the stressed form of *bonum* (§ 478) was retained later, usually spelled *boin, boine*, § 720 (cf. *Auc.* 3, 14, 6, 36).

§ 600. *Appellations.*—Late Latin *senior* *sęnior unstressed was reduced in Gallo-Roman to **sęior, whence O.F. sirę : the stressed form of the nominative *sendra* is only attested in French in the *Oaths of Strasbourg*.   O.F. *sieur* was either formed on *sire* or reduced from dialectal *signeur* (§ 422).   The early contraction of maïstrę to maistrę and of consobrinum to kusin *cosin* is possibly attributable to the use of these

words as appellations; the weakening of **a** to **e** in the first syllable of *demoiselle* is due to its frequent use in the locution *"ma damoi'selle.*

§ 601. In the Old French derivatives of *dominus* and *domina*—*danz, dame, damnedé, dancel, dameisele, dangier* (< *dominiarium*)—the vowel sound of the initial syllable is ordinarily **ā** instead of **ū**. The unrounding of ǫ blocked before a nasal is characteristic of the speech of the south-western region, (S.W. § iii) cf. *Danfront, dangerosa* 1060, *Candiacum* 1108, *Damceium* 1130 (Drevin, pp. 65, 118, 83, 99); *Troie, cante (conte) : oitante* 5628 : *pesante* 10909, but it appears unlikely that this local trait could impose itself so early on the rest of northern Gaul. More probable is the explanation suggested by Professor Meyer-Lübke (*Gr.* § 34) that the vowel **o**, weakly stressed in all these words, was early reduced to **e** (cf. **nen** < **non**), nasalised and lowered to **ā** (cf. § 447 (5) and **naie**, § 831).

§ 602. (2) *Enclisis and Proclisis.*—Monosyllabic unstressed words might be either *enclitic* or *proclitic*, i.e. so unemphatic as to be pronounced either as part of the word which preceded them or as part of the one that followed them, in either case with loss of the vowel ę. Enclisis was current when the following word began with a consonant, proclisis when it began with a vowel. Examples are:—

Enclisis.—Eulalia : *Enz enl fou* 19, *poros furet morte* 18, *nos voldret* 21 ; St. Legier : *sobrels piez* 230, *Penrel rovat* 150, *qual horal vid* 149 ; *St. Alexis : Purquem fuis* 453, *Ol poissent recovrer* 312 ; *Roland : Sim cumbatrai* 878, *Ies lur dirrai* 2919, *sin ad* 2480.

Proclisis.—Eulalia : *Qu'elle* 17 ; St. Legier : *en s'evesquet* 122, *defors l'asist* 142, etc.

With monosyllabic words in ę enclisis was obligatory in Early Old French and unemphatic *est* was included as well as the unstressed forms of the pronouns and articles (cf. *Al.,* MS. L, *sist ampairet* 10, *ço(e)st* 49). With the lessening of the intensity of the tonic stress (§§ 170, 171) the repugnance to the juxtaposition of unstressed words diminished and the practice of enclisis, moribund already in the eleventh century after words of more than one syllable, gradually died out among monosyllables also, except in the forms of the article.

[For enclitic forms of pronouns and article cf. §§ 838, 843.]

Section 3.—INFLUENCE OF POSITION IN THE SENTENCE ON VOWELS IN PERIOD I.

§ 603. (1) *Prosthetic* ę.—The initial on-glide, developed in Late Latin before the group **s** + *consonant* (§ 361), remained movable after a vowel throughout Period I (cf. *Al., ta spuse* 53, *la spuse* 102, 147, etc.), but with the twelfth century it became a fixed integral part of the word (cf. *Rol.*, Digby MS., *s'espee* 346, etc., *l'espee* 443, etc., *l'estandart* 3267, etc.

✳✳ In the northern region its movability continued later, N.E. § x.

§ 604. (2) *Effacement of Unstressed Final Vowels—Apocope.*— Already in Oldest French the juxtaposition of final unstressed ę with a vowel following on it in quick succession was avoided, i.e. final unstressed ę was slurred if it stood before a closely connected word beginning with a vowel (cf. *Eul., Ell'ent adunet* 15, *St. Legier, in su'amor* 3, *Ciel'ira* 105).

This practice led to the formation of doublets among adverbs and prepositions ending in ę (*arriere, derriere, soure, onque, ore, (i)lore, mare*), for the forms developed in *prae-vocalic* position (*arrier, derrier, sour, onc, or, lor, mar*) were early taken into use before consonants also (cf. *Rol., sur sun escut* 526, *unc mais* 1040, *unc ne* 3516, *or veit* 1029, *or remeint* 1696). On the model of *onc-onque* the forms *avueque, ilueque* were created as doublets of *avuec, iluec.*

§ 605. (3) *Elimination of Weakly Stressed Initial Vowel—Aphaeresis.* —The initial vowel sound of loan-words or proper names was sometimes run in with the definite article and then cut off, cf. O.F. *baustre* < *l'abaustre* (< *alabaster*), *boutique* (< *apotheca*), O.F. *glise* (< *eglise*), *mine* (< *hemine*), *migraine* < (*hemigrania*), *poplisie* (< *apoplexie*), *rogne* (< **aronea* (?)), O.F. *vesque* < (*evesque*), *Gilles* (< *Aegidius* (§ 645), *Guyenne* (< *Aquitania*), *Pouille* (< *Apulia*).

§ 606. *Agglutination of Articles and Prepositions.*—A word beginning with a vowel sometimes fused with a preceding word, which thus became an integral part of it. This process (known as *agglutination*), took place most commonly when words were preceded by articles or prepositions.

Examples are: (*a*) *Articles: lendemain* < O.F. *l'endemain, lendit* < *l'endit, liere* < *l'iere, Lisle* > *l'isle, lingot* < *l'ingot, loriot* < *l'oriot, luette* < *l'uette,* O.F. *Laustic* < *l'austik, lalgalife* < *l'algalife.*

In *alemele* < *la lamele* (< *laminella*), *alèze* < *la laize* (< *latia*) and *ieuse* < *li euze* (a Provençal form of *ēlicem* (dialectal)) the vowel only of the preceding form was incorporated.

In the river name *Sebre* (*Rol.* 2465, etc.) it is the article derived from *ipse* which appears to be agglutinated.

(*b*) *Prepositions: aise* < *à aise, abandon* < *à bandon, alarme* < *à l'arme, alors* < *à lors, atout* < *à tout, aval* < *à val, amont* < *à mont, dinde* < *d'Inde* (cf. § 242).

It is suggested that in a similar way the modern *tante* may be derived from *gran-t ante* (< *amita*), (*Mem. Soc. Ling. Paris,* VI, 259).

Section 4.—INFLUENCE OF POSITION IN THE PHRASE ON CONSONANTS IN PERIOD I.

§ 607. In the early period of the language words were ordinarily still, as they had been in Latin, the unit of the phrase, and it was only

among the unstressed 'tool-words' pronounced in close connection with the following word, that the pronunciation of the final consonant was modified by its position in a word-group.

§ 608. (1) In the pronunciation of the monosyllabic words aθ (< ad and *at < habet), ęθ, oθ (< *aud < apud), the final sound θ was early effaced before a consonant and voiced before a vowel, i.e eθ > ę and ęᵭ, aᵭ > a and aᵭ, etc. On the model of the doublets thus formed (especially ę, ęᵭ) analogical forms kęᵭ, nęᵭ, sęᵭ were created and used in prae-vocalic position, instead of kę, nę, sę (< quia, nec, si), cf. Eulalia, ned 7, Alexis, qued 21c, quet 13e, set 26c, net 53e. [For the subsequent effacement of ᵭ cf. § 347.]

§ 609. (2) From ibi were developed early the doublets iv, used before vowels, e.g. Oaths, nun li iv er, and i used before consonants: i was early generalised, cf. Alexis, jo i ai 30c, n'i ai 38b.

§ 610. (3) Before nasalisation set in strongly, final n in en (< in) and in mon, ton, son was often labialised to m before labial consonants, e.g. Alexis : sum pris 16c, sum voil 34b.

ent from inde was early reduced to en in prae-consonantal position and en was generalised whenever the word was unstressed in the sentence, its final n being also often labialised to m before a labial consonant, cf. em mener, Alexis, em perde 12e : at the pause ent survived into Later Old French and even longer in the northern region.

Section 5.—INFLUENCE OF POSITION IN THE PHRASE ON FINAL CONSONANTS IN PERIOD II.

[For final l and r cf. §§ 392, 400-402, for final n cf. §§ 436, 438.]

§ 611. In Later Old and Middle French the tendency to run together words closely linked in sense was at its maximum (§ 171), and modified strongly the pronunciation of final consonants. Those consonants that stood at the end of the sense-group, i.e. at a pause, were at first un-affected and retained their Old French value, but within the phrase final consonants tended to develop along the lines that had been followed earlier by consonants in the interior of words :—

(1) *Plosive* and *fricative* consonants, final of the word, that stood in the phrase before words beginning with a consonant, became *mute*, often with compensatory lengthening of the previous vowel.

(2) Final s and *unsupported* f, when they stood in the phrase before words beginning with a vowel, were voiced to z and v respectively.

Model sentences illustrating this pronunciation are given by the sixteenth-century grammarians St. Liens (1580) and H. Estienne. ' *Tou tin si ke tu fai zau zautres, vou zeste zun nome de bien.*' (St. Liens.) ' *Vou*

me dite toujours que votre pays est plu gran de beaucoup et plus abondan que le notre e que maintenan vou pourrie bien y vivre à meilleur marché que nou ne vivon depui troi mois en cete ville : mai tou ceux qui en viennet parlet bien un autre langage,' and H. Estienne adds : ' notice that in *toujours* I have retained *s* although the word is followed by a consonant, the reason being that after this word the speaker makes a slight pause ' (Th. II, 7, 11, 12).

These new tendencies in pronunciation are illustrated to some extent from the later thirteenth century on by the ' rimes leonines,' which include the consonant preceding the rhyming tonic vowels, and are described by sixteenth century grammarians. *Rose II : espousa : nous⌢a, conforté : confort⌢ai, ostelas : ostel⌢as ; ne ros : conter os ;* Cretin: *compasses : coup⌢asses, tresorier : tresor⌢hier, doubter⌢est : interest, toujours⌢or : tresor, fortune : fort⌢une, ongle(s)tordre : tinssent⌢ordre, grant port⌢as : portas, rapport(z) telz : rapportez, cordelle : accorde(z)le, des sept montz* (**dẹ sẹ mūz**) : *tous les noms* (**tu lẹ nūz**).

Sylvius (1531) : ' At the end of a word we only write but do not pronounce *s* or other consonants fully, except when a vowel follows or it be at the end of a phrase ; thus we write *les femmes sont bonnes* but we pronounce *les* with a sound cut off, *femme* without *s, son* without *t, bones.*' (Th. II, 11.)

Peletier (1549) : ' Quand nous proferons une oreson continue, nous ne sonnons point les dernieres lettres des moz fors les *rr*, de sorte qu'elles n'i servet que de tenir les sillabes longues.' (Th. II, p. 4.) ' Nous écriuons *vif, naïf, massif* . . . par *f* final : combien que nous les prononçons par *u* consone' (i.e. v), ' einsi qu'on conoèt an prononçant ces moz, *homme d'esprit inuantif é résolu.*' (Th. II, 135.) Dewes (1532) : ' And if any word endyng with an *s* have the next worde folowyng begynning with a vowell, than shall ye sounde the said *s* lyke a *z*,' p. 899.

§ 612. All final plosive and fricative consonants thus tended to have a double or triple pronunciation, a stage retained partially in the Modern French rules for ' liaison' and completely in the current pronunciation of the numerals *cinq, sept, six, dix, neuf;* cf. *nous sommes dix ; dix hommes, dix femmes* **nu sǫm dis, di zǫm, di fam.** Ordinarily, however, the final consonant of a word is pronounced in the same way before consonants and at a pause, i.e. it is either mute in both positions or sounded in both.

§ 613. *Date of Effacement of Final Consonants.*—Effacement of final consonants varied in date according to the nature of the consonant and its position in the word. The first to be affected are final **s** (**z**), a consonant that was in process of effacement in prae-consonantal position in the interior of a word (§ 377), and final *supported* plosive consonants, as these when juxtaposed to an initial consonant, were brought into the *weak* position middle of three (§ 362). Examples of effacement of these consonants in *prae-consonantal* position appear in MSS. of the later twelfth century :

Cf. *Rol.,* Digby MS., *le chefz* 44, *le freins* 2485 ; *Al., sain batesme* 29, *s'en vat* 9 ; *Rol.,* Digby MS., *Sein Gabriel* 2847, *quan l'ot* 601, *grandamage* 3479, *er frere* 1214 ; *Q.L.R. dunne saves ?*

Effacement of the final consonant in prae-consonantal position in the phrase was sufficiently marked to attract the attention of the compilers of A.N. spelling treatises. In the earliest, (middle xiii ?), *s* is said to lose its sound completely before a consonant among pronouns and verbs and *t* almost (cf. M.L.R. v, pp. 191, 192), and the slightly later *Orthographia Gallica* goes further: ' Item quociensque diccio incipiens cum consonante sequitur immediate diccionem in consonante terminantem, dum tamen sine pausa pronunciebatur, consonans ultima diccionis anterioris debet pronunciando pretermitti, verbi gracia, *mieuz vaut boyr apres manger que devant*,' Reg. viii, pp. 17, 18.

§ 614. *Simplification of Pronunciation in Middle French.*—So varying a pronunciation of the final consonants of words imposed a heavy burden on the memory and people soon began to make things easier for themselves by reducing the number of forms employed. The earliest and commonest method adopted was to use at the pause the *prae-consonantal* form, the one with effaced final consonant.

§ 615. (1) *Words ending in a Supported Consonant.*—Among the words ending with a supported consonant, e.g. *cerf, banc, champ, fort,* etc., the extension of the use of the shortened prae-consonantal form began sporadically in Later Old French and was very general in speech in Later Middle French.

Ronsard admits the rhymes: *rang : defend, gond : adonc, blond : tronc,* and re-commends rhymes like *fort : or, fard, part : char* (*Art Poét.*, p. 328). In his phonetic transcription of the lines *Et les dangiers que' ay iusques cy passez, Dont i'ay suffert, graces à dieu, assez,* Palsgrave omits not only *s* in *dangiers* but also *t* in *suffert* (p. 60). At the end of the century Tabourot permits rhymes between words in *anc : ang : ant ; onc : ong : ont : ond ; orc : ord : or,* and Lanoue states explicitly that in the rhyme *vins : echevins, s* is not pronounced (Th. II, 35). Rhymes in *St. Joan,* (e.g. *barons : dont, riens : appartient* p. 191), and other Mystery Plays, indicate that this pronunciation was current in the fifteenth century (cf. also G. Alexis I, 25, *cours ont : courront*).

[For the refusal of seventeenth-century prosodists to admit rhymes of this kind cf. Kastner, p. 43 ; for spelling-changes cf. §§ 784, 891.]

§ 616. Isolated rhymes indicating the beginnings of the use of the form with effaced consonant at the pause crop up occasionally in Old French.

(i) The form **dūn** (< **dūnk** and **dūnt**, *donc, dont*) is early attested. Coucy *dun* (< *donum*) : *don* (*donc*) (ed. Fath, p. 54) ; *St. Martin, don : don* (*dont*) 2743, and the vogue of this pronunciation, together with the similarity of the symbols used for *c* and *t*, explains the frequent graphical confusion between *donc* and *dont*. In later Middle French this pronunciation was still dominant, cf. Villon, *don : don* (*donum*) T. xxii, and the remark of Duez : ' the *c* is always mute.' In the seventeenth century the pronunciation **dūk** (> **dǭk**, § 460) was re-established in prae-vocalic position and introduced elsewhere for emphasis (cf. Th. II, p. 132). The pro-nunciation : **sęlūnk** *selonc* became obsolete in the sixteenth century.

(ii) Rhymes indicating the use of other words with effaced supported **t** and **s** appear occasionally in the late twelfth century, cf. *Troie, bor(t) : or* 23454, *nequeden : Troien* 18659 ; *G. Dôle, vert : vers* 4571, *estor : tors* 107, *bourc : amor* 323. It is, however, possible that rhymes of this type are due to some extent to the influence of the southern border dialects (e.g. Poitevin) as in these supported *t* was early effaced (cf. S.W. § 8, Appel, § 53, Gamillscheg, *Becker vol.*, p. 63).

§617. (2) *Words Ending in a Single Final Consonant.*—Among words ending with a single final consonant the pronunciation of the final consonant persisted longer at the pause (cf. rhymes with Latin words and puns such as: *inimicos : Il n'y mit qu'os, Tunc acceptabis : Tunc a sept habits*, T. p. 35 *v°*), but in uneducated speech it is evident that there was already in the later fifteenth and early sixteenth century a marked disposition to use the forms with mute consonant in this position also, cf. the rhymes employed in popular works such as mystery plays, e.g. *peril : prist, bruit : meshuy, luy : chetif, rechief : bouclier, estomac : mac* (for *mat*), *sobreset : sec* (Chatelain, p. 76, *St. Joan*, p. 191). After ẹ the effacement of **s** was particularly early, e.g. *St. Joan, hommes : comme(s)*, 599, cf. § 623.

In the later sixteenth century confirmation is also found in the description Tabourot has left of an inn sign, in which the representation of '*un os, un bouc, un duc, un monde*' stood for '*Au bout du Monde*,' Th. II, 130, and in some of the puns cited by him and others, e.g. *Iliadae curae = il y a des curez, requiescant in pace = Rê, qui est-ce ? Quentin, Passez* (T. p. 34 *v°*), *j'ai soif, bois = g. c. b.* **gẹ sẹ bẹ.**

§618. This vulgar simplification ran counter, however, not only to older tradition but also to orthography and the pronunciation of Latin, and consequently, among the grammarians and in educated speech, it met with opposition tenacious enough to lead ultimately to the retention of the sounded consonant, especially **f** and **k**, in some few words in all positions, and to retard generally the acceptance of the prae-consonantal form at the pause.

§619. (1) The prae-pause form of the word, the one with sounded consonant, was retained very generally: (i) in monosyllabic words, i.e. words whose individuality would have been almost completely destroyed by the effacement of the final consonant, e.g. *bec, coq, duc, sec, soc, trictrac, boeuf, chef, grief, nef, neuf, oeuf, soif, veuf, juif, cep, sens, vis ;* (ii) in archaic and late loan-words, e.g. *chétif, jadis, cap, dot* (Provençal, cf. Bloch), *fat* (Provençal), *julep, public*, etc.

§620. (2) A general sounding of single final consonants at the pause was still insisted on by the grammarians of the early seventeenth century. Maupas, for instance, in 1607, while warning his readers against sounding final consonants too strongly, adds 'Toutefois il est bien séant d'exprimer assez clairement toute consonne finissant la période,' and this advice is reproduced by his English translator in 1630. By the middle of the century resistance to the inevitable was, however, wearing down. Practice remained variable throughout the century but already Chifflet ruled in 1659: 'A la fin des périodes, ou quant on finit le cours des paroles pour reprendre haleine, les consonnes qui finissent le dernier mot ne sont jamais prononcez. Par exemple, "*Ne donnez pas tout.*" Prononcez *tu*, sans faire sonner le *t.*' (Th. II, 15, 92-95.)

§ 621. Conflict was fiercest about the pronunciation of final s and z, the consonants most important in flexion and weakest in popular pronunciation (§§ 613, 623). Their functional importance led the purists of the sixteenth century to urge their retention in prae-consonantal position, but here their weakness was too general to admit even temporary reinstatement and at the pause their effacement, though retarded temporarily, was accepted with that of other consonants in the middle of the seventeenth century.

Meurier (1557), 'Plusieurs ont escript de la lettre s et affirmé qu'on la doibt prononcer es substantifs pluriels, a l'opinion desquelz j'eusse condescendu, n'eust este la demesuree exception que seuffrent leurs reigles, de consideration mal fondees et hourdees, car si apres le substantif plurier ensuit un adjectif, s de l'adjectif final se prononcera et non pas du substantif. Exemple *Apportez nous les chappons rostis* ou s final de *rostis* est prononcee et non de *chappons*.' (*Wahlund Vol.*, p. 181.) H. Estienne, quoting the O.F. saying, *Qui de ses sujets est hays N'est pas seigneur de son pays*, adds: ' nor is there any doubt that they pronounced *pays* with an s as we do.' (Th. II, p. 31.)

Maupas (1607), 'A la fin des mots n'est point de maubvais grace de la (sc. s) prononcer, porveu que modérément et foiblement.' This remark is elucidated by his English translator in these terms : 'somewhat like z, as *les hommes*, which must be pronounced *lez hommez*, or very neere that sound.' Model sentences given by this latter are : '*Que faites vous ?* here s in *vous* is pronounced. *Si nou dison que nou somme iustifies, par no bonnes œuvres, san le merite de Iesu Christ, nou nou seduisons*.'

The anonymous grammarian of 1624 held more advanced views: 's final is mute before a consonant and at the end of a phrase, especially in words in *-is* as *fils*, *Paris*, *amis*; z final is lost at the end of a period and before a consonant.' (Th. II, 36.)

The modern pronunciation of *fils*, with sounded s, appears to have only begun in Paris in the eighteenth century. H. Estienne remarks : ' the common people say *fis* or *fi*,' and the anonymous grammarian cited above states explicitly '*fils* is pronounced *fi*, even before a vowel and at the end of a phrase.' (Th. II, 81.)

§ 622. Tabourot reports a misplaced use of final s among the half educated that is closely parallel to the Modern English vagaries in the use of initial h : ' s, par vulgaire ne se prononce pas au bout de chasque mot : dont toutes fois quelques autres sont si curieux, que, pour sembler bons Francois et montrer qu'ils parlent proprement, ils prononcent a tort et a travers au bout de chasque mot une s. Et diront, " *Monsieur, ic me recommandes a vous de tous mons cœur*," etc., auec tel soin qu'il semble qu'ils sifflent en l'air à chasque s.' (Th. II, p. 37.)

§ 623. *Consonants in Prae-Vocalic Position—Liaison.*—In educated speech throughout the sixteenth century final consonants, whether single or supported, were maintained when in *prae-vocalic* position in the phrase, cf. Meigret : '*il perd et gagne . . . il tond aotant de draps*,' in these ' nous oyons le t sonner ferme,' and Lanoue : '*Quand je vins pour cet effect Les Echevins avoyent fait . . .* icy on ne prononce pas l's au mot *vins*, pour ce qu'elle est suyvie d'une consonne, et à *Echevins* au contraire, pour ce que elle y a une voyelle.' (T. II, 35.)

Uneducated speech carried effacement already much further :—

(i) Final *single* consonants appear to have been ordinarily maintained when the word was prae-vocalic, e.g. in locutions like *petit͡ homme, nous͡ avons*, etc., i.e. whenever the suppression of a final consonant would have left two oral vowels in hiatus, but among words ending with

supported consonants the forms with mute final consonants (the prae-consonantal forms) were already employed freely before vowels, e.g. pẹr for pẹrt *perd*, tūn for tūnt *tond*, mọr for mort, vẹ for vẹz *vins*, etc.

(ii) Final *s* (z) in the ending *es* -ẹz was also slurred when prae-vocalic, a tendency which had its beginnings in earlier Middle French, cf. G. Tory: 'Les dames de Paris, pour la plus grande partie observent bien cette figure poetique' (elision) 'en laissant le *s* final de beaucoup de dictions, quant au lieu de dire "*nous auons disne en ung jardin et y auon menge des prunes blanches et noires, des amendes doulces et ameres . . .*" elles disent et prononcent "*nous auon disne dans ung jardin et y auon menge des prune blanche et noire, des amende doulce et amere . . .*"' (Th II, 23).

On both points educated usage was much more conservative. The effacement of *s* in the ending -*es* was peremptorily vetoed by Malherbe: '"*Tu pense éveiller*," il faut dire "*tu penses*" et n'y a point de réponse.' (Th. II, 28); and Maupas (1607) still enjoins explicitly liaison under all conditions: 'Au milieu des périodes, en fil d'oraison, si le mot suivant commence par une voyelle ou *h* muette la consonne finale se doit lier et conjoindre avec la voyelle commençant le mot suivant, comme si elle luy appartenoit.' (Th. II, 7-8.)

Here again, however, the movement was checked but not stopped, and by the middle of the seventeenth century the modern tendency to restrict the sounding of final consonants before vowels to the more closely connected word groups was clearly evident, although liaison was still practised much more extensively than in current French, cf. H.L.F. IV (i), 213-216.

In 1659 Chifflet recommends the pronunciation of -t in liaison in all verbal forms and terminations except -*ast*, (i.e. in -*ent*, -*oit*, -*oient*, -*ist*, -*ust*, *font*, *ont*, etc., *est*, *fait*, *vient*, etc.), giving as example *Ils chantent et ils rient I chante -té i rie* but elsewhere he admits it only when the following word depends or is governed by the preceding one, e.g. in '*Petit-t'enfant, Devant-t'hier* but not in *Petit et joli*', *Devant et derriere*. In the ending -*ent* Hindret (1687) only retains the pronunciation of t in verse and declamation, admitting *i doivarive* for *ils doivent arriver* in conversation: -rt he treats similarly and writes of *s* final: 'La prononciation seroit contre notre usage ordinaire . . . si on prononçoit . . . *avé vouzachevé, attendé vouzaprais, nous en avonzapri tout* . . . au lieu de dire *avez vou achevé, atandé vou aprai, nouz en navon apri tout*.' (Th .II, pp. 8, 9, 91-95.)

§ 624. The uncertainty about the absence or presence of final z led to its misuse among the half-educated, who introduced it as a sort of transition sound to obviate hiatus in locutions of the type *avant hier, a tort et a travers* which were pronounced avāzjẹr, a torz⌢e a travẹrs on the model of *bons hommes, gents inconnus*, etc., būz⌢ūmẹ(z), žāz⌢ẹkūnü(s) (Thurot, II, 60-61).

[For the practice of liaison in Modern French cf. H. Langlard, *La Liaison dans le Français*, Paris, 1928, Grammont, *Traité de Phonétique*, pp. 416-418.]

CHAPTER XVIII.

TREATMENT OF LOAN-WORDS: GREEK, FRANKISH, LATIN, ITALIAN.

Section 1.—INTRODUCTORY.

§ 625. Loan-words are apt to show irregularities in their development for they often contain sounds or groups of sounds that are unfamiliar in the sound-system of the borrowers and these are accommodated to current pronunciation by sound-substitutions—metathesis, dissimilation, replacement—or simple elimination. The contingent of Greek and Germanic loan-words in Latin, of Frankish words in Gallo-Roman and of learned loan-words (*mots savants*) in French exemplify these phenomena in different ways.

§ 626. Loan-words may be borrowed from a spoken or a written language, and in studying them the following considerations should be borne in mind: (1) The starting-point of the pronunciation of a word borrowed *orally* is the pronunciation current *at the time of the borrowing*, and the accentuation and sound system of *both* the languages concerned must be taken into account; (2) The starting-point of the pronunciation of words borrowed from a *written* source is the pronunciation accorded to that word in the language of the people borrowing it. It follows that in discussing the learned Latin loan-words the pronunciation accorded to Latin at the epoch at which the word is borrowed must always be kept in view; (3) Loan-words are normally not affected by the sound changes that have taken place in the borrowing language *before* the date at which they were introduced, but a certain amount of accommodation of words to the linguistic habits of the day is usual: for instance, terminations are ordinarily adapted to those current in the borrowers' language. Thus Germanic words borrowed in Latin and Gallo-Roman were given the ordinary endings of the time: *-us, -a, -u* (*-um*); *-are, -ire*, etc., cf. O.F. *esclou*<**sklagu̯**<Frk. *slag, blou*<**blau̯u̯**<*blao, bleve*<**blau̯a**. Abstract nouns borrowed in French from Latin words in *-itatem* received the termination **-ite̞**, e.g. *charité, légalité*, etc. (cf. *Eulalia, virginitet* 17).

§ 627. The date of a loan-word may therefore sometimes be determined approximately by its reaction to sound changes: thus the retention of *l* in the word *cultiver, multiplier*, of *s* in *chaste, juste* indicates that these words were borrowed or re-formed after the period in which ꝉ was vocalised and prae-consonantal **s** effaced (cf. § 92).

Section 2.—PRONUNCIATION OF GREEK LOAN-WORDS IN LATIN.

AUTHORITIES:

> Juret : *Manuel de Phonétique latine*, Paris, 1921.
> Meyer-Lübke : *Grammaire des Langues Romanes.*
> Grandgent : *An Introduction to Vulgar Latin.*

§ 628. The earliest Greek loan-words were borrowed orally, and in their latinisation an attempt was made to render approximately the acoustic value of the unfamiliar sounds ; later on, when the literary language was constituted and the language fixed, Greek spelling was followed as closely as possible and pronunciation was sometimes affected by spelling.

§ 629. *Consonants.*—The Greek aspirated consonants, φ, θ, χ, were rendered at first by the unaspirated breath plosives **p, t, k,** sometimes lengthened in intervocalic position :

> *purpura* < πορφύρα, *spata* < σπαθή, *tus* < θύος.

From the second century on aspiration was usually marked by the use of affixed *h*, but the aspirated pronunciation of these sounds was confined to the educated class and left no mark on later pronunciation, cf. O.F. *colp* < *colaphum* < κόλαφον, *teie* < *theca* < θήκη, *tros* < *thursus* < θύρσος, *braz* < *brachium* < βράχιων.

The pronunciation of φ as **f** is relatively late and due to the passage of the Greek sound to **f** : the spelling appears first in the graffiti of Pompeii. This pronunciation was continued in mediaeval Latin and is exemplified in the O.F. words : *faisan* (< φασιανός), *orfenes* (< ὀρφανός), *fantome* (< **fantauma* for φάντασμα).

§ 630. Initial *plosive* consonants, being perhaps weaker than the corresponding Latin ones, were sometimes rendered by their voiced counterparts, cf. O.F. *boiste* < **büxida* < πυξίδα, *jambe* < **gamba* < καμπή.

§ 631. The Greek sound ζ (**dz** ?) was rendered at first by **s** or **ss** when intervocalic, e.g. *massa* < μάζα.

In Late Latin when the sounds **dž** and **ǥ** had developed (§§ 290, 308) it was equated with them and developed in Gallo-Roman into **dž** when initial, and either **ẑ** (> ǀz) or **ɉ** (< ǥ, § 309 (ii)) when intervocalic. Cf. O.F. *jalos* **džalǫs** < **zelosus* < ζῆλος ; *batisier, bateiier* < **baptizare* < βαπτίζειν.

§ 632. *Vowels.*—Greek υ (i.e. **ü**) was latinised first as **u** ; later it was written *y* and accorded the value **i** :

> O.F. *borsa* < **bŭrsa* < βύρσα, *boiste* < **büxida* < πυξίδα, *crote* < *crŭpta* < κρύπτη, *girer* < **girare* < γυρός.

The starting-point of the O.F. word *proveire* (*presbyterum*) appears to be a late form in which ö, the Late Greek pronunciation of the sound ü, has been unrounded to ę and the prefix *pro-* substituted for *pres-*.

§ 633. Greek η was long and open, ę̄. In the words borrowed early when *quantity* was dominant, it was rendered by Latin ē and became ę, cf. *cēra* kęra < κηρός, but later on the open *quality* of the sound predominated, cf. *ecclesia* ekklęsja.

The mediaeval Greek pronunciation i̯ is reflected in O.F. *tapiz* tapits < ταπήτιον.

Section 3.—FRANKISH LOAN-WORDS.

§ 634. The Frankish sound-system contained two fricative consonants absent from the Early Gallo-Roman sound-system :

h (eliminated in Late Latin) and θ (ð).

Two others, χ and w, were used in new and unfamiliar positions.

The laryngal fricative h was acquired by the inhabitants of Northern Gaul (§ 28).

The dental fricative θ (ð) was replaced by the plosive dental t (d), cf. O.F. *honte* < **hauniθa*, *treschier* < **θriskan*, *esfreer* < ***exfridare* < **friðu*.

§ 635. In Frankish speech the velar fricative χ (graphy *h*) was in use not only in the intervocalic group χt as in Gallo-Roman faχtu < *factum* (§ 359), but also in initial position before l, r, n.

The Frankish intervocalic group χt was palatalised like the Gallo-Roman one (§ 324) : **waχta* > guaite, **faχ(i)da* > faide, but the treatment of χ in initial position varied at the different epochs at which the words were borrowed.

(i) In the earliest contingent of loan-words initial χ (*h*) was replaced by k (written *ch*), cf. O.F. *Chloevis* < *Hloðawig*, *Clotilde* < *Hlotilda*.

(ii) In the set next borrowed the constriction of the throat was replaced by the constriction of the lips, i.e. χ by f, cf. O.F. *floovenc* < **Hlodowing, flanc* < **hlanc, frime* < **hrim, froc* < **hroc*.

(iii) Later on, when the sound weakened, it either disappeared or was replaced by h, separated from the following consonant by a vocalic glide, cf. O.F. *Loewis, hanap* < **hnapp*.

The replacement of χ by f appears to have induced occasionally the converse substitution of h for f, cf. the northern place-name *Hinges* < *Finibus* (Pas de Calais) : this substitution may account for *hardes*, if it is a doublet of *fardes* as has been suggested, and a few other words, but cf. Orr, *M.L.R* xix, pp. 41-44.

§ 636. The pronunciation of the bilabial fricative w offered difficulties to the Latin-speaking peoples because the Latin weak fricative or semi-vowel w ?, u̯ ? had passed to β except after k (§ 186), and the

w-sound that developed from unstressed **u** and **o** in hiatus was used only as initial of a syllable, i.e. always after another consonant. In the Germanic loan-words in which **w** was *initial* of the *word* it was hardened to **gw** in accordance with the tendency to strengthen consonantal sounds in that position (§§ 202, 203). [For **g** < **gw** cf. § 192.]

O.F. *guarder* **gwardẹr** < **wardôn, guerre* < **werra, guaite* < **wahta, guaaignier* **gwaãṇier** < **waidanjan.*

Latin words that began with a fricative bilabial sound and were cognate with Germanic words beginning with **w**, or were associated with such words, were also given this stronger pronunciation :

O.F. *guarait* < *vervactum* + **wret* (?), *guaster* < **vastare* + **wost* (?), *guespe* < *vespa* + **wepsa* (?), *guez* < *vadum* + **waδ, guivre* < *vipera* + **wipera, gulpil* < **vulpiculum* + ***hwelp* (?).

Germanic **w** initial of a syllable or intervocalic, like Gallo-Roman **w** < **ṷ** (§§ 374 (ii), 328), developed into **v** or **ṷ** (cf. § 192) :

O.F. *espervier* < **sparwari, Baivier* < **Baiuwari, bleve* < ***blaṷa* < **blao, eschever* < **skiuhan.* [For O.F. **blọu** cf. § 481.]

✱✱ In the northern and eastern region the Frankish influence was strong enough to maintain **w** at the beginning of words, cf. *Auc. waucrant* 34, 10, *waumonnes* 30, 17 (N. § iii).

§ 637. *Treatment of Vowels.*—Frankish vowels were equated with Latin vowels and developed along their lines :

G. **ɑ** > **a**, **brɑsɑ* > ***brasa*; **ĕ** > **ẹ**, ***bĕrɑ* > ***bẹra*; **ē** > **ẹ**, **rēd* > ***rẹdṷ*; **ĭ** > **ẹ**, **hĭlt* > ***hẹltṷ*; **ī** > **i̧**, **wīsa* > ***gwisa*; **ū** > **ṷ**, **brūn* > ***brṷnṷ*; **ŭ** > **ṷ** > **ọ**, **hŭrdi* > ***họrda.*

Tonic **ō** and **ŏ** were, however, both equated with **ọ** and thus **fōdr* > ***fọdrṷ, *hŏsa* > ***họsa* (cf. § 180).

Frk. **ɑu** was equated with **ɑu**, **lɑubja* > ***laubja* (F. *loge*), **ɑi** was equated with **ɑ**, **hɑisti* > ***hasta*, **eu** was equated with **ẹṷ**, **speut* > ***espẹṷtṷ.* (Cf. Schwan-Behrens, *Altfrz. Gr.*, § 30.)

Section 4.—Treatment of Learned Loan-words in Period I.

§ 638. The importation of Latin loan-words began in Gallo-Roman even before the Carlovingian reforms differentiated markedly the vernacular from literary Latin (§§ 646, 647). These early loan-words were introduced *orally* in the speech of the clerks, and were mainly concerned with religion and the life of the Church, its services and organisation, but they comprised also technical and semi-technical terms of the 'professional' classes, the doctors and lawyers, as, for example, O.F. *avuegle, firie, mirie, quiter.*

§ 639. A few much used words in the early period are not strictly speaking loan-words, but rather words whose development was retarded by the influence of clerkly

speech. Such are: *angele, anme, crestien, diable, menestier, damner, condamner*, and possibly *huile* and *pueple*: all words used constantly in the services of the Church in the hearing of the people (cf. H.L.F. I, 292).

The Old French forms: *pais, vois, los* (habitual instead of *paiz, voiz, loθ*) appear to be derivatives from the nominative forms frequently heard in the phrases: *pax vobiscum, pax, vox, laus fit.*

§ 640. *Pronunciation of Latin in Gallo-Roman.*—In Gallo-Roman, particularly in Early Gallo-Roman, the clerks carried over into their pronunciation of Latin the tendencies that were most strongly affecting the speech of the time, and the words borrowed at this epoch ordinarily reflect these developments.   The most marked are the following :—

(1) The use of prosthetic **e** before initial groups consisting of **s** + consonant (§ 361): *escole, estudie.*

(2) The consonantalisation of **e** and **i** unstressed in hiatus before a vowel and the passage of ɟ to **dž** when retained as initial (§§ 220, 203):

O.F. *miliẹ < millia, paliẹ < pallium, linge < linea, lange < lanea, serorge < sororium.*

(3) The lowering of **i** to **ẹ** and of **ŭ** to **ǫ** (§ 179):

O.F. *batesme, evesque, moltepleiier, tomolte.*

(4) The diphthongisation and 'breaking' of the tonic, free mid vowels (§§ 225, 226, 410, 411):

O.F. *aliegre, liepre, siegle, avuegle, segrei (< secretum) ; eglise, empirie, ivuire.*

(5) The palatalisation of **g** *intervocalic* before **e** and **i** to ɟ (§§ 290, 297), of **g** *initial* + **e, i** to **dž**, of **k** *initial* and *intervocalic* + **a** to **tš** (§ 300) ; the palatalisation and assibilation of **k** *initial* + **e, i, k** + ɟ and **t** + ɟ to **t͡s** (§§ 290, 291, 306, 308) :

O.F. *fraile (< **frajele < fragilem) ;   Escoce < Scotia, sazier (< satiare), graisle* **graizlẹ** *(< **gra͡ts(e)le < gracilem) ;   chanoine, empedechier, predechier, vochier.*

(6) The voicing of intervocalic **t** to **d** and of **k** + **o, u** to **g** (§ 335), and the opening of intervocalic **d** to **ð** (§ 333) :

O.F. *chastedet, sene (< synodem); agut (< acutum), segont (< secundum).*

In proparoxytones in *-ĭcum* and in verb forms in *-ĭca, -ĭcas, -ĭcat*, etc., the velar was effaced:

O.F. *apostoliẹ < *apostolicum, chanoniẹ < *canonicum, moniẹ < *monicum, rustiẹ < rusticum, glorefie, glorefies, glorefiet, magnefie*, etc.

§ 641. (i) In early borrowed words **g** (< **g** and **k**), if brought in contact with **l** by the fall of unstressed penultimate **ŭ**, was opened and vocalised to **u̯** (cf. *sauma < sagma*, § 359) :

O.F. *rẹulẹ < reg(u)la > riulẹ, teulẹ < tēgula > tiulẹ, seulẹ < **sẹg(u)lu̯, saeculum.*

(ii) In the interior of later borrowed words **k** before **l** or **r** was voiced to **g** :

O.F. *segrei < secretum, jogleor < joculatorem, marreglier < matricularium, siegle < saeculum.*

§ 642. *Accentuation and Sound-Substitution.*—In the pronunciation of the Latin of the period and consequently in the learned loan-words, the tonic stress remained on the syllable that bore it in Late Latin, in proparoxytones as well as in paroxytones, cf. O.F. *angele* ˈandžlę, ˈidlę (*ˈidŏlum*), ˈmonję, ˈrüstję, etc. Unfamiliar groups of consonants were developed in words of this type by the slurring of the unstressed penultimate vowel and these were gradually accommodated to current pronunciation by various forms of sound-substitution or by simple elimination.

§ 643. (i) The penultimate vowel was slurred and the resultant unfamiliar consonantal groups were often dissimilated, reduced or replaced :

nm by **lm** or **rm** : O.F. *alme, arme* < *anme, merme* < **menme < *minimum, almaille, armaille* < **anmaille < *animalia, damledeu, damredeu* < *damnedeu* < *domine deu* (cf. § 369).

dn by **dr** : O.F. *ordre* < **ordne < *ordinem, Londre* < ***Londne.*

dl and **tl** by **dr** and **tr** : *esclandre* < *escandle* < *scandalum, apostre* < *apostŏlus, chapitre* < *chapitle* < *capĭtŭlum, titre.*

kn by **kr** : *diacre* < **diacne < *diacŏnum.*

vn by **vr** : *juevre* < *juevne.*

A late form ***jǫn(e)vior* džǫn(e)βjor, arising from the contamination of *junior* and *jovenior (§ 488), appears to be the starting-point of the curious O.F. forms *juenvre, gienvle* (§ 424), *giemble* (cf. *embler* < *involare*) : in these last two *juvenilis* may also play a part.

§ 644. (ii) The final syllable was discarded (sometimes only in Later Old French) : O.F. *ange* andžę < andž(ę)lę *angele, enque* (*encre* ≠ *chancre,* etc.) < *ˈ*encaustum, evesque* < *episcopum, image* < *imag(e)ne* < *imaginem, orfe* < *orf(e)ne* < *orphanum, orgue* < *org(e)ne* < *organum, terme* < *term(e)ne* < *terminum, timbre* < *tympanum, virge* < *virg(e)ne* < *virginem.*

§ 645. The *jod*-groups formed in loan-words after the palatalising period was over were modified in various ways.

(*a*) The groups **lj, nj, rj, vj,** remained at first, but suffered metathesis in Old French, ȷ becoming semi-vocalic and combining with the preceding vowel to form a diphthong :

O.F. apostoilę < apostolję, pailę < palję, *chanoine* tšanuinę < tšanǫnję, *moine* muinę < mǫnję, ruistę < rustję, estoirę < estorję < hĭstŏria, gloirę < glorję, memoirę < memorję, saivę < savję.

Early graphies, e.g. *glorie, apostolie,* etc., and the pronunciation of the English words *glory, story,* etc., indicate that the metathesis was carried through after the Norman Conquest.

[For the development of the diphthongs cf. chaps. xi and xiv.]

(*b*) **dj.**—In the intervocalic group **dj,** formed in loan-words of the eighth century, r̂ developed out of the palatalised d̂ ('son qui a toutes les facilités de se transformer en r̂'; Michaelson, p. 295, cf. below) :

O.F *envire* < *invidia, omecire* < *homicidium, estuire* < *studium, remire* < *remedium, Giries, Gilies* < *Aegidium* ; cf. also *gramaire* < **gramadȷę** < ****gramade**(γ)**ų** *gramaticum, daumaire* < *Dalmatica, artimaire* < *artem mathematicum* (?).

Recurrent borrowings gave rise to several variants of the semi-technical words *medicum* and *fĭcătum (' fig-fed '), the late word that replaced *jecur*.

From *ᵗ*fĭcătum*, a word modelled on the Greek and influenced by ᵗ*hepar*, ᵗ*hepătis* and adjectives ending in -*īdus* there arose in Late Latin or Early Romance the forms : *ᵗ*fēcătum*, *ᵗ*fĭdĭcum*, *ᵗ*fĕdĭcum* (cf. Gaston Paris, *Mél. Ling.* 535 et seqq.).

From ᵗ*fecatum* was developed the dominant modern form *foie :* ***fękătų** > ****feyădų** > ****fęȷęðę** > **feię** > **foię** (cf. O.F. **anę** < ᵗ**anătem**).

In the forms : *fege* < **fĕdicum, firie* < *fĭdicum and in *miege, mirie* < *medicum* the development is along the lines of the suffix -*aticum*, -*eticum* (§ 352), i.e. the intervocalic velar consonant was weakened and effaced and the penultimate vowel consonantalised to **ȷ** : in *fege, miege,* **fędžę, miedžę,** the earlier development of **ȷ** initial was followed and **ȷ** was strengthened to **dž** and the dental assimilated to it (cf. § 373), in the later forms, **firȷę** (< ****fidȷę**) and **mierȷę** (< ****miedȷe**), the group **dȷ** passed to **rȷ** and **r̂** as above.

In **meię** (eastern), **mię, męę** (south-western), **dȷ** passed to **ȷ** (through ** đ** ?), i.e. *medicum* > **mędȷe** > **męȷe** > **meię** or **mieȷę, mię, męę** (cf. Karl Michaëlsson : ' Le passage de *d* à *r* en Français,' *Studier i Modern Språkvetenskap,* IX, 261-298).

[Cf. H. Berger, *Les Mots d'Emprunt dans le plus ancien français,* 1899 ; G. Paris, *Les plus anciens Mots d'Emprunt du français, Mél. Ling.,* pp. 314-352.]

Section 5.—Treatment of Learned Loan-words in Old and Middle French.

§ 646. *The Carolingian Reforms.*—The reforms in Latin pronunciation instituted by Alcuin under the ægis of Charlemagne (§ 21) were dominated by orthography and Latin pronunciation was only restored in so far as spelling was a guide. Some of the grosser modifications introduced in the pronunciation of Latin under the influence of vernacular tendencies were, however, eliminated, and ' mots savants ' were in consequence marked off more sharply from ' mots populaires ' than before. The reforms, however, only became fully operative with the revival of Latin studies in the eleventh and twelfth centuries.

§ 647. The most noteworthy of the vernacular modifications that were avoided are the following :—

(1) The slurring of unstressed vowels :

O.F. *charite, verite, edefier* (xii), *segnefier* (xii) ; M.F. *cumuler* (xiv), *capituler* (xiv), *gratitude* (xv), etc.

(2) The lowering of **i** to **ę** and **ŭ** to **ǫ** :

O.F. *digne* (cf. *deignier*), *epistle, office, letice* (cf. *leece* < *laetitia*), *title, juise* (< *judicium*) ; *diluvie, fluvie, multeplier, cultiver* (cf. *coutiver*).

i was equated with **ı̨** and **ŭ** with **ų,** i.e. **ü.**

(3) The consonantalisation of **e** and **i** unstressed in hiatus : O.F. *avision, champion, crestüien, dïamant, dïalogue, odïeux, precïeus,* etc.

The palatalisation of preceding **t** and **k** before **j** was ordinarily continued, cf. O.F. *anciien < antianum, saziier < satiare.*

(4) The diphthongisation of the tonic free mid-vowels and the breaking of ę and ǫ : O.F. *apostolie, escole, rose, ivorie, estorie.*

(5) The palatalisation of the groups velar + dental : **kt, gd, ks, kl, kr** : O.F. *action, actif, affection, dicter, regle, siecle,* etc. ; M.F. *dejection, pacte, respect, acre, acrobate, examen.* (For the pronunciation of **kt** and **ks** in Later Old and Middle French, cf. § 650.)

(6) The opening and voicing of single consonants, intervocalic or before **r** and **l** : O.F. *(h)abiter, edifice, paradis, paterne ; acre, siecle.*

§ 648. Latin pronunciation, though thus ameliorated, continued to be strongly affected by the vernacular usage :

(1) *Accentuation.*—When the unstressed vowels had disappeared and accentuation of the final full syllable of words had become habitual in the vernacular (§ 223), the pronunciation of Latin and consequently of all learned loan-words was brought into conformity with this practice and all words made oxytone except those ending in -ę. Thus :—

'*dominum,* '*mensem,* '*laudem,* vi'*dete,* la'*vabo,* etc., were stressed : *domi*'*num, men*'*sem, lau*'*dem, vide*'*te, lava*'*bo,* etc. ; and the Latin words : '*fragilis,* '*facilis,* '*utilis,* '*mobilis,* '*fabrica,* '*canticum,* when borrowed, were turned into : *fragile, facile, utile, mobile, fabrique, cantique,* etc.

The shifted stress in Latin words, which is attested in the tenth century and illustrated by rhymes throughout the period, continued in spite of opposition in the Renaissance period into modern times, cf. the rhymes:
Alexis, grabatum : hum : bricun 546.—*Best., Cleopatras : arz* 1671 ; *equinoctium : demustraisun* 1881 ; *Deuteronomii : di* 2147 ; *crucis : dis* 2695, etc. ; *vale : furmé* 2295, etc.—*Villon, sexus : sus* L. xii ; *laudem : cordoen* T. vi ; *de profundis : ßis* T. lxxxiv ; *proles : balais* P.D. viii.—*Greban, via : il y a,* p. 288 ; *humiliate : tout gasté,* p. 273 ; *alter : denoter,* p. 493 ; *domini : infiny,* p. 45 ; *justum : hault ton,* p. 439—*Cretin, omnia : on y a* xlvi, 89.

Cf. also sixteenth-century puns, e.g. : *habitaculum—habit a cul long, omnia tentate —on y a tant tasté* (Tabourot), *laudanum—l'eau d'anon,* and Palsgrave's illustration of the meaning of the word *accentuer :* ' je ne puis pas accentuer a droit en la langue latine, car ma langue francoyse m'empesche.'
[Cf. J. Beardwood : *Rhymes of Latin and French Words in Old French,* Dis. Philadelphia, 1930 ; Th. II, pp. 726-729.]

§ 649. (2) *Sound Changes.*—The more important of the sound changes that left spelling untouched and continued in consequence to modify the pronunciation of Latin and the learned loan-words are the following :—

(*a*) The palatalisation of ŭ to ü (§183), e.g. *fureur, juste, multitude, nature, cumuler, diluer,* etc.

(*b*) The nasalisation and lowering of vowels, e.g. of ę̄ to ā (§ 447).

Cf. Peletier: ' Les mêtres d'école du tans passé disoêt *omnam hominam venicntam,*' Th. II, 427, the puns: *tunc beatam—tombé à temps, omnia tentate—on y a tant tasté* (Tabourot) and rhymes such as *cest an : pestem*, Cretin, lvii, 47.

(*c*) In the pronunciation of words beginning with s + consonant an on-glide still often developed, cf. *esclandre* (c. xii < *'scandalum*), *espace, esclave, estomaquer.*

(*d*) The passage of w to v (§ 189), cf. *vestale* (c. xiv).

(*e*) The palatalisation and assibilation of k and g before e, i, j and of t before i in hiatus, cf. *centre* (c. xiv), *cession* (c. xiii), *certitude* (c. xvi), *genereux* (c. xiv), *fragile* (c. xiv), *nation* (c. xii), *potion* (c. xiii), etc.

The palatalisation of k, *initial* and *intervocalic* before a ⟨ (§ 640 (5)) was not continued and is only found in the loan-words of Period I, cf. O.F. *calice, cantique, cause* (xii); *canal, calomniateur* (xiii).

§ 650. The reduction or assimilation of intervocalic groups of dental + labial, labial or velar + other consonants, e.g. dv, dm, bs, bt, ps, pt, mn, was continued and extended to ks and kt, which were no longer palatalised (§ 647 (5)):

Cf. Middle French, *aversaire, amirable, ajectif, averbe, oscur, ovier* (*obviare*), *ostination, saume, tisane* (*ptisane*), *accetter < acceptare, excete, abget < abjectum, sospet < suspectum, escommunier, escuser, espliquer, estase, estreme, teste* (*textum*), etc., *aumenter, dramme* (< *dragma*), *flemme,* (< *phlegma*), etc.

Cf. the rhymes: Villon, *ceptres : ancestres*, T. xxxv; G. Alexis, I, *Egipte : gicte*, p. 30, *sexe : cesse*, p. 19; Cretin, *infect : meffait*, vii, 35, *acceptes : cestes*, l, 195, *teste* (*texte*) : *celeste, atteste*, xxvi, 196; *actes : ingrates* (Jean le Maire); *adetre* (*adextre*) : *fenetre* (Vauquelin de la Fresnaye) *prefix : fils* (Cretin, xli, 339), *perplex ; plectz* (xliii, 22); and H. Estienne: 'Alii *escuser* . . . alii (et melius illi quidem) *excuser* proferunt,' Th. II, 341, and Palsgrave: ' *x* thorowout the frenche tonge hath suche a sounde as they gyve to *s* with them, whan he cometh bytwene two vowelles, that is to saye lyke as the latyns do sounde *z* in these words : *zona, Elizabet :* so that these wordes in frenche . . . *perplexite, chevaulx, beaulx* . . . *exemple, experience, executer* shall be sounded . . . *perplezite, chevaulz, beaulz, euzemple* . . .' p. 38.

§ 651. In Later Middle French Latin pronunciation was also often affected by the vernacular treatment of final consonants (chap. xvii, sect. 5), and prae-consonantal final s was consequently effaced. Cf. Erasmus: 'The French eliding s, when it falls between a vowel and a consonant, lengthen the preceding vowel.' (Th. II, 593, and above, § 565).

*Section 6.—*RENAISSANCE REFORMS.

§ 652. In the sixteenth century the more exact study of Latin and the criticism of foreign scholars (e.g. Erasmus in his *De recta latini*

graecique sermonis pronunciatione), led to renewed attempts to eliminate the vernacular tendencies that impaired the pronunciation of Latin. The attempts of the reformers, however, met with but a very partial success ; they were most effective, as in the earlier period, when supported by spelling. Nasalisation, for instance, continued, but the lowering of ẽ to ã was suppressed, and thus words like *semper, laudem* were pronounced: **sẽpẹr, laudẽ,** instead of **sãpẹr, laudã** as earlier (cf. § 649 and the modern pronunciation of *pensum,* **pẽsǫm**).

§ 653. In the reforms in which most success was achieved, the pronunciation of the vernacular, in particular the loan-words, was affected also :—

(1) The initial on-glide before **s** + consonant was condemned and earlier loan-words sometimes remodelled, thus : *scorpion, special, spirituel, stable* replace earlier *escorpion, especial, espirituel, estable.*

§ 654. (2) An attempt was made to restore the pronunciation of **h,** effaced ordinarily in the pronunciation of Latin as in the vernacular, cf. Scaliger : 'In my childhood this sound was not heard, but to-day lettered people pronounce it without scruple and some even in a tiresome way, for the unlearned use it in the wrong place and seem to bark it out.' (Th. II, 397.) The attempt led to the aspiration of **h** in some loan-words and proper names (e.g. *Hector*), and this ephemeral pronunciation influenced permanently the word *héros.*

§ 655. (3) Full value was attributed to the consonantal groups **bv, bs, dv, pt, ps, st, kt, ks,** etc., and this pronunciation combined with the influence of spelling, exercised very considerable influence on the pronunciation of loan-words (cf. § 744). (For the influence of the pronunciation of prae-consonantal **s** in Latin words, cf. § 379.)

Section 7.—ITALIAN LOAN-WORDS.

§ 656. As the accentuation and sound-systems of Italian differed relatively little from the French, words were adopted without much adjustment, but the following points deserve remark :

(i) The Italian sounds **ts, tš, dž,** obsolete in Middle French pronunciation, were replaced :—

(*a*) **ts** was ordinarily rendered by **s** :
altesse < *altezza, caresse* < *carezza, carrosse* < *carrozza.*

(*b*) **tš** either by **š** or **s** :
charlatan < *ciarlatino, douche* < *doccia, caprice* < *capriccio, façade* < *facciata, fantassin* < *fantaccino.*

(*c*) **dž** by **z** or **ž** :
courtisane < *cortegiana, passager* < *passeggiare.*

(ii) Words beginning with the group **s +** consonant were pronounced with an on-glide :—

escadron < squadrone, escapade < scapata, escarcelle < scarsella, escorte < scorto.

Section 8.—DOUBLETS.

§ 657. The variant forms derived from one etymon in use in the speech of one region are called *doublets*. In Old and Middle French they arose in various ways :—

§ 658. (1) A small contingent was furnished in Old and Middle French by the survival of both analogical and traditional forms, e.g. *courre : courir, loier : lier, ploier : plier, toldre, tolir, toleir*, etc., and a number were formed under the influence of syntactical phonetics (cf. chap. xvii).

§ 659. (2) In the older periods of the language, before its standardisation, doublets arose not infrequently from the use of dialectal forms in the speech of Paris (cf. §§ 74 and 75). Examples are :

beau : biau, eaue : iaue, sachier : saquer, pou : peu, lieu : leu, feu : fu, leu (lupum) : lou(p), oue : oie, coude : coute, grange : granche (cf. §§ 348-354). Modern *benêt : Benoît, français : François* are due to the Middle French vacillation between ę and wę (§ 522).

§ 660. (3) The largest contingent was furnished by the importation of loan-words. Examples are :—

(i) *Provençal.—balee : balade, cage : gabie, chable : cable, chasse : caisse (capsa), cheptel : cadeau (capitalem), chief : cap, chape : cape, fie : figue, iwel, owel* (§ 484) *: egal, laoste : langouste, voiier : viguier (vicarium) ; helme : elme, halsberc : osberc, herberge : auberge* (cf. § 54).

(ii) *Learned Loan Words.—chetif : captif, chenal : canal, chievetaigne : capitaine, cheptel : capital, combler : cumuler, disme : décime, ditier : dicter, dreit : direct, enferté : infirmité, esmer : estimer, espir : esprit, essaim : examen, forge : fabrique, façon : faction, fraile : fragile, grief : grave, ivoire : ivire (< ivuire)* (§ 640), *meuble : mobile, meuf* (§ 816) *: mode, nagier : naviguer, noël : natal, poison : potion, pareis (> parvis) : paradis, raison : ration, verté : verité, voyage : viatique, voyer : vicaire* (cf. § 53).

(iii) *Italian.—chaîne : cadene, chance : cadence* (cadentia), *charbonnée : carbonnade, chevreuil : cabriole, chevalier : cavalier, chevalerie : cavalerie, chevauchée : cavalcade, chiennaille : canaille, chariere : carriere, coutume : costume, duché : ducat, eschiver : esquiver, hautesse : altesse, maille : medaille, meschin : mesquin, pommée : pommade, prest : preste* (xvii) (cf. §§ 55-57).

Thus occasionally a single Latin word has given rise to three French words, e.g. *capitalem*, whence *cheptel, cadeau, capital ; vicarium*, whence *voyer, viguier, vicaire ; crypta*, whence O.F. *crute, crypte* (xiv), *grotte* (xvi).

[For doublets introduced in the Modern period, cf. Nyrop, *Gr.* §§ 77-79.]

CHAPTER XIX.

SOUND TABLES.

§ 661. i TONIC < LATIN AND GERMANIC ī.

Ref.	Position.	G.R.	O.F. I.	O.F. II.	Mid. F.	Mod. F.	Class.	Late	O.F. II.	Mid. F.	Mod. F.
	BLOCKED and FREE	i·	i·	i·	i·	i·	mille	mille	mil	mil	mil
§§ 451-455	before **n, m** + cons. or final	i·	i·	>ī	>ɛ̃	ɛ̃	finem	fine	fin > fin	>fɛ̃(n) *fin*	>fɛ̃ *fin*
§§ 451, 452	before **n, m** *intervocalic in Mid. Fr.*	i·	i·	>ī	>ĩ	i·	spīnā *spīna*	(e)spina	espine > epine	>epine *espine, espinne*	>epin *épine*
	Before PALATAL										
§ 452	before **ŋ** *intervocalic*	i·	i·	>ī	>ĩ	i·	lineā *linea*	linja	liŋe > liŋe *ligne*	>liŋe *ligne, lingne*	>liŋ *ligne*
§ 384	before **ĺ, ị** + cons.	i·	i·	i·	i·	i·	filius	filjus	fiĺts > fits > fis *filz, fiz*	fi(s, z) *filz*	>fi; fis *fils*
§ 405	+ *jod*	ij>	i·	i·	i·	i·	mīka *mica*	mika	mie	>mī *mie*	mi *mie*

Words or syllables bracketed are those replaced; sounds bracketed are those that are moribund or developing or varying in use in the phrase.
The modern forms included are those used in isolation, and in these vowel-length is not indicated.
A semicolon indicates a break in the development of words.

§ 662. i̯ COUNTERTONIC < LATIN AND GERMANIC ī.

Ref.	Position.	G.R.	O.F. L.	O.F. II.	Mid. F.	Mod. F.	Class.	Late.	O.F. II.	Mid. F.	Mod. F.
	BLOCKED and FREE										
§§ 451-455	before n or m + cons.	ī.	ī.	ī.	ī.	ī.	**wīllanum** / *villanum*	βillanu	vilāin>vilẹin	>vilẹ̃(n) / *vilain*	villẹ̃ / *vilain*
§§ 451, 452	before n or m *intervocalic* in Mid. F.	ī.	ī.	ī.	ī.	ī.	**hibĕrnum**	iβẹrnu	ivern; iver (§ 811)	iver / *hiver*	ivẹR / *hiver*
		ī.	ī.	>ī	>ẹ̃	ẹ̃	**kvinkvanta** / *quinquanta*	ʄinkvanta	tsinkāntẹ>sinkāntẹ / *cinkante*	>sẹkãtẹ / >	sẹkãt / *cinquante* >
		ī.	ī.	>ī	>ī.	ī.	**limare**	limare	limẹr>limẹr	>limẹ / >	limẹ / *limer*
§§ 382, 384	before ĩ, l̨, j̨ + *cons.*	ī.	ī.	ī.	ī.	ī.		*filẹʈẹlla / *filicella*	fi(ï)tsẹlẹ>fisẹlẹ / *ficele*	fisẹlẹ / *ficelle*	>fisel / *ficelle*
	BLOCKED and FREE before PALATALS										
§§ 451, 452	before ŋ *intervocalic*	ī.	ī.	>ī	>ī.	ī.			liɲi̯e(ð)ẹ>lĩɲi̯ẹẹ / *ligniee, ligniee*	>lĩɲẹ̃ / *ligniee, ligniee*	liɲẹ̃ / *lignée*
§§ 339, 404	+ *jod*	i̯ >	ī.	ī.	ī.	ī.	**titiōnem**	titsi̯onẹ	tizũn / *tison, tisun*	tizũ(n) / *tison*	>tizõ / *tison*

§ 663. LATE LATIN ẹ TONIC < LATIN AND GERMANIC ĕ, ĭ.

Ref.	Position.	G.R.	O.F. I.	O.F. II.	Mid. F.	Mod. F.	Latin. Class.	Latin. Late.	O.F. II.	Mid. F.	Mod. F.
§§ 493, 575	A. BLOCKED (in Late Latin and Early G.R.)	ẹ̆	ẹ̆	> ẹ	ẹ	ẹ	ĭllɑm	ẹllɑ	ẹlẹ > ẹlẹ *elle*	elẹ *elle*	> ẹl *elle*
	(before r in Middle French, cf. § 496)						dēbitɑ	dẹββẹtɑ	dẹtẹ > dẹtẹ *dette*	dẹtẹ *dette, debte*	> dẹt *dette*
§§ 443, 447-8	before n or m + cons.		> ẽ	> ã	ã̃	> ɑ̃	fíndere	fẹndere	fẽndrẹ > fãndrẹ *fendre, fandre*	fãdrẹ *fendre*	> fɑ̃dR *fendre*
							prehendere prẹndere	prẹndere	prẽndrẹ > prãndre *prendre, prandre*	prãdrẹ *prendre*	> prɑ̃dR *prendre*
§§ 447, 449	before n, m intervocalic in Mid. F.		> ẽ	> ã	ã̃	> a	fēminɑm	fẹmẹnɑ	fẽmẹ > fãmẹ *feme, fame*	fãmẹ *femme*	> fam *femme*
§§ 387, 542, 585	+ ɥ̯ (< ł + cons.)		> ẹɥ̯	> ö	ö	ö̞	íllos	ẹllos	ẹus > ös *els, eus, ex*	> ö (s, z) *eux, eulx*	> ö̞ *eux*
§§ 225-8, 518-25	B. FREE (in Gallo-Roman)	ei	>	ọi > ɥe > wẹ	> wẹ ...ẹ e	> {wa wɑ} e	fidem	fẹde	feiθ > foi > fụẹ *feit, foi*	> fwẹ *foi*	> fwa, fwɑ *foi*
							krētɑm *creta*	krẹtɑ	kreiẹ > kroiẹ > krụẹẹ *creide, croie*	> kr(w)ẹẹ > krẽ *croie*	kRẽ *craie*

§§	Condition			(cf. §487)			Latin					
§§ 225, 439, 467	before **n** or **m** *final*	> ei	> ẽi	> ę̃i	> ę̃ (cf. §487)	ę̃	**plēnum**	plę̃nu	'> plę̃in > plę̃in *plein*	> plę̃in > plę̃in *plein*	> plę̃n > plę̃(n) *plein*	plę̃ *plein*
§§ 225, 439, 467–470	before **n** or **m** *intervocalic*	> ei	> ẽi	> ę̃i	> ę̃ > ẹ (cf. §487)	e	**plēnam**	plę̃na	> plę̃inę > plę̃inę *pleine, pleinne*	> plę̃inę > plę̃inę *pleine, pleinne*	> plę̃nę > plę̃nę *pleine, pleinne*	> plę̃nę > plę̃nę *pleine, pleinne*
§ 418	preceded by a **palatal**	i	i	i	i	i	**kēram** *cēram*	ʃerą	tsirę > sirę *cire*	sirę *cire*	sirę *cire*	> siR *cire*
§§ 418, 452	and followed by **n** or **m** become *final*	i	i	> ī	> ę̃	ę̃	**rakēmum** *racēmum*	rąʒemu	raizin > ręzin *raisin*	> ręzę̃(n) *raisin*	> ręzę̃(n) *raisin*	Ręzę̃ *raisin*
	C. BLOCKED and FREE before palatals											
§§ 198, 494	**+ l**	ẹj̯	ẹj̯	ẹj̯	> ẽj	> ẽj	**parĭkulum** *pariculum*	parĩklu	parẽj *pareil*	> parẽj *pareil*	> parẽj *pareil*	paRẽj > paRẽj *pareil*
§§ 387, 542	**+ u̯ (< l + cons.)**	ẹj̯	> ẹ+j̯	eu̯ > ö	ö	ö	**parĭkulos** *pariculos*	parẽklos	pareuts > parös *pareulz, pareux*	> parö(s, z) *pareux*	> parö(s, z) ; *pareux*	parö(s, z) ; *pareux*
§§ 407, 439, 467,	before **ŋ** *intervocalic*	ẹ̇	> ę̃i	> ę̃i	> ę̃	> ę̃	**insĭnnĭa** *insignia*	ẽsẽŋĩa	ãsẽiŋę > ãnsẽiŋę *enseigne, enseigne*	ãsẽŋę > ãsẽŋę *enseigne, enseigne*	ãsẽŋę > ãsẽŋę *enseigne, enseigne*	ãsẽŋ *enseigne*
§§ 406, 279, 439, 467	before **ŋ** *final* and + cons.	ẹj̯	> ę̃i	> ę̃i	> ę̃	ę̃	**fiŋktum** *finctum*	feŋ(k)tu	fẽint > fẽint *feint, faint*	fẽ(t) *feint, feint*	fẽ(t) *feint, feint*	> fẽ *feint*
§§ 339, 404, 226–228, 518, 525	**+ jod**	>	ei̯ >	oi > u̯ę	we ……	> { wa / wa }	**tēktum** *tectum*	tẽxtu	teit > toit > tu̯et *teit, toict*	> twe(t) *toit, toict*	> twe(t) *toit, toict*	> twa, twa *toit*
					ę	e	**rĭgĭdam** *rigidam*	rẽjeda	reidę > roidę > ru̯edę *roide, roide*	> rwẽdę > rẽdę *roide, raide, redde*	> rwẽdę > rẽdę *roide, raide, redde*	> Rẽd *raide*

§664. L.L. ẹ TONIC < LATIN ě, ae, AND GERMANIC ě.

Ref.	Position	G.R.	O.F. I.	O.F. II.	Mid. F.	Mod. F.	Class. Latin	Late Latin	O.F. II.	Mid. F.	Mod. F.
	A. BLOCKED before **r**, cf. §§ 496, 497	ẹ	ẹ	ẹ	ẹ	ẹ	sěptem	sẹpte	sẹt	sẹt *sept*	sẹt *sept*
§§ 443; 447, 8	before **n** or **m** + *cons.*		> ē	> ã	ã	> ā	těmpŭs	tęmpŭs	tēns > tãns	> tã(s, z) *temps*	> tā *temps*
§§ 388, 539	+ ɥ (< + + *cons.*)	ẹ+	ẹ+ >	'ẹau > ẹ'au	> ẹ̣ọ	> ọ	bĕllŭs	bĕllŭs	bẹ+s > b'ẹaus > bẹ'aus *bels, beax, beaux*	> bẹọ(s, z) *beaux*	> bọ *beaux*
§§ 225, 510	**B. FREE** *become final*	> 'ie	'ie	> jẹ	jẹ	jẹ	pĕdem	pẹde	pieθ > pjẹ *piet, pie*	pjẹ *pied*	pjẹ *pied*
§§ 494, 576	+ *sounded final consonant*			⎫	> jẹr	jẹ	hěrī	ęrị	ier > jẹr *ier, hier*	> jẹr *hier*	jẹR *hier*
§§ 495, 576	+ *intervocalic consonant* (after š, ž, cf. §§ 510, 494, 495)			⎭	^	jẹ	fěra	fẹra	fiere > fjẹrẹ	fjẹrẹ	> fjẹR *fère*
§§ 225, 470-2,	before **n** or **m** (*become final*)	> 'ie	'ie	> jẹ > jẽ	> jẽ	jẽ	běne	bẹne	bien > bjẽn	> bjẽ(n) *bien*	bjẽ *bien*
§§ 225, 470-2,	before **n** or **m** *intervocalic*	> 'ie	'ie	> jẹ > jẽ	> jẽ / > jẹ	jẹ	těnent	tẹnent	t'iẹnent > tjẽnẽ(n)t *tienent, tiennent*	> tjẽnẹt > tjẹnẹ(t) *tiennent*	> tjẹn *tiennent*

		ʲieu	ʲie	> jö	jö	jö	děum	dęu	dieu > djö / dieu	djö / dieu	djö / dieu
§§ 254, 545	+ ų final	>ʲleu									
	C. Blocked and Free before Palatals										
§§ 410, 494, 510	+ l *final and intervocalic*	>ʲlej	ʲie	>ʲlej	>lej	>lej	wĕtulum / *vetulum*	βęklụ	vieʄ>vlęʄ / *vieil*	>vlęʄ / *vieil*	vlęʄ>vlęʄ / *vieil*
§§ 387, 410, 545	+ ų (< l + *cons.*)	>ʲlej	>ʲle↟	lęų>jö	jö	>jŏ	wĕtulos / *vetulos*	βęklos	vieʄts>vlęųts>vjös / *vieilz, vieux*	>vjö(s, z) / *vieux*	>vjŏ / *vieux*
§§ 410, 471	before ŋ *intervocalic*	>ʲle	ʲle	>je>lę̃	>ję̃ / >lę̃	je	tĕnĕat	tęnjat	tieŋe(θ)>tlęŋę / *tiegne*	>tlęŋe>tlęŋe ; / *tiengne, tiegne*	tlęŋ / *tiemne*
§§ 279, 410, 411, 451-3	before ŋ + *cons.*	>ʲlęʄ	>ī	>ī	>ę̃	ę̃	*enɗeŋŏs / *ingenuos*	*enɗeŋŏs	ēndžints>ănžins / *enginz, anginz*	>ăžę̃(s, z) / *enginz*	>ăžę̃ / *engins*
§§ 406, 470	before ŋ *final*	>ʲle(ŋ)	>ʲle	>je>lę̃	>jlę̃	jlę̃	tĕnĕo	tęnjo	tleŋ>tlęŋ / *tiegn, tieng*	tlę̃(n); / *tiegn;*	tlę̃ / *tiens*
§ 410, 411	+ *jod*	>ʲlej	>ī	i	i	i	(pĕjus)	*pęʲụs	pis	> pi(s, z) / *pis*	> pi / *pis*
		>ʲlej	>ī	i	i	i	lĕktum / *lectum*	lęxtụ	lit	>li(t) / *lit*	>li / *lit*

16

§ 665. LATE LATIN COUNTERTONIC ę < LATIN AND GERMANIC ĕ, æ AND ę < LATIN AND GERMANIC ĭ, ē.

Ref.	Position.	G.R.	O.F. I.	O.F. II.	Mid. F.	Mod. F.	Class. Latin.	Late Latin.	O.F. II.	Mid. F.	Mod. F.
§ 234	BLOCKED ę before r (+ cons.)	ę	ę	ę	ę	ę	pĕrsōnam	pęrsōna	persune>persune	persūne *personne*	>persǫne>peRsǫn *personne*
§ 234	ę before r (+ cons.) (cf. also §§ 496-498)	>	ę	ę	ę	ę	firmare	fęrmare	>fęrmer	>fęrme(r) *fermer*	>fęRmę *fermer*
§ 234	Elsewhere + oral cons. ę and ę — cf. also § 591, and below ę and ę + y	ę	ę	ę	ę	ę		*leβjarju *leviarium *desfakere *disfacere	ledžier>ležjer *legier* ; dę(z)faire	>ležę(r) *legier* ; defęrę *desfaire* >	ležę *léger* ; >defęR *défaire*
§§ 234, 235, 275	FREE ę and ę	ę	>ę	ę	ę>	ə	{ nępōtem / dēbēre	nępōte / dęβere	nevou>neveu> nevö *nevou, neveu* ; deveir>devoir>devyęr	nevö *neveu* ; >devwer *devoir*	nevö *neveu* ; >devwaR *devoir*
§§ 243-247	In hiatus in Old French (cf. also § 484)	ę	ə>	ə	e̽>						
§§ 447, 448, 443	before n and m + cons.	ę	>ē	>ā̃	ā̃	>ɑ̄	sĕntire / singularem	sęntire / sęngolare	sēntir>sāntir / sēngler>sāngler	>sāti(r) *sentir, santir* ; sāglię(r) *sanglier*	sɑ̄tiR *sentir* ; >sɑ̄glie, sɑ̄glije *sanglier*

§§	Position	Vowel stages	Latin / Proto-Rom.	Old French	Later	Modern French
§§ 447–449	before **n** and **m** *intervocalic in Mid F.*	e̦·/ ····· >ē/>e̦ >ā/e̦ ã/e̦> >a/ə	(minari) / *fenare *menare / *fimarium	fēner>fāner / mener *(faner, fanner / mener)*	fēne(r) fane, fanner / mene(r)	>fane *faner* / >mene *mener*
§486	between labial consonants	ü ọ̈>ü ·····ü (§543)		femier > *femier* / fömjer>fümje(r) *feumier, fumier*		fümje *fumier*
§§ 387, 541, 542	e̦+ e̦u>ọ̈ ọ̈>ü (§543)	*fe+trare *(feltrare)*	fe+trer>feutrer>fötrer *(feltrer, feutrer)* / fötrer	>fötre(r) *feutrer*	fötRe *feutrer*
§§ 388, 539, 40	e̦+ >ẹau>ẹau ẹau>eau >ọ	*belletate	be+te(θ)>beaute>beaute *(belte(t), beaute)* / >beaute	>bote *beaute*	>bote *beauté*
§§ 234, 407, 467–9	before PALATAL e̦ and before ŋ *intervocalic in Mid. F.*	e̦· >ēi>e̦i >e̦>e̦ e̦	sēniōrem / seŋore	sēŋour>seiŋōr >seiŋōr *(seŋour, seiŋgneur / seiŋōr)*	>seŋö(r)>seŋö(r) *seigneur, seingneur*	>seŋöR>seŋö(r) / >seŋöR *seigneur*
§§ 234, 279, 467, 8	before ŋ (+ cons.)	e̦i >ēi >ēi >ē ē̦	piŋktūra *(pinctura)* / peŋtura	pēintūre>peinture *peinture*	pẽtüre>pẽtüre *peinture*	pẽtüR *peinture*
§§ 234, 494	before j *intervocalic*	e̦· e̦· e̦ e̦	mēliōrem / meljore ; wigilare *(vigilare)* / βejelare	mēlior>meljour>mejour / mejör ; vigilare>vejler / βejelare	meljour>mejeur *meilleur* ; vejier>vejer *veillier*	mejör>mejöR *meilleur* ; veje(r)>veje *veiller*
§§ 339, 404, 226, 228, 518–25	+ jod	ei >oi>ue >wa {wa/wa e̦.....e̦ ə	mēdianum / mejanu ; wēktūra *(vectura)* / βextura ; frikare *(fricare)* / frẽkare	meiien>moiien>muŷēn *(mei(s)en, moi(s)en)* ; veitūre>voitūre>vuẽtüre *(veiture, voiture)* ; freier>froiler>fruẽer *(freier, froiler)*	>mwajẽ(n) / mỹẽ̦n *moyen* ; >vwẽtüre / vụẽtüre *voiture* ; >frwẽjer>freẽ(r) *frayer*	mwajẽ *moyen* ; >vwatüR *voiture* ; fRẽje *frayer*

§ 666. L.L. ɑ Tonic < Latin ă and Germanic ă̄.

Ref.	Position.	G.R.	O.F. I.	O.F. II.	Mid. F.	Mod. F.	Class.	Late.	O.F. II.	Mid. F.	Mod. F.
§ 182	A. BLOCKED in Late Latin and Early G.R.	> a	a	a	a	a	partem	parte	part	> par(t)	> paR *part*
§ 562,4 586	lengthened in Middle French				} > ɑ {		pasta	pasta	eθadžę > eažę *edage, eage* paste > pātę	aažę > āžę *eage, aage* pātę *pâte*	> až *âge* > pɑt *pâte*
§§ 443, 563, 586	before n or m + *consonant*	> a	> ã	ã	ã̄	> ɑ̃	grandem	grande	grãnt	> grã(t) *grand*	> gRɑ̃ *grand*
§§ 442-444	before n or m *intervocalic* in Middle French	> a	> ã	ã	ã >	a	laminam	lamena	lāmę	lāmę >	lam *lame*
§§ 387, 535-7	+ ṷ (< ɫ + cons.)	> aɫ	>	aṷ	> ǫ	ǫ	aɫbam	aɫba	aɫbę > aubę *albe aube*	> ǫbę *aube*	> ǫb *aube*
§ 182	B. FREE (1) in *monosyllables*	ɑ >	a	a	a	a	jɑm	jɑm	džɑ > žɑ *ja*	žɑ *ja*	žɑ *jà*
§ 231	(2) in *polysyllables*: (a) *final of word* in O.F.	> a > ę̆	ę̆.	ę̆.	e.	e.	gratum	grɑtu	grēθ > grę	grę	gRę
§ 494, 495	(b) + *final* l or *sounded* r				e.	e.	talem mare	tale mare	tel męr	> tęl męrę	tęl męR
§ 495, 576	(c) + *consonant* + ę				ę. >	e.	matrem	matre	mɛrę	męrę	> męR *mère*
§§ 233, 427-467	before n or m *final*	>	ãi	> ę̃i	> ę̃	ę̃	manūm	manu	mãin > mę̃in	> mę̃(n) *main*	> mę̃ *main*

§§		>	>āi	>ēi	>ē̦	ḝ	amat	amat	āimȩ>ēimȩ	>ȩmȩ>ȩmȩ, aime, ainme	>ȩm aime
§§ 427, 467, 8	before n or m intervocalic in Mid. F.	ȩ+ (< ł)		e̦ɥ>ieɥ / >jȭ̌	jȭ̌	jȭ̌	palos	palȯs	pȩ+s>pieus>pjȯs / *pels, piez, pieux*	pjȯ(s, z) / *pieux*	pjȯ / *pieux*
§§ 388, 545	+ u̯ (< ł)					jȭ̌					
§ 414	preceded by PALATALS final of word and after š, ž, ļ, ɲ	>ȩ>'ie	'ie	>ję	ję	ję	piętatem mandukare / *manducare*	piętate mandukare	pitieθ>pitjē mānǯier>mānžjer / *mangier*	pitjē >māžę(r) / *mangier*	pitjē >māžę / *manger*
§ 510	after š, ž, ļ, ɲ and (1) + final sounded consonants				>ȩ	ȩ	karum / *carum*	karu / *caru*	tšier>šjer / *chier*	>šer / *cher*	šęR / *cher*
§§ 494, 495, 576					>ȩ	ȩ	karam	kara	tšierę>šjerę / *chiere*	>šerę / *chiere*	šęR / *cher*
§§ 495, 576	or (2) + consonant + ȩ				>ȩ	>ȩ	kanem / *canem*	kane / *cane*	tšien>šję(n) / *chien*	>šję(n) / *chien*	>šję / *chien*
§§ 471, 510	preceded by palatals and (a) followed by nasal	>ȩ>'ie	'ie	>ję>ję̃	>ję̃	ję̃	jaket / *jacet*	jaȼet	džist>žit / *gist*	>ži(t) / *gist*	>ži / *gist*
§ 411	(b) followed by jod	>ȩj>'iej	>i	i	i	i	allium	alļu̯	aj / *ail*	aj / *ail*	aj / *ail*
§ 198	BLOCKED AND FREE before Palatal + ļ final and intervocalic	>aj	aj	aj	aj	>(aj aɥ)	palea	palja	palę / *paille*	>palę / *paille*	>paj / *paille*
§§ 387, 534-7	+ u̯ (< ļ + cons.)	>aɥ		aɥ	>o̦	o̦	*allios / *allios*	*ałļos / *allios*	ałts>auts>aus / *ailz, aux*	>o(z) / *aulx*	>o / *aulx*
§§ 198, 442-4	before ɲ intervocalic	>a	>ā̃	ā̃	ā̃>	a	montaněa	montanja	mōtāñę>mūtāñę / *montaigne, montaigne*	>mūtāñę / *montaigne*	>mō̦tañę / *montagne*
§§ 279, 466-9	before ɲ + cons.	>ai a(ɳ)	>āi	>ę̃i	>ȩ	ę̃	saɳktum / *sanctum*	saɳtu̯	sāint>sę̄int / *saint*	>sę̄(t) / *saint, sainct*	sę̄ / *saint*
§ 406	before ɲ final										
§§ 403-4, 528-9	+ jod prae-consonantal	>ai	ai	>ȩ	>ȩ	ȩ	magis	majes	mais>mę̦s / *mais, mes*	mę(s, z) / *mais*	>mȩ, mẹ / *mais*
	+ jod or i, final in Latin + jod, final or intervocalic in G.R., cf. §§ 404, 530-2	> ai	ai	>ȩ	ę̦ (§ 487)	ȩ	habeo	*ajo	ał>ę̦ / *ai, e*	ę̦ / *ai*	ę̦ / *ai*

§ 667. LATE LATIN a COUNTERTONIC < LATIN AND GERMANIC ā, ă.

Ref.	Position.	G.R.	O.F. I.	O.F. II.	Mid. F.	Mod. F.	Class.	Late.	O.F. II.	Mid. F.	Mod. F.
§ 182	BLOCKED and FREE	>a	a	a	a	a	maritum	*abbate maritu	abęθ>abę mariθ>mari	abę mari	abę abbé maRi
§§ 565,	lengthened before s effaced			ā	>	α		*bastire	bastir>bātir / bāstir	bātir>bāti(r) / bāstir	>batiR / bātir
	In hiatus in Old French, cf. §§ 242, 238, 409, 484 (ii)										
§§ 182, 442-6	before n or m + cons. in O.F. I.	a	ā	ã	ã̄	>ā	sanitatem	sanętate	sãnęθ>sãntę	>sãtę / sante	>sātę / santé
§ 444	before n or m intervocalic in Mid. F.	a	ā	ã	>	a		*annata	ãnę̈ę>ãnęę / annede, annee	>ãnę̈ / annee	ane / année
§§ 182, 387, 534-7	+ʮ (<ɫ, ḷ +cons.)	aɫ, aj	>	au	>ǫ	ǫ	saɫtare	saɫtare	saɫter>sauter	>sǫtę(r) / sauter	sǫtę / sauter

§	Condition											
§ 182, 493, 417	FREE *preceded by* PALATAL	> ę	> ę̊	ę̊	ę̊	ę̊	e		*kaβallu caballum*	tšęval > šęval *cheval*	šęval *cheval*	šęval *cheval*
§ 417	but followed by l or r or tonic e	a	a	a	a	a	a	kalēre *calere*	kalęrǫ	tšaleir > tšaloir > šalųer *chaleir, chaloir*	> šalųer *chaloir*	šalwaR *chaloir*
	BLOCKED and FREE before PALATAL											
§§ 182, 198	before ‿ inter-vocalic	a	a	a	a	a	a, a	paleărium	paljariŋ	paljier > palję *paillier*	> palję(r) *paillier*	palję > paŋę *paillier*
§§ 182, 198, 442-44	before ŋ inter-vocalic in O.F. (for *plaignant,* etc., cf. §§ 445, 941)	a	ã̄	ã̄	>	a	a	aŋŋęllos *agnellos*	aŋŋęllos	ãŋę+s > ãŋęaus > ãŋęaus *agnels, agneaus*	> ãŋęǫ(s, z) *agneaux, aingneaux*	> aŋǫ *agneaux*
§§ 279, 466-69	before ŋ + cons.	> ai	> ãi	> ę̃i	ę̃	ę̃	ę̃	saŋktītatem *sanctitatem*	saŋtętate	sãįntę(ð)ę(θ) sęįntęę ; *saintete*	sętętę *saincteté*	sętę *sainteté*
§§ 182, 404, 528-9	+ jod prae-consonantal (for **ai** in hiatus, cf. §§ 239, 531)	ai	ai	> ę̊	> ę̊	ę̊	ę̊	mansiōnem *mansionem*	masjǫne	maizun > mę̃zũn	mę̃zũ(n)	> mę̃zǫ *maison*

§ 668. ǫ TONIC < LATIN ŏ, GERMANIC ŏ AND ǒ (§ 180).

Ref.	Position.	G.R.	O.F. L.	O.F. II.	Mid. F.	Mod. F.	Latin. Class. / Late.	O.F. II.	Mid. F.	Mod. F.
§ 580	A. BLOCKED	ǫ	ǫ	ǫ	ǫ	ǫ	mŏrtem mǫrt	mǫrt	> mǫr(t)	mǫR *mort*
	(before *effaced* s)	> ǫ	> u	> ū	ǫ / > ū̃	ǫ	tŏstum tǫstǫm	tǫst > tǫt	> tǫ̃(t) *tost*	tǫ *tôt*
§§ 426, 460-2	before **n** or **m** + *cons.*	ǫɫ	ǫɫ	ǫu̯ > u	u	> ǭ u	pŏntem pǫnte	punt > pūnt	> pũn(t) *pont*	> pǭ *pont*
§§ 387, 548	+ u̯ (< ɫ + *cons.*)						fŏlles fǫlles	fǫ+s > fǫus > fus *fǫls, fǫns*	> fu(s, z) *fons*	fu *fous*
§§ 225-227, 550-553, 585	B. FREE		> 'ue	> ö̂	ö̂	< ǭ / ǫ̂	bŏvem bǫβe *bovem*	buef > bö̂f *buef, boef, beuf*	bö̂f *beuf, bœuf*	> bö̂f *boeuf*
	before **n** or **m** *final or inter-vocalic,* cf. §§ 477, 478, 599						*pǫtet	puet > pö̂t *puet, poet, peut*	> pö̂(t) *peut, peult*	pö̂ *peut*
§§ 410, 550-3, 585	C. BLOCKED and FREE before PALATALS + j *final and intervocalic*	'uoj	> 'uej	> ö̂j	öj	ö̂j > ö̂j	ŏkulum ǫklụ *oculum*	uej > ö̂j *ueil, oeil*	ö̂j *oeil*	> ö̂j > ö̂j *ocil*
							fŏlia fǫlja *folia*	fuejə > fö̂jə *fueille, feuille*	fö̂jə *fueille*	> fö̂j > fö̂j *feuille*
§§ 387, 410, 556, 7	+ u̯ (< j + *cons.*)	'ioj	> 'ue+ >	'ueu / 'ieu / > jö̂	jö̂	jǫ̈	ŏkulos ǫklǫs *oculos*	uejts > ueuts > leuts > jös *ueilz, ieus, etc.*	jö̂(s, z) *yeulx*	jö̂ *yeux*
§§ 410, 411, 515, 6	+ *jod*	'ioj	> 'uej) üi >	> wi	wi	wi	nŏktem nǫχte *noctem*	> nüit > nụit >	nwi(t) *nuict*	nwi *nuit*
							hŏdie ǫje	uii > wi *ui*	wi *hui*	wi *lui*

Ref.	Position.	G.R.	O.F. I.	O.F. II.	Mid. F.	Mod. F.	Class.	Late.	O.F. II.	Mid. F.	Mod. F.
§§ 184, 234	ǫ and ọ Blocked and Free (but cf. §582)	ǫ	>	u	u	u	tŏrmentum	tǫrmentu	> tǫrment > turmént	> turmãã(t) *tourment*	> tuRmã *tourment*
							(mŏrīrī)	*morire	mǫrir > murir *mourir*	murir > muri(r) *mourir*	> muRiR *mourir*
	(In hiatus in Old French, cf. §§ 242, 238, 409)						dūbitāre	doβetare	doter > duter	dute(r) *douter*	> dute *douter*
							nōdāre	nodare	nǫ(ð)er > nuer	nue(r) *nouer*	> nue > nwe *nouer*
§§ 426, 459-62, 464, 437	ǫ and ọ before **n** and **m** + *consonant*	ǫ	> u	> ũ	> ũ̃	> ɔ̃	fŏntānam	fǫntana	funtaine > fũntẽine *fontaine*	> fũtẽnę *fontaine*	> fõtẽn *fontaine*
							fŭndāre	fǫndare	funder > fúnder *fonder*	> fũde(r) *fonder*	> fõde *fonder*
§§ 426, 459-63	ǫ and ọ before **n** and **m** *intervocalic* in Mid. F.	ǫ	> u	> ũ	ũ	> ɔ̃ > ɔ	hŏnōrem	ǫnǫre	unour > uneur > ũnör *onour, onneur*	ũnör *honneur*	> ɔ̃nör > onör *honneur*
							dōnāre	donare	duner > dũner *onneur, onneur*	dũne(r) *donner, donner*	> dõne(r) > dõne *donner*
§§ 234, 387, 547-9	ǫ + ṷ < ł (+ cons.)	ǫł	>	qu > u	u	u	sōlidāre	sǫlędare	sǫłder > sǫuder > suder	> sudę(r) *souder, soulder*	> sudę *souder*
§ 386	ǫ + ṷ < ł (+ cons.)	ǫł	>	u	u	u	kŭłpābilem *culpabilem*	kǫłpable	kǫłpable > kupable *colpable, cupable*	kupablę *coulpable*	kupabl *coupable*
§§ 234, 426, 459-64	ǫ and ọ before **Palatal.** Before ǰ *intervocalic* (cf. also §§ 408, 465)	ǫ	> u	> ũ	ũ	> ɔ̃ > ɔ	*kǫnjāta *cuneata*	*konjata	kunję(ð)ę > kũnjeę *coigniee, coigniee*	> kũnę *coigniee*	> kõnę > konę *cognée*
§ 473	before ŋ (+ cons.)	> ǫi	> ui	> ui	> uę̃	> ǫ̃ > ǫ	pŭ̃ktūra *punctura*	pǫ̃tyra	puintũrę > puintürę *pointure*	puętürę *poincture*	> pwętüR *pointure*
§§ 184, 234	before ǰ *intervocalic*	ǫ	>	u	u	u	būllientem	bǫljente	bǫ‖(ãnt) > bujãnt *boillant, buillant*	> bujã(t) *bouillant*	> bujã *bouillant*
§§ 184, 234, 404, 518-25	+ *jod*	> ǫi	>	uį > ųę	> wę	> {wa / wa}	mŏdiŏlum	mǫjǫlų	moiuel > mųęǫl *moiuel, moieul*	mwęǫl > mwęjǫ(l) *moieul*	> mwajɔ *moyeu*
							tōnsiōnem	tǫsjǫne	tǫįzun > tųęzũn *toison*	twęzũ(n) *toison*	> twazɔ̃ *toison*

§ 670. LATE LATIN ǫ TONIC < LATIN ŏ, ŭ, GERMANIC ŭ.

Ref.	Position	G.R.	O.F. I.	O.F. II.	Mid. F.	Mod. F.	Class. Latin	Late Latin	O.F. II.	Mid. F.	Mod. F.
§ 184	A. BLOCKED (in Late Latin and Early Gallo-Roman)	ǫ	>	u	u	u	gŭttam *guttam*	gǫtta	gǫtę > gutę *gote > gute*	gutę *goutte*	> gut *goutte*
							kohortem *cohortem*	kǫrte	kǫrt > kurt *cort, curt*	kur(t) *court, cour*	> kuR *cour*
							kŭbitum *cubitum*	kǫβętu	kǫdę > kudę *cude, code*	kudę *coude, coubde*	> kud *coude*
§§ 426, 459-62, 437	before n or m + cons.	ǫ >	u	> ũ	ū̃	> ǫ̃	fŭndus *fundus*	fǫndųs	funts > fũns *funz, fonz*	> fũ(s, z) *fonds*	> fǫ̃ *fonds*
§§ 426, 459-63	before n or m inter-vocalic in Mid. F.	ǫ >	u	> ũ	ũ	> ǫ	sŭmmam *summam*	sǫmma	sumę > sũmę *some, sume, somme*	sũmę *somme*	> sǫm(ə) > sǫm *somme*
§§ 184, 386	+ ʯ (< ɫ + cons.)	ǫʯ	>	u	u	u	pŭlwěrem *pulverem*	pǫɫβęre	puɫdrę > pudrę *poldre, puldre, poudre*	pudrę *poudre, pouldre*	pudR *poudre*
§§ 225-230, 541,2 585	B. FREE	ǫu	>	ęu > ö	ö	< ǫ̈ ǫ̈	ĭllōrŭm *illorum*	ęllǫrų	lour > leur > lör *lor, lur, lour, leur*	lör *leur*	> lœR *leur*
							nōddŭm *noddum*	nǫdų	nou(θ) > neu > nö *nox(t), neu*	nö *noeud*	nö *noeud*
§§ 426, 436, 59-62	before n or m final	ǫ	> u	> ũ	ũ	> ǫ̃	dōnŭm *donum*	dǫnų	dun > dũn *don, dun*	dũ(n) *don, dun, doun*	> dǫ̃ *don*

§§		ǫ	>u	>ū	>ü	>ǫ̃ >ǫ	dǫnat	>ǫ̃>ǫ>dōnat	duneθ>dūne *done(t), dame(t), donne, dunne*	dūne *donne, doune*	>dǫ̃ne >dǫn *donne*
§§ 426, 459-64	before **n** or **m** *intervocalic* in Mid. F.	ǫ	>u	>ū	>ü	>ǫ̃ >ǫ	dǫnat	dōnat	dūne	dūne	>dǫ̃ne >dǫn *donne*
§§ 184, 489	before a *labial cons.* (for *lupum* cf. § 343)	ǫu	>u	u	u	u	lǫpa	lūpa	luvę *love, luve, louve*	luvę *louve*	>luv *louve*
§§ 198, 184	**C. Blocked and Free** before a **Palatal** + ļ	ǫ̣	^	u]	u]	>uj	konǫk(u̯)la *conocula*	kolūkula *colucula*	kęnuļę *kenoille, kenuille, kenouille*	kęnuļę *quenouille*	>kǝnuļ] > kǝnuj *quenouille*
§§ 184, 386	+ u̯ (< ļ + *cons.*)	ǫ̣	^	u	u	u	*fǫ+ɟere *fulgere*	(fu+gur)	fu]dre > fudrę *foildre, fuildre, foudre*	fudrę *foudre*	fudR *foudre*
§§ 426, 459-63	before ŋ *intervocalic* (cf. also § 465)	ǫ >	u	>ū	ū	>ǫ̃ >ǫ	βerekǫnɑ	werekūndia *verecundia*	vergunę > vergūṇę *vergoigne, vergongne, etc.*	vergūṇę *vergogne, vergongne, etc.*	>vergǭṇǝ > veRgǫṇ *vergogne*
§§ 279, 426, 473-5; § 406	{ before ŋ + *cons.* / before ŋ *final*	ǫi > / ǫ(ŋ)	>ui	>uī	>uē	>wę	pǫŋtǫ / konjǫ	puŋktum *punctum* / kūnēum *cuneum*	puint > puīnt *puint, point* / kuŋ > kuiŋ > kuīŋ *cuing, coing*	puę̃(t) *point, poinct* / >kuę̃(n) *coing*	>pwę̃ *point* / >kwę̃ *coing*
§§ 184, 339, 404, 518-25	+ *jod*	^	ǫi > ui > ųę > we			wa / wa / ę̃	nǫ̣ę / konnǫ̣ʃere	nūkem *nucem* / (kōanõskere) *cognoscere*	noits > nǫ̣es *nuis* / kunǫistrę > kūnǫ̣etrę *conoistre*	nwę̃(s, z) *noix* / kūnę̃trę *conoistre, congnoistre*	>nwɑ, nwɑ *noix* / >kǫnętR *connaître*

§671. LATE LATIN ų TONIC < LATIN AND GERMANIC ū.

Ref.	Position.	G.R.	O.F. I.	O.F. II.	Mid. F.	Mod. F.	Latin Class.	Latin Late.	O.F. II.	Mid. F.	Mod. F.
§ 183	BLOCKED and FREE	>	ü	ü	ü	ü	nūllŭm / mūrŭm	nųllų / mųrụ	nül / mür	nül / mür	nül / müR
§§ 183, 456, 457	before **n** or **m** *final* or + *cons.*	>	ü	ü >	ü̃ >	õ̥ *un*	ūnŭm	ųnų	ün > *juing*	ũn > *juing*	õ̥ *un*
§§ 183, 456, 457	before **n** or **m** *intervocalic* in Mid. F.	>	ü	ü	ü̃ > ü	ü	ūnam	ųna	üne > *nus*	üne > üne	> ün *une*
§§ 183, 386	+ **u̯** < ɫ + *cons.*	>	ü+	> ü			nūllŭs	nųllus	nü+s > nüs *nus*		
§§ 183, 407, 435, 476	BLOCKED and FREE before PALATALS; before **ŋ** *final;* before **j** *intervocalic*, cf. 407	>	üi(ŋ)	> üi	> üĩ >	w̃ẽ	jūnium	jųnjų	džũŋ > žũiŋ *juing, juign*	> žüĩn *juing*	žw̃ẽ *juin*
§§ 183, 404, 514-16	+ *jod*	>	üi	> üï ⋮ i (§ 516)	wi	wi	frūktum / *fructum*	frųxtų	früit > früit > *fruit*	frwi(t) *fruit, fruict*	fRwi *fruit*

§ 672. LATE LATIN ŭ COUNTERTONIC < LATIN AND GERMANIC ū.

Ref.	Position.	G.R.	O.F. I.	O.F. II.	Mid. F.	Mod. F.	Class.	Late.	O.F. II.	Mid. F.	Mod. F.
§ 183	Blocked and Free	>	ü	ü	ü	ü	mūrāliɑ	myrɑljɑ	müralę *muraille*	müralę *muraille*	müra]>müRɑ] *muraille*
	(for ü in hiatus, cf. §§ 238, 241)	>	ü	ü	ü	>ŏ	pūrgāre	purgɑre	purdźier>purźier *purgier*	>purźę(r) *purgier*	>püRźę *purgier*
§§ 183, 456-8	before n and m + consonant	>	ü	ü >	ū̃	>ö̃	(lūnɑe diem)	*lunęs die *lunis diem*	lüunzi *lunsdi*	lũndi *lundi* >	lɵ̃di *lundi*
§ 457	before n and m intervocalic in Mid. F.	>	ü	ü >	ũ̈	>ü	fūmāre	fumɑre	fümer	fūmęr>fümę(r) *fumer*	fümę *fumer*
§ 382	+ ų (< +,] + cons.)	>	ü+, üj	>ü	ü	ü		*pulęʝellɑ *pulicella*	püteʝellę>püselę *pucelle*	püselę *pucelle*	>püsel *pucelle*
	before] intervocalic (cf. §§ 407, 515)										
§§ 183, 404, 339, 514-16	Blocked and Free + jod	>	üi	>ųi	ẅi	ẅi	*ustʝɑrjų *ustiarium*	uisier>ẅisier *uissier*	>ẅisę(r) *huissier*	>wisę *huissier*
	[for lutter, etc., cf. § 517]				ẅi i	ẅi	*esfruxtare *exfructare*	e(z)früitier>efrụitier *esfruitier*	efrite(r) *effriter*	>efRitę *effriter*

§673. Late Latin **au** Tonic < Latin and Germanic **au.**

Ref.	Position.	G.R.	O.F. I.	O.F. II.	Mid. F.	Mod. F.	Class. Latin.	Late.	O.F.	Mid. F.	Mod. F.
§ 505	Blocked and Free	>ǫ	ǫ	ǫ	ǫ	ǫ	aurum	auru	ǫr	ǫr	ǫR
§ 579	before *intervoclic* **v** and **z**				ǫ	ǫ	pauper / kausam *causa*	pauper kausa	povrę / tšǫzę *chose* >>	povrę, pauvrę / šǫzę *chose*	povR *pauvre* / šǫz *chose*
§ 578	*in iiuatus*			>ǫ	>u	u		*gauta	džǫ(ð)ę > žǫę *joe* >	žū(ę) *joue* >	žu *joue*
§§ 505, 426, 459-62	before **n** or **m** + *cons.*	>ǫ	>ǫ>u	>ū	ū	>ǭ······ǫ	G. *haunita	hunte > hūnte *honte, hunte* >	hũtę *honte*	ǭt *honte*
§ 463	before **n** or **m** *intervocalic* in Mid. F.					ǫ	*sauma (§ 350)	sǫmę > sūmę *some, sume*	sūmę *somme*	sǫm(ə)>sǫm *somme*
§§ 505, 368, 547, 8	+ ų <(ł + *cons.*) (for *paucum* cf. § 549)	>ǫł	>ǫł>u		u	u	kaules *caules*	kaules	tšǫłs>tšǫus>šus *chols, chous, chox*	>šu(s, z) *choux*	>šu *choux*
§§ 505, 404, 518-25	Blocked and Free + *jod*	>ǫi	ǫi	>ųę	>wę	>wa / wa	gaudia	gaudja	džoię>žųęę *joie*	>žwę̃(ę) *joie*	>žwa, žwa *joie*

§ 674. Late Latin **au** Countertonic < Latin and Germanic **au.**

Ref.	Position.	G.R.	O.F. I.	O.F. II.	Mid. F.	Mod. F.	Class.	Latin. Late.	O.F. II.	Mid. F.	Mod. F.
§ 505	BLOCKED and FREE	> ǫ	ǫ	ǫ	ǫ	ǫ		*lauraríų *laurarium	lǫrier > lǫrįer *lorier*	> lǫrįę(r) *laurier*	> lǫRįę *laurier*
§ 579	before **z** or **v**			ǫ........	........ǫ	o		*ausare *ausare	ǫzęr *oser*	> ǫzę(r) *oser*	> ǫzę *oser*
§ 578	*in hiatus*			ǫ	> u	u	laudare	laudare	lǫ̌ęr > lǫer	> luę(r) *luer, louer*	> luę > lwę *louer*
§§ 505, 459-62	before **n** or **m** + consonant	> ǫ	ǫ > u	> ū̃	> ū̃	> ǭ		(G. *haunita) huntous > hūntōs *honteus, hunteus*	huntous > hūntōs	> hūtö(s, z) > *honteux*	ǭtǫ̈ *honteux*
§ 463	before **n** or **m** *intervocalic in* Mid. F.	> ǫ	ǫ > u	> ū	ū	> ǫ̃ > ǭ		*saumaríų *saumarium	sǫmier > sūmįer *somier*	> sūmįę(r) *sommier*	> sǫ̃mįę > sǫmįę *sommier*
§§ 505, 404, 518-25	BLOCKED and FREE + *jod*	> ǫi	ǫi	> y̨ę	> wę (wą)	wa (wą)		*autẹllos *aucellos (§ 187)	ǫizę+s > y̨ęzę̆aus *oisels, oiseaus, oiseax*	> węzę̆ǫ(s, z) *oiseaux, oiseaulx*	> wazǫ *oiseaux*

LABIAL CONSONANTS.

§ 675. p.

Ref.	Position.	G.R.	O.F. I.	O.F. II.	Mid. F.	Mod. F.	Class. Latin.	Late.	O.F. II.	Mid. F.	Mod. F.
§ 202	INITIAL *of word or syllable*	p	p	p	p	p	pūrum	pūrų	pür	pür	püR *pür*
§§ 611-16, 623	*Become final*	p	p	p	>—	—	ta+pam	ta+pa	ta+pę > taupę *taupe*	topę *taupe*	> tǫp *taupe*
							kampum *campum*	kampų *campu*	tšănp > šănp *champ*	> šã(p) *champ*	> šã *champ*
§§ 335, 372	INTERVOCALIC *and* + r	> v	v	v	v	v	rīpam	rīpa	rivę	rivę	> Riv *rive*
							lĕpŏrem	lĕpǫre	lievrę > ljevrę *lièvre*	> ljevrę *lièvre*	> ljevR *lièvre*
§§ 206, 335, 617-23	*Become final*	> f	f	f	(f)	f	kaput *caput*	kapų	tšief > šef *chief*	> šęf(f, v) > *chief*	šef, šę *chef*

§												
§ 366	INTERVOCALIC GROUP **pp**	>**p**	**p**	**p**	**p**	**p**	**kŭppa** *cuppa*	**koppa**	**kopę > kupę** *cope, cupe, coupe*	**kupę** *coupe*	>**kup** *coupe*
§§ 617-623	*Become final*	>**p**	**p**	>—(**p**)	**p**	—		***drappu**	**drap**	>**dra(p)** *drap*	**dRa** *drap*
§ 372	**pl** [for **pr**, cf. above]	>**bl**	**bl**	**bl**	**bl**	**bl**	**dúplum**	**dɔplu**	**doblę > dublę** *doble, duble, double*	**dublę** *double*	>**dubl** *double*
§ 373	*p before other consonants is assimilated or falls*						**sęptem**	**sępte**	**sęt**	**sęt** *sept*	**sęt** *sept*
§§ 194, 203, 305, 373	**pj**	>**ptš > tš**	**tš**	>**š**	**š**	**š**	**sapiam**	**sapja**	**satšę > sašę** *sache*	**sašę** *scache*	>**saš** *sache*
§ 364	*p middle of three before* **r**	**p**	**p**	**p**	**p**	**p**	**rũmpęre**	**rompęre**	**rumprę > rũprę** *rompre, rumpre*	>**rũprę** *rompre*	>**rõpR** *rompre*
§ 365	*Elsewhere*	>—	—	—	—	—	**kórpus** *corpus*	**korpus**	**kɔrs** *cors*	>**kɔr(s, z)** *cors*	**koR** *cors*

17

§ 676. CLASSICAL LATIN **b**, LATE LATIN **b** AND *β*.

Ref.	Position.	G.R.	O.F. I.	O.F. II.	Mid. F.	Mod. F.	Class.	Late.	O.F. II.	Mid. F.	Mod. F.
§ 202	INITIAL *of word or syllable*	b	b	b	b	b	**barbam**	**barba**	**barbę**	**barbę**	**baRb** *barbe*
§ 206, 611-16	*Become final*	> p	p	p	> —		**kŏrbum** *corbum*	**kǫrbu**	**kǫrp** *corp*		
§§ 332, 333, 343, 344	INTERVOCALIC *before* o, u *and after tonic* u	β > —	—	—	—	—	(**tabānŭm**)	**taβone*	**taun > taūn** *taon*	> **tã(n)** *taon*	> **tã** *taon*
							(**nūbes**)	**nuβa*	**nüę**	> **nü** *nue*	**nü** *nue*
§§ 332, 333, 343, 345, 372, 189	*before* e, i, a *and* r	β > v	v	v	v	v	**habēre**	**aβere**	**aveir > avoir > avụẹr**	> **avwẹr** *avoir*	> **avwaR** *avoir*
							libram	**liβra**	**livrę**	**livrę**	> **livR** *livre*

§§ 333, 343, 345, 206	*before* **e, i** *become final*	**β > v > f**	**f**	**f**			**trabem**	**traβe**	**tręf**		
§ 366	INTERVOCALIC GROUP **bb**	>	**b**	**b**	**b**	**b**		***abbate**	**abę(θ)** *abbe*	**abę** *abbe*	**abę** *abbé*
§ 372	**bl** [for **br** *cf. above*]	**bl**	**bl**	**bl**	**bl**	**bl**	**tabulam**	**tabla**	**tablę**	**tablę**	> **tabl** *table*
	before other consonants	*is assimilated or falls*					**dēbĭta**	**dęβęta**	**dętę > dętę**	**dętę** *debte*	> **dęt** *dette*
§§ 305, 203, 194, 373	**bj**	> **bdž** > **dž**	**dž**	> **ž**	**ž**	**ž**	**rŭbĕum**	**rọbjų**	**rọdžę > ružę** *roge, ruge*	**ružę** *rouge*	> **Ruž** *rouge*
§ 364	*Middle of three* + **r**	**b**	**b**	**b**	**b**	**b**	**membrum**	**membrų**	**mēmbrę > mānbrę**	**mābrę** *mambre, membre*	> **mābR** *membre*
§ 365	*Elsewhere*	> —	—	—	—	—		***presbęter** *presbyter*	**pręstrę > prētrę**	**prētrę** *prestre*	> **prętR** *prêtre*

§ 677. CLASSICAL LATIN *v w > β*, §§ 186, 187.

Ref.	Position.	G.R.	O.F. I.	O.F. II.	Mid. F.	Mod. F.	Latin — Class.	Latin — Late.	O.F. II.	Mid. F.	Mod. F.
§ 189	INITIAL of *word* or *syllable* [cf. also § 189]	β > v	v	v	v	v	**wentum** *ventum* ; **sěrwire** *servire*	βentu ; seρβire	věnt > vänt ; servir	> vã̌(t) *vent, vant* ; servi(r)	> vã̌ *vent* ; > sęRviR *servir*
§ 187 (ii)	INTERVOCALIC before **o, u** [cf. also § 188]	—	—	—	—	—	**pawōrem** *pavorem*	paоre	paour > peör *paour, paor, peeur*	> pör *peur*	> pöR *peur*
§§ 345, 372	before **e, i, a** and **r**	β > v	v	v	v	v	**lawāre** *lavare* ; **wīwere** *vivere*	laβare ; βiβ(e)re	laver ; vìvrę	> lavę(r) *laver* ; vìvrę	> lavę *laver* ; > vivR *vivre*
§§ 345, 206	(+ **e, i**) become *final*	β > v > f	f	f	f	f	**nawem** *navem*	naβe *nef*	nef	nęf (f, v) >	nęf
§ 373	INTERVOCALIC GROUP *before consonant* [cf. also § 187 (i)]	*is assimilated or falls*					**kiwitatem** *civitatem* ; **bōwes** *boves*	tʃiβetate ; boβes	tsitę(θ) > sitę *cité(ė)* ; bues > bös *bues, beus*	sitę *cite* ; bö(s, z) *boeufs*	sitę *cité* ; > bö *boeufs*
§§ 194, 203, 305	**wj** [cf. also § 187 ii (c)]	> βdž > dž	dž	> ž̌	ž̌	ž̌	**kawēa** *cavea*	kaβja	kadžę > kažę *cage*	kažę *cage*	> kaž *cage*
§§ 363, 365	*Middle of three*	> —	—	—	—	—	**pū+werem** *pulverem* ; **sěrwit** *servit*	po+βere ; serβet	po+drę > pudrę ; sęrt	pudrę *poudre* ; > sęr(t)	> pudR *poudre* ; > sęR *sert*

§678. d.

Ref.	Position.	G.R.	O.F. I.	O.F. II.	Mid. F.	Mod. F.	Class.	Latin. Late.	O.F. II.	Mid. F.	Mod. F.
§ 202	INITIAL of word or syllable in L.L. and Early G.R. [but cf. § 350]	d	d	d	d	d	dūrum mandare	durų mandare	dür māndẹr	dür >mādẹ(r)	düR >mādẹ *mander*
§§ 206, 611-16, 623	Become final	>t	t	t	>(t)	—(t)	rīgida tardum	reį(ẹ)da tardų	reidẹ>roidẹ>rųẹdẹ tart	>rwẹdẹ>rẹdẹ *roide, rede, raide* >tar(t) *tard*	>Rẹd *raide* >taR *tard*
§§ 333, 346, 347, 372	INTERVOCALIC and + r and w *Intervocalic become final*	>ð >ð>θ	^ ^	— —	— —	— —	nūdam nūdum	nųda nųdų	nūðẹ>nüẹ nūθ>nü	>nü *nue* nü	nü *nue* nü
§§ 309, 194	INITIAL GROUP dj	>dž	dž	>ž	ž	ž	diūrnum	djornų	džǫrn; žur *jorn, jor, jur*	žur *jour*	žuR *jour*
§§ 367, 194, 611-23	INTERVOCALIC GROUP d + s *final*	>ts	ts	>s	>(z)	—(z)	pēdes	pẹdes	piets>pjes *pįez*	>pjẹ(s, z) *pies, pieds*	>pjẹ *pieds*
§§ 309(ii), 339	dj *intervocalic* [for **ndj** cf. **nj**]	>j>ị					hŏdie	ǫdje>ǫje	>üi>wi *ui, hui*	wi *huy*	wi *hui*
§ 373	d + other consonant (cf. also §§ 744-766)	>—					*radītjina* *radicīna*	*radįtjįna* *radicīna*	ratsinẹ>rasinẹ *racine*	>rasinẹ *racine*	>Rasin *racine*
§ 364	MIDDLE OF THREE + r	d	d	d	d	d	mŏrdere	mǫrdere	mǫrdẹ	mǫrdẹ	>mǫRdR *mordre*
§ 365	*Elsewhere*	>—					manducare mandūkare *manducare*	manducare mandųkare	māndžier>mānžjer *mangier*	>māžẹ(r) *mangier*	māžẹ *manger*

§ 679. t.

Ref.	Position.	G.R.	O.F. I.	O.F. II.	Mid. F.	Mod. F.	Class. Latin	La:e.	O.F. II.	Mid. F.	Mod. F.
§ 202	INITIAL of word or syllable in L.L. and Early G.R. [but cf. § 350]	t	t	t	t	t	tū / pŏrta	tu / pǫrta	tü / pǫrtę	tü / portę	tü / >pǫRt *porte*
	[Fort preceded by palatal, cf. § 316]						dūbĭtāre	dopętare	dotęr > dutęr *doter*	dutę(r) *doubter*	>dutę *douter*
§§ 611-616, 623	Become final	t	t	t	>	—(t)	fŏrtem	fǫrte	fǫrt	>fǫr(t)	>fǫR *fort*
§§ 335, 346, 347, 372	INTERVOCALIC and + r, n	>d>ð	>	—	—	—	wīta *vita* / patrem	βīta / patre	vidę>vię *vide, vie* / peðrę>perę *pedre, pere*	>vi *vie* / perę	vi *vie* / per>pęR *père*
§§ 335, 346, 347	Become final	>d>ð>θ	>	—			grātum	gratų	gręθ>grę *gręt, gre*	grę	gRę *gré*
§§ 355, 356, 611-16, 623	Latin final t after consonant or unstressed e and i after consonant	t	t	t	>	—(t)	sŭnt / tĕnet	sǫnt / tęnet	sunt>sūnt / tient>tjēnt	>sū(t) *sont* / >tjē(t) *tient*	>sǭ *sont* / tjē *tient*

§§	Elsewhere	>θ	θ	>—	t	t	portat	portat	portę(θ)>portę	portę	pọRt *porte*
§§ 346, 347, 355, 6	*Elsewhere*						**portat**	portat	portę(θ)>portę	**portę** *porte*	**pọRt** *porte*
§ 366	INTERVOCALIC GROUP / tt *intervocalic*	>t	t	t	>(t)	t	(tō̆tam)	*tǫtta	tǫtę>tutę	tutę *toute*	>tut *toute*
§§ 366, 611-623	tt *become final*	>t	t	t	>(t)	—(t)	(tō̆tum)	*tǫttu	tǫt>tut	tu(t) *tout*	tu *tout*
§§ 367, 194; 611-23	t + s *final*	>ts	ts	>s	>(z)	—(z)	ad satis	ad sates	asets>asę	asę(s, z) *assez, assez, assez*	>asę *assez*
§§ 308, 194	tj *initial*	>ts	ts	>s	s	s	fortia	fǫrtja>fǫrtsja	fǫrtsę>fǫrsę	forsę *force*	>fǫRs *force*
§ 308	tj *intervocalic*	>d͡z> (j)z	z	z	z	z	ratiōnem	ratjone>ratsjone	raizun>rezūn *raison, reson*	ręzū(n) *raison*	>Ręzǫ̃ *raison*
§§ 308, 206	*Become final*	>(l)s	s	s	>(z)	—(z)	prĕtium	prętju>prętsju	>pris	>pri(s, z) *pris, prix*	>pRi *prix*
	[For tˡl cf. §§ 360, 372]										
§ 364	MIDDLE OF THREE + r / *Elsewhere*	t	t	t	t	t	aɫterum	aɫtęrų	aɫtrę>autrę	>ǫtrę *autre*	>ǫtR *autre*
§ 365	*Elsewhere*	>—	—				testimōnium	testemǫ̃nų	tę(z)muŋ>tęmuiŋ *tesmoing, tesmuing*	>tęmuę̃(n) *tesmoing*	tęmwę̃ *témoin*
	[For sts cf. § 367]										

§ 680. s.

Ref.	Position.	G.R.	O.F. I.	O.F. II.	Mid. F.	Mod. F.	Latin. Class.	Late.	O.F. II.	Mid. F.	Mod. F.
§ 202	INITIAL of word and syllable	s	s	s	s	s	sŏror	sǫror	suer > sör	sör *sœur*	sŏR *sœur*
§§ 611-623	Become final [For intervocalic **ks**, cf. § 325]	s	s	s	> —	—	ŭrsam	ǫrsa	ǫrsę > ursę	ursę *ourse*	> uRs *ourse*
							kŭrsum *cu sum*	korsų	kǫrs > kurs *cors, curs*	> kur(s, z) *cours*	> kuR *cours*
§ 334	INTERVOCALIC	> z	z	z	z	z		*ausare	ǫzęr > ǫzęr	> ǫzę(r) *oser*	> ǫzę *oser*
§§ 334, 338, 617-23	Become final	> z > s	s	s	> (z)	— (z)	risum	risų	ris	> rī(s, z) *ris, ri*	> Ri *ri*
§§ 361, 377-9	INITIAL GROUP	(e)s + cons.	>	ę + cons.	—	—	spatha	(e)spata	(e)spe(ð)ę > epęę *(e)spede, espee*	> epę *espee*	epę *épée*
§ 366	INTERVOCALIC GROUP ss intervocalic	s	s	s	s	s	prĕssa	prĕssa	pręsę *presse*	presę *presse*	> pRęs *presse*

§§ 366, 617-23	ss become final	s	s	s	>(z)	—	bassum	bassu	bas	bā(s, z) _bas_	>ba _bas_
§§ 377, 378	s before voiced cons. [For z'r cf. § 370]	>	z > ð >	—	—	—		*męskǫlare _misculare_	mę(ð)lęr > mêler _mesler, medler_	mêlę(r) _mesler_	>mêlę _mêler_
§§ 377, 378	Before breathed cons. [For sts cf. § 365, for s'r cf. § 370]	s	s	> —	—	—	fęstam	fęsta	fęstę > fêtę _feste > fête_	fêtę _feste_	>fêt _fête_
§ 314	sj	> ẑ > (i̯)z > z	z	z	z	z	mansiǫnem	masjǫne	maizun > męzũn _maison_	>męzũ(n) _maison_	>mêzõ _maison_
§ 315	ssj, stj, skj	> ŝ > (i̯)s > s	s	s	s	s	messiǫnem	messjǫne	meisun > moisũn > mmęsũn _meisson, moisson_	mwęsũ(n) _moisson_	>mwasõ _moisson_
§§ 318, 194, 617-23	s final after ḷ, ŋ	>ts	ts	>s	>(z)	(z)	filiũs	filjǫs	fits > fis _filz, fiz_	>fi(s, z) _fils, filz_	>fi; fis _fils_
§§ 367, 194, 617-23	t, d + s final	>ts	ts	>s	>(z)	(z)	ad satis	ad satęs	asets > asę _asses, assets_	>asę(s, z) _assez_	>asę _assez_
§§ 365, 194, 617-23	(r)n, (n)n + s final	>ts	ts	>s	>(z)	(z)	annos	annǫs	ãnts > ãns _anz_	>ā(s, z) _ans_	>ã _ans_
§§ 611-623	s final elsewhere	s	s	s	>(z)	(z)		*drappǫs	dras _dras_	>drā(s, z) _draps_	>dRa _draps_

§ 681. r.

Ref.	Position.	G.R.	O.F. I.	O.F. II.	Mid. F.	Mod. F.	Class. Latin	Late.	O.F. II.	Mid. F.	Mod. F.
§ 394	INITIAL of word or syllable	r	r	r	r	> R	ridere	rīdere	ri(ð)rẹ > rirẹ	rirẹ	> RiR *rire*
§ 394	INTERVOCALIC	r	r	r	r	> R	amāram / *amara*	ɑmɑrɑ	âmerẹ	> âmerẹ	> amęR *amère*
§§ 400-403	Become final / After ẹ, yẹ in poly-syllables	r	r	r …(j)	> — …z (cf. § 399)	—	pórtare	portare	pọrter	> portẹ(r) *porter*	> pọRtẹ *porter*
							operárium	operariụ	ọvrier > uvrier	> uvriẹ(r) *ouvrier*	> uvRi(j)ẹ *ouvrier*
§§ 394, 400-402	After i, ö	r	r	r	(r)	> R	sentire	sentire	sẽntir > sãntir	sãnti(r) *sentir*	> sãtiR *sentir*
								*portatọre	portẹeur > portẹör	portö(r) *porteur*	> pọRtọR *porteur*
§ 394	Elsewhere [cf. also § 401]	r	r	r	r	> R	pūrum	purụ	pūr *pur*	pür *pur*	> püR *pur*
§ 394, 366	INTERVOCALIC GROUP rr [For tr, dr cf. § 372]	rr	> r	r	r	> R	férrum	ferrụ	fẹr *fer*	fẹr *fer*	> fẹR *fer*
§ 394, 396-8	r before cons.	r	r	r (ɹ)	r (ɹ)	> R	partem	parte	part, [paɹt > pãt], *part*	par(t) *part*	> paR *part*
§ 313	rj [For -ariūm cf. § 26]	> ɾ̃ > (j)r	r	r	r	> R	warium / *varium*	βarjụ	vair > vẹr *vair*	vẹr *vair*	> vẹR̃ *vair*

PALATAL CONSONANTS.

§ 682. j.

Ref.	Position.	G.R.	O.F. I.	O.F. II.	Mid. F.	Mod. F.	Class. Latin.	Latin. Late.	O.F. II.	Mid. F.	Mod. F.
A §§ 203, 194	LATIN JOD INITIAL *of word*	>dž	dž	>ž	ž	ž	jam	ja(m)	dža>ža *ja*	ža *ja*	ža *jà*
§ 339	INTERVOCALIC	>	ị				majŭm	maịụ	maị>mẹ	mẹ, mę *mai*	mẹ *mai*
B §§ 219, 305	LATE LATIN JOD INITIAL *of syllable* *After voiced labial*	>dž	dž	>ž	ž	ž	rŭbĕum	rǫbịụ	rǫdžę>ružę *roge, ruge*	ružę *rouge*	>Ruž *rouge*
§§ 219, 305	*After breathed labial*	>tš	tš	>š	š	š	sapĭam	sapịạ	satšę>sašę *sache*	sašę *spache*	>saš *sache*
	After other consonants, cf. §§ 306-315 INTERVOCALIC, cf. §§ 339, 404, 531										
C	GALLO-ROMAN JOD, cf. §§ 339, 404, 530, 531										

VELAR CONSONANTS.

§ 683. CLASSICAL LATIN k > LATE LATIN k, ʃ.

Ref.	Position.	G.R.	O.F. I.	O.F. II.	Mid. F.	Mod. F.	Class. Latin	Late Latin	O.F. II.	Mid. F.	Mod. F.
A	Latin k + e, i, j > L.L. ʃ — INITIAL of word or syllable — k + e, i — §§ 290-292, 194	ʃ > t͡s >	ts	> s	s	s	kentum / *centum*	> ʃentʉ	tsēnt > sãnt / *cent, cant*	> sã(t) / *cent*	> sã / *cent*
			...... > (i̯)ts	> s			rūmikem / *rumicem*	romeʃe	runtsę > rũnsę / *ronce, runce*	> rũsę / *ronce*	> Rõs / *ronce*
	Become middle of three in Early G.R. [For sk + e, i, cf. § 315] — § 293	ʃ > t	t	t	t	t	karkerem / *carcerem*	karʃere	tʃartrę > ʃartrę / *chartre*	šartrę / *chartre*	
	INTERVOCALIC k + e, i — §§ 294-296	ʃ > t͡s > d͡z	> (i)z	z	z	z	plakēre / *placere*	plaʃere	plaizir > plęzir / *plaisir*	plęzi(r) / *plaisir*	> plęziR / *plaisir*
	Become final — §§ 294, 617-23	...... > (i̯)ts	...... > (i̯)ts	> s	> (z)	—(z)	pikem / *picem*	pęʃe	peits > poits / *pęiz, poiz*	> pwę(s, z) / *poix*	> pwa / *poix*
	kj — §§ 306, 194	ʃ > t͡s >	ts	> s	s	s	fakiam / *faciam*	fakjɑ	fatsę > fasę / *face*	fase / *face, fasse*	> fas / *fasse*
	Become final — §§ 611-623	......	......	> s	···(z)	—(z)	brakium / *brachium*	brakjʉ	brats > bras / *bras*	> bra(s, z) / *bras*	> bRa, bRɑ / *bras*
B	Latin k + a, au (G.R. a, au, § 182) — INITIAL of word and syllable — k + a [For Germ. k + a, e, i cf. §§ 298-300] — §§ 298-300	> ʃ > tš	tš	> š	š	š	karrūm / *carrum*	karrʉ	tʃar > ʃar / *char*	šar / *char*	> šaR / *char*
			> š		š	š	kausam / *causa*	kausa	tʃõzę > ʃõzę / *chose*	šõzę / *chose*	> šõz / *chose*
	INTERVOCALIC — Preceded by e, i — §§ 335, 302	g > γ > ʃ / j	> ĭ		1		plikat / *plicat*	plękat	pleieθ > ploię > pluęę / *pleie, plore*	> plwę / *ploye*	> plwa / *ploye*
	by a (< ɑ) — §§ 404, 531	j	j	>	i		bakam / *baca*	baka	baję / *baie*	> baię > bę / *baie*	bę / *baie*
	by o, u, au — §§ 335, 342	> g > γ > —	—	—	-	—	lŏkare / *locare*	lokare	lǫer > luęr / *louer*	> luę(r) / *louer*	> luę / *louer*

Latin **k + o, u** — developments

Sec.	Latin k + o, u	c1	c2	c3	c4	c5	Form 1	Form 2	Form 3	Form 4	Modern French
C §202	INITIAL of word and syllable	k	k	k	k	k	kórpus (*cor*)	korpos (*korpos*)	kors (*cors, corps*)	kǫr(s, z) (*cors*)	> koR (*corps*)
§§611–616, 623	Become final	k	k	k	(k)	> —(k) [cf. §619]	arkūm (*arcum*)	arku (*arku*)	ark (*arc*)	ark(k) (*arc*)	aRk (*arc*)
§364	Become middle of three in Early G.R. + l, r						kirculum (*circulum*)	ʄerk(u)lu	tsęrklę > sęrklę (*cercle*)	sęrklę (*cercle*)	> sęRkl (*cercle*)
§365	Elsewhere						pǫrkos (*porcos*)	pǫrkǫs (*porkos*)	pǫrs (*porcs*)	pǫr(s, z) (*porcs*)	> poR (*porcs*)
§§335, 340–342	INTERVOCALIC [For -ācum, -īcum, cf. §302; for -icum, -ica, cf. §352]	> g > γ —					sękūrum (*securum*)	sękuru (*sekuru*)	sęür > sęür (*seur*)	> sür (*seur*)	süR (*sûr*)
D	INITIAL Group **kl, kr** initial of word [but cf. §202]	persist				kr > kR	krętam (*creta*)	kręta (*kreta*)	kreiðę > kroię > kruęę̄ (*creiđe, croie*)	> krę̄ (*croie*)	> kRę (*craie*)
§366	INTERVOCALIC Group **kk + o, u**	>				k	sikkum (*siccum*)	sękku (*sekku*)	sęk > sęk (*sec*)	sęk (*sec*)	sęk (*sec*)
	kk + a	> tš		> š		š	sikkam (*sicca*)	sękka (*sekka*)	setšę > sęšę (*seche*)	sęšę (*seche*)	> sęš (*seche*)
§§323, 362	**kr**	> gr > γr > jʀ	r	r	> (l)r	R	lakrīmam (*lacrima*)	lakręma (*lakrema*)	lairmę > lęrmę (*larme*)	> larmę (*larme*)	> laRm (*larme*)
§325	**ks (x)** Latin [but cf. §359] Become final [For rāks nx, cf. §326] For rāks nx, cf. §359, 320	> χs > jš	s	s	> (j)s	s	laksare (*laxare*)	laχsare (*laxsare*)	laisier > lęsięr (*laisier, lessier; laissier*)	lęsę(r) (*laisser*)	lęsę (*laisser*)
	(ks final)	> χs > jš	(z)	s		> —	aksem (*axem*)	aχse (*axse*)	ais > ęs (*ais*)	> ę(s, z) (*ais*)	> ę (*ais*)
§324	**kt**	> χt > (j)t̮	t	t	> (j)t	t	traktare (*tractare*)	traχtare (*traxtare*)	traitier > tretier (*traiter; tretier*)	tretę(r) (*traiter*)	tretę (*traiter*)
§§617–23	Become final For nct, rākt cf. §§359, 320					> —(t)	faktum (*factum*)	faχtu (*faxtu*)	fait > fęt (*fait*)	> fę(t) (*faict*)	> fę (*fait*)
§322	**kl** For ku qu cf. §§187, 327–330	> ḷ (§687)									

§ 684. CLASSICAL LATIN **g** > LATE LATIN **g, γ, ǵ, j**.

Ref.	Position.	G.R.	O.F.L.	O.F.II.	Mid.F.	Mod.F.	Class.	Late.	O.F. II.	Mid. F.	Mod. F.
A	Latin **g + e, i, j** L.L. **ǵ, j** INITIAL										
§§ 290-292, 194	of word or syllable **g + e, i, j**	ǵ > dz >	dž	> ž	ž	ž	**gentem**	**ǵente**	džẽnt > žãnt *gent, jant*	> žã(t) *gent*	> žã *gent*
§ 293	*Become middle of three in Early G.R.* [For ng < ng + e, i cf. §§ 311, 687]	ǵ > d	d	d	d	d	**plangere** *plangere*	**plangere**	pláindre > pleindre *plaindre*	> plẽdre *plaindre*	> plẽdR *plaindre*
§ 297	INTERVOCALIC + e, i g > ǵ > j	....	—	—	—	—	(sĭgĭllos)	*se(i)ellos	seẽ+s > seẽ eaus	> seǫ (s, z) *sceaulx*	> sǫ *sceaux*
§ 339		.... > ĭ					(flaḡĕlla)	*flaǵellos	flaleǰs > fleḷ+eaus	flẹǫ(s, z) *flaiaulx*	> flẹǫ *fleaux*
§ 307, 339	**g + i** > jj	> j >	i	i				*esajjų *exagium	esaǰ > esẹ *essai, esse*	esẹ, esẹ *essai*	esẹ *essai*
B	Latin **g + a, au** (G.R. **a, au**, § 182) INITIAL of word and syllable **g + a, e, i** [For Germ. g+a, e, i cf. §§ 298-300]										
§§ 194, 298-300		ǵ > dž	dž	> ž	ž	ž	**ga+bĭnum**	**ga+bęnų**	dža+nę > žaunę *jalne, jaune*	> žǫnę *jaune*	> žǫn *jaune*
§ 333 § 302, 404	INTERVOCALIC > L.L. γ Preceded by e, i	> j	> ĭ	> ĭ	—	—	lĭgat	leγat	leięθ > loię > lięę; *leid, loie*	ᵛlaię > plẽ *plaie*	plẽ *plaie*
§§ 340, 341	Preceded by a	> j	ĭ	j >	{ĭj}	—	plaga	plaγa	plaję		plẹ *plaie*
§§ 340, 341	Preceded by ᵾ	> —	—	—	—	—	rūga	rųγa	rüę	> rü	Rü *rue*
§ 341	Preceded by o	> w >	v	v	v	v	*doγa *dōᵗa	*doγa	doyę > duvę	duvę	> duv *duve*

					Latin	L.L./G.R.	O.F.		Mod. Fr.
C — Latin **g + o, u**									
§ 202 INITIAL *of word and syllable*	g	g	g	g	gŭstum	gǫstʋ	gǫst > gūt *gost, grust*	> gū(t) *goust*	gu *goût*
§§ 206, 617-623 *Become final*	> k	k	> (k)	> k	lǫɐgum	lǫɐgʋ	lunk > lũnk *lonc, lunc*	> lũ(k) *long*	> lõ *long*
§ 364 *Become middle of three in Early G.R. + l, r*	g	g	g	g	ũngūla	ǫɐg(ʋ)lɐ	unglę > ũnglę	> ũglę *ongle*	> õgl *ongle*
§ 365 *Elsewhere*	> —	—	—	—	lǫɐgos	lǫɐgos	luns > lũns	> lũ(s, z) *longs*	> lõ *longs*
§§ 332, 333, 341 INTERVOCALIC > L.L. γ	—	—	—	—	augŭstum	aɣostʋ	aǫst > aut *aost, aust*	> ū(t) *aoust*	u(t) *août*
D									
§ 202 INITIAL GROUP **gl, gr** *initial of word*	gl, gr	gl, gr	gl, gr	gl, gR	grātum	gratʋ	greθ > grę	grę	gRę *gré*
§§ 323, 362 INTERVOCALIC GROUP gr > γr	..ɥr >	(l)r	r	> R	nĭgrum	nеɣrʋ	neir > noir > nųęr	nwęr *noir*	> nwaR *noir*
....r	r	r	r	> R	peregrīnum	peleɣrinʋ; peleɣrinʋ	pęlęrin > pęlęrin	> pęl(ę)rę(n) *pèlerin*	pęlRę *pèlerin*
§ 359 **gm > γm > ɥm**						*saɣmɐ > sauma	sumę > sũmę *some, sume*	sũmę *somme*	> sõm *somme*
[For **gn ɳan** cf. § 321]									
[*For L.L. or Early G.R. groups from Latin* **g** + ě *or* i + **l**, cf. § 322; **g** + **d**, cf. **i** + **d**, cf. § 316]									

NASAL CONSONANTS.

§ 685. m.

Ref.	Position.	G.R.	O.F. I.	O.F. II.	Mid. F.	Mod. F.	Latin. Class.	Latin. Late	O.F. II.	Mid. F.	Mod. F.
§ 202	INITIAL of word and syllable	m	m	m	m	m	matrem	matre	męrę	merę	> męR *mère*
	INTERVOCALIC	m	m	m	m	m	pǫma	pǫma	pume > pūmę *pome, pume*	pūmę *pomme*	> pǫmę > pǫm *pomme*
§ 435	Become final	m	∧	n	(cf. § 436)		famem	tame	fain > fęin *faim, fein*	> fę̃(n) *faim*	> fę̃ *faim*
§ 366	INTERVOCALIC GROUP mm	∧	m	m	m	m	flammam	flamma	flāmę	flāmę > *flamme*	flam *flamme*
§ 373	mn	> mm	> m	m	m	m	fēminam	fęmena	fę̃mę > fāmę *feme, fame, femme*	fāmę > *femme*	fam *femme*
§ 369	m'r	> mbr	mbr	> nbr	(§ 436)		kameram *camera*	kamera	tšãmbrę > šãnbrę *chambre*	> šãbrę *chambre*	> šãbR *chambre*
§ 369	m'l	> mbl	> mbl	> nbl	(§ 436)		kūmŭlum *cumulum*	kǫm(o)lu	kūmblę > kūnblę *comble*	> kūblę *comble*	> kǫbl *comble*
§§ 203, 305, 194	mj, mnj	> ndž	ndž	> nž	(§ 436)		sīmium	simju	sindžę > sInžę *singe*	> sę̃žę *singe*	> sę̃ž *singe*
	m before other cons.	m	m	> n	(§ 436)		kampum *campum*	kampu	tšãmp > šãnp *champ*	> šã(p) *champ*	> šã *champ*
§ 365	m middle of three	—	—	—	—	—	dōrmit	dǫrmit	dǫrt	> dǫr(t) *dort*	> dǫR *dort*

§ 686. n AND m.

Ref.	Position.	G.R.	O.F. I.	O.F. II.	Mid. F.	Mod. F.	Class. Latin.	Late.	O.F. II.	Mid. F.	Mod. F.
§ 202	**n** Initial *of word and syllable*	n	n	n	n	n	nasum	nasy	nes	> nę(s, z) *nes, nez*	> nę *nez*
§ 371	mn	mm >	> m	m	m	m	fēminam	femęna	fēmę > fāmę *feme, fame, femme*	fāmę *femme*	fam *femme*
	n Intervocalic										
§ 436	*Become final*	n	n	n	> (n)	—(n)	lūnam	lyna	lüne > lüne	> lünę	> lün *lune*
							finem	fine	fin > fin	> fę(n) *fin*	> fę *fin*
	Intervocalic Group										
§ 366	nn	> n	n	n	n	n	pinnam	penna	pēnę > pānę	pānę > *panne*	pan *panne*
§ 436	*Become final*				§ 435	§ 435	annum	anny	ān	> ã(n)	> ã *an*
§ 371	n'm	> mm	> m	m	m	m	anima	anęma	āmę *anme, ame*	āmę *âme*	ām *âme*
§ 369	n'r	> ndr	ndr	ndr	(n)dr (§ 436)	dR	pōnēre	ponere	pundrę > pūndrę	> pūdrę *pondre*	> pōdR *pondre*
	[For rn's, nn's, cf. § 365 (ii)]										
§ 311	nj, ng (< ng + e, i)	> ŋ	ŋ	ŋ	ŋ	ŋ	lineam	liŋa	liŋę > liŋę *ligne, ligne*	> liŋę *ligne*	> liŋ *ligne*
§ 321	ŋn	> ŋ	ŋ	ŋ	ŋ	ŋ	agnellos *agnellos*	aŋellos	āŋels > āŋeaus *aignels, aingneaus*	aŋę(s, z) *agneaulx*	aŋǫ *agneaux*
§§ 321, 406, 435	ŋ (< nj, ŋn) *become final*	ŋ	>	(j)ŋ >	> (n)	§ 435	balneum; bany	*baŋos	bāŋ > bāiŋ > bēiŋ *baing*	> bę(n) *baing*	> bę *bain*
§§ 311, 321	ŋ (< nj, ng, nɟ, ŋn) *become prae-consonantal*	ŋ >	(j)n	n	§ 436	§ 436	balneum		bāints > bēins *bainz*	> bę(s, z) *bains*	> bę *bains*
§§ 359, 320	nk nc + cons. > n + cons.	n	n	n	§ 436	§ 436	sanctum *sanctum*	santy	sāint > sęint *saint, seint*	> sę(t) *saint*	> sę *saint*
§ 436	n before other consonants	n	n	n	§ 436	§ 436	grandem	grande	grānt	> grā(t) *grand*	> gRã *grand*

18

§ 687. I-SOUNDS (§ 380).

Ref.	Position	G.R.	O.F. I.	O.F. II.	Mid. F.	Mod. F.	Class.	Latin. Late.	O.F. II.	Mid. F.	Mod. F.
§ 302	INITIAL *of word or syllable*	ı	ı	ı	ı	ı	lūnam	lụna	lüne > lüne	> lüne *lune*	> lün *lune*
§§ 392, 393	INTERVOCALIC	ı	ı	ı	ı	ı	alam	ala	ęlę *aile*	> ęl *aile*	> ęl *aile*
	Become final (cf. also § 812)	>	ı	ı	ı …	§ 392	malum	malụ	mal	mal	mal
§ 366	II INTERVOCALIC	>	ı	ı	ı	ı	illam	ẹlla	ẹlę > ẹlę	ẹlę *elle*	> ẹl *elle*
	Become final (cf. also § 812)	>						*kaβallụ *caballum*	tševal > ševal *cheval*	ševal *cheval*	> ševal *cheval*
§§ 322, 381	INTERVOCALIC GROUPS kl, gl	> l	l	l	l	> ı	větŭlụm; *vetulum*	βẹklụ	viel > vjel *vieil*	> vjel *vieil*	> vjel *vieil*
§§ 312, 381	lj	> l	l	l	l	> ı	filiam	filja	filę > filę *fille*	filę *fille*	> fił > fij *fille*
§§ 383-91	Early O.F. ɨ, ỉ, ị *and* ɉ + consonant										
§ 384	After ị	î, ɉ	î, ɉ, >	—	—	—	filios	fiłos	fiłts > fits > fis *filz, fiz*	> fi(s, z) > *fils*	fi ; fis *fils*
§ 386	After u, ü	ɨ, ɉ	ɨ, ɉ, >	ʮ > —	—	—	(fulgúrem)	*folgere	fo]drę > fudrę *foildre*	fudrę *foudre*	fudR *foudre*
§§ 387-8	After ǫ, a, ẹ, ę, ie, ue	ɨ, ɉ	ɨ, ɉ, >	(§§ 534-56)							

PART III.

ORTHOGRAPHY.

CHAPTER I.

PERIOD I—OLD FRENCH.

Section 1.—PERIOD DIVISION.

§ 688. The history of French spelling begins with the *Strasbourg Oaths*, the first extant document written in the vernacular, in 842.

Its history in the Middle Ages, like the history of pronunciation (§ 16), falls into two main periods, but since changes in spelling are necessarily subsequent to changes in pronunciation it is advisable to advance the limits of the two periods. Period I is therefore carried to the end of the twelfth century, Period II to the end of the seventeenth, i.e. to the publication of the *Dictionary of the Academy* in 1694.

In the earlier period spelling is, broadly speaking, phonetic in intention, if not always in performance ; in the second, scribal tradition hardened and set, and there began that conflict between the champions of phonetic representation and the traditionalists that has been carried on ever since. In France, as in England, despite the bold bid for supremacy made by the phoneticians of the sixteenth century, it was the traditionalists that carried the day, almost all along the line.

Section 2.—THE LATIN SYMBOLS.

§ 689. The aim of the scribes who first set down the vernacular in writing was to represent as closely as they could with the means at their disposal the pronunciation of their time. They were, however, all Latin-trained and consequently biassed to some extent by Latin tradition, and the symbols which they took over with their current value were wholly inadequate to represent the more complicated sound system of ninth-century vernacular speech.

§ 690. *Inadequacy of the Latin Symbols.* — In comparison with Classical Latin the Early Old French sound system, though less copious

than the Gallo-Roman, was very rich and varied.   Among the consonants

$$\text{J, ŋ, ts, dz, tš, dž, } \theta, \text{ ð and v}$$

were new sounds and consequently without symbols; a whole series of
diphthongs had been created; differentiation of the quality of the e-*sounds*
had been emphasised and a new vowel sound **ü** was in process of formation.
Unfortunately for posterity the early scribes were too timid, too much
under the domination of tradition to invent freely new symbols or new
distinguishing signs to represent these new sounds; they contented
themselves for the most part with modifying the value of the Latin
symbols and adding extra letters as distinguishing (*diacritical*) marks.
Some support for this latter procedure could be found both in Latin and
Germanic scribal tradition, for in both the symbol *h* had assumed this
function: among German scribes *dh* was a usual graphy for **ð** and in
mediæval Latin *ph* functioned as **f** and *ch* as **k** (e g. *Christus* for **Kristus**).

§ 691. *Value Accorded to the Latin Symbols.*—*i* and *u* had still both
vocalic and consonantal value and retained double value throughout the
Middle Ages : *i* represented **i, į** and **J**, *u* stood for **ų** (> **ü**), **ų** and **w** ;
both had also assumed new functions for *i* in initial position represented
dž and *u* was used for **v**.

In Merovingian times and sometimes later *i* was also sometimes used for **ę**
and *u* for **ǫ**, cf. *Fred. rigis, habitur, minsis, gluria, custudia, persunas* (Haag, pp. 843,
847) ; *Oaths, podir, dift, prindrai, returnar* (cf. § 180) : *uu* was sometimes used for **w**.

§ 692. *c* and *g* still represented ordinarily **k** and **g**, but before *e* and
i they had assumed the values, *c* of **ts** and *g* of **dž**.

'The proper sound of *c* is that before *e* and *i*, as in *cecitas*. Before all other
vowels it is pronounced like *q*, as in *cadit, codex, culpa*. The proper sound of *g* is
that before *e* and *i* as in *Georgius*. Before all other vowels it is weakened as in
Garganus, Gotthus, gula.' (Latin *Spelling Treatise* of the tenth century, cited
Beaulieux, I, pp. 24-26.)

g intervocalic before *e* and *i* might also function as **J** in Gallo-Roman, cf. MSS.
of Gregory of Tours, *agebat* for *aiebat, ingens* for *iniens* (B. p. 173) ; *Gloss. Reich.
anoget* for *anoiet* 1122, *iuorgiis* for *ivorjis* 896 ; *Eul. pagiens, regiel* for *paiiens, reiiel* 8, 12.

§ 693. *ti* and *ci* had the value of **ts** and were interchangeable (cf.
Haag, § 43).   *Gloss. Reich. anetiauerunt* 452, *anetsauerit* 510, *anetsau-
erunt* 697, *supersticiosos* 710, *superstitiones* 712.   *s* in intervocalic position
stood for **z**; *z* represented **dz** and **ts** and was used ordinarily to represent
ts, final of the word, cf. O.F. *doze, duze* for **dudzę** ; *paramenz* for **para-
ments** (*Eul.* 7).

x was used in Latin orthography only, and ordinarily with the value **s**, cf. *Fred.
ausilium, estincti, meretris ; comex, prolexs, Sexsionas* (for *Sessionas*, Haag, § 53).

Section 3.—USE OF LETTERS AS DIACRITICAL SYMBOLS IN EARLY O.F.

§ 694. **h.**—*h* was juxtaposed to a letter to indicate simply that its pro-. nunciation was not what would normally be expected under the conditions in which it stood.

(*a*) *ch.*—In early texts, under the influence of the spelling *Christus, ch* was sometimes used with the value of **k** before *e* and *i*, e.g. *Eul. chi* 12, *chielt* 13 ; *Alexis, chi* 101c, *unches* 87e, 115e, and so also occasionally in the twelfth century, cf. *Rol. chi* 596, 838, *unches* 640, 920, etc.

[For A.N. use of *ch* cf. § 1209.]

More commonly *ch* was used before *a, e, ie* to indicate **tš**, e.g. *Charles, cheval, chier*, and this value early became fixed.

(*b*) *dh* and *th.*—In the *Strasbourg Oaths dh* stands for **ð**, e.g. *aiudha, cadhuna, ludher*, and in MS. L of the *Alexis* (under English influence) *th* fulfils the same function, cf. *cuntretha* 20, *mustrethe* 71, *espethe* 72.

In the north-eastern region, as well as in Provençal, *h* was affixed to *l* and *n* to indicate a palatal pronunciation of these sounds, cf. Al. MS. V. *meruelhe* 88e, *asolhe* 101e, *senhiour* 101a, *prenhent* 102 a ; *Poème Moral, travalh, uelh, orgulh*, etc.

§ 695. **g.**—*g* (presumably with the value ɟ, § 692) was combined regularly with *n* and occasionally with *l* (e.g. *Jonas, cilg, entelgir*) to indicate the palatalisation of these sounds ; ordinarily it stood first, e.g. *segnour* for **seɲour**, *viegn* for **vieɲ**, but when the sound was final, and occasionally elsewhere, it was appended or written alone and thus **puɲ** might be written *puing* and *puig* as well as *puign* and **vieɲ**, *vieng, vieg, viegn.*

Often *i* was praeposed to *gn* and then it is difficult for us to determine whether *i* is a simple graphical device or part of a diphthong, i.e. whether *seignour* is to be interpreted **seɲour** or **seiɲour**, *oignon* **uɲūn** or **uiɲūn**, etc., and it is often only the later history of the word that determines the value of the early spelling.

§ 696. **i.**—*i* was praeposed to *l* to indicate palatalisation ; in intervocalic position *l* was then usually, but not consistently, doubled, cf. *Alexis*, MS. L. *uailant* 2c, *muiler* 4d, *bailie* 42d ; MS. P. *uaillant, moillier, baillie.*

Variant spellings of these palatal sounds were thus numerous ; in *Doomsday Book* there are ten variant spellings of the sound ɟ, nine of **ɲ**, in intervocalic position :

ɟ	-ill-	*Taillebosc*	-illi-	*Batailliae*	-lli-	*Talliebosc*	-ll-	*Tallebosc*
	-il-	*Tailebosc*	-ilg-	*Tailgebosc*	-illg-	*Taillgebosc*	-llg-	*Tallgebosc*
	-lg-	*Talgebosc*	-ilgi-	*Tailgia*				

ɲ	-ign-	*Puignant*	-gn-	*Pugnant*	-ingi-	*Puingiant*
	-ngi-	*Pungiant*	-in-	*Puinant*	-inn-	*Puinnant*
	-ini-	*Bainiart*	-nn-	*Punnant*	-ni-	*Puniant*

Section 4.—REPRESENTATION OF O.F. SOUNDS.

§ 697. *Vowels.*—ę.—The graphy used in the *Oaths of Strasbourg* to represent the obscure sound ę, developed after the final group **dr** as an off-glide, is *a* in the word *sendra* l. 7 ; *a* is used (as well as *e*) in the form derived from *fratrem : fradra* l. 3, *fradre* ll. 2, 4, 6, but unstressed ǫ (< ŭ) is still ordinarily written *o*.

In the *Eulalia e* is employed normally both to represent the sound developed as an off-glide (*sempre* 10) and for the sound derived from unstressed **a** and ǫ as well as ę (cf. *auret, bellezour* 2, *uoldrent, ueintre* 3, *diaule* 4, etc.), and *a* only occurs in words which contained it in Latin ; its use is therefore in all probability due to Latin influence. Hesitation about the way to represent the sound appears, however, to have continued to the end of Early Old French, for both *a* and *e* are found still in the oldest MS. of the *Alexis* (L, twelfth century), cf. *pedra, medra* 21a, *estra* 22e, 30e, 41b, *perdra* 41e.

§ 698. *Back and Front Labial Vowel Sounds* **u**, ǫ, ǭ, **ü**, **ö**.—The symbol *u* was given the value **ü**, but all through O.F. it was employed also with the value **u**.

The symbol *o* was used consistently for ǫ, e.g. *mort* **mǫrt**, *or* ǫr and for ǭ when it developed in *Later Old French*, §§ 579, 580 ; for *Early Old French* ǭ, (in Gallo-Roman already a high close variety of sound, §§ 180, 691), and for **u** developed out of it, *o* and *u* were both employed, *u* more consistently where the value **u** was soonest acquired, viz. before nasals (§ 426) and in West French (§ 184), e.g. *mult, molt ; tur, tor ; dun, don ; duner, doner.*

In the thirteenth century, when the range of back labial vowels was extended by the development of ǭ from earlier ǫ (§§ 579, 580), it became more than ever necessary to distinguish between these sounds, and gradually the digraph *ou* was brought into use to denote **u**. Its use is occasional in the early thirteenth century (cf. Angier, *a estrous, mourous,* etc.), but was generalised rather slowly. The starting-point lies in words of the type *mout, escoute, genouz, fous,* in which the diphthongs ǫu and ǭu had levelled to **u** (§§ 386, 548).

Prae-consonantal ɫ > ʯ (§ 385) and the symbol *l* was sometimes accorded the value ʯ, *ol* being used for *ou* **u**, *el*, *uel* for **eu**, **ueu** or **ö**, cf. *Rol. neuold* 2870 ; *Auc. Colstentinoble* 2, 39 ; Angier, *qelt, selt, velt* for **köt, söt, vöt.**

§ 699. *Consonants.*—**dž** was usually represented by *g* before *e* and *i* and by *i* before *a, o* and *u*, e.g. *gent, engin, alge, ge, gie ; iambe, ioie, donion, iuge, maniuce.*

Occasionally *i* was employed before *e* and *g* before *o* and *u*, e.g. *borieis ; goie, dongon, manguce.*

§ 700. tš was usually represented by *ch* (§ 694); **ts** was usually represented by *c* before all vowels and by *z* when final, e.g. *char, chier, franche ; cent, proece, cinc, ca, menconge, macue, co ; enz, faz, assez.*

[For the graphy *ce* cf. § 731.]

In the earliest texts *cz* and *tc* represent **ts**, e.g. *Eul. czo* 21, *manatce* 8 ; in the northern region *c* stands for **tš**, e.g. *Auc. cac*, **katš**, *cerf*, **tšẹrf**.

§ 701. **k** and **g**.—The very general attribution of the value **ts** to *c* and of **dž** to *g* (§§ 692-693) led to the employment of various devices to represent the velar sounds **k** and **g**, especially before *e* and *i :*

k functions already in the *Eulalia* (*Krist*), but was not in frequent use before the later twelfth century. When initial **gw** *gu* and **kṷ** *qu* were reduced to **g** and **k** (§ 192), the graphies *gu* and *qu* were utilised to represent **g** and **k** before *e* and *i*, cf. *longue, Aufrique* (*Africa*).

✳✳ In the northern region *gh* and *c* were often so used, e.g. *longhe ; ceval, teces* (**tẹkẹs**).

§ 702. **j** (developed out of the diphthong ¹ie, § 510) was represented by *i*, but when juxtaposed to a diphthong in **j̣**, e.g. in **ploijẹr, noijẹr**, etc. (< **pleiⁱier, ꞑeiⁱier**), it was ordinarily left unrepresented except in the northern region.

CHAPTER II.

PERIOD II—THIRTEENTH CENTURY AND MIDDLE FRENCH.

Section 1.—LEGAL AND LATINISING INFLUENCES.

[Cf. Beaulieux, *Histoire de l'Orthographe Française*, Paris, 1927.]

§ 703. In its main features the spelling of the Middle French period becomes more and more opposed to the earlier simpler system ; it loses mobility and is no longer adapted to pronunciation, becomes strongly latinised and is destined more and more to appeal to the eye of the reader.   These changes would doubtless have been brought about to some extent by the devotion to Latin that characterises this period, by the increase in the volume of vernacular literature and the introduction of printing, but they were greatly accelerated and increased by an influence of another kind—the orthographical practice of the lawyers and their clerks.   With the immense complication and variety of the legal proceedings of the later Middle Ages, when royal justice had superposed itself on feudal, and the consequent multiplication of legal documents, (cf. the list in Rabelais), the number of law clerks and official scribes swelled portentously, (' Len souloit estimer a Paris plus de soixante mille escripuains,' Guillebert de Metz), and it is the orthographical system of the lawyers (the *praticiens*), a system that is rigid, latinising, destined for the eye and not the ear and deliberately complicated, that gradually imposed itself on other scribes and was in consequence followed by the early printers (cf. Beaulieux, I, pp. 104-117).

§ 704. *Rigidity of Tradition.*—No care was taken to make spelling consistent and the scribes of the period made little attempt to modify spelling to suit the changes in pronunciation.   Very slowly the reduction of the diphthong **ie** to **e** took effect (§ 510) ; but other changes, e.g. the passage of **oi** to **wẹ** and **ẹ,** the lowering of the high nasal vowels, etc., affected spelling spasmodically only, and written evidence of the sound changes of the period is more and more only supplied by the writings of the uneducated (cf. §§ 458, 520, and section 4 below).

§ 705. *Latinising Influence.*—The Latin training of the schools had all along inclined the scribes to latinise to a certain extent, but the procedure had hitherto not been erected into a principle. This is done, however, in the earliest extant orthographical treatise, that of T. H., "student of Paris," in the late thirteenth century : ' *Item quelibet diccio gallica concordans latino, in quantum poterit, debet sequi scripturam latine,*' § 26. The tendency was strongest among the lawyers and their clerks, for they were writing alternately in French and Latin or translating from one language into the other, and they were, moreover, definitely advised by their superiors to adopt this practice to simplify their work (Beaulieux, I, p. 114).

In the earlier period the Latin influence had shown itself chiefly in its restrictive influence on the invention of symbol (§ 690), in the later time it exercised a two-fold influence, conserving and perturbing.

§ 706. (i) *Conserving Influence of Latin.*—Throughout the period the influence of Latin tended to prevent the introduction of new spellings that would represent more closely the changed pronunciation, but which were further removed from Latin orthography.

In the MSS. of later Old French the use of *e* for levelled *ai*, and of *ã* for lowered *ẽ* had gained much ground. In the sixteenth century there is still hesitation, cf. R. Estienne : *Calais* and *Calez*, *faiz* and *fez*, *fraisle* and *fresle*, *graisse* and *gresse*, *haire* and *here*, *vairole* and *verole*, etc., but under the influence of Latin the more phonetic spellings ordinarily failed to maintain themselves, except in words of non-Latin or unrecognised origin such as the following : *guère*, *guet*, *guetter*, *céans*, *léans*, *frêne*, *guéret*, *grêle*, *ménage*, *merrain*, *serment*, *vérole*, *dans*, *dedans*, *dimanche*, *panser*, *revanche*, *sangle*, *sanglier*, *sans*, *tancer*, *tanche*, *trancher*.

§ 707. (ii) *Modifying Influence.*—The chief modifications in spelling that resulted from the deliberate attempt to connect French words with Latin are the following :—

(*a*) Consonants that had become effaced, assimilated or vocalised were re-introduced :

Vocalised ł, § 385: aultre, aulx, doulce, eulx, etc.
Labial + dental, § 373 : accepter, compte, escript, sept, doubte, absoudre, obvier, etc.
Palatalised or effaced velar, Pt. II, chap. vi : craincte, faict, poinct, doigt, vingt, Magdeleine, seing (§ 406), joug (§ 341), etc.
Effaced dental, § 373 : advenir, adventure, nid, nœud, nud, pied, etc.
s and z replaced by x : paix, noix, six, voix, dix, etc.
Simplified double consonants (§ 366): abbé, belle, mettre, etc.
Not infrequently the spelling was adapted to a mistaken derivation :
scavoir ≠ scire, legs (O.F. les < lessier) ≠ lego, poids (O.F. pois) ≠ pondus, lacs (O.F. las < lats < laqueos) ≠ lacier.

§ 708. (*b*) *Vowels.*—Latin vowels were restored, spellings altered to be more suggestive of Latin forms. Palsgrave writes : *oreille, hobreau, poure,*

toreau, but R. Estienne gives alternatives : *aureille : oreille, haubereau, aubereau, taureau : toreau*, and adds to *poure :* ' Aucuns escrivent *pauvre* pour ce qu'il vient de *pauper*.'

The traditional spellings, *ele* (*esle*), *cler, per, rere*, were replaced by *aile, clair, pair, raire* (cf. § 717).

[Cf. also § 785.]

§ 709. *Distinction of Homonyms.*—The works written in the vernacular in the older period had been destined to be sung or read aloud, but the great mass of legal documents were composed to be read, and thus spelling came to be regarded more and more as a matter for the eye, a tendency that was increased when printing multiplied the number of readers.   It became therefore more and more usual to use spelling both to distinguish homonyms and to link together related words wherever possible (cf. § 1239).

Thus thirteenth-century *mes* (< *magis, missos, meos*) was differentiated into *mais, mets, mès ; pois* (< *pisum, *pēsum*) into *pois, poids ; fes* into *fais (facis), faictz (factos), faix (fascem) ; las* into *las, lacs ; pris* into *pris, prix ; seaux* (< **sitellos, *sigellos*) into *seaux, sceaux*, etc.

(For the restoration of effaced consonants before flexional *s* cf. § 809.   For the feminines *veufue, grecque*, etc., cf. § 785.)

§ 710. These various processes resulted in the introduction of a large number of superfluous letters, and this vicious tendency was strengthened by material considerations.   Payment of the copyist was ordinarily on the piece-work basis, so much per page or per number of lines, and so it was to his interest to lengthen out the words as much as possible.   This practice continued into the seventeenth century, as we learn from a passage in Sorel's *Francion :* ' L'advocat faisoit des escritures ou il ne mettoit que deux mots en une ligne pour gagner dauantage. Afin de les enfler tres-bien son clerc usoit d'une certaine ortographe ou il se trouvoit une infinité de lettres inutiles ; et croyez qu'il estoit bien ennemy de ceux qui veulent que l'on escriue comme l'on parle et que l'on mette *piez* sans un *d* et *deuoir* sans un *b*.'   (Beaulieux, I, p. 150.)

Section 2.—SPELLING IN THE SIXTEENTH AND SEVENTEENTH CENTURIES.

§ 711. The complicated spelling that resulted from these practices was taken over by the early printers : ' La détestable graphie de Rabelais ne se distingue plus de celle d'un praticien' (Beaulieux, I, p. 152), and it was unfortunately accepted by the printer-scholar Robert Estienne who used it in his two dictionaries, the *Dictionarium Latino-Gallicum* of 1538 and the *Dictionnaire François-Latin* of 1539.   As it is these two dictionaries that served as the basis not only of the early seventeenth-century dictionary of Nicot (1606), but also of the dictionary

of the Academy in 1694, the complications of Modern French spelling are explained.

§ 712. Neither the sixteenth nor the seventeenth century accepted the system without protest. The sixteenth-century phoneticians, e.g. Meigret, condemned it root and branch : ‘Car come l’ecriture ne soęt qe la vray’ imaje de la parolle, a bone ręzon on l’estimera faos’ ę abusiue, si elle ne luy ęt conforme par un assęmblemęnt de lęttres conuenantes ao batimęnt dę’ voęs.’ (*Gr.* p. 4), but the most practical reformer of the sixteenth century was Ronsard, who employed in his earlier works, up to 1565, a simplified spelling system of his own which incorporated many of Meigret’s proposals. He suppressed the symbols *y* and *x* and *z* final and many superfluous letters; made use of the *tréma*, employed the circumflex accent to replace mute *s*, and the acute accent to distinguish ę and ę from ę; *j* and *i* were also distinguished in the *Hymnes*. Ronsard, however, yielded to the opposition of the traditionalists, and in France his reforms exercised no permanent influence.

§ 713. *Seventeenth Century.*—In Holland, at that time a great centre for printing French books, Ronsard’s reforms were, however, very largely taken up and in the seventeenth century the simplifications in use in these Dutch-printed books found support in many quarters, e.g. among the *Précieuses*, (H.L.F. IV, p. 96), the grammarians of Port Royal, and some of the great authors. Corneille, for instance, who like Ronsard concerned himself with orthography, advocated various reforms, e.g. the distinction between *i* and *j* and between *u* and *v*, between *s* mute and *s* sounded, and the use of the grave accent to mark the open quality of the *e* in *accès*, *après*, etc. (*Avis au Lecteur*, *Théâtre*, 1660, cf. Beaulieux, II, pp. 64-66).

Unfortunately the majority of the Academicians were of the traditionalist school, and though in deference to the opinion of the day they accepted the simplifications most in vogue, e.g. the cedilla and the typographical distinction between *i* and *j* and between *u* and *v*, they adopted relatively little else. The principles they followed, as laid down by themselves or their secretary, Mézeray, in his *Cahiers de remarques sur l’orthographe françoise* (1675), are the following: ‘La Compagnie declare qu’elle desire suiure l’ancienne orthographe qui distingue les gents de lettres d’auec les ignorants et les simples femmes, et qu’il faut la maintenir partout, hormis dans les mots ou un long et constant usage en aura introduit une contraire.’ (cf. Beaulieux, I, 353). ‘La Compagnie s’est attachée à l’ancienne Orthographe receuë parmi tous les gens de lettres, parce qu’elle ayde à faire connoistre l’Origine des mots. C’est pourquoy elle a creu ne devoir pas authoriser le retranchement que des Particuliers, et principalement les Imprimeurs ont fait de quelques lettres . . . parce

que ce retranchement oste tous les vestiges de l'Analogie et des rapports qui sont entre les mots qui viennent du Latin, ou de quelque autre Langue.   Ainsi elle a écrit les mots *Corps, Temps* auec un *P*, et les mots *Teste, Honneste*, auec une *S*, pour faire voir qu'ils viennent du Latin . . .' ' . . . il faut reconnoistre l'Usage pour le Maistre de l'Orthographe aussi bien que du choix des mots.' (*Préface*, quoted H.L.F. IV, i, 143.)

The application of these principles had for its result that the dictionary transmitted to modern times 'une graphie déjà archaïque en 1549 et entachée de vices introduits au moyen âge par les praticiens.'   Successive editions of the dictionary accepted some of the proposed reforms (§§ 736-8), but modern French spelling is still very largely a partially phonetic representation of Later Old French pronunciation, marred by Latinisms (cf. the spellings *autre, beaux, fait, loi, plaindre, plein, fin, dieu, leur, porter, portant*, etc.; *doigt, vingt, coup, loup, temps*, etc.).

Section 3.—Representation of New Sounds.

§ 714. (1) **ö**.—The sound **ö**, developed in the course of the twelfth century mainly from the diphthongs **eu** and **ue** (§§ 542, 551), was denoted ordinarily by one of the digraphs *eu, ue, oe* or by the combination *oeu : euvre, uevre, oevre, oeuvre, preu, prue, proe, proeu* ; *oe* was employed most frequently at the beginning of a word to avoid confusion with *ve* and *ne*.

[For the use of *el* to represent ö, cf. § 698.]

§ 715. (2) *Nasal Vowels and Diphthongs.*—In early Old French the nasalisation of vowels was left unrecognised in spelling, but in the thirteenth century scribes began to mark the nasalisation of the vowels that stood before intervocalic nasal consonants by the so-called *tilde*, a wavy line placed above the vowel : *fẽme, ãmer, sãine, ãime, plẽine, siẽne, Bretãingne, ensëigne*.   Later on the *tilde* was often replaced by an additional nasal consonant : *femme, anmer, sainne, ainme, pleinne, sienne, Bretaingne, enseingne*.

Coyfurelly (c. xiv) : '*g* autem posita in medio diccionis inter vocalem et consonantem habebit sonum quasi *n* et *g* ut *compaignon, compaignie, moigne* et *maigne*. Tamen Gallici pro majori parte scribunt *n* in medio ut *compaingnon, compaingnie* . . . quod melius est.' (M.L.R. V, 187.)

(For the value of *nn, mm* in Later Middle French cf. § 728.)

Section 4.—Influence of Sound Changes on the Value of Symbols.

§ 716. Although, already in the thirteenth century, spelling was becoming too fixed to reflect rapidly the sound changes that were taking place, old notations often acquired new value.   At times there is simple confusion of symbols, but not infrequently scribes made a definite

attempt to give diacritical value to symbols that no longer fulfilled their former function.

§ 717. (1) *Vowels.*—ai > ẹ (§ 529) and the spellings *ai* and *e* were used interchangeably, first in words in which *ai* was traditional, then elsewhere to represent ẹ :

mais : mes, lais : les, faire : fere, traitier : tretier; alegre : alaigre; cher (§ 498) : *chair, per : pair, cler : clair, brese : braise, fres : frais, espes : espais.*

✷✷ § 718. In the endings *-age* **-ažẹ,** *-ache* **-ašẹ,** *-asse* **-asẹ** and wherever **a** palatalised to ẹ (E. § xv), the digraph *ai* is far more commonly used than *e*, e.g. *avantaige, saiche, portaisse,* etc.

In the western region in which **ei** was early levelled to ẹ (§ 230), the digraphs *ei* and *ai* were interchangeable with each other and with *e,* cf. *Rose,* MS. Ab., *claie* for *cleie, raie* for *reie, saie* for *seta* and *siam, saient* for *seient,* etc., *poaie* for *poeie, donaie,* etc., *otroiet* for *otroieit, conoisset,* etc., (*Intr.* pp. 199, 206) ; *St. Martin, vaile* for *veile, deite* for **dẹtẹ,** *leitre* for **lẹtrẹ,** *ceissiez* for *cessiez, Mir. Chartres voailent* for *vuelent* **vụẹlẹnt,** p. 38. Cf. also *Et. Angier,* p. 10.

The scribes of this region, copying MSS. from other parts of France, found there the spelling *oi* (< *ei*) where they themselves were pronouncing ẹ, and consequently they sometimes attribute the value ẹ to the digraph *oi,* cf. the forms *choier* = **tšẹẹr** < **kɑdēre),* *choiet, soier, Beroul, Intr.* xxxvii (cf. *Et. Ang.* p. 10).

§ 719. **ẽ > ã, ãi > ẽi.**—The nasal vowels ẽ and ã, and the nasal diphthongs **ãi** and **ẽi** fell together (§§ 448, 467), and so before nasal consonants *e* and *a, ai* and *ei* were interchangeable :

gent : jant, penser : panser, vent : vant, ame : emme, feme : fame : femme, amer : anmer : emmer, main : mein, meins (< *minus*) : *mains, plain : plein,* etc.; cf. *St. Martin, enmast* 1330, *enmer* 3754, *enmere* 6747 ; *Mir. Chartres, enneaus (aneaus), hennas (hanas),* p. 48.

§ 720. **oi > oẹ > ụẹ** (§§ 518-522) and the spellings *oi, oe, oue* become interchangeable : *boite : boiste : boette : bouette, coiffé : coeffé, coite : coete : couette, miroir : miroer : mirouer, poisle : poesle, poivre : poevre,* etc., cf. also *fouetter : foitter, reprueche : reproiche* (Walberg, *Vising vol.,* pp. 328, 329).

✷✷ In the north-eastern region where the diphthong **oẹ < oi > ö** (§ 526) the graphies *ue (oe), eu* and *oi* were interchangeable, cf. Walloon, *tuest* and *toist* (< *tost,* N.E. § ix), Walberg, *Vising vol.,* pp. 311-322.

§ 721. *o, os, or, au, eau.*—In Middle French there developed from various sources a lengthened *o* sound (§§ 396, 561, 564) and the spellings *o, os, or,* and later on *o, os, or, au, eau,* are found interchanged, either with the value **ǭ** or with the more closed sound into which lengthened **ǭ** passed (§§ 536, 580) :

donoier (loan-word from Provençal, § 54) : *dosnoier : dornoier; donoi : dosnoi : daunoi; fossier : forsier : faussier* (Gf.) ; *faux du corps : fort du corps* (Gf.) ; *for(s)borc : fosborc : fausborc; l'aulogier : l'orlogier; geolier : gaullier.*

§ 722. *Consonants.*—**ts** (written *c* and *z,* § 700) **> s** (§ 194), and the symbols *s* and *c, s* and *z, c* and *z* became interchangeable :

*cil : sil, cest : sest, ci : si, ce : se, ceinture : sainture, cengle : sangle, cidre : sidre,
genice : genisse, macon : masson, forcene : forsene, cercueil : sercueil, sauce : sausse, source :
sourse,* etc.; *nes : nez, sus : suz, foiz : fois, treilliz : treillic.*

In the termination *-ece* the value s was often indicated by the combination *sc*,
e.g. *proesce*, and this digraph was sometimes utilised in other words, cf. *Auc. laiscies*
15, 14, 6; *quesisce* 35, 15; *seusce* 40, 19.

In the sixteenth century the use of the symbol *s* for *c* was widespread among the
unlearned and by reaction *c* was frequent for *s* among the learned and half-learned,
cf. Meigret: 'Les homes de France se moquent des dames le faisant ainsi' (i.e.
using *s* for *c*): 'desquelles si nous recherchons la façon d'escrire, nous la trouuerons
beaucoup plus raysonnable et mieux poursuyuie selon l'alphabeth que celle des plus
sauans homes des nostres.' (Beaulieux, I, p. 299.)

§ 723. In Middle French z *final* was ordinarily replaced by *s* after *n*
and *r*, but *z* was very generally retained after tonic vowels (whether
following on them immediately or after mute consonants) and accorded
new values :—

(1) After ẹ the symbol *z* was given diacritical value (§ 726) and very
generally retained.

(2) Under Latin influence it was sometimes used to represent z, e.g.
Faits Rom. couzin l. 4, *vouz ai* l. 135, *az deus* l. 52, and this is the value
specifically attributed by Palsgrave to the symbol in all positions, in the
words *dez, metz, secz,* for instance, as well as in *zodiaque, breze, quatorze,*
etc. (p. 39).

[For the replacement of *s* and *z* by *x* after *u* cf. § 733.]

Section 5.—USE OF LETTERS AS DIACRITICAL SYMBOLS.

§ 724. Variations in the length and quality of vowels became frequent
in this period (Pt. II, chaps. xv, xvi), induced often by the effacement of
consonants or of ẹ, and older spellings were often deflected from their
earlier function to denote these new values.   In this way, *prae-consonantal
s* and *double e* were often used to denote length, *prae-consonantal s, final z,
double nasals* and other *double consonants,* to indicate the quality of the
e-*sounds*.

§ 725. *Prae-consonantal s.*—In the course of Old French s was effaced
when in prae-consonantal position, with compensatory lengthening of
the preceding vowel (§§ 377, 564), but the traditional spelling was
ordinarily maintained and acquired gradually a two-fold diacritical value :

(i) *s* was very generally used before a consonant to indicate vowel
lengthening and was introduced unetymologically into words with this
function :

gesne for *gēne* < *geïne; jeusne* for *jeûne* (<*jejunium*); *hasler* for *hāler; traistre,
vouste* (<*volvita*).

Cf. Péletier du Mans: 'Nous métons voulontiers céte létre (s) pour sinifier que
la sillabe êt longue.'

(ii) The spelling *s* + *consonant* served also to differentiate an **e**-sound of full value from ę *feminine*. In the tonic syllable the sound was ordinarily long and open, in the countertonic ordinarily closed :

(a) ę̄ *tonic* : esle for ę̄lę (< *ala*), *griesve, liesve*, etc. Cf. *Mir. Chartres, mestre* for **m**ę**tre** (< *mittere*), p. 6, *charreste*, p. 16, *lestre*, p. 19.

(b) ę *countertonic* an l *intertonic* : *esgal, esguille, esglise, esguiere, esvier, empescher, prescher, mesrain* (< O.F. *mairien* < *materiamen*).

Cf. Behourt : ' Pour faire sonner l'*e masculin*, on met vulgairement un *s* au lieu d'un accent, comme *meschant, estincelle, estroit*.' (Th. I, p. 39, cf. Beaulieux, I, 264-266.)

§ 726. *z final.*—In the ending *-ez, -es*(z) (< *-ates*, e.g. *bontez, -atis*, **-jatis*, e.g. *portez, fassiez, -atos*, e.g. *portez*) *z* gained diacritical value and was retained to indicate the full and close value of the preceding vowel, and its use extended to other words, e.g. *nez, rez,* **n**ę̄(s), **r**ę̄(s).

Cf. Pillot : ' Vulgo solet addi *z* sine accentu, recentiores *s* tantum addunt, retento accentu, ut *lettré, lettrés*.' (H.L.F. II, 301.)

§ 727. *ee.*—The effacement of ę final produced ordinarily lengthening of the vowel (§ 271), and *ee* began to acquire diacritical value in the sixteenth century.

Cf. Tabourot : ' Nos peres . . . au lieu d'accentuer l'*e* de l'aduerbe, y mettoient deux *éé* comme *affligéément* . . . mais comme la douceur de nostre langue n'a peu porter ce baâillement de forcée prononciation, nous nous contentons d'y mettre un *é* long.' (Th. II, 584-585.)

§ 728. *Double Nasal Consonants.*—In Early Middle French the nasalisation of a vowel before an intervocalic nasal was often marked by the doubling of the nasal (§ 715) and in Later Middle French, when the denasalisation of ę̃ (ję̃, wę̃) was far advanced (§ 440) the double nasal came to be used to indicate open quality of the preceding vowel.

Cf. Lanoue : *-emme*, ' Ceste premiere *m* ne luy sert que pour faire distinguer l'*e* qui la precede de l'*e* masculin et de l'*e* feminin, luy donnant la prononciation de la diphthongue *ai* (i.e. ę).' (Beaulieux, I, p. 269.)

§ 729. **ff, kk, ll, rr, ss, tt** (*-effe, -ecque, -elle, -erre, -esse, -ette*).—In Middle French, when tonic ę was ordinarily long and open before simplified *lengthened* consonants which were often still written double (§§ 366, 575), the doubling of the consonant came to be employed as a device for showing the open quality of the ę-sound. Robert Estienne systematised this use, and in the first edition of the Dictionary of the Academy doubling of the *l* and *t* after ę was still habitual before final ę, e.g. *achette, jette, attelle, fidelle* (cf. Beaulieux, II, 73).

Cf. Lanoue : ' Ceste terminaison (*-elle*) se deuoit escrire de droit auec une *l* seule, mais pour ce que nous n'auons point d'*e* auec marque particuliere pour estre prononcé comme la diphyongue *ai* ' (= ę), ' il faut icy adiouster ceste *l* qui lui baille ceste uertu; cependant elle ne laisse d'auoir la penultiesme breue.' ' La double *s* de ceste terminaizon ' (*-esse*), ' ne luy sert pas d'alonger sa penultieme mais d'empescher

seulement qu'on n'y lise un *z* . . . et aussi de donner a l'*e* precedent le son de la diphthongue *ai* (ę).' 'L'un de ces *t*, (in -*ette*), ne sert qu'a donner a l'*e* penultieme le son
de la diphthongue *ai* (ę).' (Beaulieux, I, 269.) Du Val: 'Souvent nous doublons l'*f*
inutilement a cause de la voyelle *e*, exemple *greffe, greffier*, que nous prononçons
graife, graifier.' (Th. I, 107, cf. also Th. I, 39-40.)

§ 730. *h* was employed as a diacritical symbol in Later Old French
and subsequently :—

(*a*) From the thirteenth century on, to obviate the ambiguity of the
symbol *u, h* was often prefixed to words beginning with this symbol
used with vocalic or semi-vocalic value, e.g. *huis, huit, huem*.

(*b*) On the model of *jehir* (< G. *jehan*) and Latin *vehere, trahere*,
h was introduced to mark hiatus in the interior of a word, e.g. *aherdre,
ahuser, trahir, cahier*.

§ 731. *e*, more rarely *i*, was introduced after the symbols *c* and *g*
before *a, o* and *u* to indicate the value s and ž, e.g. *manceunge, Oxf. Ps.*

This device was used sparingly in Early Middle French, but accepted
by Robert Estienne in 1557 : 'Souuent pour addoulcir la prolation, de
peur qu'on ne prononce le *c* comme en *Cato, condo, sicut*, on entremet
ung *e, commencea, commenceons, receut*.' (Cf. Beaulieux, II, pp. 12, 13.)

§ 732. *ng final*.—The spelling *ng* at the end of a word, which in
O.F. denoted the palatal nasal, lost value when ŋ was depalatalised in
this position (§ 435), and was then extended to the word *un* to distinguish
it from the words *nu, vu, vii* with which in MSS. it might readily be
confused.

Section 6.—INTRODUCTION OF NEW SYMBOLS.

§ 733. *x*.—In Latin MSS. a symbol 9 was much used to represent the
termination -*us* and this symbol was confused with *x* and taken over by the
scribes of the late twelfth century to represent final -*us* in vernacular
words of the type, *beaus, osteus, chevaus, fius, Deus*, etc., i.e. in words in
which the vowel preceding -*us* still retained its value : the use of the
symbol was rapidly extended to all words ending in -*us*, i.e. to words of
the type of *preus, corageus, jeus, lieus*, etc., in which *eu* had the value ö
(cf. *Auc. prex* 31, 11 ; *mervellex* 24, 15) and already in the thirteenth
century *x* was functioning as a simple equivalent of final *s* when preceded
by *u*, e.g. *angoisseux, seux* (*seuls*), *lieux*, etc. (Beaulieux, I, pp. 81-84).

Throughout Middle French there was hesitation between *x* and *s*,
but in the sixteenth century *x* became established as the sign of the plural
in words whose radicals ended in the plural in -*u*, although several
of the reformers prescribed *s*.

Meigret admitted only *s* and *z* as plural endings (p. 48), Palsgrave prescribed *x*
for all substantives ending in -*eu*, -*ou*, -*eul*, -*oul*, -*al*, -*ail*, -*eau* (pp. 180-181), and so
also the grammarians of the early seventeenth century (H.L.F. III, 282).

§ 734. *Use of the Symbol y in Middle French.*—The symbol *y* was employed very sparingly in the early Middle Ages, chiefly in loan-words and proper names, e.g. *cyrografe, Helye, Adelays,* etc., but from the thirteenth century on it began to be used with some frequency to take the place of *i* juxtaposed to *n, m, u, v,* to avoid orthographical confusions, e.g. *Haynnau, Remy, yuer* and *y* was introduced for *i < ibi* in the thirteenth century. In later Middle French its functions and use were extended, partly to secure ready intelligibility, partly because it occupied more space than *i* (§ 710).

In the dictionaries of Robert Estienne it was accorded the following functions, the first three of which were retained in the Academy's first Dictionary :—

(1) To represent Greek *v*, e.g. *cymbale, cypres.*

(2) To represent initial ɉ, e.g. *yeulx.*

(3) For intervocalic ɉ, e.g. *effrayer, noyer, ennuyer.*

(4) For *i* initial before *u* (**v**) and between *u* and *u* (**v**), e.g. *yuer, yure; suyure, cuyure.*

(5) For *i* final after vowels, and in the plurals of such words before the *s* or *z* of the flexion, e.g. *ay, lay, foy, luy, layz, delayz.*

In this last case *y* was often used more freely : e.g. *amy, demy, Ɉamyn;* it was also employed by some to replace *i* in hiatus, cf. *hayr, pays,* and also to take the place of an *i* which stood before another *i* functioning as Ž, e.g. *pyion (pigeon), myiour (mi jour), Dyion (Dijon).*

With functions so many and so diverse it is not surprising that its use was extended still further and that it is found replacing *i* in all its vocalic and semi-vocalic functions in the spelling of the half-lettered public, cf. the orthography of François I (Beaulieux, I, 273), and of Anthoine, Duc de Lorraine : ' Ma dame j'ay receu deux vos lestres et suys fort ayse de ce que vous portes byen et que estes byen traytee du Roy vostre mary. J'esperre que le ceres encores plus de iour en iour car uous la ualles et il est cy uertueulx prynce quy ne sares fayre autremant, de quoy ie loue Dieu et uous doyent byen tost ung beau fyls. . . . Priant Dieu quy, madame, vous doyent bonne vye.' (Balcarres Papers, p. 34.)

Section 7.—USE OF TYPOGRAPHICAL SIGNS.

§ 735. *Accents.*—The use of accents in Modern French has for its starting-point the use to which they were put by the Italian printers of Latin books. [For the divergent function of accents in Anglo-Norman cf. § 1211, in mediaeval MSS. cf. Beaulieux, II, 1-17.] In the Latin books printed at Lyons they were introduced early, but the first Parisian printer to adopt them is Geofroi Tory who makes use of them in his *Horae in laudem Virg. Mariae . . . ubi orthographia, puncta et accentus suis locis habentur* and in the French translation of this work *Heures . . . en bonne orthographie de poinctz, daccens et diphthongues* (1525): he also recommends their use in his *Champfleury.* Tory was quickly followed by others, but usage was at first very fluctuating as there was no fixed determination of the value to be attributed to them. Some made use of the acute accent to denote vowel length (e.g. Meigret), others to

denote ẹ closed; some, e.g. Ronsard, made use of this accent to distinguish both ẹ and ę from ẹ, writing *écrire, chés, beautés, trêue, blême, foréts;* others made this distinction by placing a grave accent above e when it was feminine (= ę), e.g. Sylvius: *grènier, vestèment, armèè.* Variation in the use of accents was also increased by the changes and variations that were taking place in the quality of the vowels (cf. Pt. II, chap. xvi).

§ 736. *Acute Accent.*—The acute accent was first used systematically to distinguish ẹ in a final syllable from ę by Robert Estienne in his edition of the *De corrupti sermonis emendatione* of Mathurin Cordier in 1530 (e.g. *trompé, corrigé, abbé, assés, venés*): its use was extended to words ending in *-ee* (ę̄ < ę̄ę) by Dolet, more slowly to ę in the interior of words, and it is only in the third edition of the Dictionary of the Academy (1740) that the full modern use is adopted.

§ 737. *Grave Accent.*—The grave accent was mainly employed in the sixteenth century to distinguish the monosyllabic words from their homonyms: e.g. *à, où, là.* Its modern use to distinguish ę from ẹ, though proposed by Corneille in the *Avis au Lecteur* which he prefixed to his *Théâtre* in 1660, was only accepted by the Academy in its third edition (1740).

§ 738. *Circumflex Accent.*—To denote the lengthening of a vowel that resulted from the contraction of two vowels or the levelling of a diphthong (§§ 561, 562) the circumflex was introduced into French by Jacques Sylvius in his work *In Linguam Gallicam Isagωge* (e.g. *âge, saûl* sül < *satullum*). This use found acceptance with other grammarians and was adopted (with exceptions) by the Academy in the first edition of its Dictionary in 1694.

Sebillet in 1549 extended the use of this accent to vowels lengthened by the effacement of prae-consonantal s (z), § 564 (e.g. *honêtte, répondîttes-vous, plaît, tôt*), but this more revolutionary procedure, although in part supported by Ronsard and his school in the sixteenth century, and by the Précieuses in the seventeenth, was rejected by the Academy in 1694, and only accepted in 1740.

According to Somaize (*Dictionnaire*, pp. 178-184) the principle followed by the Précieuses in their attempt to introduce 'une nouvelle ortographe afin que les femmes peussent ecrire aussi asseurement et aussi correctement que les hommes' was that 'all superfluous letters should be removed,' and as in Ronsard's system, the circumflex accent is used by them to replace s after the lengthened vowels ā, ō, ū, the acute when the vowel is ę, e.g. *prône, hôtel, plût, tôujours* but *téte, extréme,* etc.

§ 739. *The Cedilla.*—In Spain and later in Italy *c* was early written with *z* under it to denote the value **ts.** The symbol passed into the

south of France in the late thirteenth century and from that time on was occasionally used in MSS. French printers employed it in the printing of Spanish books, and in 1531 it was introduced by Geofroi Tory in a small treatise, entitled *Le Sacre et Couronnement de la Royne*. In spite of the recommendation afforded it by Montflory's *Briefue Doctrine pour deument escripre selon la propriete du langage françoys* (edition of 1533), its use was only popularised in the middle of the century under the influence of the translation of the *Amadis des Gaules*, by Herberay des Essarts (1540), and by the advocacy of Meigret, (Beaulieux, II, *passim*).

Section 8.—Influence of Orthography on Pronunciation.

§ 740. With the wider diffusion of education and the increased facilities for reading afforded by the printing press in the sixteenth century, orthography began to exercise an influence on pronunciation. It contributed to the conservation or restoration of l and r, *final*, §§ 392, 401, and of the final consonant of monosyllables (e.g. **kǫk, sęk, šęf, sęrf**, § 619; **žug**, *joug*, § 341), and also to the renewed pronunciation of the first consonant of many consonantal groups, which had been effaced in the normal development of the word and restored *graphically* under the influence of Latin or some other form of the word, §§ 655, 809.

§ 741. (1) *Plural Forms.*—In the plural it had become customary to introduce into the written form of the word the final consonant of the radical effaced before flexional s—**p, f, c, g, d**, consistently, **t** more variably, e.g. *champs, vifs, secs, longs, bonds, dis* and *dits (ditz)* (cf. § 809). The evidence of the rhymes and the rules and remarks of some of the grammarians make it abundantly clear, however, that in the earlier sixteenth century pronunciation was still unaffected by this practice.

Cf. Villon: *proces : ceps* L. xvii, *neufz : cheveulz* L. xxvi; Marot: *lacs : soulas, ducs : perduz, regrets : grecs, juifs : fuis, apprentifs : gentils;* Ronsard: *espics : inutils, boucs : tous, neufs : deux, cerfs : deserts, lascifs : assis;* G. Alexis, I, *nulz : nudz,* 39, *sotz : socz,* 50, (H.L.F. II, 297; Th. II, pp. 61-85).
    Peletier: 'Aucunęs lętręs s'ecriuęt aussi pour proporcionner les nons pluriers auęc leurs singuliers, commę an ces nons *cocs, laidz, naïfz, cheuaulx, noms, draps, faictz,* la ou combien quę les lętręs *c, d, f, l, m. p, ct,* nę sę facęt point ouir, toutfoęs ęlęs i seruęt pour montrer qu'iz vienet des singuliers *coc, laid, naïf, cheual, nom, drap, faict.* . . . E quant a ceus qui disęt qu'on prononcę *draps, cocs, longs,* iz ne le dirǫęt pas s'iz auǫęt bien ecoutè les Françoęs parler, quand iz disęt: les *cos* chantęt, les *dras* sont *blans, lons,* e largęs.' (*Dialogue*, pp. 51, 129; cf. § 1242, and Beaulieux, p. 337.)

§ 742. By the end of the century the consistency of the orthographical practice, combined with the influence of Latin and the widespread efface-ment of final s (§ 621) was already leading in educated speech to the establishment of the modern pronunciation in all but the most used

words, i.e. the intercalated consonant was beginning to be pronounced in the plural if it was sounded in the singular.

§ 743. The progress of the movement may be illustrated to some extent from the remarks of the grammarians Tabourot (1587) and Lanoue (1596):—

ecs : T. 'tu peux rimer avec la dite terminaison en *ais* et *ets*.' L. 'Le plurier de *sec*, qui est *secs*, se peut bien prononcer sans le *c*, comme s'il estoit escrit *ses*.'

ocs, *oucs* : T. 'tu rimeras auec *ots*, *outs*.' L. 'A grand peine se veulent ilz' (the plurals of words in *oc*), 'dessaisir du *c* pour rimer a ceux en *os*.'

efs : T. rhymes *couvrechefs, nefs, fiefs, reliefs, trefs* with *-ais*; L. still admits *chefs, meschefs, couvrechefs, clefs, fiefs* without *f*, but prescribes its pronunciation in *nefs, brefs, briefs, reliefs, griefs* (Th. II, pp. 66-71).

§ 744. (2) *Consonant Groups in other Positions.*—The influence of Latin spelling had led in many words to the graphical restoration of consonants assimilated, effaced or vocalised in speech (§ 707), and in the sixteenth century, under the combined influence of this spelling and the more correct Latin pronunciation of the time (§ 652), full value was more and more frequently given to these intrusive consonants. In the latter part of the century, indeed, the belief obtained among the educated that this fuller pronunciation was the earlier traditional form, cf. Pasquier: 'Nous veismes un des Essars qui . . . en ses dernieres traductions de Iosephe . . . nous seruit de ces mots *ammonester, contenner, sutil, calonnier, amministration* . . . ie proteste d'estre resolu et ferme en mon ancienne prononciation d'*admonnester, contemner, subtil, calomnier, administration.*' (*Lettres*, quoted Beaulieux, p. 304.) The new pronunciation, which began with easily recognised Latin loan-words, was gradually extended to others, e.g. *absoudre, obscur*, O.F. *asudre, o(s)cur*. Hesitation was most frequent among the words containing effaced prae-consonantal **s** as the fuller pronunciation of this sound found support in French dialects, (Provençal and Walloon), and in Italian and Spanish loan-words as well as Latin.

§ 745. According to the citations in Thurot, II *passim*, among the words in which fuller pronunciation of consonantal groups was coming into vogue in the sixteenth and early seventeenth century are the following:—

b + *consonant: absent, absoudre, abstenir, nonobstant, obscur, obscurcir, obseques, observer, obstinement, subsequent, abject, objet, subjet, subtil, subjuguer.*

d + *consonant: adjectif, admettre, administrer, admonester, admonition, adverbe, adversaire.*

k + **t**, *ct: affection, affecté, ectique, dicton, octroyer, aspect, correct, direct.*

m + **n:** *hymne* (for *hinne*).

p + *consonant: accepter, adoption, concepcion, corruption.*

[For **s** + *consonant* cf. § 379.]

§ 746. The hesitation of the grammarians, the conflict between spelling and traditional pronunciation, is well illustrated by the remarks

of Meigret and Bèze on *obvier*. Meigret: 'Le *b* semble quelque peu sonner en *obvier*; combien que ce n'est pas la nayve prononciation françoise. Car sans y prendre garde nous prononçons plus volontiers *ovier* que *obvier*; et n'y a point de doubte qu'au dernier *obvier* nous nous forçons, pensans que la prononciation latine nous y doyve contraindre.' Bèze: '*obvier* is pronounced almost as if it were written *ovier*.' (Th. II, 367.) The pun quoted by Tabourot: *on y a mal obvie* = *omnia malo viae* shows that the older pronunciation was still in vogue at the end of the century, but the artificial use of the *b* in this word triumphed in the seventeenth century.

In all cases there was much hesitation and the issue of the conflict between spelling and traditional pronunciation has remained in some words undetermined up to the present day: 'La lutte n'est pas encore terminée aujourd'hui; elle cessera seulement lorsque la graphie aura, inévitablement, fait prononcer tous les groupes de consonnes dans tous les mots. Un mot aussi populaire que *cheptel* (šẹtẹl) commence à être prononcé šẹptẹl par des notaires et même par des cultivateurs.' (Beaulieux, I, 305.)

PART IV.

MORPHOLOGY.

CHAPTER I.

CONTAMINATION AND ANALOGY.

Section 1.—INTRODUCTORY.

§ 747. In the sound changes treated in Part II it was mainly physiological processes that were considered (movements of the tongue, the lips, etc.), but in the modifications that flexional systems undergo, psychology plays a part of equal if not greater importance. All thought is dominated by the tendency to associate ideas—it is, indeed, an axiom with psychologists that no idea that enters consciousness remains in isolation—and no word is without links of some kind with another or others. There is always some likeness of sound or sense or function— or some contrast—to suggest an association, which is, of course, often merely ephemeral, and among words linked together in grammatical systems associations are especially strong and varied.

The associative process that modifies words or forms in isolation is termed *contamination*, the associative process that affects forms arranged in grammatical systems is called *analogy*.

Analogy plays an important part in the history of construction, but in this book the process is only considered in its influence on flexional development.

Section 2.—CONTAMINATION.

§ 748. *Contamination* (*Blending*) is the name given to the process by which a word, form or construction is directly modified by the influence of another word, form or construction with which it is associated. Contaminations may be merely ephemeral, the result of individual chance associations, (as for instance those engendered by the sequence of words in a sentence), but the contaminations that are of importance in linguistic development are those that result from associations that are more permanent and common to many.

Contaminations arise occasionally among constructions, e.g. the Old

French construction *bone chose est que de pais* is the result of a contamination between the two constructions *bone chose est que pais* and
bone chose est de pais, but it is forms and words and mainly words, that
are affected by this phenomenon.

§ 749. The basis of the association may be similarity of *sound*, e.g.
L.L. *scŭtella* < *scŭtella* + *scūtum*, but ordinarily it is the likeness or
contrast in the meaning that provokes association, or the combination of
the two factors. Thus the O.F. form *chascun* arose from the blending
of *quisque unum* with the half Greek locution *kata unum* (one by one)
and *maint* is thought to be de.ived from the blending of *magnum* and
tantum, L.L. **plusiores* from *pluriores* and *plus*, *fade* from *fatuum* and
vapidum; from the associations of opposites arose **blastimare* <
blasphemare + *aestimare*, *grief* from *gravem* + *levem*, O.F. *jus* džüs <
*ḍọsụ (<děorsum) + **sụsụ*, O.F. *ovrir* < *aperire* + *coperire*, *rendre* <
reddere + **prendere*, *virer* < *vibrare* + *gyrare*, and several forms of the
verbs *tenere* and **prendere*, *stare* and *vadere* result from the influence these
associated couples exercised on each other (§§ 931, 937, 948, 959; cf.
A. Risop, *Begriffsverwandtschaft und Sprachentwicklung*, Berlin, 1903).

§ 750. Among bi-lingual peoples contaminations are usually frequent:
in Gaul a few resulted from the contact of Latin and Celtic, e.g. O.F.
braire < *rugire* and Celtic **brag*, *criembre* < *tremere* and Celtic **crit*,
orteil < *articulum* and Celtic **ordiga* ; a more considerable number from
the contact of Gallo-Roman and Frankish speech, e.g. *brusler* < *ustulare*
+ *brennen*, *brunst*, *bruire* < *rugire* + **bragere*, *halt* < *altum* + **hōh*,
hanste < *hasta* + **hand*, *gueredon* < *donum* + **widarlon*.

[For the influence of Germanic words beginning with **w** on Latin
words associated with them, cf. § 636.]

The following additional examples may be cited, taken mainly from Period II :
aspic < *aspe* (< *aspidem*) + *basilic*, *aveindre* < *avenir* + *atteindre*, *chaisne* (*chêne*) < *chasne*
(< *cassanum*) + *fraisne* (< *fraxinum*), *cuiriee* (< *corata* or *cūrata*) + *corium*, (*cuir*),
cuistre < *coustre* (< **custor*) + *cuistre* (< *coquistro*), *exaucer* < *essaucier* (< *exaltiare*) +
exaudire, *grimper* < *griper* + *ramper*, *gauchir* < *guenchir* (< *wenkjan*) + *gauchier* (< *walkan*),
meindre < *mendre* + *meins*, *joiel*, *joial* < *joel*, *joal* (< *jocale*) + *joie*, *juillet* < O.F.
juignet + *juil* (*julium*), *ovec* < *avec* + *od* (< *apud*), *oncore* < *encore* + *onc*, *pluriel* (xvi)
< *plurier* + *pluralem*, **rancura* < *rancorem* + *cura*, *soulagier* < *sozlegier* + *soulaz*, **tur-
bulus* < *turbidus* + *turbulentus*, *tambour* < O.F. *tabour* + Ital. *tamburo*, *truite* < *troite*
+ *truie*, O.F. *uisine* < ***ocine* (< *opicina*) + *cuisine*, *ustensile* (xvii) < *utensile* + *user*.

§ 751. *Folk Etymology.*—In the special form of contamination known
as *folk-etymology*, the modification of a borrowed or unusual or archaic
word under the influence of one more familiar to the speaker, it is
mainly similarity of sound that is the determining factor, cf. *arriere-
ban* for *arban* (< **hariban*), *bascule* < O.F. *bacule* (< *baculer* formed from
bat cul) + *basse*, *courte-pointe* < O.F. *coute-pointe* (*culcita puncta*, cf. also
§ 396), *fai nèant* < *feignant*, *hausse col* for *hausse cot* (< **halskot*),

goupillon for *guipillon, poire de bon chrestien* for *poire panchresta* (Gk. = all good), *tonlieu* < O.F. *tolneu* (**toloneum* < *teloneum* + *tollere*) + *lieu*.

The modification may be orthographical only, cf. Middle French *sens dessus dessous* for *c'en dessus dessous, entretemps* for *entretant, vert de gris* for *vert de Gris* (< *Grice* pronounced **gris**).

Section 3.—ANALOGY.

§ 752. Habitual use of the process of *analogy* is made by all who acquire and use a flexional language, for all such learn to decline and conjugate on certain given models and in so doing are all the time creating 'analogical' forms; but normally one only becomes at all conscious of the nature of the process employed when a *wrong* model is followed, i.e. a model not accepted in ordinary usage, as when children say ' I catched,' ' I seed,' 'je traisais,' 'vous disez,' etc. As is often the case with operations that are familiar to all, the abstract definition is none too easy. The one given in the *New English Dictionary* runs as follows : ' Analogy is the process by which a word or words is created bearing a certain relation to a form or forms on the model of the relations existing between other forms with which it is associated.' More concise though somewhat less exact is the definition furnished by de Saussure (*Cours de Linguistique Générale*, p. 221). It runs: ' Une forme analogique est une forme faite à l'image d'une ou de plusieurs autres d'après une règle déterminée.'

As is evident from these definitions the process involves four terms or sets of terms and what is perhaps the simplest formulation of the process is a mathematical one, for analogical formations may be set out like a sum in proportion :

$$x \quad : \quad a \quad \text{as} \quad b \quad : \quad c$$

valúi, corúi : **valutum, *corutum* as **amai, audii : amatum, auditum.*
forte, grande, tele : fort, grant, tel as *bone, bele*, etc. *: bon, bel*, etc.

The analogical perfects *valúi, corúi*, etc., were created in Gallo-Roman to match the Gallo-Roman past participles **valutum, *corutum* on the model of the relation between the perfects and past participles of the Latin first and fourth conjugation.

The analogical feminine forms, *forte, grande, tele*, were created in French to match the masculine forms of these adjectives on the model of the relation borne by the many feminine adjectives in ę to their masculine counterparts.

§ 753. In the development of sounds and flexions sound change and analogy play opposed but complementary parts. The individual word is continually being modified by the action of sound change,

but the modifications wrought by this factor are gradual, development
is continuous and the word retains its identity even though no sound
remains unaltered. Unlike as they are in sound the modern words
chevaux, *chef*, *œil*, š(ə)vǫ, šęf, ǫ̈ǰ are the lineal descendants of Late Latin
caballos kaβallos, *capum* kapµ, *oculum* ǫklµ. Of the grammatical
systems into which words enter sound change is, however, recklessly
destructive, isolating form from form so that at times little remains
but a heterogeneous sequence of unrelated forms (cf. the thirteenth-
century pronunciation of the perfect of *avoir*: wę oi—ęüs *eus*—ǫt—
ęümęs—ęüstęs—ǫręnt).

Analogy, on the other hand, has no care for the individual word ;
it is continually creating afresh, replacing forms that have become out-
worn or isolated by forms that are clearer, simpler or more in accord
with an existing system : its function is to conserve or perhaps rather
re-form grammatical system, ever following in the wake of sound-
change, reconstructing rather than restoring, bringing a harmony of parts
into systems, disintegrated by the disruptive operations of sound change
or so complicated as to be a burden on the memory.

§ 754. The clear understanding of the workings of analogy, which
is essential to the comprehension of the development of flexion, is
facilitated by a comparison of this process with the related associative
one, contamination.

§ 755. (1) *Contamination*, as was seen above, results from the blending
of two partially remembered words, which come up into consciousness
together: *analogy* is a creative process, operating when memory is a
blank, either to satisfy a new need (cf. the English neologism *air-man*),
or, and this is the form we are more concerned with here, to replace a
form that is already existent in the language, but not at the moment
of speaking or writing present to the mind of the speaker or writer.
Thus the analogical forms (*je*) *fais*, *meurs*, *bous*, *veux*, etc., are not
modifications of older *faz*, *muir*, *boil*, *vueil*, etc., but brand-new forms,
created by people who have let slip the old isolated forms and who have
a feeling that there is ordinarily a relationship between a first person
and a second and third. Again, the O.F. forms *païsant*, *romant*, *pont*
are not alterations of earlier *païsenc*, *romanz*, *pon* (< *pomum*), but new
accusatives, created on the model of the much-used types ending in
-anz : -ant, *-onz : -ont*, which have impressed themselves on the memory.

§ 756. (2) In contamination only two factors are in play, for contaminated forms are produced by the direct influence of word on word,
form on form or construction on construction : analogy is a much more
complex phenomenon, one which presupposes the arrangement of words

in set patterns, for it is always concerned with words arranged in grammatical system, and is determined by the relation between words.

The analogical feminine forms *telle*, *forte*, etc., which replaced the earlier feminine forms *tel*, *fort* (cf. § 779), are not due to the simple direct influence of words like *belle*, *bonne*, etc., they are new feminine forms, created because people had begun to establish a direct relation between the formation of the feminine of adjectives and the addition of -ę to the masculine. Gallo-Roman *patri*, *baroni*, etc., are not modifications of *patres*, *barones*, etc.; they, too, are new forms created on the model of nominative plurals of the second declension, *muri*, etc., because these had come to be the dominant type in the masculine: *donne*, the Modern French form of the first person singular of the present indicative of *donner*, is an analogical form, made on the model of other forms (cf. § 898), *doins*, the Old French form of this person, results from a contamination of the two half-remembered forms **don** and ***dois** (cf. § 959).

§ 757. The generalisation of a particular analogical form may, however, be accelerated by the influence of individual words with which it is closely associated, cf. for instance, the early generalisation of the forms *commune*, *dolente*, under the influence of *une* and *lente*. In the formation of analogical forms there is, however, always present in the background the subconscious perception of a set of flexional relations. It is not, indeed, always easy to determine which of the two related processes, analogy or contamination, has been followed, and the term analogical is frequently used, conveniently if loosely, to cover both types of associative processes. In the widespread levelling of radicals that went on in Later Old and Middle French analogy is dominant (cf. chap. iv), but some forms, e.g. *veincre*, which ousted O.F. *veintre*, the strong radical *manju*—which replaced earlier ****mandu**—appear to spring from the simultaneous emergence into consciousness of the half-remembered forms *veintre : vencu*, *venqui* and *mandu : mangier*, etc., i.e. they are rather the result of contamination than analogy; similarly the Middle French forms *prins*, *print*, etc., appear to be due to the direct influence of the perfect of *tenir*.

§ 758. Analogical formations are provoked so variously that it is only possible to indicate broadly the lines likely to be followed in their creation. Memory and forgetfulness always play an important part.

§ 759. (1) *Forms Replaced.*—Forms that tend to be replaced earliest by analogical formations are those that slip the memory most readily, i.e., either those that have become isolated from the system of which they form a part by sound change or some modification of function or significance, or those that are of comparatively rare occurrence in speech. Conversely those that resist longest analogical replacement are those that are most strongly impressed on the memory, i.e. those that form part of a large, clearly defined, homogeneous system and those that are in frequent use.

The phonetic isolation of the O.F. infinitives *criembre*, *giembre*, *tortre*, *cueudre*, etc., led to their relatively early replacement by the forms

craindre, geindre, tordre, cuillir, made on other radicals of the verb or other associated groups of verbs (cf. §§ 936, 942). The disruption of the declension of substantives and adjectives with radicals ending in -l, that was occasioned by the vocalisation of this sound when brought in contact with flexional s and the subsequent levelling of the resultant diphthongs (cf. §§ 534-556) led to much analogical remaking, cf. for instance, *tieus* (< *tels*) : *tel* replaced by *tels* : *tel, cheveus* : *chevel* replaced by *cheveus* : *cheveu,* etc.

In the tenses of the subjunctive the third person singular is on the whole the one that figures most frequently in speech, mainly on account of its use in imprecation and blessing (*benedictus, maledictus sit !* deus vos adjutet ! utinam vixisset !* etc.), and it is noteworthy that in the history of these tenses the third persons have often resisted the analogical re-creation that has overtaken the other persons. Thus O.F. *seit* is derived from *sit,* O.F. *seie, seies,* etc., from L.L. analogical **siam, *sias,* etc.; *amast, finist, pleust,* etc., are etymological forms, *amasse, amasses, finisse, finisses, pleusse, pleusses,* etc., analogical (cf. §§ 952, 1046).

By the twelfth century the first and second plural of the present indicative of all verbs of the Latin third conjugation had been re-made, except those of the much used verbs *dire, faire, traire* : *dimes, dites, faimes, faites, traites ;* before the end of Old French the only forms surviving were *faites* and *dites,* remembered because of their use as imperatives as well as indicatives; and in Modern French the form *dites* has been ousted by the analogical form *disez* in those derivatives of *dire* that are of infrequent use or but rarely employed in the imperative, e.g. *contredisez, prédisez.*

§ 760. The so-called *irregular* verbs of Modern French are indeed often historically the *regular* ones, verbs so much used as to have preserved their traditional forms in spite of the disintegration of the conjugation system that has been wrought by the vicissitudes of sound change, (cf. for instance, the varying radicals of the modern verbs, *geler, mener, peser, boire, mourir, tenir, venir, vouloir,* etc.), and it is the so-called *regular* verbs (*aimer, laver, pleurer, vider, jouir,* etc.) that have been re-made analogically (§§ 882, 929).

§ 761. (2) *Models followed.*—The models followed in the creation of analogical forms are those most present to the mind of the persons creating them, i.e. those most commonly used in the speech of the time or those that are linked together in a simple and coherent system.

In the conjugation system it is the verbs of mood and the auxiliary verbs that exercise a strong influence, e.g. the starting-point of the analogical endings of the first person plural is *sumus* (cf. § 893) and the

rapid extension of the dissimilated form -*ẹa* in the imperfect indicative is mainly due to the fact that the form was developed in the conjugation of *habere, debere, bibere* and *vivere*, all much used verbs (cf. § 917). Throughout the history of the language the large, well-marked second conjugation exercised an attractive influence on the verbs belonging to the more heterogeneous third conjugation (cf. § 882), and similarly the first masculine O.F. declension (the *murus*-type) drew into itself more and more substantives, declined at first on other models (cf. §§ 789, 805).

§ 762. The models followed are not necessarily the same at all periods of the language ; to understand a choice of model it is necessary to enter into the linguistic feeling of the creating period. In Gallo-Roman, when perfects of the 'strong' type were frequent, there was created the strong analogical perfect *volsi ;* in Middle French, when the perfects of this type were out of favour, this form was replaced by the weak perfect *voulu(s)* (cf. § 1035). In the earlier stages of the language, when the subjunctive mood was still freely used, analogical subjunctive forms were created that were clearly differentiated from the indicative, e.g. *donge, muerge* (cf. § 910) ; later on the forms adopted were usually undifferentiated, e.g. *donne, meure,* etc.

§ 763. (3) The forms created by analogy do not at once supersede the earlier forms. Many, indeed, have only an ephemeral existence (cf. the form *perdesse,* employed by the poet of *Eulalia,* l. 17). All analogical forms are bound to co-exist for a period with the traditional forms that they replace, because at the time they are created there will always be some people remembering the traditional forms and using them. Co-existence may, indeed, extend over a long period : throughout Old French two strong perfects of *vouloir, voil* and *vols* were in use and three subjunctives of the verb *aler,* and *grande,* appearing in the eleventh century, has not yet finally ousted *grant* (cf. § 780).

Occasionally traditional and analogical forms are both retained and differentiated in function, cf. *fonds : fond, plier : ployer ;* ordinarily, however, after a period of co-existence, one or other form (not always the earlier traditional one), falls into disuse.

§ 764. The factors that determine the survival of an analogical form are not always now discernible : appropriateness to the system is ordinarily the most important, but the other factors that influence the life of words may play a contributory part, as, for instance, the subconscious desire to distinguish homonyms. It is this desire that in all probability contributed to the replacement of *tendrai* and *vendrai,* the O.F. futures of the verbs *tenir* and *venir,* by *tiendrai* and *viendrai,* less liable to confusion with the futures of *tendre* and *vendre.*

Section 4.—PRESERVATIVE ANALOGY.

§ 765. The analogical forms that attract attention are ordinarily ones that make a break with phonological tradition, and introduce a new form, but associative influences may serve at times negatively merely to conserve an old form and render inoperative a phonological tendency. This form of analogy, named '*Preservative Analogy*' by Professor Jespersen, the scholar who first called attention to the phenomenon, was defined by him as follows : 'A general tendency to change a sound in a certain direction may be checked in the case of some words, if there exists some other closely related form (of the same or other words), in which the sound exists under such circumstances that it is not affected by the change.' (*A Modern English Grammar*, p. 13.) This tendency operated in Middle French, when the general tendency to reduce hiatus between vowels was counteracted, not infrequently, by the influence of associated words (cf. § 238) and may be responsible for the retention of forms such as *rotulum, spatula, ovum*, etc., in Late Latin (cf. § 262).

AUTHORITIES :

F. de Saussure : *Cours de Linguistique Générale*, Pt. III, chaps. iv-vi.
J. Vendryes : *Le Langage*, Pt. II, chap. v.

CHAPTER II.

SUBSTANTIVES AND ADJECTIVES.

Section 1.—SURVEY OF DEVELOPMENT.

§ 766. *Period I.*—In the disintegration of the Latin flexions sound-change played an important part, but the re-modelling of the system was largely due to psychological factors: the desire for greater intelligibility (cf. the increased use of prepositions and the formation of the future and of the compound past tenses), the gradual modification of point of view (cf. the disappearance of the neuter gender and the re-modelling of the conjugation system, § 871), the growing inability to handle a flexional system so complicated and subtle (cf. the disappearance of the fourth and fifth declensions, of the passive voice and the deponents, etc.).

The beginnings of the disintegration and of the re-modelling it provoked lie in the Latin period [cf. Meillet, *E.L.L.* pp. 257-265].

§ 767. *Gender.*—Already in Classical Latin the *neuter* gender was only a survival, for its original function, the designation of *inanimate* objects, was obliterated (cf. Meillet, *Lg. H.* pp. 199-210): in Late Latin uncertainty in its employment increased, and among substantives its use was almost completely eliminated in the course of Period I. The distribution of masculine and feminine gender was little modified, but abstract words in *-orem* become feminine, tree-names in *-us*, masculine.

§ 768. *Declension.*—The phonological changes in process in Late Latin (§§ 179, 180, 205, 222) introduced confusion into the case system, and already in this period all distinction was beginning to disappear between the second and fourth, the fifth and third declensions, and between the forms of many of the cases (§ 786). Confusion was increased in Gallo-Roman by the slurring of unstressed vowels other than **a**, § 256, and the ever-increasing use of prepositions (§ 786), and the use of the oblique cases other than the accusative was gradually discontinued.

The Old French declension system is consequently a simple two-case one (nominative-vocative and accusative) and both case and number are

marked ordinarily by the presence or absence of the flexional symbols s or z (ts), § 796. Analogical re-modelling of the nominative forms led further to a completely new grouping of the declensions (§ 794).

§ 769. The Latin variations of radical were only preserved in the declension of adjectives in the comparative degree and of such substantives as are capable of functioning as proper nouns or appellatives (e.g. *soror, comes, homo, presbyter*). New variations of radical were, however, extensively developed by the differences that arose in the development of consonants by virtue of their varying position in a word—final, intervocalic, in group, before flexional s or varying vowels (§§ 782, 808).

§ 770. The feminine of adjectives derived from Latin three-termination adjectives, e.g. *bonus, bona, bonum*, was formed in accordance with the normal phonological development by adding -ę to the radical, while the feminine of those derived from the Latin two-termination adjectives, i.e. those that had no distinctive feminine form in Latin (e.g. *fortis, grandis, talis*) was ordinarily undistinguished in Old French, except by the presence or absence of flexional s or z.

§ 771. Except among the most used adjectives (§ 819) the synthetic forms of the comparative were replaced by the combination of the adjective in the positive degree with *plus*.

§ 772. *Period II.*—In the *written* language of the twelfth and thirteenth centuries the flexional system was maintained in relative stability, although with some slight modification. It was, however, slowly undermined by the gradual effacement of final s in prae-consonantal position, and case distinction, rendered more and more unnecessary by the fixing of the word-order, fell into complete abeyance in the central region ·in the later thirteenth and early fourteenth centuries.

The alternations of radical produced by the sound changes of the preceding period were often eliminated by analogical reformation or masked to the eye by the introduction in the spelling of the final consonants that had been effaced before flexional s (e.g. *chefs, bancs*, § 809).

By the end of the period final s was very generally mute, except in liaison (§§ 620, 621), and thus, as in Modern French, the plural number was ordinarily only distinguished in speech by the variation of the accompanying article. An age-long evolution thus reached its term (cf. Meillet, *E.L.L.* pp. 265-273).

§ 773. Under the influence of the adjectives that formed their feminine by the addition of ę, analogical feminine forms in -ę more and more frequently replaced the Old French one-termination adjectives, and by the end of the period etymological feminine forms like *grant* were only preserved in stereotyped locutions (§ 780).

Section 2.—Gender.

§ 774. *Neuter Gender*.—Already in Classical Latin there was some unsteadiness among the terminations of the neuter and in the course of the first period its use among substantives was almost completely eliminated. Masculine gender was ordinarily assumed, but neuter substantives employed frequently in the plural or with collective signification became feminine, cf. O.F. *aumaille* (< *animalia*), *bataille*, *geste*, *levre*, *peire*, *veile*. In declension the nouns becoming masculine followed ordinarily the Latin second declension, the feminines the Latin first, but neuters of the third declension in -**us** were indeclinable.

A few words survived in double form, e.g. *braz : brace, cervel : cervele, boel : boele corn : corne, grain : graine, fueil : fueille, pom : pome, raim : raime, sestier : sestiere, vaissel : vaissele ; foildre, livre,* masc. and fem. *Mer* < *mare* accommodated itself to *terra*.

The unsteadiness in the use of the neuter in Late Latin led to the attribution of neuter gender to a few masculine words, cf. O.F. *fonz* and *gluz* indeclinable (< neuters **fundus, *glutis*) and the feminine words *boele, deie, raime* derived from neuter plurals, **botella, *digita, *rama*.

§ 775. *Neuter Gender in Old French*.—Traces of the neuter plural lived on into Later Old French, especially in the plural of nouns denoting weight and measure, cf. *charre* (Rol. 33, 186), *deie* (Rol. 444 ; *Rose* I, 4605, etc.), *milie* (Rol. 587, etc.), *paire* (*Rose* II, 5408), *sestiere*.

Adjectives and participles retained the neuter form of the nominative singular, i.e. remained uninflected, when in agreement with neuter pronouns or conjugated with *estre* and used impersonally, cf. *ce m'est molt grief,* Crest. *Iv.* 141 ; *Mult lor est bel,* Villeh.; *Ce fu escrit de ma main,* Jv. The neuter nominative singular of the comparative forms of a few adjectives (e.g. *melius, pejus*) was retained in adverbial, more rarely substantival, function (*St. Alexis, del melz qui donc i eret* 4b).

Under Latin influence, particularly in translations, the nominative singular of nouns that were neuter in Latin was sometimes left uninflected, cf. *Oxf. Ps. argent, ciel, conseil, jugement* (M. pp. 87, 88).

§ 776. *Masculine and Feminine in Period I*.—Masculine and feminine substantives preserved normally their Latin gender but analogical influences occasioned a few changes in the course of Period I :

(i) Abstract substantives in -**orem,** influenced by the gender of other abstract nouns, assumed feminine gender and *flos : florem* followed suit, cf. *Lex Salica : labor clausa est,* Fred. *magnam timorem, ea pavorem, parva dolore.*

(ii) Under the influence of the termination -*us,* names of trees in -*us* became masculine and *arbor* followed suit, cf. Fred. *quendam arborem.*

(iii) *frons* and *vallis,* under the influence of *pons* and *mons,* and *aestas,* under the influence of the names of the other seasons, became masculine ; **sorice f. (for *sorex*), **berbice f. (for *vervex,* cf. § 189) appear to have been influenced by *radicem.*

§ 777. *Later Old and Middle French.*—In both Old and Middle French there was a considerable amount of fluctuation in the genders of words and double genders were relatively frequent. The main causes of this hesitation were :—

(i) *The levelling of words and suffixes under a common form :* thus the reduction of the two suffixes -**itatem** and -**itatum** to ę and of *-aginem* (in loan-words) and *-aticum* to -**ažę** *-age* led to uncertainty in the gender of such words as *comté, duché, parenté, image, eage.*

(ii) *The contrast between the traditional gender and the significance or form :* in Old French the traditionally feminine words *espie, ost, pape, profete, prison* were often made masculine ; in Middle French *personne* and *rien* began to assume masculine gender under the influence of their meaning ; *affaire, alarme, eschange, prestige* were sometimes made feminine under the influence of their terminations and *frisson, poison, soupçon* masculine.

(iii) *The analogical influence of associated words :* in Old French *dent* changes gender under the influence of *bouche*, etc. ; *art, sort,* and *val* under the influence of *mestier, destin, mont.*

(iv) *The influence of Latin :* the scholars in the Later Middle French period made a determined attempt to restore the masculine gender to the abstract nouns in *-eur* and consequently the words *erreur, honneur, humeur, odeur* and many others are masculine in Rabelais and elsewhere ; Latin gender was also given to some nouns whose gender had changed, e.g. *arbre, comete, ordre, paroi, periode,* and many borrowed Latin neuters that had become feminine under the influence of their termination were made masculine, e.g. *estude, idole, infortune, office, silence* (cf. H.L.F. II, 400-407).

With most of these words and many others uncertainty still prevailed in the seventeenth century (cf. H.L.F. IV, 2, pp. 783-807).

Section 3.—FORMATION OF THE FEMININE OF SUBSTANTIVES.

§ 778. (i) The suffix *-esse*, from L.L. *-issa*, of Greek origin (cf. *abbatissa, diaconissa*) was widely used to form feminines in Middle French, more particularly among substantives formed with the suffix -ˈ*ator,* -*aˈtore,* e.g. *abeesse, clergesse, miresse ; enchanteresse, lecheresse.*

(ii) The Latin suffix *-trix, -tricem* survived only in *empererriz* and *pecherriz ;* its borrowed form *-trice* was introduced in the sixteenth century.

(iii) The gradual effacement of final *r* and *s* in Late Middle French (§§ 400, 621) led to a confusion of the suffixes *-eur* and *-eus*, with the result that nouns in *-eur* began to form feminines in *-euse* (cf. § 400).

While Palsgrave makes no mention of such feminines, Meigret rules that 'tous denominatifs . . . come *frapeur, batteur* . . . font leurs feminins en *-euze*,' p. 41.

Section 4.—Formation of the Feminine of Adjectives.

§ 779. *Terminations.*—In Old French it was only the adjectives derived from the Latin three-termination adjectives—*bonus, bona, bonum*—that possessed a distinctive feminine form in *-ę*—*bon, bone ;* the feminine of the adjective derived from the Latin two-termination adjectives—*grandis,* m. and f., *grande,* n. —although differentiated from the masculine by case flexion in the nominative plural—*li grant ome, les granz femes*—was not ordinarily characterised by the addition of *-ę,* cf. O.F. *grant mere : granz meres, roche fort : roches forz, gentil fille, eaue bevant,* etc.

§ 780. Isolated analogical feminine forms began to be made in the first period, and a few were generalised, e.g. *comune* (± *une*), *Rol.* 1320, *dolente* (± *lente*), *Rol.* 1104, *corteise, curteisement, Rol.* 1164, but although *grande* appears in *Alexis* 610, *grandes* and *verte* in *Rol.* (*Oxf. MS.*) 302, 3656, 1569, *fole* in Crest. *Cl.* 511, *mole* in *Thebes* 477, *teles* in *Eneas* 4413, these forms and others similar were not generalised until Late Middle French. Palsgrave still mentions the forms *grant, vert,* etc., when placed before the noun, but adds : ' but if suche adjectyves come after the femynine substantyves, it is more sure to use their femynine termynation, as *ung amour especialle . . . une dame telle quelle* ' (p. 297), and the French grammarians, including Robert Estienne, only admit the etymological forms in stereotyped locutions such as *grand'chere, grand'mere, grand'rue, lettres royaux, raifort, Rochefort, Vauvert, elle se fait fort,* and in the adverbs in *-amment* and *-emment* formed from adjectives in *-ant, -ent* (cf. Beaulieux, I, 330).

§ 781. In Late Middle French the differentiation of masculine and feminine was often extended to borrowed adjectives that ended in *-ę,* e.g. *beningne, juste, oneste, publique,* and thus the analogical masculine forms, *benin, just, onest, public,* were created. From *preudefemme* (the locution modelled on *preudomme* <*prodem de homine) was drawn the feminine adjective *preude* (> *prude,* § 543), which displaced the earlier analogical feminine *preuse* (± *preuz*).

§ 782. *Radical.*—A marked divergence in the radical of the masculine and feminine forms often resulted from the sound changes occasioned by the varying vowels of the terminations. The more frequent types are :

(1) Velar radicals (§§ 300, 325) : *freis : fresche, angleis : anglesche, daneis : danesche,* etc., *larc : large, lonc : longe* lǫndžę, *lois*(<*luscum*) *: losche, sec : seche.*

(2) Dental radicals (§§ 206, 385) : *reit : reide, vuit* (< *vocitum*) *: vuide ; gris : grise ; beaus : bele, fous : fole, vieuz : vieille*.

(3) Labial radicals (§ 206): *baillif* (< **bajulivum*) *: baillive, vif : vive ; chauf : chauve, corp* (< *curvum*, § 189) *: corbe*.[1]

§ 783. Simplification began early, either (i) by the generalisation of one or other form, usually the feminine, the form more homogeneous in declension, or (ii) by the creation of analogical forms on the model of one or other radical or on associated types.

(i) The feminine forms *chauve* (Crest. *Cl.* 4772), *corbe, ferme, flasche, large* (Crest. *E.* 3182, etc.), *losche, moiste* (≠ *moist* < *muscidum*), *roide* (Crest. *P.* 8351), *vuide*, were all generalised in Old or Early Middle French.

(ii) The alternation *-eis* (*-ois*) *: -esche* was early replaced in the adjectives denoting nationality by *-ois : -oise* ≠ *cortois : cortoise* (already *Rol.* 396, *franceise*, Crest. *Cl.* 1995, *denoises*); O.F. *longe* **londžę** was also early replaced by *longue* **longę**, a form either of northern origin (§ 301), or made on the radical of *longueur*.

Baillive was retained into modern French but *jolive* was replaced by *jolie*, formed on the analogical masculine form *joli* (§ 812).

Old French *anti* is derived from *antiquum* (**antikwŭm** > **antiku*, § 187 (ii *b*) > **ānti**, § 302), the feminines *antive, antiue* from *antiqua* (**antikwa** > **āntiwę**, §§ 327, 328), and the masculine forms *antif, antiu* are formed on their model; from the masculine *grieu, griu* < *graecum* were drawn the feminines *griwe, grive, griue ;* the loan-words *grec* and *greque* appear in the twelfth century (*Troie* 92, *greque*). Derivatives formed from *graecum* with the suffix *-iscum*, *-isca* (> *-eis*, *-esche*, §§ 26, 325, 300) were also in use, e.g. *grezeis, grezesche* (< **graeciscus*, etc.), and *grieis, griesche* (formed on the radical *gri-*). From the masculine *juieu, juiu* **džüieu, džüiu** (§ 546) there was formed a feminine *juiwe* **džüiwę** > **džüivę** *juive*, and this form gave rise in turn to the masculine *juif;* from *pieus* (< **pius*, § 123) was formed *pieuse* which gradually displaced O.F. **pię** < **pīa**.

§ 784. *Variations of the Radical in Middle French.*—The sound changes of the Later Old and Middle French Period, e.g. the effacement of final consonants (§§ 400, 614-622), the modifications in the quality of the vowels (chap. xvi), the nasalisation and denasalisation of vowels (§§ 441-478), produced further very considerable differences between the masculine and feminine forms, cf. the late Middle French pronunciation of the masculine and feminine of *bavard* **bavar(t) : bavardę,** *fort* **fǫr(t) : fǫrtę,** *faux* **fǫ(s) : fǫsę,** *premier* **pręmję : pręmjęrę,** *fin* **fę̃(n) : finę,** *plein* **plę̃(n) : plęnę,** *sain* **sę̃(n) : sęnę,** *un* **ŏ̃(n) : ünę.** These differences were for the most part, however, masked by the fixity of orthographical tradition and as in Modern French indication of the varying pronunciation of the masculine and feminine forms was as a rule only given with adjectives ending in *-et, -ot, -an, -ien, -on* (e.g. *net : nette, muet : muette, complet : complette, vieillot : vieillotte, paisan : paisanne, mien : mienne, bon : bonne*), in which the doubled t indicated open quality of the preceding vowel (§ 729), the double nasal at first its nasality (§ 432 (iv)),

---

[1] In this section and throughout this chapter the colon is used to indicate related forms, masculine and feminine, singular and plural, etc.

and subsequently its open quality (§ 728).   Later on, when the use of
the grave accent was established (§ 737 and Beaulieux, II, pp. 79, 80),
it was employed in a few loan-adjectives in which the doubling of the
consonant t had not become traditional, e.g. *complet*, *discret*.

In the feminine of the adjectives in -*ein*, -*ain* the mediaeval doubled consonant
was not retained because the open quality of the vowel was indicated sufficiently by
the digraphs *ei* and *ai*.

When final supported t became mute (§ 615), graphical accordance
between masculine and feminine was restored by the substitution of *d* for
t, in the words whose Latin radical ended in *d*, e.g. *grand*, *rond*, *sourd*,
tard, or which were formed with the suffix -*art* (fem. -*arde*, § 26), e.g.
bastard, *vieillard*.

§ 785. The deliberate attempt to preserve to the eye the connection
between the masculine and the feminine (cf. § 708) produced complicated
spellings such as *pensyfue*, *veufue*, *anticque*, *grecque*, *magnificque*, etc.,
cf. Palsgrave : ' for generally there is none adjectyve of the femynyn
gendre but he hath the consonant of his masculyne, whiche he is formed
out of, except adjectyues endyng in *x*, whiche in their femynynes chaunge
x into *s*,' p. 293.

Section 5.—Declension in Late Latin and Early Gallo-Roman.

§ 786. *Case-system*.—In the extant written documents, even of the
late Empire, flexional tradition was for the most part upheld, but many
of the influences that led to the re-modelling of the declension system
in Gaul were already operative (§ 766).   Among the uneducated,
phonological changes, e.g. the levelling of ẹ and ị of ụ and ọ (§ 180), the
gradual obliteration of the quantitative differences (§ 222), the effacement
of final m (§ 205), were already resulting in a great unsteadiness in the
use of the oblique cases (e.g. of *dominum* and *domino*, *pedem* and *pede*
regis and *reges*, etc.) and confusion was increased by the extended use of
prepositions, cf. *Peregrinatio*, *de actus*, *de hoc ipsud*, *contra ipso luce*, etc.

The reduction and effacement of final unstressed vowels in the
Gallo-Roman period (§ 256) completed the disintegration, and the
oblique cases other than the accusative all fell into disuse in the course
of Gallo-Roman.

§ 787. A certain number of O.F. words contain fossilised oblique cases.   Thus
the genitive singular survives in the names of the days of the week, e.g. *lunsdi* < *lunis
diem, *juesdi* < *jovis diem* ; the ablative (locative), in some place-names, e.g. *Aix* <
Aquis, *Poitie(r)s* < *Pictavis*, *Angiers* < *Andecavis*, in adverbs in -*ment* (< *mente*),
and in a few adverbs or adverbial locutions, e.g. *ore* < *hac hora*, *lore* < *illa hora*, *ceste*
part, *cest an*, *oan* < *hoc anno*, *lues* < *loco* + *adverbial* s, *la merci De*, *mal gre vostre*,
mon vuel.   The vocative is preserved in O.F. *damne deu*.

A genitive plural in -*our* (-*or*, -*ur*) was introduced by clerks and used in the
vernacular, e.g. *ancienur* (*Al.* 1), *francur*, *paienur* (*Rol.* 1443, 1019).   It survives in
la (sc. *fête*) *Chandeleur*.

§ 788. *Declension System.*—The complications of the Latin declension system induced much analogical re-modelling; the most important modifications introduced are the following :—

§ 789. (1) The fourth and fifth declensions lost ground steadily to the second and first : *fructus, jussus, passus,* etc., followed the *murus* type ; *acies, facies, glacies* were replaced by *acia, *facia, *glacia, and *dia ranged itself by *dies* (cf. O.F. *diemanche*<*dia *domenica*).

§ 790. (2) In the third declension the *imparisyllabic* type was often simplified. The process most frequently adopted was the re-formation of nominative-vocative forms on the radical of the oblique cases, forms like *bos, caro, lac, sus, excellens,* etc., being replaced by *bovis, *carnis, *lactis, *suis, *excellentis (cf. GG. 153). The process continued in Gallo-Roman (cf. Fred. *urbis, bonetates, gentes ; Gl. Reich. papilionis, pedis, travis*), and in Old French the imparisyllabic type of declension is only retained among those words that designate persons, i.e. those used relatively often in the nominative and vocative.

A few substantives (e.g. *heres, sanguis*) re-formed the radical of their oblique cases on the nominative-vocative radical and a few feminine nouns passed into the first declension, e.g. *juventa,* *pauperta, *potesta, *tempesta.

[For the new G.R. imparisyllabic feminine type in '-a, -'ane cf. § 30.]

§ 791. (3) In the first declension, in which all distinction between the nominative and accusative singular was obliterated in Late Latin by the effacement of final **m** (§ 205), the nominative plural was re-modelled on the accusative plural and thus brought into line with the plural of the third declension. These forms in **-as** (e.g. *linguas, *filias), occasionally attested in Late Latin, were generalised in Gallo-Roman, cf. Fred. *Cartago condita est a rege et alias urbis plurimas : ut omnes vicinas gentes de ipso canerent* (Haag, 875).

§ 792. (4) In the Gallo-Roman period the nominative plural of all masculine nouns was re-modelled on the second declension and so became flexionless in Old French, cf. *Gl. Reich. folli ; Gl. Cassel, sapienti, pirpici.*

§ 793. As a consequence of all this re-modelling the forms of the nominative and accusative of *terra, virtus, nonna, pater, pons, amans, baro* that were in use in Early Gallo-Roman were presumably as follows :—

Nom.	terra	**terras**	fines	fines	**vertutes**	vertutes	nonna	**nonnanes**
Acc.	terra	terras	fine	fines	vertute	vertutes	**nonnane**	**nonnanes**

Nom.	pader	**padri**	pontes	**ponti**	**amantes**	**amanti**	baro	**baroni**
Acc.	padre	padres	ponte	pontes	amante	amantes	barone	barones

(Analogical replacements in heavy type.)

Section 6.—DECLENSION IN OLD FRENCH.

§ 794. The drastic re-modelling of the early period led to the formation of a new declension system on very simple lines. Its main
features are as follows :—

(1) It is a two-case system, the nominative being used ordinarily as
nominative and vocative, the accusative for all other purposes.

(2) The ordinary flexional symbols are *s* or *z* (value **ts**) : the distribution of these symbols is determined by the previous phonetic development of the word (§ 796).

(3) To form the accusative plural *all* substantives and adjectives,
except the indeclinables (§ 795), add *s* or *z* : *all* are flexionless in the
accusative singular.

(4) The forms used for the *nominative* vary, and according to these
variations words may be grouped into six declensions—three masculine
and three feminine. The variations are due to two causes : (i) The
survival of the *imparisyllabic* type of radical among substantives denoting
proper names, appellatives and a few adjectives in the comparative degree
(§ 819). This produced among these words a differentiation of the
radical of the nominative from that of the other cases. (ii) The presence
or absence of the flexional symbol : in the nominative *plural* all *masculine* nouns and adjectives are flexionless, all *feminine* nouns and
adjectives add **s** or **z** : in the nominative *singular* all nouns and adjectives
are flexionless if they are derived from Latin words that did not end in
s in the nominative singular (e.g. *femina, mater, magister, latro, imperator,
melior*) : all others, except the indeclinables, add **s** or **z**.

§ 795. *Indeclinables.*—As *s* and *z* were the only flexional symbols, all
pari-syllabic nouns and adjectives whose radicals ended in *s* or *z* were
indeclinable :—

(1) Words whose radicals ended in *s* in Latin, e.g. *nes* < *nasum,
meis* < *me(n)sem.*

(2) Words whose radicals ended in Old French in *z* (**ts**) or *s*, derived
from palatalised **k** or **tj**, e.g. *aprentiz, braz* (**brats** < **brakju* < *brachium*),
romanz < *romanice, tierz* < *tertium, palais* < *palatium* (§§ 295 (iii), 306,
308).

(3) All masculine substantives derived from imparisyllabic Latin
neuters ending in *-us*, e.g. *cors* < *corpus, tens* < *tempus.*

In O.F. the adjective *viez* (< *vetus*), the substantives *gluz* and *funz*, derived from
Late Latin neuter forms **glūtis, *fundus, rez* < plural *retes* (?) and *guez* (< *vadum*
+ Frk. **waδ** (?)) were also ordinarily indeclinable.

§ 796. *Distribution of Flexional* s *and* z.—z (**ts**) replaced flexional **s**
when the Latin radical ended in one of the following ways :—

(1) In **t** or **d**, because the affricated sound **ts** appears to have been
everywhere substituted for the consonantal group **t** + **s** (§ 367), e.g. **partes**

> parts *parz*, **finitus** > **finits** *finiz*, **grandis** > **grãnts** *granz*, **nūdus** > **nüts** *nuz*.

(2) In **st**, because the group **sts**, formed when the unstressed vowel was slurred, was simplified to **t** + **s** and also replaced by the affricate **ts** (§ 365 (ii)), e.g. **hŏstes** > ****ǫst-s** > **ǫts** *oz*, ***mastos** > ****mast-s** > **mats** *maz*.

(3) In **rn** or **nn**, because in the groups **rns** and **nns n** was wholly or partially denasalised to **t** and the group **t** + **s** replaced by the affricated consonant **ts** (§ 365 (ii)), e.g. **diurnos** > ****džorn-s** > **dzorts** *jorz*, **annos** > ****ann-s** > **ãnts** *anz*.

(4) In **ʃ** and **ŋ**, because final **s** brought in contact with these sounds was shifted to **ts** (§ 318), e.g. ***trapalios** > ****travaʃ-s** > **travaʃts** *travailz*, *cuneos* **kǫnjǫs** > **kuŋ-s** > **kuints** *coinz, cuinz*.

§ 797. *Paradigms of the Early Twelfth Century.*[1]

Masculine.

I. *Parisyllabic Type.*

(a)

	Singular.	Plural.	Singular.	Plural.	Neuter Sg.
Nom.	mur-s	mur	bon-s	bon	}bon
Acc.	mur	mur-s	bon	bon-s	
Nom.	an-z	an	gran-z	grant	}grant
Acc.	an	an-z	grant	gran-z	

§ 798. On this model were declined all declinable nouns and adjectives not comprised in I (b) or II, i.e. (i) all substantives and adjectives of the Latin second declension ending in -**us**, e.g. *amis : ami, fiz : fil ;* (ii) all surviving masculine parisyllabic nouns of the Latin third, fourth and fifth declensions not ending in **ę**, e.g. *pains : pain, fruiz : fruit, dis : di ;* (iii) all surviving masculine imparisyllabic nouns and adjectives that had re-made their nominative singular on the radical of the other cases (cf. § 790), e.g. *piez : pie(t), lions : lion ;* (iv) all surviving neuter nouns that had become masculine, except those whose nominative singular ended in -**us** in Latin (§ 795 (iii)), e.g. *vins : vin, nons : non ;* (v) all masculine derivative and borrowed words and all infinitives used substantivally, e.g. *vieillarz : vieillart, helmes : helme, branz : brant, plorers : plorer.*

§ 799.   (b)

	Singular.	Plural.	Singular.	Plural.	Neuter Sg.
Nom.	maïstre	maïstre	altre	altre	}altre
Acc.	maïstre	maïstre-s	altre	altre-s	
Nom.	pe(d)re	pe(d)re	tendre	tendre	}tendre
Acc.	pe(d)re	pe(d)re-s	tendre	tendre-s	

On this model were declined all parisyllabic adjectives ending in -**er** in the nominative singular in Latin and all substantives of this type denoting persons. [For names of things cf. § 805.]

---

[1] In the paradigms in this chapter heavy type is used to emphasise the flexions and variations of radical and not to denote phonetic value.

§ 800. II. *Imparisyllabic Type.*

		Singular.	Plural.	Singular.	Plural.
(1) Adjectives in synthetic comparative form (§ 819).	Nom.	**mieildre**	meillour	**pire**	peiour
	Acc.	meillour	meillour-s	peiour	peiour-s
(2) (i) Substantives in ˈ-ŏr, -ˈōrem.	Nom.	**sire**	seignour	**ancestre**	ancessour
	Acc.	seignour	seignour-s	ancessour	ancessour-s
	Nom.	**pastre**	pastour	**tra(d)itre**	tra(d)itour
	Acc.	pastour	pastour-s	tra(d)itour	tra(d)itour-s
(ii) (a) Substantives in ˈ-atŏr, -aˈtōrem.	Nom.	**empere(d)re**	empere(d)our	**trove(d)re**	trove(d)our
	Acc.	empere(d)our	empere(d)our-s	trove(d)our	trove(d)our-s
(b) Substantives in ˈ-atŏr, -aˈtōrem preceded by a palatal (§ 414).	Nom.	**pechie(d)re**	peche(d)our	**peschie(d)re**	pesche(d)our
	Acc.	peche(d)our	peche(d)our-s	pesche(d)our	pesche(d)our-s
(iii) Substantives (a) of the ˈ-o, -ˈōnem type (cf. *fel : felon, compaign : compagnon*).	Nom.	**ber**	baron	**le(d)re**	la(d)ron
	Acc.	baron	baron-s	la(d)ron	la(d)ron-s
(b) of the -ˈus, -ˈonem type (cf. *Charles Charlon*).	Nom.	**bris**	bricon	**garz**	garcon
	Acc.	bricon	bricon-s	garcon	garcon-s
(iv)	Nom.	ˈabes	abe(t)	**cuens**	conte
	Acc.	aˈbe(t)	abe-z	conte	conte-s
	Nom.	ˈenfes	enfant	**nies**	nevou(t)
	Acc.	enˈfant	enfan-z	nevou(t)	nevou-z
	Nom.	**on, uem**	ome	**prestre**	provei(d)re
	Acc.	ome	ome-s	provei(d)re	provei(d)re-s

Feminine.

§ 801. I. *Parisyllabic Type.*

(a)

	Singular.	Plural.	Singular.	Plural.
Nom.	tere	tere-s	bone	bone-s
Acc.	tere	tere-s	bone	bone-s
Nom.	me(d)re	me(d)re-s	altre	altre-s
Acc.	me(d)re	me(d)re-s	altre	altre-s

On this model were declined all feminine substantives and adjectives that ended in ę in O.F., i.e. (i) all feminine substantives and adjectives that were declined on the model of the Latin first declension in Gallo-Roman, e.g. *dame, porte, face* (§ 789), *poeste* (§ 790), *bele, fiere, dolce* (< *dulcia*) ; (ii) all feminine nouns and adjectives of the Latin third declension, whose nominative ended in -*er*, e.g. *tendre* ; (iii) all neuter plurals that had become feminine (§ 774), e.g. *fueille, levre, pome.*

(b)

§ 802.

	Singular.	Plural.	Singular.	Plural.
Nom.	flour-s	flour-s	fin-s	fin-s
Acc.	flour	flour-s	fin	fin-s
Nom.	vertu-z	vertu-z	gran-z	gran-z
Acc.	vertu(t)	vertu-z	grant	gran-z

On this model were declined all feminine parisyllabic nouns and adjectives whose radicals in Old French ended in a consonant or tonic vowel, i.e. (i) all parisyllabic nouns and adjectives of the Latin third, fourth and fifth declensions whose radicals ended in a consonant, e.g. *mains : main, forz : fort, vi(l)s : vil ;* (ii) all imparisyllabic nouns and adjectives that had re-formed their nominative singular on the radical of the other cases (§ 790) ; e.g. *amors : amor, bontez : bonte(t), amanz : amant.*

✱✱ § 803. In West French case distinction was early obliterated among the words of this type of declension and thus I(*a*) merged in I(*b*) and *flour*, etc., were declined : *flour : flour : flours : flours, vertu(t) : vertu(t) : vertuz : vertuz.*

§ 804.　　　　　　II. *Imparisyllabic Type.*

		Singular.	Plural.	Singular.	Plural.
(1) Adjectives in synthetic comparative form (§ 819).	Nom.	**graindre**	graignour-s	**pire**	peiour-s
	Acc.	graignour	graignour-s	peiour	peiour-s
(2) (i) The substantive *soror*.	Nom.	**suer**	sorour-s		
	Acc.	sorour	sorour-s		
(ii) Substantives of the G.R. type (*a*) in ꞌ-a, -ꞌanem (§ 30).	Nom.	**ante**	antain-s	**none**	nonain-s
	Acc.	antain	antain-s	nonain	nonain-s
(*b*) in ꞌ-a, -ꞌanem preceded by a *palatal* (§ 414).	Nom.	**taie**	taien-s	**Joie** (< *Gaudia*)	
	Acc.	taien	taien-s	Joien	

§ 805. *Modifications in Later Old French.*—(1) Under the influence of the second masculine declension, *s* and *z* came to be regarded as the characteristic flexion of the nominative singular masculine. Parisyllabic nominatives denoting things, e.g. *vespre*, began to be affected in the early twelfth century, those denoting persons and the imparisyllabic type a little later, cf. *Rol. Digby MS. parastres* 287, *Guenes* 277, *empereres* 661.

(2) Correct alternation of the radical in the imparisyllabic type began to give way also in the course of the twelfth century, earliest in west French, cf. *Rol. suer* acc. sg. 312 ; *Troie, suer* acc. sg. ; *baron, felons* nom. sg., *pire* nom. pl., *maires* acc. pl. ; Beroul, *home, garcons, felon* nom sg., *ber, pire, sire* acc. sg., *fel* nom. pl. (*Intr.* pp. liii, liv).

§ 806. *Disintegration of the Declension System.*—In the thirteenth century and Middle French, as in Later Latin, both phonological and syntactical factors combined to undermine the declension system. The gradual effacement of final **s** in prae-consonantal position and even elsewhere (§§ 621, 623) rendered the flexional system often inoperative ; the increasing fixity of word order made it unnecessary. Hesitation is observable first in proper nouns, in subjects placed after their verbs and in participles and adjectives used predicatively (cf. Laubscher, *The Syntactical Causes of Case Reduction*). In the Île de France and Champagne the system appears to have been maintained through most of the thirteenth century (cf. Rustebuef, the *Rôles de Taille*, and the charters emanating from Joinville's chancellerie), but in the fourteenth century it is only among the writers of the more northern region (e.g. in Jean le Bel and Froissart) that any consistency in its use is found. Villon, in his pastiche of Old French (T. 385), shows clearly that he had no understanding of the rules at all. Normally it is the accusative case that is generalised, but

in a few words employed frequently in the nominative-vocative case it was this latter form, e.g. *filz* (Wace, *fiz* acc. sg. 5461), *ancêtre, cuistre, gindre* (< *joindre* < *jŭnior*), *pâtre, peintre, prêtre, preux, queux, sire, soeur, traître*.   The form *Dieux* persisted into Late Middle French, cf. Villon, *m'ait Dieux : vieulx*, T. xvi and Th. II, 33.

✱✱ In the western region the disintegration of the declension system began earlier: already in the *Eneas* (c. 1170, south Norman), disregard of flexional *s* is occasional (some fifteen instances attested for the poet, *Intr.* p. xix); in the *Tristan* of Beroul (1190-1200) it is frequent (*Intr.* pp. li-liii).

§ 807. Confusion was brought into the use of the flexional symbols **s** and **z** by the changes in sound and spelling of Period II.   The introduction of *x* for *us* (§ 733) gradually displaced both symbols after *u*, (e.g. *beaux, chaux* for *beaus, chauz*); the passage of **ts** to **s** (§ 194) and the voicing of prae-vocalic **s** *final* to **z** (§ 611(2)) confused the use of *s* and *z*, especially as this latter symbol was sometimes given the value **z** (§ 723); lastly the frequent effacement of *final* **s** (§ 621) made the use of these symbols mainly a matter of orthography.   Palsgrave still attempts to lay down rules, although he admits 'diversite amongest the authours' (p. 181), but Meigret gives up all attempt to discriminate in their use: 'Tou' pluriers ont *s* ou *z* ou finalle' (p. 68).

✱✱ The modern distinction between *-ez* and *-és* was first proposed by Dolet: 'Tu escriras *voluptés* car *z* est le signe de *é* masculin au plurier nombre des verbes de seconde personne,' but it was only accepted by the Academy in 1762.

Section 7.—DEVELOPMENT OF RADICAL.

§ 808. The varying position which the final consonant of the radical occupied in the course of the declension produced a considerable amount of *alternation* of radical.   In the later twelfth century the most usual types are as follows:—

(i) *Labial cons.* effaced before **s**, §§ 365 (iii), 373 (**f, p,** supported **m**).	Nom.	cers	neis	vis	gas	chans	fers
	Acc.	cerf	neif	vif	gap	champ	ferm
(ii) *Velar cons.* effaced before **s**, § 365 (i).	Nom.	cos	sas	haubers	paisans	lons	
	Acc.	coc	sac	hauberc	paisanc	lonc	
(iii) Supported **n** denasalised before **s** to **t**, § 365 (ii).	Nom.	anz	jorz				
	Acc.	an	jorn				
(iv) **st** + **s** > **ts**, § 365 (ii).	Nom.	maz	paz	oz	fuz		
	Acc.	mast	past	ost	fust		
(v) **l** and **ʆ** effaced after **ɪ** before **s**, § 384.	Nom.	vis	gentis	fis	fiz		
	Acc.	vil	gentil	fil (**fiil**)	fil (**fiʆ**)		
(vi) **l** and **ʆ** vocalised before **s**, §§ 385-388.	Nom.	maus	chevaus	travauz	tieus (cf. also § 391 (1))		
	Acc.	mal	cheval	travail	tel		
	Nom.	beaus	praeaus	peaus	cheveus	conseuz	
	Acc.	bel	prael	pel	chevel	conseil	
	Nom.	fous	genouz	nus	seus		
	Acc.	fol	genoil	nul	seul		
	Nom.	vieuz	cieus	ieuz	dieus, dueus		
	Acc.	vieil	ciel	ueil	duel		

These variations in the radical provoked much re-formation— orthographical and analogical—in Later, Old and Middle French.

§ 809. *Orthographical Re-formation.*—To produce a likeness of appearance to the eye of the reader it gradually became the custom to introduce into the written form of the word the consonants that had been effaced before flexional **s.** In Anglo-Norman this practice began early (cf. *Rol. Digby MS. chefs* 44, *blancs* 110, *hastifs* 140, etc.); on the Continent this tendency shows itself more tardily and graphical omission of the consonant was still occasionally prescribed in the early sixteenth century. The introduction of **t** remained optional, e.g. *dens dents, petis petits,* but Palsgrave and all later grammarians insist on the introduction of labials and velars, e.g. *griefs, secs.*

In the later sixteenth century, pronunciation, which up to then appears to have remained entirely unaffected by this orthographical practice, began to be modified by it (cf. §§ 741-743).

Barcley, endeavouring to maintain tradition in England, writes in 1521: ' Al maner nounes of the masculyne gender endynge in the synguler nomber in *c, g,* or *f* as *blanc, vyf, long* shall be wryten in the plurell nomber with *s,* hauynge *c, g,* or *f* put awaye from them as *blans, vis, lons,*' but Meigret accepts scribal practice : ' Le *t* et le *d* final du singulier se transmet en *s* ou *z* ao plurier . . . rejettant ce *t* come trop dur è malèzé a prononcer. . . . Toutes les aotres consonantes finalles du singulier se consèruent en leur plurier, èn receuant seulement *s* ou *z.*' (Th. II, pp. 61-63.)

§ 810. *Analogical Re-formation.*—Analogical replacements began also in Later Old French. The new forms were made ordinarily on one of the radicals developed in the course of the declension of the given word, but the model selected was occasionally some other word or type of radical with which associations had established themselves owing to similarity of pronunciation or of significance or of function. The forms created were often only ephemeral and usage fluctuated greatly during the fourteenth and fifteenth centuries.

The types of analogical formations most frequently introduced are the following :—

§ 811. *Analogical Forms made on the Model of the Alternative Radical of the Word.*—(1) Nouns and adjectives whose uninflected radical ended in supported **-n,** e.g. *enfern, jorn,* were given early analogical forms without **n** (cf. Ph. Thaon, *Best. jur : onur* 249, *enfer : fer* 2903).

§ 812. (2) Nouns and adjectives whose uninflected radical ended in **-f,** were given forms without **f,** e.g. *bailli, joli, cer* (cf. Crest. *E. cer : fer* 712, Rtbf. *tré (tref): Vitré,* p. 150), but these forms were not always accepted.

§ 813. After **ts > s** (§ 194) *court* was replaced by *cour* and sometimes *mast, past,* etc., by *mas, pas,* e.g. Ex. Deguileville, *mas : pas,* 181.

§ 814. (3) Among substantives and adjectives ending in **l** and **ļ** analogical forms began to appear in the thirteenth century (cf. Rtbf., *osté* (*ostel*) *: osté*, p. 6, *leu : eu* (*oculum*), p. 129); they were made sometimes on the radical of the acc. sg.—nom. pl., e.g. *cruels, tels, ciels, conseilz, licols*, sometimes on the radical of the acc. pl.—nom. sg., e.g. *beau, peau, cheveu, genou, fou.* Before the end of the period alternation of radical had been practically eliminated among words ending in *-eau, -eil, -el* (< *-alem*), *-il*, and was moribund in words ending in *-euil* (*deuil*, etc.), *-ou ;* the only really living alternation was among words in *-al* and *ail* and a few other much used ones like *oeil*.

(i) *-el : -eaux.* Among adjectives *-el* < *-ellum* was maintained in prae-vocalic position, but elsewhere among substantives and adjectives it was replaced by *-eau*, cf. Rtbf. MS. A. *biau, trossiau.* Palsgrave considers the termination *-el* to be 'olde Romant.'

(ii) *-el* (< *-alem*) *: -ieux.* The ending *-el* was generalised in Late Middle French, but fifteenth century authors still often employ the traditional forms *tieulx, quieulx*, cf. Villon *vieulx : tieulx*, Lais 244, Ch. d'Orléans *tieulx : mieulx*, B. cvii : *yeulx*, Ch. x.

(iii) *-el* (< *ïllum*), *-eil : -eux. -eil* was generalised in Late Middle French : alternation is still employed by Charles d'Orléans (e.g. *conseulx : jeux*, B. cxx), but is not mentioned by Palsgrave : *chevel* gave way early to *cheveu* (: *neveu*, Guiart, I 2656).

(iv) *-al, -ail : -aux.* In the early sixteenth century alternation of radical was still usual among words ending in *-al, -ail* (cf. Palsgrave 180, 181), but the analogical forms in *-als, -ails* gained ground and at the end of the period Lanoue gives *bals, bocals, cals, canals, madrigals, vassals ; atirails, bails, espouvantails, gouvernails, portails, soupirails, travails.* The modern rules were finally settled later.

(v) *-eul, -euil: -eux ; -ol : -oux, -ouil : -oux.* Among words with these endings (derived from the suffixes *-eolum, -iolum, -uculum*) and in the plurals of the words *col, ciel, oeil*, there was still hesitation in the sixteenth century, increased for the words in *-eul* by the analogical influence of those in *-euil* (§ 817, i) : the forms *cielz, licolz, genouilz, oeilz* are, for instance, found in Rabelais. Modern usage was only finally determined in the next century (H.L.F. III, pp. 281-283, W. 675-678).

(vi) *-il : -is.* Among words in *-il*, e.g. *fil, vil, -il* was generalised.

§ 815. *Analogical Forms made on the Model of Associated Nouns and Adjectives.*— (1) *-anz : -an, -anz*, indecl., *-ans : -anc.* Nouns in *-anz : -an* (*tiranz : tiran*) were often re-modelled on the type *-anz : -ant* (*granz : grant*), e.g. *tiranz : tirant, Normanz : Normant ;* nouns in *-ans : -anc* (< *-ens : -enc*) (*paisans : paisanc*), and indeclinables in *-anz* (*romanz*), followed both these types, cf. O.F. *paisant, paisan, chambellant, chambellan, romant, roman.*

fonz, indecl., and *pon* (< *pomum*) followed often *pons : pont* (< *pontem*), cf. O.F. *font, pont* (*Rol. punt*, 466, etc.) ; *esforz* (indecl. < *esforcier*) and *formiz* (indecl.) followed the types *forz : fort* and *finiz : fini*, cf. O.F. *esfort, formi*.

§ 816. (2) The types *-eis : -eif* (*neis : neif, seis : seif*), *-ues : -uef* (*ues : uef*), *-is : -if*, served as a model to *seis : sei* (< *sitim*), *mues : mue* (< *modum*), *faldestueus : faldestuel, aprentis : aprentiz*, cf. O.F. *seif, muef, faldestuef, aprentif* (C. xvi, *apprenti*).

§ 817. (3) The type *-ueuz* (*-ieuz*) *: -ueil* served as a model both to the nouns in *-ueus : -uel* (*dueus : duel, chevrueus : chevruel*), and to those in *-ueus : -ueu*, (*sarcueus : sarcueu*), cf. Middle French *chevrueil, dueil, sarcueil ;* **feeil** (< *fidelem*) was early replaced by **feeļ** + **kũnseļ** *conseil*, etc., *gentil* **žãtil** by **žãtiļ** + *fil* **fiļ** (< **filium**).

Section 8.—Degrees of Comparison.

§ 818. In Late Latin the use of the adverbs *plus, magis, melius* with an adjective in the positive degree to express comparison gained ground considerably and was in Old French the normal method in use. The adverb usually employed was *plus*, but *mielz* occasionally performed this function in the early texts, cf. *St. Alexis*, 20 *melz gentils*.

§ 819. A synthetic comparative form was retained by a few of the most used adjectives, e.g. *maire : maiour ; mendre (meindre ≠ meins) : menour, meins ; mieildre : meillour, mielz ; pire : peiour, pis*.

On the model of the L.L. form *pluriores*, was formed *plusiores*, whence O.F. *pluiseur(s)*, in Middle French *plusieurs* by metathesis.

Other O.F. synthetic comparatives are: *joindre* < *jŭnior (Modern *gindre*, ẓ̧ẹdR, through žwẽndrẹ, § 475) : *gignour ; joenvre, genvre* < *jovenior § 643 : *joveignour : noaudre* < *nugalior : noaillour, noauz ; belais* < **bellatius : beleisour ; sordeis* < *sordidius : sordeiour ; halzour* < *altiorem ; forzour* < *fortiorem*.
[For declension, cf. §§ 800, 804.]

§ 820. The few superlative forms that survived, e.g. *pesme ; prueisme, proisme* < *proximum ; menmes, mermes* (cf. § 643) < *minimus ; maismes* (> *mesmes*) < *maximus*, lost superlative force and served merely as emphatic positives, a change in significance that also had its beginnings in Late Latin, cf. St. Aug. *sancta et dulcissima, Gl. Reich. optimum : valde bonum*.

The suffix -*isme* was introduced by clerks and employed to form an absolute superlative, cf. *Rol.* 2708 *altisme, Auc.* 24, 18 *grandisme*.

Section 9.—Numerals.

§ 821. The ordinary forms in use in the accusative masculine in the twelfth century were as follows :—

Cardinals : un, dous > deus, treis > trois, quatre, cinc, sis, set, uit, nuef, diz (dis, cf. § 295 (iii)), onze, doze, treze, quatorze, quinze, seze, diz et set, diz et uit, diz et nuef, vint, trente, quarante, cinquante, seisante, setante, oitante, nonante (*or* dous vinz, dous vinz et diz, etc.), cent, mil, *sg.* milie (mirie) > mile, *pl.* millier.

Ordinals : premier, altre (*or* segont), tierz, quart, quint, siste, se(d)me, ui(d)me, nuefme, disme, onzisme, dozisme, trezisme, quatorzisme, quinzisme, sezisme, diz et se(d)me, diz et ui(d)me, diz et nuefme, vintisme, etc.

§ 822.　　　*Declension of Cardinal Numerals.*

	Masculine.	Feminine.	Masculine.	Feminine.
Nom.	uns un	une unes	dui (doi)	dous > deus
Acc.	un uns	une unes	dous > deus	dous > deus

Düi is derived by mutation (§ 419) from L.L. ***düi***, modelled on the nominative plural of the second declension: Later Old French **doi** was modelled on **dous.**

Late Latin **ambi* (for *ambo*), strengthened by **dui*, was declined ordinarily: *masc.* andui (andoi) : ansdous; *fem.* ambesdous, but these forms were often replaced by analogical forms showing reciprocal influence, e.g. *masc.*, ambedui, ambesdous, *fem.*, ansdous.

Inflected forms were often supplied to *treis*, *vint*, *cent*, and more rarely *milie*, viz. trei (troi), *nom. pl.*, vinz, cenz, milies, *acc. pl.;* analogical *doues*, *fem.* was sometimes used.

Formation of Old French Forms.

§ 823. *Cardinals.*—The O.F. forms are derived from forms current in Late Latin, which had already undergone modifications of various kinds :—

(i) In *viginti* and subsequent numbers up to *centum* the stress was shifted backwards on to the preceding (significant) syllable.

(ii) Intervocalic **g** before **e** and **i** had, as usual, palatalised, opened, and disappeared (§ 297). Thus *viginti* **wigínti** > βé(j)ẹnti > **vint** (by mutation, § 419), **trigínta** > **tré(j)ẹnta** > **trēntẹ**, **nonagínta** > **nona(j)ẹnta** > **nonāntẹ**, etc., and *octoginta* was brought into line with the rest of the series.

(iii) *quinque* **kụinkụe** was dissimilated to **kịnkụe*; post-consonantal **w** was slurred in *quattuor* ***kụatt(w)or** and *septuaginta* ***sept(w)a(j)ẹnta** (§ 374 (i)) ; *doze* **dudzẹ** (§ 194) is derived from **dōdĕcim* **'dọdĕ́ẹ** levelled from **düödĕkim** *duodecim* ; *onze* **ūndzẹ** from **ŭndĕcim* **'ụndĕ́ẹ** with shortened tonic vowel (cf. Juret, p. 336).

(iv) **miljẹ** (> **milẹ**, *mille*) is a loan-word from **millia** ; it early became interchangeable with *mil.*

§ 824. *Later Old and Middle French.*—The use of *h* in *huit* is a graphical device (§ 730) ; it had no effect on pronunciation before Early Modern French ; for *ung* cf. § 732.

The spellings *treize*, *seize* for O.F. *treze*, *seze* (**trẹzẹ, sẹzẹ** < **trẹdzẹ, sẹdzẹ**, §§ 194, 575) were introduced in Middle French, cf. Meigret, ' *seze* qu'aucuns escrivent *seize*,' cf. Th. I, 341.

§ 825. *Ordinals.*—*Segont* is an early borrowed form (§ 640) ; *uidme* and *nuefme* are derived from the forms **octimum*, **novimum* formed analogically on *septimum* ; *onzisme* and *dozisme* are formed on *onze* and *doze.*

The forms in *-isme* (*-iesme*) that have replaced the older forms from *tierz* to *nuefme* inclusive, made their appearance in the later twelfth century (cf. Crestien, *E. cinquismes* 2991, *huitismes* 1699), and by the

sixteenth century the numeral system, apart from the continued use of *tiers* and *quart*, was that of Modern French.

The suffix *-isme* was taken over from *disme*. In the south-western region in which ẹ *tonic* + *palatal* resulted in **ie** (i.e. where *decimum* > *diesme*, S.W. § i) the numeral suffix in use was *-iesme* (cf. *Rou, diesme* 7549; *Troie*, MS. variants *onziesme, unziesme* 8119). In the later twelfth century this form of the suffix spread over the whole western region and in the thirteenth century it became general (cf. Rtbf., *cinquieme*, p. 179, l. 40, *disiesmes*, p. 183, l. 62).

[Cf. Vising, Observations sur les nombres ordinaux des langues romanes, *Rom.* L., pp. 481-498.]

CHAPTER III.

PRONOUNS.

Section 1.—INTRODUCTORY.

§ 826. Pronouns are tool-words and as such liable to the influence of sentence stress and position in the sentence ; variant forms—stressed and unstressed, proclitic and enclitic, prae-consonantal and prae-vocalic—are in consequence frequent.

The case system was preserved more fully than among substantives, but there was much analogical re-formation—the pronouns of the first person often influencing those of the other persons, and the relative the demonstrative.

Forms were sometimes simplified, e.g. those of the relative and interrogative : the pronoun **is** early became obsolete and **ipse** survived into Old French only in fossilised phrases and in its derivative *met-ipsimum*, § 850. From *hoc, ille* and *iste* strengthened by *ecce* the Old French demonstrative pronouns and adjectives were derived, from *ille* uncompounded the pronoun of the third person and the article.

Section 2.—PERSONAL PRONOUNS OF THE FIRST AND SECOND PERSON —REFLEXIVE PRONOUNS.

§ 827. Under the influence of varying sentence stress syntactical doublets developed of the pronouns *ego, me, te, se*, but of *nos* and *vos* the only forms in use in Old French were **nǫs > nus, vǫs > vus.**

The absence of diphthongisation in these forms is not easy to explain : some scholars look upon them as unstressed forms generalised ; Professor Meyer-Lübke suggests that they may be forms developed in prae-consonantal position, e.g. *nos sumus, vos videtis*, as in this position the vowel was blocked (*Gr.* § 264).

§ 828.   *Twelfth Century Paradigms.*

	Singular.		*Plural.*
		First Person.	
	Stressed.	*Unstressed.*	*Stressed and Unstressed.*
Nom.	gie džję, ge džę	je džę ⎫	nos, nus (nǫs > nus)
Acc.	mei, moi (mei > moi)	me mę ⎭	

Second Person.

	Stressed.	*Unstressed.*	*Stressed and Unstressed.*
Nom.	tu	tu	
Acc.	tei, toi (**tei > toi**)	te tẹ	vos, vus (**vọs > vus**)

Reflexive, Singular and Plural.

	Stressed	*Unstressed*
Acc.	sei, soi (**sei > soi**)	se sẹ
Dat.		

An unstressed form te (tẹ), nom. sg., either weakened from tü or formed on džẹ *je* in *dis-je*, etc., appeared in the thirteenth century and is still recorded by Sylvius in the sixteenth: ' *u*, Hannonii . . . quandoque elidunt ut *t'es sage pro tu es sage.*' (Th. I, 279.)

§ 829. **ego** *stressed.*—The development of ****ẹo**, the early Gallo-Roman form of **ĕgo** (§ 341), was complicated by variations of stress, sentence position and dialect. In the region comprising the centre, south-west and south-east, the *stressed* forms developed were *gie* and *ge* džjẹ, džẹ, which became obsolete in the early fifteenth century.

Cf. Crestien, E. *congie : ferai gie* 2921, *logie : lo gie* 4005 ; *Rose* I, *rent gie : pie* 1925, *estoie gie : songie* 2449 ; Rtbf. *ferai gie : enragie*, p. 220, l. 557, *ai gie : forjugie*, p. 215, l. 358, Christ. *Pis.* II, *je : congie*, p. 245, l. 690, *songie*, p. 250, l. 882.

The stages of development appear to be :—
(1) **ˡẹo > ˡieo** by normal diphthongisation of the tonic vowel, § 225.
(2) **ˡieo > įẹu** by shift of stress in the diphthong **ˡie**, §§ 510, 512.
(3) **įẹu > džjẹ > džẹ** by the closing of initial **j** to **dž**, § 203, and effacement of final vowel. Effacement of **u** *final* is found in the south-western region, § 255, and may have been facilitated in the case of the pronoun by sentence position (**džjẹ(u)** e(θ) **tü**, *ieu et tu*, etc.).

** § 830. In the northern region the stressed form was **džu**, N. § xxiii (graphy in Picard *jou*, in Walloon *ju*, N.E. § xv) : this form may either be the unstressed form generalised or be derived from earlier **ˡieo** reduced to **ˡio** (in the same way as the triphthong **ˡieu** was reduced to **ˡiu** in this region, § 546) and subsequently developed to **jọ > džọ > džu**.
** In thirteenth century Norman a nasalised form *jen* žẽn (cf. *cen*, § 849) was developed from **džẹ** standing before *ne* or *meisme*, e.g. in phrases of the type *je ne sui*.

[Cf. Rydberg, I, §§ 115-129.]

§ 831. **ego** *unstressed.*—Gallo-Roman ****ẹo** unstressed passed early to **jọ**, whence **džọ** ; from this form and from **džẹ** in unstressed function arose unstressed **džẹ** *je*, attested metrically in the *Chanson de Roland* by the elision of the vowel (e.g. ll. 246, 254, 2406, etc.) and in rhyme in the later twelfth century (e.g. *Troie, criem ge : vienge*, 8469).

Old French *oie* and *naie* (*Eracles, oie : veoie* 537, *Rom. Ham. naie : esmaie*) contain unstressed **ẹo* combined early with *hoc* and *non*.

** § 832. In the western region (as in Provençal) an unstressed form *os*, *us* developed from *vos* (S.W. § x), cf. *Rose* II, 7950, etc., Beroul, 424, 1243, 2815, etc.
** In the northern region *mihi* lived on contracted into **mi**, and **ti** and **si** were formed on its model, N. § xxiv.

Section 3.—Pronoun of the Third Person—Article.

§ 833.   *Paradigms of the Early Twelfth Century.*

Pronoun.

	Masculine.				*Feminine.*				*Neuter.*
	Singular.		*Plural.*		*Singular.*		*Plural.*		*Singular.*
	Stressed.	Unstressed.	Stressed.	Unstressed.	Stressed.	Unstressed.	Stressed.	Unstressed.	Unstressed.
Nom.	il	il	il	il	ele	ele	eles	eles	
Acc.	lui	lo, lu, le	els	les	li	la	eles	les	lo, lu, le
		(lu > lẹ)							**(lu > lẹ)**
Dat.	lui	li	lour, leur		li	li	lour, leur		
			(lour > leur)				**(lour > leur)**		

§ 834.   **Article.**

	Masculine.		*Feminine.*	
	Singular.	*Plural.*	*Singular.*	*Plural.*
Nom.	li	li	la	les
Acc.	lo, lu, le	les	la	les
	(lu > lẹ)			

Enclitic forms—

al	als > as	a la	als > as
del	dels > des	de la	dels > des
enl > el	els > es	en la	els > es

Unstressed forms of *ille* were sometimes used with demonstrative value in Old French, e.g. *la* for *celle* (*Rol.* 3145, *Gormont* 276, *Gerbert* 3082); *li* for *cil* (*Rol.* 1444, *Gerbert* 4171), cf. Jenkins, *Mod. Phil.* xvi, 131. A neuter form *el* survived combined with *non* and *o* in O.F. *nenel, nenal, oel, oal* (cf. G. Paris, *Rom.* xxiii, 161-176).

[For later development of *els* cf. §§ 387, 542, of *ele, eles*, § 493, of *leur* § 542.]

§ 835. *Formation of Old French Forms.*—The forms of the demonstratives were considerably modified by analogy in Late Latin, and the development of the pronoun *ille*, uncompounded, was influenced strongly in Period I by varying sentence stress and position in the sentence.

§ 836. *Analogical Replacements.*

(1) The neuter forms *illud, ipsud, istud* were replaced by *illu, *ipsu, *istu.

(2) Under the combined influence of the relative pronoun *qui* and of the nominative plural the forms of the nominative singular were replaced by forms ending in -i and thus *elli, *epsi, *esti replaced ẹllẹ, ẹpsẹ, ẹstẹ and in these forms the tonic vowel was mutated to i (§ 419), cf. O.F. il, is, ist.

(3) Under the influence of the dative forms *cui* and *huic*, new dative forms *ellui, *epsui, *estui were created and these gave rise to the feminine counterparts *ellei (*illaei), *epsei, *estei, formed on the alternative dative

forms *illae*, etc., GG. § 390 ; -ẹi, the tonic syllable of these feminine
forms, developed in the normal way through -iei to i̥ (§§ 410, 411), and
thus *ẹllẹi > (ẹl)li, *eccellei **(ẹk)t͡sẹllẹi > tsẹli, celi, **(ẹk)t͡sẹstẹi >
tsẹsti *cesti*.

§ 837. *Influence of Sentence Stress.*—The uncompounded forms, used
with weakened demonstrative force, were often accorded relatively slight
stress in the sentence and the initial syllable was then weakened and
slurred : thus *ẹlli̥ > li, *ẹllu̥ > lu > lẹ, *ẹlla > la, etc.

§ 838. *Influence of Position in the Sentence.*—The pronunciation of
both the stressed and unstressed forms was liable to modification when
a preceding closely associated word ended in a vowel :—

(i) In Gallo-Roman stressed and unstressed forms following such
words lost their initial syllable (§ 605), and these shortened forms
were sometimes generalised ; thus, for instance, **de *ẹllu̥i > de lüi, de
*ẹllẹi > de li**, etc., and similarly *qui illum videt* ku̥i illûm wĭdẹt >
ku̥i (ẹl)lu̥ βẹdẹt, etc.

(ii) Unstressed masculine or neuter forms standing between a word
ending in a vowel and another beginning with a consonant became
enclitic, i.e. lost their vowel sound and joined on to the preceding word
(cf. § 602) : **ki lu βẹdẹt > kil veit, **sic los βẹdẹt > sis veit, **en tẹrre
lu mettent > ẽn terrẹl metẹnt, **de lẹ mu̥r > del mür, **de los mu̥rs >
deꝉs mürs > des mürs ; **a lẹ mu̥r > al mür, **a los murs > **aꝉs
mürs > as mürs, *en lu mür > enl mür > el mür, **en los mu̥rs > eꝉs
mürs > es mürs, **contre le mu̥r > contrẹl mür.**

Throughout Early Old French the enclitic forms of masculine and
neuter pronouns *me, te, se, le* and *les* were ordinarily employed after
monosyllabic words ending with a vowel—*ja, je, jo, ne, lui, qui, quei, se,
si, tu*—e.g. *Al.* MS. L. *luin, sil* 20 *e, nel* 24*b, e, jol* 31*e, jos* 41*e*, but the
phonetic changes of the twelfth century (the vocalisation of ꝉ and
the effacement of prae-consonantal **s** (**z**)), often obscured the significance of these forms, and in the thirteenth century the commonest types
only were still employed—*nel* (*neu, nu, nou*), *jel* (*jeu, ju*), *sel* (*seu*), *si*(*l*),
nes, jes, ses—and these also become obsolete in the early fourteenth
century.

Already in the eleventh century little use was made of enclisis after
polysyllabic words ending in a vowel and examples are rare in the
twelfth century, except in texts of the south-western region, e.g.,

Thebes : destrel, fairel, jostel, Intr. lxxi, *Chron. Norm. contres, entres*, etc.

Les might become enclitic before a word beginning with a vowel, cf. *Rol.* 3882.

✶✶ § 839. *Local Variants.*—The stressed feminine form **li** varied with the
development of the group ẹ + *jod* (§ 412) : in the eastern and north-eastern region it
was *lei*, N.E. § i, E. § x, in the south-western *lie* or *lei*, S.W. § i.

✱✱ In the western region *el* (< * *illu*) survived as neuter nominative form and *ele* was often reduced to *el* (W. § xiv).

✱✱ In the northern region a dative form *les* (< *illis*) survived, N.E. § xv and *la* was reduced to *le* (cf. N. § xii). [For the use of *li* as the nominative feminine of the article cf. N. § xii.] In the eastern and southern region **lu** *lou* persisted into the thirteenth century, E. § xxv, S.C. § xvi.

§ 840. *Later Old and Middle French.*

(1) *Lui and li.*—In the course of the thirteenth century *lui* **lw̃i** (< **lüi** § 515) was often reduced to **li** (§ 516), and consequently the masculine and feminine forms were confused. In Middle French the stressed feminine accusative *li* was replaced by *ele* formed on *eles* and *li* fell into disuse.

§ 841. (2) **il** *Singular and Plural.*—In *prae-consonantal* position the **l** of **il** was effaced in the later twelfth century (cf. § 392) and in consequence *qu'il* and *qui, s'il* and *si* became homophonous in this position and were often confused (*St. Martin,* 1986 *dist qu'i n'i estereit,* 2952 *ne cuit qu'i portassont,* 4617 *Et s'i les chacot; Parisian charters* (XIII): *i le plera, i nous sembla* (Rydberg, II, 995). Effacement continued in the sixteenth century (cf. Tabourot, *quanto vini statera = quand au vin il se tastera*), and although under the influence of Latin and spelling an attempt was made to restore the pronunciation of final **l** in prae-consonantal position, it is still sometimes omitted in conversation (cf. Thurot, II, p. 141, Nyrop, *Man.* § 47 and *below* § 1204).

St. Liens: 'Some (and I am of the number) pronounce the *l* of *il*, without reference to the following consonant, as e.g. *il convient, il dit* . . . the courtiers, however, do not pronounce *l* in such locutions'; H. Estienne: 'I know that there are not lacking people who give no sound to *l* in *puisqu'il t'a pleu* but pronounce it *puisqu'i t'a pleu ;* but this pronunciation, taken from the common people, should be absolutely rejected'; but Chifflet (1659): 'Le pronom *il* ne sonne point l'*l* devant les consonnes, comme *il dit,* prononcez *i dit,* ny aux interrogations, quoy qui suive: comme *que dit-il ?* lisez *que dit i? parle t'il à vous ?* lisez *parle ti à vous ?* ' (Th. II, 141.)

§ 842. (3) *Ilz, Nominative Plural.*—In the fourteenth century, when the accusative plural of substantives was being generalised, the nominative plural *il* began to be written *ilz* (± *filz*). In prae-vocalic position the pronunciation **iz** slowly gained ground, but the traditional pronunciation of the word **i** + *consonant,* **il** + *vowel* persisted into the seventeenth century.

✱✱ Peletier wrote *iz* consistently, but Bèze kept to the traditional pronunciation : ' *s* ' (in *ils*) 'is always mute, whether before a vowel or a consonant, as in *ils ont dit, ils disent,* which are pronounced as if written *il ont dit, i disent,*' pp. 79-80; cf. also Duez : 'Before a vowel *ils* is spoken in two ways, namely as *il* by the common man, who leaves *s* out and *is* by most of the lettered people and those in the schools. . . . All the same the first is the most usual pronunciation.' In the later seventeenth century *iz* + *vowel* triumphs, cf. Hindret : 'dans le discours soutenu on ne fait sonner que l's, . . . *iz ont, iz esperent* . . . Dans le discours familier cet usage est fort partagé, car il y a bien des gens qui prononcent regulierement . . . et il en y a d'autres, qui, trouvant cette prononciation trop affectée, s'en tiennent à l'usage le plus commun, c'est à dire qu'ils mangent l's finale et que, faisant sonner l'*l* . . . ils prononcent *il ont* . . . Cette manière de prononcer est bien autant ridicule et défectueuse que celle de *j'avons*.' (Th. II, 79, 80.)

§ 843. (4) *Article.*—In prae-consonantal position **al** was vocalised to **au,** and on its model, in the thirteenth century, the earlier enclitic form **as** was replaced by **aus.** When **del** and **el** were in prae-consonantal position their final **-l** was also vocalised and the preceding vowel rounded either to ö, *eu* (in the north-western and west central region) or to ǫ (in the eastern, east central and northern region, § 502); western ö, like unstressed ö in **afübler,** etc. (§ 543), was raised to **ü;** eastern and northern ǫ raised to **u** (§ 184). In the central region both pronunciations were current (cf. *Rose* II, *du mains : humains, dou leur : douleur, u vis : fu vis, ou sein : vous ain, Intr.* pp. 290-291); in Later Middle French **dü** and **u** *ou* were the forms generalised, but in the sixteenth century the contracted forms of *en,* often confused with those of *a,* fell gradually into disuse (cf. Rydberg, *Krit. Jb.* VI, i, 225 ; Huguet, *Rabelais,* pp. 53, 54).

Section 4.—DEMONSTRATIVE PRONOUNS AND ADJECTIVES.

§ 844. *Compounded Forms.*—In Late Latin the demonstrative pronouns gradually lost force and were often strengthened by combination with the particle *ecce* (cf. Aug. '*Abscessit enim, et ecce hic est. Cum ecce illi, qui missi erant, reperint . . .*'), and it is these compounded forms that are the starting-point of the Old French demonstrative pronouns and adjectives : *cil, cist, ço.* The initial syllable of these strengthened forms was slurred early, under conditions not yet fully determined, but in the course of Early Old French the analogical forms *icil, icist, iço* were created under the influence of the adverb *ici,* itself formed under the influence of the adverbs *(i)luec* (< *illo loco*) and *(i)lore* (< *illa hora*), cf. Kjellmann, *Vising vol.* pp. 161-172, and Foulet, *Rom.* xlvi, pp. 571-577).

§ 845. *Paradigms of* cil *and* cist *in the Early Twelfth Century.*

	Masculine.			*Feminine.*			*Neuter.*
	Singular.		*Plural.*	*Singular.*		*Plural.*	*Singular.*
Nom.	cil,	icil	cil, icil	cele,	icele	celes, iceles	cel
Acc.	⎰cel,	icel	cels, icels	⎰cele,	icele	celes, iceles	cel
	⎱ce'lui,	ice'lui		⎱ce'li,	ice'li		
Dat.	ce'lui,	ice'lui		ce'li,	ice'li		
Nom.	cist,	icist	cist, icist	ceste,	iceste	⎰cestes, icestes	cest
						⎱cez, icez	
Acc.	⎰cest,	icest	cez, icez	⎰ceste,	iceste	⎰cestes, icestes	cest
	⎱ces'tui,	ices'tui		⎱ces'ti,	ices'ti	⎱cez, icez	
Dat.	ces'tui,	ices'tui		ces'ti,	ices'ti		

[For the forms *cil, celui, celi,* etc., cf. § 836; for the opening of ę in L.O.F. cf. §§ 493, 575 ; for the effacement of s cf. § 377.

✱✱ For northern *cis,* n. sg. cf. N. § xxvi; for *cilh, ilh* cf. N.E. § xv; for *caus, ciaus,* cf. N. § xvii, E. § ix, S.C. § xi; for *chil,* etc., *chist,* etc., cf. N. § 1.]

§ 846. *Later Old and Middle French.*—The neuter form *cel* early became obsolete, except in the locution *puet cel estre.*

The feminine form *cez* **tsęts,** shortened form of *cestes* **tsęstęs** (cf. *noz* < *nostres*), was generalised before the later twelfth century, except in the western region where *cestes* persisted into Late Middle French, cf. Huguet, *Syntaxe de Rabelais,* p. 88. In Middle French the masculine singular *cest* **sęt** < **tsęst** (§§ 377, 575) was reduced to **sę** or **sę**, when prae-consonantal, and these forms, under the influence of the article **lę,** began to be reduced to **sę** in the sixteenth century (**sę** Péletier, **sę** Ramus). The spelling *cest* persisted into Modern French ; *cet* and *cette* **sęt, sętę** were very generally reduced between vowels to **st** and **st(ę)** in conversation in Later Middle French, cf. *asteure* for *a ceste heure* (Th. I, p. 210).

The accusative forms were slowly generalised in Late Middle French, but *cil* remained in use in the earlier part of the sixteenth century.

The forms derived from **ecciste* began to be more and more restricted to the adjectival function, those from **eccille* to the pronominal. The addition of the adverbs *ci* and *la,* to indicate more clearly the demonstrative force, began in the thirteenth century.

Iceluy, icelle, etc., persisted into Modern French but were already beginning to appear pedantic in the sixteenth century.

Cf. Meigret : ' dę'qels toutefoęs le courtizant n'uze pas communemęnt ; çe sont plutót relatifs uzurpez par lę'praticięns pour lę'qels nous uzons de *le, la, lęs . . .* combien qę *içeluy* e *içęlle* ręmplisset mieus un papier,' Gr. p. 75, and Huguet, *op. cit.* pp. 88-94.

§ 847.　　　　*Paradigms of the Sixteenth Century.*

Pronoun.

Masculine.		*Feminine.*	
Singular.	*Plural.*	*Singular.*	*Plural.*
celui, celui-cy, -la	ceulx, ceulx-cy, ceulx-la	celle, celle-cy, celle-la	celles, celles-cy, celles-la
[iceluy, cil, cestuy, cestuy-cy, cestuy-la]	[iceulx, etc.]	[icelle, etc.] [ceste, etc.]	[icelles, etc.]

Adjective.

Masculine.		*Feminine.*	
Singular.	*Plural.*	*Singular.*	*Plural.*
cest, cet, ce	cez, ces	ceste, cete	cez, [cestes]
[cestuy, (i)-celui, cil]		[(i)-celle]	

[Forms in brackets those falling into disuse either in that particular function or altogether.]

§ 848. *co, ce.*—The Old French neuter pronoun **tsǫ** *co, ceo* is developed from the compounded neuter pronoun *ecce hoc,* but in the region

in which the stressed form of *ego* developed into **džję** or **džę** *gie, ge* (the region comprising the south-centre, south-west and south-east, § 829) this form was replaced by **tsę** (**tsję**), written *ce, cie, cei*, which persisted into the sixteenth century, cf. Jean le Maire, *pensé : en ce* (p. 67, l. 383). In the less stressed positions in the sentence the stressed forms were reduced to **tsę** *ce*, whose existence is attested metrically, (by elision of the vowel), in the later twelfth century and in rhyme in the early thirteenth, (*Escoufle, en est ce : hautece* 1615, *por tou ce : courouce* 7085, Rtbf. *je croi en ce : creance*, pp. 243, 257, cf. Rydberg, § 142).

The strengthened forms *ceci, cela* appear in the fourteenth century.

✶✶ § 849. In the northern region **tsǫ** became **tsu** or **tšu** (written *cou, chou* in Picard, *cu, chu* in Walloon) : in Normandy a nasalised form **tsēn** *cen* developed before words beginning with a nasal (cf. *jen*, § 830) ; another stressed form that survived into the sixteenth century and had considerable extension, particularly in the south-east, was *ceu*, which may, however, be derived from *cel* (cf. for all these forms Rydberg, II, pp. 619-786, H.L.F. I, 426).

§ 850. *Uncompounded Forms of hic, iste, ipse.*—By the end of the eleventh century the uncompounded forms of *hic, iste, ipse* had become obsolete except in derivatives or stereotyped phrases.

Uncompounded *hoc* survived in the phrases *oie < hoc ego* (§ 831), *o tu, o il, o el* (cf. § 834), *o nos, o vos* and in combination with the prepositions *ab, pro, sine* in *avuec* (whence *aveuc, av(ų)ec*, §§ 551, 553), *poruec, senuec*.

Uncompounded *ipse* survived in the fossilised phrases *en es le pas, en es l'oure*, and the feminine *esse* was used by Philippe de Thaon in the phrase *en esse la chariere*, *Comp.* 1433, *Best.* 1087. Out of the emphatic form **ipsimum*, strengthened by the particle *met* (**se met ipse, *se met ipsimum*), was developed O.F. *medesme* **mę(ð)ęzmę** (*< męmę*), and **mę(ð)izmę**, the latter formed under the influence of **is**, the mutated nominative form of *ipse* (§§ 419, 836). From *nec ipse* and *nec *ipsi* were derived similarly the two words *neës* and *neïs*, early reduced to *nes* and *nis*.

Forms derived from uncompounded *iste* appear in the *Oaths, Alexis* 41e (MS. P) and not infrequently in *Troie* (cf. H. Ganzlin, *Die Pronomina demonstrativa im Altfrz.*, 1888).

Section 5.—POSSESSIVE PRONOUNS AND ADJECTIVES.

§ 851　　　　*Paradigms of Later Old French.*

[Analogical forms of this period in italics.]

A. Pronouns of the Singular.

Stressed.

	Masculine.		*Feminine.*	
	Singular.	*Plural.*	*Singular.*	*Plural.*
First Person.				
Nom.	miens	mien	meie > moie *mienne*	meies > moies *miennes*
Acc.	mien	miens	meie > moie *mienne*	meies > moies *miennes*

Stressed.

Masculine.		Feminine.	
Singular.	*Plural.*	*Singular.*	*Plural.*

Second Person.

Nom.	tuens	tuen	toue > teue, *toie,*	toues > teues, *toies,*
	tiens	*tien*	*tienne*	*tiennes*
Acc.	tuen	tuens	toue > teue, *toie,*	toues > teues, *toies,*
	tien	*tiens*	*tienne*	*tiennes*

Similarly *suens, soue.*

Unstressed.

First Person.

| Nom. | mes | mi | ma, *mon* | mes |
| Acc. | mon | mes | ma, *mon* | mes |

Second Person.

| Nom. | tes | ti | ta, *ton* | tes |
| Acc. | ton | tes | ta, *ton* | tes |

Similarly *ses, sa.*

§ 852.   **B. Pronouns of the Plural.**

Stressed and Unstressed.

Masculine.		Feminine.	
Singular.	*Plural.*	*Singular.*	*Plural.*

First Person.

| Nom. | nostre | nostre | nostre | nostres, noz |
| Acc. | nostre | nostres, noz | nostre | nostres, noz |

Similarly *vostre.*

Third Person.

leur < lour < (il)lōrum *indeclinable.*

✳✳ § 853. In the western region much used forms of the unstressed nominative singular of the pronouns of the singular were **mis, tis, sis,** formed on the nominative plural **mi, ti, si** ; for south-central *mian, mianne,* etc., cf. § 472, S.C. § vi.

✳✳ In the northern region **ma, ta, sa,** were reduced to mę, tę, sę, *mon, ton, son* to *men, ten, sen* (N. § xii), and from nǫs (< nǫts, *noz,* cf. § 365 (ii)), there was built up a complete declension, masc. **nos : no, no : nos;** fem. **nos : no, nos : nos,** and later on *noe : noes,* cf. N. § xxv; for *mei, tei, sei* in the north-east cf. N.E. § xv.

§ 854. *Development of the Old French Forms.*

(i) *Differentiation of Tonic Vowels.*—In Late Latin, in accordance with the tendency to differentiate tonic vowels from juxtaposed unstressed ones of similar or very similar articulation (cf. § 131), the forms *męa, *męas, *tǫos, *tǫǫm, *sǫos, *sǫǫm, were differentiated to *mẹa, *mẹas, *tǫos, *tǫǫm, *sǫǫs, *sǫǫm.

§ 855. (ii) *Influence of Stress.*—(a) Under the influence of sentence stress double forms were developed in Late Latin and in the less stressed

forms the tonic vowel, become unstressed, was gradually slurred and thus ˈmẹμs > mẹos > mos, ˈmẹμm > mẹom > mọm, ˈmẹa > mẹa > ma, etc.   Subsequently *mos, tos, sos, mas, tas, sas* were reduced to *mes, tes, ses.*

Monosyllabic forms are cited by Virgilius Maro, a Gallic grammarian of the fifth century : ' Sunt et alia pronomina quae in latinitate ussitate non habentur et tamen indubie recipiuntur . . . ut *mus* . . . *mum* . . *mi* . . . *mos* . . . *ma* . . . *mas* . . . et *tus* pro *tuus*.'   (Cf. § 10 and Rydberg, I, 244.)

(*b*) In the course of Gallo-Roman the tonic vowels of the stressed forms were diphthongised and later differentiated in the ordinary way (cf. §§ 225, 226), e.g. *mẹom > **mieon > mien > mjēn (cf. § 510 and the place-name *Brienne < Brĕŏna*), *tọọm > **tuoon > tuon > tuen, *mẹa > meiẹ > moiẹ, *tọa > touẹ > teuẹ > töẹ.

§ 856. *Analogical Modifications.*—An analogical influence was exercised at one time or another : (i) by the forms of the first person on those of the other persons, (ii) by the accusative singular on the other cases, (iii) by the masculine forms on the feminine.

§ 857. (i) *Influence of the First Person.*—(*a*) The forms of the second person plural *vester, vestrum, vestra,* etc., were replaced in Late Latin by *voster, *vostru, *vostra,* etc., formed on the model of *noster,* etc.

(*b*) In the course of the twelfth century the feminine forms *toie, soie,* etc., were formed on the model of *moie,* etc., and in the later twelfth century the masculine forms *tuen, tuens, suen, suens* began to give way to *tien, tiens, sien, siens,* formed on the model of *mien, miens* (cf. *Cor. L.* xliv, liii, *sien,* Rtbf. *siens : biens, Conte Poit.* 68).

§ 858. (ii) *Influence of the Accusative Singular.*—(*a*) Before the twelfth century the declension of the stressed masculine forms of the pronouns of the singular had been entirely re-modelled on the form of the accusative singular and thus *miens, mien* had replaced the stressed forms derived from *mẹos, *mẹi and *tuens, tuen, suens, suen* those derived from the stressed forms *tọọs, tui, *sọọs, sui.

The existence of etymological stressed forms in the early period is attested for the first person : (*a*) by the use of *meos* in the *Strasbourg Oaths* and of *mei* in the north-east, (*b*) by the analogical northern French feminine form *mieue* (*miue,* § 546), modelled on earlier **mieus** (< **mẹos**), cf. N. § xxv.

§ 859. (iii) *Influence of the Masculine.*—In the thirteenth century the stressed forms of the feminine (*moie, teue,* etc.) began to give way to the analogical forms *mienne, tienne, sienne,* etc., formed on the model of the masculine.   The etymological feminine forms become rare in the fifteenth century.

§ 860. In the thirteenth century the use of phrases such as *bon*(*e*) *amie* appear to have provoked the use of the masculine form *mon* before feminine words beginning with a vowel, (*Rose* II, *mon art, son image*) ;

the extension of this form was facilitated by the frequency of double genders in Old French (§ 777), but it was not consistent until Later Middle French: modern *ma mie* (< *m'amie*) is a relic of the older usage.

§ 861. *Levelling of the Old French Declension.*—Case distinction among the possessives was gradually eliminated by the generalisation of the forms of the accusative on the same lines and at the same period as among substantives, i.e. in the course of the later thirteenth and fourteenth centuries.

In this same period inflected *leur* (*leurs*) began to replace *leur* in the plural (Boileaue, *leurs mestiers*, p. 157); its use was general, though not consistent, in Middle French (H.L.F. I, 424).

Section 6.—RELATIVE AND INTERROGATIVE PRONOUNS.

§ 862. A thinning out of the forms of the relative and interrogative pronouns began in Late Latin and the only ones that lived on into Old French were *qui, quem, cui, quid* and the adjective *qualis*.

qui and *quem* function as feminines in inscriptions of the fourth and fifth centuries, *qui*, nominative plural feminine, is not attested till a little later; *quis* began to be replaced by *qui* in Late Latin, *quid* begins to oust *quod* in the seventh century, (Rydberg, I, 342 et seqq.).

§ 863.   *Paradigms of the Early Twelfth Century.*

Pronouns.

Masculine and Feminine.				Neuter.		
Stressed.		*Unstressed.*		*Stressed.*		*Unstressed.*
Nom. qui	**ki**	qui	**ki**	} quei(t) quoi		que(t)
Acc. cui		que	**kę**	} **kweiθ > koi**		**kęθ > kę**
küi > kẅi						
Dat. cui	a cui					
Gen. cui, dont, de cui						

§ 864. Latin *qui* **kụi > ki** in the Gallo-Roman period (*Eul. chi* 12); the dative *cui* **küi** (< **kūī**) passed through **kẅi** to **ki** in the course of the twelfth century (§§ 515, 516). [For the confusion of *qui* and *qu'il* cf. § 841; for the spelling *chi* cf. § 694, for *ki, ke*, § 701.]

In the central region *qui* began to replace the neuter nominative *que* in the early thirteenth century; in eastern and western French *que* was maintained and its use extended to the feminine, more rarely the masculine, and in Later Middle French this use became very general (cf. Huguet, *Rabelais*, pp. 116-117).

The use of *quoi* was also extended, first to indefinite antecedents and things and then to persons. The relative adverb *ou* was also given relative function and in Later Middle French there was some confusion between *d'ou* and *dont*, i.e. between **du** and **dū** (§ 616).

Liquels (cf. below) came into use as an interrogative pronoun in the early twelfth century (cf. *Rol.* 735, 1387, 2553, etc.); as a relative in the later part of this century.

§ 865. *Adjective.*

	Singular.		*Plural.*	
	Masculine and Feminine.	*Neuter.*	*Masculine.*	*Feminine.*
Nom.	quels	quel	quel	quels
Acc.	quel	quel	quels	quels

§ 866. The analogical feminine form *quele* appears in the later twelfth century (e.g. Guernes, 1217), but *quel* is still used in attributive function in the early sixteenth century (§ 780); *quels* ke̜ɫs passed to kɪeus (> kjös) in the course of the twelfth century, (§ 388): analogical *quels* ke̜ls (< ke̜ls) appears in the same century and is the form usually employed in later Middle French though *quieus* is still occasional in the fifteenth century.

[For the pronunciation kẽs *quels*, ke̜ke̜ *quelque* cf. § 391 (i).]

§ 867. *Paradigms of the Early Sixteenth Century.*

Masculine, Feminine, Neuter.

Nom. qui, lequel, etc., que (unstressed).
Acc. qui, lequel, etc., quoi, que (unstressed).
Dat. a qui, auquel, etc., a quoy, ou.
Gen. de qui, duquel, etc., de quoy, dont, d'ou.

The delimitation of the spheres of these forms belongs to the seventeenth century, cf. H.L.F. II, pp. 318, 422-425, III (1), pp. 293, 294.

Section 7.—INDEFINITE PRONOUNS.

§ 868. Late Latin *tottus (< tōtus with emphatic lengthening of the consonant (?), Juret, p. 154) was declined as follows:—

	Masculine.		*Feminine.*	
Nom.	toz	tuit	tote	totes
Acc.	tot	toz	tote	totes

Tuit (tüit < to̜ttį with mutated vowel and metathesis of i̯, § 419) was sometimes replaced in Later Old French by to̜t, formed on the model of the other forms.

§ 869. *Chascun* (< *quisque unum* contaminated with the hybrid *kata unum*, § 749, O.F. *chedun, cheun, Oaths cadhuna*) served as both adjective and pronoun; the adjective *chasque*, formed from *chascun* on the model of *quelque—quelqu'un*), is occasional in Old French (e.g. Crest. *Cl.* 3326), but was not frequent before the sixteenth century.

§ 870. O.F. *autrui, nului (nelui)* were formed on *celui*; *on* is derived from *hŏmo* unstressed, O.F. *uem* from *hŏmo* stressed, O.F. e̜l from L.L. *alu (*ale ?) for *aliud*.

CHAPTER IV.

VERBS.

Section 1.—Survey of Development.

§ 871. *Late Latin and Gallo-Roman.*—The Latin conjugation system was maintained more fully than the declension system, but even more profoundly modified. Sound-change exercised its disintegrating influence, more especially in Gallo-Roman (§ 873), but the more fundamental changes were psychological in origin and had their beginnings in Late Latin. Forms that no longer served a function were discarded (e.g. the supines, the deponents); those that had become isolated or worn out were replaced by forms that were more in harmony with the system or more readily intelligible (e.g. the periphrases of *habere* and *esse* with the infinitive or past participle). The system was also modified by the creation of new forms fitted to express more fully shades of meaning that had become important, and thus a conjugation system that had served mainly to express the extent to which actions were completed was turned into one constructed to express more particularly *tense*, the stage of time at which an action takes place [cf. Meillet, *E.L.L.*, pp. 257-265].

§ 872. The more important of the changes that led to these results may be summarised as follows :—

(i) The forms of the deponent conjugation and the passive voice became obsolete, the former being replaced by active forms, the latter by the periphrasis of **esse** (***essere**) with the past participle. A certain unsteadiness in the use of the deponent forms is observable all through Latin (GG. §§ 113, 409) and isolated examples of the replacement of the passive by the periphrasis occur in the Latin of the Church Fathers, e.g. St. Augustine, *permissa est accedere*, (GG. § 112).

(ii) The supines fell into disuse, cf. St. Aug., *cum veneris ad bibere*, (GG. § 103).

(iii) The idea of futurity was more and more frequently expressed by periphrases such as the combination of the infinitive of the verb with the present or past tenses of the verbs *habere, velle, ire*, and the traditional forms gradually fell into disuse, except the much used future of *esse*.

In Gaul the periphrasis most in favour was that of the *infinitive* + *habere*, found functioning as a future in Late Latin, e.g. *unde mihi dare habes aquam vivam ; exire habebat* (GG. § 127 ; cf. also E. § xxviii).

(iv) The periphrasis of *habere* and the past participle slowly assumed tense value, the beginnings of the shift being also attested in Late Latin, cf. St. Aug., *metuo enim ne vos habeam fatigatos* (GG. § 122). On the model of the deponent verbs neuter verbs began to form past tenses with the past participle and *esse*.

(v) The function of the pluperfect was modified : in the subjunctive it gradually assumed simple past function and displaced the imperfect in most parts of the Empire ; in the indicative it acquired double value, that of simple past tense and of conditional. In northern Gaul the indicative forms became obsolete in the course of the eleventh century, except in the south-western region and Anglo-Norman.

The only examples attested in the twelfth century in continental French are *dure* (< *debuerat*) : *aventure, Thebes* 8557, and more doubtfully '*deuret*, Gormont 633, both with the conditional value that survived in Provençal. In Early Old French its use is frequent, mainly with simple past value, cf. *Eul. roveret, furet, auret, voldret, St. Legier, presdra*, etc., *Ste Euphrosine vire (viderat)*, 679. The *Vie de St. Alexis* contains examples of its use in both functions : (*a*) simple past *firet*, MS. L, xxv (*e*) : (*b*) conditional *sore (sapuerat)* and *oure (habuerat)*, MS. V, xcviii (*c*), (*e*).

§ 873. *Gallo-Roman.*—Sound-change (e.g. the levelling of -ĕŏ and ĭŏ, -ĕa and -ĭa under jo and ja, § 220, of ĭĕ under ę, § 220, of *amare, amarem, amaverim*, under *amare*), brought about a certain amount of confusion among the endings and conjugation systems in Late Latin, and this factor became much more disintegrating in Gallo-Roman, when the expiratory accent had been reinforced by the Germanic influence and palatalisation was at its height, (Pt. II, chaps. v and vi). To this period mainly may be assigned :—

(1) The gradual formation of a new conjugation system, the modern French *second*, from the Latin inchoative (inceptive) verbs with infix *sc*, *dormīscere*, etc. (§ 880).

(2) The reduction and effacement of unstressed **e, i, o, u** (§ 256) and consequent obliteration of the differences in the terminations of the present stem tenses in the Latin conjugations II, III, IV, which combine to form the *third* conjugation in French (§ 876).

(3) A drastic re-modelling of the types and terminations of the perfect indicative (and pluperfect subjunctive) that had for its result the formation of two main types of perfects : (*a*) *weak*, stressed throughout on the termination ; (*b*) *strong*, stressed in at least three persons on the radical (section 13).

(4) The development of much variety of radical (sections 8-10).

§ 874. *Early Old French.*—In the course of Early Old French terminations were somewhat further simplified :—

(i) An analogical termination -**ons** (≠ **sons** < **sumus**) was generalised in the first person plural of the present indicative and future, and frequently used in the present subjunctive and other tenses.

(ii) -*ez*, -*iez* (<-**atis**) were generalised in the second person plural of the present indicative and imperative, and used frequently elsewhere.

(iii) In the imperfect indicative and subjunctive and in the present subjunctive of *avoir* and a few other verbs the sequence of personal termination, -ę, -ęs, -t was established in the singular, §§ 917, 1046, 953, 955.

(iv) -**ānt,** the ending of the present participle and gerund of the first conjugation was adopted in other conjugations, § 921.

§ 875. In *Later Old and Middle French* simplification of radical and termination was carried much further :—

(i) In the first conjugation all types of vocalic alternation of radical, except ę—ę, were gradually eliminated by the generalisation of one or other radical ; by the end of the sixteenth century this process was almost complete (§§ 929, 930).

(ii) The new second conjugation was extended at the cost of the third and many of the more isolated forms of the third conjugation, e.g. infinitives such as *veintre, tortre, criembre,* futures like *cueudrai, baudrai, gerrai, harrai,* first persons such as *boif, serf, muir, vueil,* etc., were replaced by forms made more in harmony with the system to which they belonged.

(iii) The types of perfects were early reduced by the absorption into the weak **i**-*perfect* type of the perfects derived from verbs conjugated on the model of -*dedi* (§ 1006) and in the course of Middle French all alternation of stress in the strong perfects was eliminated either by the action of sound-change or by analogical re-formations or by both combined.   By the end of the period the types of perfect in use were those remaining in Modern French (sect. xvi).

(iv) In the first person of the present indicative and in the singular of the present subjunctive of the first conjugation, the etymological forms which were becoming more and more isolated from others by the influence of the sound-changes in process, were replaced by analogical forms in -ę. These forms make their appearance in the twelfth century and became general in Middle French (§§ 898, 909).

(v) In the first person of the present indicative of the third conjugation analogical -*s* (*z*) made its appearance in the early thirteenth century and was gradually extended to the first person of the perfects in -*i* and -*u* and of the imperfect indicative.   The influence of Latin retarded somewhat its extension in Late Middle French, but by the end of the

period the use of -s was general in the perfects and frequent, though not consistent in the present indicative and imperfect (§§ 899-902).

(vi) In the thirteenth century the ending -ions was developed in the subjunctive present from the contamination of -ons and -iens ; the endings -ons -ions, -ez -iez were generalised throughout the present stem tenses, but the modern differentiation of the terminations -ons and -ions, -ez and -iez in the present indicative and subjunctive was not consistently observed until the seventeenth century (§§ 907, 908).

(vii) In the first and second persons plural of the imperfect subjunctive of the first conjugation the ordinary Old French endings -issons (-issions), -issiez were only finally ousted by analogical -assions, -assiez in the later sixteenth century (§ 1044).

Section 2.—CLASSIFICATION OF CONJUGATIONS.

§ 876. In the course of Period I the differences between the terminations of the present stem tenses of the Latin second, third and fourth conjugations were obliterated by the reduction and effacement of unstressed vowels (§ 256) and the influence of analogy (§ 874) ; a new type was, however, developed out of the Latin inchoative (inceptive) verbs (§ 880), and there remained consequently in French *three* conjugations, two living and relatively homogeneous, the modern *first* and *second*, a *third*, heterogeneous and moribund, that comprised all verbs not included in the other two.

The customary modern French division into four conjugations has no real correspondence with usage but is based on Latin grammar and the terminations of the infinitive present.

§ 877. *Conjugation I* is derived from the Latin first conjugation. In Old French it was subdivided into two : (*a*) verbs whose infinitive ended in **-er**, e.g. *amer, durer, porter* ; (*b*) verbs whose infinitive ended in **-ier**, e.g. *aidier, cuidier, laissier*, viz. those verbs whose radical ended with a palatal or palatalised consonant in Gallo-Roman, because under the influence of such sounds **a** tonic free developed to ie (§ 414). The verbs in this sub-division were differentiated from the others in all the terminations in which **a** tonic free was preceded by a palatal sound, i.e. in the *past participle*, e.g. *laiss*-ie, the second person plural of the *present* of the *indicative* (and by extension of the subjunctive), e.g. *laiss*-iez, and in the third person plural of the perfect *laiss*-ierent. In the course of Middle French the difference was eliminated either by the normal reduction of ɪę to ę after the consonants š, ž, ɟ and ŋ (§ 510, *manger, chercher, conseiller, gagner*, etc.), or by the analogical re-formation of the terminations on the more common type (*laisser, aider*, etc.). The spellings *-ier*, etc., were only finally given up in the seventeenth century.

✱✱ In the northern and north-eastern region in which ˡie was reduced to i (N. §§ vii, xxxi), the termination *-ir*, etc., sometimes replaced *-ier*, etc. (cf. F. p. 212).

§ 878. *Conjugation I included:*

(1) Verbs derived from the Latin first conjugation, e.g. *amer, chanter, laissier.*

(2) Verbs derived from Germanic verbs in *-an* and *-ôn*, and more rarely from those in *-jan*, e.g. *guier* < **wîtan, espier* (< Prov. *espiar*) < **spehôn, guaaignier* < **waidanjan.*

(3) Derivatives and Latin loan-words of the first conjugation, e.g. *avesprer, mercier, enluminer, glorefier.*

§ 879. In the course of Middle French a few verbs were brought over from conjugation III under the influence of isolated associative influences. Thus O.F. *espelir* (<G. **spellôn), secourre* (<*subcutere), puir* (<**putire), tistre* (<*texere), tossir* (<*tûssire*), were replaced by *espeler, secouer, puer, tisser, tousser* under the influence of *appeler, nouer, tuer, glisser, pousser,* respectively.

In Middle and Early Modern French *recouvrer* and *recouvrir* were often confused (cf. Vgl. *Rem.* I, p. 69, F. p. 214); some loan-words (*afligir, contribuir,* etc.) and a few others (e.g. *grondir, sangloutir*) were replaced by new formations and the forms *cueille, cueilles,* etc. (§ 943) led to the formation of an infinitive form *cueiller* (cf. Vgl. *Rem.* II, 259).

§ 880. *Conjugation II,* infinitive termination **-ir,** was developed out of the Latin inchoative (inceptive) verbs, i.e. those verbs to which the use of the infix *-sc-* gave originally the significance of change of state or of beginning of action. The infix was originally used with verbs of all conjugations, cf. *irascere, parēscere, cognōscere, dormīscere,* but in Gaul and some other parts of the Roman Empire it attached itself more and more exclusively to the present stem tenses of the fourth conjugation, lost all significance and became a simple flexional element. When placed before the palatal vowels **e** and **i** (e.g. in *finiscebam, finiscentem, finiscis,* etc.) **isk** was palatalised to **iŝ** (> **is,** § 315) and the palatalised form was generalised in all the parts of the verb in which the infix had secured a place, i.e. throughout the present indicative and subjunctive as well as in the imperfect indicative, gerund and present participle.

§ 881. *Conjugation II included:*

(1) The verbs of Latin origin that had adopted this infix, e.g. *florir, norrir, porrir.*

(2) Verbs of Germanic origin derived from verbs in *-jan* and occasionally others, e.g. *choisir* < **kausjan, honir* < **haunjan, jehir* < **jehan.*

(3) Derivative verbs (especially those formed from adjectives), and Latin loanwords from conjugations II, III, IV, e.g. *asservir* (<*servum), baillir, blanchir, nercir, marchir* (< **marka); agir, relenquir.*

§ 882. *Conjugation III,* which included all verbs not comprised in conjugations II and III, had no organic unity and lost ground to conjugation II throughout the history of the language. The verbs mainly affected were those with infinitives in **-ir,** many of which had double forms already in Old French. Others were given analogical forms in Middle French and there was still uncertainty about the conjugation of some of the verbs in *-ir* in the seventeenth century (cf. H.L.F. IV, 719, etc.).

Double forms are attested of the following Old French verbs: *boillir, covir* (< *cupire*), *cropir, emplir, (a)ferir, glotir, guerpir, haïr, joïr, marir, norrir, offrir, partir, resplendir, soffrir, sortir, vertir* and. their compounds, cf. *Oxf. Ps. emples, raemplist; Rol. guerpisset; Chron. Norm. guert, guerpe; Oxf. Ps. esjoent,* Rtbf. *esjoie,* Cam. Ps. *esjoisse; Al. revert,* Rol. *convertisset.*

Inchoative forms of *haïr* made their appearance in the twelfth century (*Oxf. Ps. haissanz*), but the traditional forms were still preponderant in the sixteenth century (cf. §§ 960, 962 and verb table, p. 395). In the sixteenth century Palsgrave places *accroupir, deguerpir, (en)fouir, gloutir, gemir, jouir, merir, nourrir, vertir* entirely in conjugation II, but he attributes mixed forms to *emplir, marchir, partir, sentir, sortir, vestir* and their compounds; [for *benir* and *maudire* cf. §§ 960, 961].

Cf. Risop, *Studien zur Geschichte der Französischen Konjugation auf* -ir, Halle, 1891, F. §§ 13-17.

§ 883. *Conjugation III (infinitive terminations* -ir, -eir (> -oir), -rę) included :

(1) The surviving verbs of conjugations II and III, e.g. *deveir, valeir, defendre.*

(2) The surviving verbs of conjugation IV that had not adopted the infix -*sc*-, e.g. *oïr, sentir.*

(3) A few early borrowed verbs of Germanic origin, e.g. *espelir, guerpir* < **werpjan, haïr* < **hatjan,* and a few of clerkly origin, e.g. *beneïr, esvanuïr* (formed on *esvanuit*).

Interchange of the infinitive termination was frequent among verbs in this conjugation, induced in a few verbs by the action of sound-change, more often by associative influences.

§ 884. *Extension of the Termination* -ir.—(i) In verbs whose radicals ended in a palatal consonant in Gallo-Roman the termination -ęre was raised to -ir (§ 418), cf. O.F. *leisir* < *licere, plaisir* < *placere, taisir* < *tacere, moisir* < *mūcere, gesir.*

(ii) Already in Late Latin some of the i-*verbs* of the third conjugation began to adopt forms of the fourth, e.g. **cupire, *fodire, *fugire, *morire, *rapire* (GG. § 400, F. p. 5), and with the levelling of the terminations -ĕo, -ĕam, -io, -iam, etc., to the common forms -jo, -ja, etc. (§ 220) exchange of infinitive termination was extended to *complēre, implēre, florēre, gaudēre, merēre, putēre, putrēre, repoenitēre,* cf. O.F. *(a)complir, emplir, florir, joïr, merir, puïr, porrir, repentir.*

(iii) The anomalous infinitive forms *offerre, sufferre* were re-formed on the model of *aperire* and *co-operire; *fallire* was formed on *salire, *tollire* on *bullire.*

(iv) In the course of Period I ***teneir* was replaced by *tenir* ≠ *venir* (*tenire,* Form. Andecavenses; *tenoir* still occasional in O.F., cf. F. p. 223). In Middle French *courre* was replaced by *courir* ≠ *mourir, querre* by *querir* ≠ *ferir.*

The forms *chaïr, seïr, veïr* were of frequent use in Old French, especially in the northern region; the infinitive forms *suivir* and *venquir* were formed ≠ of the perfects *suivi* and *venqui, suïr* and *eschuïr* (*eschiver*) ≠ *fuïr* and the futures *circoncirai, clofirai, desconfirai, ocirai, souffirai* gave rise to the infinitives *circoncir, clofir, desconfir, ocir, souffir* in the thirteenth century (cf. Risop, *Studien,* 23).

§ 885. *Extension of the Infinitive Termination* -eir.—The anomalous forms *posse, velle* were early replaced by **potēre, *volēre* (≠ *potĕbam, potui, volebam, volui,* etc.), **cadēre* and **sapēre* were formed under the influence of *habēre, pluĕre* gave place to **plovēre.* In Later Old French *receivre,* etc., were replaced by *recevoir,* etc. ≠ *devoir* and *falloir* was formed ≠ *chaloir* and *valoir* in the fifteenth century.

§ 886. *Extension of the Infinitive Termination* -rę.—The infinitives **augĕre* (O.F. *aoire*), **docĕre, *mordĕre, *ridĕre, *respondĕre, *tergĕre, *torcĕre* (O.F. *tortre*) began early to replace *mordēre,* etc., and **essēre* displaced *esse.* Before the thirteenth century *plaisir, taisir* were replaced by *plaire, taire* (≠ *faire*), *luisir* and *nuisir* by *luire, nuire* (≠ *cuire*).

22

The future forms *ardrai*, *(a)saudrai*, *baudrai*, *boudrai*, *faudrai*, *istrai*, *(re)main-drai*, *semondrai*, *toudrai* gave rise to the O.F. infinitives *ardre*, *(a)saudre*, *baudre*, *boudre*, *faudre*, *istre*, *(re)maindre*, *semondre*, *toudre* for *ardoir*, *(a)saillir*, etc.

Section 3.—Terminations of the Present Indicative.

Paradigms of the Early Twelfth Century.

§ 887. *Conjugation I.*

Infinitive in **-er** *dur*-er, *entr*-er.			*Infinitive in* **-ier** *lei*-ier, *repair*-ier.	
—	*dur*	*entre*	*lei*	*repaire*
-ęs	*dur*-es	*entr*-es	*lei*-es	*repair*-es
-ęθ	*dur*-e(t)	*entr*-e(t)	*lei*-e(t)	*repair*-e(t)
-uns	*dur*-ons	*entr*-ons	*lei*-ons	*repair*-ons
-ęts **-iets**	*dur*-ez	*entr*-ez	*lei*-iez	*repair*-iez
-ęnt	*dur*-ent	*entr*-ent	*lei*-ent	*repair*-ent

§ 888. *Conjugation II.* *pun*-ir.

-is	*pun*-is	**-isuns**	*pun*-issons
-is	*pun*-is	**-isęts, -isiets**	*pun*-issez, *pun*-issiez
-ist	*pun*-ist	**-isęnt**	*pun*-issent

§ 889. *Conjugation III.*

	Infinitive in **-ir** *dorm*-ir.		*Infinitive in* **-eir** *ve(d)*-eir.	*Infinitive in* **-rę** *quer*-re.
—	*dorm*	*offre*	*vei*	*quier*
-s, -ts	*dor*-s	*offre*-s	*vei*-z	*quier*-s
-t (θ, § 356)	*dor*-t	*offre*-(t)	*vei*-t	*quier*-t
-uns	*dorm*-ons	*offr*-ons	*ve(d)*-ons	*quer*-ons
-ęts	*dorm*-ez	*offr*-ez	*ve(d)*-ez	*quer*-ez
-ęnt	*dorm*-ent	*offr*-ent	*vei(d)*-ent	*quier*-ent

Formation and Development of the Old French Forms.

§ 890. *Second Person Singular.*—*z* (**ts**) was the normal flexion of the third conjugation among all verbs whose radicals ended in **d, t, ʃ, ŋ** (§§ 318, 367), e.g. *creiz, hez, puez, venz, cueilz, plainz*; it was occasion-ally adopted by other verbs, e.g. *sez, deiz* (≠ *hez, creiz*), cf. *Et. Angier*, 60, 61. The symbol *z* lost all value when **ts** became **s** (§ 194) but its use persisted into the sixteenth century and was occasionally extended.

[For the effacement of s in the termination -ęs cf. § 623, F. p. 185.]

§ 891. *Third Person Singular.*—In the first conjugation **t** > **θ** and was effaced before the middle of the twelfth century (§ 346): in the other conjugations **t** remained into Old French II unless the radical required a supporting vowel, § 356, but was gradually effaced in prae-

consonantal position, more particularly after **r** and the nasal sounds (e.g. in *mort, ront, veint*, etc., § 615). In consequence of this pronunciation the spelling of this person in the verbs in *-aindre, -eindre, -oindre, -endre, -ondre, -ardre, -erdre, -ordre* and in *vaincre* was often modelled on the radical of the infinitive in Later Middle French, cf. Greban, *Mystere: prend* and *prent, deffend, estand, remord*.

Meigret admits *vainq* but, like Palsgrave (p. 396), disapproves of the substitution of **d** for **t**; 'ne faot pas estimer qe la tierse pẹrsone retiene le *d*, pour le *t*, come font aojourdhuy noz ecriueins contre l'ançiene coutume, qi ecriuent *pẹrd, fẹnd, tond,* pour *pẹrt, fẹnt, tont:* vu qe la prononçiaçíon le nou' montre, qant le vocable suyuant comẹnçe par voyẹlle: come *il pẹrt ẹ gañe . . . il tont aotant de draps q'un marchant ẹn vẹnt a la foẹre;* ẹ'quels tous, nous oyons le *t* soner fẹrme, tout einsi q'ẹn *dit, fẹt, conoẹt.*' (*Gr.* pp. 108, 109.)

§ 892. *Interrogative Forms.*—The pronunciation of **t** final in liaison in the interrogative forms of the third person of the plural of all conjugations, and of the singular of the second and third conjugations, led to its introduction into the interrogative form of the third singular of the first conjugation in Later Middle French.

The traditional form is still metrically attested in Villon, T. 1816. *Pour qui amasse il? Pour les siens*, but in the sixteenth century Péletier affirms: 'Nous disons *dine ti? ira ti?* e ecriuons *dine-il? ira-il?*' (Th. II, 141, cf. § 841.)

§ 893. *First Person Plural.*—The forms *faimes, dimes* lived on into the twelfth century, but in all other verbs the Latin endings were replaced in the course of Period I by the stressed termination **uns** *-ons, -uns* and its variants *-omes, -umes, -om, -um*. The starting-point of **-uns** appears to be O.F. *sons* **suns < sumus,** which may have served first as the model for the first person plural of the verbs whose third person plural ended in **-unt** *-ont*, e.g. *estons, alons, avons* (cf. M.L. *Gr.* § 292).

[For suggested Frankish influence cf. § 30 (ii); for use as first singular cf. § 74.]

✱✱ § 894. The absence of **-s** final which characterises this termination in the western region (*-om, -um, -on*, W. § xv), characterises also the endings employed in this person in Provençal (*-am, -em*) and is possibly due to a desire to restrict **s** to the second person. The ending *-on* was sometimes employed in francien, cf. Rtbf. 251, 1279, *amendon: bandon*, but its use there died out in the fifteenth century.

✱✱ § 895. The termination *-omes* (*-umes*) was probably introduced under the influence of *somes*, the alternative form of the first person singular of the present indicative of *estre* (§ 952). It is first attested in the N.E. (*Jonas, posciomes*) and in Later Old French was chiefly found in that region, but its use in the twelfth century was widespread, cf. *Rol.* 391, *avriumes; Eneas*, 6693 *disomes;* Crestien, *Cl. Intr.* p. lviii, (cf. for discussion and variant explanations, M.L. *Zts. frz. Spr. u. Lit.* XLIV, pp. 91-93, and Lorentz, *Die erste Pers. Plur. des Verbums in Altfrz* 1886).

The consistent use of the termination *-em* in *Alexis*, MS. V, (*auem* 107*b, poem* 124*b, serem* 105*e, Arch. Rom.* xiii, p. 64), indicates that the introduction of *-ons* was relatively late in the north-eastern region.

§ 896. *Second Person Plural.*—Apart from *estes, dites, faites*, and in the twelfth century *traites*, the only Latin endings that survived in the central and western region in this person were those proper to the first

conjugation, i.e. -*ez* and -*iez*, the latter developed from -*atis* preceded by a palatal or palatalised consonant (§ 414). In the fifteenth century, when ję was reduced to ę after the consonants ž, š, ʝ, ŋ (§ 510), -*ez* (ę(z)) was generalised.

[For the Middle French spelling cf. §§ 726, 807.]

✳✳ In the eastern region -*oiz* (< -eits < -ētis) persisted as well as a termination -*iz* -its < -ītis, [cf. E. § xxvi, M.L. *Zts. frz. Spr. u. Lit.* XLIV, pp. 88, 89].

§ 897. *Third Person Plural.*—Unstressed -**ant**, -**ent**, -**unt** all resulted in -**ęnt**, which was reduced to -**ęt** (< -ę̄t) in the late thirteenth century (§ 437) : before the end of the sixteenth century t final was ceasing to be pronounced at the pause as well as in prae-consonantal position (§§ 614, 615) and in the course of the next century it became mute in conversation before vowels (H.L.F. III (1), 321, F. § 97 ; cf. also § 623).

Cf. Tabourot (1587) : ' Pour le regard des noms, tu ne les sçaurois contrerimer en sorte que ce soit auec les verbes, combien qu'il y ait peu de différence quant à la prononciation : comme '' *Plusieurs me blasment Pour une dame* '' ; ny aussi avec le plurier : '' *Aucuns me blasment D'aimer les dames.*'' ' (Th. II, p. 99.)
[For termination-stressed forms cf. § 1048 ; for the extension -*ois* cf. E. § xxxi.]

Analogical Extension of ę and s in the First Person in Later Old and Middle French.

§ 898. *Conjugation I.*—The first person was flexionless in Old French, -**ę** being only in use among the verbs which had radicals requiring a supporting vowel, viz. paroxytone radicals ending in -**dž**, *plosive* + r or l, e.g. *enrage, repaire* < *repatrio, semble*, § 257, or proparoxytone radicals that had not been early reduced to paroxytones, e.g. *dote, juge*, § 259. Under the combined influence of these verbs and of the second and third persons of the tense, analogical forms in -ę began to make their appearance in the later twelfth century and became general in the later fourteenth century ; the isolation of the flexionless forms, which was increased by the tendency to efface final consonants (§§ 614-617), contributed to the rapid extension of the ending. Cf. Beroul, *someille* 1402, *grate* 3728 ; *Rose* I, metrically attested thirteen examples with -ę, twenty-three without (*Intr.* p. 315).

When the radicals no longer required an ę in Old French, analogical forms without it are not infrequent, e.g. *dot*, Beroul 2839, *desir*, *Rose* I, 2494.
In the interrogative form of all first persons, when in Late Middle French the stress shifted on to the final syllable, ę became ę and was written *ei* and *ay* as well as *e*, e.g. *Chansons XV, feussei-je* (cf. Rydberg, II, 654, Vgl. I, 343-344). In the sixteenth century verbs of the third conjugation were sometimes given a similar interrogative form, e.g. *entendé-je ? menté-je ? perdé-je ?* (cf. F. pp. 194, 195).

§ 899. *Conjugation III.*—The first person was flexionless in Old French, the forms which end in *s* or *z* (e.g. *faz, creis, conois, puis*) being ordinarily those in which *s* or *z* was a part of the radical. Analogical

forms in **ts** and **s** appear in the twelfth century ; these were formed at first ∓ *faz* **fats** and ended in -*z* (*guaz*, *Rol.* 515), but the group of verbs whose first persons ended in -*s* (*puis, creis, conois, finis*, etc.) also served as a model (*Rose* I, *tiens, viens, atens, sens*, etc.), and when in the thirteenth century **ts** became **s** (§ 194), the use of **s**-forms gained ground, their vogue being increased by the relative isolation of the flexionless forms ; in Greban's *Passion* the proportion is still, however, only 1 : 2 (F. p. 181).

The use of *s* and *z* was not at first confined to the third conjugation, cf. *Rose* I, *ains, acors*, and in Late Middle French *je parles, achettes, confesses* (F. p. 182).

The verbs whose radicals ended in a group of consonants requiring a supporting vowel ended in ẹ, e.g. *cuevre, offre, souffre*.

✱✱ § 900. In the northern region, where *facio* developed into **fatš** *fach* (§ 306), analogical first persons were formed ending in **tš**, graphy *ch* or *c*, cf. *Auc. siec*, 10, 21, *atenc*, 40, 18 (N. § xxviii).

✱✱ In the western region analogical forms of the first person were made on the model of verbs whose radical ended in -*c* **k** (✱✱*planc*, ✱✱*sorc*, ✱✱*aerc*, §§ 938, 941), e.g. *Rol. moerc* 1122, *Oxf. Ps. vienc*, (M. 20), cf. § 910, W. § xvii, *Et. Angier*, pp. 34, 35, 60.

§ 901. *Extension of* -**s** *to other tenses.*—The growing dislike of hiatus increased the vogue of the forms in -**s** and in Middle French it began to be adopted in other tenses also : (i) in the first person of the perfects in -**i** and -**ü** (*senti-s, valu-s, du-s*) where its introduction was facilitated by the forms of the **s**-*perfects* (*fis, mis, pris*, etc.) ; (ii) in the first person singular of the imperfect indicative, e.g. *duroi(e)s, sentoi(e)s ;* (iii) in *soi(e)s*, the first person of the present subjunctive of *estre*.

§ 902. In the sixteenth century the extension of first person singular forms in -*s* received a temporary set-back owing to the prejudices of the scholars, who, influenced by Latin, viewed **s** as the flexion proper to the second person only : the paradigms given by Meigret, for instance, contain fewer forms in -*s* than those furnished by Palsgrave. By the beginning of the seventeenth century, however, **s** was established in the first person of all perfects in -**i** and -**ü**, and by the middle of the century it was usual in the imperfect indicative and in the form *sois ;* in the present indicative hesitation continued throughout the century, but by this time the question had become mainly one of spelling, except when liaison was made.

Sebillet : ' Tu te dois garder de mettre *s* aux premieres personnes singulieres des verbes de quelque moeuf ou temps qu'ils soient : comme *ie voy*, . . . *ie aimoye*, . . . *ie rendi ;* ce que tu verras aujourd'huy observé des sauans en leurs escritures : et la raison t'enseigne que tu le dois observer ainsi, à cause que *s* est note de seconde personne aux Grecs et aux Latins : et doit estre à nous, qui tenons d'eux la pluspart du bien que nous auons.' Ramus : ' Pour ne point tomber en une deplaisante concurrence de voyelles nous interposons quelque fois . . . une *s* comme . . . *ie ris et pleure* pour . . . *ie ri et pleure* non pas que . . . *s* soit a telle personne, mais pour tant qu'il plaict ainsi a l'oreille.' Tabourot : ' les premieres personnes en *oi* ou *oie* se peuuent librement terminer en -*ois*, quand une voyelle suit : comme *ie diray* pour la douceur du vers *i'aimois une belle femme* plustost que simplement *i'aimoy une belle*

femme ou *i'aimoye une belle femme.* Et ainsi en usent tous nos poètes.' H. Estienne :
' There are many who write and pronounce *i'alloys a la ville*, who not only do not
pronounce *s* in *i'alloi dehors* but also do not write it.' (Th. II, 40-44 ; cf. also Ronsard,
Art Poétique, VII, 333.)

The treatment of the question by Vaugelas is characteristic : ' *ie crois, ie fais, ie
dis, ie crains*. . . . Quelques-uns ont creu qu'il falloit oster l's finale de la premiere
personne, et escrire, *ie croy, ie fay, ie dy, ie crain*, etc., changeant l'*i* en *y*, selon le
genie de nostre langue, qui aime fort l'usage des *y* grecs à la fin de la pluspart des
mots terminez en i, et qu'il falloit écrire ainsi la premiere personne pour la distinguer
d'auec la seconde, *tu crois, tu fais*, etc. Il est certain que la raison le voudroit, pour
oster toute equiuoque, et pour la richesse et la beauté de la langue ; mais on pratique
le contraire, et l'on ne met point de difference ordinairement entre ces deux personnes.
. . . Ce n'est pas que ce fust une faute, quand on osteroit l's mais il est beaucoup
mieux de la mettre tousjours dans la prose. . . . Nos Poëtes se seruent de l'un et de
l'autre à la fin du vers, pour la commodité de la rime ; M. de Malherbe a fait rimer
au preterit parfait definy, *couury*, auec *Iury*. . . . C'est contre l'usage de nostre langue,
qui ne le permet qu'à la premiere personne du present de l'indicatif, et non pas aux
autre temps. . . . A mon auis, ce qui a fait prendre l's, c'est que l'on a voulu euiter
la frequente cacophonie que cette premiere personne faisoit auec tous les mots, qui
commencent par une voyelle, car pour ceux qui commencent par une consonne, l's,
qui precede ne se prononce pas. Mais il ne s'agit pas d'examiner s'il y a raison ou
non, il suffit d'alleguer l'vsage, qui ne souffre point de replique,' I, 226.

The Academy, in its comment in 1704, prescribed, with an equally characteristic
lack of historical knowledge, *scay* and *voy* without *s*, *fais, dis, crains, prens*, etc., with *s*,
' to denote the length of the vowel in these forms ' (cf. § 567) ; and left the use of *s*
optional in *conoi(s), aperçoi(s), croi(s), doi(s), conceuoi(s)*.

[Cf. also H.L.F. III (1), pp. 318-321.]

Section 4.—Terminations of the Present Subjunctive.

Paradigms of the Early Twelfth Century.

§ 903. *Conjugation I.*

Infinitive in **-er** *dur-*er, *entr-*er.			*Infinitive in* **-ier** *lei-*ier, *repair-*ier.	
—	*dur*	*entre*	*lei*	*repaire*
-s, ts	*dur-*s	*entre-*s	*lei-*s	*repaire -*s
-t, (θ, § 356)	*dur-*t	*entre-*(t)	*lei-*t	*repaire-*(t)
-uns	*dur-*ons	*entr-*ons	*lei-*ons	*repair-*ons
-ẹts, -iets	*dur-*ez	*entr-*ez	*lei-*iez	*repair-*iez
-ẹnt	*dur-*ent	*entr-*ent	*lei-*ent	*repair-*ent

§ 904. *Conjugation II.*

Infinitive in **-ir** *pun-*ir.

-isẹ	*pun-*isse
-isẹs	*pun-*isses
-isẹ(θ)	*pun-*isse(t)
-isuns, (-isiens ?)	*pun-*issons
-isiets, -isẹts	*pun-*issiez
-isẹnt	*pun-*issent

§ 905. *Conjugation III.*

Infinitive in **-ir** *dorm-*ir, *in* **-eir** *ve(d)-*eir,
in **-rẹ** *quer-*rẹ.

-ẹ	*dorm-*e	*vei-*e	*quier-*e
-ẹs	*dorm-*es	*vei-*es	*quier-*es
-ẹ(θ)	*dorm-*e(t)	*vei-*e(t)	*quier-*e(t)
-uns, (-iens ?)	*dorm-*ons	*vei-*ons	*quer-*ons
-ẹts, -iets	*dorm-*ez	*vei-*iez	*quer-*ez
-ẹnt	*dorm-*ent	*vei-*ent	*quier-*ent

Formation of Old French Forms.

§ 906. *Second Person Singular.*—*z* (**ts**) was the normal flexion of all verbs of the first conjugation whose radicals ended in **d, t** (§ 367), **ļ**, and **ŋ** (§ 318), **rn** or **nn** (§ 365 (ii)), cf. O.F. *neuz* (< *nodes*), *porz, conseilz, deinz* (< *dignes*), *torz* (< *tornes*).

§ 907. *First Person Plural.*—In the extant works of the western region in the twelfth century the etymological forms of the first person plural are already superseded by the analogical forms of the present indicative : *-ons, -uns, -om, -um, -omes, -umes,* cf. *Rol. dejetuns* 226, *perduns* 45, 59, etc., but in the eastern and northern region and probably the central, *-iens*, developed from ***jamŭs** <-**ĕamus, -iamus** and from **-amus** preceded by a palatal or palatalised consonant (§ 414) remained in use (E. § xxvi). This form gained ground in the central region in the later thirteenth and fourteenth centuries, and preponderates in Parisian documents of the fourteenth century (cf. *Ord. des Rois : acordiens et octroiens, aiens, faciens,* etc., *Archiv* lxv, 90). From the contamination of the two forms *-iens* and *-ons* there arose at this time the form *-ions* which became general in the later fifteenth century and was accepted by most of the sixteenth-century grammarians, although *-ons* remained in use through the century (cf. H.L.F. II, 341-342).

§ 908. *Second Person Plural.*—In the central and western region the forms ordinarily in use were *-ez* -**ẹts** (< **atis**) and *-iez* -**ịets** (< -**ĕatis, -iatis** and **-atis** preceded by a palatal or palatalised consonant, § 414) : in Old French **-iez** was extended to verbs with such radicals and only these. Its generalisation in Middle French followed on the adoption of *-ions* in the first person plural, and though *-ez* is still frequent in the sixteenth century *-iez* is the only termination prescribed by the grammarians of that time (cf. H.L.F. II, 341).

✳✳ *-oiz* (< **-eits** < **-ẹtis**) continued in use in O.F. II (*Cam. Ps. recunteiz,* 47, 14), more particularly in the eastern region, cf. Crest. E. *parloiz : droiz* 173, E. § xxvi.

[For the use of **t** and **θ** in the third person singular cf. § 356; for the ending of the third person plural cf. § 897; for dialectal termination-stressed forms cf. §§ 1048, E. § xxix, S.C. § xix, S.W. xi.]

§ 909. *Extension of Forms in* -**ẹ** *in Conjugation I.*—In the singular of the subjunctive of the first conjugation, as in the first person singular of the indicative (§ 898), -**ẹ** was at first only in use in the terminations of the verbs whose radicals required a supporting vowel, or had been proparoxytone in Gallo-Roman, §§ 257-259, e.g. *entre, semble, repaire, dote,* etc., but under the combined influence of the verbs of this type and of the subjunctive of the other conjugations analogical forms in -**ẹ** made their appearance in the early twelfth century, cf. *Rol. merciet* 519, *Brendan, Intr.* clxxii. The isolation of the traditional forms, which was

greatly increased by the sound-changes of the Later Old French period, gave impetus to the adoption of the analogical forms, and they became general in the course of the fourteenth century, latest in the much used third person.

> *Rose* I, Pres. Subj. 1 : two examples with analogical -*e*, three without.
>   3 : no examples with analogical -*e*, twenty without.
> *Rose* II, Pres. Subj. 1 : six examples with analogical -*e*, six without.
>   3 : eighteen examples with analogical -*e*, over eighty without.
>   (*Intr.* pp. 325, 326.)

As in the first person singular of the indicative analogical forms without -ę were sometimes adopted by verbs which had earlier required it, cf. *chevalzt*, *Rol.* 2109, *culzt*, *Rol.* 1682, *repairt*, *Oxf. Ps.* (M. 24), *dot*, Crestien, *E.* 3876.

In stereotyped phrases etymological forms survived into and even beyond the sixteenth century, e.g. *Dieu te gard!*, *Le diable m'emport!*, *Dieu t'ait!*, *M'ait Dieux!*, written sometimes *Medieus* or *Medieu*, (cf. F. pp. 198-199).

✱✱ § 910.—In Old French there was a marked tendency to differentiate the forms of the subjunctive in a characteristic way. In West French use was made of the infix -*ge* **džę**, adopted from verbs in which -**džę** was the normal development of the radical (§ 300), e.g. *aerge* (**aderga* < *aderiga*), *sorge*, *lerge*, *plange*, etc., cf. *Rol. alge* 288, etc., *moerge* 359, *moerjum* 1518 ; *Troie, prenge : venge* 12227, *vienge : criem ge* 12903, etc., W. § xvii ; in the north and east the model followed was the subjunctive of *faire*, **fatsę** or **fatšę** (§ 306), and -*che* or -*ce*, later -*sse*, was adopted, cf. Mousket, *mence : diemence ; Ombre, messiece : piece, mece : destrece ; Ps. Lor. messe* (N. § xxix) ; in the east and south-east forms in -*oie* (≠ *soie*) and -*oisse* (-*oie*+-*sse*) were employed (E. § xxxi).

In the central region forms in -*ge* and -*ce* are occasional, e.g. Rtbf. *griece* (**grevet*): *piece*, Elis. 1834, Guiart, *eschiece : niece* 2667, cf. *Rose, Intr.* p. 327.

Section 5.—TERMINATIONS OF THE IMPERATIVE.

§ 911. Of the Latin terminations of the imperative only the second person singular was preserved : the second plural was replaced by the indicative, which was also used as the optative in the first person plural.

Conjugation I.				*Conjugation II.*
dur-e	*entre*	*lei*-e	*repaire*	*pun*-is
dur-ez	*entr*-ez	*lei*-iez	*repair*-iez	*pun*-issiez, *pun*-issez

Conjugation III.

dorm	*vei*	*quier*	*di*	*fai*
dorm-ez	*ve*-ez	*quer*-ez	*di*-tes	*fai*-tes

[For the radical cf. below ; for the shortened forms (*a*)*gar*, *aga*, *dor*, *pren*, *ser*, etc., cf. § 937 ; for *di* and *fai* cf. § 357, for *va* cf. § 959.]

§ 912. In the conjugation of the verbs *avoir*, *estre*, *savoir*, *voleir* the subjunctive forms were in use, and remained dominant throughout Old and Middle French, although forms of *savoir* and *vouloir* modelled on the indicative are occasional, e.g. *ses*, *veulx* (cf. also § 957).

§ 913. *Extension of Flexional* -*s*.—In Later Old French analogical forms in -*s* (*z*) began to be formed in the second person singular in con-

jugation III under the combined influence of forms such as *aies*, *soies*, *saches*, *vueilles*, the second person singular of the imperative of conjugation II (*punis*) and of the indicative present of conjugation III, (*Alexis* MS. L. *Oz* xiva; *Auc. Os* xxii, 15; cf. *vas*, *Al.* MS. L. 11*b*).

In Middle French there was much fluctuation, increased by the frequent effacement of final -s (§§ 621, 623), and the question became very largely one of scribal tradition. In this period: (i) *s* is frequently extended to the first conjugation, cf. *Mir. N.D.* aymes, donnes, vas, etc., Villon, *luttes* T. 1700, *reculles* T. 1708; (ii) the subjunctive forms *aies*, *soies*, *saches*, *vueilles*, when functioning as imperatives, are often docked of their final *s*.

In the sixteenth century Meigret prescribed the modern rule for the first conjugation (*Gr.* pp. 126, 127) but fluctuations continued through the century (cf. H.L.F. II, 327-329, F. § 106).

Palsgrave's rules illustrate the uncertainty of the time : ' if the seconde parson of the present indycatyve have a vowell afore *s*, outher alone or in a dyphthonge, they use ever, in the imperatyve, to put the *s* away, as ... *va, dy, fay, voy*. But if the sayd person indycatyve ende in a consonant, though, for the moste parte, they ever leave out *s*, to sayeng *pren, ren, sort, met*, yet I fynde them also with *s*, as *prens, rens, sorts, mets*' (pp. 398-399).

Section 6.—TERMINATIONS OF THE IMPERFECT INDICATIVE.

Paradigms of the Twelfth Century.

✶✶ § 914. *Conjugation I.*

		West French.		East French.	
-ọụẹ,	-ọẹ	port-oue,	port-oe	-ẹvẹ	port-eve
-ọụẹs,	-ọẹs	port-oues,	port-oes	-ẹvẹs	port-eves
-ọụt,	-ọt	port-out,	port-ot	-ẹvẹ(θ)	port-eve
-ïiens,	-ïuns	port-ïiens,	port-ïons	-ïiens	port-ïiens
-ïiets		port-ïiez		-ïiez	port-ïiez
-ọụẹnt,	-ọẹnt	port-ouent,	port-oent	-ẹvẹnt	port-event.

§ 915. *Conjugations II and III.*

-eịẹ	> -oịẹ	pun-iss-eie	> pun-iss-oie	dorm-eie	> dorm-oie
-eịẹs	> -oịẹs	pun-iss-eies	> pun-iss-oies	dorm-eies	> dorm-oies
-eịt	> -oịt	pun-iss-eit	> pun-iss-oit	dorm-eit	> dorm-oit
-ïiens,	-ïuns	pun-iss-ïiens,	pun-iss-ïons	dorm-ïiens,	dorm-ïons
-ïiets		pun-iss-ïiez		dorm-ïiez	
-eịẹnt	> -oịẹnt	pun-iss-eient	> pun-iss-oient	dorm-eient	> dorm-oient.

§ 916. *Conjugation I.*—The imperfect is little used in Old French, and in the central and northern region the forms of the first conjugation have for the most part already been superseded by those derived from the termination -*ebam* by the time attesting documents containing them

are extant.   A few examples of the third person singular of this type are preserved and these end as in western French in *-ot*, e.g. Rtbf. *amot : mot*, p. 130, l. 167.

The eastern development is the normal one found in the sound sequence **-aba** (cf. **fęvę < faba**) and it is modified to **-ievę** after a palatal in the ordinary way (e.g. *mangieve*, cf. § 414).   The western development is that ordinarily found in this region in the sound sequence **-aµa** (cf. § 483).   In both regions these terminations were supplanted by that of the other conjugations before the fourteenth century (cf. W. Müller, *Beiträge zur Geschichte des Imperf. Ind. im Altfrz.* 1904, Darmstadt).

⁑ In the eastern region there also survived into the thirteenth century a termination **-ivę**, etc., derived from a Late Latin form **-ibam**, made on **-ire**, etc., cf. E. § xxvii, M.L. *Einf.* § 171.

⁑ The development of the western endings was influenced by the forms of the strong **u**-perfects (§ 1020): (1) the form of the third singular, *out, pout*, etc., appears to have been the model for the termination **-oµt**, which replaced Early O.F. **-oµeθ** (cf. *Passion*, 48*b*, *uuardouet*); (2) in Later Old French the diphthongal forms of 1-3 and 6, (e.g. *Rou* II, 1776 *laissout : Herolt*) were replaced by **-ǫę, -ǫęs, -ǫt, -ǫęnt** ÷ the later perfect forms **ǫt, pǫt**, etc. (§ 1025), cf. Marie Fr., *Fables : semblot : mot*, 34, 45; Beroul, *amot : esjot* 2519, *gardo(i)t : tripot* 4347.   Where **ǫu** is differentiated to **eu**, N. § viii, a termination *-eue, -eut, -euent* is found, cf. F. p. 236.

§ 917. *Conjugations II and III.*—The terminations of the second and third conjugations are derived from the Latin second conjugation, which absorbed **iēbam** in Late Latin (§ 945); the forms *-ebam, -ebas*, etc., *-ęβα, *-ęβαs, etc., § 333, were, it is thought, dissimilated to **-ęa**, etc., in the conjugation of the imperfect of verbs with labial radicals (*habebam, debebam, bibebam, vivebam*, etc.) and this dissimilated form was extended to other verbs, GG. § 421.

In the earliest Old French texts the termination of the third person singular was *-eiet* **-eięθ** (*Eul. sostendreiet* 16, *Jonas, doceiet*, etc.): before the end of Period I the similarity of the terminations *-eie, -eies, -eiet* to the sequence of forms in the present subjunctive of *estre—seie, seies, seit*—led to the replacement of **-eięθ** by **-eit**, cf. *Al. aveit* 334, *deveit* 77, *serveit* 336.

The development of the tonic vowel *ei* is normal: **ei > oi > ǫę > ę** (attested first in the late thirteenth century, finally accepted only in the seventeenth, §§ 519, 522, Vgl. I, 185).   Under the influence of the third person singular final **-ę** in hiatus began to be disregarded in the thirteenth century, earliest in the northern region, e.g. *P. Mor. sarroi* 98*c*, *voldroi* 167*c*, etc., cf. Tobler, *Frz. Versbau³*, pp. 41, 42; its complete effacement was very general in the sixteenth century (§ 271): Palsgrave still prefers *-oye*, but Meigret only differentiates between the third singular *estoit* and the third plural *estoient* by the length of the vowel in the latter, writing *etoęt* and *etoȩ̄t*.

[For the use of s in the first person cf. §§ 901, 902; for the effacement of **nt** cf. § 897; for dialectal termination-stressed forms of the third person plural cf. § 1048; for dialectal ę < ei cf. W. § vi, S.C. § iv.]

§ 918. *First and Second Persons Plural.*—In the western region -*iiens* was replaced by -*iuns* (-*ium*, etc., cf. § 893) in the twelfth century (cf. *Rol. avium* 1547, *avriumes* 391, *Oxf. Ps. recordiums*) and in the thirteenth century these forms became general in the central region. Both -*ions* and -*iiez* became monosyllabic by the consonantalisation of intertonic i in the same century (§ 267).

§ 919. The development of these terminations offers some difficulty. The oldest forms appear to be -*eiiens*, -*eiiez* (eɹⁱiens(?), eɹⁱiets(?)), and the most plausible explanation of them is that the hiatus created in the Late Latin forms by the disappearance of the intervocalic labial consonant was maintained relatively late under the influence of the other persons (-ⁱęa, -ⁱęas, etc.), and obviated, not, as earlier, by the consonantalisation of the unstressed vowel in hiatus, but by the development of an intervocalic palatal glide, under whose influence tonic a was raised to ę and diphthongised to ⁱie in the normal way (§ 414): *-ęamǫs > **-ęjamǫs > -eɹⁱiens, *-ęatęs > **-ęjatęs> -eɹⁱiets (cf. O.F. *seiiens* seɹiens < *sęamǫs). The subsequent raising of intertonic ę to i was presumably provoked by the influence of the following palatal consonant (cf. *pavillon* paviɹūn < paveɹun, § 422): *charrier* (< *charreier*, § 927) shows a parallel development.

✱✱ In the northern region -*iens* persisted late and, contaminated with -*umes*, gave rise to an ending -*iemes* (cf. N. § xxvii, and for a variant explanation, Meyer-Lübke, *Zts. frz. Spr. u. Lit.* XLIV, pp. 93-95). In this same region the terminations became monosyllabic relatively early (cf. *Auc. aferries*, 14, 25 and N. § xi; for eastern forms, cf. E. § xxix).

§ 920. *Estre.*—In the conjugation of the verb *estre* the analogical imperfect *esteie* was already in use in Old French I but the etymological forms derived from Latin *eram*, etc., lived on, those of the most used persons into the fourteenth century. In the twelfth century the forms in use were: *iere, ere; ieres, eres; iere, ere, ert; eriiens, erions; eriiez; ierent, erent.*

The undiphthongised forms, which assonate with ę < a tonic free, appear to have been influenced by the radical of the pluperfect of the first conjugation (*roveret, ameret*, etc., § 231). The forms *erïiens, erïons; eriiez* are infrequent except in the more southern region, where they gave rise to the forms *ereie, ereies, ereit, ereient* (*Et. Angier*, pp. 46-47).

Section 7.—PRESENT PARTICIPLE AND GERUND.

§ 921. In the forms derived from the Latin gerund and present participle the termination of the first conjugation was generalised in the course of Old French I, cf. *Alexis, vailant* 8, *remanant* 9, *vivant* 39. (For the feminine and the declension of the present participle cf. §§ 779, 780, 790, 797, 802.)

✱✱ In the south-eastern and south-western region (cf. Provençal) the ending -*ent* (< *entem* and -*endō*) is sometimes found (e.g. *Troie, manent : argent* 26668). [For the extension of the palatalised radical cf. § 949.]

Section 8.—Variations in the Radical of the Present-Stem Tenses due to Incidence of Stress.

§ 922. Much variation in the radicals of the Old French verb was produced by the sound-changes that took place in Period I. The chief factors operative were :—

(1) The varying accentuation of the Latin verb.

(2) The influence of position in the word on the development of consonants.

(3) The varying development of the velar consonants.

(4) The influence of *jod*, developed from unstressed **e** and **i** in hiatus.

§ 923. In the conjugation of the Latin verb the main stress may fall either on the *radical*, e.g. in ˈa*mo*, ˈa*mas*, ˈa*mat*, ˈa*mant*, ˈa*ma*, ˈa*mem*, ˈmo*neo*, ˈau*dio*, etc., or on the *termination*, e.g. aˈma*re*, aˈma*mus*, aˈma*tis*, aˈme*mus*, etc. Forms stressed on the radical are called *strong*, those stressed on the termination *weak*.

In the present stem tenses of the Latin verb the stress fell on the radical :—

(i) In *all* conjugations, in the singular and third person plural of the present indicative and subjunctive and in the singular of the imperative.

(ii) In the *third* conjugation, in the infinitive present, in the first and second persons plural of the present indicative and in the second person plural of the imperative. In the indicative and imperative this type of termination was very generally replaced by stressed forms before Old French II, §§ 893, 896.

§ 924. Owing to the way in which the development of vowels was affected by the presence or absence of stress (Pt. II, chap. v), its varying incidence in the conjugation of the verb produced variations both in the number of syllables in the radical and in the form of the vowels, and these variations often led to modifications in the development of the final consonant of the radical. The systematic variation in the *number* of *syllables* in the radical provoked by the incidence of stress is termed *syllabic alternation ;* the systematic variation in the *vowel* of the radical provoked in this way is called variously *vocalic* or *vowel alternation, vowel gradation* and *apophony*. In this book the term *vocalic alternation* is used.

§ 925. *Syllabic Alternation* is found among verbs containing *poly-syllabic* radicals in which the last syllable is *long*, for in the conjugation of verbs of this type this syllable persisted when stressed and fell when

unstressed, unless its vowel was required as a supporting vowel (cf. § 926 (2)): *pa'raulo > parọl, *parau'lare > parlẹr. The marked disparity between the radicals that was thus produced led to the early re-formation of all but the most commonly used verbs, and double radicals of this type are only found in more or less consistent use in Old French II in the conjugation of the following verbs :—

aid-*ier* < adjū'ṭ-*are* aiu-*e* ajuẹ < a'djūt-*at* (*aïe* by the unrounding of ü by ȷ, § 424)

*a*raisn-*ier* < **adratjō'n-are* *a*rai'son-*e* < **adra'tjōn-at*

*de*raisn-*ier* < **deratjō'n-are* *de*rai'son-*e* < **dera'tjōn-at*

disn-*er* < **dis(je)jū'n-are* des'jun-*e* < **dis(je)'jūn-at*

mang-*ier* < mandū'c-*are* man'ju-*e* (**mān'džü-ẹ** < **man'dūcat** contaminated with the weak radical **mandž-**)

parl-*er* < **parau'l-are* pa'rol-*e* < **pa'raul-at*

In the fifteenth century *aidier ẹdier* was still conjugated on the two radicals *aid-* ẹd- and aïd- (< **aid-** contaminated with aï-) and Palsgrave cites *je desjune, je manjeue* and *je parole*. Modern French *déjeuner* is a derivative of the substantive *jeûne*.

Double radicals are occasionally found in Old French in the conjugation of the verbs *assaisnier* (**adsatiōnare*), *empoisnier* (< **impotiōnare*), *mincier* (< **minūtiare*), *percier* (< **pertūsiare*).

§ 926. *Vocalic Alternation* is frequent among verbs containing a monosyllabic radical, occasional in others.

(1) *Monosyllabic Radicals.*—Alternation was induced in all verb-radicals containing vowels whose development was modified by variations of stress. These include radicals containing, in Late Latin :—

(i) ẹ, ẹ, ọ, ọ and **a**, when *free* and unmodified by other sounds (§§ 225, 226, 231).

(ii) ẹ, ẹ, **a** when *free* and followed by a nasal consonant (§§ 225, 427, 439).

(iii) ẹ and ọ when followed by a palatal or palatalised consonant (§§ 410, 411).

(iv) **a** *free* when preceded by a palatal (§ 414).

(v) ẹ blocked by double consonant, if reduced in countertonic syllables to ẹ in Period I (§ 234).

(2) *Polysyllabic Radicals.*—Vocalic alternation was induced when the radical ended in a group of consonants that required the mainten-ance of a preceding atonic vowel (§ 257), e.g. **calumniare, *corruptiare,* or contained an intertonic vowel reduced to ẹ in Old French (§ 251). The normal types found in twelfth-century French are as follows :—

Late Latin Vowel	Conditions	Alternation Strong	Alternation Weak	Conjugation I.	Conjugation III.
	Monosyllabic Radicals.				
a	§ 231, *free*	ę	a	leve, laver	pert, pareir
	§ 227, *free + nasal*	āi	ā	aime, amer	maint, maneir
	§ 414, *free preceded by palatal*	ie	ę		chiet, cheeir
	§ 415, *free preceded and followed by palatal*	i	ę	conchie, concheer	gist, gesir
ę	§ 225, *free*	ie	ę	lieve, lever	siet, seeir
	§ 225, *free + nasal*	ie	ę		crient, cremant
	§ 411, *free + palatal*	i	ei(>oi)	prie, preiier	ist, eissir
ẹ	$\begin{cases} § 225 \\ § 226 \end{cases}$ *free*	ei(>oi)	ę	esfreie, esfreer	
	§ 439, *free + nasal*	ēi	$\begin{cases} ę \\ ē(>ā) \end{cases}$	meine, mener feine, faner (§ 449)	
	§ 575, *blocked + double cons.*	ę(>ẹ)	ę(>ẹ)		met, metons
ǫ	$\begin{cases} § 225 \\ § 226 \end{cases}$ *free*	ue	ǫ(>u)	trueve, trover	$\begin{cases}\text{muet, moveir}\\\text{duelt (§ 387),}\\\text{doleir}\end{cases}$
	§ 411, *free + palatal*	üi	oi	enuie, enoiier	
	§ 410, *free and blocked +] (§§ 387, 556)*	ue	ǫ(>u)		cueilt, coillir
	§ 234, *blocked*	ǫ	ǫ(>u)	aproche, aprochier	
ọ	$\begin{cases} § 225 \\ § 226 \end{cases}$ *free*	ou(>eu)	ǫ(>u)	ploure, plorer	coust, cosdre
	Polysyllabic Radicals.				
a	(§ 251)	a	e	travaille, traveillier	
ę, ẹ	(§ 575) + *double cons.*	ę, ę(>ẹ)	ę	apele, apeler halete, haleter	
ẹ	(§ 422) + *palatal cons.*	ei(>oi)	ei>i	charreie, charrier	
ǫ	(§ 257) *blocked*	ǫ(>u)	ę	coroce, corecier	
ǫ	(§ 257) *blocked + nasal*	ǫ(>ū)	ē(>ā)	chalonge, chalengier	

[For the phonetic development of the vowels in these radicals in Later Old and Middle French cf. Part II, chaps. x, xi, xiv.]

§ 927. Broadly speaking vocalic alternation was observed with marked consistency in the written French of the twelfth century and was even extended analogically to two small groups of verbs which were etymologically conjugated on one radical:—

(1) On the model of verbs of the type *prie : preiier, prise : preisier,* the alternation **i : ei** was carried into the conjugation of the *one*-radical verbs in -*eiier* (< ę + *jod*), e.g. *leiier, pleiier, freiier,* cf. *Rol. lient* 3738, 3965.

In the conjugation of the verbs formed with the suffix **-**ejare** (*charreier*, etc., § 631), the influence exercised by palatal consonants on preceding intertonic ę (§ 422) led to the development of the alternation *ei (oi) -i* in the course of Old French and the weak radical -**i** was early extended, cf. *Rol. flambient* 3659, *otri,* 3202.

(2) The alternation **ŏ** *ue* : **u** *ou* or ǫ was often used in the conjugation of *courre, soffrir, offrir* and *moillier,* the forms *kuert, sueffre, ueffre* being formed on the model of *muert, cuevre, uevre,* and *mueil* on *dueil, vueil,* etc.

In the conjugation of *engeignier* (< **ingeniare*) three radicals developed, two strong and one weak: *engiegn-* **ēndžieŋ-** (< ę *tonic* + ŋ *intervocalic and final*, § 410), *engin-* **ēndžin-** (< ę *tonic* + ŋ *prae-consonantal*, § 411), *engeign-* **ēndžeŋ-** (< ę *intertonic* + ŋ *intervocalic*); this last became **āndžiŋ-** in Later O.F. (§ 422) and was early generalised (cf. *Rol.* 95, *engignent*). In the conjugation of *aproismier* (*adproximare) the strong radical *apruisme* (**aprüizm-**, § 411) was sometimes reduced to *aprizm-* (§ 516) and this radical often extended, e.g. *Oxf. Ps. aprismerent* (M. 42); in the conjugation of *baer* (*badare) the strong radical was generalised and **beẹr** > **beję**, *bayer*, (§ 239); *corecier* was either replaced by *corocier* or shortened to *corcier*.

Levelling of Radicals.

§ 928. Before the twelfth century vocalic alternation had been already eliminated in the conjugation of the verbs *cuire* and *nuire*, in *lire* (≠ *dire*) and in *valeir*, and was threatened in *chaleir* and *travaillier* (cf. *Rol. chielt* (MS. *chelt*) 2411, *chalt* 227, 1405, etc.; *Oxf. Ps. travaillie*, etc., M. p. 56). Isolated examples of the extension of one radical or the other became more and more frequent in the twelfth century, cf. Crest. *E. apuier* 3215, *ennuier* 2615, *issue* 1673, *prisoient* 761; *proie* 6505; *Rol.* (*Digby MS.*) *annuiez* 2484, *apuier* 500, *aproeciez* 2800, *cumperee* 449, *issut* 2667, *prium* 3808, and when variation was increased by the vocalisation of prae-consonantal ᴨ and ʝ, analogical re-formation became frequent, especially in the first conjugation.

§ 929. In the *first* conjugation levelling became very general in Middle French and turned ordinarily in favour of the weak radical, this being the one employed in the greater number of forms; the strong radical was, however, generalised: (i) if it was supported by a related or associated word, cf. *pleurer—pleurs, ennuyer—ennui, v(u)idier—v(u)ide, aprocher, empirer, envoyer, priser*; (ii) if impressed on the memory by frequency of use in a particular phrase: the phrase *je te pri, je le ni*, for instance, led to the generalisation of the radicals *pri-; ni-* and most other verbs with the alternation **i : oi** followed suit. By the sixteenth century vocalic alternation was rare in this conjugation except among verbs that retained or adopted one of the following alternations :—

(i) ę : ẹ, e.g. *pese : peser.*

(ii) ö (*eu*) : **u** (*ou*), e.g. *treuve : trouver, preuve : prouver.*

(iii) ę (ę̄) : **a** (ā), e.g. *declere* (*declaire*) : *declarer, aime : amer.*

The last two alternations were eliminated in the course of the sixteenth century; the first was extended by further vowel levelling and analogical re-formation and in the seventeenth century it was, as now, the only living vocalic alternation in this conjugation.

§ 930. The alternation ę : ẹ is etymological in the conjugation of verbs whose strong radicals are derived from the following types :—

(i) Later O.F. ę from L.L. ẹ and ę *blocked*, e.g. *apelle : apeler*, **apęlę : apẹlę**.

(ii) Later O.F. ję (< ʲie) preceded by š or ž and followed by **l** or **r** (§ 510), e.g. *gele : geler*, **žęlę** (< žʲẹlę) : **žẹlę**.

(iii) Later O.F. wę (< oi) levelled to ẹ in Middle French (§ 522), e.g. *pese : peser*, **pęzę** (< poizę) : **pẹzę**.

(iv) O.F. **ẽi**, levelled to **ẹ̃** and denasalised in late Middle French (§§ 467, 468), e.g. *meine : mener*, **mẹ̃nẹ : mẹnẹ.**

Under the influence of these verbs this alternation was extended analogically to the verbs which had earlier alternation in ɪᵉ : ẹ (not preceded by š or ž), e.g. *leve : lever*, **lẹvẹ** (for lɪᵉvẹ) : **lẹvẹ,** *creve : crever.*

It was also adopted in the verb *achater*, O.F. I *achate : achater*, O.F. II *achate : acheter*, **ašatẹ : ašẹtẹr** (§ 266) and *achete : acheter*, **ašẹtẹ : ašẹtẹ** (± *jete : jeter*, etc., *Rose* II, *achete : mete* 8667 ; Palsgrave still *achatte*, etc. ; cf. § 1058).

The spelling of these verbs was still often traditional in the sixteenth century. Palsgrave gives : *creue : crieue, esleue : eslieue, mayne : mene*, '*je poyse* or *je pese*, *whiche* is the more used in common speche.'

[For further details cf. verb tables and F. §§ 27, 28.]

§ 931. *Third Conjugation.*—In the conjugation of *veoir* the use in the present participle of the strong radical began early (cf. *Rol.* 287, *veiant*) ; its generalisation took place only in Middle French (F. 62) ; in the conjugation of *croire* levelling was relatively late and in most verbs vocalic alternation was preserved through Middle French (cf. verb tables).

The imperative *veez* **vẹẹts** was early shortened to **vẹts** *vez*. In the course of the twelfth century **mẹt-**, the strong radical of **mẹtṛẹ,** opened to **mẹt-** (§ 575), and in the sixteenth century replaced the earlier weak radical **mẹt-** (F. 61). In Late Middle French the strong radicals of *devoir* and *boire*, *doiv-* and *boiv-*, were often carried into the weak forms (cf. *doibuez*, Rab. I, 7, *il boiuoit*, etc.), and the weak radical of *boire* which had been labialised to **ö** (*eu*) and raised to **ü** (§ 486) was often substituted for the strong radical, e.g. *ilz beuvent ;* in the conjugation of *cosdre, escorre, secorre* the alternation **u** (*ou*) : **ö** (*eu*) was eliminated (Crest. *Yv. cost : cost (constet)*, 5423), in the conjugation of other verbs with this alternation (e.g. *douloir, mouvoir, moudre*) both radicals were often used indiscriminately in Later Middle French.

✶✶ Over a widespread region which included Champagne and the South-Centre the forms *veign, veingne, vaign, vaigne* (**vẹiŋ** > **vẹ̃n,** § 435, **vẹ̃ŋẹ**), *teign, teingne* were substituted for the etymological forms (*viegn, viegne*, etc.) under the influence of the weak palatalised forms *veingniez*, etc., and the palatalised forms of *prendre, preign, preigne*, etc., cf. Rtbf. *secrestain : tain*, p. 129, l. 117, *vain : je vain*, p. 142, l. 725, *veingne : enseingne*, p. 37, l. 71, Villon, *tiengne : Bretaigne* T. 1632, cf. S.C. § xx ; for northern *tign, vign*, etc., cf. N. §§ vii and xviii.

Section 9.—VARIATIONS IN THE RADICAL DUE TO THE DEVELOP-MENT OF THE FINAL CONSONANT OF THE RADICAL.

§ 932. The slurring of unstressed final **e, i, o, u** brought the final consonants of the verb radical into continually varying positions in the conjugation of the present tenses : intervocalic consonants became final or first of a group, initial became final or middle of a group, and their development varied accordingly (§§ 202, 205, 206, 209).

Labial and Dental Radicals.

§ 933. To illustrate the main types of variation in twelfth-century French theoretical paradigms of the present indicative of *bibere, claudere, *cremere, rumpere, subcutere, molere*, and the present subjunctive of *crepare, amare, consiliare, appellare, salvare, tornare*, are subjoined.

Single intervocalic consonants.

beif	crief	b and p *intervocalic* become *final*, §§ 333, 335, 343, 344.
beis	cries ⎫	
beit	criet ⎭	b and p *intervocalic* become *prae-consonantal*, § 373.
bevons	crevons ⎫	
bevez	crevez ⎬	b and p *intervocalic* and remaining so, § 344.
beivent	crievent ⎭	
beivre		b + r, § 372.
aim, ain	criem, crien	m *intervocalic* become *final*, § 435.
ains	criens ⎫	
aint	crient ⎭	m *intervocalic* become *prae-consonantal* + *dental.*
amons	cremons ⎫	
amez	cremez ⎬	m *intervocalic* and remaining so.
aiment	criement ⎭	
	criembre	m in the group **m'r**, § 369.
clo(t)	socou(t)	d and t *intervocalic* become *final*, §§ 333, 335, 346.
cloz	socouz ⎫	
clot	socout ⎭	d and t *intervocalic* become *prae-consonantal*, §§ 367, 373.
clo(d)ons	soco(d)ons ⎫	
clo(d)ez	soco(d)ez ⎬	d and t *intervocalic* and remaining so, §§ 333, 335, 346.
clo(d)ent	socou(d)ent ⎭	
clo(d)re	socou(d)re	d and t + r, § 372.

Supported labial and dental.

romp	sauf	torn	initial **p, w, n** become *final.*
rons	saus	torz ⎫	
ront	saut	tort ⎭	initial **p, w, n** become *middle of three*, § 365.
rompons	sauvons	tornons ⎫	
rompez	sauvez	tornez ⎬	initial **p, w, n** remaining *initial.*
rompent	sauvent	tornent ⎭	

l, ɫ and ʝ

apel	conseil	muel	l and ʝ become *final.*
apeaus	conseuz	mueus ⎫	
apeaut	conseut	mueut ⎭	l and ʝ become *prae-consonantal*, §§ 387, 388.
apelons	conseillons	molons ⎫	
apelez	conseilliez	molez ⎬	l and ʝ remaining *intervocalic.*
apelent	conseillent	muelent ⎭	
		moudre	l and ʝ become *prae-consonantal* + r, §§ 370, 385.

[Cf. also *baillier: bail—bauz—baut*, etc.; *parol, parous, parout*, etc.]

Levelling of Old French Radicals.

§ 934. Analogical forms replaced the most isolated forms before the twelfth century and became more and more frequent, but the two forms, analogical and etymological, often co-existed for a considerable period.

In the *first* conjugation the isolated forms produced in the first person singular of the present indicative and in the singular of the present subjunctive were replaced by analogical forms ending in ę, made ordinarily on the radical that was in use in the second and third persons singular: *Ind. Pres.* 1: *Rose* I, *conseille, meine, Rose* II, *eschape, garde*; *Subj.* 3, *Rose* II, *s'esveille, parole, claime, Intr.* pp. 315, 326, cf. §§ 898, 909.

23

§ 935. In the *third* conjugation analogical forms were sometimes made on the strong radical of other persons, sometimes on the weak radical and sometimes on the radical of an associated verb or group of verbs. The isolated forms of the first person singular of the present indicative early lost final consonants in *prae-consonantal* position (cf. *dor gie*, Rose, 20, 483) and were gradually replaced by forms ending in -s made on the radical of the second and third persons singular (e.g. *Rose* II, MS. Ha, *sens, criens, veus* (for *vueil*), cf. § 899).

§ 936. *Labial Radicals.*—(i) The forms with final labial (*boif, recoif, serf,* etc., pres. ind. 1 and imper. 2) were replaced at first by forms made on the radical of the second and third persons singular, e.g. *boi, recoi, ser,* later on by forms made on this radical but ending in -s, e.g. *bois, recois, sers* (§§ 899, 913) : *sol* and *soil* (≠ *tol, toil*) were introduced in prae-literary times in place of ** *solf* and *sous* appears in the fourteenth century. [For *pruis* and *truis* cf. § 955.]

(ii) The infinitive form *escrivre* was re-modelled on *dire, lire, boivre* on *croire,* (*escrire : dire,* Eneas 7891, *boire : acroire,* Feuillée 797) ; *criembre, giembre, priembre, raiembre* (< * *reademere*) were early re-modelled on the group *ceindre, peindre, plaindre,* etc., and in the thirteenth century the radical of the present stem tenses began to follow suit (*Rol.* crendrai 257, 791, *creint* 2740, *Cam. Ps.* criendre, reinderat, raendrat, Eneas geindre 8244, *Rose* I *crien, crient, Rose* II *craing, craint, craindre, craindraie,* etc., *Intr.* p. 329).

(iii) In the conjugation of *soldre* and its derivatives the weak radical ** *solv-* was replaced before Later Old French by *sol* ± the weak radical of *sol-eir, tol-dre, vol-eir* (cf. verb tables) ; the modern weak radical *solv-* is a borrowed form, attested first in the later fourteenth century (e.g. *absolvons* in 1361). The sixteenth century made use of the radicals : *sol-, solv-,* and *soud- ;* (cf. Kirsch, W., *Zur Geschichte des consonantischen Stammauslauts im Präsens und den davon abgeleiteten Zeiten im Altfranz.,* Heidelberg, 1897, H.L.F. III (i), 313).

§ 937. *Dental Radicals.*—The effacement of the *single intervocalic dental* (§ 346) brought the weak radical of the verbs containing it into hiatus with the terminations and it was re-modelled in all verbs except *rire, escourre* and *secourre,* § 879. In Old French *circoncions,* etc., *ocions, ociez,* etc., were replaced by *circoncisons, ocisons, ocisez,* etc. ≠ *disons, lisons,* etc. ; *clouons, clouez* (< *clore*) were re-formed on the radical *clos-,* used in the past participle and perfect : [for *pouvoir,* etc., cf. § 954, for *seoir, cheoir,* § 963, for *ouir* cf. § 950].

Supported Dental.—Under the influence of *tenir* (§ 749) *prend-,* the weak radical of *prendre,* was replaced by *pren-,* except in the northern region, and the similarity of the forms *pondre* (< *ponere*) and *respondre* (< * *respondĕre*) and of *pont,* etc., and *respont,* etc., led to a frequent

interchange of radicals in the conjugation of these verbs (cf. *responeit* for *respondeit*, *Rou* 5955) : the radical *pond-* was gradually generalised, but etymological forms of the verb *pondre* were still current in the sixteenth century (cf. Meigret : '. . . les uns dizet *ponons*, *ponez ponent*. Les aotres dizet *pondons*,' etc., p. 109).

[For the spelling of the third person singular in Late Middle French cf. § 891.]

In the imperative singular and indicative present the forms with effaced dental, i.e. the prae-consonantal forms, were often generalised, cf. *pren*, *Auc.* 2, 19 ; *ren toy* Ch. d'O. R. ccxvi ; *gar*, *agar* (reduced to *aga*, cf. § 76).

Velar Radicals.

§ 938. Since the whole range of Latin vowels was represented in the terminations of the Latin verb, the development of radicals ending in velar consonants was very varied (Pt. II, chap. vi). The theoretical forms of the chief types in late twelfth century French are as follows :—

[*Forms in square brackets are theoretical forms already replaced.*]

First Conjugation.

Infinitive.	Present Indicative. 1 and 3		Present Subjunctive. 3	Present Participle.
Single Velar (§§ 294, 295, 302, 341).				
precare—preiier	[prieu]	prie	[prist]	preiant
locare—loer	lieu	luee	[luist]	loant
exsucare—essuer	essu	essue	[essuist]	essuant
Supported Velar (§§ 206, 291, 300, 349).				
circare—cerchier	[cerc]	cerche	cerzt	cerchant
collocare—[colgier]	[colc]	colche	[colzet]	[colgant]
judicare—jugier	juge	[juche, cf. § 352]	[juzet]	jugant

Third Conjugation.

Single Velar (§§ 294, 295, 302, 306 ; 323, 341, 342).				
placere—plaisir	plaz	plaist	place	plais(ant)
dūcere—duire	[du]	duist	due	duis(ant)
*destrūgere—destruire	[destru]	destruit	[destrue]	destrui(ant)
lĕgere—lire	li	lit	[lie]	[lei-(ant)]
*tragere—traire	[trou]	trait [3 pl. tront]	traie	trai(ant)
Supported Velar (§§ 206, 291, 293, 300, 312, 349).				
plangere—plaindre	[planc]	plaint	[plange]	plaign(ant)
surgere—sordre	[sorc]	sort	sorge	sorg(ant)
				sordžant
vincere—veintre	[venc]	[veinst]	[venche]	[venz(ant)]
*torcere—tortre	[torc]	tort	[torche]	[torz(ant)]
collĭgĕre—cueildre	[colc]	cueilt	[colge]	coill(ant)
coillir (§ 759)				

Levelling of Radicals.

§ 939. *Conjugation I.*—The more isolated forms—the first singular of the present indicative and the singular of the present subjunctive— were for the most part re-modelled on the radical of the second and third persons singular of the present indicative before the twelfth century, and those surviving into this century in the course of Later Old French ; *essuer* early adopted the radical *essui-* (under the influence of *ennui-, apui-* or by glide development (§ 239)); *manjuce*, etc., replaced *manjuiz*, etc., *Oxf. Ps. manjucent* (M. p. 25).

The etymological forms of the first person of the indicative of *joer* and *loer* occur occasionally (forms supported by an associated noun), e.g. *Best. Guill. jou gieu : lieu*, and with analogical extension, *Oxf. Ps. aliut* (M. p. 24), *Auc. liués*, xxiv, 47, but the weak radical was early generalised.

The forms of the subjunctive had some vogue in the twelfth century, cf. *Rol. chevalzt* 2109, *culzt* 2682, *Oxf. Ps. curuist, escerst, esdrest* (M. p. 24); in the north-eastern region forms of this type even provoked others, e.g. *desirst, parolst*.

§ 940. *Conjugation III.*—(1) *Radicals with Single Velar.*—Before the twelfth century the radical *lis-* (≠ *dis-*, weak radical of *dire*) had been generalised in the conjugation of *lire*, cf. *Rol.* 802 *lisent ;* in the conjugation of *duire, -struire* and their compounds the radicals *du-* and *stru-* were early replaced, first by *dui-* and *strui-*, later by *duis-* and *struis-* (cf. Crest. *Cl. conduie : enuie* 268, Wace, *Brut. destruient : fuient* 6311, *Chev. II Esp.* 12336, *deduisent, Ille et Gal. destruisent* 4473, but *conduye, Mist. V. Test.* 3853).

In Late Middle French there was some confusion between forms in *-ise, -isons, -uise, -uisons*, etc., and *-isse, -issons, -uisse, -uissons*, e.g. Palsgr. *deduisse, deduissons* (cf. F. p. 33). The only attested etymological *jod* forms are : (*a*) (once only) *plaz, Song. Sol. plastz* 42, *jacet.* F. 70; (*b*) in Later O.F. *tace, place*, (Froissart, *Mel. place,* 14,824) but already *taises, plaiset*, etc., *Oxf. Ps.*

§ 941. (2) *Radicals ending in Supported Velar Consonants.*—(i) *Verbs in -aindre, -eindre, -oindre.* (*a*) The etymological forms of the first singular of the present indicative and those of the present subjunctive were replaced before the twelfth century by forms made on the model of those in which ng + e or i had palatalised to ŋ, e.g. *plaign* **plāŋ** (> **plāiŋ** > **plē**, § 406) ≠ *plaignant* **plāŋānt**, etc., *peign* **pēiŋ** (> **pę̄**, § 406) ≠ *peigne* **pēiŋ̨** (§ 407); *oign* **ūŋ** ≠ *oignant* **uŋant**, etc., cf. § 465).

The previous existence of the etymological forms is attested for the western region by the use of analogical forms in *-c* and *-ge*, which appear to have been made on their model (cf. *Rol.* 1122 *moerc*, 1485 *alge* and §§ 900, 910).

(*b*) The weak radical of the verbs in *-eindre* (*ceindre, peindre*, etc.) developed on normal lines : ę + ŋ *intervocalic* > ēiŋ (§ 407) > ę̄ŋ > ęŋ (§§ 467, 469) but the weak radicals of the verbs in *-aindre* (*plaindre*, etc.) and *-oindre* (*joindre, oindre*, etc.) were re-modelled under the com-

bined influence of dialectal variants (§ 408) and the forms in which ŋ
in prae-consonantal position had disintegrated into ĭn, § 311 (e.g. *plaindre*,
oindre) : thus the radical āŋ (e.g. *plaignant* plāŋănt) was displaced by ę̄
(< āi, e.g. plęŋ ănt) in the course of Middle French and Meigret mentions
this radical only (p. 109), and the weak radical ūŋ (*oignant* ūŋănt) was
replaced by -u̯ę̄ (u̯ęŋ ā(t)) in the course of the seventeenth century, § 465.

In Middle French at times and in the northern region earlier and more consistently
(cf. *Dial. Greg. estraindans, foindans*), the weak radical of these verbs was formed
on the infinitive; Palsgrave admits *nous ceindons, ils ceindent, nous estaindons, nous
attayndons, que je atteynde*.

§ 942. (ii) *-erdre, -ordre, -ortre*. In the conjugation of the verbs
aerdre, terdre, sordre, tortre, (tordre ≠ mordre), the dominance of the
radical of the infinitive was early accepted, cf. *Rol. surdent* 2975, *Oxf.
Ps. resurdent, aerde*, (M. pp. 20, 26), Crest. *E. detordre* 3810, *Cl.
tordent* 5811, *Ren.* VIII, 367, *estorte* (MS. *estorde*) : *porte*, Va, 1017
estorde : morde, Rose II, *detortant* 8861, *detortez* 9107.

§ 943. (iii) In the conjugation of *veintre* the radicals in use in the
early twelfth century were *venc-, venqu-* vĕnk- (*vencu, venqui* and also
venquant, venquons, venquez, venquent, venque, etc., *venqueie*, etc.) and
vĕin- (*veintre, veins* and *veint ≠ veins, feint*, etc.). From the contamination of these forms arose vĕink- (*veinc, vainc-, veinqu-, vainqu-*), Crest. *C.
vainc* 4160, *E. vaincu* 1149, *vainqui* 1249, *Troie veinquent* 19028, and
veincre replaced *veintre* in the early thirteenth century. In the conjugation of *cueudre* (*cuillir*, § 759) the forms *cueil : cueille*, etc., early displaced
**colc* and **colge ;* in the course of Period II the vowel of the strong
radical was generalised (*Rol. Digby MS. recuillir* 2965, *requeillit* 3210)
and the forms with vocalised ǀ (*keus, kieus, keut, kieut*) were gradually
replaced by analogical *cueilles, cueille*, (*Cor. Loois, acueille* 1485, *acuelt*
2687, but Plsgr. still *cueilx, (re)cueilt ;* for *cueiller*, cf. § 879).

Section 10.—VARIATIONS IN THE RADICAL DUE TO THE INFLUENCE
OF jod.

§ 944. The consonantalisation of unstressed ĕ and ĭ in hiatus before
a vowel (§ 220) provoked the palatalisation or modification of all preceding consonants (§§ 303-315) and these in turn often modified the
preceding vowel (Pt. II, chap. x.) ; much variety of radical is consequently found in Old French among the surviving *jod*-forms.

The terminations that contained unstressed ĕ and ĭ in hiatus in the
Latin verb are : (1) in the *second* and *fourth* conjugations and in the
-io verbs of the *third* conjugation, (a) the first person singular of the
present indicative, e.g. *moneo, audio, capio*, (b) the present subjunctive,
e.g. *moneam, audiam, capiam*, etc. ; (2) in the *fourth* conjugation and

in the -*io* verbs of the *third*: (*a*) the imperfect indicative, gerund and present participle, e.g. *audiebam, audiendum, audientem, capiebam*, etc., (*b*) the third person plural of the present indicative, e.g. *audiunt, capiunt*.

§ 945. In the course of Late Latin or Early Romance the forms of the second set were all modified. In the forms of (2) (*a*) iē was levelled to ẹ (§ 220), and **audiēbam** > *audẹβα, **audiendum** > *audẹndụ, **audientem** > *audẹnte; in the third person plural of the present indicative the *jod*-forms were all re-modelled: e.g. **sapiŭnt** was replaced by *sapụnt, **dormiŭnt** by *dormụnt, **sentiŭnt** by *sentụnt.

§ 946. Among the *jod*-forms of the first group there was a considerable amount of analogical re-modelling.

Labial Radicals.—In the conjugation of the verbs with labial radicals used frequently with auxiliary value—*habere, debere, sapere*—the group *labial + jod* was reduced to ɉ and thus *abjo, *dēbjo, *sapjo > *ajo, *dejo, *sajo and *abja, etc., *dēbja, etc. > *aja, *deja etc., but the radicals of the present subjunctive of *sapere* (less used in auxiliary function), and of *stupere* were maintained and developed normally into O.F. **satše** *sache,* **estǫtše** *estoche* (§ 305, *estueche ǂ estuet, estuisse ǂ puisse*); the jod-forms of all other verbs were early re-modelled, cf. O.F. *muef, serf, receif, dorm*, derived from *movo, *servo, *recipo, *dormo.

§ 947. *Dental and Velar Radicals.*—In the conjugation of verbs with dental and velar radicals jod-forms were only maintained in the most used verbs and in those whose radicals ended in **l** and **n**, consonants easily palatalised: (i) *Dental radicals* (§§ 309, 311-313), *joïr, oïr, seeir, veeïr; boillir, chaleir, doleir, oleir, saillir, soleir, valeir, voleir; maneir, respondre, somondre, tenir, venir; ferir, merir, morir, pareir.* (ii) *Velar radicals* (§§ 306, 307), *foïr, faire, plaire, taire, gésir* (but cf. § 940).

[For forms cf. verb table.]

§ 948. *Analogical Extension of jod-forms.*—In isolated cases, when verbs came under the influence of associated verbs or forms, analogical *jod*-forms were created. In Late Latin the replacement of *velle* by *volere* led to the creation of *voljo, *volja, etc., and these forms provoked **moljo, **molja, etc., **tolljo, **tollja, etc., **solljo, **sollja (from *solvere*); *ponjo and *ponja were made ǂ *responnjo, *responnja (< respondeo, respondeam), **prennjo : **prennja ǂ *tenjo : *tenja ; O.F. *aille, fail : faille ǂ chaille, sail : saille, vail : vaille ; doign : doigne ǂ somoign : somoigne (<submoneo, submoneam) ; pruis : pruisse, ruis : ruisse (rover < rogare), truis : truisse ǂ puis : puisse* (§ 955).

§ 949. In the conjugation of verbs whose present subjunctive was used with imperative (optative) force, the palatalised radical was intro-

duced into the forms of the gerund and present participle: *ayant*, *puis-sant*, *sachant* (concurrent with *savant*), *vaillant*, *vueillant*. In the conjugation of the O.F. verbs derived from *bullire* and *salire* the pala-talised radical *boill-*, *saill-* displaced etymological *bol-* and *sal-* in all the forms in which the *l* had not vocalised: in the conjugation of *falir* (*fallire) the two radicals *faill-* and *fal-* were both generalised and received specialised meaning in Middle French: *jaillir*, O.F. *jalir* followed in the wake of *saillir* and *faillir*.

§ 950. *Levelling of Radicals.*—In the course of Later Old French the use of the palatalised radicals *oi-*, *joi-* was extended in the conjuga-tion of *oïr* and *joïr*, under the influence of the forms of *veoir* and of the substantive *joie*, and the forms *oiant*, *ois*, *oit*, *oions*, *oiez*, *oient*, *oioie*, *joiant*, *jois*, etc., appear in the later twelfth century. In the same period forms of *joïr* were created ≠ the second conjugation and these were generalised before the sixteenth century. *Foïr* (*fouir* < *fūgīre) retained its double radical **fu-** and **füi-** (§ 420) into the seventeenth century.

Most of the palatalised jod-forms of the first person singular of the present indicative (e.g. *preing*, *muir*, *boil*, etc.) were superseded in the course of Later Old French by forms made ≠ the second and third persons singular; with the dentalisation of final ŋ (§ 435), *tiegn* and *viegn* tjēŋ, vjēŋ developed into tję̄(n), vję̄(n) and *vueil* and *dueil* alone survived into the sixteenth century (cf. § 957). In the present sub-junctive the palatalised forms were longer lived, but sporadic analogical forms appear early, (*Oxf. Ps. plaiset*, *taises*, *Leis Guill.* 10, *deive* ≠ *deivent*, etc.), and apart from those that survive in Modern French the only palatalised ones in use in the sixteenth century were *asoille*, *doie*, *doint*, *ouie*, *prengne*, *tiengne*, *viengne*, *vaillons*, *vailliez*, *veuillons*, *veuillies*, and all those in use in this tense were in competition with the analogical formations that replaced them, (cf. § 957 and for *taign*, *vaign*, cf. § 931).

' C'est une faute familiere aux Courtisans, hommes et femmes de dire *preigne* pour *prenne* . . . et *vieigne* pour *vienne*.' (Vgl. *Rem.* I, 143); 'Il n'y a plus que le bas peuple qui dise *ieigne* pour *vienne*; mais beaucoup de femmes disent encore *preigne* pour *prenne*. . . . On doit prendre soin pour l'éviter.' (T. Corneille.)

Section 11.—Anomalous Presents.

§ 951.

estre		aveir	
sui	seie	ai	aie
ies, es	seies	as	aies
est	seit	a(t)	aie(t), ait
somes, esmes	seiiens, seions	avons	aiiens, aions
estes	seiiez	avez	aiiez
sont	seient	ont	aient

§ 952. The form *sui* appears to have been influenced by *fui* but is not yet fully explained : **ęs** is an unstressed form.

sons, the normal development of *sumus* and the starting-point of the termination *-ons* (§ 893) is attested, but rarely, in central and northern texts (e.g. Rtbf. 135, 383, and Froissart) : the dissyllabic forms *estes* and *somes* appear to be due to the combined influence of preservative analogy (**estęs** for ****ets** *ez* < ****ests**) and the forms *dites, faites, traites, dimes, faimes, esmes* (< ****esimus**, formed early on the radical of the second persons *es* and *estis*).

All the forms of the subjunctive of *estre*, except the third singular, are derived from an analogical type ***sia, *sias,** etc., formed early on the model of the subjunctive of the third conjugation : the conservation of the monosyllabic form of the third singular (with plosive final **t**) is perhaps due to the frequency of its use in imprecation and blessing, (cf. § 759 and the pronunciation of modern emphatic exclamatory *soit !*).

The weak radical **sei-** is due either to the influence of the strong forms or to the development of a palatal glide between the **ę** of the radical and juxtaposed **a,** (cf. § 919).

[For later *sois* from *soie* and *soies* cf. §§ 901, 902.]

§ 953. The forms of the singular of the present tense of *aveir* and its present subjunctive are derived from Latin short forms ***ājo, *ās, *āt, *aja,** etc. (§§ 121, 946) : *ont* appears to be derived from ***aunt,** shortened form of ***a(β)ųnt** for **aβent** < **habent ; ait,** which early replaced **aięθ,** is modelled on **seit** (*Alexis*, 508, MS. L. *aiet*, MSS. A, P, S *ait ;* cf. also ll. 185, 599).

§ 954.

poeir			trover	
puis	puisse		truis	truisse
puez	puisses		trueves	truisses
puet	puisse(t), puist		trueve(t)	truisse(t), truist
poöns	poissiens, puissiens		trovons	troissiens, truissiens
	poissons, puissons			troissons, truissons
poëz	poissiez, puissiez		trovez	troissiez, truissiez
pueënt	puissent		truevent	truissent

§ 955. The origin of the forms *puis, puisse*, etc., has been the subject of much discussion : the most plausible theory appears to be that the forms of the Latin subjunctive were early replaced by ***pǫssjɑ, *pǫssjɑs,** etc., under the influence of subjunctive forms of conjugations II and IV (***monjɑ, *audjɑ**), and that under their influence ***pǫssų** was replaced by ***pǫssjo** (> **püis,** §§ 410, 411).

The strong radical **püis-** was early introduced into the first and second plural of the present subjunctive, and under the influence of the verb-sequences **seię, seięs, seit, aie, aies, ait** (§ 953) the mono-syllabic

form **püist** was created which served in its turn as a model for the anomalous forms **doinst, doint, voist, trüist, prüist, rüist.**

The anomalous forms of **poëir** early served as a model for the first singular of the present indicative and for the subjunctive present of the verbs *rover* (< *rogare*, § 341), *prover, trover,* (*reu* < *rogo, true*(*f*)*s* occasional only) ; these forms were later replaced by forms made on the weak radicals of these verbs.

The other forms of **poeir** are derived from the L.L. analogical forms **¹pǫtes, *¹pǫtet, *po¹tęmus, *po¹tętis, *¹pǫtent,* forms made on the model of the Latin second conjugation on the radical **pǫt-**, which was in use in other tenses of the verb (*potebam, potens, potui*). A labial glide, (**w** > **v**), appears to have developed in some of the forms in which the radical was in hiatus, e.g. in *poant*, **puãnt**, *poons*, **puũns**, *poez*, **puęs**, *peuent*, **pöęnt**, and in Later Middle French the radicals **puv-** and **pöv-** were established under the influence of the form of *mouvoir*.

The forms *peult, peulent*, used in Middle French, are modelled on the corresponding forms of *vouloir* : [for dialectal **puęnt**, cf. § 552].

§ 956.	voleir		saveir	
vueil	vueille	sai	sache	
vuels, vueus	vueilles	ses	saches	
vuelt, vueut	vueille(t)	set	sache(t)	
volons	voilliens, voillons	savons	sachiens, sachons	
volez	voilliez	savez	sachiez	
vuelent	vueillent	sevent	sachent	

§ 957. The O.F. forms of *voleir* are derived from the analogical forms introduced in Late Latin on the model of the second conjugation (§ 885). In the first person analogical forms were made in Period II (*vuel* xii², *veu* xiv), but *vueil* continued in use into the sixteenth century : ' Mes aojourd'huy nou' dizons plu' voulęntiers *veu* ou *veus*, *deul* ou *duels*,' (Meigret, p. 104).

In the first and second persons plural of the subjunctive the vowel of the strong radical was early introduced and in Late Middle French the analogical forms *voulions, vouliez* were created, (and similarly *valions, valiez* for *vaillons, vailliez*). In the imperative *veuillez* persisted longer.

[For O.F. *voil, voille*, etc., cf. § 554 ; for the later development of **ue, ue⊣**, cf. §§ 551, 557.]

sai (< L.L. **saɟo*, § 946) levelled to **sę** in the course of Later Old French (§ 529). In Later Middle French the close quality of the vowel was often modified in the three persons of the singular of *savoir* and of *haïr* under the influence of the forms of *faire* (**fę(s)**, **fęt**), and the spelling *ai* was generalised (cf. Villon, T. 1909 *scet : cessoit*, T. 1603 *hait : deshait*). Analogical *savent* appeared in the later twelfth century

(*Chron. Norm.* I, 1758) but only ousted **sęvęnt** (*scevent, scaivent*) < O.F. **sęvęnt** in the sixteenth century (H.L.F. II, p. 348).

✻✻ In the western region *sache* **satšę** was sometimes replaced by *sace* **satsę** (± **fatsę**, *face*): for *saiche*, etc., cf. § 423, for the spelling *sc* cf. § 707.

§ 958.   aler.   ester.   doner.

vois	voise, aille	estois	estoise	doins, doign	doinse, doigne
vas	voises, ailles	estas	estoises	dones	doinses, doignes
vait, (va)	voise(t), aille(t)	esta(t)	estoise(t)	done(t)	doinse(t), doigne(t)
	voist, alt	estait	estoist		doinst, doint, dont
alons	voisons, aillons	estons		donons	doinsons, doignons
	voisiens, ailliens				doinsiens, doigniens
alez	voisiez, ailliez	estez		donez	doinsiez, doigniez
vont	voisent, aillent	estont	estoisent	donent	doinsent, doignent

§ 959. In the conjugation of *vadere* short forms began to be developed in Late Latin (e.g. imper. *va*, cf. § 121), and these forms are the starting-point of Old French: **vas** (± ***va**), **vait** < ***va**(d)**it**, **vunt** < ***va**(d)**unt**; analogical **va**(θ) was early introduced ± *vas*, *estat* and *at* (< *habet*). The later development of *vois* is normal: **vǫis** > **vųęs** > **vwęs** > **vę(s)**, written *vais* (§§ 519, 522).

Meigret still gives '*je voe* ou *je voes*,' Gr. p. 104, Ramus *vay* or *voe* (Th. I, 325). In Middle French *vois* was sometimes replaced by *vas* ± *vas, va*; *aille* only finally supplanted *voise*, etc., in the later sixteenth century.

The formation of *vois* is still under discussion. The most plausible theory appears to be that in Gallo-Roman an analogical form, ****vausjo**, ****vauẑo** (?), was formed on ****vao** ± ****trasjo**, ****traẑo** (?) < **tra(n)sěo**.

estois, estait, estont and the subjunctive *estoise* are modelled on the corresponding forms of *aler*; *estace, estaces*, etc. (± *face*) sometimes replace *estoise*, etc.; [for *esta*(*t*), cf. § 182].

doins results from the contamination of **dǫn** (< **dōno**), and a presumed form ***dǫis**, developed like **vǫis** from analogical ****dao** (± ***vao**); **duŋ** *doing*, **duŋę** *doigne* are from types ****dǫnjo**, ****dǫnja** made ± ****monjo**, **monja** < **moněo**, **moněam**; **dunt** *dont* is from **dōnet**.

[For *voist, estoist, doinst, doint*, cf. § 955.]

§ 960.

faire.		haïr.	
faz	face	he, haz	hee, hace
fais	faces	hez	hees, haces
fait	face(t)	het	hee(t), hace(t)
faimes,	faciens,	haons	haiens, haciens
faisons	facons		haons, hacons
faites	faciez	haez	haez, haciez
font	facent	heent	heent, hacent

dire.		beneïstre, beneïr (xiii).	
di	die	bene(d)i(s)	bene(d)ie, bene(d)isse
dis	dies	bene(d)is	bene(d)ies, bene(d)isses
dit	die(t)	bene(d)ist	bene(d)ie, bene(d)isse
dimes	diiens	bene(d)ions	bene(d)ions
dions	dions	bene(d)issons	bene(d)issons
dites	diiez	bene(d)iez	bene(d)iez
		bene(d)issiez	bene(d)issiez
dient	dient	bene(d)ient	bene(d)ient
		bene(d)issent	bene(d)issent

§ 961. *dire, faire.*—The radical of the forms **di, dit, dimes, dites, fait, faimes, faites** is that of the imperative (**di, fai,** § 911) and the infinitives : *font* is derived from *faunt (< *facunt ; for **fęęnt** in *Jonas,* cf. *Zts. Rom. Ph.* xxi, 401). *faz* began to be replaced by *fais* (± *fais, fait*) in the thirteenth century (cf. *Rose* I, *fais : fais* < *fascem* 1941, but Deguileville, *fas : mas,* 7144), *faimes* and *dimes* by *faisons, dioms* in the twelfth (*faisons,* Wace, *Rou.* 8932, *Q.L.R. ; benediums, Oxf. Ps.* M. p. 19). The analogical forms *disons, disent, dise,* etc. (± *diseie, disant,* etc.), appear in the thirteenth century but the etymological forms were not obsolete in the seventeenth.

' Au singulier, *quoy que l'on die,* est fort en usage, et en parlant et en escrivant, bien que *quoy que l'on dise* ne soit pas mal dit ; Mais *quoy qu'ils dient,* au pluriel ne semble si bon a plusieurs que *quoy qu'ils disent;* je voudroie user indifferemment de l'un et de l'autre. Il y en a qui disent *quoy que vous diiez,* mais il est insupportable.' Vgl. *Rem.* II, 38. The analogical forms *contredisez, medisez, maudissez* were established by the seventeenth century.

In the sixteenth century the radical **fęz-** was shortened to **fǝz-** under the influence of the future (**fǝrę,** *ferai,* etc.). Meigret gives only **fęzant, fęzons, fęzoet,** etc., and Bèze condemns the pronunciation **fǝzā** *fesant* as a ' vitium vulgi Parisiensium,' but Ramus allows **fǝzā** (cf. Th. I, 313).

In the conjugation of *maldire* the radical **diz-** *dis-* obtained early some extension but in the main the forms in use in Old French were those of *dire.* In Later Middle French, under the influence of *beneïr* the verb was gradually drawn over into conjugation II and sometimes given the infinitive *maudir* and *maleïr,* but the two earlier radicals **di-** and **diz-** were still in use in the sixteenth and seventeenth centuries, (F. p. 125).

The O.F. infinitive *beneïstre* and the past participle *benę(d)eit* appear to be derived from Early Gallo-Roman ****beneditsěre,** ****benedęχtμ** maintained unshortened under clerkly influence, (cf. § 638). The O.F. forms are sometimes those of *dire* but forms in *-iss,* made on the model of the second conjugation, appear early, cf. *Rol. beneissent* 3667, *Oxf. Ps. beneissum* (*Ind.*), *beneisse* (Subj. 3), *benedis* (Imper. 2) ; in the later twelfth century the infinitive *beneïr* and the past participle *beneï* were introduced and *benit* was formed ± *maudit* (Renclus, *Mis.* cxciv). Some of the older forms, e.g. the subjunctive *benie,* persisted in Early Modern French, (F. 124).

§ 962. *haïr.*—The forms **hę, hęę,** etc., were derived from ****hato,** ****hata,** etc. ; *haz* **hats** and *hace* **hatsę** were modelled on *faz* and *face.* In

Middle French forms with a glide development—*hayons, hayez, haye*—
displaced the earlier ones and continued in use into Modern French
together with the analogical forms of second conjugation type, *haïssons,
haissez*, etc., that also made their appearance in Middle French.

Palsgrave mentions a form in -**iss** only in the present subjunctive, ' que *je haye* or
haysse'; Meigret admits '*hayons aosi bien que haissons*'; Malherbe condemned the
use made by Desportes of *hayez* and *hayant*, (cf. Brunot, *Doctrine*, 414). In the
singular *haïs* and *haït* were also employed in the sixteenth century; for hęt, *hait*,
cf. § 957.

§ 963. se(d)eir   che(d)eir, cha(d)eir.

sie	sië,	sie(d)e	chie(t)	chie(d)e
siez	siës,	sie(d)es	chiez	chie(d)es
siet	sië(t),	sie(d)e(t)	chiet	chie(d)e(t)
se(d)ons	seiiens, seions,	se(d)ons	che(d)ons, cha(d)ons	che(d)ons, cha(d)ons cheiens, chaiens
se(d)ez	seiiez,	se(d)ez	che(d)ez, cha(d)ez	che(d)ez, cha(d)ez
sieënt	siënt,	sie(d)ent	chie(d)ent	chie(d)ent

In the conjugation of *sedere* four radicals appear to have developed,
sieъ̆- and sęъ̆- from sĕd- strong and weak, si- (§ 411) and sei- from *sęj-
(< *sędj-) strong and weak; in the northern and eastern region si-
developed also out of s'ieë, etc. (N. § v) and an infinitive *assire* was in
use. In the course of Period II the use of the radical sei- (> soi-) was
extended in both strong and weak forms under the influence of the
forms of *veoir*; sję- (< s'ie-) was often replaced by sę- under the influence of *che-*, šę- (cf. below) and a new radical *sis- siz-* was introduced
under the influence of forms of *gesir* (*gisent, gisons*, etc.). The radical
sę- became obsolete: in the infinitive its vowel was slurred and elsewhere it was replaced by one of the other radicals, all of which remained
in indiscriminate use in the sixteenth century; [for further details cf.
F. pp. 155-158].
In the course of Period II the radical *chie* tšję- (< tš'ie-, § 414)
developed normally to šę- (§ 510) and was often used in the weak forms,
and the radicals *choi-* and *chai-* were introduced under the influence of
the forms of *seoir, veoir* and *avoir* (*aie*, etc.): *che-* šę- gradually became
obsolete.

✳✳ In the northern and eastern region *chiee*, tšieę, etc., was reduced to tšię
(cf. N. § v), and *cheïr, chaïr* (≠ pf. *cheï* ?) and *seïr* often replaced *cheoir* and *seoir*. In
the western region the infinitive forms of these verbs and of *veeir* are sometimes
written *choier, soier, voier* (e.g. Beroul), *choeir, soeir, voeir* (: *poeir*) (e.g. *Rose* II),
possibly by metathesis or to represent a pronunciation šuęęr, sueęr, vuęęr, or
šuęr, suęr, vuęr (?).

Section 12.—First and Second Future (Conditional).

§ 964. *Paradigms of the Early Twelfth Century.*

Future.

First Conjugation.	Second Conjugation.	Third Conjugation.		III(b).	III(c).
		III(a).			
porter-*ai*	punir-*ai*	orr-*ai*	offr**ẹ**r-*ai*	devr-*ai*	bevr-*ai*
porter-*as*	punir-*as*	orr-*as*	offr**ẹ**r-*as*	devr-*as*	bevr-*as*
porter-*a(t)*	punir-*a(t)*	orr-*a(t)*	offr**ẹ**r-*a(t)*	devr-*a(t)*	bevr-*a(t)*
porter-*ons*	punir-*ons*	orr-*ons*	offr**ẹ**r-*ons*	devr-*ons*	bevr-*ons*
porter-*eiz, -ez*	punir-*eiz, -ez*	orr-*eiz, -ez*	offr**ẹ**r-*eiz, -ez*	devr-*eiz, -ez*	bevr-*eiz, -ez*
porter-*ont*	punir-*ont*	orr-*ont*	offr**ẹ**r-*ont*	devr-*ont*	bevr-*ont*

Second Future (Conditional).

First Conjugation.	Second Conjugation.	III(a).		III(b).	III(c).
porter-*eie*	punir-*eie*	orr-*eie*	offr**ẹ**r-*eie*	devr-*eie*	bevr-*eie*
porter-*eies*	punir-*eies*	orr-*eies*	offr**ẹ**r-*eies*	devr-*eies*	bevr-*eies*
etc.	etc.	etc.	etc.	etc.	etc.

(Cf. for the endings of the Second Future the Imperfect Indicative, §§ 917-919.)

§ 965. The first and second future are derived from the periphrases formed of the infinitive of the verb with the present and imperfect tenses of *habere :* ***portare *ajo,** etc., **portare (*a β)ẹa,** etc. (§ 872 (iii)).

In northern Gaul these forms fused early into a unity (cf. Fred. : '*Et ille respondebat:* "*Non dabo*". *Justinianus dicebat :* "*Daras*,"' Haag, p. 888), and the weak forms of *habere* were curtailed by the suppression of the first syllable.

[For the development of the strong forms of *habere* cf. § 953.]

Personal Endings of the Future.

§ 966. *First Person Singular.*—In the course of Later Old French **-ai** passed through -ẹi to -ẹ (§§ 529, 533) and was written sometimes *ei* or *e*.

In the Orléanais and in West French where the diphthong **ei** early passed to **ẹ** (W. § vi, S.C. § iv), the terminations of the future and conditional were sometimes confused and the spelling -*oi* used in the future and -*aie* in the conditional (cf. *Rose* I, *Intr.* pp. 197-199).

§ 967. *Second Person Plural.*—The ending -*ez* (O.F. -**ẹts**), derived from **-atis,** had already been extended to the future in the early twelfth century in western French, cf. *Rol. laisse* V : *irez, porterez : mer, citez,* etc., *laisse* VI : *ireiz, portereiz : reiz, meis,* etc.

Outside the western region the etymological form held its ground longer and it is probable that the termination -**ẹs,** in use with 'some Parisians' (Meigret), was the outcome of this form : **-eits** > -**oits** > -**wẹs** > -**ẹs** (§§ 519, 522).

Radical.

§ 968. *Accentuation.*—When the periphrasis of the infinitive with *habere* became a unity (§ 965) accentuation adjusted itself to the normal word-stress (§ 218) and ''por'tαre *'αjo, ''pu'nīre *'αjo, ''de'bĕre *'αjo, 'currĕre *'αjo, ''αu'dīre *'*ajo* were stressed **''portα'rαjo, **''puni'rαjo, **''debe'rαjo, **''curre'rαjo, **''αudi'rαjo: thus in all conjugations the infinitive *termination* became *unstressed* and the infinitive *radical* became *secondary stressed.*

§ 969. *Development of the Termination of the Infinitive.*—The infinitive termination, become unstressed, developed in the ordinary way that intertonic vowels developed (§§ 251, 256), **a** being reduced to ę, and **e, i, o, u** being slurred unless required as supporting vowels, in which case they were reduced to ę, cf. O.F. **portęrai; devrai, currai, orrai; covręrai, offręrai.**

§ 970. In the *first* conjugation the modifications were mainly phonological.

(i) In the course of Early Old French intertonic ę (< **a**) was effaced between **r-r, n-r** (§ 253) and thus the futures of *durer, doner, torner,* etc., were reduced to *durrai, donrai, torrai;* subsequently **n'r** was often assimilated to **rr** and thus **dun(ę)rai > durrai, men(ę)rai > merrai,** etc. Analogical forms made on the infinitive were, however, already in use in the conjugation of many verbs in Later Old French, e.g. *finerai, sonerai,* and the shortened futures of the most used verbs, still current in the sixteenth century, became obsolete in the next.

> Vaugelas condemns *lairay,* etc., and considers *donray* and *dorray* ‘des monstres dans la langue.’ (I, 210.)
>
> ę was also not infrequently slurred in the conjugation of verbs with radicals ending in **t** and **d,** e.g. *acatrai, demandrai* (H.L.F. II, 360).

(ii) In Middle French ę began to be effaced when it stood in hiatus with the countertonic vowel, (e.g. *lou(e)rai, ennui(e)rai,* etc.), and in the sixteenth century it was completely mute (§ 270).

> Cf. **Bèze:** ‘In quibusdam futuris verborum exteritur *e,* ut *envoirai, ennuirai, essuirai, loûrai* pro integris *envoijerai, ennuijerai, essuijerai, louerai.*’ (p. 94.)

§ 971. In the *second* and *third* conjugations modifications were mainly analogical.

(i) In conjugation II the consistent use of the vowel i in other tenses led to an early use of forms in *-irai,* etc., which were generalised before Later Old French, cf. O.F. *finirai, punirai,* etc.

(ii) In conjugation III (*a*) the same tendency showed itself, but later and with less general acceptance. In Later Old French analogical forms were established in *dormir, partir, sentir, vertir, repentir (partrai, repentrai* occasional only), and were adopted by other verbs in the course of Middle French (cf. verb table).

§ 972. Among verbs with radicals ending in *-fr* and *-vr* the intertonic vowel was retained as a supporting vowel, e.g. *offrerai, covrerai*, and in Later Old and Middle French there was a tendency to extend this type of future among verbs with radicals ending in **ļ**, e.g. *assaillerai, bouillerai, cueillerai, faillerai*, and thus secure forms in which the final consonant of the infinitive radical remained intact. [For details, cf. Risop, *Studien*, pp. 60, 61.]

✶✶ In the northern region forms with intertonic **ę**, retained or developed, were frequent among verbs with radicals ending in **d, t, v**, e.g. *prenderai, parterai, receverai, serverai*. In the same region metathesis was also common, cf. *enterrai* < *entrerai, coverrai*, etc., N. § xxii.

§ 973. *Radical of Verb.*—(1) *Vowel.*—The adjustment of stress mentioned above made the verb radical a secondary stressed syllable in the future and conditional of all conjugations and it is consequently the *weak* radical that is found ordinarily in these tenses, cf. O.F. *amerai, leverai, preierai, plorrai, enveerai, harrai, eistrai, crembrai, devrai, crerrai, savrai, tendrai, vendrai.* An analogical influence was, however, often exercised by the strong radical, especially when it was the radical of the infinitive, and in the course of Later Old and Middle French many analogical forms were created, some of which secured acceptance, e.g. *boirai, croirai, cueudrai, girrai* (§ 979), *istrai, sierai, maindrai, perrai* (≠ *pert* < *paret*), *tiendrai, viendrai* (cf. § 764), *voirrai* (frequent in the sixteenth century). The verbs of the first conjugation that adopted the strong radical in the infinitive (§ 929), adopted it also in the future and conditional, e.g. *aimerai, pleurerai, prierai*, etc.

[For the modern futures of the type *lèverai, gèlerai*, cf. H.L.F. IV (2), p. 709.]

enveerai was early replaced by *envoierai* (≠ *envoie*, etc.); this form was contracted in the ordinary way to *envoirai* (§ 970 (ii)) and pronounced in Late Middle French **āvwęrę** and **āvęrę** (§§ 519, 522); under the influence of the future of *voir* the latter form became dominant.

Throughout Old French the forms *lirai, cuirai, nuirai* are so consistent that it is probable that the shift of stress that took place in these tenses and turned the periphrasis into a unity, took place *after* the period in which tonic **ę** and **ǫ** were 'broken' under the influence of following palatal sounds (§§ 410, 411), and thus the radical employed in them is the strong one.

§ 974. (2) *Consonant.*—In conjugation III the slurring of the intertonic vowel brought the final consonant of the radical in contact with **r** and the consonantal groups thus formed followed the normal development of such groups in intervocalic position. Examples are :—

Labial + **r** (§§ 369, 372): **p'r, b'r > vr**, e.g. *avrai, savrai* (cf. § 976), *bevrai;* **m'r > mbr**, e.g. *crembrai* (cf. § 936).

Dental + **r** (§§ 369, 370, 372): **t'r, d'r > ðr > rr**, *harrai, crerrai, orrai;* **r'r > rr**, *corrai, ferrai;* **n'r > ndr**, *tendrai, vendrai;* **ꝉr** and **ļr > ꝉdr > ųdr**, *vaudrai, voudrai, cuildrai (cueudrai).*

Supported velar + **r** (§ 293): **nk(e)r > ịntr**, *veintrai, feindrai, plaindrai;* **rk(e)r > rtr**, *tortrai* (§ 942); **rg(e)r > rdr**, *sordrai;* **sk(e)r > ịstr**, *naistrai, eistrai.*

[For further examples cf. verb table.]

§ 975. The isolation of many of these forms provoked early a considerable amount of analogical re-formation, especially among verbs of III (*a*), (cf. *Oxf. Ps. esjoirunt*, M. 14, Crest. *Cl.* MS. V, *issiront*). Before the sixteenth century the forms *cueudrai*, *guarrai*, *jorrai*, *toudrai* had been replaced by forms in *-irai* or *-erai* (§ 971), and the grammarians of the time cite not only (*as*)*sailleray*, *bouillirai*, *faillirai*, *faillerai*, *hairai*, *hayerai*, *issirai* as alternative forms to (*as*)*saudrai*, *boudrai*, *faudrai*, *harrai*, *istrai*, but also *courrerai*, *mourrerai*, *quererai*. The final settlement belongs to the next century (cf. H.L.F. IV (2), 709).

✱✱ For the northern forms *faurrai*, *baurrai* for *baudrai* (⁎ *faudrai* for *baillerai*, etc.), *verrai* for *vendrai*, etc., cf. N. § xiii.

§ 976. *Anomalous Futures.—Avoir, savoir.*—The O.F. future forms *avrai*, *savrai* and the northern *arai*, *sarai*, which were also current in Paris (cf. Tabourot's pun *Tartara : tard ara*), persisted into the later sixteenth century, and were only slowly displaced by the modern forms *aurai*, *saurai* (ǫrę, sǫrę), which appear to be a court or literary introduction from the south. For a divergent view of the origin of the modern future of *avoir*, cf. R.P.F. 1922, p. 173.

These forms are first mentioned by Sylvius in 1531 ; they figure occasionally in the letters of the Duchess of Guise, p. 25, *ares*, *ore*, p. 95, *saries*, *sores* (*Guise Letters*, 1537-48), and are given as alternative forms by Meigret : ' *auoer* e *sauoer* . . . peuuet ajouter a l'*a* preçedant un *o* pour fére diphthonge, de sorte qe nou'dizons *j'arey* e *j'aorey*, *je sarey* e *saorey*,' p. 125 (cf. § 537). Bèze (1584), who mentions the three forms *avrai*, *arai*, *aurai*, still gives preference to *arai : '* the which forms are to be pronounced with simple *a*, not with the diphthong *au* ' (p. 70).

§ 977. *Estre.*—The etymological future of *estre* continued in use into the fourteenth century : *ier*, *er* (unstressed) ; *iers*, *ers ; iert*, *ert ; iermes*, *ermes ; ierent*, *erent*, but the forms *serai* and *estrai* (<*esseraio*) were also current. The loss of the initial syllable in *serai*, etc., appears to have been provoked by the combined influence of the forms of the verb that began with initial s (*sum*, *sumus*, *siam*) and of words like (*e*)*spede*, (*e*)*spose*, (*e*)*scole*, (*e*)*steindre*, in which the initial glide-sound was still movable in Period I (§ 361).

§ 978. *Faire.—ferai* is derived from a L.L. shortened form **fare*. The reduction of the countertonic vowel to ę appears to be due to the frequent use of the form in phrases of the type ✱✱*síc farái*, ✱✱*nón farái*, ✱✱*ió farái*, etc., in which the initial syllable lost its ordinary stress.

§ 979. *Gesir.—girrai* and *gerrai*, the future forms of *gesir*, were formed analogically : *girrai* on *gi*(*s*)*t*, the third person singular of the present indicative (§§ 410, 411), *gerrai* ⁎ *cherrai*, the future of *cheoir*.

[Cf. J. Bröhan, *Die Futurbildungen im Altfrz.*, 1889.]

Section 13.—FORMATION OF OLD FRENCH PERFECTS.

Types of Perfects.

§ 980. In Classical Latin four methods of formation of perfects were employed :—

(1) Reduplication, e.g. *do, dedi ; sto, steti ; curro, cucurri.*

(2) The addition of the terminations of the perfect to the present stem, which normally underwent a vocalic modification, e.g. *fŭgio, fūgi ; sĕdeo, sēdi ; prehendo, prehendi ; vĕnio, vēni ; vĭnco, vīci.*

(3) The use of the infix **-s-** attached to the radical, e.g. *scribo, scripsi ; ardeo, arsi ; rego, rexi* (**rek-si**) ; *plango, planxi.*

(4) The use of the infix **ŭ** or **ṷ** attached either (*a*) to the radical, or (*b*) to a thematic vowel, e.g. (*a*) *moneo, monŭī ; habeo, habŭī ; moveo, mōvī* (**mŏṷ-ĕo : mōṷṷī**, cf. Wahlgren, *Et.* 16/17) ; (*b*) *amo, am-a-vi ; delĕo, del-ē-vi.*

§ 981. In all these types the position of the accent varied from person to person and in the third person plural three varieties were in use :—

a'mavī, ama'vīstī, a'mavĭt, a'mavĭmus, ama'vĭstis, ama'vērunt—ama'vēre—
                                                                    a'mavĕrunt.
'monŭī, monŭ'īstī, 'monŭit, mo'nŭĭmus, monŭ'istis, monŭ'ērunt—monŭ'ēre—
                                                                    mo'nŭĕrunt.
'arsī, ar'sĭstī, 'arsit, 'arsĭmus, ar'sĭstis, ar'sērunt—ar'sēre—'arsĕrunt.

The type in *-ĕrunt*, existent but little used in Classical Latin, (Meillet, *E.L.L.* p. 124), gained ground in Late Latin.

§ 982. In Old French there were eight types of perfects, divided by incidence of stress into two classes, called *weak* and *strong*, each class comprising four sub-divisions. The *weak* perfects, those stressed throughout on the termination, comprised :—

(i) The **a**-*type :* a'mai, a'mas, etc., derived from type 4 (*b*), ama(v)i.

(ii) The **i**-*type :* sen'ti, sen'tis, etc., derived from type 4 (*b*), audi(v)i, etc.

(iii) The **u**-*type :* co'rui, co'rus, co'rut, etc., a new formation (§ 985).

(iv) The '*dedi*' type, e.g. per'di, per'dis, per'die(t), etc., a new formation (§ 984).

The *strong* perfects, those stressed on the radical in three or more persons, comprise :—

(i) The **i**-type : *vi, veĭs,* derived from type 2.

(ii) The **s**-type : *mis, mesis,* etc., derived from type 3.

(iii) The **u**-type : *dui, deus,* etc., derived from type 4(*a*).

(iv) The perfect of the verb *estre,* 'fui, 'fus, etc., strong throughout.

[For paradigms, cf. below.]

24

§ 983. The broad features of the re-modelling of the Latin types are as follows : (1) The first two types and the *-evi* type, moribund in Classical Latin, went out of use in Late Latin, with the exception of the perfects *dedi, steti, feci, veni, vidi, fui,* the surviving verbs being given perfects of other types :—

(a) **absconsi, *cadedi* or **cadui, *cursi* and **currui, *fallii, *stetui* and **stavi, *morsi, *punxi, *tanxi.* (b) **fendii, *fodii, *fugii, *rumpii, *vertii ; *bibui, *cepui, *jecui, *legui* or **lexi, *plovui ; *franxi* and **fregui, *fusi, *impinxi, *occisi, *pre(n)si, *raempsi, *respo(n)si, *sessi* or **sedui, *solsi, *volsi ;* [cf. Wahlgren, *Et. passim*].

§ 984. (2) The compounds of *do* (*perdo, reddo, trado,* etc.) re-formed their perfects *¹perdidi,* etc., on the simple verb, e.g. **per¹dẹdi,* etc. (cf. *perdedi,* C.I.L. III, 8447, *reddedit, ib.* V, 6464), and these forms were the starting-point for the new weak perfect (iv), the ' dedi ' type of perfect (§ 1003), that was adopted first by verbs with radicals ending in **-d** and **-t** and then extended to others (§ 1038), cf. Greg. *crededit, tradedit,* etc. (B, p. 490), Fred. *ostendedit, spondedit,* etc. (Haag, 890).

Like *cado, credo* was given an alternative strong **u**-*perfect* (**¹crẹdụi*), under the influence of its new participle **credūtus.*

§ 985. (3) The rapid extension of the new weak type of past participle in *-ūtum* (§ 1050), and the tendency to secure conformity between perfect and past participle led to the creation of a new weak perfect type in **-ụ** *stressed,* and this type received much extension among verbs with radicals in **l, m, n, r,** e.g. ***co¹rui, **do¹lui, **cre¹mui, **pa¹rui ;* impf. subj. ***corusse, **dolusse,* etc. (cf. Wahlgren, *Etude,* 171-175).

§ 986. (4) New forms were created for the deponent and semi-deponent verbs, e.g. **gaudii, *morii* or **morui, *nascui, *sequii,* etc. ; anomalous forms were replaced by others more in conformity with the systems in vogue and thus **crepai, *crepatus, *secai, *secatus, *vetai, vetatus ; *ersi, *sorsi ; tolsi, *tollui* or **tollii* took the place of *crepui, crepĭtus, secui, sectus, vetui, vetĭtus ; erexi, sorrexi ; sustuli.*

§ 987. Associative influences of various types led to much re-modelling of individual verbs. A weak perfect **estai,* etc., was formed to match the infinitive and past participle of *stare ;* weak perfects in *-¹i* were occasionally created on the weak forms of perfects, e.g. **co¹si, *tex¹i* on **co¹sisti, tex¹isti* (§ 374 ; cf. also § 1038). Some new formations were due to the influence exercised by individual verbs : thus **sapui* was formed on *habui, *quesi* on **presi, **crensi* on ***raensi* (§ 983), **franxi* and **tanxi* on *planxi, *punxi* on *junxi ;* O.F. *luis, nuis* on *duis,* etc. ; in others it was the form of the infinitive that determined the line followed, and thus **fo¹dii, *fo¹gii* were modelled on **fodire, *fogire* : the commonest cause of analogical replacement appears to have been, however, the desire to secure conformity between the associated forms perfect

and past participle, cf. above the formation of the weak *u*-perfects and
the perfects *fusi*, *occisi*, *presi*, *responsi*, *morsi*, *sorsi*, *sēsi*, all created
under the influence of their s-*participles*, *fusum*, *occisum*, etc.

The radical was sometimes influenced by that of the present stem tenses, cf.
prensi (for *pressi*, ✠ *premo*, etc.), *posi* (§ 374, ✠ *pono*, etc.).

§ 988 *Re-distribution of Stress.*—The re-distribution of stress that led
to the formation of the two main types of Old French perfects, the weak
and strong, was brought about as follows :—

§ 989. (i) In the perfects of the types -*avi* and -*ivi* (-αι̯i, -iι̯i), in
which the position of the stress varied between the termination and the
thematic vowels α and i, the effacement of the intervening infix ι̯ (begun
in Classical Latin) was carried further, and the thematic vowels were
brought into hiatus with the vowels of the termination, α + i̯ *final*
becoming αi, α + ę, α + ę, i̯ + i̯, i̯ + ę, i̯ + ę contracting to ᾱ and ī
respectively : αma(ι̯)ī > **αmai, αma(ι̯)istī > **αmᾱs(t), αma(ι̯)ĕrunt
> **αmᾱrent, sentiī > *sentī, sentī(ι̯)istī > **sentīs(t), sentī(ι̯)ĕrunt
> **sentirent. In this way stress was brought uniformly on to the
terminations in these types.

In the third person singular two terminations appear to have been current in
Late Latin : (1) -ᾱt, in Gaul, Rhaetia and Roumania, (2) αut (< αι̯(i)t, with
vocalised ι̯) elsewhere (cf. Gamillscheg, *Zts.frz. Spr.*, LVI, p. 110).

§ 990. (ii) In the third person plural the type -'ĕrunt (§ 981) was
generalised, and in the u-*perfects* the accentuation of this person was
brought into conformity with that of the third person singular, i.e.
'debu̯ĕrunt, 'monu̯ĕrunt replaced de'bŭĕrunt, mo'nŭĕrunt.

§ 991. (iii) In the course of Gallo-Roman the accentuation of the
first person plural of the strong perfects and of the ' *dedi* ' type was
adapted to that of the second plural, cf. O.F. ve'imes, ar'simes, de'umes,
per'dimes.

§ 992. *Influence of Mutation.*—As both the first and second persons
of the perfect ended in -ī, mutation of the preceding tonic vowel was
induced whenever it was ę or ǫ (§ 419), and whenever mutation occurred
in these persons the mutated vowel was carried subsequently into the
persons most closely associated in form with them.

§ 993. (i) In the *first* person singular of the strong perfects *radicals*
in ę and ǫ were mutated to i and ü respectively, e.g. *pręsi* > pris,
feci *fęti* > fis, *debui* dębui > **diwwi, fūi > *fu̯i > füi, *movui* mǫu̯i
(§ 980) > **müwi and the two other strong forms, the *third* persons
singular and plural, were re-formed on this mutated radical, cf. Old
French prist : prisdręnt, fist : firęnt, düt : düręnt (§ 1025), müt : müręnt.

§ 994. (ii) In the *second* person singular mutation took place in the
termination -ęsti̯ (< istī) which developed to -ist in the G.R. types,

weak (iv), strong (i), (ii), (iii), cf. O.F. **perdis** < *__perdedęsti__, **vẹis** <
*__βịdẹsti__ (§ 156 (vi)), **arsis** < *__arsẹsti__, **oüs** < **__awwist__ < *__aβwẹsti__ <
habŭisti (§ 1027), and the *first* and *second* persons plural were re-formed
on this mutated radical, cf. O.F. **perdimes, perdistes, vẹimęs, vẹistęs,
arsimęs, arsistęs, oümęs, oüstęs** (< **__awwịmes__, **__awwịstęs__, § 1027).
Under the influence of these forms the terminations of the Imperfect
Subjunctive of verbs of these types were also re-formed (§ 1043).

Personal Endings.

§ 995.

Latin.	Old French.
-ī	—
-stī	-s
-t	-(θ), t
-mŭs	-męs
-stis	-stęs
-rŭnt	-ręnt.

§ 996. *First Person Singular.*—In the first person singular Latin **ị**
final was slurred after a consonant, cf. O.F. **ars, plains, viθ**, merged in
preceding tonic **ị**, cf. O.F. **sēnti, perdi** < **pęrdiei**, § 1006, combined in a
diphthong with other preceding tonic vowels, cf. O.F. **portai, valüi, düi**,
§§ 254, 1025, **pọi**, § 1025.

[For the introduction and extension of **-s**, cf. §§ 901, 902 ; of **tš** (*c, ch*)
in Picard, cf. N. § xxviii.]

§ 997. *Second Person Singular.*—After the slurring of the final unstressed vowel in Gallo-Roman the termination of the second person
singular (**-ast, -ist, -üst, -st**) ran counter to the normal distribution of
personal endings in the other tenses, for in these **s** was characteristic of
the second person and **t** of the third, and this lack of conformity,
together with the effacement of final **t** in the inverted form before the
personal pronoun, (**portas**(t) **tü ? finis**(t) **tü ?**) led to the replacement
of the endings **__-ast, **__-ist, **__-üst, **__-st, by **-as, -is, -üs, -s** in prae-
literary times.

§ 998. *Third Person Singular.*—In the third person singular Latin
t final developed along normal lines (§ 356): it was preserved in
Old French in the *strong* perfects (cf. O.F. **arst, mist, vit, düt, ǫut**,
etc.), but opened to **θ** and effaced in the weak perfects (cf. O.F. **amaθ,
sĕntiθ, valüθ, perdieθ** (< **__perdę(d)et**, § 1006). In the early thirteenth
century, however, under the influence of the strong perfects, the weak
terminations **-i** and **-ü** (*fini, perdi, valu*) and the form **fü** began to be
replaced by **-it, -üt** and **füt**, and these later on were generalised (cf.
Angier, *dit : assentit, franchit, dut : morut, fut*, etc., *Etude*, pp. 61, 62).

999. *First and Second Persons Plural.*—In Middle French when prae-consonantal s was mute, *s* was often introduced into the first person plural ± the second plural, e.g. *portasmes, sentismes, veismes*, etc., and is prescribed in the *Orthographia Gallica* (MSS. CO, *rule* 21, p. 9).

The endings -mẹs, -stẹs have not yet been fully explained: for the possible influence of preservative analogy in the second person (-astẹs for **-ats, *az* < **-a(s)ts, etc., § 365 (ii)) and of early proparoxytone forms such as *vĭdĭmus, scrĭpsĭmus* in the first, cf. M.L. *Gr.* § 329.

** In the north-eastern region an etymological termination -ins is occasional, e.g. Froissart, *Meliador, desins*, 22312, cf. F. p. 268.

Section 14.—Weak Perfects in Period II.

Paradigms of the Early Twelfth Century.

§ 1000. I. **a**-*type :* dur-er, laiss-ier.   § 1001. II. **i**-*type :* sentir.

-ai	*dur*-ai	*laiss*-ai		-i	*sent*-i
-as	*dur*-as	*laiss*-as		-is	*sent*-is
-a(θ)	*dur*-a(t)	*laiss*-a(t)		-i(θ)	*sent*-i(t)
-āmẹs	*dur*-ames	*laiss*-ames		-imẹs	*sent*-imes
-astẹs	*dur*-astes	*laiss*-astes		-istẹs	*sent*-istes
{ -ẹrẹnt { -ierẹnt	*dur*-erent	*laiss*-ierent		-irẹnt	*sent*-irent.

§ 1002. III. **u**-*type.*   § 1003. IV. 'dẹdi-*type.*

-üi	*val*-ui		-i	*perd*-i
-üs	*val*-us		-is	*perd*-is
-ü(θ)	*val*-u(t)		-ie(θ)	*perd*-ie(t)
-ümẹs	*val*-umes		-imẹs	*perd*-imes
-üstẹs	*val*-ustes		-istẹs	*perd*-istes
-ürẹnt	*val*-urent		-ierẹnt	*perd*-ierent.

§ 1004. *Type I* comprised: (i) L.L. perfects of this type, e.g. *amai, crevai, lavai, seiai, veai* (§ 986), *estai* (§ 987); (ii) the perfects of loan verbs and of verbs of new formation in conjugation I, e.g. *guardai, finai, glorefiai.*

Type II comprised: (i) L.L. perfects of this type, e.g. *senti, joï, sivi* (§ 986), *fendi, foï* (< *fodii and *fugii), *rompi, verti* (§§ 983, 987); (ii) the perfects of verbs of conjugation II, e.g. *fini, puni;* (iii) a few perfects of verbs in conjugation III, especially those with infinitives in *-ir*, e.g. *haï, coilli, offri.* Before the twelfth century the strong perfect forms of *cosdre* and *tistre* had also been replaced by weak ones of this type (cf. § 987, and Wahlgren, *Et.* pp. 131, 186, 7).

Type III comprised mainly perfects of verbs with past participles in *-utus*, e.g. *corui, morui, valui* (§ 985).

There was some interchange between types II and III, especially in Middle French. Type III gained ground under the influence of the past participles in ü and alternative perfects *cousis : cousus, feris : ferus, tissis : tissus* are cited by sixteenth-century grammarians, with preference ordinarily for the older forms in -i (cf. Vgl. *Rem.* II, 391, Wahlgren, *Et.* pp. 131, 182-187); *courir, secourir* and *mourir*, on the other hand, were sometimes given perfects in -i.

Type IV comprised ordinarily (i) the compounds of *do*, e.g. *perdi, rendi ;* (ii) verbs whose radical ended in **d** or **t**, e.g. *bati, descendi, espandi ;* (iii) the anomalous perfects of *iraistre, naistre, vivre, veintre* (§ 1038); (iv) a few others with *-utum* participles, e.g. *rompi, sivi.*

✱✱ In the south-west and east, as in Provençal, the type was considerably extended.

§ 1005. *Formation and Development of the Old French Forms.*— Types I and II are derived from the Latin perfects in *-avi* and *-ivi*, with the modifications set forth above (§ 989). In accordance with these, the two perfects appear to have been conjugated in Early Gallo-Roman as follows :—

> *am*-ai, *am*-āsti, *am*-āt (§ 989), *am*-āmus, *am*-āstes, *am*-ārunt.
>
> *fin*-ī, *fin*-īstī, *fin*-īt, *fin*-īmus, *fin*-īstes, *fin*-īrunt.

Cf. St. Greg. *edocastī, deuastastis, memoramus, vocitamus* (B. p. 440), Fred. *judicat, regnat, denumerat, speramus* (Haag, p. 889).

In the third person singular the vowel **a** (**ɑ** ?) was retained under the influence of the sequence *ai, as, at* and of the other persons of the singular of this tense, and in *-ames* under the influence of *-astes.*

§ 1006. In the strong forms of type IV the second **d** was early dissimilated and the dissimilated forms extended to other verbs. In the first person singular **-ęi** passed through **-iei** to **i** (§§ 410, 411), and **-ęt** and **-ęrent** developed normally to **-ie(θ)** and **-ieręnt** (cf. *Troie : pendié : pecchie* 26883, *Chron. Norm. responudie : noncie, St. Martin, rompie : pie* 2321, *atendierent : charreerent* 5345).

In the central and northern region the forms in **-ie** were displaced by those in **-i** before the end of the twelfth century (cf. Wolterstorff, H. *Das Perfekt der zweiten schwachen Conjugation im Altfrz.*, Halle, 1882).

✱✱ In the eastern, southern, and south-western zone, i.e. in the region in which **ęi** developed to **ei** or **ie** (S.W. § i), the characteristic forms of this type had more vitality and sometimes served as a model for the other persons of the tense, and for the imperfect subjunctive, cf. *Oxf. Ps., confundies, vendies,* (M. pp. 43, 44), *Gormunt, perdiest, venquiest,* laisses xi, xii. [For the survival of this type into Middle and even Modern French, cf. Wahlgren, *Et.* pp. 104-111.]

§ 1007. *Modifications in Later Old and Middle French.*—Type I.— In the fourteenth century **-ięręnt** (< **ieręnt**) began to be replaced by **-ęręnt**, and the process was hastened in the fifteenth century by the reduction of **-ięręnt** to **-ęręnt** after **ĵ, ŋ, š** and **ž** (§ 510).

§ 1008. In Later Middle French two attempts were made to simplify the terminations of type A : both had their beginning in the north-eastern region.

(i) The termination of the third person plural **-ęręnt** was replaced by **-aręnt** (╪ *-ames, -a(s)tes*) and this form was even prescribed by one or two early grammarians, e.g. Sylvius, and used in some sixteenth-century works, e.g. the first edition of Du Bellay's *Deffense* (cf. H.L.F. II, 338, F. p. 248).

(ii) The terminations of type II were sometimes employed instead of those of type I: this encroachment began in the northern region in the course of Old French II, among verbs in which the termination of the third person plural was *-ierent*, pronounced there -ˈi(e)rẹnt (§ 513, N. § xxxi). In the sixteenth century it had a very considerable extension in Paris and elsewhere (cf. Rabelais, *arrachit* I, xxxvi, 313, *tranchit* xlv, 36, F. § 129). The grammarians, fortified by Latin influence, exercised their influence against these forms and were successful in causing their rejection (§§ 74, 76); cf. Palsgrave, ' Where I fynde in Alayn Chartier *donismes* and *enfermismes* . . . that is nat to be folowed ' (p. 393). Sylvius, ' The perfect of the first conjugation ends in *ai*, *as*, *at*. Some, however, prefer to end in *-i*, *-is*, *-it*. . . . You will hear both pronounced at Paris, but the first approves itself to most people because it is nearer the Latin.' (F. § 129, H.L.F. II, 326-328.)

§ 1009. *Type III.*—The passage of the diphthong üï to ẅï (§ 515) isolated the first persons of this type and analogical forms made on the other persons make their appearance in the thirteenth century, e.g. *valu(s)*.

Section 15.—Strong Perfects in Later Old French.

Type I.—i-Perfects.

§ 1010. *Twelfth Century Paradigms*—

vi(t)	*vin*	*voil*
ve(d)-is	*ven*-is	*vol*-is
vi-t	*vin*-t	*vol*-t
ve(d)-imes	*ven*-imes	*vol*-imes
ve(d)-istes	*ven*-istes	*vol*-istes
vi(d)r-ent	*vindr*-ent	*voldr*-ent

§ 1011. This class of perfects comprised in Old French: (i) the Latin perfects *veni* and *vidi*, (ii) the perfect of *tenir*, formed on the model of *venir*, (iii) the perfect of *voleir*, brought into conformity with this type by the early assimilation of consonantalised ŭ to preceding l (*volui* *wọlwi > **vọlli > vọil (§ 254), *voluisti* *wolwisti > **vollisti > volis(t), etc. (§ 374)).

A few isolated examples of other verbs conjugated on this model are found, e.g. *solt* (<*soluit*), *Rol.* 352, *soult*, *Q.L.R.*, *valist* (*valuisset* (?)), Renclus, *Car.* lii, 7, (cf. Wahlgren, *Et.* p. 172).

In the conjugation of **voleir** the s-perfect type was also frequently used, especially in the weak forms and the imperfect subjunctive, cf. *Al.* MSS. A and P, *volsisse*, L, *volisse* 41(*b*), and similar weak forms of the perfect and the imperfect subjunctive of *tenir* and *venir* (*tensis*, etc., *tensisse*) were formed in the thirteenth century (Angier, *Et. tensist*, p. 43).

✳✳ In the north-eastern region there was a different treatment of the groups **nw**, **lw**, and in the third person singular the forms *tinve(t)*, *vinve(t)* (< **venuit + tenuit) and in the subj. impf. *vowist*, *vowissent* are attested, cf. F. p. 315.

Type II.—s-Perfects.

§ 1012. *Twelfth Century Paradigms.*

A. Vowel Radical (s *intervocalic*).				**B.** Consonant Radical (ss and s *supported*).	

mi-s	*mi*-s	*fi*-s	*me*-s	*plain*-s	*dui*-s
{ mę-zis	*me*-sis	*fe*-sis } *ma*-sis		*plain*-sis	{ *dui*-ssis
{ mę-is	*me*-ïs	*fe*-ïs }			{ *dui*-sis
mist	*mi*-st	*fi*-st	*me*-st	*plain*-st	*dui*-st
{ mę-zimęs	*me*-simes	*fe*-simes } *ma*-simes		*plain*-simes	{ *dui*-ssimes
{ mę-imęs	*me*-ïmes	*fe*-ïmes }			{ *dui*-simes
{ mę-zistęs	*me*-sistes	*fe*-sistes } *ma*-sistes		*plain*-sistes	{ *dui*-ssistes
{ mę-istęs	*me*-ïstes	*fe*-ïstes }			{ *dui*-sistes
{ mi-zdręnt	*mi*-sdrent	*fi*-strent *me*-sdrent } *plain*-strent			*dui*-strent
{ mi-stręnt	*mi*-strent	*fi*-rent *me*-strent }			
{ mi-ręnt	*mi*-rent				

§ 1013. *Type* **A** comprised: (1) the remaining Late Latin s-*perfects* of those verbs whose radicals ended in a vowel, e.g. **mi-si**, ***ma-si**, ***clo-si**, ***prēsi**, ***posi** (§§ 987, 374); (ii) the perfects of the verbs *dire*, *despire*, *lire*, whose strong forms conformed to this type and whose weak forms were re-made analogically on **męzis**, **pręzis**, etc., before the twelfth century; (iii) the perfect of *faire*, whose divergent forms **fiz, **feisis, etc., were also re-made.

[For full list cf. verb tables.]
The type was sometimes extended to early loan-words of Germanic origin, e.g. *guaris : guaresis : guarist, maris : maresis*, etc. (cf. *Etude Angier*, p. 43).

§ 1014. In all verbs of this type, except *clore*, the weak and strong radicals were differentiated by vocalic alternation : among verbs with radicals in ę (e.g. ***pręsi**) the alternation i—ę was induced by the mutation of the vowel of the first person and its analogical extension to the other strong forms (§ 993); among verbs with radicals in i (**mīsī**) the alternation i—ę was due to the dissimilation of the countertonic vowel i to ę in the weak forms (§ 156 (vi)); in the perfects of *maneir* and *rere* alternation was due to the influence exercised by stress on the development of a *free* (§ 231).

The strong persons of *maneir* were not infrequently modelled on those of *metre* and the weak persons on the radical *main* (*mainsis*, etc.). The strong radical was sometimes generalised in perfects of the type *mis* and *fis*, e.g. *Oxf. Ps. despisis, eslisis, disis* (M. p. 49). In the strong forms of the perfect of *pondre* the radicals **pun** (≠ *pondre*), **pǫ-** and **pü-** (< **pǫ-** (§ 987) mutated) were all in use, e.g. *repuns* (*Oxf. Ps.*), (*re*)*post*, (*Auc.* 20, 3), (*re*)*pust* (: *fust*, F. p. 283).

§ 1015. In the weak persons of this type, **s**, being *intervocalic*, was voiced to **z**, e.g. **misisti** > **mę-zis(t)**, *mesis*(t), etc., but under the influence of perfects of type **B** (and of earlier **deissis (?), etc.) **z** (**s**) was sometimes replaced by **s** (**ss**).

§ 1016. *Type* **B** comprised the perfects of those verbs whose radicals ended in Latin in a consonant (except *dixi, despexi, lexi*) ; it included consequently those verbs in which the final consonant of the radical had been completely assimilated to **s**, e.g. *escris*, or palatalised, e.g. *duis, cuis, trais*, as well as those in which the final consonant persisted into Old French, e.g. *ars, plains, sols*.   In all these the intervocalic consonant of the weak forms was normally **s** (*ss*), but under the influence of type **A s** (*ss*) was not infrequently replaced by **z** (*s*) in the conjugation of the verbs of type **B** (ii), i.e. the verbs in which **s** was intervocalic in Old French, e.g. **düizis, eskrẹzis**.

[For full list cf. verb tables.]

§ 1017. Except in the perfect of *escrivre* there was no vocalic alternation in this type, and in the conjugation of this perfect, the weak forms *escressis (escresis), escressimes*, etc., were often replaced by analogical *escrissis (escrisis)*, etc.

The forms of some perfects were occasionally influenced by radicals of other parts of the verb, e.g. *Oxf. Ps. crienstrent* (M. pp. 49, 50).

§ 1018. *Third Person Plural*.—In the third person plural three types developed :—

(i) Among verbs in whose radical **s** was intervocalic in Latin and consequently voiced (§ 334), the ending **-zdrẹnt**, e.g. **mizdrẹnt, prizdrẹnt, klozdrent,** *closdrent*.

(ii) Among verbs in whose radical **s** was lengthened or supported in Latin the ending **-strent**, e.g. **eskristrẹnt, arstrẹnt, plāinstrẹnt, distrẹnt.**

(iii) In the perfect of *facere*, both **fistrẹnt** and **firent : fistrẹnt** from L.L. **fẹferụnt*, with **k** palatalised in Late Latin and subsequently shifted forward to **t͡s** (> **s**, §§ 290-295), **firẹnt** from early shortened **¹fẹkrụnt.*

[For the vowel **i** cf. § 993.]

Between the forms **-zdrẹnt** and **-strẹnt** there was early some interchange but **-strẹnt** became dominant in Later Old French (cf. *St. Legier, fisdren* 62, *Al.* MS. L, *pristrent* 80, MS. P, *mistrent* 30).

✱✱ For northern *misent, dissent*, etc., cf. N. § xxx.

§ 1019. *Modifications in Type A in Later Old French*.—In the course of the later twelfth and thirteenth centuries *type* **A** was re-modelled under the influence of the perfects of *veoir* and *faire*.

(i) On the model of the weak forms of the perfect of *veoir* (**vẹ-is, vẹ-imẹs, vẹ-istẹs**), the weak forms of the perfects of verbs of this type and the forms of the imperfect subjunctive began to be replaced by forms without intervocalic **z** (**s**), cf. *Rol. feïstes* 1708, 1723, Crest. *meïstes, meïst, meïssiez*, etc., *Q.L.R. feïs, oceïs*, etc.   A tendency to dissimilate the two s-*sounds* may have contributed to this change, especially in the imperfect subjunctive, in which it is earliest attested, cf. *feïssent, St. Leg.* 54, *Oxf. Ps.* (M. 52).   In the northern region the etymological forms remained dominant into the later fourteenth century.

(ii) Under the combined influence of *virent* and *firent* analogical *mirent, prirent*, etc. were introduced in the later twelfth century (Crest. *virent : prirent, E.* 3087), but the etymological forms continued in use into the fifteenth century, cf. Chr. Pis. *distrent*, Comm. *misdrent*, p. 18, l. 1, *mistrent*, p. 25, l. 21.

Type III.—u-Perfects.

§ 1020. *Twelfth Century Paradigms—*

A	B	C
oi	düi	müi
o-üs, ẹ-üs	dẹ-üs, dọ-üs	mọ-üs, mẹ-üs
ọut, ọt	düt	müt
o-ümẹs, ẹ-ümẹs	dẹ-ümẹs, dọ-ümẹs	mọ-ümẹs, mẹ-ümẹs
o-üstẹs, ẹ-üstẹs	dẹ-üstẹs, dọ-üstẹs	mọüstẹs, mẹüstẹs
ọurẹnt, ọrẹnt	dürent	mürẹnt

§ 1021. The Old French strong perfect of the **u**-type was derived from the Latin **u**-perfect, but the type was only retained by verbs possessing radicals ending in plosive and fricative consonants other than **s**. The verbs with radicals ending in **l, n, m, r, s** either lost early the characteristic labial sound in their phonetic development (e.g. **volli, *cosi* (<*consŭi*), **texi, *posi*, § 374) or were re-formed, (e.g. **co'rui, *va'lui, *somo'nui* or **somonsi*).

[For full list cf. verb tables.]

§ 1022. *Type* **A** comprised the perfects of Late Latin verbs with radicals in **a**, (*habui, pavi, placui, sapui, tacui*) and *potui ; type* **B** comprised the Late Latin perfects with radicals in **ẹ**, e.g. *crevi, debui, licuit ; *bebui, *-cepui, *credui, *fregui* (*Eneas, frut*, 4502), **jecui, *legui, *stetui* (§§ 983, 984); *type* **C** those with radicals in **ọ**, *cognōvi, mōvi* (§ 980(4)), *stŭpuit* and the perfects of *nuire* and *ploveir* (§ 983).

Before tonic **u** and **ü**, **ọ** *countertonic* was often dissimilated to **ẹ** (§ 490) and **ẹ** *countertonic* rounded to **ọ** (§ 484), and thus types **B** and **C** early fell together. The spelling *e* was kept, but **ẹ** was reduced to **ẹ** and probably rounded and fronted to a weak ö-sound (§ 275).

In Old French the perfects of *choir* and *sivre* were also sometimes modelled on type **B**, cf. *Rou. decheurent : jurent* I, 1042, *aconsurent : esmurent* 1039; *sut : conut* Beroul 1541 and so still Rabelais *aconceurent*, I, ch. 25, l. 55, and Mod. Fr. *déchut, échut* (cf. Wahlgren, *Et.* pp. 179, 180, 198-203).

§ 1023. *Development of Old French Forms.*—In this type of perfect **ŭ** in hiatus consonantalised to **w** in Late Latin (§ 220) and the salient feature of its development is the influence exercised by this sound on the consonants and vowels juxtaposed to it.

[For the influence of mutation cf. §§ 992-994.]

§ 1024. (1) In contact with **w** the final consonant of the radical was assimilated or effaced (§ 374), e.g. habŭī > *abwi̯ > **awwi̯, habŭit > **awwet, habŭĕrunt > **awweru̯nt (§ 990), dēbŭi > **di̯wwi̯, plakŭi *plakwi̯ > **pla̯wwi̯, crēdŭi *kre̯dwi̯ > **kri̯wwi̯.

Alternative forms of the weak persons of the perfect of pŏtŭī are frequent in Old French, e.g. Jonas *podist*, Crest. *Iv.* 264, *poïsse*, etc., Marie Fr. *poïst*, F. 378, *Rose* II, *poïsse, poïst, poïssent, Intr.* 327 : these are derived from a type in which the intervocalic group **tw** was early reduced to **t** (cf. **sw**, § 374), and consequently opened to ð and effaced : pŏtŭisti > *po̯twi̯sti̯ > **po̯ti̯sti̯ > po(ð)is.

§ 1025. (2) In contact with **w**, preceding *tonic* **a** and **i** were rounded to ǫ and ü respectively (cf. § 481) ; **w** was combined in a diphthong with preceding ǫ in the third persons singular and plural and elsewhere merged in the vowel it rounded.

**awwi̯ < habŭī > ǫi̯, **awwet < habŭit > ǫut, **awwĕru̯nt < habŭĕrunt > ǫu̯re̯nt, **di̯wwi̯ < dēbŭī > düi, **diwwet (§ 993) > düt, **diwwĕru̯nt (§ 993) > düre̯nt.

In the later twelfth century, (under the influence of the first person ?), the diphthongal forms in **-ǫut, -ǫu̯re̯nt** were replaced by forms in **-ǫt** and **-ǫre̯nt**, cf. Wace, *Rou.* II, *Herolt : out* 1776 : *plout* 2900 ; Crest. *E. mot : ot* 385, *ot* (*audit*) *: ot* 324.

§ 1026. (3) In contact with **w** preceding countertonic **a** was rounded to **o** (§ 481): habŭisti > **awwi̯sti̯ > oüs.

[For *doüs*, etc., cf. § 1022.]

§ 1027. (4) In contact with **w**, **i̯**, the tonic vowel of the stressed terminations (developed by mutation in the second person singular, introduced analogically in the other two persons, § 994) was rounded to ü (§ 480), e.g. **awwi̯sti̯ < habŭisti > oüs, **awwi̯ste̯s > oüste̯s, **dewwi̯sti̯ < dēbŭisti > deüs(t).

Some scholars attribute the rounded vowel of these terminations to the analogical influence exercised by the strong perfect of *estre* (fŭi, etc.).

✹✹ § 1028. In the north-eastern region **w** exercised no rounding influence and the types developed were : *au : awis : aut : awimes : awistes : aurent, diu : dewis : diut : dewimes : dewistes : diurent, mu : mowis : mut : mowimes : mowistes : murent, pou : powis : pout*, etc. (cf. *Eul. auret* 20, *awisset* 27, *Dial. Greg. tau, taut, plaurent, estiut, biurent, P. Mor. diut* 116d, 324b) : subsequently e̯ was rounded to ö, ǫ fronted to the same sound and the vowel ö, written *eu*, was often introduced into the weak persons of type A, e.g. euïs, euïmes, euïstes (cf. Suchier, ' Die Mundart des Leode-garliedes,' *Zts. Rom. Ph.* II, 255 et seqq. ; republished by L. Spitzer in *Meisterwerke der Rom. Sprachwissenschaft*, 1929, pp. 290-349).

✹✹ § 1029. In the Picard region, in which the diphthong ǫu was differentiated to eu (> ö) (§ 549), ǫut, ǫu̯rent, etc. > eut, eurent and later ö(t), öre̯(n)t, cf. Auc. *eut* 20, 1, Renclus, *Mis. eut, peut* (< *pavit*) : *keut, seut* (*solet*), xlviii (N. § viii) ; in Normandy, also, where eü > ö, beüs, etc. > bös, etc., and this pronunciation had some currency in Paris in the sixteenth century, (cf. Thurot I, p. 518, F. p. 319).

Section 16.—-STRONG PERFECTS IN MIDDLE FRENCH.

§ 1030. The conjugation of the strong perfects was disintegrated by the sound-changes that took place in the course of the thirteenth century in Middle French, and alternation of stress, the fundamental characteristic of these perfects, was gradually eliminated. The process, begun by the corrosive influence of sound-change, was completed by analogical re-formation when alternation had begun to appear anomalous.

Sound-Changes.

§ 1031. (1) Effacement of prae-consonantal **s** (§ 377) obliterated the characteristic sound of the **s**-perfects in the third persons, e.g. **prist > prit, pristrent > pritrent, plainst > plaint, plainstrent > plaintrent** and in type **B** the third singular became in consequence homophonous with the third singular of the present indicative. The plural forms persisted into the late fifteenth century, e.g. Commines *misdrent, mistrent.*

§ 1032. (2) Levelling of diphthongs resulted in the isolation of the first person singular of the **u**-perfects, e.g. o̧i > wȩ (§ 519), düi > dẅi, müi > mẅi (§ 515), and these forms were gradually replaced by forms made on the model of other persons of the tense, e.g. *o(s)* or *eu(s)* ü(s) for *oi*, *po(s)* or *pü(s)* for *poi*, *du(s)* and *mu(s)* for *dui* and *mui* (cf. W. Essler, *Zur Geschichte der ŭi-Perfecta*, Darmstadt, 1905). The third persons singular and plural of *type* A (e.g. *ot, orent*), now isolated, were replaced by analogical forms made on the model of the weak radical and the other **u**-perfects, cf. G. Guiart I, *ut : mourut* 725, *purent : furent* 351, etc., and Essler, *op. cit.*

In types **B** and **C** analogical forms of the first person are attested in the early thirteenth century, in type **A** only in Middle French, F. p. 317.

1033. (3) The effacement of countertonic ȩ in hiatus (§ 243) obliterated alternation of stress in the conjugation of the perfect of *veoir* and the **u**-*perfects* and also in the **s**-*perfects* which had the vocalic alternation ȩ : i, e.g. *eus* ȩüs > ü(s), *eumes* ȩümes > ümes, *eustes* ȩütes > ütes, *meis* > mis, *mȩimes* > mimes, *meistes* mȩites > mites, *vȩis* > vis. This development, accelerated by the influence of the strong forms, appears to have reached its term in the early fifteenth century but the traditional spelling of these forms (*eus, meis, veis* etc.) was continued long after and very commonly influenced the spelling of the old strong forms, cf. Mid. Fr. *deut, deurent, meit, veit,* etc.

Analogical Re-formation.

§ 1034. The weak forms of the perfects of *venir* and *tenir* (*venis, venimes, venistes,* etc.), began to give way to forms modelled on the strong persons in the fifteenth century, and *vinmes, vintes,* etc., in their turn gave rise to the third plurals *vinrent* and *tinrent*, which finally

replaced older *vindrent* and *tindrent* in the seventeenth century, cf. Vgl. I, 182.

Cf. Palsgrave: ' . . . of *je tyns* and *vins* . . . cometh *tinsmes* and *vinsmes* rather than *tenismes* and *venismes*, thoughe these latter be more used.' (pp. 396, 397).

✶✶ [For Picard *tinrent*, *vinrent*, cf. N. § xiii.]

§ 1035. Under the combined influence of the past participle *voulu* and the perfect of *valoir* the Old French perfects of *vouloir* were gradually replaced by the modern weak **u**-*perfect*. This is attested in the north-east in the early thirteenth century, but in francien the traditional forms remained dominant into the late fifteenth century.

In Villon the proportion of traditional forms to the new analogical is 5 : 3, in Charles d'Orléans 6 : 11, in the Cent Nouvelles Nouvelles 32 : 34 (Wahlgren, *Et.* p. 217). In the conjugation of *veoir*, *venir* and *tenir* weak perfects in -**u** made their appearance also early in the north-east and under the influence of the past participle the perfect *pourvu(s)* established itself in Late Middle French and there was some hesitation about *prévu(s)*, (cf. Vgl. *Rem.* II, 74, W. *Et.* pp. 214-216, F. p. 324).

§ 1036. In the course of the thirteenth century and Middle French the remaining **s**-*perfects* were for the most part re-made on the weak **i**-*perfect* type, but on varying radicals : *clore* made *clou-i(s)* or *clos-i(s)*, *traire*, *traï(s)* or *traïs-i(s)* ; the verbs in -*ardre*, -*erdre*, -*ordre* early adopted the radical of the infinitive (e.g. Deschamps, *ardit*, *ardirent*) ; the verbs in -*ure* (≠ the past participle) adopted the radical of the strong persons, (e.g. Charles d'Orléans, (*tu*) *conclus*, Commines, *conclusmes*, Wahlgren, *Et.* p. 219) ; *escrire* and the verbs in -*aindre*, -*eindre*, -*oindre* re-formed their perfects on the weak radical of the present tenses (e.g. Joinville, *ceigny*, *estraignimes*, *constreignirent*) ; *cuire* and the verbs in -*uire*, on the weak radical of the perfect (e.g. *conduisirent*, Adenes, *Cleomades*, *destruisit*, Deschamps).

Meigret admits *ceigni* but rejects *deduisis* and *detruisis*, p. 118.

[Cf. E. Dietz, *Zur Geschichte der frz.*, **si**- *und* **i**-*perfecta*, Diss. Heidelberg, 1911, R. Ekblom, *Étude sur l'extinction des verbes au prétérit en* -**si** *et en* -**ui** *en français*, Thèse, Upsal. 1918.]

§ 1037. Many verbs had alternative perfects in Old French, e.g. *criembre*, *ester*, *lire*, *voleir*, and in Middle French analogical forms were frequent: widespread and early, especially in the northern region, were the analogical weak **i**-*perfects* made on the radical of the infinitives in -*aindre*, -*eindre*, -*oindre*, cf. Froissart, *contraindi*, *joindi*. *Mir*, *Chartres*, *estaindrent*, p. 209, Palsgrave (p. 387) admits *attayndis*, *estayndis* and enjoins *fayndrent*, *payngdrent*, *playngdrent* ≠ *fayndre*, etc. (cf. F. p. 287).

The perfect of *prendre* was often influenced by the perfect of *tenir* and conjugated *prin(s)*, *prins*, *print*, *primes* (Mgr.)—*prinsmes* or *prenismes* (Plsgr.), *prittes* or *printes* (Mgr.)—*prinstes* (Plsgr.), *priret*, *prindret*, *prinret* (Mgr.)—*prindrent* (Plsgr.).

Pondre was early given a weak perfect *pondi* (≠ *respondi*, Cam. *Ps. repondirent*) ; later on *pondu*, *ponni(s)* and *ponnu(s)* are all found (W. *Et.* pp. 121, 122) and a like variety is accorded to *manoir* and *somonoir* (cf. Tables and W. *Et.* pp. 123, 124).

Throughout Middle French but more especially in the works of the less educated and in the regions in which literary tradition was weak or relatively little affected by francien, e.g. in the north-east, analogical formations were of very great variety,

usually weak, e.g. *teni*, *veni* (W. p. 132), *prennis*, *esconsi*, *disi*, *escrisi*, *metti*, *moury*, *veii*, etc. (F. *passim*), but occasionally strong, e.g. *vouls*, 2 p. sg. (Greban), *voulstes* (Chr. Pis.), *osmes* (± *os*, *habui*), *destruismes*, *destruites* (F. 289, 291, 318) : for further details cf. verb tables and F. pp. 287, 289-295, 297, 320, 327-329.

Section 17.—Anomalous Perfects.

§ 1038. The O.F. verbs *iraistre*, *naistre*, *vivre*, *veintre* (< *vincere*), and sometimes *beneïstre*, formed weak perfects on the radicals : **irask-** (*irasqu-*), **nask-** (*nasqu-*), **vesk-** (*vesqu-*), **venk-** (*venqu-*). Type IV, the model first followed, was early replaced by type II.

nasqu-i (*irasqu*-i)	*vesqu*-i (*benesqu*-i)	*venqu*-i
nasqu-is	*vesqu*-is	*venqu*-is
{ *nasqu*-ie(t)	*vesqu*-ie(t)	*venqu*-ie(t) }
{ *nasqu*-i(t)	*vesqu*-i(t)	*venqu*-i(t) }
nasqu-imes	*vesqu*-imes	*venqu*-imes
nasqu-istes	*vesqu*-istes	*venqu*-istes
{ *nasqu*-ierent	*vesqu*-ierent	*venqu*-ierent }
{ *nasqu*-irent	*vesqu*-irent	*venqu*-irent }

In Late Middle French the modern weak **u**-*perfect vescus*, etc., was made on the model of the past participle but *vesquis* only became obsolete in the seventeenth century, (cf. Vgl. *Rem.* I. pp. 196, 197 ; Wahlgren, *Et.* pp. 209-213 ; H.L.F. II. 339).

These perfects are all of Romance origin and the **-dedi** type appears to be the earlier : *venqui* was formed on the radical of the analogical past participle *vencu* (*vincutum) ; the starting-point of *irasqui*, *nasqui* and *vesqui* appears to be the weak forms of older strong perfects, e.g. ****nas'kwis** < ***nɑ.skŭ'isti**, the adoption of the type being facilitated by the influence of the past participles, *irascu* and *nascu* being in use in Old French together with *iré* and *né*. The radical **vesk-** appears to have been developed by metathesis in the weak persons of the Latin perfect : *vixisti* ***βęksisti** > ****vęskis(tį)** ; (cf. the Provençal perfects *elesquet* and *tesquet*, §§ 374, 1021, Wahlgren, *Et.* pp. 182-184, and for a variant explanation M.L. *Gr. Rom.* II. § 289). The perfect forms *resurrexis*, etc., are learned loan-words.

Section 18.—Imperfect Subjunctive.

Paradigms of the Twelfth Century.

§ 1039. *Weak Perfects*—

a-*type.*	i-*type.*	u-*type.*	dẹdi-*type.*
dur -asse	*sent* -isse	*val* -usse	*perd* -isse
dur -asses	*sent* -isses	*val* -usses	*perd* -isses
dur -ast	*sent* -ist	*val* -ust	*perd* -ist
dur { -issons	*sent* { -issons	*val* { -ussons	*perd* { -issons
{ -issiens	{ -issiens	{ -ussiens	{ -issiens
dur { -isseiz	*sent* { -isseiz	*val* { -usseiz	*perd* { -isseiz
{ -issez	{ -issez	{ -ussez	{ -issez
{ -issiez	{ -issiez	{ -ussiez	{ -issiez
dur -assent	*sent* -issent	*val* -ussent	*perd* -issent

§ 1040. *Strong Perfects—*

i-*type.*		s-*type.*		u-*type.*		*estre.*	
ve(d)	-isse	*mes*	-isse	*o*	-usse	*fu*	-sse
ve(d)	-isses	*mes*	-isses	*o*	-usses	*fu*	-sses
ve(d)	-ist	*mes*	-ist	*o*	-ust	*fu*	-st
ve(d)	{-issons / -issiens	*mes*	{-issons / -issiens	*o*	{-ussons / -ussiens	*fu*	{-ssons / -ssiens
ve(d)	{-isseiz / -issez / -issiez	*mes*	{-isseiz / -issez / -issiez	*o*	{-ussiez / -ussez / -ussiez	*fu*	{-sseiz / -ssez / -ssiez
ve(d)	-issent	*mes*	-issent	*o*	-ussent	*fu*	-ssent

§ 1041. The imperfect subjunctive is derived from the Latin pluperfect subjunctive. Its development follows the lines of the termination-stressed forms of the perfect indicative and is often directly influenced by them.

Radical.

§ 1042. In all verbs, except the verb *estre*, the tense was stressed throughout on the termination, and the radical employed was the weak one, i.e. the radical developed in the termination-stressed forms of the perfects: cf. O.F. am-*asse*, proi-*asse*, plor-*asse*, voi-*dasse*; ve-*isse*, mes-*isse*, mas-*isse*, de-*usse*, mo-*usse*, etc. (cf. *sect.* 8 above, §§ 1014, 1022, 1026).

[For later phonetic development and analogical replacements of radicals, cf. sections 8 and 16 above.]

Terminations.

§ 1043. *Stressed Vowel.*—The stressed vowel of the singular and the third person plural is always the same as the stressed vowel of the weak forms of the perfect: amasse, sentisse, perdisse, valüsse, veisse, mesisse, oüsse.

In the conjugation of verbs forming their perfects on the *weak* a- and i-types (*amasse, sentisse*), this similarity is due to similarity of phonological development: ɑmɑ(w)isse > amas(ę) (§ 1046), sentiissem > sentis(ę). The terminations -*isse* and -*üsse*, in use in the *dedi*-perfects and the *strong* perfects, are analogical in origin, etymological -ęsę (< *perde(d)issem* (cf. Eulalia *perdesse* 17), *vidïssem, misïssem, habüïssem*) having been in all types replaced by -ısę, under the combined influence of the weak i-type (*sentisse*) and the weak persons of the perfects (*perdis, veïs, mesis,* etc., §§ 992, 994). In the forms of the strong u-type as in the perfect (§ 1027), į was subsequently labialised to ü by juxtaposed preceding w : **awisset > oüst; (for the weak ü-type, *valusse,* cf. § 985).

✶✶ [For eastern -*aisse*, etc., cf. E. § xv ; for north-eastern unrounded forms such as *awisse, deuisse,* etc., cf. § 1028, N.E. § xvii.]

§ 1044. *Unstressed Intertonic Vowel.*—In the terminations of all types in conjugations II and III, the vowel in the intertonic syllable of the terminations of the first and second plural is always the same as the stressed vowel in the other terminations, the obscured vowel which

would normally have developed having been analogically replaced, cf. O.F. sentissons, valüssons, veïssons, mesïssons, oüssons.

In the terminations of these persons in the *first* conjugation, etymological forms with ę (< reduced unstressed ǝ) are occasional (cf. Crest. MS. C, *E. obliessiez* 3913, *L. leisessiez* 5475; *St. Martin* 6699, *menessunt : malades sunt*, etc.; *Et. Angier* 46), but the forms ordinarily in use in the twelfth century were **-issons, -issiez**, etc., made on the model of *sentissons, perdissons, veissons, mesissons*, etc., cf. *Rol. meslisez* 257, *Auc. amissies* 14, 18, *alissies* 22, 35. The modern forms *-assions, -assiez*, formed on the other persons of the tense, made an early appearance in Anglo-Norman (§ 1306), but were only finally adopted in French in the later sixteenth and early seventeenth century.

In 1561 Pillot still explicitly prescribes *aymissons, aymissiez*; Robert Estienne also only mentions forms of this type but his son Henri writes: ' I am aware that my father wrote *aimissons* and *aimissiez*, but yet I know that in speaking he used *aimassions, aimassiez*, and although he gave directions for both to be put in his grammar the second form was omitted.' (Th. I, 237, F. § 173.) The explanation of the older forms furnished by Peletier is as follows: ' Mais depuis que les français ont esté en paix, ils ont commencé à parler plus doucement, et si j'osois dire, plus mollement. Ne les avons-nus pas vus si sujets a leurs dames, qu'ils eussent cuidé estre peché mortel de prononcer autrement qu'elles . . . Et de là est venu *aimissions, parlissions, donnissions*.' (*Dialogue*, p. 132.)

§ 1045. As in the perfect, § 1007 (ii), there was a widespread tendency to replace all the forms in *-asse* of the first conjugation by forms in *-isse*, cf. Tabourot: ' Ces mots' *aymasse*, etc., ' sont rudes et . . . quelques-uns pour plus doux son de la langue les mettent en *-isse* . . .' According to Meigret, however, such forms are ' faotes qui n'ont jamais été reçues par les homes bien apriz en la lange Françoeze.' (Cf. Th. I, 238, F. p. 338.)

§ 1046. *Personal Endings.*—*Singular.*—Under the influence of the endings of the present subjunctive of conjugations II and III (*puniss-ę, puniss-ęs, puniss-ę(θ), dorm-ę*, etc.) analogical forms in -ę, -ęs, -ę (θ) early came into use in the singular of the imperfect subjunctive of conjugations II and III (*Eulalia, perdesse* 17, *awisset* 27); before the eleventh century like forms were established in the first and second persons of all conjugations, cf. *Alexis* L, *volisse* 41 b, *repairasses, reconfortasses* 78 d, e, but not in the more used third person in which the etymological forms held their own (cf. § 759).

§ 1047. *Plural.*—In the first and second persons plural the *personal* terminations in use in the later twelfth century were those of the present subjunctive (§§ 907, 908), i.e. in west French *-um (-om, -on)* and *-iens ; -iez* and *-ez*, in the east and north and probably the centre *-oms (-ons)* and *-iens ; -eiz* (> *-oïs*), *-ez* and *-iez*. In the central region in the thirteenth century the use of *-ons* and *-iens* produced *-ions* in this tense as in the present subjunctive and in the second person *-iez* was generalised.

✱✱ § 1048. The termination of the third person plural was sometimes brought into line with the terminations of the first and second persons by shift of stress or re-modelling, in all regions except the Centre and Normandy. The forms varied. In the east, south-east and south-centre -ˈient (± -iens), was the form preferred, in the south-west -ont (-ˈūnt ± -ˈūns ons), and -ant (-ˈānt < -ˈent stressed, nasalised and lowered). These stressed forms are attested earliest, and in Old French most frequently, in the imperfect subjunctive (cf. *Erec*, l. 1449, and Foerster's note, Angier, *Étude*, p. 44 and note); they are found also occasionally in the present indicative, more frequently in the present subjunctive and, in the eastern region especially, in the imperfect indicative (E. § xxix, S.C. § xix, S.W. § xi).

[Cf. W. Söderhjelm, *Ueber Akzentverschiebung in der 3. Pers. Pl. im Altfrz.* 1895, M.L. *Gr. Fr.* § 288 ; for their survival in the modern period, cf. F. § 4.]

Section 19.—PAST PARTICIPLES.

§ 1049. *Types.*—The suffixes -tus and -sus, added either directly to the radical or to the thematic vowel, produced in Latin six types of participial terminations : -ˈātum, *am*-ātum, -ˈętum, *del*-ētum, -ˈītum, *aud*-ītum, ˈ-ītum, *pos*-ītum, ˈ-tum, *planc*-tum, ˈ-sum, *clau*-sum. Of these ✱-ętu became obsolete in Late Latin together with the perfect in -*evi* ; the others survived and gave rise to four types in Old French : two *weak*— -*e*(*t*), -*ie*(*t*), -ę (θ), -ie(θ)(< -ˈātum) and -*i*(*t*), -ˈi(θ)(<-ˈītum), e.g. *porte*(*t*), *laissie*(*t*), *senti*(*t*), and two *strong*— -t (< ˈ-ītum and ˈ-tum) and -s (<ˈ-sum), e.g. *plain-t*, *pos-t*, *clo-s*, *ri-s*.

There was some extension of both strong types in Late Latin and Gallo-Roman, cf. O.F. *muete* < ✱*movita*, *tolt* < ✱*tollitu*, *solt* (< ✱*solvitu*), *volt* (< ✱*volvitu*) and the substantives *falte, fente*.

§ 1050. Two new weak types were subsequently developed, -*u*(*t*) -ü(θ) and -eit. (1) In Late Latin the participles of verbs with radicals ending in -u, e.g. *secū-tus, battū-tus, consū-tus, statū-tus* were the starting-point of a stressed participial termination -ųtų that spread rapidly among verbs with u-*perfects*, e.g. ✱*debutum*, ✱*habutum*, ✱*molutum*, ✱*movutum*, ✱*nocutum*, ✱*volutum*, and was subsequently extended to other verbs with participles in -ītum, in particular to those whose perfects were being formed on the new ' -*dedi* ' model, e.g. ✱✱*perdutum*, ✱✱*vendutum*, ✱✱*vencutum* (cf. Wahlgren, *Et.* pp. 21, 22).

§ 1051. (2) On the model of *collectum*, a participle in frequent use in the church service, an analogical participle, ✱*tollectum*, was formed for the associated verb *tollere*, and the influence of these two forms, together with that of *adjectum* and the clerkly participle *benedictum* (benęδeit), led to the adoption of the type by a few verbs, e.g. *chaeit, seeit, remaneit*.

✱✱ The extension of this type appears to be greatest in the eastern region, the region in which lĕctum became leit (§ 412), cf. Wahlgren, *Et.* pp. 36, 37.

§ 1052. Various causes combined to induce a considerable amount of interchange of types.

(1) The tendency, operative at all periods of the language, to bring the formation of the past participle into conformity with the perfect (Wahlgren, *Et. passim*). To Late Latin is ascribed the analogical form **torsus*, made on the model of the perfect *torsi ;* to the Gallo-Roman period, O.F. *aers, pos, quis* (§ 1055), *sols, sors, respons, vols* (*volvere*), made on the model of the perfects **aersi, *posi, *quesi, *solsi, *sorsi, *responsi, *volsi ;* (cf. also O.F. *remasu*).

§ 1053. (2) The bias in favour of the more distinctive weak terminations, a bias that gained in strength with the isolation often induced among the strong forms by their phonetic development. In the prae-literary period ***sens* and ***vers* were replaced by *senti* and *verti, **fent, **respons* and ***vent* by *fendu, respondu* and *vendu ;* in the course of Old French *coilleit, lit* (< *lectum*), *rot* (< *ruptum*) and *seü* (< *secutum*) gave place to *coilli, leü, rompu* and *suivi ;* in the course of Middle French *mors* yielded to *mordu* and *tors* and *tort* to *tordu, pont* (§ 1054), and *tont* to *pondu* and *tondu.* Many of the earlier etymological strong participles survived as feminine substantives, e.g. *dete* (< *debita*), *fente, muete* (< **movita*), *vente* (< *vendita*).

§ 1054. (3) The associative influence exercised by one verb or group of verbs on another. Thus, for example, the similarity of many of the forms of *sentir* and *repentir* with those of *vendre, pendre,* etc., led to the formation of the participles *sentu, repentu ; boulu* (cf. F. p. 363) appears to have owed its existence to *moulu, somons* to *respons* (Wahlgren, *Et.* p. 40), *pont* to *tont, prient* to *crient* (**cremĭtu*), and Middle French *tins* to *prins,* itself formed analogically on the analogical perfect *prins* (§ 1037). O.F. *luit* and *nuit* were formed under the combined influence of the O.F. infinitives *luire, nuire* and the participles *cuit* and *duit.*

[For additional examples of analogical forms of all types cf. the Verb Tables and F. chap. iv, § 3. As among the perfects the freest formations are ordinarily cited from the northern and north-eastern region, cf. § 1037.]

§ 1055. *Analogical Modifications of Radical.*—The vowel of the radical of the participle was sometimes brought into conformity with that of other parts of the verb, especially the perfect. The participles *dictum, missum, *presu* (< *prehensum*), **quesu, sěssum* were re-made on the radical of the perfect, cf. O.F. *dit, mis, pris, quis, sis* (cf. the substantives *mes, message*) and the participles *fictum, impactum, pictum, strictum* on the radical of other parts of the verb, cf. O.F. *feint, empeint, peint, estreint ;*

O.F. *frait* and *post* were replaced by *fraint* and *pont* (*fraindre* and *pondre*), O.F. *crient*, *prient* by *craint*, *preint* (§ 936).

[For *bouilli*, *cueilli*, *sailli*, cf. § 949.]

§ 1056. Participles in *-ūtum* were formed either on the radical of the present stem tenses, e.g. **vedutu* or of the perfect, e.g. **pavutu*. Their development followed the ordinary lines :—

(i) The final consonant of the radical, if intervocalic **k, g, b, w** was effaced in Gallo-Roman (§§ 341, 342, 343), if intervocalic **t** or **d** in the course of Early Old French (§ 346), cf. O.F. **seü** < **secutum**, **leü** < ***legutu**, **deü** < ***debutu**, **peü** < ***pɑwutu**, **veð̃üθ** < ***vedutu**, **esteð̃üθ** < ***statutum** : **seü** and (re)**ceü**, the participles of *savoir* and of (re)*ceivre* etc., conformed to this type.

(ii) In juxtaposition with tonic **ü**, **a** was fronted to **e** (< ę̈), § 421, and **ǫ** dissimilated to **ę** (> ę̈), § 490 ; in the course of the thirteenth century and Middle French **ę** was effaced (§ 243), but the traditional spellings *deu*, *receu*, *veu*, etc., were long retained.

Pareir and other verbs with radicals ending in **r** sometimes formed participles in -ę̈ü, e.g. *Al. apareüde*, 82 d.

✱✱ In the northern region these participles were not infrequently influenced by the strong perfects (§ 1028), cf. O.F. *esliut*, *eslieut*, *deciut*, *decieut* for *esleü*, *deceü*, cf. N.E. § xviii ; and a labial glide was sometimes developed in the feminine form, e.g. *decheuwe* (F. p. 351, N.E. § xiv).
In the western region **ę** was sometimes rounded to **ǫ** before tonic **ü** (§ 484), cf. *Rol.* *oüt* 864, and in Later Middle French **ę̈ü** was contracted to **ö**, § 245, cf. Cretin, *veu* (**vidutum*) : *veu* (*votum*), 128, 903.

§ 1057. *Modifications in Middle French.*—In the pronunciation of the participles whose radical ended in **t** or **s** (*dit*, *luit*, *mis*, *ris*, etc.) the final consonant became very generally mute in the course of Middle French (§§ 614-621) and those participles which had rarely used feminine forms or were themselves little employed were brought into conformity in their spelling with this pronunciation and the more usual type of participle ending, e.g. *lui(t)*, *nui(t)*, *souffi(t)* (< *suffectum*) ; *ri(s)*, *conclu(s)*, *exclu(s)* (cf. Verb Tables). In the spelling of the other participles ending in *t* or *s*, whose feminines were more frequently used—*cuit*, *dit*, *conduit*, etc., *confit*, etc., *destruit*, etc., *assis*, *clos*, *mis*, *quis* and *perclus* the etymological consonant was retained, although spellings such as *destruy*, *assy*, *confi*, *qui*, etc., are occasionally found.

LATER OLD FRENCH.

The forms included in this table are those first attested or commonly in use in Later Old French; those marked with an asterisk are formed in accordance with normal practice but not attested in the sources consulted; forms bracketed ( ) are those that appear only to have come into use in the thirteenth century; for verbs with ordinary vocalic alternation cf. Section 5 and Index.

Dialectal forms, e.g. subjunctive forms in -ge and -ce (§ 910), are not ordinarily included.

Spelling.—The spelling employed is that of the Later Twelfth Century. The normal sound-changes of the period that resulted in a change in spelling (e.g. **ei** > **oi**, **ou** > **eu**, **ǫ** > **u**) are noted once only in the infinitive form or in the person in which the sound affected first occurs in the table.

O.F. **ǫ** (> **u**) is represented by *o*, the diphthong *ue* by *ue*; the sounds **ɵ** and **ð** are not indicated; **ŋ** final is written *gn*.

In the indicative present the first and third persons are cited; in the subjunctive present the third person singular; in the weak perfects the first person singular; in the strong perfects the first and second persons singular; in the perfects of the sixteenth century ordinarily only the first person. Other persons are indicated by a prefixed number. Analogical forms created in Old French are separated from others by a semi-colon.

§ 1058. CONJUGATION I.

Infinitive.	Participles.	Present Indicative.	Present Subjunctive.	Future.	Perfect.
achater > (acheter)	achaté > (acheté)	achat; (achet) achate; (achete)	achat	achaterai > (acheterai)	achatai > (achetai)
aidier; (aïder); aiuer	aidié	*aju > aï ajue > aïe; aide	3. ajut > aït	aiderai	aidai
aler	alé	§ 958 Imper. 2. va	§ 958	irai	alai
amer	amé	aim > ain aime	3. aint	amerai	amai
comparer [< *conparare] (comprer)	comparé (compré)	comper compere; (compre)	3. compert	comparrai, § 970; comperrai	comparai
demorer, demurer	demoré	demuer demuere; demore	3. demuert; demort	demorra, § 970	demorai
doner, duner	doné	§ 958 done	§ 958	donrai > dorrai, § 970	donai
engeignier > engignier, § 927	engeignié, > engignié	*engign > (engin) engeigne; engigne	3. engint	engeignerai > engignerai	engeignai > engignai
eschever; eschiver; eschuir; (eschivir)	eschevé; eschivé	*eschiu eschive; (eschieve)	eschiut > eschieut	escheverai; eschiverai	eschevai; eschivai

Present Indicative extra forms:
		achatons > (achetons) achatent; (achetent)			
		aidons ajuent > aïent; aïdent			
		amons aiment			
		comparons, (comprons) comperent			
		demorons demuerent			
		donons donent			
		engeignons, > engignons engeignent; engignent			
		eschevons eschivent			

SIXTEENTH CENTURY
(according to Palsgrave).

§ 1058. *Forms with M. prefixed are from Meigret; forms with Mz. prefixed are cited by G. Manz, Das Verbum nach den frz. Grammatiken v. 1500-1768; those with L. prefixed from Lanoue (1596), cited by Manz; those with B. from H.L.F. vol. ii. The numbers in the Infinitive column indicate the page in Palsgrave; forms in square brackets are those becoming obsolete.*

Infinitive.	Participles.	Present Indicative.	Present Subjunctive.	Future.	Perfect.
achapter 451 acheter	achapté	achapte, L. achette	achapte	achapteray	achaptay
ayder 583	aidé	ayde ayde aydons aydent	ayde ayde (se mayt Dieu)	aideray	ayday
aller 123	allé	vas, M. voę, voęs, L. vay, vois vas va allons allez vont	1. voyse, aille 2. voyses, ailles 3. voyse, aille 4. aillions, Mz. aillons, allions 6. voisent, aillent	yray	allay
aimer B. amer	aimé B. amé	aime aimons	aime	aimerai	aimai
comparer, comparoyr 399, 400, 401, 415, 455	comparu	compare		comperray, comparerai	comparus
demourer 394, 414, 401, 530 B. demeurer	demouré	demeure B. demoure demourons	demeure	demour(e)rai Mz. demourrai, demeur(e)rai	demouray
donner 392, 393	donné	donne donnons	1. donne 3. donne, doynt	donray, donneray Mz. dorray	donnay
enguyner, 446 *first conjugation*		enguyne			
eschiever 541 *first conjugation*	eschievé	eschieve			

§ 1058. Conjugation I (*cont.*). Later Old French.

Infinitive.	Participles.	Present Indicative.	Present Subjunctive.	Future.	Perfect.
ester, arester	esté; esteñ	§ 958	§ 958	esterai	estui, estai
geter, geitier; giter (§ 324)	geté; gité	get, git; giet geté, gite; giete / getons getent, gitent; gietent	3. get, git; giet	geterai	getai
joer; juer	joé	geu, gi(e)u geue; gi(e)ue; joe / joons geuent; gi(e)uent; joent	§§ 938, 9, jot	joerai	joai
laier	*pres. part.* laiant	lai lait,¹ aie *Imper.* 2. lai / laient	3. laie	lairai > lerai, lerrai *2nd fut.:* lairoie > lerroie	
lever	levé	lief; (lieve) lieve / levons lievent	3. liet	leverai	levai
loer, luer aloer, aluer; (aleuer)	loé	§ 939 luee; li(e)ue; loe / loons luent; li(e)uent; loent	3. §938, li(e)ut; lot	loerai	loai
mangier	mangié	manju, §925; manjuz; manjue / manjons manjuent	3. manjust; man-juce; manjue	mangerai	manjai
mener	mené	mein, main meine, maine / menons meinent, mainent	3. meint, maint	menrai, merrai, § 970	menai
ovret, uvrer	ovré	uevre uevre / ovrons uevrent	3. uevre	overai, overrai	ovrai
parler	parlé	§ 925	§§ 925, 933	parlerai	parlai
peser	pesé	peis > pois; poise / pesons poisent	3. poist	peserai	pesai
prover, *see* trover					
rover, *see* trover					
trover, truver	trové	§ 954	§ 954	troverai	trovai

SIXTEENTH CENTURY.

ester (obsolete)						
jecter 477	jecté	jecte	jectons	jecte	jecteray	jectay
[laier] 401					layrra *condit.* larroit	
louer *first conjugation*						
lever, liesver 436, 464, 665, 684	levé, liesvé	liesve, lieve, leve, § 930	levons	lieve	leveray, lieveray	levai
manger 400, 540, 722, 102	mangé	1. mange, mangeue 3. mange, mangeut	mangeons mangent mangeuent	mange, mangeue, mangeusse	mangeray	mangeay, mengeus
mener 604, 401, 466	mené	mayne, mene, § 930	menons, maynons	mayne, mene	meneray, menray, mayneray Mz. marray	menay
oeuvrer 784	oeuvré	oeuvre	oeuvrons	oeuvre	oeuvreray	oeuvray
parler 727	parlé	parle, parolle	parlons	parle	parlerai	parlai
peser 778	pesé	poyse, pese	pesons	poyse, pese	peseray	pesay
prouver, *see trouver*						
rouver (*obsolete*)						
secouer, *see escorre*						
trouver 394, 550	trouvé	trouve, treuve	trouvons	trouve, treuve	trouverai	trouvay
Mz. treuver	B. treuvé					

§ 1059. Conjugation III.

Weak Perfects in -i. Later Old French.

Infinitive.	Participles.	Present Indicative.	Present Subjunctive.	Future.	Perfect.
bolir § 949; boillir buillir; (boudre)	boli; boilli; (boulu)	boil / bolt > bout // bolons; boillons bolent; boillent	3. boille	boldrai; boildrai > boudrai	boli; boilli; (3. bolut)
bruire; bruir	bruit bruiant	3. bruit // bruient	3. bruie	3. bruira	
chaeir > chaoir, cheëir > cheoir; chaïr, cheïr	chaü, cheü chaï't, cheï't	§ 963	§ 963	charrai, cherrai	chaï, cheï
coillir, cuillir; cueillir, § 943, queillir; cuedre; (queillier)	coilli; cuilli; coillu; (queillie)	cueil, queil; coil; (cueille, § 943) cueilt, quelt > queut keut, quieut, kieut; (cueille) // coillons; cueillons, cueillent, queillent; (coillent)	3. cueille; (coille)	coildrai; cueildrai keudrai; (cueillerai) § 971	coilli; cueilli
cosdre, cusdre, coudre; queu(s)dre, keudre	cosu; cosi	*queus / queust; cost // *cosons queusent; cosent	*queuse; couse	cosdrai	cosi
covrir, cuvrir	covert; (covri)	*cuevre / cuevre // covrons cuevrent	3. cuevre	covrerai, coverrai	covri
eissir > oissir; issir	eissu; issu; eissi; issi	*is / ist // eissons; (issons) issent	3. isse	eistrai; istrai	eissi; issi
emplir	empli; (emplu)	emple / emple; emplist // emplons emplent	3. emple; 3. emplisse	emplerai; emplirai	empli
falir; faillir (§ 949)	failli	fail / falt > faut // faillons falent; faillent	3. faille	faldrai > faudrai	fali; failli

Weak Perfects in -i. Sixteenth Century.

Infinitive.	Participles.	Present Indicative.		Present Subjunctive.	Future.	Perfect.
bouillir 459, 716 boudre	bouily	bouils, bouls M. bous bouilt, M. bout	bouillons, Mz. boulons,	bouille	bouilyray	bouilis
bruyre 473, 694	bruy, bruyt	bruis	bruyons	bruye	bruyray	bruys
cheoyr 544, 604	cheu, cheut B. f. cheutte	cheoys, choys M. ches chiet, M. chet	cheons M. chayons M. chayent, B. cheent	cheoye M. chaye	cherray	cheys, cheus
circuyre 491, 485	circuyt	circuys	circuyons	circuye	circuyray	circuys
cueillir 560, 779, 394 Mz. cueiller	cueilly	cueilx, cueuls, cueulx (re)cueilt B. cueult, cueille	cueillons	cueille	cueilliray L. cueilleray	cueillis
cousdre, cousir 399, 725	cousu	cous	cousons	couse	coudray, Mz. couseray (xvii)	cousis M. couzus
couvrir 499	couvert	couvers M. ceuvre, couvre	couverons couvrent	couvre	couvreray	couvris
yssir 593 M. issir, itre, Mz. istre	issy, issu	ys yst	issons	ysse	ystray B. yssiroit	yssys
emplyr, (remplir) 549	emply	emplys	emplys	emplysse	empliray	emplys
faillir 543, 571	failly	faulx fault	faillons	faille	fauldray M. faillirey faodrey	faillys *Impf. Subj.* faillisse faulsisse

§ 1059. CONJUGATION III (cont.). LATER OLD FRENCH.

Infinitive.	Participles.	Present Indicative.	Present Subjunctive.	Future.	Perfect.
ferir	feru	fier / fiert / ferons / fierent	3. fire; fiere	ferrai	feri
foïr, fuir [*fugīre] fuire [fŭgĕre]	foï	fui / fuit / fuions / fuient	3. fuie	fuirai	foï
foïr, fuir [fodere]	foï	*fue / fuet / foons / fueent	3. fuee	forrai; foïrai	foï
guerpir, gerpir	guerpi	guerp; guerpis; guert; guerpist / guerpons; guerpissons guerpent; guerpissent	3. guerpe; guerpisse	guerperai; guerpirai	1. guerpi, 2. guerpis; guerpesis, § 1013
haïr	haï; haänt; (haïssant) § 884	§ 960	§ 960	harrai, harai; (haïrai)	haï
joïr	joï; joiant; joïant (joïssant) § 882	1. joi, 2. joz, 3. jot; joïst / joons; joïssons joez joet; joient; joïssent	3. joie; joïsse	jorrai; joïrai	joï
merir	meri	mir; mier *miert / merons *mierent	3. mire; merisse	merirai	meri
offrir, see soffrir					
oïr	oï oant; oiant	1. oi, 2. oz, 3. ot; Imper. 2. o; oi; oz / oons; oions oez; oiez oent; oient	3. oie	orrai; (oïrai)	oï
ovrir, see covrir					
partir	parti	part / part; partons; (partissons) partent; partissent	3. parte; (partisse)	partrai; partirai	parti

SIXTEENTH CENTURY.

faloyr 419, 413	fallu	fault		faille	fauldra	fallut *Impf. Subj.* fallust, faulsist
ferir 723, 739	feru	fiers fiert	ferons, M. ferons	fiere	ferray Mz. feriray	ferus M. feris
fuyr, fouyr 552	fuy	fuys	fuions	fuye	fuyray	fuys
fouyr 516	fouy	fouys	fouyssons	fouysse	fouyrai	fouys
guerpir 477	guerpy	guerpis	guerpissons	guerpisse	guerpyrai	guerpys
hayr 579 Mz. heir	hay Mz. hayant, haïssant	hays, M. hę, hęs, Mz. hay, hai hayt, M. hęt Mz. haït	hayons M. haïssons, hayons Mz. heons, heions, heent, M. haïssent	haye B. haïsse	hayeray, herray Mz. haïray	hays Mz. hei
(res)jouyr 683	resjouy	resjouis	resjouissons	resjouysse	resjouyrai	resjouys
meryr 513	mery	merys	merissons	merisse	merirai	merys
offrir 645	offert	offers offre	offrons	offre	offrirai	offrys
ouyr 583	ouy *Impf. Ind.* oyoye	os, M. oę, oęs ot, M. oęt	oyons oyent	ouye	orray M. orrey, oïrey	ouys
ouvrir, *see* couvrir						
partir 653	parti	pars, partys (*trans,*) part	partons, partissons (*trans,*)	parte, partisse (*trans,*)	partiray	parti
puyr 736 Mz. (xvii) puer (§ 879)	puy	pus put	puons	pue	pueray Mz. puray	puis
resplendir 703	resplendi	resplendis, [resplens], [resplend] resplendist, [resplend]	resplendissons	resplendisse	resplendiray	resplendys

§ 1059. CONJUGATION III (cont.). LATER OLD FRENCH.

Infinitive.	Participles.	Present Indicative.	Present Subjunctive.	Future.	Perfect.
resplendir, resplandir	resplendi; resplendant; resplendissant	*resplent; resplent; resplendist / resplendons; (resplendissons)	3. resplende; resplendist	resplendiray	resplendi
respondre, respundre	respons; respondu	respoign; respon respont / respondons; responons respondent; responent	3. respoigne; responde	respondrai	1. respondi 3. respondiet; respondi respost
rompre, rumpre	rot; rompu	*romp ront / *rompons rompent	3. rompe	romprai	1. rompi 3. rompiet, rompi
salir; saillir (§ 949)	sailli	*sail salt, saut / saillons salent; saillent	3. saille	saudray; (sailleray); (sailliray)	sali ; sailli
sentir	senti, sentu	sent sent / sentons sentent	3. sente	sentiray	senti
sivre, § 328, sievre, siure, sieure, seure; suïr; sivir	seü; sivi, etc. sewant> sevant; sivant; suiant	§§ 328, 329	§§ 328, 329	sivrai, siurai, s(j)eurai	sewi > sevi; sivi; suï 3. sewi > sevi; sivi; suï; sut (§ 1022)
soffrir, suffrir	soffert; (sofri)	soffre; suefre, § 927; (sofris) sofre; suefre; (sofrist) / sofrons sofrent; suefrent	3. sofre; suefre	sofrerai, soferrai; (sofrirai)	sofri
sortir, resortir	sorti	*sort sort / *sortons sortent	3. sorte	sortirai	sorti
tistre	teissu; tissu	tis tist / *teissons; tissons tissent	3. tisse	tistrai	teissi, tissi
toudre; tolir	tolu; toleit	toil, tol tolt > tout, tot (§ 391) / *tolons tolent	3. toille	toldrai > toudrai	toli; tols; (tolui)
tondre	tondu	*tont tont / *tondons tondent	3. tonde	tondrai	tondi
vestir	vesti; vestu	vest vest / *vestons vestent	3. veste	vesterai; vestirai	vesti

SIXTEENTH CENTURY.

	responnu	respons respont	responnons responnent	responne	respondray	respondis
respondre 432						
rompre 463	rompu	romps M. rons (roms, rom) M. ront (romt, rompt)	rompons	rompe	romperay M. romprey	rompis
saillir (assaillyr, tressaillir) 606, 492; 437, 570; 734	sailly	sauls, assaulx M. [saos] Mz. assaille, assaillis M. [saot] Mz. assaille, assaillist	saillons	saille	sailliray, sailleray sauldray	saillys
sentir 547	senti, Mz. (xvii) sentu	sens sent	sentons sentent	sente	sentiray	sentys
suyvre, (en)suyvir (aconcepvoir, § 1022) 553 M. suyvir, suyvre	suyvy B. suy, Mz.suyt; aconceu	suis, M. suy, suys M. suyt	suivons	suyve	suyveray M. suyvrey, [suyvirey]	suyvis, suyvy H. aconceut aconceurent
souffrir 742	souffert Mz. souffri	souffers M. soufre, seufre	souffrons	souffre	souffriray	souffrys
sortir (assortir, conj. II.) 492	sorty	sors	sortissons	sorte	sortiray	sortis
tistre 779 M. [titre tissir] Mz. (xvii) tisser (§ 879)	tissu	tys, M. obs. tist, M. obs.	tissons	tisse	tistray Mz. tissiray, (xvii) tisseray	tissis
tollyr, touldre 747, 399	tollu, Mz. tolli Mz. tollant, tollissant	toles (sic) Mz. [toul] Mz. [toult]	tolons Mz. [toulent]	tolle	touleray	tolus Mz. tollis Impf. Subj. que je tollisse
tondre 702, 397	tondu	tons M. tont	tondons tondent	tonde, tonse	tonderay	tondis Impf. Subj. tonsisse, tondisse
vestir 488	vestu, Mz. vesti Mz. vestant, vestissant	vests Mz. (xvii) vestis vest Mz. (xvii) vestist	Mz. vestons, (xvii) vestissons	veste	vestiray Mz. vesteray	vestys

§ 1060. Weak Perfects in -u. LATER OLD FRENCH.

Infinitive.	Participles.	Present Indicative.	Present Subjunctive.	Future.	Perfect.
chaleir > chaloir	chalu	chielt; chalt	chaille	chaldra > chaudra	chalut *Impf. Subj.* chalust; chalsist
corre, curre; (courir)	coru; coreü	cor; keur (§ 927) cort; keurt corons corent; keurent	core; keure	corra	corui; cori
doleir, duleir > doloir, duloir; (deuloir)	dolu	dueil duelt > deut, dieut dolons duelent	dueille	doldrai > doudrai; (deudrai)	dolui
moldre > moudre	molu; mols	*muel; mueil muelt; (molt) molons muelent	muele; mueille	moldrai > moudrai	1. molui, mols 2. molsis
morir, murir	mort	muir muert morons muerent	muire; (meure)	morrai	morui; mori
oleir > oloir	*Impf.* oloit	3. uelt > eut uelent	uelle		
pareir > paroir	paru; pareü	pair > per pert parons perent	paire	parrai	parui
soleir, suleir > soloir, suloir	solu	sueil, soil suelt solons suelent	sueille, soille		1. solui 2. solus 3. solut, solt
somondre, sumundre	*see* s-perfects				
valeir > valoir	valu valant; vaillant; valissant	vail valt valons valent	vaille	valdrai > vaudrai	valui *Impf. Subj.* valsisse; valusse

Sixteenth Century.

				chaille Mz. chale	chauldra Mz. chaura	M. challut Impf. Subj.
chaloyr 475, 413, 398	chalu Mz. chalant, chaillant	chault		chaille Mz. chale	chauldra Mz. chaura	M. challut *Impf. Subj.* chaulsist, chaillist, Mz. chalusse
courir, (secourir) [courre] 693, 393 ; 724 Mz. [coeurre]	couru	cours court, Mz. cueurt		coure	couray Mz. coureray	cours, *(sic)* secouris
doulor 420, 725	doulu *Impf. Ind.* Mz. doulois, deuillois, deulois	deuls, deulx M. [deuil], deul, deuls deult	doulons, M. deulons Mz. deuillons doulent, deuillent, M. deuillent	dueille	dueilleray, douleray M. deulerey, deulrey, deuldrey	doulus, Mz. deulis, deuillis
mouldre 575 M. mouldre, meuldre	moulu	mouls, Mz. meulds	moulons, M. mulons Mz. meulons M. meulent, Mz. moulent	moulle, Mz. (xvii) meule	mouldray, Mz. meudray	moulus Mz. moulis
mourir 515	mort	meurs, M. meurs, meur	mourons, Mz. meurons	meure	mourray	mourus
(ap)paroir, comparoir apparoistre, comparoistre 433, 104	apparu *Impf. Ind.* apparissoye, apparoye Mz. apperoye	apers Mz. apparoy apert	apparons Mz. apperons, apparoissons apparent, apperent	appare, appere	apparray, apperray, aperay	aparus
souloyr 431, 103	*Def.*; M. solu *Impf. Ind.* souloye	seulx seult	soulons seulent, soulent	*Def.*	*Def.*	soulus
valoir 431	valu	vaulx	valons	vaille Mz. vale 4. M. vaillions	vauldray	valus *Impf. Subj.* valusse, vaulsisse

§ 1061. **Strong Perfects in -i** (§ 1010). LATER OLD FRENCH.

Infinitive.	Participles.	Present Indicative.	Present Subjunctive.	Future.	Perfect.
tenir	tenu	tiegn; teign, taign / tient / tenons / tienent	tiegne; ** tigne; teigne, taigne, §931	tendrai	1. tin / 2. tenis
veeir 〉 **veoir**	veü / veant; / veiant 〉 voiant	voi / voit / *Imper.* 2. pl. veez, vez. / veons; (voions) / voient	voie	verrai	1. vi / 2. veïs
venir	venu	viegn; veign, vaign / vient / venons / vienent	viegne; ** vigne; veigne, vaigne, §931	vendrai	1. vin / 2. venis
voleir, vuleir 〉 **voloir, vuloir**	volu; / volant; / vueillant	vueil, voil / vuelt 〉 veut, (§ 556) / ** viaut, § 501 / volons / vuelent	vueille, voille	voldrai 〉 voudrai	1. voil; vols / 2. volis; volsis (voulu(s) xiv, § 1035)

SIXTEENTH CENTURY.

tenir (abstenir) 586, 415, 396	tenu B. tins	tiens M. tien, tiens	tenons (abs)tiennent	tiengne abstienne Mz. teigne, tienne	tiendray	1. tins 4. tinsmes, [tenisnes] M. 1. tins, tin 2. tins 4. tinmes 6. tindrent Mz. (xvii) tindrent
veoir, (pourveoir) 707, 668, 392	veu	voys	voyons Mz. [veons]	voye, voy	verray, voyrray pourvoyrai, pourvoyerai M. pourveyrey pourvoyerey	vis M. vi(s) M. pourvu
venir, (advenir) 131, 396, 492	venu	viens vient	venons	viengne, Mz. veigne, vienne	viendrai	(cf. tenir) *Impf. Subj.* vinsse, venisse
vouloyr 104, 402	voulu	vueil, veulx M. [veuil], veu(s) veult	voulons veullent	vueille 4. vueillons	vouldray	voulus, § 1036 [3. sg. voult] M. voulu(s), *Subj. Impf.* voulsisse, voulusse

26

§ 1062. **S-Perfects** (§ 1012). LATER OLD FRENCH.

Type A. *Vocalic Radicals.*

Infinitive.	Participles.	Present Indicative.	Present Subjunctive.	Future.	Perfect.
clore	clos	*clo / clot ; cloons / cloent	cloe	clorai	clos; (cloï) / 2. closis; (clois)
conclure	conclus	*conclu / conclut ; *concluons / conclut / concluent	conclue		conclus / 2. conclusis
despire	despit	*despis / despist ; despisons / despisent	despise	despirai	despis / 2. despesis, despeïs
dire	dit	§ 960	§ 960	dirai	dis / 2. desis ; deïs ; disis
maudire	maudit	maudi / maudit ; maudions (maudissons) / maudient (maudissent)	maudie / maudisse	maudirai	maudis / 2. maudesis ; maudisis
faire	fait	§ 960	§ 960	ferai	fis / 2. fesis ; feïs
frire	frit	*fri / frit ; *frions / frient	frie	frirai	fris / 2. fresis
maneir > manoir ; maindre	mes ; remasu	maign, (main(s)) / maint ; manons / mainent	maigne	maindrai	mes ; (mains), 2. masis ; (mainsis)

§ 1062. **S-Perfects.** Sixteenth Century.

Type A.

Infinitive.	Participles.	Present Indicative.		Present Subjunctive.	Future.	Perfect.
clore, (esclore) 397, 488, 703	closy, clos Mz. closant, cloant	clos, M. clo(s) clost, M. clot	closons, [clouons], M. (e)cloons, B. (es)clouent	close, Mz. cloe	clorray	closys, clouys, Mz. clois
conclure 493	conclu, conclud	conclus	concluons	conclue, conclue, conclude	conclueray, conclu-ray, concluderay	conclus *Impf. Subj.* conclusisse
despire	*obsolete*					
dire 397, 398, 696, 753	dit, dict	dis dit	disons, dissons dictes, dittez disent; Mz. dient	die, dise M. die dies die dizyons dizyez dizent	diray	dis 2. dis *Impf. Subj.* disse, disisse
frire 568	fryt	frys	frions; Mz. frisons	frie	friray	frys
mauldire 417 Mz. maudir	mauldict	maudis	mauldissons mauldissent Mz. maudisent	mauldie F. maudisse	mauldiray	mauldys 2. mauldys
faire 97, 617	faict *Pres. Part.* M. fęzant, § 961	fais, M. fę(s) fais, M. fęs fait, M. fęt	faisons, M. fęzons faictes, M. fęttes font	face, M. fasse	feray Mz. fairay	fis 2. fis
(re)mayndre (re)manoyr 684, 399	*def.*	remayne	remainons	remaigne	remayndray	remainys *Impf. Subj.* remainysse

§ 1062. S-Perfects, Type A (*cont.*). LATER OLD FRENCH.

Infinitive.	Participles.	Present Indicative.	Present Subjunctive.	Future.	Perfect.
metre	mis	met met metons metent	mette	metrai	mis 2. mesis ; meïs
ocire	ocis (ocisant)	oci ocit ocions ; (ocisons) ocient ; (ocisent)	ocie	ocirai	ocis 2. ocesis ; oceïs
prendre > prandre	pris	prent, pren ; preing, praing § 948 prent *Imper.* pren, § 937 prenons, prendons (§ 937) prenent, prendent (§ 937)	prenne ; preigne, praigne, prende (§ 937)	prendrai	pris 2. presis ; preïs
querre ; (querir, *attested* 1307)	quis	quier quiert querons quierent	quiere	querrai	quis 2. quesis ; queïs
rere	res *raant ; reant	*re ret *raons reent	ree	*rarai	res 2. rasis
rire	ris	ri rit rions rient	rie	rirai	ris 2. resis ; reïs
(as)seeir > (as)seoir ; (as)seïr ; (assire)	sis seant ; seiant > soiant	§ 963	§ 963	serrai	sis 2. sesis ; seïs

SIXTEENTH CENTURY.

mettre 671, 565	mys	mets, prommais M. męs, mę	mettons, M. mêtons, § 931	mette	mettray	mis 2. mis
occire 397, 598 Mz. occir	occy, § 1057	occis	occisons, F. occions (xvii)	occise, occie	occiray	occis 2. occis *Impf. Subj.* occisisse
prendre 746, 94, 96	prins (cf. §1054) M. pris	prens	prenons, prennons prennez prennent Mz. prenent	preigne, preingne preignons M. prene	prendray	§ 1037 *Impf. Subj.* prinsse, prennisse, prennisse
querir, querre (conquerre) 708; 494	quis	quiers	querons	quiere conquise	querrai	quis 2. quis *Impf. Subj.* quisse conquisisse
rayre 701, 397, 662	*def.* Mz. rez	rays raist	raysons Mz. reons, rayons	raise, (rase)	*def.* (raseray) Mz. [rairay]	rasys *Impf. Subj.* rasisse
rire 604 soubzrire, 722	ry, § 1057 Mz. ris soubzris	rys	rions	rie	rieray M. rirey	risis *Impf. Subj.* risisse
rassayr (*sic*), seoyr, asseoyr 136, 445, 618, 713, 719 Mz. sir	sye, assis	seoys, assis, asseys, M. assie, Mz. assieds siet, seoyt M. assit	seons, rassions M. seyons, sions, Mz. soyons, sisons, M. seyent, sient, Mz. seent, assisent	sye, assie Mz. siee, seie, see	seyerai, assieray syera M. serrey Mz. siray, sieray, seeray, (xvii), soiray	asseys *Impf. Subj.* asseisse rassisisse

§ 1063. **S-Perfects**, *Type* **B.** *Consonant Radicals.* LATER OLD FRENCH.

Infinitive.	Participles.	Present Indicative.	Present Subjunctive.	Future.	Perfect.
ascondre, abscondre escondre	ascons ; abscondu				escos 3. escost
aërdre, aherdre ; aerdeir	aërs aerdant	*aërc aërt / aerdons aerdent, aergent	aerde, aerge	aerdrai	aers ; (aerdi) 2. aersis
aoire (*obs.* xiii²)	aoit	3. aoit ; aoist	aoise aoisent		3. aoist
ardeir > ardoir ; ardre	ars	*arge art / ardons ardent	arge ; arde	ardrai	ars 2. arsis
ataindre	ataint	ataign ataint / ataignons ataignent	ataigne	ataindrai	atains 2. atainsis
braire, *see* traire					
ceindre, caindre	ceint	*ceign ceint / ceignons ceignent	ceigne,	ceindrai	ceins 2. ceinsis
criembre ; criendre ; (craindre, § 936) ; cremeir ; cremir	crient ; cremu	criem > crien ; (craing) crient ; (craint, § 936) / cremons (§ 936) criement (§ 936)	crieme (§ 936)	crembrai ; creindrai ; criendrai (§ 936)	crens ; criens ; cremui ; cremi 2. crensis ; cremus cremus
cuire, quire	cuit	queu 3. cuist ; cuit / cuisons cuisent	cuise	cuirai	cuis 2. cuissis cuisis
destreindre, *see* ceindre					
destruire, *see* duire					
duire [ducĕre, § 886]	duit	*du ; dui duit / duions ; duisons duient ; duisent	due ; duie ; duise	duirai	duis 2. duissis ; duisis
duire [docĕre, § 886]	duit	3. duit / duisent	duise	duirai	3. duist
empeindre, *see* ceindre					

SIXTEENTH CENTURY.

abscondre, 584	abscondy	abscons	absconsons	absconde	abscondray	abscondis
adherdre, 486 (olde Romant worde)	adhert	adhers	adherdons	adherde	adherdray	adherdis
ardre, ardoyr, 460, 399, M. art	ars, M. art	ars / art	ardons	arde	ardray / Mz. arderai	ardis
attaindre 439, 680, 397	attaynct	attayngs	attayngnons, attayndons, § 941 / attayngnent	attaingne, attaynde	attaindray	attaingnis, attaindys / 6. attayn(g)drent / M. ateñirent
brayre 462, 694	*Impf. Ind.* brayoyt	brais, brayt	M. brayons / M. brayent			M. brahyey, L. brayi
ceingdre 566, 397	ceyngt	ceingns / ceingt	ceyndons, § 941 / M. ceñons / ceyndent, M. ceñent	ceigne	ceyngdray	ceingnis / cein(g)drent
craindre, cremyr (craingner, Romant.) 528, 399, 397	craint [craignu]	crayngs	craignons / M. creñons	craingne	crayndrai	craignis, [craignus] / crayn(g)drent / M. creñirent
cuire, 595, 716, 133	cuyt	cuyts / cuit	cuisons	cuise	cuyrai	cuisis, / Mz. cuy
destruire, *see* duire						
(con)duire 493, 466, 420	conduict	conduis	conduisons / deduissons	conduise, deduisse	conduiray	1. conduis, produisis / 6. Mz. duyrent, duisirent / *Impf. Subj.* conduisse, conduisisse

§ 1063. **S-Perfects,** *Type* **B.** *(cont.).* LATER OLD FRENCH.

Infinitive.	Participles.	Present Indicative.	Present Subjunctive.	Future.	Perfect.
escurre > esqueurre; escorre, rescourre, socourre	escos	*esqueu; *esco / esqueut; escot escoons / esqueuent; escoent	esqueue; escoe	escorrai	escos / 2. escossis; escosis
escrive; (escrire, § 936)	escrit	*escrif / escrit escrivons; escrisons / escrivent; escrisent	escrive	escrivrai (escrirai)	escris (§ 1017) / 2. escressis; escrissis
espardre, *see* ardre					
esteindre } *see* esteindre } ceindre feindre					
fraindre giembre, *see* criembre	frait; / fraint	*fraign / fraint fraignons / fraignent	fraigne	fraindrai	frains / 2. frainsis
joindre	joint	*joign / joint joignons / joignent	joigne	joindrai	joins / 2. joinsis
luire, § 886 luisir	luit	3. luist, luit luisent	luise	luirai	luis; luisi / 2. luisis
moldre (mulgere) (*obs. xv*)	mos			moudrai	mols / 2. molsis
mordre	mors	mort / mort mordons / mordent	morde	mordrai	mors / 2. morsis
nuire, *see* § 1066					

SIXTEENTH CENTURY.

escouer, secouer (escouyr, Romant.) 700 (§ 879) rescourre 687 (cf. W. Et. pp. 73-4)	escoué secoué / Def. Mz. (xvii) recoux, recous	escoue, [escoux] escoue / rescous, Mz. recou Mz. recout	escouons escouent	escoue / Def.	escoueray, [escourray] / Def. Mz. (xvii) recouray	escouai, Mz. recouis 3. escoua, escouyt Def.
escrire 785, 396	escript	escrips	escripvons	escripve	escripray	escrips, escripvis M. escrivi(s),
esparser 730 / faindre, see ceindre 543	esparsé F. epart espars (Rab.)	espars	esparsons	esparse	esparseray	esparsis
enfraindre refraindre (refrenir) 464, 682, 397	enfraynt, refrainct	enfrayns	enfraygnons refrenons Mz. enfreindons	enfraigne	enfraindray	enfraygnis, Mz. enfreindi 6. refrayn(g)drent, M. refreñirent
gemyr 575	gemy	gemys	gemissons	gemisse	gemiray	gemys
joindre 593	joinct	joyngs	joignons M. joïons	joingne	joindray	joingnys 6. join(g)drent M. joñirent
(re)luyre 568, 703	luyt reluy (§ 1057)	luis	luisons	luyse	luyray	luys Impf. Subj. luysisse
(a)mordre 456	mort M. mors, mordu	mors	mordons	morde	morderay	mordis

§ 1063. **S-Perfects,** *Type* **B.** *(cont.).* Later Old French.

Infinitive.	Participles.	Present Indicative.	Present Subjunctive.	Future.	Perfect.
oindre, *see* joindre peindre, *see* ceindre plaindre, *see* fraindre poindre, *see* joindre					
(re)pondre, (re)pundre	post; pos, pus; pons; (ponu); pondu	*pon pont ponons; (pondons) ponent; (pondent)	ponne; poigne; (ponde)	pondrai	pos; pus; pons; 2. posis; ponsis 1. pondi; pontúi (ponni, xiv)
priembre, *see* criembre					
raiembre; raembre; raeindre, raaindre § 936	raent; raient; raeint, raint raemant	*raiem raient; (reimt) *Imper.* 2. reeim raemons; (raembons) (raiment, reimbent r(a)embent	*raieme; reaime; (raimbe)	raembrai; raiembrai; raeindrai	raens; raiens 2. raensis, raeinsis 3. raemst; raienst
(a)soldre > (a)soudre (§§ 936, 948)	(a)solt > (a)sout; (a)sols > (a)sous; (a)solu	(a)soil, (a)sol, (a)solt > asout (a)solons (a)solent	(a)soille	(a)soldrai	(a)sols 2. (a)solsis
somoneir, sumuneir > semonoir; somondre, semondre	somons	somoign, (semon) somont, semont somonons somonent	somoigne	somondrai	somons 2. somonsis somonúi
sordre, surdre	sors sorjant; sordant	*sorc sort sorjons; sordons sorgent; sordent	sorge ; sorde	sordrai	sors 2. sorsis
terdre, *see* aerdre					
tortre; tuertre; (§ 410), tordre	tort, tors tortant; tordant	*torc 3. tort, tuert tortons; tordons tortent; tordent	torte; torde	tortrai; tuertrai; tordrai	tors; tuers 2. torsis
traire	trait	1. trai 2. trais 3. trait traions traites; traiez traient	traie	trairai	trais 2. traisis
voldre (*obs. xiv*)	volt, vols				3. volst

oindre, (432) *see* joindre						
peindre(651)*see* ceindre						
(com)plaindre 491, 397	plain(g)ct	plaings	playngnons M. pleñons	plaingne	plain(g)dray	plaingnis 6.playn(g)drent M. pleñirent
poindre, (666), *see* joindre						
pondre, [repostre] 601, 584 Mz. ponre	ponnu Mz. pondu, Mz. pond	pons	ponnons M. ponons, pondons, M. ponent, pondent	ponne Mz. ponde	pondray	ponnys, M. ponu, Mz. pondis
(em)prayndre, *see* ataindre						
(as)souldre 438	(as)soulu, (as)souls B. [resoultes]	(as)souls, absoulx	(as)soulons, M. soudons, solvons (as)soulent, M. soudent, solvent	(as)soylle, Mz. (xvii) (ab)soude	(as)souldray	(as)soulus, (as)souls
semondre 454, 725	semons Mz. semonnu, semond	semons	semonons, Mz. semondons semonent	semonne Mz. semoigne	semondray	semons, semonnis, Mz. semondi
sourdre 692, 730	sourdy, sours Mz. sourdu	sours sourt	sourdons	sourde	sourdyray, sourderay	sourdys
(re)tordre 764	tors Mz. tordu	tors	tordons	torde	torderay	tordis
trayre, abstraire 526, 577, 453	tray, trayct, abstrahy	trays, abstrahys	traions, trayons abstrahisons Mz. treons	traye, abstrahye	trayerai, retrayrai abstrahirai	trays, abstrahys, M. trahyey

§ 1064. **u-Perfects** (§ 1019). LATER OLD FRENCH.

A. *Type.*

Infinitive.	Participles.	Present Indicative.	Present Subjunctive.	Future.	Perfect.
aveir > avoir	oü, eü	§ 951	§ 951	avrai, § 976	oi 2. oüs, eüs
paistre	poü, peü	pais paist	paisse	paistrai	poi 2. poüs, peüs
		paissons paissent			
plaisir; plaire	ploü, pleü	plaz; plais plaist > plest	place; plaise	plairai	ploi 2. ploüs, pleüs
		plaisons plaisent			
poeir > pooir	poü, peü poant; puissant	§ 954	§ 954	porrai	poi 2. poüs, peüs pois
saveir > savoir	soü, seü savant; sachant	sai set	sache	savrai	soi 2. soüs, seüs
		savons sevent			
taisir taire } *see* plaire		§ 940			

§ 1064. **u-Perfects.** Sixteenth Century.

A *Type.*

Infinitive.	Participles.	Present Indicative.	Present Subjunctive.	Future.	Perfect.
avoyr 107	eü M. u	ay / a — avons, ont	1. aye 3. ayt, aye M. aye, ęyt	avrai M. arey, aorey	eus M. us
(re)paistre 546-547	(re)peu M. pu	(re)pays, M. pęs, pę (re)payst — (re)paissons	(re)paisse	(re)paystray	(re)peus M. pu
plaire 660	pleu M. plu	plays plaist, playt — playsons	plaise	plairay	pleus M. plu
pouvoyr 105, 402	peu M. pu	1 puys, peulx M. puy, puys, puys, peus 2 puys, peulx, M. peus 3 peult, M. peut — pouons, M. pouvons pouez, M. pouvez peuvent, Mz. peuent, peu(s)lent	1. puysse 3. puist, puysse	pourray	peus M. pu
scavoyr 474, 600, 135	sceu M. su saichant Mz. s(c)avant	scay, M. sçy, sé M. sęs, scaîs M. sęt, scait — scavons M. savent B. scevent	scaiche M. sache	scavray M. sarey, saorey	sceus M. su
tayre 587	teu M. tu	tays — taysons	tayse	tayrray	teus, taysis M. tu

§ 1065. **u-Perfects** (§ 1019). LATER OLD FRENCH.

B *Type.*

Infinitive.	Participles.	Present Indicative.	Present Subjunctive.	Future.	Perfect.
aperceivre, *see receivre*					
beivre > boivre; (boire, § 936)	beü, boü	boif; boi / boï boit	boive	bevrai; (boirai)	bui 2. beüs, boüs
conceivre } *see receivre* concevoir } *see receivre*					
creire > croire	creü	croi croit	croie	crerai crerrai	creï, crui 2. creüs, creüs
creistre > croistre	creü	crois croist	croisse	croistrai	cruï 2. creüs
deceivre, *see receivre*					
deveir > devoir	deü, doü	dei > doi doit	doie; doive	devrai	dui 2. deüs, doüs
ester	§ 1058				
gesir	geü gesant; gisant	gis gist	jace, § 940; gise	gerrai; girrai	juï; gis 2. geüs; gesis
leisir > loisir	leü	loist	loise		lut
lire	lit, leü	li lit	lise	lirai	luï; lis 2. leüs; lesis; lisis

ramenteveir
  > ramentevoir;
ramenteivre
  > ramentoivre
	ramenteü	ramentoif
		ramentoit
			ramentoive	ramentevrai	ramentui
					2. ramenteüs

receivre > recoivre; receveir > recevoir	receü	recoif; recoi recoit *Imper.* 2. recoif	recoive	recevrai	recuï 2. receüs

SIXTEENTH CENTURY.

Infinitive.	Participles.	Present Indicative.	Present Subjunctive.	Future.	Perfect.
apercevoir, *see* recevoir					
boyre 529, 519	beu, M. bu / M. buvant / Mz. beuvant, boyvant	boys, boy / boyt	beuvons, M. buvons, / Mz. boivons / boyvent, M. buvent / Mz. beuvent	boyve	buray, boyray, buveray / Mz. beuvray, bevray	beus / M. bu
croyre 447, 392, 394	creu, M. cru	croys, croy	croyons	croye	croyray / [creroye]	creus / M. cru
croystre 576	creu, M. cru	croys	croyssons	croysse	croystray	creus / M. cru
decevoir, *see* recevoir					
debvoyr 106, 650	deu, M. du / Mz. devant, doivant	1. doybs, doy / 2. doybz / 3. doy(b)t	devons / devez, doibvez / doyvent	1. doye, doyve / 4. doyions	deveray / M. devrey / B. doibvray	deus / M. du
gesir 610, 398 / M. jir *obs.*, Mz. gire	geu / M. ju, / Mz. gesy	gis / gist	gisons	gisse, gyse	gerray / Mz. giray, gesiray	geus, M. ju(s) / Mz. gesy, gisi / *Impf. Subj.* / gisisse
loisir	*Impf. Ind.* / Mz. loisoit	Mz. loist		Mz. loyse	Mz. [loysera]	Mz. [loisit]
lire, eslire 681, 398, 484	leu / M. lu	lis	lisons	(es)lise, eslie	liray	lis, lisis, / eslus / *Impf. Subj.* / (es)lysisse / eslusse
ramentevoyr 474, 396, 398, 635	ramentu	ramenteve (sic) / ramenteve	ramentevons / ramentevent	ramenteve	ramenteveray	ramentus / ramentevay
recepvoir 680, 392	receu	recoys, recoy	recepvons	recoyve	receveray / M. recevrey	receus

§ 1066. **u-Perfects** (§ 1019). LATER OLD FRENCH.

C *Type.*

Infinitive.	Participles.	Present Indicative.	Present Subjunctive.	Future.	Perfect.
conoistre, cunuistre quenoistre, (§ 490)	coneü, conoü	conois, conoist; conoissons, conoissent	conoisse	conoistrai	conui, 2. conoüs, coneüs
estoveir, estuveir > estovoir	estoü, esteü	estuet	estuece, estuisse; estuist	estovra	estut
moveir, muveir > movoir	moü, meü	muef, muet, *Imper.* 2. muef; movons, muevent	mueve	movrai	mui, 2. moüs, meüs
nuisir; nuire (§ 888)	noü, neü; nuit	*nuis, nuist, nuit; nuisons, nuisent	nuise	nuirai	nui, 2. noüs, neüs; nuis (§ 987), 2. nuisis
ploveir, pluveir > plovoir	ploü, pleü	pluet	plueve	plovra	plut

§ 1066. **u-Perfects** (§ 1019). SIXTEENTH CENTURY.

C Type.

Infinitive.	Past Participle.	Present Indicative.		Present Subjunctive.	Future.	Perfect.
congnoistre 600 estovoir, *obs.*	congneu	congnoys M. conoęs, conoę	congnoissons	congnoisse	congnoistray	congneus
mouvoyr 635, 641	meu	meus, meuve, mouve M. meu, meus	meuvons, M. mouvons Mz. mouvont, meuvent	meuve, Mz. mouve	mouveray Mz. meuveray, mouvray	meus
nuyre 644	nuy, § 1057 Mz. nuyt	nuys	nuysons	nuyse	nuyray	nuys
plouvoyr 678 M. plouvoer, pluvoer	pleu *Impf.* pluvoyt	pleut	M. pleuvons, pluvons M. pleuvent, pluvent	pleuve	plouvera M. pluvrey	pleut

27

§ 1067. **Anomalous Perfects** (§ 1039). LATER OLD FRENCH.

Infinitive.	Participles.	Present Indicative.	Present Subjunctive.	Future.	Perfect.
beneïstre, benoïstre; beneïr	beneeit, beneoit; benit; beneïssant	§ 960; *Imper.* 2 beneï, beneïs	§ 960	beneïstrai	beneesqui; cf. § 1038; beneï
iraistre, *see* naistre					
naistre	ne; nascu; naissu	nais; naist; naissons; naissent	naisse	naistrai	§ 1038
veintre, vaintre; (veincre, vaintre); (venquir)	vencu; veincu	*venc; veinc; veint; venquons; veinquons; venquent; veinquent	venque; veinque	veintrai; (veincrai)	§ 1038
vivre	vescu	vif; vit; vivons; vivent	vive	vivrai	§ 1038

SIXTEENTH CENTURY.

Infinitive.	Past Participle.	Present Indicative.		Present Subjunctive.	Future.	Perfect.
benyr, benoistre 457 Mz. beni(s)tre iraistre, *obs.*	beny, benoyst, Mz. benit	benys	benissons Mz. benissent, benient	benisse, Mz. benie	benirai	benis
naystre 127 Mz. nasquir	ne	nays nayst	naissons naissent	naisse	naistray Mz. naquirai	nasquis
vaincre 648	vaincu	vaincs M. veinc, veincs M. veinq	vainquissons M. veincons M. veinqent	vaincue	vaincray	vainquys M. veinqi
vivre 612 Mz. vesquir	vescu	vis M. vi, vis	vivons	vive	viveray	vesquis, vescus M. veqi

PART V.

ANGLO-NORMAN.

CHAPTER I.

INTRODUCTORY.

Section 1.—EXTERNAL HISTORY.

§ 1068. French speech had some vogue in England before the Norman Conquest (cf. *Vising*, p. 8), and the number of immigrants that followed William and the closeness of the relations established with his Continental domains rapidly extended its use. The number of French knights provided with fiefs at this time is put at five thousand and immigration continued through the century; the French religious orders, Cluniac, Cistercian, Augustinian, formed branches in England—by the end of the reign of Henry I. their number is put at more than a hundred (*Vising*, p. 11); bishops and abbots and monks were translated freely, John of Salisbury, for instance, became Bishop of Chartres, Peter of Blois held many offices in England; the great French schools and later on the University of Paris attracted large numbers of English scholars. The settlers, moreover, were not drawn only from the nobility and the Church: the father of Thomas à Becket was from Rouen, his mother from Caen, and an anonymous biographer adds: 'Many natives of the chief Norman cities, Rouen and Caen, removed to London and chose them out a dwelling there because it was a fit place for their trade and better stored with the goods in which they were wont to deal.' French thus became the language of the mercantile communities and so continued officially in the thirteenth century and long after, as may be seen from the extant municipal laws and ordinances of the merchant guilds, all of which are in French or Latin (cf. the *Oak Book of Southampton*, I, *Introduction*). The accession of the Angevin dynasty and the development of trade, particularly the trade in wine, between their more southern domains and ports such as Southampton, led to the establishment of French also as the maritime language (cf. P. Studer, *Oak Book of Southampton, Supplement*, pp. 8, 9, and §§ 1186, 1195-1199).

In the later twelfth century the assize of *novel disseisin*, which gave all freeholders access to a royal, i.e. French-speaking, Court contributed

to the extension of French speech in the rural districts also (cf. Pollock and Maitland, *History of English Law*, I, (2), pp. 83, 84).

The vogue of French literature in England is attested by the number of Anglo-Norman MSS., and the encouragement given to literature and learning by the Court, the Church and the nobles, great and small, led to a relatively large output of French works in England, mainly didactic, religious, historical or narrative but also dramatic (cf. *Vising*, Part II).

§ 1069. With the loss of Normandy and the adjacent provinces in the beginning of the thirteenth century insular life became less closely bound up with Continental; the barons were forced to choose between their English and French domains, and those who chose the former were soon brought to throw in their lot wholeheartedly with the rest of the population; the incapacity of John and his son and Henry's Gascon favourites brought together nobles and middle class and the welding together of these classes, begun in this way, was completed by the national wars engaged in under the Edwards against the Scotch and finally the French. The fame of the university of Oxford and its great teachers Grosseteste and Duns Scotus rendered less usual the sojourn at Paris undertaken previously by so many English clerks.

Trade relations were maintained at something like their former intensity, but with the close of the century the importance of the wool trade deflected the main body of trade to the Low Countries (cf. §§ 1186, 1200).

The change in relations with the Continent and still more the modification in outlook and attitude that it induced led naturally to a wider use of English among the classes that had hitherto been mainly French-speaking. Significant is the fact that the proclamation of 1258 was issued by Henry III to 'all his faithful, learned and lay,' in both French and English, and towards the end of the century we learn from the author of *Arthour and Merlin* that he had seen many a nobleman who could not speak a word of French (*Vising*, p. 21).

In the spheres in which the use of French was most firmly established, however, in literature, law and education, its displacement went but slowly.

§ 1070. At the court French remained in use up to the reign of Henry IV, the first king whose mother-tongue was English, and the social prestige of the language of the conquerors was long maintained, [cf. Robert of Gloucester's chronicle (end xiii. ?), 'If a man does not know French he is little esteemed'].[1] The great variety of English local speech led,

---

[1] Ranulf Higden, writing in the middle of the fourteenth century, still comments on the way the country people ape their betters in the use of French: . . . 'gentil men children beeth i-taught to speke Frensche from the tyme that they beeth i-rokked in here cradel . . . and uplondisshe men (rurales) wil likne hym self to gentil men, and fondeth with greet besynesse for to speke Frensce, for to be i-tolde of.' *Polychronicon*, II, pp. 159, 161 (Trevisa's translation).

moreover, to the retention of Anglo-Norman as a convenient common form, cf. the remark of the fourteenth-century chronicler Ranulf Higden (II, chap. 59), reproduced by his English translator as follows : 'for a man of Kente, southern, western and northern men speken Frensshe al lyke in soune and speche, but they can not speke theyr Englyssh so.'

§ 1071. The voluminous didactic literature and the romances of the fourteenth century were still for the most part composed in French : Nicholas Bozon, for example, as late as *c.* 1300, makes use of it in his translation from Latin, 'En comun langage pur amis, Ke de clergie ne ount apris', (cf. *Vising*, pp. 15-18), and the rather blatantly national romance of *Richard Cœur de Lyon*, the hero held to outshine Charle-magne and Roland, was englished only at the end of the century.

§ 1072. In legal literature the use of French was rather increased than diminished as it was used instead of Latin in the many documents of new type that arose, e.g. in the Parliament Rolls which begin at the end of the century and in the Statute Rolls, e.g. in the *Statute of Gloucester*, enrolled in 1278, and in the so-called *Year Books*, that unparalleled series of partially verbatim reports of cases that lawyers began to make and preserve for their own instruction from the later thirteenth century on, beginning in 1285 and continuing after 1293 with little interruption to the reign of Henry VIII.   In legal works of older type the introduction of French went slowly, but the first legal treatise, the summary attributed to the lawyer Britton, goes back to the later thirteenth century.

§ 1073. In the next century the use of English gained ground more rapidly, in spite of more deliberate efforts to enforce the use and acquire-ment of French.   The students at Oxford were bidden to speak either French or Latin, and the teaching of French was given some encourage-ment by the university (Rashdall, *Universities of Europe*, II, 2, pp. 459, 460); for political purposes it was resolved in the parliament of Edward III : 'que tout seigneur, baron, chevalier et honestes hommes de bonnes villes mesissent cure et dilligence de estruire et aprendre leurs enfans le langhe françoise par quoy il en fuissent plus able et plus coustumier ens leur gheires.' Efforts were made to enable scribes to master the intricacies of spelling and to check the deterioration of Anglo-Norman.   The first spelling treatise composed by T. H., student of Paris, in the later thirteenth century and revised by Coyfurelly of Orléans, was soon followed by the better known *Orthographia Gallica*, xiii-xiv.   The first French grammar, the *Donait François* of John Barton appeared *c.* 1400 and *Maneres de Langage* multiplied, the earliest *c.* 1396 (cf. *Intr. Orth. Gall.* pp. xii-xvi). These efforts were, however, of little avail.

§ 1074. In education, where French remained dominant and was the medium of instruction in the schools until the middle of the fourteenth

century, what appears to have been an Oxford reform brought about its displacement. At that time, as we learn in the chronicle of Trevisa, Fellow of Stapledon Hall (the present Exeter College), John of Cornwall, the master who taught grammar to Founder's kin at Merton College, first made his pupils construe in English instead of in French, and his method was carried on by Richard Pencriche, the Head of another Hall.[1]

§ 1075. In 1362 English is allowed in the Courts on the ground that ' la lange Franceis . . . est trope desconue,' and in the latter part of the century we hear from William of Nassyngton that ' Bothe lered and lewed, old and yonge, Alle understonden english tonge.' (*Speculum Vitae*, cited *Vising*, p. 22.) The few authors of the fifteenth century who, like Gower, still make use of French in literary compositions, model their usage as closely as they can on the speech of France—or rather Paris, and are Anglo-French rather than Anglo-Norman.[2]

§ 1076. The last stronghold of the older traditional language was the law. The proclamation of 1258 (§ 1069) remained a dead letter, and in legal documents French with Latin continued in use throughout the thirteenth century. In the fourteenth century petitions to Parliament began to be presented in English and its proceedings to be held in that language. The earliest evidence of this is a passage in the latest version of Froissart's Chronicle which describes the proceedings in the Parliament of 1337 : ' Adonc se leva uns clers d'Engletere, licensiiés en drois et en lois, et moult bien pourveus de trois langages, de latin, de françois et dou langage englois. . . . Si parla atempréement et remoustra tout en hault, et en englois, a la fin que il fust mieuls entendus de toute gens, car tous jours sçut on mieuls ce que on voelt dire et proposer ens ou langage ou on est d'enfance introduit qu'en un aultre, tous les poins et les articles desquels messires Robers d'Artois les . . . avoit enfourmés.' (MS. de Rome, Vol. I, p. 360.) Statutes were enrolled in English from the accession of Richard III on, but the first legal text-book in English was composed in the sixteenth century only, and in the courts and records French was even longer lived. Under Henry VIII, it is true, the

---

[1] Barton's preface, while indicating the continued vogue of French among the upper classes, makes it plain that it is an acquired language : ' Pour ceo que les bones gens du Roiaume d'Engleterre sont embrasez a sçavoir lire et escrire, entendre et parler droit François afin qu'ils puissent entre comuner ove lour voisins, c'est a dire les bones gens du roiaume de France, et ainsi pour ce que les leys d'Engleterre pour le graigneur partie et aussi beaucoup de bones choses sont misez en François, et aussi bien pres tous les seigneurs et toutes les dames en mesme roiaume d'Engleterre volentiers s'entrescrivent en romance, trenecessaire je cuide estre aus Englois de sçavoir la droite nature de François.' (*Donait*, p. 25.)

[2] For a discussion of the terms Anglo-Norman and Anglo-French, cf. P. Studer, pp. 4-16.

'barbarous tong and old French, whych now serveth to no purpose else,' was condemned, but the remedy proposed was a return to good French, and the use of *Law French*, the technical form of Anglo-Norman, persisted and found staunch defenders in the seventeenth and even eighteenth centuries : 'for really the law is scarcely expressible properly in English, and, when it is done, it must be *Françoise*, or very uncouth.' (Roger North, 1633-1734.)

[Authorities : * J. Vising, *Anglo-Norman Language and Literature*, London and Oxford, 1923 ; P. Studer, *The Study of Anglo-Norman*, Oxford, 1920 ; O. H. Prior, Preface to *Cambridge Anglo-Norman Texts*, Cambridge, 1924.

On the history of *Law French :* Pollock and Maitland, *History of English Law*, I, (2), pp. 38-65 ; * Maitland, *Year Books of Edward II* (Selden Soc.), Vol. I, pp. xxxii-lxxxi; cf. also D. Legge, *Year Books*, Vol. XX.]

Section 2.—Period Division.

§ 1077. The history of Anglo-Norman falls into two main periods. The first, the period of development, extends roughly up to the end of the first third or middle of the thirteenth century, i.e. up to the time when the loss of the French provinces (1203-4) had begun to exercise an influence on the use of the language and when a well-defined national movement against it had begun.   In this period it is still possible to regard Anglo-Norman as a dialect of French, i.e. as a living local form of speech, handed down from generation to generation, albeit one that was progressively modified by the peculiar conditions in which it found itself; it is in this period consequently possible to trace a real development in linguistic usage.   In the second period, the period of degeneracy, when insular French was cut off from its base and more and more restricted in use, it gradually became a 'dead' language, one that had ceased to be the mother-tongue of anybody and had always to be taught ; a 'faus franceis d'Angletere,' a sort of 'Low French,' characterised by a more and more indiscriminate use of words, sounds and forms, but half-known, markedly similar in its debasement to the 'Low Latin' of the Merovingian period in Gaul.

The first period may be conveniently sub-divided into two.   In Early Anglo-Norman, i.e. in the first fifty or sixty years after the Conquest, the French of England differed but little from that in vogue in the west of France ; it was still in the main the language of the invaders and their offspring.   In the later twelfth and early thirteenth century, when it was being widely used by people of mixed parentage or of pure English descent, it was modified with ever-increasing rapidity under the combined influence of the English speech habits and the

relative isolation in which it found itself, but it is striking how often the modifications attested in Anglo-Norman find parallels either in continental dialects or in later francien.

In the later twelfth century the cleavage between insular and Continental French is marked enough to induce authors, who like Marie de France and Guernes de Pont Ste. Maxence are of French origin, to emphasise their French origin (§ 59). In the next century Anglo-Norman is not infrequently a subject of jest. In Philippe of Beaumanoir's *Jehan and Blonde* the subject is lightly touched on; Blonde, unlike her father, the Earl of Oxford, had not had the advantage of residence in France and in consequence ' Un peu paroit a son langage, Que ne fut pas nee a Pontoise,' but all deficiencies in her accent are rapidly remedied under the able tuition of her French lover Jehan : ' De maint jeu a juer l'aprist. Et en millour françois la mist Qu'ele n'estoit quant a li vint.' In the fabliau of the *Deux Anglois et l'Anel*, which turns upon the Anglo-Norman confusion of ŋ with n (of *asnel* and *agnel*, both **aṇel** (?) in Anglo-Norman), the fun is broader, but the joke is carried furthest in the episode of Renart as jongleur in Branch Ib of the *Roman de Renart*, ll. 2350-2530, in which Renart feigns to be an English jongleur. Here some of the thirteenth-century Anglo-Norman traits are reproduced with some exaggeration, e.g. the confusion of ü and u, and incidentally of the perfect *fut* (*fuit*), and parts of the verb *foutre ;* the suppression of unstressed final ę (*sir* for *sire, enseign* for *enseigne,* etc.) and initial a- (*pelez* for *apelez*) ; the extension of the endings of the first conjugation (*perdez* for *perduz, diser* for *dire*), and in addition a use of case and verb form more like modern pidgin-English than the Anglo-Norman of that date.

Section 3.—GENERAL CHARACTERISTICS OF ANGLO-NORMAN.

§ 1078. Although the relations between England and the Continent remained very close in the early period, the French spoken in England was from the first relatively isolated and was not long in showing the combination of conservatism and neologism that ordinarily characterises a speech that is severed from its parent stock, cf., for instance, Canadian French. Sounds, forms, words, locutions and graphies, discarded on the Continent, sometimes lingered on in insular speech, while, on the other hand, the weakening of tradition among the settlers and their descendants allowed an acceleration of pace in other changes and much freedom of analogical creation, cf. below and the *Vie de St. Gilles*, Intr. pp. xvii-xxiii.

It must always be borne in mind that the basis of Anglo-Norman is the *speech* of France and that it is the *spoken* language that exercised influence on its development in the first main period. Since orthographical tradition was at that time relatively weak in insular French (§ 1222), the written form of words was more readily modified than on the Continent and this fact must be taken into account in considering the apparent precocity of some of the linguistic changes in Anglo-Norman (cf. §§ 1131-1135, 1201-1203, 1284, 1292).

§ 1079. The instability of speech induced in these ways was, however, greatly increased by a variety of other factors :—

(1) The men who settled in England came from all parts of William's

domains, and thus from the outset the language introduced, though predominantly western, was more variegated than any form of local speech in use on the Continent.

(2) The French of the eleventh century was still a rapidly changing speech and modifications continued throughout Later Old French although slackened down (§§ 1095-1103); Anglo-Norman was affected variously by many of these modifications.

(3) French in England was brought in contact with another idiom, one spoken by a people with a very different organic basis (§§ 1110-1112), and one, moreover, that was also honey-combed with local divergences and was also rapidly changing.

(4) Literary production in England was largely dominated by Continental fashion; educated Englishmen very generally passed through Paris University (§ 63); political and trade relations continued close but with varying regions of France (§ 1186) and thus Continental French, written and spoken, the speech of Paris and of the northern region, as well as the whole of the western region, exercised a continuous but variable influence on insular French.

§ 1080. These varying factors all contribute to render the development of French speech in England an intricate problem, and the difficulty in unravelling it is greatly increased by two others: (1) the extreme instability of the spelling (§ 1205) and (2) the unsatisfactory character of many of the edited texts. Neglect to distinguish between spelling and pronunciation has vitiated much of the work previously done on the subject, (it is, for instance, a radical defect in the book that embodies the valuable work done by M. Tanquerey on the conjugation system); neglect to publish texts with complete accuracy and regard for orthographical problems often renders difficult exact observation of linguistic change. Much spade work remains to be done before the course of development can be accurately determined.

CHAPTER II.

PHONOLOGY.

Section 1.—INTRODUCTORY.

§ 1081. From what has been said it is evident that any one who attempts to trace the development of the pronunciation of French in England must understand the sound-system of the language introduced by the conquerors and the changes in process at the time of introduction and in the period subsequent, and that one must also take account of the influence exercised by English speech habits, of the varying relation in which England stood to the Continent and the influence of isolation. The first two of these subjects have been treated in the earlier part of this book but, for convenience, short summaries are included in this part as well as a general characterisation of the English sound-system and of the main changes in process in Early Middle English.

Section 2.—CHARACTERISATION OF THE FRENCH INTRODUCED.

[For eleventh-century French cf. §§ 166-168 above and section 6 below.]

§ 1082. Mercenaries flocked to William's standard from many parts of France, but the bulk of his followers were drawn from his own domains —Normandy and Maine—and from Brittany, which acknowledged his suzerainty. The French introduced was therefore predominantly western, but western with a northern element, because it must be remembered that before the establishment of the Normans in France, the northern half of the territory assigned to them formed a part of the region in which the northern form of French was spoken (§§ 37, 1320).

§ 1083. *Western Characteristics* (cf. below, §§ 1326, 1327).—(1) The vowel ǫ had already moved up to **u**, the place left vacant by the palatalisation of L.L. **u** to **ü** (§§ 183, 184); thus Early Old French **tǫt, dǫlour, angǫịsẹ** were being pronounced **tut, dulur, anguịsẹ**.

§ 1084. (2) As in the northern region the nasal vowel **ē** remained unlowered before **n** (W. § viii), cf. English loan-words such as *gentle, amend, defend,* etc.

§ 1085. (3) The tonic stress being relatively weak and early lessened in this region (§§ 17, 1326), the course followed in the levelling of diphthongs differed somewhat from that taken in francien (W. §§ i-vii) :—

(i) The diphthongs ǫu and ei remained undifferentiated (W. §§ v, vi) and levelled gradually to u and ę; ǫu to u in the course of the eleventh century (W. § v), ei to ę in Later Old French (W. § vi). Thus Early Old French **flour** became **flur** in the western region, **fleur** (> flȫr) in francien (§§ 226, 542); Early Old French **eir** (* **herem**) > remained **eir** in the western region and was levelled subsequently to ęr, but in francien it was differentiated to **oir** and passed to ųęr (§§ 226, 519).

(ii) In the more southern part of the region the diphthong **ai** was already levelling to ę when prae-consonantal (W. § ii), the diphthong **ie** to ję (W. § i) and the triphthongs ꞌieu and ꞌuęu to jęu and ųęu; thus francien **mais, faire** were being pronounced męis, fęirę or męs, fęrę, francien pꞌie(θ), tš̑ꞌier *chier*, pjęθ, tš̑ję̑r, francien dꞌieu, fꞌueu, djęu, fųęu.

§ 1086. (4) In francien š̑ developed ordinarily a palatal glide in front of itself; in the western region no such glide developed after ü (W. § x): G.R. üš̑ (< * **üstiŭm**) > ꞌüis in francien, üs in the western region.
[For later developments cf. §§ 1326, 1330.]

§ 1087. *Northern Characteristics.*—The northern traits that appear to have had some vogue in insular speech are the following :—

(1) A certain tardiness in the development of the ǫ and ų-sounds, ų not yet being fully palatalised to ü (§ 183, cf. Waters, *Brendan*, p. cl), ǫ not yet raised as far as u (§ 184).

§ 1088. (2) As in western French the continued differentiation of ē + n from ā (N. § xx, and cf. § 1084).

§ 1089. (3) A lowered pronunciation of ę before ɫ + *consonant,* which led to the development of the triphthong -ęau < -ęɫ, e.g. ęaus (< *illos*), *ceaus,* tsęaus, cf. *Brendan,* pp. cxli, cxlii, N. § xvii.

§ 1090. (4) A greater intensity of tonic stress which induced :—

(i) The reduction of the triphthongs ꞌieu and ꞌüeu to ꞌiu and ü, respectively, e.g. **liu** for **lieu, fü** < **fueu** (N. § vi, cf. *Boeve,* p. 204).

(ii) The reduction of ꞌieẹ̈ and ꞌueẹ̈ to ꞌię̈ and ꞌuę̈ respectively : **maisnię** < **maisnieę, ruę** < **rueę** (N. § v, cf. *Boeve,* p. 202).

(iii) As in francien (§ 226) the differentiation of the diphthongs **ei** and **ou** to **oi** and **eu** respectively.

(iv) The relatively early instability of ę in hiatus, N. § x.

§ 1091. (5) The retention of the velar articulation of k and g initial before Latin a, N. § i, cf. *Rol. Digby MS. castel* 4, *embrunket* 3505, etc., *Boeve,* p. 235, and English loan-words, *cark, cart, cat, catch, cancel, pluck,* etc.

§ 1092. (6) The passage of ts̑ (< Latin **kj, tj** *initial*, **k** *initial* + **e** and **i**, N. § i) to ts̆ instead of **ts**, §§ 291, 306, 308, cf. *Boeve*, p. 233, and the English loan-words, *cherries, chive, fashion*, etc.

§ 1093. (7) Retention of initial **w** in words of Germanic origin, e.g. *warder, walcrer*, cf. English loan-words, *wafer, wager, war*, etc., N. § iii.

§ 1094. (8) A tardiness in the development of intervocalic s̑ (< **sk** + **e, i** and **sj, ssj, stj**, § 315, N. § xvi).
[For later Old French developments cf. Section 11.]

Section 3.—Sound-Changes in Process in Old French.

§ 1095. In the later eleventh century important sound-changes were in process in French, and although the literary and social influences of the twelfth century had begun to exercise a retarding influence, the evolution of the language continued to be relatively rapid. In the period in which England was closely connected with France and its language a living dialect of French, Anglo-Norman participated, ordinarily, in these changes, especially the western ones; in the later period, when insular speech was more isolated (§ 1069), the influence exercised on it by contemporary Continental changes was superficial only. The more important of these *later* modifications are considered in Section 11: those that affected both Continental speech and Anglo-Norman in the early period may be summarised as follows: all varied locally in pace and extension. Their influence is considered below in Sections 11 and 12.

§ 1096. (1) *Sound-Changes in Process in the Late Eleventh Century.*— The more general changes which were in process in the late eleventh century are the following :—

(i) A gradual diminution in the intensity of the tonic stress and consequent gradual levelling of diphthongs (cf. §§ 223, 508).

(ii) The closer grouping of words bound together in closely connected locutions or phrases and a consequent gradual modification of the pronunciation of final consonants within the locution or phrase (§§ 170, 171).

(iii) The increasing influence exercised by nasal consonants on the vowels preceding them (§§ 434, 448).

In continental speech all these tendencies appear to have increased in strength in Later Old French; in Anglo-Norman the first and last were checked or modified under English influence, cf. §§ 1151, 1154-1169.

§ 1097. The more limited sound-changes that were in process in the late eleventh century are the following :—

(i) The vocalisation (or effacement) of ꝉ and ɉ prae-consonantal (§§ 383-388), and the development of vocalic glides between these sounds and ę and ę̄ (§ 388).

(ii) The effacement of ð and θ (§§ 346, 347).

(iii) The reduction of the consonantal groups: **gw** and **kw** (§ 192). ð + *consonant* (§ 372), **z** + *consonant* (§ 377).

(iv) In west French the beginning of the levelling of diphthongs: **ai** to ę (§ 533), ˡie to ɪę (§ 512).

§ 1098. (2) *Sound-Changes that had their Beginnings in the Twelfth or Early Thirteenth Centuries.*—(i) Shift of value among the e-sounds: in the twelfth century the passage of ę̆ (< Latin ē, ĭ *blocked*, §§ 179, 180) to ę̄ (§ 575); in the early thirteenth century, in western French, the opening of ę̄ (< Latin a *tonic free*, § 231) to ę̄ before **r** and **l** (§§ 494, 495): **mę̄trę > mę̄trę̄, ę̆lę̄ (< *ęlla < ĭlla) and ę̄lę̄ (< ɑlɑ) > ę̄lę̄, pę̆rę̄ > pę̄rę̄.**

§ 1099. (ii) Levelling of diphthongs :—

eu > ö (§ 542), **ɪeu > ɪö** (§ 545), **ǫu > u,** (§ 548).

ˡ**ue > ö** or **wę** (§§ 551, 553), **ueu > ö** or **ɪö** (§ 556).

ˡ**üi > ẃi** (§ 515), **oi** and **ui > ẃę** (§ 519), **ăi** and **ēi > ę̄i** (§ 467).

ˡ**ęau > eˡau** (§ 539) and in the northern region **iau (> ɪau)** (§ 540).

§ 1100. (iii) The gradual effacement or syneresis of the weaker vowels in hiatus (§§ 242, 243, 268).

§ 1101. (iv) The passage of ǭ (< ð + s + *consonant*, § 580, + z, § 569, or in hiatus, § 578) to ǫ and later in the south-western region to **u**: **tǫst > tǭt > tǭt > tūt** (*toust*), § 581.

§ 1102. (v) In the northern region the shift of **ts** to **s** in the twelfth century (N. § xxi) and in the thirteenth century a general shift of **ts** to **s**, of **tš** to **š**, and of **dž** to **ž** (§ 194).

§ 1103. (vi) The reduction of **s** + *consonant* (§ 377) and more variably of **r** + *consonant* (§ 396).

Section 4.—CONSERVATISM IN PRONUNCIATION.

§ 1104. The relative isolation of insular speech led to a certain conservatism in the French spoken in England, sounds being sometimes retained at the stage at which they were introduced longer than on the Continent. This influence was only felt ordinarily in conjunction with the influence exercised by the English speech habits and is considered below, but the following characteristics of Anglo-Norman speech may be ascribed directly to it :—

§ 1105. (1) The recently borrowed loan-words containing the Latin suffixes *-arium*, *-erium*, *-orium*, introduced with the pronunciation *-arje*, *-erje*, *-orje* (cf. § 645), persisted late in this form in Anglo-Norman and gave rise to the English forms in *-ary*, *-ery*, *-ory*, e.g. *contrary*, *mystery*, *history*.

§ 1106. (2) In the late eleventh century prosthetic **e**, developed in words beginning with **s +** *consonant* (cf. § 361), had not yet become a fixed and integral part of the word (cf. § 603); its movability persisted in Early Anglo-Norman. as in the northern region, N.E. § x (cf. *Q.L.R. li speriz*, p. 31, *sa spee*, etc.), and contributed to the instability that characterises the initial syllable of words in this dialect (cf. § 1137).

§ 1107. (3) The descending type of diphthong, which was dominant in eleventh-century French (cf. § 507), persisted longer in Anglo-Norman than in western French. The influence of Northern French and English, however, contributed to this result, and the discussion of the subject will be found below in §§ 1154-1169.

§ 1108. The vocalisation of prae-consonantal **ł** and **ʝ** appears to have been somewhat retarded and the development of vocalic glides that accompanied this process to some extent checked, §§ 1162-1169.

§ 1109. (4) In Continental French of the twelfth century there was a tendency to dissimilate countertonic **u** from tonic **u**, but in Anglo-Norman the older form was ordinarily retained, e.g. *sucours*, *sulunc*, *sumuns*, *sujurn* (§ 131).

[Cf. also §§ 1150, 1177-1181.]

Section 5.—ENGLISH INFLUENCE.

§ 1110. The strongest factor in the growing instability of Anglo-Norman pronunciation was undoubtedly the influence of English speech habits. Displacement, together with contact with a foreign tongue, shook tradition, and the acquirement of French by people with a different organic basis induced gradually many modifications. The most disturbing factor in the English speech-habits was the heavy tonic stress, its intensity in all periods, its position in the later, and under its influence the development of diphthongs and the less stressed syllables was very considerably modified (cf. below, §§ 1130-1140, 1154). Sound-changes were sometimes accelerated, sometimes retarded, sometimes deflected, and already in the first period, and much more in the second, new developments proper only to Anglo-Norman made their appearance.

Consonantal sounds that were unfamiliar to the English were early modified, for example the affricate **ts** (§ 1183) and the palatal sounds **ʝ** and **ɲ** and post-consonantal **ʝ** (§§ 1182, 1155); those that were moribund or rather ephemeral in French were sometimes retained longer than on

the Continent if they had a place in the English sound-system, for instance the dental fricatives θ and ð, and the velars χ and w (§§ 1177, 1178, 1180, 1181). Among the vowels the changes induced were on the whole more gradual and more complex, as in both languages pronunciation was changing rapidly and much diversified locally. Those changes that were on the lines of English changes were accelerated (§§ 1152, 1158, 1173); those that found no support in English speech-habits were retarded or perturbed (§§ 1162, 1164, 1165, 1169); processes unfamiliar in Middle English (such as nasalisation), were gradually given up (§§ 1150-1152); others not found in Continental French were introduced under English influence (§§ 1156 (iii), 1163, 1170, and 1185).

[For the possible influence of English dialects on Anglo-Norman, cf. Prior, *Preface to Cambridge Anglo-Norman Texts*, pp. xx-xxvi and *Romania*, xlix, pp. 177-185.]

Section 6.—Comparison of Old French and Middle English Sound-Systems.

§ 1111. A brief comparison of the salient features of the accentual and sound-systems of Later Old French and Early Middle English and a short summary of the more important M.E. sound-changes will best serve to explain the lines followed by the English influence. Both languages, it must be remembered, were much diversified locally and rapidly changing.

§ 1112. *Old French of the Late Eleventh Century.*—The stress fell upon the last or last but one syllable of the word. Its intensity had lessened considerably in the western region (§ 223), and the new tendency to link together words closely connected in thought was already operative, making the phrase the unit of the sentence instead of the word (§ 170). This tendency was already beginning to modify the pronunciation of final consonants (§ 611).

Quantity and quality appear to play no part in the differentiation of vowels other than the e-sounds (§ 573, but cf. Pt. II, chap. xv and § 586).

Nasalisation was clearly audible in the pronunciation of the low vowels **a** and **e** and of the diphthongs **ai** and **ei** when they stood before nasal consonants (§ 434).

Diphthongs were abundant, all falling, but in the western region levelling had set in (§§ 508, 1326).

In unstressed syllables the vowel ordinarily in use was ę, possibly slightly labialised in the vicinity of labial sounds (§ 275).

The range of consonants was considerable and *palatals* were relatively numerous. Intervocalic groups of consonants were relatively rare and among the ones in use the groups + and ʝ + *consonant*, z + *consonant*, ðr and ðl were in process of reduction (§§ 383-388, 377, 372).

No double consonants were pronounced except possibly **rr** (§ 366).

WESTERN AND NORTHERN FRENCH SOUND-SYSTEM IN THE LATE
ELEVENTH CENTURY.

[Sounds in square brackets northern only.]

§ 1113. *Consonants.*

	Labial.		Dental.				Denti-Palatal.		Palatal.	Velar.	Uvular.	Lar-yngal.
	Bi-labial.	Labio-dental.	Dental.	Alevolar.	Palatalised Denal.	Palatalised Alveolar.	Post-Alveolar.	Prae-Palatal.				
Plosive	p b		t d							k g		
Affricate			ts dz					tš dž				
Nasal	m		n							ŋ		
Lateral			l ɬ							ʎ	(ɬ)	
Trilled				r								
Fricative	w	f v	s z θ ð			[ŝ]				ʝ	(w)	h
Semi-vowel	(ɥ)									i̯	ʮ	

§ 1114. *Vowels.*   [For î cf. § 382 (4).]

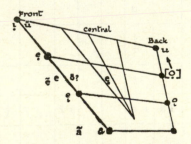

Diphthongs, ai, ei, ǫi, [ǫi], ui, üi; ʼue, [ʼie]; ʼui, [ęu < ou], i̯ęu, [ʼi(e)u].
The vocalisation of ɬ (§ 385) was inducing the formation of ʼau, ʼǫu, ęu, ęau
(ęu, § 1162), ęeu (ęu, § 1162), ʼueu (ʼüeu).

28

§ 1115. *Early Middle English.*—Stress was strong and fell ordinarily upon the root syllable of words, i.e. on the first syllable in words not beginning with a prefix.

The word formed ordinarily the sentence unit and retained its individuality in the sentence.

Pure vowels were strongly differentiated by quantity and quality.

There was no audible nasalisation of vowels.

Diphthongs were few, for the O.E. diphthongs had for the most part been levelled and the new ones formed in M.E. by the vocalisation of the open consonants were only incipient.

The range of consonants was considerable, but it was the *velar* consonants that were relatively numerous.

Intervocalic groups of consonants were of varying type and relatively frequent : double consonants were still in use.

EARLY MIDDLE ENGLISH SOUND-SYSTEM.

§. 1116. *Consonants.*

	Labial.		Dental.				Denti-Palatal.		Palatal.	Velar.	Uvular.	Laryngal.
	Bi-labial.	Labio-dental.	Dental.	Alveolar.	Palatalised Dental.	Palatalised Alveolar.	Post-Alveolar.	Prae-Palatal.				
Plosive	p b			t d						k g		
Affricate								tš dž				
Nasal	m			n						ŋ		
Lateral				l ł						(ł)		
Trilled				r								
Fricative	w	f v	θ ð	s z				š ž	ç ʝ	x γ (w)		h
Semi-vowel	(ɥ)									ɥ		

§ 1117. *Vowels.*

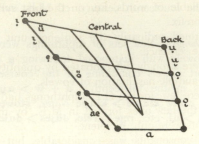

The vowels **a, ẹ, ọ, ü, i, ö** (< ¹**ēo** and ¹**ĕo**) were differentiated by length; the O.E. diphthongs **ēa** and **ēo** had levelled in the course of the eleventh century to **ę̄** and **ō** or **ŏ** (Luick, §§ 356, 357); **æ** was levelling to **ę** or regionally **a** (Luick, §§ 361, 362).

Diphthongs. **ai, ęi, au, ọu, ęu** (> ¹**iu**).

Section 7.—SOUND-CHANGES IN MIDDLE ENGLISH.

§ 1118. The sound-changes of the Middle English period affected mainly the pronunciation of vowels and the syllabic value of words; the quantity of vowels was modified as well as the quality, but as it is the qualitative changes that affected Anglo-Norman most strongly it is only these that will be mentioned here—and only those that appear to have influenced French speech.

[For quantitative changes, cf. Wyld, §§ 173-177, Luick, §§ 385-395, 429, Jespersen, Pt. I, chap. iv.]

§ 1119. *Pure Vowels.*—In Early Middle English (before 1200 in the north, Luick, § 378), *short closed* **ę̆** and **ŏ̦** were opened, unless influenced by juxtaposed consonants: **ę̆ > ĕ, ŏ̦ > ŏ, ęi > ẹi, ęu > ẹu, ọu > ǫu,** e.g. **mę̆te > mĕte, hǫ̆rs > hŏrs, węi > wẹi, fǫur > fọur** (Luick, §§ 378, 379).

§ 1120. In Early Middle English **a** *long* ordinarily velarised further and rounded to **ọ̦**, *stan* **stān > stọ̄n** (Wyld, § 156, Luick, § 369).

§ 1121. The unrounding of **ü,** *long* and *short,* begun in some districts in Old English, continued regionally (Wyld, § 158, Luick, § 397), and **ö** (< **eo,** *long* and *short*) was unrounded to **ę** *long* (Wyld, § 168, Luick, § 357).

§ 1122. In the course of Later Middle English **ọ** *long* was gradually raised to **u** *long* (Wyld, § 163).

§ 1123. Before **r** in the same syllable with itself ę was sometimes lowered to **a** in the fourteenth century, cf. M.E. *starre* < M.E. *sterre* (Luick, § 430).

§ 1124. *Diphthongs.*—New sets of diphthongs were formed by the combination of vowels with juxtaposed following ʮ (< w or γ) and ɉ (< χ or γ), short vowels combining in the course of the twelfth century, long ones in the thirteenth : **a + w > aʮ, eo + w > eʮ, o + w > oʮ,** e.g. *clawe* **klawe > klaʮe** *clawe,* **stowe > stoʮe** *stowe ;* **e + ɉ > ei, ae + ɉ > ai,** etc., **reɉe > reie, daɉes > daies** (Luick, §§ 372, 373, 399-401).

§ 1125. Many diphthongs were levelled in Later Middle English :—

(i) The stressed element was sometimes either further differentiated from the unstressed or assimilated to it and thus **eʮ >** became either **iʮ** or **üʮ (> ǖ)** and **iʮ** more rarely **üʮ (> ǖ),** e.g. **ręwen ręʮen > riʮen** or **rüen, stiward > stiʮard > stüard** (Luick, §§ 399, 407 (3)). The spelling with *w* was very generally retained.

(ii) The less stressed second element was not infrequently effaced before homophonous consonants :—

(*a*) Diphthongs in **-ʮ,** e.g. **aʮ, eʮ, iʮ** levelled to **ā, ē, i** before the *labial* and *labialised* consonants **tš** and **dž** (cf. Luick, § 427).

(*b*) Diphthongs in **-ɉ,** e.g. **ai, ei, ui, üi** levelled to **a, e, u, ü** before **tš, ntš, š,** and also before **s +** *consonant,* cf. M.E. *mastre, frusshen, punchon* (Luick, § 427).

§ 1126. *Unstressed Vowels.*—Throughout the period there was a tendency to reduce unstressed syllables under certain conditions :—

(i) Unstressed **e** and **i** *in hiatus* with preceding tonic vowels combined with these in a diphthong or merged in them, cf. M.E. **foūr <** *fower,* M.E. **maïster < maeȝester,** M.E. **twīs < twies** (Luick, § 453).

(ii) *Unstressed interconsonantal* vowels were often slurred when the consonants juxtaposed combined readily in groups, cf. M.E. *beforn < beforen, kindom < cynedōm, webstere < webbestere, heonne < he(o)nane, forlorne < forlorene, monkes < munecas* (Luick, §§ 456, 457).

(iii) *Final* **e** was slurred after a consonant when the preceding syllable bore the secondary stress, cf. M.E. *lafdi < hláefdìȝe, drinking < dríncènde* (Luick, § 456).

§ 1127. Unstressed ę *pretonic* and *post-tonic* was raised to **i** in the course of the twelfth and thirteenth centuries, cf. M.E. *biginnen, biforen, wallis, askid,* etc. (Luick, §§ 442, 460).

§ 1128. *Consonants.*—The fricative consonants ɉ, **w, v** tended to open into semi-vowels :—

(i) *Prae-consonantal* and *intervocalic* ȷ and **w** opened to i̯ and u̯ respectively in Early Middle English, cf. above § 1124.

(ii) In the course of the thirteenth and fourteenth centuries v, preceding a consonant in the interior of a word, opened to u̯ which either merged in the preceding vowel or combined with it in a diphthong, cf. M.E. *lordes* < *lovrdes* (Luick, § 428).

§ 1129. In the consonantal groups consisting of *fricative* consonants + **r, l, n, m**, in the interior of a word and in the *post-tonic* group **ls**, a vocalic glide (e) developed in the course of the later twelfth and thirteenth centuries, cf. M.E. *evere* < *evre*, *develes* < *devles*, *boseme* < *bosme*, *redeles* < *redels* (Luick, §§ 448, 449).

Section 8.—INFLUENCE OF INTENSIFIED TONIC STRESS ON UNSTRESSED VOWELS.

§ 1130. Under the influence of the English speech-habits the main expiratory accent was intensified considerably and under this influence the development of the less stressed syllables was very considerably modified : (i) reductions carried out in francien only in Middle or Modern French were considerably accelerated and thus ę became unstable in *all* positions before the middle of the thirteenth century ; (ii) secondary stressed syllables lost value and their vowels were sometimes assimilated to the tonic vowel, sometimes confused or slurred ; (iii) unstressed and secondary stressed ę was sometimes raised (cf. § 1140).

Very similar developments are found in Middle English (§§ 1126, 1127) and some find parallels in the north and north-east of France, the region in which the tonic stress was strongest, N. §§ iv, x, xi, N.E. § vi. Graphical suppression of *e* often followed on its effacement.

(1) *Acceleration of Reductions of Unstressed Syllables.*

[For Continental French cf. Pt. II, chap. v, sections 7 and 9 ; for effacement of unstressed **e** in Middle English, cf. § 1126.]

§ 1131. *Vowels in Hiatus.*—(i) Countertonic vowels coalesced with juxtaposed tonic vowels that were homophonous or nearly so in the course of the twelfth century :—

a : a, a : ā > a, ā : *Q.L.R. asmer* < *aasmer* (< *aesmer* < **adaestimare*), *granter* < *graanter* (< **credentare*), (cf. also *aler* for *a aler*, *Brendan*, 160).

u : u, u : ū > u, ū : *cule* < *cuule, espunter* < *espuunter* (< *espaenter*, § 239, *Boeve*, p. 178), *runz* (*rotundus*) *Q.L.R.* (cf. also *Brendan*, *õus* 1604, *põust* 1658, *õusum* 766, *Intr.* p. xlviii, Late A.N. *pums* (< *puums*), T. p. 194).

e (ę) : ę, ę : ē > (ę̄, ẽ) *Q.L.R. veaus* < *veeaus, Donnei, lel* < *leel, sete* < *seete* (< *saiete*), *leinz* < *leeinz* (< *laienz*).

a : e, a : ēi > e, ēi : *Q.L.R. cheles* < *chaeles, cheines* < *chaeines.*

[For ę : ę cf. § 1139 ; for verb-forms cf. §§ 1287, 1288.]

§ 1132. (ii) Intertonic and countertonic ę, in hiatus with *following* tonic vowels, and intertonic ę in hiatus with *preceding* countertonic vowels, were ordinarily effaced in the course of the later twelfth century :—

-ęur < -atōrem > -ur, -ęūrę < -atūra > -ürę: *Q.L.R. vesture* < *vesteüre*, II, 18, *bonurez* I, 1 cf. also *emperur* < *empereür, prechur, alure*, St. *Edmund, salurez* 3952, etc. ; *sur* < *seür, juner* < *jeüner*.

[For verb-forms cf. §§ 1287-1289 ; for retention or re-introduction of forms with ę under Continental influence cf. § 1194; for graphical suppression of *e* cf. *Boeve*, p. 178.]

§ 1133. (iii) Final ę, in hiatus with a preceding tonic vowel, was ordinarily effaced in the course of the later twelfth and early thirteenth centuries, earliest when ę was juxtaposed to tonic -ę or ę (< **ai** or **ei** ; cf. *Boeve*, p. l).

ęę > ē̦ : espęę > espē̦, ęę (< **aetatem**) > ē̦, portęę > portē̦.

ęę > ē̦ : aię > ęę > ē̦, **veraię** > vręę > vrē̦ ; seię > sęę > sē̦, **porreię** > porręę > porrē̦.

ię > ī : mię > mī, finię > finī.

uę > ū : rūę > ru (*roue*).

üę > ǖ : rüę > rü.

[For verb-forms cf. § 1292 ; for retention or re-introduction of ę under Continental influence cf. § 1194 ; for graphical suppression of *e* cf. *Boeve*, p. 181.]

§ 1134. (iv) Intertonic and countertonic **i** in hiatus with following tonic vowels consonantalised early (cf. N. § xi) and **ję** was reduced here as elsewhere to ę : *Fantosme* **vjāndę** < **viāndę**; **purrjęts** *purriętz* < **purriëts.**

(*Diable* was frequently replaced by *deable* or *daiable* (**dęablę**), under the influence of English *defol* and **deable** levelled to **dęblę**, cf. *deble : fieble* (§ 1223), *Purg. Patr.* 575.)

In *interconsonantal* position the effacement of ę began also in the twelfth century, earliest in the forms *fras, frat, frez*, etc. (*Brendan*, p. xlvii, cf. *Boeve*, p. 178).

Later on the effacement of ę in this position was often restricted by the dislike of sound-groups consisting of *consonant* + **r** (cf. § 1173).

§ 1135. *Final post-consonantal* ę began to become unstable in the thirteenth century and was more and more frequently effaced (cf. Suchier, *St. Auban*, pp. 36-37, N.E. § vi).   Words with and without final ę are already grouped together in the same laisses in *Boeve*, laisse cx, *derere, eyre : destrer, mounter*, etc., pp. 181, 182 ; cf. also Bozon, *Char, derer : cher* 29, *sens : il pens* 115, *escris : mespris* (3 sg.) 503, *sal* (for *salle*) : *mal* 395.

The late twelfth century form *sir* for *sire* is presumably a prae-vocalic form generalised.   [For graphical suppression of *e* cf. *Boeve*, p. 181.]

§ 1136. (2) *Other Modifications.*—The predominance of the tonic syllable in the pronunciation of the word led to some further modifications of the less stressed syllables :

§ 1137. (i) Initial syllables were more and more frequently weakened and slurred : *acater* > *cater*, *afubler* > *fubler*, *acoillir* > *coillir*, *apeler* > *peler*, *areignes* > *reignes*, *achoison* > *choison*, *e(s)maier* > *maier*, *e(s)chape* > *chape*, etc. (cf. *Boeve*, xliii-xliv, Such. *St. Aub.* 34-35). The process was facilitated by the syneresis of preposition and initial a- (cf. § 242), by the instability of prosthetic e (cf. § 1106), and the growing hesitation about word division, cf. *la chaison* for *l'achaison*, *la vant pie* for *l'avant pie*, *lo spital* for *l'ospital.*

§ 1138. (ii) Prefixes were often interchanged, e.g. *amaier*, *affraier* for *e(s)maier*, *e(s)fraier*, *envalez* for *avalez*, *aplaé* for *empleié* (cf. *Boeve*, xliv and §§ 1152, 1177).

§ 1139. (iii) Unstressed and secondary stressed vowels were more often assimilated to the tonic ones, e.g. *busuign, espurun, musure, provost, trubucher, acravanté, assagé (assegié)*, (cf. *Boeve*, p. 177) : ẹ-ę was differentiated to i-e, e.g. **bier** < **bẹęr** (< *badare* infl. by the strong radical, § 927).

§ 1140. (iv) Weakly stressed vowels, e.g. final or intertonic ę, were sometimes raised to i in Later Anglo-Norman, cf. *Ipom. ostilee, leidiment, Boeve*, MS. D, *cheynis, gagis*, pp. 183, 177, and above, § 1127.
[For *chival, orison*, etc., cf. §§ 1200, N. § xviii.]

Section 9.—PRONUNCIATION OF VOWELS.

§ 1141. *Labial Vowels.*—The French sound-system of the late eleventh century contained three labial vowels. In the western region these were ǫ, u, ü (§ 1083); in the northern the two highest were apparently still nearer Early Old French ǫ and u (§ 1087) : the western pronunciation was, however, dominant in Anglo-Norman.

In the twelfth century ö was added by the levelling of the diphthongs **ue** (§ 551) and **eu** (§ 542).

In the later twelfth and thirteenth centuries ǫ developed out of ǭ, lengthened by the effacement of s (§ 580) before ž, z or v (§ 579) or in hiatus (§ 578).

§ 1142. **ü.**—In English speech there was much divergence in the use and quality of the ü and u-sounds (cf. Luick, § 412) ; in French there was divergence in the extent of the palatalisation of the ü- sound (cf. § 183). The result was a very varying pronunciation of the sound ü, conditioned, apparently, mainly by the local variations of the sound in English.

(i) Velarisation of ü to u appears early and is frequent, e.g. *Brendan*, *murs : flurs*, etc., (*Intr.* cxlix, cl) ; *Adam, criator : dur* 231 ; *Boeve*, laisse clxxxv, *ducz : venus : joius : tuz*. It appears to be this pronunciation that is most in vogue in the northern region, in which English ü was strongly palatalised and so differentiated from French ü.

(ii) In the midlands and south, ü appears to have been ordinarily retained and later developed into **ju,** the line of development followed by Middle English **iw** and **eow** (§ 1125), cf. spellings such as Bozon, *Contes, vewe* (< *veue*) 56, *fyute* 27, and the Modern English pronunciation of *duke, pew* (< A.N. **pü** < **püi**), *puny* (< *puis nez*), etc.

(iii) Occasionally, and early, unrounding to **i** is found (the process followed in the tenth and eleventh centuries in many regions in the development of O.E. **ü**, cf. Luick, § 287), e.g. *lune : embolisme Comp.* 191 ; *Oak Book, pelire* (for *pelure*), *alym* (*Suppl.* p. 23, cf. *aubin*, § 458), Modern English *pedigree* (< *pied de grue*).

§ 1143. ö.—In Later Anglo-Norman Later O.F. ö (< **ue, eu,** §§ 542, 551), like English ö (< **eo**, § 1121), was sometimes unrounded to **e,** cf. Modern English *jeopardy* **džepędi** < **džöparti** *jeuparti*.

§ 1144. ǫ > u.—In Later Anglo-Norman, as in southern and (south-) western French (§ 581), ǫ lengthened and closed through ọ to u before **v, š** and effaced **s,** cf. *toust, ouste* (< *tost, oste*), *Boeve*, p. 110 ; Bozon, *houtele,* (*hostel*), *O.* 144, *ouster, Contes*, p. 91, *pouches, Char,* 458.

[For M.E. passage of ǫ to u cf. § 1122.]

§ 1145. *Oral Vowels.*—The three e-sounds (ĕ, ę̆, ẹ̆) in use in tonic syllables in Early Old French were reduced to two in the course of the twelfth century in Anglo-Norman as in Continental French (§ 575) by the opening of ĕ (< L.L. ę *blocked*) to ę, earliest before **r** + *consonant* : *Brendan, cerne : verne* 8734, Adgar, *recet : net, ancele : bele* (cf. Vising, 'Die e-Laute im Reime der A. N. Dichter des xii[ten] Jahrhunderts,' *Zts. frz. Spr.* XXXIX, 1-17, and above, § 1118).

§ 1146. In west French ę̆ (< **a** tonic free) began to open to ę before **l** and **r** in the course of the thirteenth century (W. § ix). In Anglo-Norman this tendency showed itself perceptibly earlier, cf. Thomas, *leele : damisele* 1375 ; *Dermot, retraire : manere* 388 (cf. Vising, op. cit. p. 8). English influence may have been influential in the acceleration of the opening of ę before **l,** but not apparently before **r,** for in this position both in the native English words and in Anglo-Norman loan-words in English, Early Middle English appears to have used ę.

§ 1147. In Later Anglo-Norman as in Later Middle English (§ 1123) and Middle French (§ 496) ę tended to open to a before r, cf. Boeve, 532 *sarrez* (*serrez*), *Lettres A.F.* No. 6 *sarra* (*sera*). As on the Continent (§ 497) this pronunciation appears to have provoked a reaction for spellings in which *e* replaces *a* before *r* are not uncommon, e.g. *erceveske, mercher* (Boeve, p. 172).

§ 1148. The Later Anglo-Norman palatalisation of **a** to **ę** (spelling *e*, *ai*) needs further investigation, for it may be due to the influence of the Continental (dialectal) palatalisation of **a** to **ę** before š, ž and **s** (E. § xv) or to the more general palatalisation of **a** that had its beginnings in Middle English (cf. Wyld, §§ 219, 225).

§ 1149. *Nasalised Vowels.*—In the western region in the late eleventh century the nasalisation of the low vowels **a** and **e** and their diphthongs **ai** and **ei** had become audible before nasal consonants in all positions in a word, although less complete before nasal consonants that were inter-vocalic (§ 432). Prae-consonantal nasal consonants were not as yet absorbed in the vowels they had nasalised (§ 436), but final and prae-consonantal **m** was already dentalising to **n,** except possibly before labial consonants (§ 435).

In the course of the twelfth century audible nasalisation was extended to **u** and **ję** (e.g. **mūnt, bjēn**), and later on to the high vowels **i** and **ü** (§§ 434, 452, 456, 464, 471).

§ 1150. In Early Middle English the audible nasalisation of vowels was unfamiliar and it seems probable that in Early Anglo-Norman the process was retarded and consequently neither carried ordinarily to the point of absorption of the nasal consonant in the nasal vowel in final and præ-consonantal positions, nor extended to the vowels **i** and **ü**. Dentalisation of final **m** to **n** may also have been checked.

Persistence of the præ-consonantal nasal consonant is indicated by the relatively frequent use of *m* before labial consonants, e.g. *emfes* (Boeve, p. 216).

§ 1151. In Later Anglo-Norman the nasalisation of the low vowels was gradually lessened also, but it is difficult to determine with any accuracy the date of the complete disappearance of the phenomenon, as few rhymes are really significant, those sometimes quoted to attest it —between words containing vowels before intervocalic and final nasals (e.g. between *plein, main* **plēn, męn** and *pleine, meine* **plęn(ę), pēn(ę)**)— being valueless for this purpose because in Old French vowels were nasalised before intervocalic nasals as well as elsewhere (§ 432). A rule of the *Orthographia Gallica* appears to indicate continuance of nasalisation at the date of its composition, the late thirteenth century : ' *Bone mulieres, bones femmes* et debent sonari *bons femmes* et tunc *n* [debet] sonari semi-plene . . . ,' C.O. 51, p. 15, and this rule is not contradicted by the use of rhymes between -*uns*, -*unt* and -*us*, -*ut* (W. Wadington *veums : gelus, seums : nus,* cf. Tanquerey, p. 188) or the confusion between *religiuns* and *religius* (Bozon, *Char*, 202, *Plainte* 87) because in Middle

French the nasalisation of ū appears also to have been often disregarded (§ 464). Rhymes employed by Langtoft, who couples *estey(e)nt* and *fesey(e)nt* with *ceint* (Tanquerey, p. 270), are possibly more significant and it is probable that by the middle of the fourteenth century denasalisation was very general.

A weakness or disappearance of nasalisation is also indicated by the rather frequent suppression of the prae-consonantal nasal consonant in Later Anglo-Norman, e.g. *Ipomedon*, MS. A, *quoites, cutent, remet* (*remanet*), *meit* (*manet*), *vettre* (*veintre*), etc., cf. *Boeve*, p. 217, and by the tendency to denasalise partially prae-consonantal **m** to **p**, not only in borrowed words such as *dampner*, but also in the termination *-oms* **-ums,** e.g. *priomps, osomps* (*Literae Cantuarienses* 1363), T. p. 181.

§ 1152. *Velarisation of* ā.—In the spelling of words containing ā (which was ordinarily in Anglo-Norman, as in western French, distinct from ẹ̄, cf. W. § viii) the graphy *aun* comes into use in the early thirteenth century in words in which the vowel was pronounced in the same syllable as the nasal consonant, e.g. First *Prose Lapidary* (XIII[1]), *enchauntement*, p. 97, *braunches, luisaunte*, p. 98. Examples are found in the French loan-words in Middle English texts (e.g. the *Ancren Riwle*), as well as in Anglo-Norman texts.

The value of this spelling is not yet determined, but it is probable that it represents the gradual velarisation and rounding of the sound through ā̆ to ǭ: (ɔ:), the stage reached in Later Anglo-Norman, to judge from spellings found in both Anglo-Norman and Middle English MSS., e.g. Bozon, *Contes*, pp. xxxviii, 169 *daunyer, dauneour* for earlier *donier, doneour* (A.N. forms of O.F. loan-words from the southern French, cf. § 54), Bozon, *Char*, 246, *esquinauncye*, MS. C, and *la quinoncie̜*, MS. O ; *Ayenbite of Inwyt, chonge, penonce* (cf. Prior, *A.N. Texts*, p. xxiii).

Middle English, in which ā̆ also velarised and rounded, § 1120, probably contributed to this velarisation, but a like development of ā is attested in Later Middle French in the western and northern regions of France (cf. W. § viii, N. § xx, and *Kastner Miscellany*, pp. 401-402).

[Cf. for variant interpretations of the spelling, Luick, 414 (2), Wyld, *Short History of English* (3), § 184, Menger, 48, Prior, xxii-xxiii ; and for the use of *au* to represent ǭ, cf. § 536.]

§ 1153. *Velarisation of* **a** *before effaced* **s.**—It seems probable that the effacement of prae-consonantal **s** induced compensatory lengthening of the previous vowel in Anglo-Norman as in Continental French (cf. § 564), and this appears to have been followed by an early velarisation of **a** to **ɑ** and even ǭ̄, for in late Anglo-Norman spellings such as *chaustel, bauston, tauster, portaustes, trovaustes* are not infrequent (cf. *Boeve*, 173, Tanquerey, 204), the spelling **au** being apparently carried over from the

representation of ā (§ 1152).   This velarised pronunciation appears to be
that indicated in rules H. 32 and C.O. 67 in the *Orthographia Gallica* :
'Et a la foithe escriveretz *s* en lieu de *u* come *ascun, blasmer*, etc., et
serra sone *aucun* (i.e. ǭkün (?)).' H. 32, p. 8.

[For velarisation of ā in later Continental French cf. § 586.]

Diphthongs.

§ 1154.   In eleventh-century French of the northern region, as
was noted above, diphthongs remained intact and falling; in the
western region levelling had begun, both by mutual association of the
two elements (**ai** > ẹ, W. § ii), and by shift of stress and consonantalisation of the first element ('**ie** > ɪẹ, W. § i); in Later Old French
levelling went on in both regions by both processes (§§ 509-556).   The
diphthongs of the English sound-system were also all descending, and
levelling was in process here also but it proceeded mainly by assimilation
or by the effacement of the second element (§ 1125).   In Anglo-Norman,
as may be expected, levelling of diphthongs is as marked as in Old
French, but the processes mainly employed are those in vogue in Middle
English—assimilation and effacement of the second element—and shift
of stress plays a less important part than on the Continent.

§ 1155.   '**ie**.—In the western region '**ie** was passing to ɪẹ at the time
of the Conquest (cf. W. § i), and in the more south-westerly region ɪẹ was
levelling to ẹ in the early twelfth century (cf. W. § i); the use of ɪ after
consonants was unfamiliar in English speech and consequently the passage of ɪẹ to ẹ and of ɪē to ē was greatly accelerated in insular French
and from the later twelfth century on becomes a marked feature of
Anglo-Norman, cf. Comput, *marchels : icels* 551 ; *Debat, desconseillee : nee*,
presenter : mestier, etc. (Vising, 'Die e-Laute im Reime der A. N.
Dichter,' *Zts. frz. Spr. u. Lit.* XXXIX, 11-14, *Boeve*, p. 203).
[For the northern reduction of '**ie** to **i** cf. § 513 ; for the re-introduction of ɪe < **ie** cf. § 1189.]

§ 1156.   '**ue**.—In twelfth-century French '**ue**, a falling diphthong in the
late eleventh century, was gradually levelled to ö in the central region,
to ö or **u** in the northern and to ɥẹ (> ẹ) in the western (§§ 551-554,
W. § vii).   In Anglo-Norman three pronunciations became current :
(i) '**ue** was retained as a falling diphthong and subsequently levelled to
u (written *u* or *o*), e.g. *Q.L.R. repruce, jufnes, estuce ; Brendan* MSS.
buf, bofs, iluches, ilokes, muvet, movet, puple, fuilles, foilles, orgul, orgoil
(cf. Waters, p. 159) ; Bozon, *Char, fure* (< *fuerre*) : *cure, sure*, 85.
(ii) Western French ɥẹ was adopted, especially after **k** or **g**, cf.
quer : penser (**kɥẹr** < **kuer** : **pēnsẹr**), (cf. Vising, op. cit. 8) ; Angier,

muere : tere, demuere : requerre, veil (< *vueil* v**ụẹ**]) : *soleil, Etude,* p. 16 ; *St. Auban, duel, lincel : el, ostel,* etc., laisse xxxviii.

(iii) Central and northern ö was also adopted, (spelling *ue, oe, eo,* e.g. *queur, peuple, peot,* etc., cf. *Boeve,* p. 28).

In later Anglo-Norman the reduced form e is also not infrequent, derived either from (**ụ**)**ẹ** (§ 553) or from ö, unrounded under English influence (§ 1121), e.g. *Cam. A.N. Texts,* C, *ef* < *uef* 53, *evre, preve* 851, Bozon, *Char, contrevent* (< *contruevent*) 355, (cf. Modern English *contrive*).

§ 1157. *Diphthongs in -i.*—**ai** *prae-consonantal,* which was maintained as a falling diphthong in Northern French of the eleventh century (§ 533), was already then passing through **ẹi** to **ẹ** in the western region, (W. § ii), and it is this latter pronunciation which was dominant in Anglo-Norman, e.g. *Comp. beste : paistre,* Gaimar, *terre : faire,* (cf. Suchier, *Gr.* 27 (*c*)).

ai *final* and *in hiatus.*—In Northern French **ai** (**aɪ** ?) *final* and *in hiatus* was maintained ; in Western French pronunciation appears to have varied regionally between **ai**, **ẹ** and **ẹ** (§§ 530-533) : in Anglo-Norman **ai** (**aɪ** ?) and **ẹ** (**ẹi** ?) appear to have been used indiscriminately, and in the later period **ai** was often reduced to **a** : Chardri, *truvai : mei,* S.D. 1209, *Boeve, sai : mei, curtays,* etc., *Sermon, saie (seta) : raie* 1360, *sai, (sei) : lai* 400, *Lettres A.F. eons, ehoms, eye,* Nos. 19, 30, 68 ; *ael,* No. 68, *pae* 13, etc., *osera ge* 40 (cf. *Boeve,* p. 195, N. § vii, and for reduction in Middle English, § 1125).

§ 1158. ei, (as in the western region (W. § 6) but more rapidly), was levelled to **ẹ** in the course of the late twelfth and thirteenth century, e.g. Simund, *estre : crestre* ; Chardri, *tollet : deget, tere : crere* (cf. Vising, op. cit. p. 16). The M.E. opening of **ẹi** to **ẹi** (§ 1119) may have contributed to this result.

[For Continental French **oi** < **ei** cf. § 226 ; for the infinitive termination *-eir* cf. § 1309.]

§ 1159. The nasal diphthongs **ãi** and **ẽi** developed as in the western and central region (§ 466) but rather more rapidly :—

(1) In the first half of the twelfth century **ãi** and **ẽi** fell together under a common sound, presumably **ẹ̃i**, e.g. *Brend. funtaines : pleines* 1002.

(2) In the later twelfth century **ẹ̃i** was levelled to **ẹ̃** and in the thirteenth century the spellings *ein, ain, en* are interchangeable, (§ 1224), cf. *Adam, defens : mains* 149, Gaimar, *meins : tens* (cf. Matzke, p. 645).

§ 1160. ¹**üi**, introduced as a falling diphthong (§ 515), was ordinarily levelled early to **ü** (**u**, § 1142), e.g. *Brendan, ru(i)stes : justes* 41, Chardri,

Jos. cestu : aparceu 219, *lu : venu* 937, *nut* (*nuit*) *: dut* 2783. After **k**, as on the Continent (§ 503), the stress shifted ordinarily and *cui* **küi** > **kẅi, küirę** > **kẅirę**, and as in western French (W. § iv) this shift is also sometimes found elsewhere, cf. *destruire : ire, Best.* 805, *quire* (*cuire*) *: sire, Brend.* 1579.

[For -**üs** < -**üŝ** cf. § 1086.]

§ 1161. **ǫi** and **ui** (**ǫi**).—In the diphthong derived from the combination of Early Old French **ǫ** with **ɪ** two pronunciations appear to have had vogue : **'ui** and **'ǫi**, the first presumably western, the second northern (§§ 1083, 1087). The M.E. tendency to eliminate the palatal element of diphthongs in -**ɪ** before certain consonants (§ 1125) appears sometimes to have modified their development.

(i) **'ui**, introduced as a falling diphthong, was levelled to **u**, cf. Adgar, *croiz : deduiz*, p. 60, l. 79, *Hue Linc. chanoin : procession, croiz : Jus* (Uhlemann, p. 585), but after **k** and **g** and in unstressed syllables stress was sometimes shifted and **wi** subsequently reduced to **i**, thus O.F. *anguisse* **āng'uisę** > **āngwisę,** *kuilte* **kuiltę** (< **kuɪtę,** § 1182) > **kwiltę,** (*re*)*cuillir,* (**rę**)**kuilir** (< (**re**)**kuɪir,** § 1182) > (**rę**)**kwilir,** (*re*)*quillir, cunuissant* **kunuisant** > **kun(w)isant.**

(ii) **ǫi** fell in with **ǫi** (< **au** + **ɪ** and **ei,** § 226) in the later twelfth century, e.g. Chardri, *Jos. croix : foiz* 2847, and remained as a falling diphthong except when influenced by the Continental change to **ųę,** § 519.

[For spelling cf. §§ 1223, 1226.]

§ 1162. Diphthongs and triphthongs in -**ų** were formed in Continental French :—

(1) In the course of Period I, by the combination of **ę, i, ie, ue** with **ų** from vocalised prae-consonantal **w** and **γ** (§§ 328, 359) and with **ų** *final* (§ 254), e.g. **siut, riulę** (< **ręulę**), **Dieu,** *cieu* **tsieu, *fueu,** **sarkueu** (< **sarkǫfų**), § 341.

(2) In the course of the eleventh and twelfth centuries by the combination of the vowels **a, ę, ĕ, ē, ǫ, 'ie, 'ue** with -**ų** from vocalised prae-consonantal **ɫ** and **ʝ** (§§ 387, 388): **a + ų, ĕ + ų, ǫ + ų** resulting in the diphthongs **au, eu, ǫu; ĕ + ų, ē + ų, 'ie + ų, 'ue + ų, 'üe + ų** in the triphthongs **'ęau, 'ieu, 'ueu, 'üeu.**

In the development of this second set of diphthongs and triphthongs divergence arose between insular and ordinary French usage mainly because the stage reached on the Continent in the late eleventh century persisted late in Anglo-Norman, the diphthongs **ęų** and **ēų** remaining without glide developments (cf. the spellings *beus, beute, teus,* etc.) and the triphthongs **'ieu, 'ueu, 'üeu** continuing stressed on the first element. The influence of northern French pronunciation, N. § vii, and of English contributed to this tardiness in development.

§ 1163. **au.**   The diphthong **au** remained at first but was ordinarily reduced in Later Anglo-Norman to **a** (**ɑ** ?) before labial and labialised consonants (i.e. **tš** and **dž**, cf. § 1125), *Lettres A.F.*, *savement*, Nos. 1, 162, *saf* 164, *Boeve*, *chivachier* 1022, etc.

§ 1164. **ĕu** and **ēu.**   The diphthong **ēu** from **ẹ** (< a *tonic free*) + **ɫ** persisted ordinarily as **ēy̆** (ct. § 388) and like **ĕy̆** from **ĕ** *blocked* + **ɫ** was labialised to **ö** (cf. § 542), e.g. *St. Auban*, *teus*, *morteus : jieus : eus*, etc., xl, *St. George*, *teus : deus* (*dĕōs*) 344, *deus* (*dŭōs*) *: ceus* 279, *eus* 608.

§ 1165. **ẹy̆** and **'ẹau** (< **ẹ** + **ɫ**) :

(1) When **ẹy̆** was retained it was either levelled to **ö** like **ĕy̆**, e.g. *St. Auban*, *nuveus*, *aigneus : jieus*, *Deus*, etc., xl, and later on unrounded to **ẹ**, cf. Modern English *Beauchamp* **Bitšam**, or, like M.E. **ẹy̆**, it was differentiated to **iu > ju** (§ 1125), cf. Modern English *ewer* (< *ewiere*), *sewer* (< *sewiere*), *beauty*.

(2) When the triphthong **'ẹau** was developed as in Continental French, (§ 388), stress was sometimes shifted and **'ẹau** became **au,** e.g. *Cam. Ps. ruissals*, *Q.L.R. helme* and *halme* (< *healme*), cʳ. § 539. Occasionally, as in northern French (N. § viii), **'ẹau** was differentiated to **iau.**

§ 1166. **'iu** passed early to **ju** which was often reduced to **u,** e.g. *sut* < *siut*, *rule* < *riule*, *lu* < *liu*, cf. *Boeve*, p. 204.

§ 1167. **ọu** (< **ọ** + **ɫ**) was levelled to **u** as in Continental French (§ 548), e.g. **fọus** < **fus.**

§ 1168. **'ieu.**   The triphthong **'ieu** was sometimes, as in western and central French (§ 545), levelled to **jö** (> **ö**), e.g. *St. Auban*, *jieus : eus* xl; more often as in the northern region (N. § vi) reduced to **'iu,** which passed ordinarily through **ju** to **u, lieu > liu > lu,** *gieu* **džieu > džiu > džu** *giu.*   The spelling *iw* found when **iu** was in hiatus, e.g. *R. Phil. ciwe* 297, *Adgar, Gywesse*, p. 25, 184, is probably a simple graphy for **ju** (cf. § 1125).

§ 1169. **'ueu.**   The earlier triphthong **ueu** (**üeu** (?)) (< **ue** + **y̆** final) was either labialised to **ö** (§ 556) or as in northern French (N. § vi) reduced to **ü** (> **u**), cf. *Adgar, fu : ennu*, p. 26, *St. Georges, fu : vertu* 219, *St. Auban sarcu : lu* (*lupum*).

The later triphthong **'ueu** (< **ue** + *vocalised* **ɫ** and **ɫ̦**, § 387) remained ordinarily undifferentiated to **'ieu** (§§ 556, 557), and was either levelled to **ö** (spelling *ueu, oeu, oe, eo*, etc., § 1229) or reduced to **u,** (spelling *u, o, ou*), e.g. *Adgar, genuilz : oilz*, p. 84, 103, *Chardri, ouz* (for *oculos*), S.D. 1164 : ue**ɫ** appears also to have been sometimes reduced to **ʲue,** whence **y̆ẹ,** written at times *oi* (§ 1223), cf. *Boeve*, MS. D, *vois* for earlier *vuels* 2616, *voit* (*vuelt*) 979, etc.

Quantitative Differentiation.

§ 1170. In Early Old French quantitative differences appear to have played no part in the differentiation of any vowels except the e-*sounds* (§§ 573, 233), but in the course of Later Old and Middle French vowels appear to have been lengthened by the effacement of following consonants, (e.g. *prae-consonantal* s, z, § 564) or *unstressed* ę (§ 562). In Middle English most vowels were differentiated by length (§ 1115) and quantitative differences appear to have been gradually established in Later Anglo-Norman, mainly on the lines of the English quantitative differences, i.e. long vowel in open syllables, short vowel in blocked ones : *māle, frēre, rōbe—tĕns, entĕnt* (cf. Luick, § 413). There was, however, some hesitation—

(1) Before single consonants, e.g. *bĕk, nĕt, bŭt.*

(2) Before the affricates tš and dž, e.g. *rŏche, lŏge.*

(3) Before such intervocalic groups of consonants as might be pronounced as initial of the following syllable, e.g. *prŏfre.*

(4) Before r + *consonant,* e.g. *părt.*

Secondary stressed vowels appear to have been ordinarily pronounced short.

[For the use of double consonants to indicate short or shortened vowels cf. § 1217 ; for the use of double vowels to indicate long or lengthened vowels cf. § 1235 ; for the use of inorganic s to indicate lengthened vowels cf. § 1236.]

Glide Developments.

§ 1171. *Vowels in Hiatus.*—Anglo-Norman moved more rapidly than Continental French in the reduction of vowels in hiatus (§ 1130) but when in any words hiatus was retained or when, under Continental influence (§ 1194), a fuller pronunciation of juxtaposed vowels was attempted, the process was often facilitated by the development of an intervocalic glide sound, ȷ between palatal vowels, w between or after the rounded velar vowels ; e.g. *deveyer < deveër (devetare), leyens < leënz (illac intus), seyens, espeie, jorneie, feie < feē (fata) ; cowardie, cordewan, owe < oë appower < appoer (*appodiare), nuwe* (cf. *Boeve*, pp. 220, 237, 238).

In this tendency Anglo-Norman resembles the French of the north-eastern region (cf. N.E. § xiv).

[For the graphical intercalation of *h* cf. § 1237.]

§ 1172. i and e + r.—On the Continent, particularly in the western region, there was a tendency to facilitate the juxtaposition of i to r by the development of a low vocalic glide (W. § xi), e.g. *cierge, vierge, dierre, ociere* and in Anglo-Norman the same practice is observable not only between i and r (e.g. *dierre, fierent* for *firent*) but also between ę̄ and

r in words in which the high value of the vowel ę was maintained or introduced under Continental influence, e.g. frę̧erę̧ (cf. Modern English *friar*).

§ 1173. **v, f, t, d + r.**—As in the northern region of France (N. § xiii) and to some extent in Middle English (§ 1129), the juxtaposition of **v, f, t, d** and **r** was disliked and often obviated by the development of an intervening vocalic glide ; between voiced consonants and **r** this practice was already in vogue in the later twelfth century, cf. *Q.L.R. severad* 1, 2, *deseniveras* 15, *overouent* 3, 13 ; *Boeves*, B. *averai, vinderent, perderez, ankeres* (*ancres*), etc., p. 179.

<h3 align="center">Section 10.—CONSONANTS.</h3>

§ 1174. Consonantal sounds in the sound-system of the late eleventh and twelfth centuries, which were discarded or modified on the Continent, persisted later in Anglo-Norman when they found support in the English sound-system : consonants which found no such support were gradually modified.

Consonants Maintained.

§ 1175. **θ and ð.**—The western French sound-system of the late eleventh century still included **θ** and **ð**, derived from two sources :—

(i) Gallo-Roman **t** and **d** *intervocalic* or **+ r, l, v**, or *final* under certain conditions (§§ 333, 335, 372, 356), e.g. *vide* **viðę̧** (< *vita*), *pedre* **peðrę̧**, *vedve* **veðvę̧**, *feit* **feiθ**, *portet* **portę̧θ, portę̧θ.**

(ii) Eleventh century prae-consonantal **z** (< **s**) + *voiced consonants* and from **s + f** (§§ 377, 378), e.g. *medler* **meðler**, *adne* **aðnę̧**, *idle* **iðlę̧**, **eðreiier.**

§ 1176. The treatment of the sounds **θ** and **ð** in words of the first type in Anglo-Norman appears to be approximately that found in Western French, the Continental region in which they appear to have persisted latest (§ 347). Both sounds appear to have become obsolete in the beginning of the twelfth century, for they play no part in the rhymes of the *Bestiaire*, cf. *vie : Marie, mue : manjue, fei : lei, ni* (< *nidum) : autresi, signefie : Marie* ; on the other hand, the verbal termination -ę̧ < -ę̧θ so often retains syllabic value before words beginning with a vowel in the earlier Anglo-Norman texts, that it would appear that the disuse of **θ** was relatively recent, and this conclusion is supported by the spelling of English loan-words, in which a final dental sound (**ð** or **θ**) is often represented by **d, ð, th** or **þ**, (Behrens, p. 175). To judge from the frequent use of *d* to represent the final sound, e.g. *ad, fud, oïd, vertud*, **θ** was voiced to **ð** before effacement.

§ 1177. The more recently developed prae-consonantal ð-*sound*
appears to have been, however, longer lived than on the Continent :—

(i) The use of the symbol *d* is very consistent in the best early A.N.
MSS., e.g. *Q.L.R. adnes* ix, 3, *chaidne* x, 3, *podnee* xv, 20, *vadlez* xxvi, 23.

(ii) Before labial and dental consonants ð appears to have been
nasalised and preserved (e.g. **enbaïr** for **eðbaïr** < **ezbaïr**, Walberg, *Best.*
lxvi-lxvii), and thus to have contributed to the confusion of the prefixes
es- and *en-*, cf. *Orth. Gall.* C.O. 74, p. 8, ' Item aliquando scribetis *s* in
loco *n*, ut *espernez* pro *enpernez.*'

(iii) English loan-words such as *meddle* (< **meðlẹr**), *medlar* (**meðlier,**
*mespilarium) contain this sound hardened to **d.**

§ 1178. χ and ɪ.—In the development of the groups **z** and **s** +
consonant, **z** and **s** appear to have been frequently either palatalised
or velarised in the eleventh or twelfth centuries (§ 378). On the
Continent this stage was evidently ephemeral, but in Anglo-Norman,
where these consonants found support in the English sound-system, it
left evident trace :—

(i) The palatal fricative ɪ, developed in the groups **zl** and **zn,** induced
the palatalisation of the preceding dental consonants, and thus *isle* **izlẹ**
> **iɪẹ,** *disner* **diznẹr** > **diɲẹr,** cf. *Best. ille : eisille, bruille : uille* and the
spellings *digner, maignee, eimes* (Walberg, *Best.* lxvi).

(ii) The fricatives ç and χ, developed in the group **st,** persisted in
Anglo-Norman into the late thirteenth or fourteenth century, cf. the
spellings *osaht, vousiht, fuht,* etc. (Tanquerey, p. 122, Behrens, pp. 183,
184, § 1216, and the gloss of the *Orthographia Gallica :* ' Et quant *s* est
joynt a la *t* ele avera le soun de *h*, come *est*, *plest* serront sonez *eght,
pleght.*' H. 35, p. 8, cf. H. 91, C.O. 18).

§ 1179. ɫ.—The vocalisation of ɫ (< ɫ and] + *consonant*) was far
advanced at the time of the Norman Conquest and followed ordinarily
in Anglo-Norman the same lines as on the Continent : one or two doublets
among the English loan-words, e.g. M.E. *quyltes, cowltes* (Mod. Eng.
quilt, counterpane), indicate that the final stage of the vocalisation of]
was, however, reached somewhat tardily in insular speech, (cf. also
§§ 1108, 1162, 1164, 1165, 1169).

§ 1180. **w.**—In Continental French of the eleventh and twelfth centuries the fricative labio-velar **w** was effaced after **k** and **g** and shifted to
v or vocalised elsewhere (cf. § 192) ; in Anglo-Norman it appears to have
persisted later ; cf. (i) the spellings *gw, gu, qu, w,* still frequent in MSS.
of the thirteenth and fourteenth centuries, *Boeve*, p. 236, MS. B, *gwenchent,
gwerer*; *Brendan*, p. 166, D, *ewe, ewage, liwe ;* (ii) the pronunciation of
English loan-words such as *squash, squat, ewer, sewer* (< *exaquaria).

[For retention of *initial* **w** cf. § 1093.]

§ 1181. **tš** and **dž**.—The retention of these sounds in the English loan-words (e.g. *judge, John, chance, cheer*) and the use of the symbols *gg, cch* in later Anglo-Norman (*Boeve*, 236, 240), make it probable that these sounds were retained longer in insular speech than on the Continent (cf. § 194), but in Later Anglo-Norman as in Middle French **š** and **ž** were used, the pronunciation **š** being sometimes indicated by the spelling *sch*, e.g. *Oak Book*, II, 16 *aschaut* (*achate*), I, 24 *proschayn*, II, 100 *schochiz* (*choses*).

Consonants Modified.

§ 1182. **ʎ, ŋ**.—The absence of the palatal sounds **ʎ** and **ŋ** in the English sound-system led to early modification of these sounds and they are ordinarily resolved into dental **l** and **n** preceded by a palatal glide. The process began in Early Anglo-Norman, cf. *Brendan, eisil : cil, ːoleil : peil, plein : desdeign, feignent : peinent* (*Intr.* cliv, clvii), but the pronunciation appears to have varied for some time, if one may judge from the practice of individual writers (cf. Menger, § 36). The diphthongs formed in this way developed along ordinary lines (§ 1157-1161) and thus **soleil** and **travail** > **solẹl** and **travẹl, muntāŋẹ** > **muntẹnẹ** (< **muntāinẹ**).

In later Anglo-Norman the occasional confusion of *veier* (*videre*) and *veillier* (T. p. 408) indicates a reduction of **ʎ** to **j**, a curious anticipation of Modern French (cf. § 106).

§ 1183. **ts**.—In western and central French the shift of **ts** to **s** appears to have taken place only in the late twelfth or thirteenth century (§ 194); in the northern region it was earlier (N. § xxi) and also in Middle English. In Anglo-Norman the shift also appears early, cf. *Best. tens : dedenz, meis : feiz, avis : criz, Intr.* p. lxiv, but the practice of individual writers varied for some time.

§ 1184. **r + consonant**.—In Anglo-Norman, as in some regions of France (§ 396) and in Middle English, prae-consonantal **r** was sometimes effaced, cf. *Best. sage : large* 7, *cors : enclos* 291, *Intr.* p. lv, Bozon, *Ste. Agnes, abaundonent : retournent* 61.

§ 1185. **v + consonant**.—In Middle English in the late thirteenth and fourteenth centuries prae-consonantal **v** was ordinarily vocalised to **ṳ**, which either merged in the preceding vowel or combined with it in a diphthong (§ 1128); these processes were sometimes extended to Anglo-Norman, cf. *poure* and *pore < povre, keure chef < keuvre chef, keure fu < keuvre fu* (§ 927 (ii)), *culurs < culuvr(e)s*, *Boeve*, MS. D, 923. [For the late Anglo-Norman doubling of consonants cf. § 1217.]

Section 11.—INFLUENCE OF CONTINENTAL DIALECTS.

§ 1186. The political and commercial relations between England and the Continent went through many changes after the Conquest and these are reflected to some extent in Anglo-Norman pronunciation and still more in Anglo-Norman spelling.

In the twelfth century the accession of the Angevin dynasty and the marriage of Henry II with Eleanor of Aquitaine introduced for a time a close relation between England and the more southerly region of western France. In the later thirteenth century the ties between England and the northern region were strengthened: Ponthieu passed into the possession of the English royal house in 1279 and the wool trade with Flanders grew steadily in magnitude.

Throughout the period, but more especially in the thirteenth and fourteenth centuries, the growing importance of Paris and its speech (§§ 60-65) increased the influence exercised by francien on Anglo-Norman and led in the later fourteenth century to the displacement of Anglo-Norman in literary works by French or Anglo-French.

Influence of Francien.

§ 1187. The influence of francien was strong enough, especially when supported by the northern pronunciation, to influence spelling considerably and to introduce some forms and pronunciations that displaced, partially or wholly, those current in Anglo-Norman which were of western origin.

§ 1188. (1) **oi** for **ei** or **e**.—**oi**, the central and northern French form of the diphthong **ei** (§ 226, W. § vi), sometimes displaced A.N. ẹ < **ei**, e.g. **loial** for earlier lẹạl or lẹẹl (> lẹ̄l), **esploit** for **espleit** (> e(s)plẹt).

Occasionally in the later thirteenth and fourteenth centuries the shift of **oi** to ǫẹ (> wẹ) was also introduced, cf. Bozon, *angweyse*, *Bonté*, 182, and Modern English *squeamish* < O.F. *escoimous*.

§ 1189. (2) **ie, ịe** for **ẹ**.—In spelling, and presumably sometimes in pronunciation, an attempt was made to replace ẹ (ẹ), the A.N. reduced form of **ịe** < the earlier diphthong **ie**, by *ie* (ịe), cf. *Orth. Gall.*, Rule I.

Diccio Gallice dictata habens sillabam primam vel mediam in *e* stricto ore pronunciatam requirit hanc litteram *i* ante *e* (pronunciari) verbi gracia *bien, dieu, mieuz, trechier* (= tres chier), mier. (T. 1, p. 2.)

§ 1190. (3) ẹ̈, the central and northern pronunciation of the **e**-*sound* derived from Latin **a** tonic free before **r** and **l** (§ 1146), replaced sometimes the A.N. pronunciation ẹ, e.g, **frẹrẹ, pẹrẹ, tẹl** for **frẹr(ẹ), pẹr(ẹ), tẹl.**

[For the spelling *ie* cf. § 1223.]

§ 1191. (4) ęu, the twelfth-century central and northern pronuncia-tion of the diphthong ǫu (§ 1085), displaced sometimes the A.N. pro-nunciation u (< ǫu), cf. *Q.L.R. male veue*, *Brendan* B, *deus, leus (lupos)*, p. 158, and Modern English *nephew, lure* (< *leurre*).

[For the passage of ęu to ju cf. § 1125.]

§ 1192. (5) ā for ē.—ā, the lowered pronunciation of ē in use in the central and eastern regions (§ 448), sometimes displaced the western and northern unlowered sound, cf. *Boeve*, laisses vii, xxxv, xxxvii, in which ē and ā are combined and Modern English *pansy, dandelion*.

§ 1193. *Effacement of* r *Final.*—In western French *final* r appears ordinarily to have maintained its articulation (§ 402), but in the eastern and central region it became fricative and was often effaced after the higher vowels ę (ję) and i (§ 400), and in this region the terminations -*er* and -*ez*, -*jer* and -*jers* fell together under ę (§ 401). In Anglo-Norman, as in western French, the articulation of final r was ordinarily maintained and preceding ę opened to ę (§ 402); but in the later period, under the influence of francien, a variant pronunciation, -ę for -**er**, is not infrequent, e.g. in *Boeve*, where both pronunciations appear to be ad-mitted : -ęr in laisses xxi, lv in which *acoler, trover, dreiturer* assonate with *mer, cher, quer*, etc., ę in laisses xvi, liii in which -*er* and -*es* are coupled together.

§ 1194. *Vowels in Hiatus.*—Continental French went more slowly than Anglo-Norman in the reduction of unstressed vowels in hiatus (§ 1130) and one sometimes finds in Later Anglo-Norman a fuller pronunciation of the weaker vowels under the influence of the more conservative Continental speech ; this pronunciation which is sometimes indicated by the intercalation of *h* (§ 1237), appears to have led sometimes to the development of ju glide sounds between the juxtaposed vowels, cf. above, § 1171.

Influence of the South-Western Region.

§ 1195. Isolated forms in the works of some of the writers of the later twelfth and early thirteenth centuries indicate contact with the speech of the south-western region : Anjou, Maine, Touraine :

§ 1196. (1) Spellings such as *s(i)event, s(i)evre, pois, oistre, noit, trois, puesse*, for *sivent, sivre, puis, uistre, nuit, truis, puisse*, in which the product of the group ę and ǫ + *jod* takes one of the forms **ie** or **ei, ue** or **oi** which are proper to the speech of this region (S.W. § i), cf. also *beivre : queivre* (< *kueivre* < **copreum*, Brendan 1416).

§ 1197. (2) Forms in which final t (< the Latin group kt) has dis-appeared, e.g. *lai, plai, entresai, vui, qui*, for *lait, plait, entresait, vuit, quit*, cf. S.W. viii and *Best.* pp. lix, lx.

§ 1198. (3) Isolated forms resulting from a variant treatment of the group **4t** (S.W. § vii), e.g. *avuiltre(s)*, *Q.L.R.* xxvi. 19 ; cf. also *luiriez* (*loθr), *Best.* 177 in which the group **θr** is treated like *intervocalic* **tr** in Provençal.

§ 1199. Of greater importance, in all probability, is the influence that the speech of this region may have exercised on two more wide-spread traits : the effacement of final supported **t** (cf. § 616) ; and the reduction of ȷȩ to ȩ (W. § i), for in both these developments the speech of the more southern region was in advance of that of the rest of France, cf. above, §§ 612, 512, and Gamillscheg and Meyer-Lübke, *Becker Festschrift*, pp. 63 and 135.

Influence of the Northern Region on Later Anglo-Norman.

§ 1200. The closer political and commercial relations entertained with Ponthieu and Flanders in the later thirteenth and fourteenth centuries encouraged the use of northern forms in insular speech and spelling.   Among these may be mentioned :—

(1) Forms in which **a** was palatalised by following **ž** and **s**, e.g. *saige, trespaissent*, cf. E. § xv.

(2) Forms in which countertonic ȩ had been raised to **i** by preceding **tš** or following **ȷ, ʃ, ŋ** (N. § xviii) and in which intertonic **e** had been raised similarly by following **ŝ** and **ẑ** (N. § xviii), e.g. *chival, chivalerie, chiminee* (*Boeve*, p. 177), *fïë, fïeë* (<*vicata), cf. § 422 ; *orison, venison, damisele*, cf. *Boeve*, pp. 200, 205. [For verb forms cf. below, chap. 5.]

Section 12.—INFLUENCE OF SYNTACTICAL PHONETICS.

§ 1201. In Later Old French the newly-developed practice of running together words linked together in the phrase (§§ 171, 611) was already leading to the effacement of final consonants in prae-consonantal position within the phrase.   The consonants first affected were the supported final consonants, final **s** (**z**) and final **l** after **i** (§§ 613, 615, 621, 392).

In Anglo-Norman this tendency made itself evident early because Anglo-Norman spelling was more readily affected by pronunciation than the Continental (§ 1222).

§ 1202. (1) *Final supported consonants :* **k, t, p, f.**—In words such as *donc, grant, champ, cerf* the final supported consonant began to be slurred in prae-consonantal position within the phrase in the later twelfth century. In the south-western region the tendency was increased by the influence of the French spoken in the region further south, in which final **t** was more generally effaced (§ 616, S.W. § viii).   This pronunciation may have accelerated the process in Anglo-Norman, for in MSS. of the later twelfth century there is a noticeable tendency to omit final **t** in this position, cf. *Rol. Digby MS.* ier 556, *quan* 601, *mor* 2030, *sein* 2847, *fier* (< *fiert*) 3603, and Thomas in the *Romance of Horn* allows himself to include

sumun (for *sumunt*) in laisses in *-un*, cf. also *Q.L.R. dun ne me revelai. . ?*
In the thirteenth century the tendency is more pronounced, and in *Boeve*
words such as *donk, Bradmound, mound* are included in the rhymed laisses
in *-un* (xviii, etc.), *sanc, champ* in laisses in *-ant* (xxvii, clxiv).

[For the interchange of final *d* and *t* cf. § 1233.]

§ 1203. (2) *Final Unsupported* s (z).—Effacement of unsupported
final **s** and **z** in prae-consonantal position within the phrase began also
in Later Old French (§ 613), and is represented already in the *Digby
MS.* of *Roland*, e.g. *le chefs* 44, *si cumpainz* 324, *mi sire* 636, etc.; **s** (z ?)
is also occasionally omitted after **ę**, e.g. *fesime* 419, *este* 3497. Rhymes
indicating the extension of this effacement to words used at the pause
begin in the thirteenth century, (cf. *Boeve*, viii, *afie* for *afies* in a rhymed
laisse, xvi, xxviii), and in the fourteenth century graphical effacement is
frequent (*Boeve*, p. 226).

[For absence of flectional **s** cf. § 1246; for the endings -ęz and -ęr
cf. § 1193; for the confusion of *sus* and *sur* cf. § 401.]

§ 1204. (3) *Final* l.—As in Continental French **l** final was effaced in
the thirteenth century after **i** when in prae-consonantal position within
the phrase (§ 841), cf. *Lettres A.F. i ne pount, i ne soient* (1283), *Orth.
Gall.* H. 64: 'Item altrefoithe [escriuerez] *y* litteram pur *si* come *y
vous plęst*,' (p. 14), and Bozon, *Contes, I ne pas* for *Il n'est pas*, p. 62.

In later Anglo-Norman effacement of prae-consonantal **l** was also
very general after **e**, e.g. in *cel* (*Boeve*, 2033, *se chastel*), *nel* (< *ne le*), *del*
and also in *al*, cf. *Boeve*, p. 212.

CHAPTER III.

ORTHOGRAPHY.

Section 1.—INTRODUCTORY.

§ 1205. The unstable and motley character of Anglo-Norman ortho-graphy is the result of several factors. The scribal traditions of three schools conflicted—English, French and Latin ; variant forms were numerous, and though a few eleventh-century archaisms were preserved tradition was weaker than on the Continent and this led at times to a relatively rapid recognition of sound-changes and, especially in Later Anglo-Norman, to a most disconcerting interchange of symbols used with shifted value.

Section 2.—ARCHAISMS.

§ 1206. Early Anglo-Norman MSS. preserve some ways of represent-ing sounds that early became obsolete on the Continent :—

§ 1207-8. (1) The representation of ę by *a*, e.g. *Alexis*, MS. L, *estra* 30*e*, *altra* 32*a*, *perdra* 41*e*, cf. § 697.

§ 1209. (2) Use of the digraph *ch* to represent **k** before **i** and **e**, cf. *Eulalia*, *chi* for **ki**, 12 : this spelling, usual in the *Oxford Psalter*, is found at times in other texts, e.g. *Rol. Digby MS. chi* 596, 838, *unches* 640, 920, etc., *Brendan*, MS. D, *unches, iluches, dunches, unchores*, p. 172, *Q.L.R. alches*, (cf. § 694).

§ 1210. (3) The representation of final ð by *d* (cf. above, § 1176). In Early Old French the use of *d* for ð was occasional, e.g. *Eul. ned* 7, *qued* 14, *St. Legier, fied* 24, *fud* 28, etc., *pordud* 161, etc. In early Anglo-Norman texts such as *Brendan*, MS. A, its use is frequent, especially after stressed vowels, *abed, cited, feid, vertud, l(i)ed, ad* (< *habet* and -*at*), -*id* (-*itum*, -*iit*), -*ed* (-*atum*), -*ud* (-*utum*, -*uit*), p. 167. In the words *ad* (*habet*) and *od* (*apud*) this spelling was retained because it served to distinguish these words from homonyms, cf. *Orth. Gall. O.* 82, 83, p. 14.

§ 1211. The relatively systematic use of accents in some of the early A.N. MSS. may also be mentioned in this connection, cf. Lincke, *Die Accente in Oxforder und Cambridger Psalter sowie in anderen altfrz. Hss.*, Erlangen, 1886, and Beaulieux, pp. 7-17.

Section 3.—Varying Scribal Tradition.

§ 1212. *English.*—(i) The levelling of the O.E. diphthong **ea** to ę in the eleventh century (§ 1117) led occasionally to the use of the digraph *ea* for ę, cf. *Alexis*, MS. L, *seat* for *set* (< *septem*); *Adam, deavee* (for *desvee*) 357; Bozon, *Contes, eagle*, p. 139, *Char, freavele* 55 (cf. Menger, p. 46).

§ 1213. (ii) The rounding of **eo** to ö (§ 1117) induced occasionally the use of *eo* to represent ö, cf. *Rol. deol* 929, Bozon, *Contes, eops, eol, eols* for ös < *opus*, öl < *oculum*, ös < *oculos*; the unrounding of ö to ę (§ 1121) led to the occasional use of *eo* for ę, cf. *Cam. Ps. feorm, Boeve, ceoly* 216.

§ 1214. In the representation of the group **ĭu** derived from **ĭw** and ęw (§§ 1124, 1125) English scribes continued the older spelling (e.g. *Tiwesdai, hewe*) and this spelling was sometimes similarly used by late Anglo-Norman scribes, e.g. Bozon, *Contes, viwe*, p. 74, *vewe*, p. 99, *mangiwe*, p. 109.

§ 1215. (iii) Anglo-Norman scribes made some use of the digraph **th** for ð, more rarely θ, cf. *Brendan*, MS. A, *vetheir, fetheilz, veuthes, ethez* (p. 169); *Alexis*, MS. L, *mustrethe, espethe, mandethe* 15 *a, b, c*, etc. (cf. Menger, § 39). Very occasional is the use of the O.E. symbol ð, e.g. *fieðe, Lois Guillaume.*

§ 1216. (iv) To represent the sound χ (< s + t, § 1178), Anglo-Norman scribes had recourse to the English symbols **h** and occasionally *gh* or *sh*, e.g. *miht, conuht, eshtel*, cf. above, § 1178, and Menger, p. 102.

§ 1217. (v) In Middle English the doubling of a consonant came to be used as an orthographical device to indicate the short vowel (cf. Jespersen, *Gr.* § 4, 91), and this practice, combined with the Middle French use of a doubled consonant to indicate ę, § 729, led to the use of doubled consonants in Later Anglo-Norman to indicate short, open vowels, e.g. *Boeve*, MS. B, *gibbet, suffres, mette, gette, occis*, etc., cf. *Boeve*, pp. 239, 240, and § 1170.

[For *cch* and *gg* cf. § 1181; for Latin influence cf. § 707.]

§ 1218. *Latin.*—The influence of Latin spelling made itself felt chiefly in Anglo-Norman as on the Continent, in the use of double consonants and in the restoration of letters representing sounds effaced or modified, e.g. *occire, occis, saiettes*, etc., *saincte, corps, oeps* (*opus*), *sept*, etc. The earliest spelling treatises enforce respect for the Latin etyma: 'Item

quelibet diccio gallica concordans latino in quantum poterit debet sequi scriptura latini.' (*Tract. Orth.* (*M.L.R.* V, p. 193), cf. also *Orth. Graph.* C.O. 85, p. 16, T. xxvi, and §§ 707-710, 809.)

§ 1219. In some MSS. the digraph *ae* functions as ę, apparently under Latin influence, e.g. *St. Auban, saet (septem)* 359, *(sapit)* 1568, *saerree* 509, *saerpent* 522, *raedde* 788, cf. Menger, p. 65 ; Angier, *maes, plaest, aeve, Et. Angier,* p. 11.

[For the influence of Latin orthography on verb-forms cf. §§ 1294-1297.]

§ 1220. *Later Old French.*—(i) The use of the digraph *ou* for **u** began on the Continent in the late twelfth century (§ 698) ; it is occasional already in Angier (*Et.* p. 18), and was adopted, though tardily, by Anglo-Norman scribes, who employed it, (alternatively with *u* and *o*), for **u** nasalised as well as **u** oral and for **u** derived from earlier **ü, üi** and **ui** and occasionally also in the diphthong **ui**, cf. *Purg. Patr.* (MS. H), *jour* 61, *priour* 62, etc., *plusour* 110 ; *noun* 49, *resoun* 70, *hounte* 91, etc., *soucher* (< sūctiare) 297 ; *Sermon, pounz (pugnos)* 121 ; *St. Auban, oui (hodie)* 1647, cf. T. p. 477.

§ 1221. (ii) *x* was adopted by some of the later scribes to represent **s** after **u**, (§ 733), e.g Bozon, *Contes, ceaux, porceaux, queux, auxint,* etc.

Section 4.—INFLUENCE OF SOUND-CHANGE ON THE VALUE OF SYMBOLS.

§ 1222. *Interchange of Symbols.*—Anglo-Norman scribes, relatively little versed in French tradition, often represent current pronunciation more immediately and simply than their Continental compeers. The effacement of prae-consonantal **s**, for instance, and of final consonants and of ę is early recognised in their notation of words and 'phonetic' spellings such as *e* for *est* and *ait, dekes, jekes* for *desque, jesque, sein* or *sen* for *saint, setes* for *saietes, ser, ver* for *seeir, veeir* are not uncommon.

Unfortunately for us, however, the attempts made to represent pronunciation are more often than not 'semi-phonetic' and not 'phonetic,' i.e. they are of the type found so often among partially educated people who are attempting to write a language with a half-known traditional orthography. For all such persons, the symbols or combinations of symbols used to represent any given sound are more or less interchangeable in value and we find consequently that the later Anglo-Norman scribes made just such an indiscriminate use of the traditional Old French symbols as is found to-day in the letters of French peasants, who use, for instance, any one of the notations -*e*, -*ee*, -*er*, -*ez*, -*ai* to represent final ę.

[For a similar use of symbols in less educated Continental French cf. §§ 722, 734.]

§ 1223. *Representation of the* e-*sounds.*—As soon as the diphthongs **ai, ei, ie** were levelled the symbols representing them became interchangeable with themselves, with the symbol *e* and with the English symbols *ea* and *eo* (§§ 1212, 1213). Interchange was often facilitated by associative influences; the endings *-ere* and *-iere*, for instance, are early confused, Angier writes *emperiere, jugliere* ÷ *jugiere*, etc., and *pel, tel, quel* were often replaced by *piel, tiel, quiel* or *pieu, tieu, quieu* under the influence of the forms *pieus, tieus, quieus.*

Since **ai** and **ei** levelled through ẹi to ẹ (§§ 1157, 1158), the digraphs *ai* and *ei*, together with English *ea* and Latin *ae* (§ 1219), were kept ordinarily for ę, e.g. *fait, feit, fet, feat, faet; seit, sait, set, seat, saet,* etc.

As **ie** and English ẹo levelled to ẹ (§§ 1155, 1121) the digraphs *ie* and *eo* were usually used for ẹ, e.g. *set* (< *sapit*), *siet, seot.*

Confusion in the value of these two sets of symbols was, however, early occasioned by the passage of ẹ to ę before l and r (§ 1146), and by the attempt to re-introduce the pronunciation ję (§ 1189), and in Later Anglo-Norman the significance of the digraph *ie* is very varying.

In the thirteenth century when the diphthong **oi** passed to ụę and later to ę (§§ 519, 522), the digraph *oi* was also given the value ụę and ę (cf. *Boeve*, MS. B, *estoit* for *estuet*, MS. D, *voit* for *vuet, poyt*, p. 207), and then vęt (< *videt* and *vadit*) might be written *vet, veit, vait, voit, voet, vest* (§ 1236), *veet* (§ 1235), and sometimes with loss of *t*: *vai, vei, voi* and sęt < *sapit*, often pronounced sęt ÷ fęt might be written *set, siet, seet, seot, seit, soit, seat, saet.*

[For the use of *-ee* for ẹ and ę cf. 1235.]

§ 1224. ẽ.—The representation of ẽ, (< ãi, ẽi (j)ẽi §§ 1155, 1159) varied also between *e, ei, ai, ie,* e.g. *ben, bein, bien, graindre, greindre, grendre* (*Boeve*, pp. 185, 196, 203).

§ 1225. *Representation of the Labial Vowels.*—(i) ọ, ǫ, u, ü : In early western French, it must be remembered, the sound-system appears to have comprised the vowels ọ, u and ü (and not ǫ, § 1083) : ọ was always represented by *o*, ü by *u* and **u** in the earlier MSS. ordinarily by *u* (cf. MSS. C and S of the *Comput*, L and O of the *Bestiaire*) ; *o* was however also used under the influence of Latin and the northern and francien tradition and gained ground in Later Anglo-Norman. In Later Anglo-Norman *ou* tended to replace both *o* and *u* (§ 1220).

§ 1226. In the pronunciation of the diphthong **ui** (< earlier ǫi) there was some hesitation (§ 1161) and in its representation etymology often appears to have been the determining influence; *ui* was frequent in *anguisse, fruissier*, etc., *oi* usual in *voiz* (and on its model *croiz*) and not infrequent elsewhere.

§ 1227. When the diphthongs üi and iü were levelled to ü, the symbols *u, ui* and *iu* became interchangeable, cf. *Brendan*, MSS., *pus, cunduz, lu* (for *lui*), *su, utme*, etc., p. 160, *cunuit, pluis, sius* (for *sus*), p. 153.

The velarisation of ü to u (§ 1142) and the levelling of 'ue to u (§ 1156) brought in further alternatives, and thus in Later Anglo-Norman **put** < O.F. **puet** and **pǫut** might be written *puet, puot, put, pot, pout, puit* (cf. also §§ 1282, 1288).

§ 1228. The vocalisation of ɫ and prae-consonantal ʃ to ʮ led early to the use of *ol* in prae-consonantal position with the value **u**, cf. *Rol. Digby MS., neuold* for *nevoud* **nęvu**; *Boeve*, MS. D, *provolt* 2859 for *provost* **pruvut** (cf. § 1144).

§ 1229. (ii) ö.—The sound ö, developed in the course of the twelfth century from **ue** (§ 551), **ueu** (§ 555) and **eu** (§ 541), was represented very variously :

(*a*) *eu, ue* and *oe*, the digraphs in use when **eu** and **ue** were still diphthongal (§ 714), were retained.

[For their distribution in early MSS. cf. Suchier, *Gr.* § 28; for *uo* cf. § 1207.]

(*b*) The digraph *eo*, adopted under English influence (cf. § 1213), is frequent in some early MSS., e.g. *Cambridge Psalter, Q.L.R.*, and occasional throughout Anglo-Norman, e.g. *Oak Book, illeoques, veot, Suppl.* p. 28.

(*c*) In early MSS. special symbols were occasionally employed, cf. § 551, Suchier, *Gr.* § 28.

§ 1230. *gn* and *n*.—The passage of ŋ to ĩn (§ 1182) led to the use of *gn* for intervocalic *n*, a use prescribed by the *Orthographia Gallica* after *i*, e.g. in *certaignement*, H. 96, C.O. 92, p. 28.

§ 1231. **ts, s**.—The shift of **ts** to **s** (cf. § 1183) led, as in French (cf. § 722), to an interchange of the symbols *s, z, c, sc* (*ts, tz*) in Later Anglo-Norman (cf. Vising, *Purg. Patr.* p. 11, *Boeve*, pp. 225, 233). Thus the spellings *lez, sez, suz, amiz* may stand for *les, ses, sus, amis ; ce, ci, cil, ces, cist, ici, cemeines*, for *se, si, sil, ses, sist, issi, semeines ; sa, si, seinte, asser, pessa, lessoun*, for *ca, ci, ceinte, acer* (< *acier*), *peca* (< *piece a*), *lecoun*. The intercalation of the final (mute) consonant of the radical brought in the use of *ts* and *tz*, and the author of the *Orthographia Gallica* and his commentators endeavour in vain to systematise the use of flexional *s, z, ts* and *tz* in plural forms.

These rules prescribe the continued use of *z* in the plural : (i) in the endings of all participles, adjectives and verbs, with the exception of all first persons plural and the first and second persons plural of the perfect ; (ii) all substantives ending in *ee* or *e* (i.e. ę or ę̈), e.g. *bountez, feez* (< *faiz*), *eisnez ;* (iii) all substantives ending in *t*, e.g. *tenemenz*, but *ts* and *tz* allowed ; (iv) all substantives ending in *l* (< ʃ), e.g. *genulz, filz*, pp. 6-7.

§ 1232. The effacement of final consonants, §§ 1201-1204, provoked much graphical confusion, final consonants being not only sometimes omitted, ibid., but also at times interchanged or wrongly introduced, cf. *Boeve*, MS. B, 63 *branc* for *brant*, etc., MS. D, l. 3733, *kanc* for *kant;* *Brendan*, MS. A, *Perrunt, Nerunt, cardunt; Rol. Digby MS. barunt*, l. 1889; *jas, bens, comons*, cited in *Boeve*, p. 228 (cf. Addenda).

§ 1233. Characteristic of Later Anglo-Norman is the use of final supported *d* for *t* (cf. *Brendan*, p. 167, *Boeve*, p. 221). This practice appears to be often graphical only, occasioned by the influence of Latin or associated forms, as in *grand, mund (mundum), secund, reguard, Richard, cald, freid*. But the spelling is not confined to words of this type, cf. *mund (montem)*, and the pronunciation of such words in Modern English, together with the parallel development found in others of English origin, e.g. *lend, pound, sound* (Jespersen, §§ 7, 61), make it probable that in Later Anglo-Norman this spelling was in accord with pronunciation and that final **n** (lengthened by the effacement of **-t** (?) or by denasalisation of the previous vowel (?)) had been partially denasalised to **nd**.

§ 1234. *Diacritical use of Symbols.*—As in Continental French, some attempt was made to utilise as diacritical symbols, the letters that were relatively little used or represented effaced sounds.

§ 1235. *ee.*—When ẹ, in hiatus with preceding tonic ẹ, was completely effaced in pronunciation (§ 1133), the spelling *ee* was employed to distinguish ẹ (ẹ̄) final from ẹ, cf. *Orth. Gall.* II, T. 3 : 'Praeterea diccio terminata in *e* plene pronunciata debet scribi cum *ee* geminatis, verbi gracia *donee, amee*.' (Cf. also *Intr.* p. vi.) According to Vising the use of this device is not frequent before the fourteenth century, although sporadic instances of *-ee* for *e* occur from the later twelfth century on, (*Purg. Patr.* p. 11).

From the middle of the thirteenth century on the double *ee* appears also to have been used to indicate a lengthened open ẹ̄, e.g. in *pees* (< *pais*), *tees* (< *taces*), *pleet* (< *plait*), *neestre* (< *naistre*), cf. Vising, *Purg. Patr.* p. 11.

§ 1236. **s.**—Tradition maintained ordinarily prae-consonantal **s** after it had become mute, and in Later Anglo-Norman it is sometimes used (as on the Continent, § 725) to denote lengthened ẹ (e.g. in *ovesques* (≠ *evesqes*), *fest* for fẹ̄t (*fait*)), sometimes to indicate lengthened velarised ā, cf. § 1153.

§ 1237. *h.*—As in Continental French, § 730, but rather more extensively, *h* was employed to indicate hiatus between vowels, e.g. *Lettres A.F.* No. 30, *pohoms, ehoms* 38, *avohisons*, Bozon, *O., juhe* (for

jue < *jocat*) 58, *suihez, courtehours* (< *couretours*) 230, *charruhers* 315 (cf. *Boeve*, p. 239, and above, § 1194).

[For the doubling of consonants cf. § 1217.]

§ 1238. *Use of Inorganic Letters.*—The effacement of unstressed vowels, particularly ẹ, of prae-consonantal **s, z, ð, +,]** and of final consonants led to the frequent intrusion of inorganic letters in Later Anglo-Norman spelling, e.g. *meur* for *mur* (< *murum*), *veneu, foreste, lece* (*eslais*) ; *veient* for *veint, aienz* for *ainz ; fidle* for *fille* (≠ *idle*, cf. § 1177) ; *meisne* for *meine, cest* for *set* (but cf. § 1236) ; *voils* for *vois, voildie* for *voidie, voisdie, out* for *ou* (cf. *Boeve, Appendix*, passim).

The number of spellings thus rendered possible may be illustrated by the variant spellings of A.N. **fu** (< O.F. **füθ** < **fuit**) : *fut, fud, fu, feut, fust* (§ 1236), *feust, fuit* (§ 1160), *fuist, fuht* (§ 1178), and all these variants, except *fud*, may also function for **fu** < Early O.F. **füst** < **fuisset**.

§ 1239. *Distinction of Homonyms.*—The compilers of the various spelling treatises made some attempt to bring order into this chaos and thus the *Orthographia Gallica* contains rules to enable scribes to utilise variant spellings to distinguish homonyms, cf. C.O. 50, p. 14 : ' Item diversitas scripture facit differenciam aliquarum diccionum quamvis in voce sint consimiles, verbi gracia : *ciel, seel* (< *salem*), *seal* (< **sigellum*) ; *cerf* and *serf, teindre* and *tendre ; . . . aymer, amer ; veel* (< **vitellum*), *viel* (< **veclum*) ; *veile, veille ; . . . nief* (< *navem*), *neif* (< *nivem*), *neof ; piel* (< *palum*), *peel* (< *pellem*).' (Etyma inserted.)   Cf. also C.O. 90, p. 17, ' Item habetur diversitas inter *estreym* (*strawe*) et *estreyn* (*hansel*).' Attempts such as these, however, touched but the fringe of the question and effected but little, and it was only the official legal scribes who were able to build up any form of orthographical tradition (cf. § 703).

CHAPTER IV.

DECLENSION.

Section 1.—INTRODUCTORY.

§ 1240. The factors that undermined the pronunciation of French in England were also active in the disintegration of the Old French flexional system, but their influence took effect on somewhat varying lines. The declension system of *substantives and adjectives*, in which the case-system was already threatened in western French in the twelfth century (cf. W. § xii), was early shaken by contact with the English system, and its complete disintegration was completed in the thirteenth century by the sound-changes of the time, in particular by the frequent effacement of final s and of ę. Among the *pronouns* English influence was relatively slight and the systems more resistant, but the combined influence of the sound-changes of the period and of the variant Continental dialectal forms that had been introduced provoked much instability in Later Anglo-Norman.

Section 2.—DECLENSION OF SUBSTANTIVES AND ADJECTIVES.

§ 1241. *Declension in Early Anglo-Norman.*—As in western French (cf. W. § xiii) the nominative case of feminine substantives and adjectives was normally uninflected, cf. *Brendan, rien : bien, grant : espant, mort : fort (Intr.* clxv). The neuter singular of adjectives and participles referring to neuter pronouns was also left uninflected as in Continental French (*Brendan*, clxv), as was also, under Latin influence, the nominative singular of nouns that were neuter in Latin (cf. § 806 and Laubscher, *The Syntactical Causes of Case Reduction*, chap. ii).

[For the early passage of **ts** to **s** and consequent graphical confusions, cf. § 1231.]

§ 1242. *Analogical Formations.*—(i) From the middle of the twelfth century on, or even earlier, there showed itself a marked tendency to introduce the final consonant of the uninflected radical before flexional s, cf. *Rol. Digby MS. vifs* 746, *osbercs* 994, etc., *colps* 1013, etc., *Q.L.R. prestz*, p. 14, *serfs* 16, *salfs* 20, etc., cf. *Intr. Brend.* p. clxv.

The use of these consonants was at first and for long (as on the Continent, cf. § 741) graphical only, cf. *Div. Mund.*, *secks : fres* 123, *blancs : anz* 319, *Orthographia Gallica*, C.O. 51, p. 15 : 'Item sciatis quod hee littere *c, d, e, f, g, l, n, p, s*, et *t* debent mutari in sono et non in scriptura . . . *Vifs hommes* loquatur *vys hommes* et sic de similibus.'

§ 1243. (ii) In the same period begins the extension of flexional s to the nominative singular of masculine nouns in -ę, cf. *Brend.* clxiv, *peres, leres, faitres.*

§ 1244. (iii) Free use of analogical feminine adjectives in -ę characterises also Early Anglo-Norman, e.g. Phil. Thaon, *brieve, uele, tele, ardante, tranchante*, etc. ; *Brendan, Intr.* clxv-clxvi, *forte, grande, tele, curante.*

All these three types of analogical formations were employed also on the Continent (cf. §§ 809, 805, 780), but all came into vogue there more slowly than in Anglo-Norman.

§ 1245. *Archaisms.*—Some older etymological forms, e.g. words in *rm*, *rn*, persisted late in Anglo-Norman, cf. *Boeve*, B. *verm* 946, *corn* 559, *enfern* 1247, cf. § 811 and *Boeve*, App. pp. 215, 216.

§ 1246. *Disintegration of Declension.*—(i) Contact with a different flexional system accelerated greatly the disintegration of the declension system that was only just beginning to show itself in western French (cf. W. § xii). The earliest Anglo-Norman writer, Philippe de Thaon, already ' permitted himself to infringe the rules' (cf. Walberg, *Best.* lxviii), and although the extent to which Anglo-Norman writers allowed themselves such liberties varied a certain amount, disintegration became marked as early as the beginning of the thirteenth century. Normally (as later on the Continent), generalisation went in favour of the accusative forms, the much used nominatives alone excepted (e.g. *fiz, suer, pire*), but there was some unsteadiness even there (cf. Vising, *St. Pat.* p. 10), and in Later Anglo-Norman the use of *s* (*z*) was often indiscriminate, cf. *Boeve*, B. acc. sg. *soun parentez, contrediz, pez* (*pedem*), *costez, criz, hardis, defiez, obliez*, acc. pl. *mer, parent, serjant, plener, Intr.* xviii, xix, *St. Pat.* 557, acc. sg. *veus : puis* (*puits*).

It must, however, be remembered that in Later Anglo-Norman the use of flexional *s* (*z* or *x*) was in the main merely a matter of spelling, s final being very generally mute (cf. § 1203). Noticeable at that time is the tendency to omit final *s* in the plural of adjectives standing before their nouns, e.g. *bele mains, veu dras, diverse culurs* (cf. Vising, *Purg. Patr.* pp. 11, 12). In all probability pronunciation and the influence of the uninflected adjective in English both contributed to this practice.

§ 1247. (ii) In the later period unsteadiness in the use of -ę *final* (cf. § 1135) led to the introduction of plurals in -*es* (-*is*, § 1140), such as *boves, coupes, hanapes, manteles, panis, gagis, matines, urses* (cf. *Boeve*, xv, 183), *cheminis, voisinis* (Bozon, *Char*, MS. O), *veisinez, fines, seintez* (*Contes*); (cf. also above, § 1127).

Section 3.—PERSONAL PRONOUNS.

§ 1248. Both central and northern forms of **ego** were current in twelfth-century Anglo-Norman, i.e. stressed **džɪ̯ę, džę** *gie, ge, je,* un-stressed **džę** *ge, je,* (cf. Chardri, *pri je : marché, demant je : cungé*) and stressed **džu** *jou, jo,* unstressed **džu** *jo,* e.g. *Alexis,* L, *Rol. Digby MS., Q.L.R.* (cf. §§ 829-831). The forms *jeo* and *ceo,* according to a rule in the *Orthographia Gallica,* appear to be ordinarily graphical variants of the forms *je* and *ce* **džę** and **sę,** and the relatively rare form *joe* (e.g. *Donnei des Amants, joe : roe*) is probably also a graphical variant of *jou* **džu,** that was brought into use when *final* ę in hiatus had become mute (cf. the spelling *rous* for *roues, Purg. Patr.* MS. H, 403, and above §§ 1133, 1238).

'Item ille sillabe *je ce, jeo ceo,* indifferenter possunt scribi cum *c-e-o* vel *cc* sine *o*' (C.O. 8), 'per *e* sine *o* ut *je, ce*' (H. 90). This value is also attested by the occasional use of *ceo* for *se* (< *si*) and *ces,* e.g. *Boeve,* 1574 *ceo jeo fusse,* 701 *ceo chevaus.*

§ 1249. *Dialectal Forms.*—The shortened west French form **us** for **vus** is occasionally used in the twelfth century (cf. S.W. § x, Chardri, *Donnei,* and Menger, p. 115). In Later Anglo-Norman the northern form **mi** (cf. N. § xxiv) is also occasional.

§ 1250. Phonological changes brought some confusion into the dative and accusative forms of the pronouns of the *third person.*

(i) The Anglo-Norman reduction of ˈüi to ü and the velarisation of ü (§§ 1160, 1142) obliterated the distinction between the stressed accusative *lui* (**lüi**) and the archaic unstressed accusative *lu* (**lu**), cf. Menger, p. 116.

(ii) The Continental shift of stress in the diphthong **üi** and subsequent reduction of **wi** to **i,** which was also introduced (cf. § 1160), obliterated the distinction between **lüi** and **li,** i.e. between the stressed and unstressed forms of the dative masculine and between the masculine and feminine dative, and in Later Anglo-Norman the use of *lui* and *li* became indiscriminate (cf. *Boeve,* p. xxi).

§ 1251. *Ele* and *el,* the western form of *ele,* were both current (cf. W. § 14, *Best.* lxxiv, Menger, p. 116). The use of the archaic neuter pronoun *el,* outside the combinations *oel, oal, nenal,* appears to be confined to *St. Brendan* (*Intr.* clxvi, cf. *Et. Angier,* p. 32).

In Later Anglo-Norman *il* (*ils*) sometimes replaced *ele* (*eles*),

(cf. Menger, p. 117), and *cil* was used for *il* (cf. *Orth. Gall.* H. 44(*a*), p. 20), possibly under English influence; *le* and *la* functioned sometimes as *li*, and the northern use of *les* as a dative pronoun (N. § xv) led to a confusion between *les* and *lur* in the fourteenth century, (cf. Vising, *Purg. Patr.* p. 60, *Boeve*, xxii).

[For **i** for **il** and *ne* for *nel* (*ne le*) cf. § 1204.]

Section 4.—ARTICLE.

§ 1252. *Variant Forms.*—(i) In the masculine accusative singular *le* and older *lu* were both in use in the twelfth century, the latter more especially in locutions of the type *la fille lu rei* (cf. Menger, 111, Rydberg, 497, and E. § xxv, S.C. § xxi, S.W. § x).

(ii) The enclitic forms *as, al, des, del* were retained late, (but cf. below).

(iii) Under the influence of the northern speech, (N. § xii), the feminine **la** was often reduced to **le**, especially in the later period, cf. *Boeve*, p. xiii.

§ 1253. *Disintegration of Declension.*—The use of **li** masculine nominative singular and plural early became unstable, and in later Anglo-Norman there is much confusion among the forms :—

(i) *Le—les* became the more usual forms for nominative and accusative masculine but *li* and *ly* were still fairly frequent in the nominative and occasional in the accusative (*Boeve*, xi); *le* for *les*, with effaced **s** (**z**) (§ 1203), is found in the plural feminine and masculine, *Oak Book, le jour soient* I, 40, *le genz* I 42, *le malades* I, 26, *contre le estatutz* I, 62, etc. (cf. *Boeve*, xii, xiii, 226).

(ii) Under the influence of the forms of the pronoun of the third person the form *lui* came into use in both nominative and accusative singular. In the accusative this form is probably a graphical variant for older **lu** (cf. § 1250 (i)) ; in the nominative it is more likely to be a variant of older **li**, influenced by the thirteenth-century confusion of the pronoun forms **lwi** and **li** (cf. § 1250 (ii) and *Purg. Patr.* p. 56).

(iii) Characteristic of Later Anglo-Norman is the replacement of the enclitic forms *al, u, as, del, deu, des* by the separate words *a le, a les*, etc., cf. *Oak Book, Suppl.* pp. 39, 40.

[For the effacement of **l** and **s** in *al, as, del, des* cf. § 1203-1204.]

Section 5.—DEMONSTRATIVE PRONOUNS.

§ 1254. *Variant Forms.*—The ordinary forms in use in Early Anglo-Norman were those of the Continent, with and without analogical initial **i-** (cf. § 844)—*cist* and *icist*, etc., *cil* and *icil*, etc., *co, ce* and *ico, ice*—but throughout Anglo-Norman the older forms, those without initial **i**, predominated.

§ 1255. In the early period the neuter forms *cel* and *cest* were not infrequent (cf. *Brendan*, clxvii, Menger, p. 117). The use of *esse* < *ipsa*

is confined to the *Comput*, that of *ist* to Angier.   As in western French
(cf. § 846) the feminine plural *cestes* persisted.

§ 1256. The northern forms of *els* and *icels*, with lowered vowel, are
frequently found, e.g. *Brendan, iceals, ceais* (cf. § 1089); in Later Anglo-
Norman *eaux* and *iceaux* are looked upon as orthographical variants of
eux and *ceux*, cf. *Orth. Gall.*, '. . . *ceaux, deaux* scribendo *ea* pro *e* . . .'
H. 89, C.O. 49, p. 5.

[For *ceo* and *coe* cf. § 1248; for *ceoly* and *iceols* cf. § 1213, *Boeve*,
p. 818; for *si, se* for *cil, cel*, cf. § 1204.]

§ 1257. *Later Anglo-Norman.*—The nominative form *cist* early became
infrequent and in some texts (e.g. *Q.L.R.*), *cez* (**ses** < **tsẹts**) and *cels*
(**ses** < **tsẹ(l)s**?) early fell together.

§ 1258. The nominative *cil* lived on, but in the plural, more rarely
in the singular, it was more and more frequently replaced by the accusative forms.   The rules in the *Orthographia Gallica* indicate much confusion in the use of the demonstrative forms, but the continuance of the
old distinction of function between derivatives of *ille* and *iste* is certainly
indicated in the rules H. 45(*a*) and C.O. 76, p. 21 : ' Mes si les chosez sont
presentz ou sunt nomez overtement en present, *ceaux* tornera en *cestes*.'

§ 1259. In the thirteenth century the neuter pronoun *co*, presumably
under English influence, began to function as an adjective, cf. Adam,
294, *co bien, Boeve*, xxv, *Black Prince*, xlii.

Section 6.—Possessive Adjectives and Pronouns.

§ 1260. The forms introduced were the usual western forms and
consequently the unstressed nominative singular of the singular pronouns
was more frequently *mis, tis, sis* § 853, (e.g. *Cam. Ps., Q.L.R.*) than *mes,
tes, ses*, (e.g. *Oxf. Ps.*).

Under northern influence *me, te, se* occasionally replaced *ma, ta, sa*
(cf. N. § xii, Menger, § 59).

§ 1261. *Later Anglo-Norman.*—Sound-changes led to frequent
modifications in the spelling :—

(i) The unstressed nominative singular forms were reduced to *mi, ti,
si*, or *me, te, se* by the effacement of final **s** when prae-consonantal (cf.
§ 1203), and when **ts** shifted to **s** (§ 1231), **sẹ** and **sẹs** were spelled *ce* and
ces (cf. above and *Boeve*, xxiii).   [For the spelling *moun, toun, soun*, cf.
§§ 1220, 1225.]

(ii) Stressed *meie (moie), tue, sue* were written *mei (mai, moi), tu, su*
when final **ẹ** in hiatus became mute (§ 1133); **mien** was early levelled
to **men** (§ 1155); *tuen* and *suen* persisted late.   The spelling *teon, seon,*
(*seone, Oak Bk. Sup.* p. 42) represents probably **tẹn, sẹn**, etc., forms with **ŏ**
unrounded, (§ 1143) or made on the model of *men*.

(iii) In prae-consonantal position nǫs and vǫs (< nǫts, vǫts *noz*, *voz*)
passed to nu(s) and vu(s) (cf. § 1144) and were often written *nous*, *vous*,
cf. Bozon, *Char*, 557, *O*. 139, 250.

Section 7.—RELATIVE AND INTERROGATIVE PRONOUNS.

§ 1262. The extension of the use of *que* for *qui* in the nominative
singular feminine and masculine showed itself early and became very
general in the thirteenth century (cf. § 864, Menger, § 60, *Boeve*, xxv).

The spellings *ki* and *ke* appeared in the later twelfth century
(§ 701, *Psalter* MSS., *Q.L.R.*); kI for earlier küi *cui* (through kẅi) is
rather later; [for *chi* cf. § 1209].

In later Anglo-Norman *quel*, and more frequently *queux*, functioned
as relative pronouns.

Section 8.—INDEFINITE PRONOUNS.

§ 1263. In the late thirteenth century the form *ascun* was introduced
modelled on *chascun* (cf. § 1153, Vising, *Purg. Patr.* p. 57).

CHAPTER V.

CONJUGATION SYSTEM.

[Cf. F. J. Tanquerey, *L'Evolution du Verbe en Anglo-Français* (xiie-xive siècles), Paris, 1915 : a work valuable for the large amount of information it presents, but requiring great precaution in use.]

Section 1.—INTRODUCTORY.

§ 1264. The gradual disintegration of the conjugation system, which becomes a marked feature of late Anglo-Norman, is the result of a combination of causes. The Old French conjugation system was characterised by its wealth of forms and relatively rapid evolution (cf. §§ 874, 875); its complexity was increased in Anglo-Norman by the co-existence of western French forms with those belonging to the speech of other parts of France, by freedom of analogical formation and (graphically) by the motley character of Anglo-Norman spelling (cf. chap. iii). This great variety of form led to an instability of tradition, which was increased by the disintegrating influence exercised by the numerous sound-changes that took place in Continental French and Anglo-Norman.

The conjugation system of Later Anglo-Norman contains, like the sound-system, occasional archaisms, but its outstanding characteristics are its wealth of analogical forms, its simplifying tendencies, and the ever-growing lack of discrimination shown in the use of variant forms. Contact with the English flexional system accelerated disintegration, but exercised little positive influence on the conjugation system (cf. § 29).

Section 2.—ARCHAISMS.

§ 1265. It is not yet possible to determine with any degree of accuracy the date at which forms became wholly obsolete either in Continental French or in Anglo-Norman, but it appears that some of the older forms, introduced in the eleventh century and displaced early on the Continent by analogical formations, survived later in insular speech. Among these may be noted :—

§ 1266. (1) The use of the ending *-em*, *-iem* in the first person plural of the present subjunctive in the *Oxford Psalter* (cf. §§ 893, 895).

§ 1267. (2) The continued use of the west French termination of the imperfect indicative of the first conjugation, *-oue, -out, -ouent*, cf. below, § 1277 and T. p. 554.

§ 1268. (3) The continued use of the older forms of the third persons of the strong *u*-perfects of the first type, e.g. *out, ourent, pout, plourent*, etc. (cf. § 1025, Uhlemann, p. 588). (These forms may, however, be merely graphical varieties of analogical forms in **u** (< ü), § 1285.)

§ 1269. (4) The occasional use of forms of first and second persons of the imperfect subjunctive of the first conjugation in *-essons, -essez*, (cf. § 1044), e.g. *moillessez*, Bozon, *Contes, delivressons, paiessez*, T. p. 664.

§ 1270. (5) The use of *faimes* (*feimes*), *esmes* (*eimes*) in the thirteenth century; the continuance of the forms *vait* (*vet, veit, voit, vest*), *veintre, descrivre* and the participles *aresteu, toleit* (*tolet*) in the fourteenth century. [Cf. also §§ 1277, 1301, 1304, 1305.]

Section 3.—Variety of Forms Introduced.

§ 1271. The conjugation system introduced was predominantly western, but the influence of northern and central French is perceptible, particularly in the later period.

§ 1272. *Termination of the First Person Plural.*— *-om* and *-um*, the western forms of the first person plural (W. § xv), and *-oms, -ons*, the more usual central and northern form, were current in early Anglo-Norman, but the western forms greatly predominated; *-ons* (*-uns, -ouns, -oms, -ums, oums, omps*, § 1151) gained ground in the later thirteenth century and was dominant in the fourteenth (T. pp. 181-191, *Orth. Gall.* p. iv), but not to the exclusion of *-um* (*-om, -oun, -oum*).

In the later period, under northern influence, *-omes* (*-umes*, N. § xxvii), occasional throughout, became more frequent and both *-iens* and *-iemes* were employed in the imperfect of the indicative and subjunctive and in the conditional (§ 919, T. pp. 162-165, 195-197).

[For the late analogical forms *-eimes, -eions, -eioms*, cf. § 1313; for the second person plural cf. §§ 1283, 1295, 1303, 1313.]

§ 1273. *Termination of the Third Person Plural.*—In the third person plural of the imperfect subjunctive forms stressed on the termination were sometimes used, possibly under the influence of south-western French: *Q.L.R.* xiii, *soüssant* 3, *venissant* 12, *fussant* 3; *Boeve, portassant* 1747 in a laisse in *-ant; Purg. Patr. orient: nient, portent: forment; Apocalypse, pensount : fount* (cf. *Intr. Purg. Patr.* p. 13; S.W. § xi).

§ 1274. The *first person singular* of the present indicative terminates sometimes as in west French (W. § xvii) in analogical **k** (*c, g*), e.g. *Oxf. Ps. vienc, sustinc, Q.L.R. requierc, tienc, vienc*; (cent. xiv) *enprenk, recommaunk* (cf. T. 39-44, *Et. Angier*, pp. 34, 35).

§ 1275. The extension -ge (W. § xvii) was in common use in the early period among verbs of the first and third conjugation whose radicals ended in **r, n, l,** e.g. *Oxf. Ps. alge, donge, parolge, curge, crenget, quergent, repunge* (cf. *Et. Angier*, p. 40); in the later period its use persisted among verbs with radicals in **r** and a few others, e.g. *apperge, curge, demurge, jurge, moerge, plurge, remorge, tourge, prenge, parouge* (T. 351-358).

§ 1276. The extension -ce (§ 910) was not infrequent in the present subjunctive of the verbs *cheeir, seeir* (*chiece, siece*) in the early period; in the later period these same forms and a few others are occasionally employed under northern influence, sometimes spelled in *s, sc* or *ss* instead of *s,* e.g. *chiese, siesce,* N. § xxix, T. pp. 348-350.

§ 1277. The western forms of the termination of the *imperfect indicative* of the *first* conjugation (W. § xvi) were dominant in the first period, the tonic vowel at first diphthongal (*-ouë, -out, -ouënt, -oue, -out, ouent*), but from the middle of the twelfth century on the forms *-oë, -ot, -oënt* (cf. Gaimar, *parloent : loent* 3749) were also employed as on the Continent (§ 916), though never to the exclusion of the older type (cf. § 1267). The use of these terminations continued longer in Anglo-Norman than in written Continental French, but the first beginnings of its replacement by the termination of the other conjugations are found in the later twelfth and early thirteenth centuries, e.g. Adgar, *aleit : esteit.*

In this same period the first analogical extension of these first conjugation endings to other conjugations is also found, e.g. Adgar, *streinout : out* p. 3, *tenout : alout* xxx, 109 ; Angier, *obeissot : comandot* 81 v. This tendency becomes more frequent in Later Anglo-Norman, and in the fourteenth century these terminations, though not in frequent use, are employed indiscriminately, T. 550-564.

The passage of **ou** to **u** (§ 1167) accounts for the spelling *-ut* (*-eut,* cf. § 1238) found occasionally in this tense, e.g. *Ipomedon,* MS. A, *reconfortut, quidut,* T. p. 555, cf. also § 1285.

§ 1278. *Weak perfect* forms of the south-western type in *-iet, -ierent* (cf. S.W. § xii) were occasionally used in the first period, e.g. *Oxf. Ps. perdies, deperdiet, deperdierent,* etc., Meister, pp. 43-44 ; *Brendan,* MS. D, *perderent, siwerent* (Appendix, § 70). Forms of this type may have contributed to the later confusion of the terminations *-erent, -ierent, -irent,* § 1314.

§ 1279. In the *weak persons* of the *strong* **u**-*perfect* forms and the imperfect subjunctive of this type, the west French labialised radical (*doüs, doüsse,* etc., cf. W. § xviii) and the central (*deüs, deüsse,* etc.) were both in use : both were reduced in the later period to **-us, -us(e),** etc., cf. above, §§ 1131, 1132.

In Late Anglo-Norman northern forms of these perfects and of the participles that went with them were introduced, e.g. *sciut*, (*scieut, scieust*), *deciut, aperciut* (cf. N.E. §§ xvii, xviii and T. 613, 609).

§ 1280. In Continental French there was considerable variety of termination among *past participles* (cf. § 1052) and this was increased in Anglo-Norman ; hesitation continued between the endings -i and -ü (O.F. *senti* and *sentu, feri : feru, reverti : revertu*, etc., *nez : nascu, remes : remasu, toli : tolu : toleit, aresté : aresteu*, cf. §§ 1053, 1054) and in later Anglo-Norman the use of these two terminations becomes very indiscriminate, e.g. (*cum*)*bati, corrumpi, respondi, aresti ; gettu, assaillu, bannu, fournu, offendu* (cf. T. 484, 485).

[For the extension of the termination of the first conjugation cf. §§ 1314, 1315.]

Section 4.—INFLUENCE OF SOUND-CHANGES.

§ 1281. As was seen above (§§ 1095, 1110), insular speech was affected by the Continental sound-changes that had their beginning in the eleventh or twelfth centuries, but the course followed by these changes was not infrequently accelerated, retarded or perturbed. The Anglo-Norman conjugation system was consequently affected by sound-change in a rather different way from the Continental and the divergence was often increased to the eye by the variegated orthography employed.

§ 1282. The *effacement of prae-consonantal* s and z (§§ 377, 378) led to much confusion in the spelling of the verb forms in the later period, cf. *Brendan*, MS. A, *dist*, present ind. and p. part. ; *St. Edmund, vest* for *vet* (*vait*) ; *Boeve*, MS. D, *sest* for *set* and *seit; Purg. Patr. voit* for *voist*, etc. ; *dust, tust* for the perfect (cf. Vising, *Purg. Patr.* 12, T. 115).

The use of inorganic *s* in certain forms is even prescribed by the *Orthographia Gallica :* 'Item in presenti et in preterito tempore inter *i, e, o, u* et *t* debet *s* scribi ut *est* . . . . *tost, lust*, etc. . . . et in preterito inter *a* et *t* ut *amast*,' C.O. 96, p. 8 ; the endings -*ast* and -*a*, -*ist* and -*i*, -*ust* and -*u* were thus confused.

[For -*aht*, -*iht*, cf. §§ 1118, 1216 ; for -*aust* cf. § 1153 ; for the possible use of *s* as a diacritical sign cf. § 1236.]

§ 1283. *Passage of* ts (z) *to* s.—In the early period the occasional use of *z* for *s* in the second person singular of the present indicative of conjugation III, the subjunctive of I (e.g. *faiz, diz, moz < moves, sez < sapis, deiz, declinz*, cf. T. pp. 66-68) is probably, as in the Continental French of the period (cf. § 890), the result of analogical influence. In the later twelfth and thirteenth century confusion was brought into the use of the symbols *s* and *z* by the relatively early passage of ts to s (cf.

§ 1183), and in the later period *z* is sometimes used for *s* as well as *s* for *z* : the *Orthographia Gallica*, for instance, prescribes *dytez, fetez* (*Rule* IV). In the second person plural the spelling *tz* was introduced about the middle of the fourteenth century, e.g. Bozon, *Contes, veretz*, p. 28, (T. 209).

[For the effacement of final **s** and other consonants, cf. §§ 1201-1204.]

§ 1284. The levelling of the diphthongs **ai** and **ei** to ę in the later twelfth century (§§ 1157, 1158) led to an interchange of the graphies *ai, ei* and *e* in the terminations -*ai*, -*eie*, -*eies*, -*eit*, -*eient*, and the verb forms *aie, aies, ait, aient, seie, seies, seit, seient, seioms, seiez*, e.g. *disaie, disait, diset, saie, saies*, etc., *seoms, serree* (for *serreie*), etc.　Combined with the effacement of ę in hiatus after tonic vowels (cf. § 1133) this levelling obliterated the difference between the termination of the first person of the imperfect and conditional (-*eie*) and the future and perfect of the first conjugation (-*ai*), cf. the spellings : future 1. *rencontrei, garrei, avere*, etc. ; perfect 1. *chaungey, chaunge ;* imperfect 1. *poai*, etc.

In the fourteenth century the spelling *oi* which was extensively employed for *ei* under Continental influence (cf. § 1188) was carried over to the perfect and future also and thus *dirai* and *direie* might both be written *dir(r)ai, dir(r)aie, dir(r)ei, dir(r)eie, dir(r)oi, dir(r)oie, dir(r)e* (cf. T. 44-60, 63, 64, 359).

§ 1285. The **u**-*sounds*.—In Later Anglo-Norman the sounds **u**, **ü** (§ 1142), **ǫu** (§ 1167), **üi** (§ 1160) had all fallen together under **u** and this sound might be represented by *u, ou* (§ 1220), *ui, eu* (§ 1288) ; thus **düt** pronounced **dut** might be written *dut, dout, duit, deut*, **portǫut** pronounced **portut** (§ 1167) *portout, portut, porteut*, and there was thus confusion in the endings of the **u**-perfects and between these and the terminations of the imperfect indicative of the first conjugation (cf. § 1277).

§ 1286. *Effacement of* ę.—The relatively early effacement of ę in Anglo-Norman (§§ 1132-1135) affected greatly the conjugation of the verb, for this sound played an important part in flexion and radical.

Radical.

§ 1287. ę *in hiatus.*—ę *countertonic* stood in hiatus with a following tonic or intertonic vowel in the following forms :—

(i) In the radicals of the weak forms of verbs with radicals ending in ę, e.g. sęeir, vęeir.

(ii) In the radicals of the weak forms of the perfect of vęeir, of the *s-perfects* of type A, in their later twelfth-century form (§ 1019), and in the imperfect subjunctive of verbs with perfects of these types, e.g. vęis, vęimęs, vęistęs, pręis, pręimęs, pręistęs, vęissę, pręissę.

(iii) In the radicals of the weak forms of the strong **u**-*perfects* and in the imperfect subjunctive of verbs with perfects formed on this model, e.g. **dęüs, dęümęs, dęüstęs, dęüssę.**

(iv) In the weak past participles of verbs whose radicals ended in an effaced consonant, e.g. **dęü, bęü,** etc., *cheeit,* **tšęeit** or **tšęeit.**

§ 1288. Effacement of **ę** in these forms began in the later twelfth century (§ 1132), and was very general in the thirteenth century, e.g. *ver* (<*veeir*) *St. Auban, Dermot* 476, *v(e)issiez* Fantosme, *v(e)u* Gaimar 1447, Thomas, *f(e)istes, pr(e)imes, d(e)istes* Chardri, *cr(e)umes St. Auban* (cf. T. 643-645, 690-694, 620-626, 667-684, 495-516).

The frequent retention of effaced **ę** in spelling led to its introduction into associated forms, e.g. the strong forms of the perfects, *preit, deut, eut,* and in weak past participles with radicals ending in a consonant, e.g. *rendeu, defendeu, veneu* (T. 475).

In Later Anglo-Norman forms in which the syllabic value of **ę** was retained were sometimes introduced under Continental influence, and *h* was sometimes then intercalated to indicate the hiatus, e.g. *dehu, recehu* (cf. § 1237 and T. 518).

[For syneresis of vowels in *oüs, oüsse, poüst,* etc., cf. above, § 1131.]

§ 1289. **ę** *intertonic* stood in hiatus with the preceding countertonic vowel in the future and conditional of verbs whose radicals ended in a vowel, e.g. **lięrai, luęrai.** Effacement began in the later twelfth century and was very general in the thirteenth, *St. Edmond, salurez* 3952, (§ 1132, T. p. 702).

In Late Anglo-Norman inorganic *e* was sometimes introduced in forms such as *escundierai, plaiera* (*Boeve,* 181, T. 731).

§ 1290. *Interconsonantal* **ę.**—Two tendencies conflicted in Anglo-Norman : the tendency to efface unstressed **ę** in interconsonantal position (§ 1134), and the tendency to develop a vocalic glide between interconsonantal groups consisting of *consonant* + r (cf. § 1173). Effacement showed itself earliest and was commonest between *breathed* consonants and r ; the glide development began in the later twelfth century and was at first most frequent between *voiced* consonants and r (cf. § 1173), e.g. *St. Br. fras* 426, etc., *frat* 367, etc., *frez* 553, etc., *truv(e)rat* 246, 412, *resuscitrai* 1567 (Intr. clxxiv) ; *Ps. d'Oxf. estreinderat, solderat, baterunt ; Q.L.R. deverad* v, 11, *saverez* vi, 3, *enuinderas* xvi, 4, etc. ; *Ps. d'Ar. receivere.* The lengthened forms gained ground in the thirteenth century and were dominant in the fourteenth but shortened forms were still occasional, e.g. Rymer, *mostra, delivra* (T. 722-732).

§ 1291. In Late Anglo-Norman, in the termination of the infinitive of verbs of conjugation III (*c*), this same tendency, combined with the

effacement of final unstressed ę (cf. § 1135), led to the development of forms in unstressed -er, e.g. Bozon, de′fender < de′fendere, ′metter ; Langtoft, at′tender, ′oynder, ′render (T. 419-423).

Terminations.

§ 1292. ę *in hiatus.*—ę stood in hiatus with the *preceding* tonic vowel in the following terminations :—

(i) In persons 2, 3, 6 of the present indicative and in the second person singular of the imperative of verbs of the first conjugation with radicals ending in a vowel, e.g. **esmaięs, otreięs, krięs, lwęs.**

(ii) In persons 1, 2, 3, 6 of the present subjunctive of verbs of conjugation III whose radicals ended in a vowel, e.g. **aię, deię, veię, seię, oię.**

(iii) In persons 1, 2, 6 of the imperfect indicative, in the terminations **-ǫuę, -ǫuęs, -ǫuęnt, -eię, -eięs, -eięnt.**

In the terminations **-eię, -eięs, -eięnt** effacement began in the later twelfth century (cf. § 917) ; it became general in all these forms in the thirteenth century, e.g. *Oxf. Ps. ferei* 39, 11 ; Adgar, *requerreint ;* Chardri, *di(e)nt, po(e)nt, esmai(e)nt, sei(e)nt ;* Adgar, *esmai, vou* for *esmaie, voue* (T. 131, 266-269, 367).

§ 1293. ę *final after a Consonant.*—Post-consonantal ę was in use as a termination (cf. §§ 898, 909, 1046), (i) in the second and third persons singular of the present indicative and in the second person singular of the imperative of verbs of the first conjugation with radicals ending in a consonant (*gardes, getes, apeles,* etc.) ; (ii) in the singular of the present subjunctive of verbs of the third conjugation whose radicals ended in a consonant (*rende, deive*) ; (iii) in the first and second persons of the imperfect subjunctive (*amasse, deusse*).

Except in shortened imperative forms such as *aur, gard, Ps. Cam.,* effacement of ę began only in the thirteenth century, first among verbs with dental radicals, e.g. *get,* Robert Gretham, *confound* (subj.) *: ont,* etc., *Boeve,* 497, etc. (§ 1135, T. pp. 126-133, 365-368). Shortened forms became more frequent in the fourteenth century and the retention of *e* in spelling led to its intrusion in other verbal forms, e.g. Bozon, *batte, mette, voile* for *bat, met, voil* (§ 1238, T. 26-30, 126-140).

Section 5.—INFLUENCE OF THE LATIN SPELLING.

§ 1294. Some forms in both periods are attributable to the influence of the spelling of Latin forms ; these may often be the expansion of the symbols used by earlier scribes to abbreviate endings.

§ 1295. (1) The use of the termination *-et, -ed* in the second plural of the *imperative* is occasional in the first period and is probably due to the influence of the Latin forms, e.g. *Brendan,* A. *prenget, seet,* D. *mettet* (*App.* p. 180), *Cam. Ps. seied, corned,* etc. (T. 207, 208).

In later Anglo-Norman the use of this spelling became indiscriminate and not infrequent, cf. *Boeve, fuet* (imper.), *usseit, fuseit, resemblet* (T. 208), Bozon, *Char, pernet, afyet, lerret*, etc. (p. xv), *Cam. A.N. Texts*, C. *Sachet, voleth, purreth, aveth, poeth, Intr.* p. 11. The graphy *th* found here and sometimes elsewhere may be due to the influence of the M.E., southern and Kentish form of flexion (cf. Prior, *Cam. A.N. Texts*, pp. 10, 11).

§ 1296. (2) The use of *-us* for unstressed *-es* in the first person plural, e.g. *sumus, levamus, esperamus*, is not infrequent (cf. Vising, *Char*, xv, T. 167-169).

§ 1297. (3) The use of *-unt* (*-ont*, more rarely *-ount*) *unstressed* in the third person plural appears to have begun under the influence of the Latin verb, for it is used most frequently at first in the perfect and present tenses in which it would have been employed in Latin, e.g. Gaimar, MS. L, *reuserunt, menerunt*; its use, however, became indiscriminate, e.g. Bozon, *Contes, parlont, enpernont*, T. 249 (cf. T. 242-253, Vising, *Purg. Patr.* 13).

[For *-unt, -ont* stressed cf. above §§ 1048, 1273.]

Section 6.—ANALOGICAL CHANGES COMMON TO INSULAR AND CONTINENTAL FRENCH.

§ 1298. The Anglo-Norman conjugation system was affected by the analogical replacements that were introduced on the Continent in the eleventh and twelfth centuries (§§ 874, 875) which were in the main simplifications among radicals, terminations and perfects, but even in the early period insular speech was also characterised by a use of analogical forms that was freer than that accepted on the mainland, the less usual or more isolated forms being more often replaced by others made on the model of much used verbs or of the first conjugation.

In the early period these forms were on the lines followed in the similar but rarer Continental forms, but in the thirteenth century the influence of the first conjugation gained ground and began to exercise an influence that became more and more subversive of the whole system ; in Later Anglo-Norman earlier freedom became licence, and forms were created that appear to us monstrous but which are not without parallels in Middle French, particularly in the north-east and east in which tradition was weakest, cf. §§ 1037, 1312.

Personal Endings.

§ 1299. Extension of ę in conjugation I (cf. §§ 898, 909).

(i) *First Person Singular of the Present Indicative.*—Two analogical forms of the first person of the present indicative in ę (§ 898) are

found in *St. Brendan, demeine* 1308, *lie* 1457, but forms of this kind still remain isolated in works of the later twelfth century (*parole, Cam. Ps., parole, prie, Q.L.R.*, T. p. 9), and it is only in Later Anglo-Norman that they become frequent; at that period they are often graphical only because ę has become mute, §§ 1133, 1135.

As in Continental French (§ 898), an early analogical reduction of ę is also occasional, e.g. *repair, Brendan*, 1364; *desir*, Adgar, ix, 113; *jug, Q.L.R.* I, 16, 7, (cf. T. pp. 24, 25).

§ 1300. (ii) *Singular of the Present Subjunctive.*—In the first and second persons of the present subjunctive analogical forms in ę came early into use (e.g. *Br. esmaie* 226, *crie* 1252, *nie* 1458) and secured extension rapidly; in the *Oxford Psalter* their use is already consistent (Meister, pp. 23, 24).

In the more used third person both introduction and extension of such forms was (as on the Continent, § 909) relatively slow. The earliest examples appear in the *Oxford Psalter* (six examples with ę, *embrive, espeire, cunferme, loed, profite, salved*, to twenty-nine without); and traditional forms remained dominant throughout the first period (T. pp. 306-316).

In the later period -ę was ordinarily without syllabic value, but its use became more frequent as forms containing it (e.g. *sauve, garde, amende*) preserved their radicals intact.

§ 1301. *Analogical z and s:* (i) *First Person Singular Present Indicative.*—The use of analogical forms of the first person singular of the third conjugation in *z* and *s* (§ 899) is occasional in Early Anglo-Norman, e.g. *Rol. Digby MS. guaz* (≠ *faz*) 515, Simund de Freine, *sez* (*sedeo*). In later Anglo-Norman forms of this type still remained infrequent but, as on the Continent, *s* was occasionally extended to the first person of the perfects, e.g. *chaïs*, Adgar, viii, 233, and even to the first person of the present indicative of the first conjugation, e.g. *Boeve, otriz* 3254, cf. § 901, T. 34-39, 589, 599-601.

§ 1302. (ii) *Second Person Singular of the Imperative.*—Occasional analogical forms in -*z* (cf. § 913) appear early, e.g. *oz, Al.* MS. L, 66; *recreiz, Rol. Digby MS.* 3892, (cf. T. p. 373). In Late Anglo-Norman, when final *s* was mute, there is occasionally graphical confusion, and forms in which *s* is part of the radical are written without it, e.g. *te* (< *tes* < *tais*, T. 372).

§ 1303. Replacement of -*eiz*.—In the second person plural the ending -*eiz* was early replaced in western French by -*ez* or -*iez* (§§ 908, 967); it is rare in Anglo-Norman except in early MSS. in which it is occasionally used in the future, subjunctive or imperative, e.g. *Oxf. Ps. orreiz* 94, 7, *saceiz* 93, 8 (cf. T. 215-217).

§ 1304. *Strong* s-*perfect.*—(i) The later twelfth-century replacement of forms containing intervocalic *s* (**z**) by forms without this sound (*meïs, meïmes, meïstes, meïsse* for *mesis, mesimes, mesistes, mesisse,* § 1019) found place in contemporary Anglo-Norman, *Oxf. Ps. seïmes* 136, 1, *Cam. Ps. seïs, Q.L.R. requeïstes, esleïstes,* p. 22, *feïst* 23, *feïs* 29, etc. In Later Anglo-Norman forms of this type were more and more frequently employed but in the fourteenth century there was a slight recrudescence of the forms with intervocalic *s,* under the influence of northern French where such forms were longer preserved (N. § xxx, cf. T. pp. 641, 642).

(ii) The replacement of the forms of the third person plural in -(s)t**ŗent,** -(z)dr**ŗent** by those in -ir**ŗent** (§ 1019 (ii)) went more slowly than on the Continent; in the early period they remained sparse, and though frequent in Later Anglo-Norman they never completely ousted those of the earlier type, cf. *Year Books, misterent, quisterent, mittrent, pritrent, pleinterent* (T. pp. 647-651).

(iii) As in Continental French this type of perfect was sometimes extended to verbs whose perfects were more ordinarily formed on the weak **i**-*model: Oxf. Ps. establisis, guerpesis,* M. p. 45, Bozon, *Contes, vendisist* 103, *perdesist* 129 (T. p. 655 and § 1013).

§ 1305. *Strong* u-*perfects.*—The replacement of the forms in -*out,* -*ourent* by analogical forms in -*ot,* -*orent* (§ 1025) was tardy in Anglo-Norman (§ 1268), but in t' e introduction of forms in -*ut* and -*urent* for these types (§ 1032) insular speech rather anticipated Continental usage, the earliest example, *turent,* appearing in the *Oxford Psalter* 106, 29, cf. also Thomas, *ut : murut,* Adgar, *pleut : receut* (T. 606-609). It must be remembered, however, that these Anglo-Norman forms may be only graphical, because in the later twelfth century the diphthong **ọu** had levelled to **u** and **ü** had velarised to the same sound (§ 1285).

All three forms of the termination remained in use in Later Anglo-Norman -*ot,* -*out,* -*ut* (-*eut*), and under northern influence forms such as *tiut, sciut, tieut, scieut,* N.E. § xvii (*tieust, scieust,* § 1282), were also occasionally employed (§ 1279, T. 613).

§ 1306. *Imperfect Subjunctive I.*—In Late Middle French the termination of the first and second plural of the imperfect subjunctive of the first conjugation began to be re-made on the radical of the other persons and thus -*issons,* -*issions,* -*issez,* -*issiez,* were gradually replaced by -*assons,* -*assions,* -*assez,* -*assiez* (cf. § 1044). In Anglo-Norman analogical forms of this type appear in the later fourteenth century and thus forestall somewhat those attested on the Continent, e.g. Bozon, *Contes* (MS. A), 15, *chauntassez;* Rymer (1360), *cessassons, delaissassons,* etc. (T. p. 665).

[For forms in -*essons,* -*esses,* cf. § 1269.]

Section 7.—ANALOGICAL FORMATIONS PROPER TO ANGLO-NORMAN.

§ 1307. The analogical formations proper to Anglo-Norman are for the most part simplifying in tendency and induced by the preponderance of much-used forms or of types such as the first conjugation. In Later Anglo-Norman the growing confusion of endings and forms indicates the gradual disintegration of the whole system.

Period I.

§ 1308. In Period I the system remained stable and the characteristic Anglo-Norman analogical forms are relatively few in number. They fall into two categories :—

§ 1309. (1) *Influence of the First Conjugation.*—In the Later twelfth century the infinitive termination *-eir* began to be replaced by *-er*, e.g. *Q.L.R. veer, seer, tamer ; St. Gilles, maneir : aprismer*, 1623 (T. pp. 390-410).

As the terminations **-eir** and **-er** were falling together under **-er** in this period (§§ 1158, 1146), this replacement is possibly graphical only.

§ 1310. (2) *Influence of much-used Verbs.*—In the later part of the first period analogical influence was exercised by the verbs *veeir, curir, mettre* on those associated with them by sound, cf. the forms *enveit* (for *enveie*), *Arundel Ps.*, etc. (T. 123), and later *ottreit, nait* (T. 123-125), *demurt, hunurt, plurt* ≠ *curt* (T. 125), *plurut* ≠ *curut* (T. 629), *gettre, get* ≠ *mettre, met* (T. 127), *(re)mist*, etc., for *(re)mest* ≠ *mist, etc.* (cf. § 1014) ; *uvrir* and *uvrer, recuvrir* and *recuvrer* were also often confused.

Period II.

§ 1311. *Radical.*—(i) Characteristic of Later Anglo-Norman is the tendency to simplify the conjugation system by generalising one or other radical and in particular the palatalised radical of the present subjunctive (a tendency already noticeable in Gallo-Roman, cf. § 949). Examples are : Bozon, *Contes, facez*, ind. pres. 2, p. 41, *faceoms*, ind. pres. 4, p. 45, *facent*, ind. pres. 6, p. 27, *doynt*, ind. pres. 3, p. 32 ; cf. also *fierge* for *fiert, meorgent* for *meorent*, (cf. T. 280, 281) ; MS. of *Black Prince, voilleit, voilloir, vailli*, etc., *viegnent, veignent* (for *vienent*), *preigniez* (for *prenez*), p. xliv.

§ 1312. (ii) In later Anglo-Norman, as occasionally in Middle French, § 1037, the third person plural of the perfect of verbs in *-eindre, -eindre, -oindre ; endre, -ondre, -ordre, -ordre*, was influenced by the infinitive, cf. the perfect forms *joindrent, esteindrent, ardrent*, etc. (T. pp. 653, 654).

§ 1313. *Terminations.*—(i) In the imperfect indicative the traditional forms in *-ium*, etc., *-ïez* (§ 918), were sometimes replaced, by the forms *-eiums, (-eyum, -oium, -eons), -eiez (-oiez, -eez)* under the influence of the other terminations, e.g. *esteyum, esteyons, estoium, estoiez, purreiez* (T. 191-193, 218, 219, cf. E. § xxix) and in Later Anglo-Norman

the termination *-eimes* was introduced under the influence of the northern *-iemes* (N. § xxvii), cf. Tanquerey, pp. 164, 165.

(ii) The spelling *faceoms*, *demangeoms*, etc., in which *e* is a graphical device (§ 731), led to its graphical introduction in other forms in late documents, e.g. *establisseoms*, *eusseoms*, *mandeoms* (T. 193).

§ 1314. *Influence of the First Conjugation.*—(i) In the early thirteenth century there began to show itself a tendency to replace the terminations *-ir*, *-irent*, *-i*, *-ie* by forms of the first conjugation, cf. Guischart, *plaiser : asaier*, *Boeve*, *plaiser*, *morer*, *revener* (p. xxviii); *Dermot*, *assenté : hué* 2371, *Boeve*, 2583, *seisé : engulez*, etc.: *guerperent : chanterent*, *isserent : ressemblerent*, cf. T. 411-418, 477-482, 577-582, Vising, *Purg. Patr.* p. 54.

The adoption of these forms was facilitated by the existence of dialectal variants: (*a*) The south-western perfects in *-iet* and *-ierent* (S.W. § xii); (*b*) The northern reduction of **ieę** to **ię** (*laissiee* to *laissie*) (N. § v); (*c*) The northern retention of the descending diphthong '*ie* and reduction to **i** (cf. N. § vii).

In legal Anglo-Norman of the fourteenth century *aconpler*, *establer*, *oyer* were the established forms, but the use of the variant terminations was often indiscriminate, cf. Bozon, *Contes*, *donir*, *gardir*, *pledir ; soilli*, *engressi*.

§ 1315. (ii) In Later Anglo-Norman the first conjugation extended its influence much further. The forms *tistrer*, *despiserent*, *aparerent*, *combata*, *entenda*, *erda*, *sourda*, figure in the *Contes* of Bozon, and Tanquerey cites *treyerent*, *coniserent*, *pleynerent* (p. 583), *diserent*, *feserent* (p. 654), *treia* (for *traist*), *rescua*, *issa*, *conissa*, *abatates*, *poames*, *poast* (pp. 586, 587). The pitch ignorance reaches in the fifteenth century is illustrated by the paradigms given in Harleyan MS. 4971, where the perfect of *vouloir* and the imperfect subjunctive of *faire* are conjugated as follows: '*jeo volay*, *tu voillastes*, *cil voillast*, *nous volasmes*, *vous voilastes ; que jeo fesace*, *tu fesacet*, *cil fesast*, *nous fesaceons*, *vous fesacez*, *ceux fesacent ; que jeo avace*, etc.' (*Intr. Orth. Gall.* p. vii).

§ 1316. *Confusion of Types and Tenses.*—Among perfects and past participles there was much confusion of type in Later Anglo-Norman. Tanquerey cites, for example, *purrust* (*pourrir*), *tenut*, *manjurent* (p. 630); *crustrent* (for *crurent*), *sustrent*, etc. (p. 656).

[For past participles cf. § 1280.]

In this period also, the forms of the perfect and the conditional were sometimes confused, for example, *purra*, *purroient*, replace *put*, *purent ;* the syntactical difference between the imperfect and perfect tense was also gradually obliterated and often only one of these two tenses was retained or else a hybrid tense compact of the two, cf. Maitland, *Year Book*, p. lxi, and *Black Prince*, p. xlv.

§ 1317. PHONOLOGY.

	Period I.		Period II.	
	1066–*c.* 1130.	*c.* 1130–*c.* 1230.	*c.* 1230–.	
Vowels				
§ 1142	ü > { u i		ü > ɪu	§ 1142
§ 1145		ĕ blocked > ę		
§ 1146		ĕ + l and r > ę		
§ 1155		je > ę		
§ 1156		ᶦue > { u wę ö	ð unrounds to e	§ 1143
§ 1160	üi > { ü(> u) wi			
§ 1161		ui < { u wi		
§ 1158	ẹi > ęi	> ę		
§ 1159	ǎi ẽi } > ęĩ	> ẽ	} ẽ denasalises	§ 1151
§ 1084	ē retained unlowered			
			ā > ā̆ and denasalises	§§ 1151,2
		a + effaced s > ā > ɑ		§ 1153
		ǫ + effaced s > ǭ > ǫ > u		§ 1144
§§ 1097, 1179	prae-consonantal ɫ vocalises			
§§ 1162, 1164, 5		ęu, ęu > ö, ęu > ɪu		
§ 1165		eau > { au iau		
§ 1167		ǫu > u		
§ 1168		ᶦieu > ɪö or ɪu	u-*diphthongs* differen-	§ 1163
§ 1169		ᶦueu > ö or u	tiated before labials	
§ 1131	Coalescence of juxta-posed homophonous vowels	consonantalisation of i in hiatus		§ 1134
§ 1132		Effacement of ę before tonic vowels		
§ 1132		Effacement of ę after ct. vowels		
§ 1132		Effacement of ę intertonic		
§ 1133		Effacement of ę final in hiatus with tonic vowels		
			Effacement of final post-con-sonantal ę	§ 1135
			Aphaeresis of initial syllable	§ 1137
			Quantitative differen-tiation of vowels	§ 1170
Consonants				
§§ 1175, 1176	Effacement of ð *inter-vocalic* and θ *final*			
§ 1177	Effacement of ð *prae-consonantal*			
			Effacement of *prae-consonantal* χ (< s)	§ 1178
§ 1182	Replacement of ʎ and ŋ by ɪl and ɪn			
§ 1183	Passage of ts to s			
			Passage of tš and dž to š and ž	§ 1181
§ 1171		Development of intervocalic glides		
§§ 1201-1204		Effacement of *final supported* consonants and *final* s and sometimes r and l		
			Vocalisation of v + cons.	§ 1185

§ 1318. DECLENSION.

	Period I.		Period II.	
	1066–c. 1130.	c. 1130–c. 1230.	c. 1230–.	
§ 1244	Analogical feminines in ę			
§ 1243	Analogical nom. sg. masc. in s			
§ 1246		Disintegration of declension		
			Plurals in -es (-is)	§ 1247
§ 1252	Retention of lu, acc. masc. of article			
			Confusion of forms of article and pronoun	§ 1253
			Confusion of il and ele	§ 1251
			Confusion of il and cil	§ 1251
§ 1248		Use of variant forms of ego		
§§ 1260, 1261		Use of variant forms of spelling of possessives		
§ 1256		Use of variant forms of illos and ecce-illos		
§ 1259		Extension of neuter ceo		
§ 1262		Extension of use of neuter que		
			Extension of use of quel and queux	§ 1262

§ 1319. CONJUGATION.

	Period I.		Period II.
	1066–c. 1130.	c. 1130–c. 1230.	c. 1230–.
	Retention of Early Western Forms.		
§ 1272	(a) Termination of first plural in -um (-om, etc.)		
§ 1267	(b) „ „ impf. ind. I. in -oue, -oues, -out, -ouent		
§§ 1275, 1274	(c) Use of subjunctive present in -ge, ind. pres. i. in -c		
	Tardiness in Generalising Analogical Continental Forms.		
§ 1277	(a) Terminations of impf. ind. in -oe, -oes, -ot, -oent		
§ 1268	(b) „ „ 3rd persons of strong u-perfects in -ot, -orent		
§ 1304	(c) „ „ 3rd pl. of strong s-perfects in -irent (for -i(s)trent)		
§ 1301	(d) Flexional s (z) in first sg. of pres. ind.		

CONJUGATION (*cont.*).

	Period I.		Period II.	
	1066–*c.* 1130.	*c.* 1130–*c.* 1230.	*c.* 1230–.	
§ 1298	*Free Recourse to Analogy.*			
		Influence Conjugation I.		
§ 1309		Replacement of *-eir* by *-er*		
§ 1314			Replacement of *-ir, -irent, -i, -ie* by forms of conj. I.	
			Generalisation of forms of conj. I.	§ 1314
			Early use of forms *-assons, -assez* in impf. subj. I.	§ 1306
§ 1310		Analogical influence of much used verbs		
			Generalisation of palatalised radical	§ 1311
			Increasing indiscriminate use of forms of perfects	§§ 1315, 1316
			Confusion of forms of perfects and conditional	§§ 1312, 1316
			Use of termination *-unt*, etc., in 3rd pl.	§ 1297
			Use of terminations *-eiums*, etc. *-eiez*, etc., in impf. ind.	§ 1313
		Influence of A.N. Sound-Changes.		
		Instability of ę in *hiatus* :		
§§ 1287-1289		(*a*) in radical: *vis* for *veĩs, veir* for *veĕir*, etc.		
§ 1292		(*b*) in terminations : *ferei* for *fereiĕ*, etc., *fereint* for *fereiĕnt*, *di(e)nt* for *diĕnt*, etc.		
§ 1290		Instability of ę *interconsonantal* : *frai* for *ferai*, etc.		
§ 1293			Instability of ę *final post-consonantal* : *chant* for *chante*, etc.	
§ 1173		Use of interconsonantal glide ę		
§ 1284		Levelling of **ai** and **ei** to ę confuses endings *-ai* and *-eie*		
§ 1285		Levelling of **ou** and **ü** to **u** leads to use of *-ut*, *-urent* for *-out, -ourent*		
§ 1282		Effacement of *prae-consonantal* **s** leads to free inorganic use		

LIST OF TEXTS CITED.

[For full details and for bibliography cf. Vising, to whom references are given.]

Early XII.

V. 64. COMPUT. *Der Computus* des Philippe de Thaun, ed. E. Mall.
V. 65. BESTIAIRE, PH. *Le Bestiaire* de Philippe de Thaun, ed. E. Walberg.
V. 10. BRENDAN. *The Anglo-Norman Voyage of St. Brendan*, by Benedeit, ed.
        E. G. R. Waters, Oxford, 1928.

Middle XII.

V. 1.   OXF. PS. *Libri Psalmorum Versio Antiqua Gallica e cod. MS. in Bibl.
        Bodl. asservato*, ed. F. Michel, cf., (Meister, J. H. *Die Flexion im
        Oxforder Psalter;* abbreviated title M.).
V. 1.   ARUNDEL PS. Ed. Beyer, *Zts. rom. Ph.* XI, XII.
V. 2.   CAM. PS. *Le Livre des Psaumes d'après les MSS. de Cambridge et de Paris*,
        ed. F. Michel.
V. 27. ADAM. *Le Mystère d'Adam*, ed. P. Studer.
V. 61. GAIMAR. *Estorie des Engleis*, by Geffrey Gaimar, ed. (1) T. Wright;
        (2) T. Duffus Hardy and Trice-Martin.

Late XII.

V. 13. ADGAR. *Adgars Marienlegenden*, (1) ed. Neuhaus; (2) ed. Herbert.
V. 25. ROM. ROM. *Le Roman des Romans*, ed Tanquerey.
V. 53. DONNEI. *Donnei des Amants*, ed. G. Paris.
V. 14. ST. EDMUND. *La Vie St. Edmund le Rei*, by Denis Pyramus, ed. Ravenel.
V. 62. FANTOSME. *Chronique* de Jordan Fantosme, ed. Michel.
V. 22. GUISCHART. *Sermon en Vers*, de Guischart de Beauliu, ed. Gabrielson.
V. 32. IPOMEDON. By Hue de Rotelande, ed. Kölbing und Koschwitz.
V. 5.   Q.L.R. *Li Quatre Livre des Reis*, ed. Curtius.
V. 15. ST. GILLES. *La Vie de St. Gilles* de Guillaume de Berneville, ed. G.
        Paris.
V. 16. ST. GEORGE, R. PHIL. *Les Oeuvres de Simund de Freine (La Vie de St.
        Georges* and *Le Roman de Philosophie)*, ed. Matzke, S.A.T.F.
V. 30. THOMAS. *Tristan*, ed. Bédier.

Early XIII.

V. 108. ANGIER. *Vie de St. Grégoire*, ed. Cloran. Cf. M. K. Pope, *Étude sur la
         langue de frère Angier*, Paris, 1903.
V. 115. AUBAN. *La Vie de St. Auban*, ed. R. Atkinson. Cf. Suchier, *Ueber die
         Matthaeus Paris zugeschriebene Vie de St. Auban*, Halle, 1876, Uhle-
         mann, *Rom. St.* iv.
V. 20, 21, 56. CHARDRI. *Chardry's Josaphaz, Set Dormanz und Petit Plet*, ed.
         Koch.
V. 292. DERMOT. *The Song of Dermot and the Earl*, ed. Orpen.
V. 104. PURG. PATR. *Le Purgatoire de St. Patrice*, ed. Vising, Göteborg, 1916.

Middle XIII.

V. 213. BOEVE. *Der Anglonormannische Boeve de Haumtone*, ed. Stimming.

V. 146. SERMON EN VERS, ed. Tanquerey.

Later XIII.

V. 158. WADINGTON. *Manuel des Pechez*, by Wilham de Wadington.

V. 395. OAK BOOK. *The Oak Book of Southampton* (chaps. iv and v), ed. P. Studer.

XIII-XIV.

V. 368. BOZON, CONTES. *Les Contes Moralisés* de Nicole Bozon, ed. L. Toulmin Smith et P. Meyer, Paris, 1889. S.A.T.F.

BÓZON, BONTÉ. *De la Bonté des Femmes*, ed. Paul Meyer, *Contes*, pp. xxxiii-xli.

V. 287. BOZON, CHAR and O. *Deux Poèmes* de Nicholas Bozon, *Le Char d'Orgueil*, *La Lettre de l'Empereur Orgueil*, ed. J. Vising, Göteborg, 1919.

V. 357. BOZON, PLAINTE. *La Plainte d'Amour*, ed. Vising.

V. 134. BOZON, STE. AGNES, ed. Paul Meyer, *Contes*, pp. xlviii-lii.

LETTRES A.F. *Recueil de Lettres Anglo-Françaises* (1265-1399), ed. F. Tanquerey, Paris, 1916.

Early XIV.

DIV. MUNDI. *Divisiones Mundi* in *Cambridge A.N. Texts*, ed. O. H. Prior, Cambridge, 1924.

V. 377. LANGTOFT. *Chronicle of Pierre de Langtoft*, ed. T. Wright, 1866.

V. 395. OAK BOOK II. *The Rolls of Oleron*, chap. ix, p. 54.

XIII and XIV.

V. 335. RYMER. *Foedera, Conventiones, Litterae.*

V. 396. YEAR BOOKS. *Year Books of the reign of Edward II*, vol. i, ed. Maitland, vol. xx, ed. Legge and Holdsworth, Selden Society.

LIST OF MANUSCRIPTS CITED.

[For full details cf. editions or Vising, pp. 88-100, to whom references are given.]

Twelfth Century.

Doomsday Book, Exchequer and *Exon.* (1086); (cf. article of F. Hildebrand, cited § 39).

V. 165. *Oxford Psalter.* Early or middle XII.

Roland, Digby MS. According to Samaran between 1130 and 1150.

V. 300. *Cambridge Psalter.* XII² (*c.* 1160).

V. 94. *Arundel Psalter.* XII².

Alexis, MS. L. XII.

V. 400. *Adam.* XII².

V. 36. $\begin{cases} Bestiaire, \text{ MS. L} \\ Comput, \text{ MS. C} \end{cases}$ XII².

V. 353. *Q.L.R.* XII² (*c.* 1175).

Early Thirteenth Century.

V. 374. *St. Brendan*, B. *c.* 1200 (cf. Waters, *Intr.* p. xii).
V. 368. *Angier.* Early XIII, *Dialogues*, 1212, *Vie de St. Grégoire*, 1214.
V. 318. *St. Brendan*, D. XIII¹ (cf. Waters, *Intr.* p. xiv).
V. 101. *Comput*, S. XIII¹.
V. 82. *Guischart.* XIII¹.
V. 332. *Leis Guillaume.* XIII¹.
            First Anglo-Norman Prose Lapidary (in *Anglo-Norman Lapidaries*, ed.
            P. Studer and J. Evans), Paris, 1924.

Middle Thirteenth Century.

V. 341. *St. Auban.*
V. 45. *St. Brendan*, A. (Cf. Waters, *Intr.* note on p. ix.)

Later Thirteenth Century.

V. 393. *Boeve*, D.
V. 12. *Gaimar.*

Fourteenth Century.

V. 325. *Oak Book of Southampton*, I. *c.* 1300.
V. 129. *Bozon, Contes*, A. Middle XIV.
V. 307.   *Contes*, B. XIV¹.
V. 59.   *Char.* XIV¹.
V. 51.   *Ste. Agnes.* XIV¹.
V. 307.   *Bonté des Femmes.* XIV¹.
V. 60.   *Plainte d'Amour.* XIV¹.
V. 51. *St. Edmund.* XIV¹.
            Divisiones Mundi. XIV¹.
V. 136, 86, 219. *Orthographia Gallica*, MSS. T, H, C. XIV².
V. 204. *Orthographia Gallica*, MS. O. XV¹.
            Black Prince. End XIV.

[For A.N. grammatical treatises cf. p. xxv.]

ABBREVIATED TITLES OF MODERN WORKS ON ANGLO-NORMAN.

BEHRENS. *Beiträge zur Geschichte der Frz. Sprache in England*, von D. Behrens, Heilbronn, 1886. (*Frz. Studien* v, 2.)
BUSCH. *Laut- und Formenlehre der anglonorm. Sprache des XIV Jahrhunderts*, von E. Busch, Greifswald, 1887.
MAITLAND. *Year Books of Edward II*, vol. i, Selden Society.
MENGER. *The Anglo-Norman Dialect, a Manual of its Phonology and Morphology*, by L. E. Menger, Columbia University Press, 1904.
SAMARAN. *Etude Paléographique du MS. d'Oxford* (in *La Chanson de Roland, Réproduction phototypique*, ed. Laborde, Roxburghe Club, 1932).
T. Tanquerey, F. J. *L'Évolution du Verbe en Anglo-Français*, Paris, 1915.
V. Vising, J. *Anglo-Norman Language and Literature*, London and Oxford, 1923.

APPENDIX.

Conspectus of Dialectal Traits, Mainly of the Later Old French Period.

H. Morf, *Zur Sprachlichen Gliederung Frankreichs*, Berlin, 1911 ; H. Suchier, *Die Französische und Provenzalische Sprache und ihre Mundarten*, Strassburg, 1911 (with valuable maps). [For the modern patois cf. E. Herzog, *Neufranzösische Dialekttexte*, Leipzig, 1914 ; J. Gilliéron et E. Edmont, *Atlas Linguistique de la France*, Paris, 1903-1910 ; D. Behrens, *Bibliographie des Patois Gallo-Romans*, 2nd ed. par E. Rabiet, 1893, (Frz. St. N.F. I), and D. Behrens and J. Jung, *Bibliographie der frz. Patoisforschung für die Jahre 1892-1902*, Z.F.S.L. xxv ; A. Dauzat, *Les Patois*, Paris, 1907.]

§ 1320. Northern Region. N.

[Cf. Wilmotte, ‘Etudes de Dialectologie Wallonne,’ *Rom.* xvii-xix, Marchot, *Zts. frz. Spr. u. Litt.* xxxix, pp. 144-153 (Marchot I), xli, 233-236 (Marchot II), the introductions to the following texts, especially Suchier’s edition of *Aucassin et Nicolete*, Doutrepont, *Etude linguistique sur Jacques de Hemricourt et son Epoque*, 1892, and E. G. Wahlgren, *Observations sur les Verbes à Parfaits Faibles*, 1931.]

Illustrative Texts and MSS. :—

(i) *Early Old French.—*
Cent. ix : *Eulalia ;* provenance vicinity of Valenciennes ; MS. end ix.
Cent. x : *Jonah Sermon = Jonas ;* provenance north-eastern.
Cent. xi-xii : *Alexis*, MS. V, pub. Rajna, *Arch. Rom.* XIII, pp. 3-10, 51-53.

(ii) *Late Twelfth and Early Thirteenth Centuries.—*
Le Jeu de St. Nicolas de Jean Bodel = *St. Nic. ;* provenance Arras.
Aucassin und Nicolete = Auc. ; provenance Hainault (?) ; MS. end xiii.
Li Romans de Carité et Miserere du Renclus de Moiliens = *Renclus ;* provenance vicinity of Amiens (?).
Poème Moral = P. Mor. ; provenance north-eastern ; MS. early xiii.
Li Dialoge Gregoire lo Pape ; provenance Liège ; Extract in Studer-Waters = *Ex. Greg.*

(iii) *Thirteenth and Fourteenth Centuries.*—

    Le Jeu de Robin et Marion de Adam le Bossu = *Jeu Rob.* ; provenance Arras.

    Le Jeu de la Feuillée de Adam le Bossu = *Feuillée* ; provenance Arras.

    Chronique Rimée de Philippe Mousket; provenance Tournai. Examples from Studer-Waters = *Ex. Mousket.*

    Chronique de Jean Froissart; provenance Hainault. Extract in Studer-Waters = *Ex. Froiss.*

(iv) *Fifteenth Century.*—

    Mystères et Moralités = *Mysteres* XV ; provenance, District of Liège ; MS. cent. xv.

The northern region included broadly Wallonia (French-speaking Belgium), Artois and Picardy, and in the characteristics developed early north Normandy also (cf. §§ 37, 1326, 1327).

The linguistic features that characterise this region and more particularly the north-western are the following :—

Phonology.

§ i. The retention of the velar articulation of initial **k** and **g** before Gallo-Roman **a, e, i** (§§ 298, 301) and the shift of **ts** [< *initial* **k** + Latin **e, i** (§§ 290, 291), **kj** (306) and initial **tj** (§ 308)] to **tš** instead of **ts**, § 292, cf. *Eul. cose, kose, Auc. kaitive, aforkent, ganbe, gardin,* Renclus, *kier, trenkier, markeandise,* St. Nic. *Aufrique: rique* 227, *Jake: vaque* 155, Renclus, *avanchier, princhier, pieche, blieche, Jeu Rob. noches: boches* 656. Originally characteristic of the whole northern region, including north Normandy (cf. the place-names *Caen, Fécamp*), this pronunciation lost ground both in Normandy and in the north-eastern region before the end of Later Old French, (cf. Morf, *op. cit.* p. 21).

[For the retention of countertonic **a** free after **k** and **g** cf. § 417; for spelling cf. § 701.]

§ ii. The greater intensity of the Frankish influence (§ 17). To this influence the following traits may be ascribed :—

§ iii. (1) The retention of initial **w** in Germanic loan-words and in the Latin words contaminated with them and in E.O.F. *intervocalic* **w**, e.g. *Auc. waucrer* 34, 10, *waumoner* 30, 17, *Ex. Froiss. wape* 26, *Mysteres* XV, *wastelet, sewisse* (*Intr.* pp. lxiii, lxiv) ; (cf. § 636).

§ iv. (2) A strengthening of the tonic stress that affected the development of both tonic and unstressed vowels, (cf. also the north-eastern developments, N.E. (iii)). Weakly stressed vowels were reduced or early slurred and the heavier tonic stress led to the retention of falling diphthongs and triphthongs to a relatively late date and thus influenced their development in various ways :—

§ v. *Diphthongs and Triphthongs.*—(*a*) The diphthongs ˡie and ˡue, when juxtaposed to ę, were ordinarily reduced to i and u respectively, so that ˡieę > ˡię, ˡueę > uę : *Auc. lië* (< *liee, laeta*) 32, 20, *puïe* (< *puiee*) 20, 13, *Jeu Rob. blechie : mie* 75, Renclus, *roe* (**ruę**) (< *ruee, rŏta*) *: loe, Car.* cvii, *P. Mor. puent* (< *pueent*), p. 63.

[Cf. also E. § iii and §§ 513, 552.]

§ vi. (*b*) The triphthongs ˡieu and ˡüeu (§§ 544 (1), (2), (3), 545, 555 (1), 556) were reduced to iu and ü respectively : *Auc. liu* (< *lieu*) 12, 33, *miue* 2, 21, *fu* (< **fueu) 4, 8, *pule* (< *pueule*, § 557), *Jeu Rob. ju : venu* 440, *Ex. Mousket, fu : fu* 13, Renclus, *gius, sius* (*sequis) *: pius, vius* (< *vilis*), *Car.* lxii, cf. *Intr.* pp. cxx, cxxi and §§ 546, 557.

§ vii. (*c*) The diphthongs ˡie, ˡue, ˡai, ˡoi were not infrequently reduced to their first (stressed) element : *Auc. destrir* 10, 21, *civres* 10, 7, *P. Mor. derrir, Pire, bin, tine* (< *tiene*), *murt* (< *muert*), *bur* < *buer, Myst.* XV, *querir : acompagnir, sentir*(*e*) *: aydier, Auc. frales* 2, 7, *fare* 5, 25, *Ex. Greg. trast* 78, *pirre* 82, *P. Mor. glore, anoe* < *anoie,* cf. *Intr.* pp. 58, 75, 76, cf. §§ 513, 533, 554.

§ viii. (*d*) In the northern region the triphthong ęau was differentiated to iau and the diphthong ǫu either to au or eu : *Auc. biax* 1, 3, *damoisiax* 2, 10, *Ex. Froiss. yawe* 27, *Auc. faus* (*follis*) 3, 7, *peu* 2, 40, *eut* 20, 1, *seut* 40, 9, *seurent* 38, 7, *Feuillée, taut* (*tollit*) *: faut* 459, *Ren.* II, 882, *vautrés* (*voltulatus), (§§ 539, 540, 549, 1029 ; but cf. N.E. § viii).

§ ix. (*e*) The diphthongs ai and āi were retained relatively late in the northern region (§§ 469, 533) and ēi apparently lowered to āi (cf. Matzke, P.M.L.A. xxi, pp. 661-668).

[For the diphthongisation of ę < a *tonic* free cf. N.E. § iv and § 232.]

§ x. *Atonic Vowels.*—(*a*) ę became early unstable when in hiatus before a vowel, e.g. *Auc. vesture* for *vesteure* 12, 16, *benois* for *beneois* 24, 61, *P. Mor. guaniet, juner, juglors, desconu, pecchors* (*Intr.* pp. 85-86), cf. § 268.

§ xi. (*b*) i in hiatus with e, as for instance in the terminations of the first and second person plural of the impf. ind. and conditional, was early consonantalised, e.g. *Auc. afferriès* 25, 14 (3-syll.), cf. §§ 267, 918.

§ xii. (*c*) The unstressed forms of the feminine of the article and of the possessive pronoun *la, ma, ta, sa, mon, ton, son* were reduced to *le, me,* etc., *men,* etc., e.g. *Auc.* 2, *le vile* 4, *le face* 13, *te tere* 21 ; 10, *men pere* 67, *sen cors* 68, §§ 839, 853. The similarity between the masculine and feminine forms of the accusative singular that was thus induced led to the use of **li** for **la** in the nominative singular, e.g. *Auc.* 5, 18 *li vostre amie.*

§ xiii. *Other Characteristics Developed in Period I.*—Retention of
the intervocalic consonantal groups **m'l, n'r, l'r** without denasalisation
of **m** or **n** (§ 369), or development of an interconsonantal glide (§ 370) :
Auc. asanlent for *assamblent* 21, 1, *tenront* 26, 20, *vinrent* 27, 17, *sorrai*
for *soldrai* 24, 58, *Feuillée, courre : pourre*, (*pulverem*) 736, *sanle* (*sembla*) :
estranle (*estrangle*) 1088 ; cf. Marchot I, pp. 146, 147, II, p. 237.
Reduction of the O.F. groups **vr, dr, tr** by the development of a vocalic
interconsonantal glide, e.g. *metera, avera*, or the elimination of **v**, e.g.
ara, sara, cf. §§ 972, 976.

§ xiv. Opening of the labial consonant in the intervocalic groups
pl, bl, e.g. *pule, Auc.* 16, 15, *diaule < diable, Eul.* 3, *covenaulement, Ex.
Bern.* 11, *taule < tabula* ; cf. § 372 and Marchot I, 146, 147.

§ xv. Retention of final **t** unsupported after tonic vowels (cf.
§ 356), e.g. *vertut, gret*, cf. *Jeu Rob. piet : siet* 197, *P. Mor. vertut :
mut* (*multum*) 44, *Ex. Froiss. donnet* 45, *piet* 68.

§ xvi. Retention of intervocalic **ẑ**, intervocalic and final **ŝ** into Early
Old French and subsequent shift to **ž** or **š** and later **χ**, without development of preceding palatal glide, (spelling sometimes *x*), *Jonas, posciomes,
escit, Eulalia, lazsier* 125, *Ps. Lorr. moixon, tixerant, Intr.* p. xlii (cf.
§§ 314, 315, E. § v, Marchot I, 147-149, M.L. *Gr. Rom.* I, § 511,
Wahlgren, *Parfaits Faibles*, pp. 65-67, 92, 93).

§ xvii. Lowering of **ę** to **ẹ** or **a** before **ɫ** and **ǰ** + *cons.* cf. § 501, e.g.
Ex. Greg. eaz 84, *Auc. caviax, ciax*, Renclus, *Mis. aus* (< *illos*) : *tem-
poraus* li : *maus*, cxxvi, *Jeu Rob. consaut : vaut* 393, cf. E. § ix.

§ xviii. Palatalisation of countertonic **ę** to **i** before **ǰ, ŋ** and **ǰ** and
after **tš**, and of intertonic **ę** before **ŝ** and **ẑ** (§ 422), e.g. *signour, vigniens*
(*veniamus*), *villier* (*vigilare*), *chival, orizon, ochison*, cf. E. § ii.

[For the palatalisation of **a** before denti-palatals and dentals cf. E. § xv.]

§ xix. Velarisation and vocalisation of prae-consonantal **ĭ** and **ǰ**
after **i** (§ 391 (4)), *Auc. fix* 8, 26, *gentix* 27, 2, Renclus, *Car. fius,
vius* (*vilis*) *: pius*, lxii, *Jeu Rob. courtieus* (< *courtils*, § 123) : *mieus*, 240.

§ xx. *Characteristics Developed in the Course of Old French.*—
(*a*) Retention of the unlowered pronunciation of **ē** (§ 450), cf. *P. Mor. Intr.*
p. 56 ; (*b*) subsequent velarisation of **ā** to **ā̲ > ǭ** (**ū**) (§ 446), cf. *Mysteres*
XV, *Mahon : an, enfan : monde, Intr.* cf. xxiii, W. § 1328 (*d*).

[For the movability of *prosthetic* **ę** cf. N.E. § x ; for the relative tardiness of
ü < ü̲ and **u < ǫ**, cf. §§ 183, 184, N.E. § ii ; for **buēn** (*boin*) cf. § 599 ; for *ent* (< *inde*)
cf. § 610.]

§ xxi. Early shift of **ts** to **s** (§ 195), cf. *Auc. enfans, petis, bras*, etc.,
St. Nic. confes : fais (*factos*), *os : os* (*hostes*) 125, *nous : genous* 153.

§ xxii. Frequency of metathesis of r: *Auc. deffrema* 12, 30, *enterries* 6, 22 (cf. *Auc.* p. 72).

Morphology.

§ xxiii. *Pronouns: Personal.*—(*a*) The stressed form derived from *ego* was ordinarily *jou* **džu** (§ 830), cf. *Auc. jou : nous, dox*, etc., 27, 11.

§ xxiv. (*b*) *illis* survived as *les*, cf. N.E. § xv ; *mihi* survived as *mi* and **ti** and **si** were formed on its model (§ 832), e.g. *Auc. mi* 2, 25, *ti* 8, 18, *Feuillée, mi : li* 153.

§ xxv. *Possessive.*—(*a*) The analogical stressed forms *mieue, miue, tieue, tiue* (§ 858, N. § vi), were retained in Later Old French, e.g. *Auc. miue* 2, 21, *siue* 10, 65.

(*b*) A complete declension system was formed on the accusative plural forms *noz, voz* (§ 853), *Auc. nos damoisiax* (n. sg.), 22, 11, *no cantefable* 41, 24, *Feuillée, voe : loe* 429.

§ xxvi. *Demonstratives.*—Under the influence of the first declension masculine, flexional s was added to the n. sg. masc. first of *cist* and then of *cil*, and the two forms **tsi(ꝉ)s** and **tsis** (<**tsists**) fell together under *cis* **tsis** (>**sis**), e.g. *iciz, Ex. Greg.* 91, *Auc. cis* n. sg. 22, 32.

[For *cou* **tsu** and *chou* **tšu** (< *ecce hoc*) cf. § 849 and N. § i.]

§ xxvii. *Verbs.*—The termination *-omes*, (§ 895), was current but *-iens*, (§§ 907, 919), continued in use in the first person plural of the present and imperfect subjunctive, imperfect indicative and conditional and *-iemes* was formed ꝉ *omes*, e.g. *Ex. Mousket, sommes : repairomes* 33, *Auc. estiiens* 22, 29, *Mysteres* XV, *auiens, sauiens, Intr.* lxxxiii, *St. Nic. donriemmes* 1119, *cuidiemes* 1159.

[For relatively late use of the termination *-em* in the North-East cf. § 895.]

§ xxviii. On the model of **fatš**, *fach, fac* the first person singular of the present indicative adopted the ending **tš**, *ch, c* and this was sometimes extended to the perfect, e.g. *Auc. siec* 10, 21, *atenc* 40, 18, *buc* 24, 51, (§ 900).

§ xxix. The present subjunctive was sometimes formed ꝉ *face* **fatšę**, cf. § 910, e.g. *Feuillée, rabaches : baches (battuas)* 552, *meche (mittat) : Rikeche* 655.

§ xxx. In the third person plural of the s-*perfects* of type A the forms in use were ordinarily **mizęnt**, *misent*, etc., **fisęnt**, *fissent*, modelled apparently on G.R. forms of the third person singular (**mizet**(?), **fitset**(?), cf. F. p. 284): z and s (*s* and *ss*) were often interchanged, e.g. *Auc. missent* 18, 19, *prissent* 34, 35, 36, *fisent* 34, 13. In the weak persons forms with intervocalic *s* persisted late, §§ 1018, 1019.

§ xxxi. The reduction of ¹ie to i (N. § 7) reduced the terminations -¹ier and -¹ierent of the first conjugation to -ir and -irent (cf. *Auc.* App. p. 82 and F. p. 212): this led in the perfect to the replacement of the terminations of the first conjugation by those of the second, cf. §§ 877, 1008 (ii), F. § 129.

[For the forms *eut, seut,* etc. < ǫut, sǫut cf. above, N. § viii and § 1029; for the strong participles, **biut**, etc., cf. § 1056, N.E. § xviii, for the weak radicals *ceindi, plaindi,* etc., cf. §§ 941, 1037; for conservatism in declension, cf. § 806.]

§ 1321. NORTH-EASTERN REGION.　N.E.

The north-eastern (Walloon) region has in addition to characteristics common to the whole northern region, the following traits, many of which it shares with the eastern region :—

Phonology.

§ i. *Absence of Breaking.*—No diphthongisation of *tonic* ę and ǫ appears to be provoked ordinarily by the influence of a following palatal sound (cf. §§ 410-412): before **ɟ** the vowels ę and ǫ often appear un-diphthongised, cf. *Eul. melz* 16, *Auc. voil* 6, 34, *foille* 19, 14, with **ɟ** they combine in the diphthongs **ei** and **oi**, cf. *Eul raneiet* 6, *lei* < **ellei* 13, *coist* 20, *Al.* MS. V, *peiz* 86*b*, *Ex. Greg. proi* 34, *boie* 99, *Ex. Bern. enoytes* 24, *deleit* 111, etc., *P. Mor. anoie : joie* 291*d*, etc., (cf. M.L. *Gr. Rom.* I, §§ 160, 191, *Rom.* xvii, p. 556).

[Cf. also E. x.]

§ ii. **u** palatalised relatively late to **ü** (§ 183), especially before nasals: Renclus, *Mis. une : corone* 34, 9, *P. Mor. mut (multum) : vertut, devenut* 44; *Mysteres* XV, *Intr.* p. xliii.

[For **u** (*ou*) < ǫ *tonic free* + **r**, cf. § 230 (ii), E. § xviii.]

§ iii. The tonic stress appears to have been strongest in this region and to have modified the development of tonic and atonic vowels :—

(*a*) *Tonic* ę and ǫ diphthongised when blocked as well as when free, ę generally, ǫ before r and s (§ 225) : *Ex. Froiss. peniel* 23, *apries* 69, *viespres* 70, *Mysteres* XV, *infier, diestre, pierte,* p. xxxiii, cf. G. Paris, *Mem. Soc. Ling,* I, p. 292.

§ iv. (*b*) *Tonic free* ę̄ (< G.R. **a** *tonic free*) diphthongised to **ei** (§ 232): *Al.* MS. V, *demeneir* 86*a*, *giteir* 86*b*, *meire* 94*a*, *Ex. Greg. boteir* 19, *espaventeiz* 25, *demeneie* 28, cf. § 232 and Wahlgren, *Parfaits Faibles,* p. 50.

§ v. (c) In proparoxytones the post-tonic unstressed vowels were often reduced more strongly than in other regions, e.g. *nat* < *natica*, cf. § 261, *Marchot, Phonétique*, p. 93, Hornung, *Die Behandlung der lat. Proparoxytona in den Vogesen und im Wallonischen*, Pr. Strassburg, 1902, *Zts. Ph. rom*. XXVII, 233.

§ vi. (d) ę *final* after consonants became earlier unstable than in francien (§ 273) and appears to have been no longer pronounced in the fifteenth century, *Mysteres* XV, *Intr*. pp. lv, lvi, Th. I, p. 166.

§ vii. (e) The diphthong **üi** was retained late and ordinarily reduced to **ü** *Ex. Bern. destrure* 84, *Mysteres* XV, *plus, concluis : bruis* (*bruits*), *Intr*. p. xliv (§ 517, E. § xiii).

§ viii. (f) The Old French triphthong -'ęau was retained late and ordinarily reduced to -ę in Middle French (§ 540), cf. *Geste Liege, pasture(a)s : malvais, Mysteres* XV, pp xvi, xxvi.

§ ix. The diphthong **uę** < **oi,** (like earlier 'ue < 'uo, § 550), labialised to **ö,** *eu* in Middle French, (§ 526), e.g. *meus* (*mensem*) (Doutrepont, 306), and the spellings *ue, oe, eu, oi* became interchangeable, (Wahlgren, *Vising vol*. pp. 313-327).

§ x. Prosthetic **e,** § 603, remained long unstable, e.g. *Ex. Greg. stuit* 35, *P. Mor. sperance, stuet*, etc., *Intr*. p. 83.

§ xi. Intervocalic **w** of the Gallo-Roman Period (< frk. **w** and L.L. **ŭ** consonantalised) ordinarily remained **w** (§ 192, iii) and exercised no rounding influence on vowels (§ 482, cf. Marchot I, 150), cf. **hawę** < **hαwα** (*houe*), **kawę** < **kαwα** (*choue*), and the forms of the strong **u**-*perfects* (§ 1028 and xvii below).

§ xii. In the Latin intervocalic group *qu* **kų** there was no palatalisation after front vowels (§§ 328, 330) and **g** (< **k**) was assimilated to **w,** cf. **awę** < ****awwa** < **αkųα** *aqua, Ex. Froiss. sieuent* 9, *sieuist* 58.

§ xiii. Before the breathed consonants **k, p** and **t** (§ 378) **s** persisted and in Middle French **st** final was often reduced to **s,** *Mysteres* XV, *request : pres, Intr*. lvi.

§ xiv. (a) In the course of Old French labial and palatal glides were often developed between vowels in hiatus (§ 239), e.g. *pawour, awiree, Mysteres* XV, p. xlix, *loweie*, p. xxxii, *veyut*, p. lxx; *decheüwe, parcreuwe*, F. p. 351. The form *souue, Eul*. 29, appears to be an early instance of this tendency.

(b) Between **u** and **r** + *consonant* a vocalic glide developed (§ 500), and subsequently 'ue > uę and was sometimes written *oi*, e.g. *juer* **žuer** < *jur* **žur** > **žuęr** *joir, P. Mor*. 402d, etc., *estuer* 466c; cf. § 720, Wahlgren, *Vising vol*. pp. 319-323.

Morphology.

§ xv. *Pronouns.*—(i) A dative form **les** < **illis** survived into the fourteenth century, cf. Tobler, *Mél.* I, 13, p. 113.

(ii) Palatalised *nominative* forms *ilh* i], *cilh* tsi] developed when **ẹlli* was in hiatus, cf. Marchot II, 239, 240.

(iii) **džu,** the stressed form of *ego* (N. § xxiv), is ordinarily written *ju*, and *cou* **tsu,** *cu*, § 849, (cf. Rydberg, pp. 628-634).

(iv) In the *nom. pl.* of the possessive, *mei* was retained and *tei* and *sei* formed on its model, e.g. *Ex. Greg. sei* 108, cf. Marchot II, p. 241.

§ xvi. *Verbs.*—In the imperfect indicative the terminations derived from -**abam,** etc., -**ẹvẹ** (-**eivẹ,** N.E. § iv) and after palatals -**ievẹ,** were retained, cf. *P. Mor. menevent* 382*a*, *quidievent* 531*a*, cf. § 916, E. § xxvii.

§ xvii. In the perfect and the imperfect subjunctive of the strong **u-***type*, **w** intervocalic exercised no rounding influence and was retained when intervocalic, vocalised to **ü** when prae-consonantal or final, e.g. *Ex. Greg. stiut* 35, *giut* 36, *Ex. Mousket euist* 95, cf. § 1028.

[For *estieut, dieut,* etc., with glide development, cf. § 123; for *tinve, vinve,* cf. § 1011.]

§ xviii. Under the influence of the perfect forms *biut, stiut,* etc., past participles of the type *biut* (> *bieut* or *but*) were created, e.g. *Ex. Greg. criuz* 56, *conut* 65, *Auc. jut* 18, 6, (cf. Suchier, article cited and § 1028).

[For the O.F. forms *desirst, parolst,* etc., cf. § 939; for the use in Middle French of the termination -*arent* for -*erent* and of perfects in -*i*, -*is*, -*it*, etc., for -*ai*, -*as*, -*a*, etc., cf. § 1008, N. § xxxi; for the termination -*ins* cf. § 999; for analogical forms of perfects cf. § 1037. For the O.F. use of *lh* and *nh* for] and ŋ cf. § 694.]

§ 1322. EASTERN REGION. E.

The eastern region includes the dialects of Lorraine and Burgundy, the former being often closely linked with the north-east, the latter with the south-central.

Illustrative Texts :—

Li Sermon St. Bernard, XII², provenance Metz. Examples from Studer-Waters = *Ex. Bern.*

Lorraine Psalter = *Ps. Lorr.*, fourteenth century MS.

Burgundian Charters, thirteenth and fourteenth century, ed. Philipon, *Rom.* XXXIX, XLI, 'Les Parlers du duché de Bourgogne.'

Lyoner Ysopet, ed. W. Foerster, 1882.

[Cf. Ch. Bruneau, 'Les Parlers lorrains anciens et modernes : Bibliographie critique (1908-1924),' *R. Lg. R.* I, and also Wahlgren, 'Sur la question de l'i, dite parasite,' *Vising vol.* pp. 290-335.]

Phonology.

The eastern region and more particularly the Lorraine dialect, where the Germanic influence was strong, shared with the north and north-eastern region the following characteristics :—

(i) The retention of Germanic initial **w**, (Lorraine only), (N. § iii).

(ii) The palatalisation of countertonic ẹ to ı before **j, J** and **ŋ** and of intertonic ẹ to ı before **ŝ** and **ẑ**, (N. § xviii).

(iii) The reduction of 'i̯eẹ to 'i̯ẹ and of 'u̯eẹ to 'u̯ẹ, (N. § v).

(iv) The diphthongisation of ẹ < **a** *tonic free*, § 232 and N.E. § iv.

(v) The retention of **ŝ** and subsequent shift to **š**, (N. § xvi).

(vi) The retention of final **t** unsupported, (Lorraine only), (N. § xv).

(vii) The opening of prae-consonantal **b** to **u̯**, (N. § xiv).

(viii) Retention of group **n'r** without de-nasalisation to **ndr** and of **lr** without development of glide **d**, N. § xiii.

This region shared with the north-eastern :—

(ix) The lowering of ẹ (**je, u̯e**) before **ł** and **J** + *consonant* to **a** (§ 501, N. § xvii and S.C. § xi).

(x) The absence of the breaking of ẹ and ǫ by a following palatal consonant (N.E. § i).

(xi) The treatment of unstressed post-tonic vowels, (N.E. § v).

(xii) The tardiness of the palatalisation of **u** to **ü**, (N.E. § ii).

(xiii) The late retention of **üı** and its ultimate reduction to **ü** (not **w̌ı**), (N.E. § vii).

(xiv) The diphthongisation of tonic *blocked* ẹ and ǫ, (Lorraine only), (N.E. § iii (*a*)).

Other characteristics of the eastern region, some of them common to the south centre, are the following :—

§ xv. In the course of Old French **a** palatalised to ẹ in Lorraine before the denti-palatals **tš** and **dž** and the dentals **ts, s, t, d** and sometimes **r**, (spelling *ai, ei* or *e*), e.g. *Ps. Lorr. vaiches* vi, 20, *veches* 8, 7, *ait* (*habet*) 22, 2, *malaides* 6, 2, *maleides* 104, 37, *wairde* 126 1, *perle* (cf. *Intr.* xiii, xv, Wahlgren, *Parfaits Faibles*, pp. 28-30, 38-42). Before the denti-palatals this palatalisation extended over the south-eastern and the whole northern region, cf. Regnier, (Aucerre), *scay-ge : courage, message* 595, *plaige* (*plege*) : *hostage* 844, *Jeu Rob. outraige : ai je* 145. Palatalised forms such as *sayche, saige* are not infrequent also in texts from other regions, (cf. *St. Joan, messaige* 197, *villaige* 203, etc.), cf. § 423, Wahlgren, *Parfaits Faibles*, pp. 50-53, 76-78, and *Vising vol.* pp. 301-306.

§ xvi. Before **ł** and **bł** the a-sound appears to have been velarised, (spelling *au*), § 502 (iii), cf. *Ps. Lorr. tauble* 22, 5, 40, 9, *maul* 7, 4, *loiaul* 88, 37.

§ xvii. ę̆ blocked was lowered through ę̆ to **a**, cf. **espas** < **espęs** (**spissum**), **mat** < **męt** (**mitte**), e.g. *Ex. Bern. mattent* 38, *charaz* 66, cf. *Ps. Lorr. Intr.* p. xxxii, Wahlgren, *Parfaits Faibles*, pp. 45, 46.

In Burgundy ę̆ *blocked* was sometimes diphthongised to **ei**, differentiated to **oi** and reduced to **o**, e.g. **soc** < **sec**, **promot** < **promet** (cf. *Rom.* xxxix, pp. 516, 517, xli, pp. 580-582).

[For the early lowering of ę to a before r cf. § 496.]

§ xviii. The diphthongisation of ǫ *tonic free* to **ou** was checked in the whole eastern region by following r and ǫ raised to **u** (§§ 230 (ii), 184); *Ex. Bern. plours* 14, *dolors* 31, etc., *Ps. Lorr. plusour, lour*, *Ex. Greg. pluisors* 3, *hore* 103, *Rom.* p. xli, 584.

§ xix. When **ei** followed a *labial* consonant, differentiation to **oi** was not checked by a following nasal consonant (§ 439): *Ps. Lorr. moinnes* (*minas) 79, 1, *poinne, Prologue*, p. 2, 17.

§ xx. Before a consonant, particularly in Lorraine, ɫ and ʆ were effaced and not vocalised (§ 391 (3)); *Ps. Lorr. sauour* 9, 15, *papieires* (*palpebras*) 10, 4, *Ex. Bern. miez* (*mieuz*) 47.

§ xxi. After the high vowels ę, **i**, **u**, **r** *final* began to be effaced in the thirteenth century (cf. § 401).

§ xxii. Before ʆ a palatal glide was developed after **a** and **ę**, the diphthong **ai** subsequently levelling to ę, the diphthong **ei** differentiating to **oi** (§ 408 (3), (4)): *Ps. Lorr. traveil* 106, 12, *entreilles* 50, 10, *consoil* 12, 2, *soloil* 49, 1, cf. S.C. § xii and also § 423.

§ xxiii. (*a*) Before ŋ a palatal glide was developed after **a** and **u** (< ǫ), the diphthong **āi** levelling subsequently to ę̃, the diphthong **ui** to ų̃ę̃ (§§ 408, 445, 475): *Ps. Lorr. monteingne* vii, 11, cf. S.C. § xiii.

(*b*) Before ŋ (< ɴ) ę was raised to **i**, *Ps. Lorr. cinct* (*cinctum*) 108, 18.

[For progressive nasalisation cf. § 429.]

§ xxiv. In the south-eastern region ǭ (< **au** and ǫ blocked) before **z**, **š** and effaced **s** closed through ǫ to **u** (*ou*) in the fourteenth century: *Rom.* xli, p. 585, *chouses, cloux* (*clausum*), (cf. § 581, and S.C. § xiv).

[Cf. for other S.E. traits: (1) the early levelling of **ai** to ę, § 533; (2) the relatively early lowering of ī to ē and of ų̃ī to ų̃ę̃, §§ 454, 475; (3) the palatalisation of γ (< **k**) between **au** and **a**, § 302; (4) the reduction of **mn** *intervocalic* to **n**, § 371 and S.W. § iv; (5) the early effacement of ð, θ, cf. § 347; (6) the assibilation of intervocalic **r**, § 399, S.C. § xv.

Morphology.

§ xxv. The eastern region is characterised to some extent by conservatism in its flexion :—

(*a*) In the accusative singular of the article and the unstressed pronoun of the third person, the form *lu* (*lo, lou*) was retained into the thirteenth century (*Ex. Bern. lo* ll. 10, 19, etc., *lou* 74).

[For O.F. *ceu* (<*cel ?* or *co ?*) cf. § 849.]

§ xxvi. (*b*) In the first person plural of the subjunctive present and imperfect *-iens* continued in use as in the northern region (N. § xxvii), and in the second person plural the etymological endings *-oiz* (< *eiz*) and *-iz* (*-its* < *-itis*) also persisted (§ 896) : *-oiz* was sometimes reduced to *-oz*, St. *Bern. prennoz*, l. 104, cf. *Rom.* xxxix, p.-517 and N. § vii.

§ xxvii. (*c*) In Later Old French the termination *-eve* (*-eive*), *-ieve* continued in use in the imperfect indicative of the first conjugation, *Ex. Bern. preievet* 54, *orevet* 61, cf. § 916, and among the verbs in **-ir** and **-ier** a form in **-ive** (< L.L. *-ibat*, cf. § 916) was also employed, e.g. *Ex. Bern. ferivet* 61, *aparillivent* 88.

§ xxviii. (*d*) The periphrasis *infinitive* + *ire* (§ 872 (iii)) survived into Later Old French, *Ex. Bern. furberit* 30, *serit* 31.

§ xxix. *Characteristics Developed in the Course of Old French.*— (*a*) A frequent use of termination-stressed forms in the third person plural (§ 1048): the commonest form is *-ient* ≠ *iens* (jēns > jāns) e.g. *Ps. Lorr.* subj. pres. *chantient* 137, 5, *disient* 39, 16, impf. ind. *chantient* 68, 10, *faisient* 113, 4, but *-ant* and *-ont* were also current (*Rom.* xli, 591, 5, 6) ; in the imperfect indicative in the fourteenth century *-aint, -eint, -oint,* were also employed, shortened from *-aient, -eient, -oient,* e.g. *usaint, veneint, soffroint, Rom.* xli, 598.

(*b*) In the imperfect indicative and conditional the terminations of the first and second persons plural were sometimes influenced in the fourteenth century by those of the other persons and thus *-eiens* (*-eins*), *-oiens* (*-oins*) were in use as well as *-iens, -iez,* e.g. *tenoiens, teneiens, Rom.* xli, 591, 2.

§ xxx. In Period II **-ęrent,** the third person plural of the perfect of the first conjugation, was often replaced by **-arent** ≠ the other terminations of the tense ; the likeness of the terminations of the singular of this tense to those of the future and the present indicative of *avoir* led to its replacement by *-ont,* **-ūnt** (*chantont*) and this termination was sometimes extended to other types of perfects, e.g. *fuyont, vendont,* cf. M.L. *Gr. Rom.* II, § 272.

[For the extension of the endings **-i, -is,** etc., to conjugation I cf. above, N. § xxxi.]

§ xxxi. In the present subjunctive extended forms in *-oisse* (≠ *conoisse ?*) were employed (cf. § 910): *Ps. Lorr. perloisse* 16, 4,

luisoisse xv, 31, *movoisse* 95, 11, *confessoissent* 106, 8, *Intr.* pp. lvii-ix. In Burgundy an extension *-oi-* is also found in the present indicative and in the present subjunctive, e.g. *entrois, lassois,* ind. pres., *tornoit, entroient,* subj. pres., *Rom.* xxxix, 517, xli, 596-600.

[For the use of past participles in *-eit* cf. § 1051 ; for the extension of perfects of the *dedi* type cf. §§ 1004, 1006, S.W. § xii.]

§ 1323. The Central Region.

The central region includes the speech of Champagne (east-central), the Orléanais (south-central) and the Île de France (francien). The speech of the Île de France is the subject of this book.

§ 1324. Champagne.

Champagne, the passage-way between the valleys of the Rhone and Saône and the central region was throughout the middle ages without cultural unity. 'La Champagne du Nord, celle de Reims, comme dit Grégoire de Tours, suit des destinées à part ; elle touche à la Picardie, lui ressemble par la forme de ses maisons de culture aux grandes cours intérieures. Les monuments d'époque préhistorique montrent d'étroits rapports avec la Belgique, presque pas avec la Bourgogne. Ses destinées plus tard sont liées à celles de la grande region picarde. Au contraire le faisceau des rivières méridionales a son centre politique à Troyes ; il est en rapports, par les passages de l'Auxois, avec la Bourgogne et le Sud-est ' (Vidal de la Blache in Lavisse, *Hist. Fr.* I, p. 123.)

In its linguistic development Champagne shows the lack of unity that characterises its cultural history. The speech of the northern part of the province is linked with the northern and north-eastern region ; the speech of the eastern with Lorraine, of the southern with Burgundy and the western is but little differentiated from the Île de France.

Illustrative Texts are the works of :—

    Joinville, late xiii ; provenance East Champagne.

    Crestien de Troies, cent. xii^2 ; provenance South Champagne.

    Guiot de Provins, early xiii ; provenance West Champagne,

    [Cf. the prefaces of the editors of these texts : de Wailly in his edition of Joinville in 1883 or in his Mémoire sur la langue de Joinville in vol. xxvi of the *Mémoires de l'Académie des Inscriptions ;* W. Förster in his first edition of *Cliges* in 1888, and Ch. Bruneau, 'La Champagne : dialecte ancien et patois moderne (Bibliographie critique),' *R. Lg. R.* V, pp. 71-175.]

§ 1325. SOUTH-CENTRE.   S.C.

Illustrative Texts.—

Roman de la Rose, ed. Langlois, S.A.T.F.
   Rose I, by Guillaume de Lorris, 1225-1240 (?).
   Rose II, by Jean de Meung, 1275-1280.
Saint Joan of Orléans = *St. Joan;* fifteenth century, selected and
   edited by J. Evans and P. Studer, Oxford, 1926.
Cf. F. M. Auler, *Der Dialect der Provinzen Orléanais und Perche im
   13 Jhdt.*, Bonn, 1888, and especially the account of the
   language of the *Roman de la Rose*, given by E. Langlois in his
   edition of this text, vol. i, pp. 185-348.

Phonology in Later Old French.—The phonological divergences that
appear in Later Old French between the south central and central region
are in the main developed in the course of Old French : in the Early
Period the two regions appear to have followed much the same
development.

The Orléanais of the twelfth and thirteenth centuries had in common
with francien :—

§ i. The lowering of ē to ā (§ 448), cf. *Rose* I, *au vent : devant* 2521,
fui enz : joianz 633, etc.

§ ii. The differentiation of ǫu to eu (§ 226), cf. *Rose* I, *corajeus : jeus*
2185, *veriteus : osteus* 1111, etc.

§ iii. Of the diphthong ʹue both the francien and the western development are found (§§ 551, 553) : *Rose* II, *meurent : demeurent, esveil : vueil,*
(*Intr.* pp. 217, 229).

In common with the western region the Orléanais had the following
characteristics :—

§ iv. ei escaped the differentiation to oi (§ 226) and monophthongised
through ęi to ę, § 230 (spelling *eiʹ, e, ai*) : *Rose* II, *valeir : à l'air,*
veire : necessaire, ameie : aie, Intr. pp. 198-200, (W. § vi).

§ v. ai in all positions was early levelled through ęi to ę or ę, §§ 528-
533, *Rose Intr.* pp. 197-200, W. § ii and S.E. (cf. E. § xxiv).

§ vi. ʹie and ʹue shifted early to ję and ųę (§§ 512, 553, W. §§ i, vii)
and were nasalised in consequence early enough to share in the lowering
of ē to ā (§§ 472, 478) : ʹmien > mjęn > mjān, *Rose, Intr.* p. 212.

§ vii. ę and ję opened early to ę, ję (§§ 494, 495, 577, W. §§ i, ix) ;
ję and ję were early reduced to ę and ę after š, ž,], ŋ, (§ 512).

§ viii. A vocalic glide was often developed between i and intervocalic r (§ 500) : *Rose* II, *ocierre : pierre* 6181 : *Pierre* 1181, *Intr.*
267 ; cf. W. § xi.

§ ix. γ (< **k** *intervocalic*) palatalised to ɉ between ****au** and ****a** (§ 302) : **pauka** > **poię**, e.g. *Rose* I, **poi : poi** (*potui*) 709, cf. § 302, S.W. § v and S.E.

[For the velarisation of ę by following ɫ cf. § 502.]

In common with the region lying to the east (Burgundian and South Champagne) the Orléanais had the following characteristics :—

§ x. **a** palatalised to **ę** before **š** and **ž** (spelling *ai* or *e*) : *saiche, saige, visaige*, e.g. *St. Joan, coraige, dommaige* 330, 2, cf. § 423 and E. § xv.

§ xi. Before ɫ and ʝ + *cons.* ię and ɥę were lowered to ʝa and ɥa : *miauz* (*mieuz*), *diaut* (< *duelt*), *Rose, Intr.* pp. 233, 234, cf. § 501, N. § xvii and E. ix.

§ xii. Between **a** and **ę** and ʝ a palatal glide developed, § 408 (3), (4), and **ai** and **ei** were ordinarily both levelled to **ę**, before the fourteenth century, cf. Guiart, *Cornoaille : s'apareille* 8003, *Rose, Intr.* p. 230, etc., and E. § xxii ; cf. also § 423.

§ xiii. Between **a** and **ŋ** a palatal glide developed and as in the eastern region the diphthong **ãi** fell in with **ẽi** (> **ę̃** §§ 408, 445), cf. *Rose* I, *enseigne : Bretaigne, Intr.* p. 195, etc., cf. E. § xxiii.

[For the effacement of ɫ after ǫ and ę̃ cf. § 391 (1), (2).]

Middle French.—In the course of Middle French, as in the south-east :—

§ xiv. **ǫ** (< **au**) before **š** and **ǫ** (< **ǫ** blocked) before **ž** and effaced **s** closed through **ǫ** to **u** (*ou*) (§ 581, E. § xxiv and S.W.) : *St. Joan, propoux : tous* 329 : *foulx* 1503, *touche : poche* 1684, *clos : tous* 1880.

§ xv. Intervocalic and final **r** were assibilated to **z** (§§ 399, 402).

[For the relatively early lowering of ī to ę̃ and of ɥī to ɥę̃ cf. §§ 454, 475.]

Morphology.—As in the western region :—

§ xvi. The termination of the first person plural is often *-on* (§ 894) : e.g. *Rose* II, *Neron : lairon* 6185 : *trouveron* 6439, W. § xv.

§ xvii. The terminations of the imperfect indicative of the first conjugation—**-ǫę, -ǫęs, -ǫt, -ǫęnt** (§ 916)—continued in use in the thirteenth century, e.g. *Rose, amot : a mot* 4185, *regnot : regne ot* 5535, W. § xvi.

§ xviii. The extension *-ge* is employed at times in the present subjunctive (§ 910) : *Rose, Intr.* p. 327, W. § xvii.

As in the south-eastern region :—

§ xix. Termination-stressed forms of the third person plural are used in *-ient* (§ 1048) and also, especially in the imperfect indicative and subjunctive, in *-eint, -aint, -oint* (< *-ei(e)nt, -ai(e)nt, -oi(e)nt* (?)) : *Rose, Intr.* pp. 318, 325, cf. E. § xxix.

§ xx. The palatalised forms of the verbs *tenir* and *venir* are *veign* (*vaign*), *veigne* (*vaigne*) : *Rose* I, *coveigne : remaigne* 2571, *compaigne : teigne* 255 (§ 931).

§ xxi. The acc. sg. masc. of the article is sometimes **lu** (*lo*, *lou*) (cf. § 834) : *Rose* II, *lou sens : vous en* 7989, *profes : lo fes* 4449, *Intr.* p. 290 ; cf. E. § xxv.

§ 1326. WESTERN REGION. W.

The western region included broadly Anjou, Maine, Touraine, Brittany, Lower Normandy, and to some extent Upper Normandy, but it must be borne in mind that the region that became Upper Normandy (*La Haute Normandie*) was in its early development (up to its occupation by the Normans in the tenth century) linked more closely with the northern region than with the western and shared in some of the northern traits (cf. § 37 and N. §§ i, ii, iv, v, viii and x).

This group of dialects is sometimes called *north-western* to distinguish it from the more southerly group, which includes the dialects of Poitou, Aunis, Saintonge and the Angoumois, the group intermediate, on the west, between southern and northern French, cf. § 1329.

Illustrative Texts :—

Chanson de Roland = *Rol.;* provenance still undetermined but probably to the east centre of this region ; *c.* 1110-1120 ; MS. (A.N.), *c.* 1170.

Epistre de St. Estienne, early xii ; provenance South Touraine (?).

Roman de Thèbes = Thebes, c. 1150 ; provenance south-west.

Roman de Troie = Troie, c. 1165 ; provenance Touraine.

Chronique des ducs de Normandie = Chron. Norm., c. 1175 ; provenance Touraine.

Livre des Manieres = Livre Man., end xii ; provenance Brittany or South Normandy.

Wace, *Roman de Rou = Rou*, 1160-75 ; provenance South Norman.

Beroul, Tristan = Beroul, c. end xii ; provenance South (?) Norman.

Sermon en Vers, xii ; provenance North Norman.

Angier, *Dialogues de St. Gregoire*, 1212, *Vie de St. Gregoire*, 1214, = *Angier* ; provenance south-western.

Péan Gatineau, *La Vie Monseignor Saint Martin de Tours = St. Martin*, middle xiii ; provenance Touraine.

Jehan le Marchant, *Le Livre des Miracles Notre Dame de Chartres*, cent. xiii = *Mir. Chartres.*

Cf. Drevin, *Die frz. Sprachelemente in den lateinischen Urkunden des 11. und 12. Jahrhundertes (aus Haute-Bretagne und Maine)*,

Goerlich, *Die Nordwestlichen Dialekte der Langue d'Oil*, M. K. Pope, *Étude sur la langue de Frère Angier*, Paris, 1903.

[For regional dissertations on Normandy cf. Wahlgren, *Parfaits Faibles*, pp. 98-124, and the general bibliography given above.]

The dialectal characteristics of this region are less marked than those of the north and east and for the most part appear to have had a relatively late beginning. It is the region in which the Frankish settlement was least intense (§ 17), and the most characteristic trait of its phonology in Old French is the relatively early levelling of diphthongs, a development that is probably indicative of a relatively early diminution of the tonic stress, never so strong here as in the northern region (cf. §§ 223, 261). This levelling is sometimes on the same lines as in francien, but perceptibly earlier, sometimes on rather different lines (§ 508).

§ i. *Levelling of Diphthongs on the same Lines as in Francien.*— ie > i̯e in the course of the eleventh century and shift of stress was quickly followed by a reduction of i̯e to ẹ (§ 512). In the more southern part of the region (Touraine and Anjou) the reduction to ẹ was probably hastened by the influence of Poitevin, the neighbouring dialect to the south, as here there was ordinarily no diphthongisation of ẹ tonic free under stress accent (cf. § 229). The quality of the ẹ-sound was, in this region as elsewhere, at first closed, but in the course of the twelfth and thirteenth centuries the sound began to open, first under the influence of following r or l (§§ 494, 495), this change also beginning earliest in the more southern part of the region (cf. *Et. Angier*, pp. 54-57, S.C. § vii).

§ ii. ai > ẹ.—In prae-consonantal position the levelling of this diphthong also began in the eleventh century in this region and appears to have become general in the more southern part before the middle of the twelfth century; ai (< a + i̯ *intervocalic* and *final*) also levelled in the course of Later Old French through ei to ẹ, e.g. Troie *raie : baleie* 11352, *Mir. Chartres*, *verai : rei*, p. 44 (cf. § 533 and S.C. § v).

§ iii. ãi > ẽi > ẹ̃.—In the south-western region levelling of this diphthong also began early (§ 469). Drevin cites forms in documents of the late eleventh and early twelfth century with the spellings *ei* and *e* for *ai*, e.g. *Sent* for *saint* 1080, *Campen* for *Campano* 1115, *Septenis* c. 1110, *Septene* c. 1150, *Sainfridus* for *Seinfridus* 1110; and the author of *Thebes* rhymes *rien : germain* 6807, *bien : vain* 8487, *crieme : aime* 4977.

§ iv. üi > w̃i.—Shift of stress in the diphthong üi appears to have begun in this region in the early twelfth century (§ 517): it is first attested in *Gormont* (*iceli < icelui* in an i-assonance), and in the

Bestiaire, deduire rhymes with *ire* 805 ; cf. also *Troie, destruire : martire* 2643, *ocire* 9637, *respit : nuit* 24783, etc.

§ v. *Levelling of Diphthongs on Lines Divergent from Francien.*— The diphthong ǫu < ǫ tonic free (§ 225) remained undifferentiated and appears to have been levelled to **u** before the end of the eleventh century (§ 230). In all the twelfth century poems of this region the sound assonates and rhymes with ǫ tonic blocked and was already, in all probability, pronounced **u**. Cf. *Roland*, laisses xxxii, lxi, lxviii, etc. ; *Troie, dous (dŭōs) : vous* 13167, 27027, *proz : toz* 207, *dolor : estor* 255, *jor* 331, *sous* (< *solus*) *: nos* 429.

§ vi. The diphthong **ei** (< ę tonic free and ę + *jod*) also remained undifferentiated (§§ 226, 230) and was gradually levelled through ęi to ę in the course of Later Old French, cf. *Troie, raie : baleie* 11352, *traient : baleient* 12015, Angier, *celestre : crestre, cerre* (< *ceire*) *: querre, Mir. Chartres, aperceive : l'eive* (< *aqua*), p. 56 (cf. *Et. Angier*, pp. 10, 11 and S.C. § iv).

§ vii. The diphthong ¹**ue** (< ǫ tonic free and < ǫ + J) was levelled to **wę** instead of **ö** in the course of the twelfth century (cf. § 553).

Other *Phonological* characteristics proper to the whole region are :—

§ viii. As in the northern region (N. § xx) ē was lowered to ā before the labial nasal but remained at the stage ē before **n** and thus **tempus > tāns, femina > fāmę** or **fēnnę** (S.W. §. iv), but **fēndre** remained **fēndre,** etc. In Normandy ā as in Northern French (N. § xx) was subsequently velarised (§§ 446, 1328 (*d*)).

§ ix. ę̄ (< a *tonic free*) opened to ę in the thirteenth century before sounded consonants (§§ 494, 495, 577, S.C. § vii).

§ x. When palatalised **s** *final* followed *tonic* **ü** the palatal glide, ordinarily developed by this sound (§ 315), was merged in the preceding vowel : thus **-üŝ > -üs** not **-üis,** e.g. **ųstjų > üs, *pertųsjų > pertüs.*

§ xi. After the high vowel į a glide *e-sound* was developed before **r** *intervocalic* as well as before **r** *prae-consonantal* (§ 500), and the resultant diphthong ¹**ie** was sometimes levelled to ıę: *Clef d'Amor, desirre : querre* 2699, *derre* (< *dire*) *: aquerre* 1305 (cf. *Et. Angier*, pp. 14, 15, S.C. § viii).

[For the relatively early shift of ǫ to **u** cf. § 184 ; for the rounding of **a** free to ǫ by intervocalic **ų** (< v) and of ę countertonic to ǫ by tonic **ü** cf. §§ 483, 484 ; for the relatively late retention of **ð** and **θ** cf. § 347 ; for the persistence of *final* **r** cf. § 402 ; for the contraction of **ęü** to **ö,** cf. §§ 245, 1328 (2).]

Morphological Characteristics.

§ xii. Early disintegration of the declension system (§ 806), cf. Beroul, *Intr.* xlix-lvi, *Et. Angier*, pp. 58, 59.

§ xiii. Early obliteration of case distinction in the nominative singular feminine of type I (cf. *fin, flur,* etc., § 803).

§ xiv. The survival of the neuter pronouns *el, cel* (*Et. Angier*, p. 32) and the shortening of the pronoun **ele** to **el** and more rarely of **eles** to **els**, cf. *Troie, el* 171, 172, 200, etc., *els* 509, 2198 (§ 839).

[For **al** from **el** cf. § 834 and Görlich, N.W., p. 70; for *jen* **žẹn** for *je* **žẹ** cf. § 830 ; for *cen* **sẹn** for *ce* **sẹ** cf. § 849 ; for f. pl. *cestes* cf. § 846; for n. sg. *mis*, etc., cf. § 853.]

§ xv. The use of the termination *-om* (*-on*) or *-um* in the first person plural of the present tenses, and of *-ïom* (*-ïon*), *-ium* in the imperfect indicative and conditional in place of *-ons, -ïons* (§ 894) ; the early generalisation of these forms in place of *-iens* and of *-ez* in place of *-eiz*, cf. *Thebes, Intr.* cii, *Troie* vi, 143, S.C. § xvi and § 967.

§ xvi. The retention of the terminations derived from those of the imperfect indicative of the first Latin conjugation and the form these terminations have assumed, i.e. *-oue, -oe : -oues, -oes : -out, -ot : -ouent, -oent*, (§§ 345, 483, 914, 916, S.C. § xvii).

§ xvii. The use of *c*, **k** in the present indicative (§ 900), and of *-ge*, **-džẹ** in the subjunctive present, § 910, more especially in the southern region, cf. S.C. § xviii, *Etude Angier*, pp. 35, 40, 160.

§ xviii. The use of labialised radicals in **u**-perfects of **B**-type, e.g. **doüssẹ**, §§ 484, 1022.

[For *sace* **satsẹ** cf. § 957 ; for *choier, choer*, etc., cf. § 963.]

§ 1327. SOUTH-WESTERN REGION. S.W.

The more southern part of the western region is also characterised by a considerable number of traits that differentiate its speech from that of the more northern part, i.e. from upper Normandy, and often connect it with the speech of the region that lies further south or south-east.

[For the early levelling of the diphthongs **ai, ãi, ei, ẽi, ie, ui**, cf. above.]

§ i. *Phonology.*—The triphthongs that resulted from the breaking of tonic **ẹ** and **ǫ** by following *jod* (§§ 410-412) were not developed in the same way as in the centre and north, **iej** being reduced to **ie** or **ei, uej** being reduced to **ue** or **ei**, cf. *Angier, seivent* (< **sequunt*) : *deceivent* (*Et. Angier*, pp. 14, 20) ; *Livre Man. sofere : deire* (< *docere*), cvi, cf. cvii, cxiii; *St. Martin, peres : peres* (*pejor + s*) 137, *seit* (<**sequit*) : *seit* (< *sapit*) 1337, *Beroul, liez* (**lectos*) 703, *lie* (*illaei*) 284, etc. (cf. § 328 and also Görlich, N.W. pp. 31-34, 49-51).

§ ii. **a** free was often retained before **l** [**ɬ** (?)], and **ɬ** *final* vocalised after it, cf. §§ 232, 502 (ii), 382, e.g. *Troie, tal : cheval* 3821, *taus* < *vassaus* 2227.

§ iii. **ǫ** was early unrounded to **a** (**ɑ**)? before **m** and nasalised to **ã** (**ɑ̃**)? e.g. *Troie, cante* (*comitem*) : *ante* 176 ; *Chron. Norm. cante* (*computum*) : *seixante* (4818 cf. § 601).

§ iv. **mn** in intervocalic position was often assimilated to **nn** (§ 371), e.g. Beroul, *fenne* (MS. feme) : *reigne* 883, etc. ; *St. Martin, fenne : Vienne* 5533 (cf. also S.E.).

§ v. γ (< intervocalic **g** < **k**, cf. § 335) was palatalised to **j** between **au** and **a**, cf. *oie* < **auca*, *poie* < *pauca*, (whence masculine *poi*), (§ 302), e.g. *Troie, poie : Troie* 16343 (cf. § 302 and S.C. § ix).

§ vi. In parts of this region prae-consonantal **J** was simplified to **ꞁ** instead of vocalising to **ɥ** (§ 391 (5)); in Brittany and Maine it velarised and vocalised to **ɥ** after **i**, cf. *fiuz* (> *fieus* § 123) < *filius*, cf. Görlich, N.W. pp. 56, 58.

§ vii. In the intervocalic group **4t, 4** was palatalised (§ 319), and also reduced to **j**, e.g. Beroul, *voitre* (< *voltre* < **voltulat*) *: coite* 3685, Angier, *avoitre* (*adulterum*), *Voitour* < *Volturnum* (*Et. Angier*, p. 25); *voitrer* is cited by Palsgrave, (*je me voystre*, p. 771) and attested in the forms of Rabelais, cf. *voytrans*, I, 24. (Cf. Millardet, *Linguistique et Dialectologie Romanes*, pp. 272, 274.)

§ viii. In words of the type *plait, vuit* (< **vŏcĭtum*), *cuit* (< **cūgito*), and in words ending in supported **t**, e.g. *dont*, **t** was sometimes effaced as in the region to the south and derivatives (*quier, vuier*) were made from these forms (cf. Gamillscheg, *Becker vol.* p. 63): *Chron. Norm. plai : fai* 6483, *delai* 16252, *voi : enoi* 21798, *St. Martin, vuie : fuie* 7649; (cf. also § 616 and *Best. Intr.* lix-lxi).

§ ix. The tonic stress, being relatively less intense in this region, the syncope of the unstressed penultimate vowels took place relatively later than in the more northern and eastern region and was consequently preceded by the voicing of intervocalic **k** to **g** and of **t** to **d** in words of the type **gabita, *granica, *basilica*, cf. O.F. *jade, grange, basoge* (cf. §§ 17, 223, 352, 353, and authorities mentioned).

[For the reduction of ꞁie-u to ꞁie cf. § 255; for the breaking of ǫ blocked by r̂ cf. §§ 293, 410; for the velarisation of ę̆ to o by 4 cf. § 502; for the early effacement of *prae-consonantal* **s** cf. § 378; for the development of palatal glides before **ꞁ** and **ŋ** cf. § 408, S.C. §§ xii, xiii; for the closing of ǫ to u (*ou*) before š, s, z, cf. S.C. § xiv.]

§ x. *Morphology.*—Pronouns.—**vus** < **vǫs** unstressed and enclitic was reduced to **ɥs** (§ 832), *Troie* 1458, *sos* for *si vos*, Beroul 424, 1243, 2815, etc.; cf. Fabri 'en bas normant on dit *ou estous . . . que dictous, que faictous ?*' (Th. I, 175).

[For *le* enclitic after polysyllables cf. § 838; for the persistence of the form *lou* cf. S.C. § xxi.]

§ xi. *Verbs.*—The termination of the third person plural of the imperfect subjunctive was often stressed on the final syllable, both *-ant* and *-ont* being employed (§ 1048), e.g. *Thebes, deissant : enfant* (13 examples in the poem); *Troie, passissant : aparissant* 11569, *St. Martin, menessunt : ileques sunt* 5961, *venissunt : i sunt* 7821, cf. *Et. Angier*, p. 44, Th. II, p. 142, S.C. § xix.

§ xii. Weak perfects of the *dedi-* type had considerable extension, e.g. *St. Martin, vesquié : arcevesquié* 513, *rompié : pié* 2321 (§§ 1004, 1006, E. § xxxi).

§ xiii. Verbal forms in *-ent* (<*-entem* and *-endo*) are occasional (§ 921). [For *ereie, erions*, etc., cf. § 920.]

§ 1328. *Western French in the Sixteenth Century.*—According to the remarks of the sixteenth and seventeenth grammarians, cited by Thurot, the western dialects of that period, and more particularly the Norman, were characterised by the following traits :—

(1) The use of ẹ < O.F. *ei* instead of francien wẹ < O.F. *oi*, e.g. fẹ (*fai*) for fwẹ *foi* (Th. I, p. 374, cf. §§ 230, 523, W. § vi).

(2) The combination of *eü* (ẹü) in the sound ö, § 245 : 'All of which nouns and participles,' *blesseure, deu, peu, seur,* 'the Chartrains and Normans like the Aquitanians pronounce with a diphthong,' Bèze, p. 52.

(3) The continuance of a diphthongal pronunciation of **au** (§ 537), cf. Hindret (1687), *fra-oude, cha-oud,* Th. I, 429.

(4) **r** final continued to be sounded after **e** (< O.F. ẹ), e.g. in the infinitives of the first conjugation and in words in -ör -*eur*, e.g. *monsieur* (§ 402, Th. II, p. 165).

(5) Variations in the treatment of nasal sounds :—

(*a*) **n** in final position continued to be pronounced and was carried on in liaison (§ 438, cf. Th. II, 425, 551, 553, 555, 559).

(*b*) Nasalisation of **ā** and **ū** (*o*) before an intervocalic nasal was retained through the seventeenth century (§ 440), e.g. *can-ne* for *cane, bon-ne* (Th. II, 447, 522).

(*c*) ī was retained unlowered into the seventeenth century (cf. §§ 452, 454, Th. II, 480).

(*d*) **ā** was velarised to ū̄ > ō̄ (*au*), § 446.

(*e*) ẹ final was nasalised to ẹ̄ and often lowered to ā, cf. Dangeau (1694), 'Les Normans font passer' (l'*e* fēminin), 'par le nés et lui donent un son qui aproche de la voyèlle nasale *an* ou de la voyèle nasale *ein*.' (cf. § 275, Th. I, 165).

Palsgrave's account of the sound possibly finds its explanation in this provincial development.

§ 1329. SOUTHERN BORDER DIALECTS.

For the dialects that lie between the regions of the Langues d'Oc and d'Oïl students are referred to the general bibliography and the following authorities :—

(1) The border group on the western side of France, (sometimes called *south-western*) : E. Goerlich, *Die Südwestlichen Dialecte der Langue d'Oïl* (*Poitou, Aunis, Saintonge and Angoumois*), Heilbronn, 1882. On Poitevin in particular cf. the article by E. Gamillscheg in the *Becker volume*, pp. 50-74, and also §§ 34, 416, 1327, W. §§ i, xii, xiv.

(2) The border dialect on the eastern side of France, the dialect of Franche-Comté : W. Förster's Introduction to the *Lyoner Yzopet*, text published in the *Altfrz. Bibliothek*, v, Heilbronn, 1882, Extract in Studer-Waters, No. 49 ; *Die beiden Bücher der Makkabäer* (Roman. Bibl. No. 2), ed. E. Goerlich (with Appendix by W. Foerster), Halle, 1888 ; for the modern patois cf. Wahlgren, *Parfaits Faibles*, pp. 15, 16.

INDEXES OF WORDS.

English words and verbs are listed separately ; Latin words are included in the French list, distinguished by italics. French words are cited in Modern French spelling ; if obsolete, in their latest form. Old French spellings and dialectal variants are added if they are of particular interest. Old French forms or spellings markedly divergent are given cross-references. Northern forms with *ch* or *k* for *c* are not ordinarily entered.

The numbers refer to the paragraphs : those in heavy type refer to the tables of sound-changes or of verbs ; those in italics to paragraphs that explain the words or forms in question, although these are not themselves mentioned.

Related forms—*masculine* and *feminine, singular* and *plural*—are separated by dashes.

A single asterisk denotes a Late Latin or Germanic etymon ; a double asterisk denotes a dialectal variant ; *m.* = masculine, *f.* = feminine, *neut.* = neuter, *sg.* = singular, *pl.* = plural, *pr.* = pronoun, *art.* = article, *str.* = stressed, *unstr.* = unstressed, *v.a.* = vocalic alternation.

INDEX OF FRENCH AND LATIN WORDS
(*exclusive of verbs*).

A.

à, 737.
abandon, 606.
abbé, 366, **667**, 676, 736, 800, A.N. 1210.
abbesse, 558, 561, 778.
abject, 650, 745.
abois, 487.
absent, 745.
accueil, 553.
achaison, cf. ochoison.
ache, 258.
acier, A.N. 1231.
âcre, 647
acrobate, 647.
actif, 647.
action, 647.
Adam, 435.
adjectif, 650, 745.
administration, 744.
admirable, 650.
admonition, 745.
adne, cf. âne.
adoption, 745.
adverbe, 650, 745.

adversaire, 650, 745.
affaire, 777.
affecté, 745.
affection, 647, 745.
âge, 194, 203, 244, 352, 561, **666**, 738, 777.
agneau ; agnel—agneaus ; **anel ; agniaus, aigneaus, 321, 442, **445, **667**, 686, *N.* § *viii*, A.N. 1077, 1165.
aïeul, **aiol, eol, 187, 530, 531, **533, **554*, A.N. 1157.
aigle, 54, A.N. 1212.
aigrette, 54.
aigu, agu, 640.
aiguière, 725.
aiguille ; aguille, 407, 514, 515, 725.
ail, *sg.* and *pl.*, 312, 382, 387, **666**, 707.
aile, ele, 182, 231, 494, 589, 687, 708, 725, A.N. 1098.
ainçois, 525.
aîné, ainzné, 218, 433, A.N. 1231.
ainsi, ainsin, 75, 455.
aire, 26, 190, 313, 404.
ais, 9, 325, 359, 404, **683.**
aise, 217, 242, 250, 606.
aisément, 270, 562, 592.

Aisne, 296.
**aissieu, essieu, **391.
Aix, 787.
alarme, 57, 606, 777.
albâtre, 605.
alerte, 57.
alezan, 58.
algalife, 606.
algarade, 58.
allègre, 640, 717.
alleu, 25.
allure, 562, A.N. 1132.
alme, cf. âme.
alors, 604, 606.
altesse, 656, 660.
alumelle, 606.
alun, A.N. 1142.
amant (m. and f.), 792, 802.
âme, alme, arme, 371, 442, 639, 643, 686, 719.
amer (amarum)—amère, 33, 34, 401, 442, 495, 681, 715.
ami (sg. and p.), 302, 429, 442, 616, 734, 798.
amitié, 295, 296, 316, 414.
ammoniac, 397.
amont, 606.
**amour, 54, 230, 802.
an (sg. and pl.), 39, 41, 365, 429, 432, 436, 442, **680**, 686, 796, 797, 808.
ancele, A.N. 1145.
ancessour ; cf. ancêtre.
ancêtre, 257, 370, 800, 806.
ancien, 267, 647.
ancienour, 787.
ancre, A.N. 1173.
andui, 822 ; cf. deux.
ane (anatem), 645.
âne, asne, adne, 259, 354, 378, A.N. 1175, 1177.
anel, asnel, A.N. 1077.
ange, angele, 639, 641, 644.
Angers, **Aungers, **446, 787.
anglais—anglaise, angleis—anglesche, 26, 522, 523, 782.
angle, 221.
angoisse, 184, 315, A.N. 1083, 1161, 1188, 1226.
angoisseux, 733.
anneau, 719.
année, 429, 432, 440, 442, **667**.
ante—antain, 804 ; cf. tante.
anti ; antif—antive, antie, 328, 783.
antique, 785.
anvel, 220, 374.
août, 242, 341, 505, 537, 684.
apoplexie, 605.
apostoile, apostolie, 640, 647.
apôtre, 643, 645.

apprenti ; apprentiz (m. and f.), 795, 816.
après ; **apries, 373, N.E. § iii.
**araigne, **408, A.N. 1137.
**araignée, **445.
arbre, 250, 363, 364, 397, 776, 777.
arc, **683.**
arche, 194, 300.
archer, 86.
archevêque, 1147.
architecture, 57.
architrave, 57.
arçon, 306.
ardemment, 444.
argent, 194, 291.
arme, cf. âme.
armée, 251, 735.
armoire, 487.
armure, 251, 269.
arpent, 6.
arquebuse, 57.
arrêt, 564.
arrière, arrier, 274, 603.
arrière-ban, 751.
arroi, 522.
arrosoir, 520.
art, 777.
artichaut, 92, 535.
artimaire, 645.
asne, asnel ; cf. âne, anel.
aspect, 745.
asperge, 497, 498.
aspic, 750.
assez, 231, **679, 680**, 700, 736.
asteure, 846.
atgier, 25.
atout, 606.
attirail, 814.
au, aux, al, als, as, 834, 843, A.N. 1252, 1253.
aube, 387, **666.**
auberge, 28, 54, 660 ; cf. herberge.
Aubigny, 6.
aubin, aubun, 458.
aucun, ascun, 536, A.N. 1153, 1263.
aulnaie, 522.
aulogier, cf. orlogier.
aumaille, 643, 774.
aumône, 580, 593.
aumuce, 86.
aune, 258.
auques, alches, A.N. 1209.
aussi, auxint, 535, 536, A.N. 1221.
autant, 535, 560.
autel, auter, 398, 535.
auteur, 536.
automne, 456.
autre, altre, 363, 364, 382, 387, 534, 535, 536, 560, 590, **679**, 707, 799, 801, 821, A.N. 1208.

bonté, bounté (*sg.* and *pl.*), 350, 426, 459, 463, 573, 588, 726, 790, 802, A.N. 1152.
borne, bosne, 378.
bouche, 300.
bouée, boie, 520.
boueux, 238.
bouffu, 57.
boulevard, 497, 498.
Boulogne, 426, 459.
bourg, 184, 206, 326.
bourgeois, 418, 699.
bourse, 632.
boutique, 605.
boyau; boel—boeaus, **boiaus, 239, 409, **540, 774.
brague, 54.
braise, brese, 231, 576, 637, 708, 717, 723.
branche, A.N. 1152.
brant, branc, 798, A.N. 1232.
bras, 306, 629, **683**, 774, 795.
brasse, 774.
brebis, 189, 776.
bref (*m.* and *f.*), 344, 743; brieve, A.N. 1244.
brese, cf. braise.
Bretagne, **Bretaigne, 445, 715, E. § xxiii, S.C. § xiii.
breuil, 6, 9.
breuvage, bevrage, 486.
bribe, 70.
bricon—bris, 800.
briga, § 9.
Brion, 435.
bris, cf. bricon.
broigne, 25.
brouillard, 397.
brume, 183.
brun, 183, 637.
brut, 274.
bruyère, 6.
buer, **bur, 599, N. § vii.
buie, **boie, N.E. § i.
burlesque, 57.
Bû-sur Rouvres, 42.
busuign, A.N. 1139; cf. besoin.

C.

çà, 357, 700.
cabane, 54.
câble, 54, 660; cf. chable.
cabriole, 660.
cadastre, 54.
cadeau, 54, 660.
cadenas, 54.
cadence, 57, 660.
cadène, 660; cf. chaîne.

cadet, 54.
Caen, 6, 242, N. § 1.
cage, 188, 305, 660, **677.**
cahier, 531, 730.
caille, 570.
caisse, 54, 660.
Calais, 706.
caleçon, 272.
calibre, 55.
canaille, 660.
canal, 660; cf. chenal.
Candy, 601.
cane, quenne (*kinn*), 25.
canne (*canna*), **1330.
cap, 54, 619, 660.
**capanna, cavanna*, 345.
cape, 660.
capitaine, 660.
capital, 660.
caporal, 57.
caprice, 656.
captif, 660; cf. chétif.
carat, 55.
carbonnade, 660.
caresse, 656.
carnaval, 57.
carrefour, 257, 272.
carrière, 660; cf. chariere.
carrosse, 656.
casenier, 55.
casse, 55.
cassette, 55.
catarrhe, 497, 569.
cause, 569; cf. chose.
cavalcade, 660.
cavalerie, 57, 660.
cavalier, 660.
ce, cest, icest, 844-847, A.N. 1254, 1255.
ce (*ecce hoc*), co, cou, czo, **chou, **chu, **cen, 700, 844, 848, **849, A.N. 1248, 1254, 1259, N. § xxvi, N.E. § xv, W. § xiv.
céans, caienz, 239, 302, 531, 706, A.N. 1171.
cédille, 58.
ceinture, 722.
ceire (*cicer*), cerre, W. § vi.
cel, *neuter*, 836, 844, 845, 846, 849, A.N. 1255, W. § xiv.
cel, *m.*, icel, 844-847, A.N. 1204.
celi, *dat. f.*, iceli, 836, 845, A.N. 1213.
celle, icelle, 834, 844-847; celle-cy, celle-là, 846, 847.
celui, icelui, celi, 836, 844-847, A.N. 1213, W. § iv, A.N. 1213; celui-cy, celui-là, 846, 847.
cembel, 54.

coute, coilte, 293, A.N. 1161, 1179, courtepointe, 751 ; cf. couette.
coutume, 372, 660.
couvre-chef, cuevre chief ; cf. chef.
craie, croie, 522, **663, 683.**
crainte, 707.
création, 570.
criard, 238.
crieme, *subst.*, W. § iii.
crierie, 270.
crieur, 238.
crique, 25.
Crisciacus, Criscecus, 416.
crois, creis, 522.
croissant, 522.
croix, 184, 523, 525, A.N. 1161.
croute, 629 ; cf. crypte.
cruel, 814.
crypte, 660 ; cf. croute.
cuens, quens, 477, 769, 800 ; cf. comte.
cuillère, 402, 407.
cuir, 313, 515, 750.
cuisine, 454, 750.
cuisse, 325.
cuistre, 750, 806.
cuivre, **queivre, 313, 734, *S.W.* § *1*, A.N. 1196.
cul—cus, 392.
curée, cuiriee, **517, 750.
cygne, cisne, 295, 378.
cymbale, 734.
cyprès, 734.

D.

daintiers, deintie, 321, 404.
dam, dan (*damnum*), 442.
damas, 397.
dame, 601, 801.
damnedé, dam(p)neḍeu, 369, 601, 787.
dancel, 601.
Danfront, 601.
danger, 510, 601.
danois—danoise, daneis—danesche, 26, 522, 782, 783.
dans, 706.
danz (*dominus*), 601.
dard, 25.
dartre, 498.
daumaire, 645.
deavé, cf. desvé.
décime, 660.
dedans, 706.
déjection, 647.
délai, 734.
delit, **deleit, N.E. § 1.
demain, 453, 468.
demeure, A.N. 1156.
demi, 734.

demoiselle, damoisele, **damisele, 228, 252, 257, **422, 518, 519, 600, 601, A.N. 1146, 1200.
Deneuvres, 6.
Denevre, 6.
denrée, 253, 272, 369.
dent, 777, 808.
déplaisir, 400.
dernier, 272.
derrière, derrier, 274, 603, A.V. 1135.
des, dels, 834, A.N. 1253.
désordre, 591.
desque, deke, A.N. 1222.
dessus, 247.
destin, 777.
destre, **diestre, 359, N.E. § iii.
destrier, **destrir, 379, N. § vii.
destruction, 379.
desvé, 378, A.N. 1212.
dette, debte, 229, 250, 353, 373, 573, **663, 676,** 718.
deugie, dougie, 349, ***502.*
deuil ; duel—dueus, dieus, **501, 550, 551, **553, 555, 557, 808, 814, 817, A.N. 1156, 1212.
deux ; dui, doi—dous, 254, 419, 541, 542, 821, 822, W. § v, A.N. 1164, 1191.
Dèvre, **553.
di (*diem*), 789, 798.
diable, **diaule, **deable, **deble, 241, 639, 697, N. § xiv, A.N. 1134.
diacre, 643.
dialogue, 647.
diamant, 647.
diantre, 241.
diapre, 310.
dicton, 745.
dieu, de, **diu, 115, 198, 227, 254, 544, 545, 546, **664,** 733, 806, *N.* § *vi*, A.N. 1085, 1162, 1189.
diffusément, 592.
digne, 647.
Dijon, 734.
diluvie, 647.
dimanche, 352, 706, 789.
dîme, **diesme, 259, 296, 660, 821, **825.
Dinan, 435.
dinde, 606.
dîner, disner, digner, 400, A.N. 1178.
direct, 660, 745.
discret—discrète, 784.
dit, dict, 741.
dix, diz, dis, 295, 612, 707, 821.
dix-huit, diz et uit, 821.
dix-huitième, diz et ui(d)me, 821.
dix-neuf, diz et nuef, 821.
dix-neuvième, diz et nuefme, 821.

mois, meis, **meus, 359, 523, 525, **526, 795, N.E. § ix.
moisson (*mŭscionem), **moixon, N. § xvi.
moisson (*messionem), 315, **680**.
moite, 353.
moitié, 190, 316, 414, 518, 519.
mon, **men—mes, 610, 851, **853, 855, 860, A.N. 1261, N. § xii.
monnaie, 522.
monnayeur, 239.
monsieur, 75, 401.
mont, 464, 777, A.N. 1169, 1202, 1232.
montagne, **monteingne, 198, 311, 430, 432, 442, 445, **666**, E. § xxiii, S.C. § *xiii*, A.N. 1182.
mort, **muert, **225, 590, 623, **668**.
mortel—mortieus (*m.* and *f.*), 234, 392, 594, A.N. 1164.
mot, 629.
mou ; mol—mous ; **mos, 76, **391, 590 ; molle, *f.*, 780.
mouchoir, 400, 520.
moule, 372.
moult, mut, munt, 386, 464, 698.
moyen—moyenne, **meianne, 470, **472, 521, **665**.
moyeu, **669** ; m. d'œuf, 393.
muet—muette, 784.
multitude, 649.
mur (*subst.*), 202, 243, 256, **671**, 797, A.N. 1142, 1238.
mûr, 421, 484.
muraille, 391, **672**.
mûrier, 543.
musure, cf. mesure.
mystère, 1105.

N.

nacelle, 373.
nache, **nat, N.E. § v.
naie (*non ego*), 831.
naif, 238, 741.
Nantes, 446.
napperon, 272.
narquois, 71.
natal, 660.
nation, 570, 649.
nature, 649.
nautonier, 54.
ne, nen, non, 599.
nécessaire, 592.
neës, neïs, nes, nis, 850.
nef (*sg.* and *pl.*), 189, 344, 576, **677**, 743, A.N. 1239.
nel (*ne le*), neu, **nou—nes (*ne les*), **502, 838.
Nemours, 398.

nenal, nenel, 834, A.N. 1251.
nenni, nennil, 429, 599.
net—nette, 259, 589, 784, A.N. 1270.
netun, cf. lutin.
neuf, nuef, 612, 619, 821, A.N. 1239.
neveu, nevold, 234, **665**, 628, 800, A.N. 1228.
nez, 231, 338, 588, 686, 722, 726, 795.
ni, ne, ned, 357, 392, 598, 608, A.N. 1210.
nid, 707.
nièce, 410.
nies, cf. neveu.
Nithart, 26.
noaillour, cf. noaudre.
noaudre, noauz, 819.
noce, **nuece, **noche, 410, N. § 1.
Noël, 231, 238, 392, 660.
noeud, **670**, 707.
noif (*nivem*), 808, 816, A.N. 1239.
noir, 323, 523, **684**.
noise, 314.
noix, 295, 518, 519, 525, **670**, 707.
nom, 435, 741, 798.
nombre, 369.
nonante, 821.
nonne—nonnain, 792, 804.
nonobstant, 745.
Normand, 446, 815.
notre, nostre ; nos, noz, **no—**noe, 852, **853, A.N. 1261, N. § xxv.
nôtre, nostre ; nôtres, 377, 564, 580, **581, 590, 852, A.N. 1144.
nou, cf. nel.
noueux, 238.
nourrice, 499.
nourriture, norreture, 257, A.N. 1134.
nous, 827, 828.
nouveau, A.N. 1165.
nu—nue, 206, 333, 346, 367, 707, 796.
nue, 343, **676**, **678**, A.N. 1121.
nuefme, 821, 825.
nuit, 411, 515, **668**, A.N. 1160, 1196.
nuiton, cf. lutin.
nul—nus, nuls, 202, 382, 386, **671**, 808.
nului, 870.

O.

oal, oel, 834, A.N. 1251.
oan, 787.
objet, 745.
obscur ; oscur, 373, 565, 650, 744.
obsèques, 745.
obstination, 650.
obstinément, 745.

R.

racine, 291, 373, **678.**
rade, 231.
radeau, 54.
rai, 281, 309, 339, 404.
raide, reit-reide, **663, 678,** 782, 783,
 A.N. 1219.
raideur, 591.
raie, roie (*riga*), 282, 718.
raifort, 780.
raim, 774.
raime, 774.
raine, 246.
raisin, 418, 451, **663.**
raison, 308, 404, 660, **679,** A.N. 1210.
rancure, 750.
rare, 570 ; cf. rerement.
ration, 660.
rayon, 531.
rebours, 397.
rebouteur, 401.
recet, A.N. 1145.
Rectum, 9.
rédemption, p. 30, n. 1.
regard, A.N. 1232.
regiel, cf. royal.
registre, 379.
règle, 647.
reigne, cf. araigne.
reille, 322 ; cf. riule.
reine, roine, 235, 246, 284, 297, 454.
relief, 743.
religieux, A.N. 1151.
religion, A.N. 1151.
remire, 645.
Remy, 310.
Renard, 26, 28.
rêne, resne, 372.
reproche, reprueche, reproiche, 720,
 A.N. 1156.
rerement, 218 ; cf. rare.
rescousse, 379.
rescrit, 379.
respect, 647.
restriction, 379.
rets, 795.
revanche, 706.
rêveur, 400.
rez, 726.
Rhône, Rosne, 372.
ribaud, 26.
richard, 26 ; Richard, A.N. 1233.
riche (*m.* and *f.*), **rique, N. § i.
rien, 470, 777, W. § iii.
rime, 372.
ris, 206.
riule (*regula*), 641, A.N. 1162, 1166 ;
 cf. reille.

rive, 335, 344, 345, **675.**
rivus, 187.
robe, A.N. 1170.
roche, A.N. 1170.
Rochefort, 780.
rogne, 605.
roi, 114, 246, 256, 297, 523, 589.
Roland, 372.
rôle, 765.
romain, 468.
roman ; romanz, 755, 795, 815.
ronce, 295, 351, **683.**
rond—ronde, 242, 784, A.N. 1131.
rose, 579, 647.
rossignol, 54.
roue, rueë, 552, N. § v, A.N. 1090, 1133.
Rouen, 6, 9, 341, 478.
rouet, 238.
rouge, 194, 203, 258, 305, 373, **676, 682.**
route, 332, 366, 373.
royal, regiel, 404, 521, 780.
rue, 333, 341, **684,** A.N. 1133.
ruine, 241.
ruisseau, *187,* A.N. 1165.
ruiste, 640, 642, 645, A.N. 1160.
ruse, 569.

S.

sa, **se—ses, 851, **853, 855, A.N.
 1260, 1261, N. § xii.
sac—sas, 326, 808.
sade, 353.
sage, **saige, 423, E. § xv, S.C. § x,
 A.N. 1200.
sagma, cf. somme.
saiete, seate, sete, 297, 404, A.N. 1131,
 1218, 1222.
sain, 715, 784.
saint, sain, sen, 359, 466, **666,** 686,
 W. § iii, A.N. 1218, 1222.
sainteté, **667.**
saisine, 454.
saison, 569.
saive, savie, 645.
salle, 382, 502, A.N. 1135.
saloir, 400.
sang, 790.
sangle, 364, 706, 722.
sanglier, 363, 447, **665,** 706.
sangsue, 341.
sans, 597, 706.
santé, **667.**
sanve, 354.
Saône, 342.
sarcelle, 498.
satisfaction, 379.
sauce, 722.

INDEX OF ENGLISH WORDS.

531

INDEX OF VERBS AND VERBAL FORMS.

v.a. stands for *vocalic alternation ;* a semi-colon between infinitive forms indicates that one or other is analogical.

abattre, cf. battre.

aboyer ; *radical,* 239, **487 ;** *pr. pt.* 239.

abscondre, escondre, ascondre, **1063 ;** *pf.* 983.

absoudre, asoldre, 707, 745 ; cf. soudre.

abstenir, 745 ; cf. tenir.

accabler, 242.

accentuer, 648.

accepter, 650, 707, 745.

accointer, 473.

accomplir, 884, A.N. 1314.

accroupir, cf. croupir.

accueillir ; acoillir, ****coillir,** A.N. 1137 ; cf. cueillir.

acheter, achater, ****acater ; 1058 ;** *radical,* 930 ; *inf.* 236, 266, 373, 930, A.N. 1137, 1181 ; *pr. ind.* 729, 899, 930 ; *fut. and cond.* 970.

achever ; *radical, v.a.* **ie** (>**ie̜**)—**e̜,** 926 ; *pr. ind.* 576.

aconsuivre, cf. suivre.

acraventer, A.N. 1139.

admonester, 379, 744, 745.

adouber, 366.

aerdre ; **1063 ;** *radical,* 942 ; *inf.* 293, 730, 942 ; *pr. ind.* 217, 900 ; *pr. subj.* 910, 942 ; *pf.* 986, A.N. 1315 ; *p. pt.* 1052.

aesmer, aasmer, A.N. 1131.

afaitier, 324.

aferir, cf. férir.

affliger, afligir, 879.

affraier, cf. effrayer.

affubler ; *inf. 486 ;* A.N. 1137.

agarder ; *imp.* aga, 76 (2), 937 ; cf. garder.

agir, 881.

aider ; aïdier ; **1058 ;** *radical,* 925 ; *inf.* 190, 217, 281, 316, 350, 414, 529, 877, 925 ; *pr. ind.* 217, 925 ; *pr. subj.* 424, 759, 909.

aimer, amer, **1058 ;** *radical,* 140, 760, 926, 933, 934, 973 ; *inf.* 214, 216, 432, 719, 877, 878, 926 ; *pr. ind.*

214, 432, 466, 666, 715, 899, 926, 929, 934 ; *pr. subj.* 140, 466, 933, 934 ; *impf. ind.* 483 ; *fut. and cond.* 973 ; *pf.* 254, 980, 998, 1004, 1005 ; *impf. subj.* 719, 759, 1042, 1043, 1044, A.N. 1282.

ajuger, 373.

aller, aler ; **1058 ;** *radical,* 749, 948 ; *inf.* 32 ; *imper.* 913 ; *pr. ind.* 147, 356, 893, 958, 959, A.N. 1223, 1270, 1282 ; *pr. subj.* 570, 910, 941, 948, 958, 959, A.N. 1275, 1282.

allier, 217 ; cf. lier.

allouer ; *inf.* 217 ; cf. louer.

amender ; *pr. subj.* A.N. 1300.

anessier (*Gl. Reich.* anetsare), 693.

aoire (*adaugere*) ; **1063 ;** *inf.* 886.

aorer ; *radical, v.a.* **eu** (>**ö**)—**o̜**(>**u**) ; *imper.* A.N. 1293.

apercevoir ; aperceivre ; cf. recevoir.

apparoir, cf. paroir.

appeler ; *radical,* 926, 929, 933, 934 ; *inf.* 926, 929 ; *pr. ind.* 926, 929 ; *pr. subj.* 356, 388, 934.

apprimer, cf. aproismier.

approcher ; *radical, v.a.* **o̜** (**ue**)—**o̜**>**u,** 410, 926, 928, 929 ; *inf.* 926, 929 ; *pr. ind.* 410, 926 ; *p. pt.* 928.

appuyer, apoier ; *radical, v.a.* **üi—oi,** 928 ; *inf.* 928, A.N. 1171.

aproismier ; aprismer ; *radical, v.a.* **üi** (>**i**)—**oi,** 516, 927 ; *inf.* 927 ; *pr. ind.* 516, 927 ; *pf.* 927.

araisnier, deraisnier ; *radical,* 925 ; *inf.* 925 ; *pr. ind.* 925.

ardoir ; ardre ; **1063 ;** *radical,* 947 ; *pr. subj.* 347 ; *pf.* 370, 991, 994, 996, 998, 1016, 1018, 1036, A.N. 1312.

arracher, 349.

arrêter, cf. ester.

ascondre, cf. abscondre.

assaillir, 367 ; cf. also saillir.

assaisnier, 925.

assembler, cf. sembler.

asseoir, cf. seoir.

deignier, cf. daigner.
déjeuner, 925.
délivrer, cf. livrer.
demander ; *fut.* 970.
démener, 217 ; cf. mener.
demeurer ; demorer ; *radical, v.a.* **ue** (>**ö**)—**ǫ**(>**u**) ; *pr. ind.* A.N. 1310 ; *pr. subj.* A.N. 1275.
deraisnier, cf. araisnier.
descendre ; *pf.* 1004.
désirer ; *pr. ind.* 898, W. § xi, A.N. 1299 ; *pr. subj.* 939.
desjuner, cf. dîner.
despire ; **1062** ; *pf.* 1014, A.N. 1315.
détruire, construire ; **1063** ; *radical,* 938 ; *inf.* 938, A.N. 1160 ; *pr. pt.* 938 ; *pr. ind.* 938, 940 ; *pr. subj.* 938 ; *pf.* 1036, 1037 ; *p. pt.* 1057.
devoir ; **1065** ; *radical,* 931, 946, 973 ; *inf.* 216, 234, 665, 710, 883 ; *pr. ind.* 204, 256, 258, 356, 373, 522, 691, 890, 931, 946, A.N. 1283 ; *pr. subj.* 946, 950 ; *impf. ind.* 761 ; *fut. and cond.* 256, 964, 969, 973, A.N. 1290 ; *pf.* 243, 374, 419, 901, 982, 991, 993, 996, 998, 1020, 1022-8, 1032, 1033, A.N. 1279, 1282, 1285, 1288 ; *impf. subj.* 484, 1042, A.N. 1279 ; *p. pt.* 243, 343, 484, 1056, A.N. 1288 ; *plupf. ind.* 872.
dicter, 647, 660.
diluer, 649.
dîner, disner ; *radical,* 925 ; *inf.* 925, A.N. 1178 ; *pr. ind.* 925.
dire, ****dierre** ; contredire, escondire, prédire ; **1062** ; *inf.* 759, W. § xi, S.C. § *viii,* A.N. 1077, 1172 ; *pr. pt.* 294, 334 ; *imper.* 357, 759, 911 ; *pr. ind.* 258, 566, 759, 895, 896, 902, 960, 961, A.N. 1282, 1283, 1292 ; *pr. subj.* 960, 961, E. § xxviii ; *impf. ind.* A.N. 1284 ; *fut. and cond.* A.N. 1284, 1289 ; *pf.* 370, 998, 1013, 1014, 1018, 1037, A.N. 1288, 1315 ; *impf. subj.* S.W. § xi ; *p. pt.* 1055, A.N. 1282.
ditier, 660.
diviser, deviser, 127, 129.
donner ; *radical,* 948 ; *inf.* 459, 669, A.N. 1314 ; *pr. ind.* 461, 670, 948, **958,** 959, A.N. 1275, 1311 ; *pr. subj.* 762, 948, 950, **958,** 959 ; *fut. and cond.* 253, 272, 369, 970, N. § xxvii ; *pf.* 1008.
donoier, daunyer, 721, A.N. 1152.
dormir ; *radical,* 935, 946 ; *inf.* 234, 889 ; *imper.* 911 ; *pr. ind.* 685, 889, 935, 945 ; *pr. subj.* 905 ; *impf. ind.* 915 ; *fut. and cond.* 971.

douloir ; deuloir ; **1060** ; *radical, v.a.* **ö**—**u**, ****501, 555, 556,** 926, 931, *933,* 947 ; *inf.* 926, 931 ; *pr. ind.* 926, S.C. § xi ; *fut. and cond.* 599 ; *pf.* 985.
douter ; *inf.* 184, 350, 679 ; *pr. ind.* 898 ; *pr. subj.* 909.
dresser, drecier, esdrecier, 216 ; *pr. subj.* 939.
duire, conduire, déduire ; **1063** ; *radical,* 938 ; *inf.* 515, 938 ; *pr. pt.* 515, 938 ; *pr. ind.* 938, 940 ; *pr. subj.* 938, 940 ; *fut. and cond.* 399 ; *pf.* 1012, 1016, 1036 ; *p. pt.* 1057.
duire (*docēre), **1063** ; *inf.* 886, S.W. § i.
duper, 70.
durer ; *inf.* 183, 887 ; *imper.* 911 ; *pr. ind.* 887 ; *pr. subj.* 903 ; *fut. and cond.* 970 ; *pf.* 1000 ; *impf. subj.* 1039.

ébahir, A.N. 1177.
écarteler, esquarterer, 129.
échapper, chaper, 377, A.N. 1137.
échoir, cf. choir.
éclore, cf. clore.
écouter ; *inf.* 386 ; *pr. ind.* 390.
écrire ; escrivre, décrire ; **1063** ; *radical,* 936 ; *inf.* 936, A.N. 1270 ; *pr. ind.* 566 ; *pf.* 1016, 1017, 1018, 1036, 1037 ; *p. pt.* 707.
édifier, 647.
effrayer, esfreer, affraier ; *radical, v.a.* **ei** (>**oi**)—**ę**, 926, *239, 523* ; *inf.* 634, 734, 926, A.N. 1138, 1175 ; *pr. ind.* 926.
effriter, 516, 672.
élever, cf. lever.
élire, cf. lire.
éloigner ; *radical,* 465 ; *inf.* 465.
embler ; *inf.* 189, 217, 365 ; *pr. ind.* 217.
embronchier, embronkier, A.N. 1091.
emmener, 138, 444, *610* ; cf. also mener.
empêcher, 42, 640, 725.
empeindre ; *1063* ; *pf.* 983 ; *p. pt.* 1055.
empirer ; empeirier ; *radical, v.a.* **i—ei** (>**oi**), 929 ; *inf.* 228, 256, 317, 929.
emplir, raemplir, **1059** ; *inf.* 882, 884 ; *pr. ind.* 882.
employer, A.N. 1138.
empoisnier, 925.
emporter, cf. porter.
empreindre, cf. priembre.
emprendre, A.N. 1177 ; cf. also prendre.

SUBJECT INDEX.

Numerals in heavy type indicate paragraphs that contain definitions, paradigms or tables of sounds or verbs. Abbreviations: at. = atonic, ct. = countertonic, intert. = intertonic, interv. = intervocalic, dial. = dialectal, adj. = adjective, subst. = substantive, rep. = representation; cf. also p. 507.

Double consonants are entered after single ones; β after **b, ð, θ** and **ɟ** after **d, dž** after **dz,** γ after **g, ʄ** after **t̂, š** after **ŝ, tš** after **ts, ž** after **z.**

A

ɑ—*sounds,* 99, 101 ; sonority, 261 (ii), 352 ; infl. on word devel. 261, 352.

ɑ̆, Latin, 157 ; frk. 637 ; pal. to **a, §** 182.

a, G.R. (< Latin and frk. **ɑ**) : devel. : *tonic,* **666,** (cf. diphthongisation) ; Prov. 32 ; Frpr. 33 ; *ct.* **667** ; *at.* 250, 251, 253, 970, cf. **ę** : infl. nasals, 427, cf. nasalisation and **ã, ãi** ; labial. in G.R. 481-483 ; lengthening in Mid. Fr. 561, 564, 569, 570 ; pal. in G.R. 413, 414, in O.F. ******423 ; infl. **ʝ** and **ŋ,** 406, 408, and cf. palatalisation, raising ; velarisation : in O.F. ******502, in Mod. Fr. 177, 586, in A.N. 1153.

a—*glide :* intercons. 635 ; between **ę** and **ʊ,** 388, 501, A.N. 1162, 1165.

ã, ɑ̃, 96 ; **ã,** O. and Mid. Fr. : rep. 715, 719, A.N. 1152 ; sources, 442, 448, 449, 601 ; date, 434, 448, 449 ; denasalisation, 444 ; lengthening by absorption of foll. nasal, 437, 563 ; velarisation in Mod. Fr. 443 ; dialectal, 446, N. § xx, 1328, A.N. 1152 ; treatment of loan-words, 649, 652.

a, graphy, 697, A.N. 1208.

-a, -anem, suffix, cf. *-ain.*

-a, -at, -ad, **-a, -a**θ : term. fut., 3, 121, 182, 953 ; term. pf. I, 3, 989, 998, 1005.

ablative : disuse, 768, 786 ; survivals, 787.

-able, suffix, 372, N. § xiv ; velarisation, ******382, ******502, E. § xvi.

Academy, 196, 688, 711, 713, 729, 734, 736, 902.

Accent, **118** ; varieties, 118, 119 ; musical accent in Latin, 210 ; in Mod. Fr. 121 ; expiratory accent in L.L. 153, 210, 217.

position : Latin, 211, 212 ; L.L. 214, 216, 217 ; French, 215, 218, 223 ; loan-words, 642, 648.

shift of stress : phonetic causes, 214, 216, 503, 510, 515, ******517, 519, 545, 553, 556 ; associative influence, 823, 990, 991 ; syntactical phonetics, 213, 837, 835 ; loan-words, 215, 648.

intensity : in Latin, 219 ; in frk. 27 ; regional variations in O.F. 223, 261, 508, 1085, 1090, W. § 1, N. § iv, N.E. § iii, E. § xiv, M.E. and A.N. 1110 ; diminishing intensity in Period II, 170, 223, 508, 602, A.N. 1096.

influence of word accent : in Latin, 219-222 ; in Period I, 223-235, 248-264 ; in A.N. 1130-1140 ; in the conjugation system, cf. vocalic alternation ; influence of sentence accent in Period I, 121, 596-602, 827, 829, 831, 835, 837, 855, 863, 870, 920, 952, 953, 959, 978.

Accents, 725-727, 735 ; acute, 712, **736** ; circumflex, 712, **738** ; grave, 713, **737** ; use in mediaeval MSS. 735, A.N. 735, 1211 ; by Italian printers, 735 ; French printers, 735-738.

Accusative : generalisation in L.L. 768 ; in Mid. Fr. 772, 806 ; replacement of nom. pl. I by acc. pl. in L.L. and G.R. 791.

Acquirement of language, 151.

-ade, suffix, 58.

Adjectives : form. of fem. 770, 779-785 ; anal. fem. 752, 756, 773, 780, 783, 866, A.N. 1244 ; anal. masc. 781, 783 ; generalisation of fem. 783 ; neuter 775.

544

alternation of radical in masc. and fem. : O.F. 782, Mid. Fr. 784 ; levelling, 783, graphical, 784, 785. form. of comparative, 771, 818 ; survival of synthetic comp. 769, 771, **819** ; superl. 820 ; cf. declension, gender, syntactical phonetics, -*eur* : -*euse*, -*isme*.

Adverbial -*s*, 597.

Adverbs : syntactical doublets, 596, 599, 604, 275 ; in -*ment* : accentuation, 218 ; in -*ément*, 270, 592, 727 ; in -*amment*, -*emment*, 444, 780.

æ, vowel, 99, 1114 ; **æ,** diphthong : Latin, 504 ; G.R. 233, 427.

ae, graphy, 504, A.N. 1219.

Aetheria, 11.

Affricated consonants, **98** (vi), 106(*b*); became fricative in O.F. II, 194, 195, N. § xxi, A.N. 1102, 1181.

-*age*, suffix, 203, 352 ; dial. palatalisation, ******423, 718, E. § xv, S.C. § x.

Agglutination of articles and prepositions, 606.

ai, diphthong, frk. 637 ; O.F. I. : sources and devel. 404, 528, 529; dialectal variant, 408 ; Period II : sources and development, 530-532, A.N. 1157 ; spelling, 533, 717, A.N. 1223.

aï : L.L. 254 ; Mid. Fr. : sources, 237, 424 ; syneresis, 242.

ai, graphy, 468, 706, 708, 717, 718, 957.

āi : sources, 404 (6), 406, ******408, 427 ; devel. 467-469 ; rep. 715, 719, 784, A.N. 1224.

-*ai*, term. fut., 1, 529, 946, 953, 964, 965, 966, W. § vi, S.C. § v, A.N. 1284 ; term. pf. I, 1, 529, 533, 989, 996, A.N. 1284 ; cf. fut. and pf.

-*aiche*, -*aige*, graphies, 718.

-*aient*, term. impf. ind. and condit., 6, 271, 897, **917** ; spelling, 718, A.N. 1223, 1284 ; cf. impf. ind.

-*ain* : -*e* (-*anem* : -*a*), 30, 793, 804.

-*aire*, O.F. -*aire*, 645, A.N. 1105.

-*ais*, suffix, O.F. -*eis*, -*ois*, 26, 523 ; fem. 782, 783.

-*ais*, impf. ind. and condit. 1, 2, 901, 902, **917** ; spelling, ******718, ******966, A.N. 1284 ; cf. impf. ind.

-*aisse*, graphy, 717.

-*ait*, term. impf. ind. and condit. 3, **917** ; spelling, ******717, A.N. 1223, 1284 ; cf. impf. ind.

Albigensian Crusade, 47.

Alcuin, 21, 646.

Alexis, cf. *St. Alexis*.

Alternation of radical, cf. vocalic and syllabic alternation.

Alternation of stress, cf. perfects, strong radical, syllabic alternation.

Alveolar consonants, **106.**

-*am*, -*amm*, -*an*, -*anm*, *ann*, graphies, 715, 719.

-*âmes*, term. pf. I, 4, 999, 1000, 1005.

Amuïssement, cf. effacement.

Analogy : nature and conditions, *93*, Pt. IV, chap. 1 ; analogical forms, 214, 393, 400, 419, 444, 510, 582, 591, 658, 768, 772, 783, 788-92, 810-817 ; in numerals, 822, 823, 825 ; pronouns, 826, 828, 832, 835, 836, 844, 846, 853, 856-861, 868, 870 ; conjugation, Pt. IV, chap. 4, *passim :* free use in Anglo-Norman, 1078, 1242-1244, 1246, 1264, 1298-1316 ; cf. preservative analogy.

Angevin dynasty, 1068, 1186.

Anglo-French, 1075.

Anglo-Norman, 59, 77, Pt. V, cf. accent, analogy, conservatism, conjugation system, declension system, orthography, francien, Western and Northern French, English, etc.

Anglo-Saxon Chronicle, 347.

Anjou, 223, 1326, 1327.

Anne of Russia, signature, 235.

Anomalous verbs, 884 (ii), 885, 920, 951-963, 976, 1038.

-*ant*, term. gerund and pr. pt. 874, 921 ; fem. 779, 780, A.N. 1244 ; decl. 793, 798, 802 ; cf. -*ent*.

-*ant*, analog. subst. ending, 815.

Ante-penultimate syllable, 211 ; cf. effacement, proparoxytone, accent, (shift of stress).

Aosta, Val d', 33.

Aphaeresis, **605,** 837, 838, 844, 977, A.N. 1137.

Apocope, 274, 597, 598, **604,** 606.

Apophony, cf. vocalic alternation.

Appellatives : shortenings, 121, 596, 600, 601 ; retention nom. 769, 794.

Appendix Probi, 10, 185, 186, 187, 205, 220, 262, 359, 360.

Aquitanians, 31, 1328.

Archaic words, pronunciation of, 379, 619.

Archaism in A.N., cf. conservatism.

Architecture, Gothic (*française*) and Norman (*romane*), 44.

-*ard* : -*arde*, suffix, O.F. -*art* : -*arde*, 26, 784 ; spelling, 784.

Argot, 70.

Armorica, 1, 14.

Ars Consentii, 10.

Article : origin and development, 826, 837, 843 ; influence of pronoun of third person, 1253 ; O.F. declension, 834, dialectal variants, N. § xii,

35

neuter : function in Latin, 767 ; occasional extension, 774 ; replacement, 766, 767, 774, 798, 801 ; Lat. neuts. in *-us*, 795, 798 ; in *-ud*, 836.

    survival in O.F. : neut. pl. 774, 775 ; pts. and adjs. 775 ; pronouns, 833, 839, 845, 846, 850, 863, A.N. 1251, 1255, 1262.

    Lat. influence in O.F. 775, 1241.

Generalisation : of acc. forms, 768, 806 ; nom. forms, 806 ; one or other syntactical doublet, 596-600, 607-610, 614-619 ; analogical forms, 757, 763, 764 ; and cf. Pt. IV, *passim.*

Genitive case : gradual disuse of, 768, 786 ; survivals, 787 ; clerkly use of gen. pl. 787 ; cf. *leur.*

Gerbert, 44.

Germanic invasions, 17 ; cf. Burgundian, Frankish, Goths, Norse, Saxon.

gg, graphy, A.N. 1181.

gh, graphy, 701.

gi, graphy, 731 ; confused with *di*, 310.

Gilliéron, 38, 147, 379.

gj, palatalisation, 307, cf. **ɖ.**

gl, init. of syllable : effacement of **g** after **r**, 365, persistence elsewhere, 364 ; interv. : palatalisation, 322, vocalisation of **g** in loan-words, 641.

Glides, 122, **123** ; vocalic : on-glides, 361, 603 ; in loan-words, 640, 649, 653 ; off-glides, 258 ; intercons. 635, ****972**, N. § xiii, A.N. 1173 ; before **J**, 407, ****408**, **ŋ**, 406-408, **r**, 500, S.C. § viii, W. § xi, A.N. 1172, N.E. § xiv, **ʯ**, 388, ****501**, A.N. 1162, 1164.

    consonantal : intercons. 123, 370, 1018, N. §§ xiii, xxx ; interv. 239, A.N. 1171 ; 919, 939, 952, N.E. xiv, A.N. 1171 ; 544, ****391** ; cf. **a, e, J, w** and *cuirs.*

Glossary of Cassel, 39.

Glossary of Reichenau, 19, 22, 39, 260, 345, 426, 505, 693, 820.

Glosses, Hebrew, 91, 275, 519.

Gloucester, Statute of, 1072.

gn, graphy for **ɲn** in Latin, 137, 321 ; for **ŋ**, 695.

Gothic, Goths (Visigoths), 14 (v), 17, 18.

gr, interv.: palatalisation, 323 ; reduction to **r**, 323.

Graffiti, cf. inscriptions.

Grammarians, 79, 80, 713, A.N. 1073 ; influence, 81, 82, 196, 618, 620, 621,

623, 740-746 ; discernment of quantitative and qualitative differences in vowels, 558, 559, 583-586 ; cf. education, orthography, Latin.

Graphical similarity, cf. Addenda.

Graphie inverse, 90.

Greek : influence on Latin, 4 ; treatment of Grk. sounds in Latin, 628-633 ; Grk. transliterations, 12 ; mediaeval Grk. ị < ē, 633.

Gregory of Tours, 20, 39, 304, 336, 692.

gu, graphy, 701.

Guernes de Pont Ste. Maxence, 59.

Guise Letters, 458, 734, 976.

gw, initial, 636, A.N. 1180; L.L. interv. group, 374, 1024.

H.

h, 98 ; effacement of Latin **h**, 185, 634 ; introduction of initial **h** in frk. and G.R. words, 28, 634 ; replacement of frk. initial χ by **h**, 635 ; effacement of frk. **h** in interior of words, 28 ; absence in Provençal, 28 ; effacement of O.F. **h** in Mid. Fr. 81, 196 ; **h** *aspiré*, 108, 196 ; onomatopeiic, 142.

h : use as diacritical sign in Grk. words, 629, Germanic, 690, O.F. I, 694, 730, A.N. 1237 ; as graphical device before initial **u, w, ü, ẅ**, 730, 824.

Hainault, 69.

Hebrew elegies, 91, 464, 522.

Hebrew glosses, 91, 275, 519.

Henri IV, 68.

Henry I, 1067.

Henry II, 1186.

Henry III, 1068, 1069.

Henry IV, 1070.

Henry VIII, 1072, 1076.

Hiatus, **115** ; avoidance by elision when words end in **ę** in O.F. 604 ; frequency of internal hiatus in Period II, 237.

    tendency to eliminate hiatus under influence of expiratory accent : in Latin by consonantalisation of atonic **ĕ, ĭ, ŏ, ŭ**, 220 ; in Mid. Fr. : by consonantalisation, 241, 267, syneresis, 242, 244, 245, effacement, 243, 268-271, 604, glide development, 239, N.E. § xiv, A.N. § 1171.

    differentiation of vowels in hiatus, 131, 234, 854 ; dislike of hiatus increases vogue of anal. term. *-s* in first person of verbs, 901, 902.

    graphical use of *h* to indicate hiatus, 730, A.N. 1237.

Prefixes : frk. infl. 26 ; accentuation, 217, 266; aphaeresis and confusion in A.N. 1137, 1138.

Prepositions, use of in L.L. 768, 786 ; devel. 596, 597, 604, 606.

Present participle : termination, 921 ; radical, 949 ; declension, 793, 802 ; fem. 779, 802; present tenses, cf. Addenda.

Preservative analogy, 188, 238, **765**, 952.

Printers : Dutch, 713 ; Italian, 735, 739 ; Spanish, 739 ; French, 711, 735, 739 ; traditionalism of 16th century French printers, 703, 711, 712, 713 ; influence of printing on use of vernacular, 51 ; cf. orthography.

Proclisis, proclitic, 602, 826.

Progressive assimilation, cf. assimilation ; progressive nasalisation, cf. nasalisation.

Pronouns, Pt. IV, chap. iii ; cf. analogy, aphaeresis, enclisis, proclisis, mutation, particles, word-list.

Proparoxytones, **212** ; shift of stress in L.L. 214 ; in G.R. vb. forms, 990, 991 ; in loan-words of Period II, 648 ; retention in loan-words of Period I, 214, 642 ; distribution of stress in Latin proparoxytones, 248 ; persistence of final unstressed vowel, 259 ; loss of penult. vowel in L.L. and Early G.R. 221, 262, in Later G.R. 250 ; cf. 261-264.

Prosody, cf. versification.

Prosthetic **e**, 361, 603, 640, 649, 653 ; movability in O.F. I, 603 ; in Northern French, N.E. § x ; in A.N. 1106 ; influence on development of future of *être*, 977.

Provençal (Langue d'Oc), 15, **31**, **32** ; extension, 32 ; causes of divergence from French, 31 ; relatively slow linguistic development, 43 ; retention of undiphthongised tonic free **a**, **ę**, **ǫ**, 32, 229; of Latin **au**, 43 ; cf. 976, of interv. **b** (< **p**), **d** (< **t**), **g** (< **k** + **a**, **o**, **u**), 43, of vb. endings -*am*, -*em*, 893, -*ent*, 921 ; existence of " breaking," 412 ; passage of **ǫ** to **u**, 43 ; absence of diphthongisation of tonic free **ę**, **ǫ**, 229, of Germ. **h** initial, 28, of palatalis. of velars before **a**, ****301**; infl. on French vocabulary, cf. loan-words.

Provincialisms, cf. dialects.

Psychology, part played in linguistic development, 93, 143, 145, 147, Pt. IV, chap. 1.

Puns, use in attesting pronunciation, 433, 444, 458, 617, 648, 976.

pw, L.L. interv. group, 374, 1024.

Q.

qu, graphy, 701 ; cf. **kw**.

Quality of vowels, **99** ; differentiation in L.L. 154, 179, 198 ; differentiation of **ę**-sounds in O.F. 573 ; of **o**-sounds in Period II, 579, 580 ; of **ö**-sounds and **ɑ**-sounds, xvi-xvii, 585, 586, Mod. Fr. 571, 572 ; recognition of differentiation by grammarians, 583-586; cf. **ɑ**-sounds, **e**-sounds, **o**-sounds, **ö**-sounds, lowering, raising, palatalisation, velarisation.

Quantity of vowels, **118** ; modifications in L.L. 154, 179, 198, 222 ; quantitative differences in **e**-sounds in O.F. 233 ; modifications in Mid. Fr. cf. lengthening of vowels.

influence on position of accent in Latin, 212 ; on quality in Period II, 199, 575, 579, 580, 586, A.N. 1153, on grammatical forms, 559, 562, 566, 567.

attitude of poets and prosodists in Later Mid. Fr. 558 ; representation in Period II, 724, 725, 727, 738, A.N. 1235, 1236.

R.

r-sounds, 98 (**iii**) ; devel. **681** ; dissimilation, **127** ; metathesis, 124, N. § xxii.

r, dental (alveolar), trilled, **106** (*a*) ; often fricative in O.F. cf. **ɹ** ; lowering influence on vowels, Pt. II, chap. 13.

ɹ, dental (alveolar), fricative, **106** (**a**) ; devel. in O.F. 395 ; assim. and effacement when prae-cons. 396, 397, A.N. 1184 ; graphical intrusion, 398, 721 ; assibilation of interv. 399, of final, ****401** ; effacement of final, 400, 401, A.N. 1193.

R, uvular, trilled, **107**, 394 ; development in cent. xvii, 394, 498 ; raising influence on vowels, 498.

ȓ, **111** ; sources : **rj**, 313 ; **jr**, 317 ; **đ** in early loan-words, 645 ; devel. 190, 279 (ii), cf. palatalisation ; influence on preceding tonic **ę** and **ǫ**, 410, 411 ; cf. also ****293**.

rr, **113** ; sources in O.F. : Latin **rr**, G.R. **ȏr**, 372, O.F. I, **n'r**, 369 ; simplification, 366, 372 ; lengthening influence, 569.

Savoyard accent of Vaugelas, 69.

Saxons in France, 21, 25.

sc, graphy for **s**, 722.

Scaliger, 654.

Sebillet, 271, 391, 738, 902.

Second person plural : ind. pr. 874, 875 (vi), 896 ; subj. pr. 875 (vi), 908 ; imper. 874, 911, A.N. 1295 ; impf. ind. and condit. 267, 918, N. § xi ; fut. 967 ; pf. 999 ; impf. subj. 1044, 1047, A.N. 1306 ; Mod. Fr. spelling, 807 ; A.N. 1295 ; survival of pr. ind. of Lat. III, 896, 961, A.N. 1270 ; cf. *-assiez, -âtes, -ez, -iez, -issez, -îtes, -oiz, -ûtes.*

Second person singular : ind. pres. 623, 890 ; subj. pres. 906 ; imper. 911, 913, A.N. 1293, 1302 ; impf. ind. and condit. 917 ; pf. 997 ; impf. subj. 1046 ; cf. **ẹ, -s, -ts**(*z*).

Secondary stress, cf. countertonic.

Semantics, 93.

Semi-vowels, **100** ; representation, 100 ; cf. **ị, ụ,** and consonantalisation, vocalisation, levelling of diphthongs, glides.

Sentence-accent (stress), 119 ; cf. syntactical phonetics.

Serlo, Italian architect, 57.

Shortened forms of words, cf. syntactical phonetics.

Sibilants, hissing sounds, cf. **s, z, š, ž, tš, dž, ts.**

Sibilet, cf. Sebillet.

sk, *sc*, Latin intervocalic group : metathesis before **o, u,** 325 ; palatalisation before **a, e, i,** 325, 880.

    O.F. interv. and final group, cf. **s** prae-cons.

Social differentiation, 70-76, 141 ; effect on language in cent. xvi, 72, 497, 622, 624 ; cf. vulgarisms.

Sonority of vowels ; influence on devel. of words, 249, 251, 261, 352.

Sorel, 710.

Sound-change : basis, **747** ; predisposing conditions and causes, 116, 117, 120, 122, 148-151, 1078-9 ; general characteristics, 141-147 ; cf. sound substitution.

    part played in linguistic develop. 753, Pts. IV, V, *passim,* and cf. analogy.

    rapidity in G.R. 19, 23, 35, 149, 150, 159, in A.N. 1078-1080, 1110, 1130 ; gradual slackening in Period II, 44-48, 78, 79, 82, 169, 1095 ; cf. education, grammarians, printing.

Sound laws : nature, 143 ; difficulty in correct formulation, 144, 145.

Sound substitution, **142,** 293, 360, 367, 498, 505 ; in loan-words, 625 ; Gk. 629-632 ; frk. 635 ; Italian, 656 ; Latin, 642, 643 ; cf. dissimilation, metathesis.

Sound-systems : Latin, 154-155, 157, 158, 380 ; G.R. 161, 167, 168 ; Early O.F. 161, 167, 168, 1111-1114 ; Early Mid. Fr. 174, 175, 580 ; Late sixteenth cent. 587 ; Early Mod. Fr. 174, 175 ; Early M. E. 1115-1117.

    modifications : Class. Lat. 154, 155 ; G.R. 160, 161 (1), (2), 163, 164 ; O.F. I, 166 ; Period II, 172, 173, 381, 1096-1102 ; Mod Fr. 177 ; for A.N. cf. Pt. V, *passim.*

Sounds, **94 ;** formation, 95-114 ; variability, 116.

South-central region, 1325.

Southern Gaul, Southern France (*pays de Langue d'Oc*), 31, 205, 229, 330 ; cf. Provençal.

South-western French, synopsis of traits, 1327 ; influence on A.N. 1144, 1195-1199, 1278.

Spanish, 15 ; diphthongisation of **ẹ, ọ** tonic free, 229 ; influence on French vocabulary, 58 ; French printing, 739 ; use of French in Spain, 88.

Speed of speech : influence on pronunciation, 120, 171 (4), 223, 236-247, 265-273.

Standard language, 146, 151 ; cf. Paris, vulgarisms.

Stopped consonants, **98** ; cf. plosives.

Strasbourg, Oaths of, 22, 39, 260, 336, 505, 600, 609, 688, 691, 697, 850, 858, 869.

Stress, cf. accent.

Strong perfects, **982** ; cf. perfects.

Strong position of initial cons. **202 ;** influence on their develop. 28, 202, 203, 362, 636.

Strong radicals (verbal), **923** ; cf. vocalic alternation ; generalisation of, 928, 929, 931, 935, 943, 977.

Subjunctive, 762, Pt. IV, ch. 4, sects. 4, 8-10, 18 ; Pt. V, chap. 5.

Suffixes : use in L.L. 5 ; frk. influence, 26 ; cf. also individual suffixes.

Suisse romande, 33.

Supported final cons. cf. final cons.

Supporting vowel (*voyelle d'appui*), **257** ; devel. 256-258, 356, 891, 898, 909, 972 ; effacement of intert. in Period II, 272, A.N. 1134 ; of final in Mod. Fr. 273 ; dial. N.E.